Latin America
New World, Third World

Latin America
New World, Third World

STEPHEN CLISSOLD

PRAEGER PUBLISHERS
New York · Washington · London

Published in the United States of America in 1972

Praeger Publishers, Inc.
111 Fourth Avenue, New York, N.Y. 10003, U.S.A.
5 Cromwell Place, London, S.W.7, England

© 1972 by The Pall Mall Press, London, England
Library of Congress Catalog Card Number: 72–117472

Printed in Great Britain

Contents

Acknowledgements   ix

The Amerindian World   1

The beginning of civilization – the Maya – Teotihuacán and the Toltecs – the Aztecs – the Pre-Inca civilizations – the Incas

The Iberian Imprint   25

The first discoveries and conquests – the conquest of Mexico – the conquest of Peru – Spanish and Portuguese expansion – strategy and tactics – social, legal and religious features of the Conquest – the fusion of races – patterns of Spanish colonial life – Portuguese colonization – mining and agriculture – civil and ecclesiastical administration – prelude to emancipation – Britain and the independence movement – Miranda the Precursor – Bolívar the Liberator – San Martín and the campaigns in Argentina and Chile – the end of Spanish rule in South America – Mexico's struggle for independence – prospects and problems of nationhood

The Twenty Republics   77

1   Mexico   79

Santa Anna and the loss of Texas – the reforms of Juárez and the empire of Maximilian – the age of Porfirio Díaz – the Mexican Revolution – the Revolution institutionalized – Cárdenas and his successors

2   Central America and Panama   96

Guatemala – Nicaragua – Honduras – El Salvador – Costa Rica – Panama

3   Haiti and the Dominican Republic   114

Haiti – the Dominican Republic

4 Cuba   124
Cuba before Castro – the Cuban Revolution

5 Venezuela   137
The age of the *caudillos* – from dictatorship to democracy

6 Colombia   144
Liberals versus Conservatives – the National Front

7 Ecuador   151

8 Peru   155
The post-independence period – the War of the Pacific and after – army, oligarchy and APRA – revolution by military fiat

9 Bolivia   164
Caudillos and tin barons – Nationalism and Revolution

10 Chile   172
The nineteenth-century republic – Chile since 1891 – the Christian Democrat experiment – Popular Unity in power

11 Argentina   180
The age of Rosas – the forging of the nation – the Perón regime – the search for a new role

12 Paraguay   191

13 Uruguay   194

14 Brazil   198
The Empire – the Republic – the Vargas period – the post-Vargas decade – Brazil under military rule

The Latin American Scene   213
1 The Social Structure   215
The ruling élite – the middle sectors – the urban working class – the *campesinos* – the Indian problem – the negro elements – European and Asian immigration – the population explosion

2 Institutions 228

The *hacienda* system – the Church – the military – the universities – the trade
unions

3 Economic Problems 255

Agriculture: (i) stagnation – causes and cures   (ii) food crops   (iii) coffee
(iv) sugar   (v) other products; – mining and minerals: (i) oil   (ii) copper
(iii) tin; – transport – industry – the role of foreign capital – the inflation
problem – foreign trade – development prospects

4 Political Forces 286

Constitutions – *caudillos* – President, Government, and Parliament – political
parties: (i) traditional parties   (ii) populist parties   (iii) Christian Democracy   (iv) Communists and Socialists   (v) other revolutionary groups

5 Patterns of Thought and Culture 306

The Indian strands – the Iberian strands – the African strand – cultural
emancipation and the quest for identity – 'Civilization and Barbarism' – the
shadow of the Colossus – new perspectives

6 Inter-American and International Relations 320

Territorial and other disputes – Pan-Americanism and the Inter-American
system – the Organization of American States – economic integration: (i) the
Latin American Free Trade Association (LAFTA)   (ii) the Central American Common Market (CACM)   (iii) new subregional groups   (iv) other
organizations; – the role of the United States – the Alliance for Progress –
Great Britain – the EEC countries – Spain – the Soviet Union – Japan –
Latin America and the world

Table of Basic Data 347

Main Events 1945-1971 349

Abbreviations 354

Glossary 359

Bibliography 366

Index 375

Acknowledgements

I am indebted to a number of friends for kindly reading through and commenting upon parts of this book in manuscript. My special thanks are due to Professor Alistair Hennessy, Mr. Hugh Holley, Sir Robert Marett, Professor J. C. J. Metford, Dr. Andrew Pearse, Professor Hugh Thomas, and Professor Doreen Warriner.

S.C.

The Amerindian World

The beginning of civilization

There seems little doubt that man first came to the American continent from Asia. Primitive hunters pursued their prey over the tongue of land linking Siberia with Alaska, before the waters of the Bering Straits had separated the two continents, and pushed across the land mass of what is now Canada, the United States and Mexico, and over the narrow isthmus of Central America before fanning out into the vast spaces to the south. The examination of ancient spear- and arrow-heads, and of human bones which can be subjected to radio-carbon dating, has been pushing back our estimate of the date at which this process began and the length of its duration. It now seems that the first men may have reached America around 25–30,000 years ago or perhaps even earlier, and that the descendants of these and other migratory groups spread throughout its length and breadth to reach Tierra del Fuego, at its southernmost tip, some 18,000 years, or 600 generations, later. The mongoloid features, straight black hair, and red or copper-coloured skins of the Amerindians of today are the bio-physical heritage of these Asian migrants.

Many millennia later—perhaps about eight thousand years ago—some groups began to seek their livelihood by planting and cultivating food-crops instead of simply gathering wild plants and seeds or hunting animals. With the development of pottery, carving, and architecture, and later of metal-working and weaving, they left artifacts from which we can form some idea of the whereabouts and nature of these beginnings of settled life. Archaic cultures bloomed and withered in a great variety of forms and places, some of them in conditions which today seem least likely to nurture civilization—the rain forests of Central America, the sandy deserts of the Pacific coast, and the desolate wastes of the high Andean plateau. Whether their development was stimulated by cultural influences which may have reached America from across the Pacific or the Atlantic long before the coming of the Spaniards is still hotly debated by scholars; Thor Heyerdahl's recent Atlantic journey in a papyrus-reed boat has emphasized the possibility of this. There have certainly been found in Central America great numbers of pre-Columbian terracotta heads apparently modelled from Negroid and European, as well as from Asiatic types quite dissimilar to those from which the Amerindians appear to have sprung. However this may be, with or without external stimuli, some communities evolved high cultures showing remarkable sophistication in their arts, religious beliefs, and social organization. Some remained at the stone-age level and none progressed beyond the stage of bronze-age civilization. Surprisingly, their achievements were accomplished without the use of the wheel, so basic elsewhere for transport and building—the wheel was known as a toy, but its practical possibilities do not seem to have occurred to them. They did not have any domestic animal higher than the llama; nor did they possess any form of writing more serviceable than the Mayan glyphs or the Mexicans' picture-writing. At the coming of the Spaniards, two remarkable and very dissimilar high cultures were in full flower—the 'empires' of the Aztecs and the Incas—whilst others had already flowered and faded.

On the evidence at present available—for fresh discoveries are constantly calling for a revision of our assumptions and many sites still remain to be excavated—it looks as if the oldest centre of civilized life in Middle America, and probably in the whole western hemisphere, developed in the torrid coastal zone to the south of Vera Cruz and in adjacent Tabasco during the period 1200–400 BC. We know almost nothing about this ancient people, not even the name by which they called themselves. Archaeologists refer to them as 'Olmecs' and to their culture as that of La Venta, after the island in a coastal mangrove swamp where they raised a large clay pyramid and several lesser mounds and left some of the most striking and enigmatic vestiges of their religion—gigantic stone heads, eight feet or more in height and many tons in weight, whose rather negroid features curiously combine the chubbiness of a baby with the snarl of a wild beast. Archaeologists now tend to believe that these Olmec heads are not modelled from any human prototype but portray the mythical offspring of human mother and jaguar, a beast regarded with awe for its strength and ferocity. A remarkable carving depicting the union of a jaguar and a woman has been found, together with several gigantic heads carved from basalt blocks, at a site at San Lorenzo which may be even older than La Venta. The same jaguar 'baby-face' emblem is also found on jade figurines and pendants discovered in other parts of Middle America, often hundreds of miles from La Venta, suggesting that the Olmecs spread their culture widely by trade or conquest. Other Olmec centres survived the destruction of La Venta, and at one of these, at Tres Zapotes some hundred miles away, there has survived the oldest dated monument yet discovered in the New World (though some artifacts are known to be very much older), the fragment of a stone column or stele bearing a hieroglyph which, in the 'Long Count' calendar later elaborated by the Maya, bears a date corresponding to the year 31 BC. It thus seems possible that the Olmec should be credited with the invention of the calendar, and perhaps of hieroglyphic writing too, in the New World, and that theirs was the mother culture nourishing the various high cultures which were later to bloom in that area. The strange carved figures of dancers, with their accompanying hieroglyphs, which are the oldest monuments of the Zapotecs' impressive mountain-top site at Monte Albán, in the Mexican state of Oaxaca, may well be of Olmec derivation. The same influence can certainly be traced in the ruined monuments of Izapan, in the torrid border country between Mexico and Guatemala, which seem transitional between the Olmec and the Maya cultures. At a site further to the west

(El Baúl), well into the territory of modern Guatemala, an Izapan stele has been found bearing the date corresponding to 36 AD—still two and a half centuries before the earliest Maya dated inscriptions. On the outskirts of Guatemala City itself, and now submerged by the expanding capital, are the ruins of Kaminaljuyú, a once important cultural centre whose remains denote a blending of Izapan influence with a sculptural style which was later to be carried to perfection by the Maya.

The Maya

The Maya inhabited a million and a quarter square miles between the Caribbean and the Pacific, the area now covered by Guatemala and adjacent parts of British Honduras, Mexico, El Salvador, and Honduras. The heartland of their civilization was what is now the low-lying tropical rain-forests of Guatemala's province of Petén, where the 'slash-and-burn' method of agriculture, still practised in the area today, was evolved—a technique at first sight primitive and wasteful, since it involves clearing a patch of land and then abandoning it for a new clearing when the ground becomes exhausted, but actually well suited to light, easily eroded tropical soils. Cultivated in this way, the land can be made productive, for one man's plot or *milpa* may support a dozen people. This method of cultivation released a large labour force for work on the ceremonial centres and great pyramids, whose ruins rise impressively and mysteriously today over the ocean of the jungle. The crop grown on the *milpas* was Indian corn or maize, evolved from the cross-pollination of indigenous wild plants to become the staple food of pre-Columbian Middle America and the most important item in the Indians' diet of maize, beans, chilli-peppers, tomatoes, and squashes. The *tortillas* eaten throughout Middle America today are probably prepared after the fashion of the ancient Maya; the maize kernels being left to soak overnight in a solution of lime and water before being ground into a dough, kneaded into a thin pancake, and then toasted on a clay griddle over a slow fire. The many myths and legends current about the origins of maize attest its importance for Amerindian civilization. *Popol Vuh*, the sacred book of the Quiché Indians, relates how the gods first tried to fashion human beings out of mud, then from wood, and finally succeeded only when they kneaded them out of maize-dough. (See page 307.)

Recent archaeological discoveries and research have gradually been modifying our picture of Maya life and achievements. It used to be thought that this gifted stone-age people was an essentially peace-loving race, ruled by a wise and benevolent priesthood, and dwelling in cities built around the temple pyramids. The partial decipherment of Maya hieroglyphs, and discoveries such as those of the dramatic wall-paintings at Bonampak and the funerary crypt in the Temple of Inscriptions at Palenque, strongly suggest that the Maya were formidable fighters ruled by secular kings who caused at least some of the great pyramids to be reared as their funeral monuments, in much the same way as did the Egyptian Pharaohs. Their 'cities' could be more properly described as straggling ceremonial centres, often covering many square miles, and comprising a complex of causeways, patios, pyramids, palaces, and other public buildings, the exact nature of which is not yet clear to us, as well as clusters of simple private dwellings, but little which indicates the regular streets and other features of a settled urban community. Though they did not constitute the ruling class, the priests certainly played a most important role in omen-reading, record-keeping, and ritual, as determined by the passage of the seasons and the conjunction of the heavenly bodies. The patient observation and recording of the latter, with their assumed power over human affairs for good or evil, led to the elaboration of the Maya's cosmography and their most astonishingly original and sophisticated achievement—the calendar. Though its basic concept may have been invented by the Olmecs, no other people has equalled the Maya in their obsession with the mystery of time present, time past, and time future, or gone to such lengths to plot its course. Not only men, but the gods themselves, were identified according to the birth-date assigned to each of them. All human activities were regulated as far as possible according to the favourable or unfavourable prognostications of the almanac. Past events were recorded, probably by individual reigns, on the intricately carved stone columns or stelae which are to be found on all the principal Maya sites.

The numerical system in use by the Maya was simple and flexible, its only symbols being a dot for one, a bar for five, and a stylized shell for nought. These symbols were grouped in vertical columns, read from the bottom upwards, their value increasing in multiples of twenty according to their relative positions. Thus, the figure 8 would appear as ⦁⦁⦁, the total number of days in a year (by our reckoning) as

$$(18 \times 20 = 360)$$
$$(= 5)$$
$$\text{Total} = 365$$

and the number of years which have elapsed between the birth of Christ and the year in which this book was written as

$$(4 \times 400 = 1600)$$
$$(18 \times 20 = 360)$$
$$(= 11)$$
$$\text{Total} = 1971$$

The calendar itself was far too complicated to be described here except in briefest outline. It was formed basically of two interlocking cycles. One consisted of twenty named days multiplied by thirteen of the numerals listed above to give a total '260-day count'—a system still in use in remote parts of Middle America. The other cycle, consisting of eighteen 'months' of twenty days each, plus five ill-omened days at the end, made up a 'vague' year of 365 days (as compared with the true solar year of about $365\frac{1}{4}$ days). The two cycles interlocked to produce the 'calendar round' of 52 years. Where a longer time span needed to be indicated, as in the stelae inscriptions, the 'Long Count' was used—an elaborate system for calculating time in units respectively equivalent to 20, 360, 7,200 and 144,000 days, and comprising a 'Grand

Cycle' of nearly 5,200 years. Like other ancient peoples of Latin America, the Maya believed in the periodic destruction and recreation of the cosmos at the close of every Grand Cycle. According to their calculations, our present universe was held to have come into existence in the year equivalent to 3113 BC (much as the Fundamentalists held that Adam had been created and placed in the Garden of Eden in 4004 BC) and was due for annihilation on Christmas Eve, 2011 AD—a prophecy of doom which we who live under the shadow of nuclear destruction are in no position to laugh off.

If the intricacies of the Maya calendar can now be fairly well understood, their method of glyph-writing has still not yet yielded up all its secrets. Thanks largely to the work of the Russian scholar Knorosov, it is now however known that the Maya script is not to be read by means of a simple 'alphabet', such as that drawn up by Bishop Landa, the sixteenth-century Spanish historian, but is more in the nature of a syllabary combining phonetic elements with semantic or ideographic concepts derived from primitive picture-writing. Furthermore, it has been discovered that Maya inscriptions, which were formerly assumed to be exclusively concerned with religious and calendrical matters, also served to record historical events. Nor has the Maya script survived only in carved inscriptions. They also wrote in 'books' or scrolls made from strips of bark which were coated with gesso and folded like screens. In his zeal to root out idolatry, Bishop Landa ordered the destruction of all these 'books', only three of which, dealing with ritual and astronomical exegesis, are known to have escaped the holocaust and survived to our day. There have also come down to us certain texts originally written in Maya and later translated into Spanish, such as the esoteric jumble of genealogies and religious lore known as the *Book of Chilam Balam*, and the *Popol Vuh*, or *Book of the People*, with its creation myths and entertaining legends (see page 307). There are but few crumbs of historical fact to be found in this strangely spiced fare, and for a reconstruction of Maya history we must turn to the evidence of the stelae, the temple pyramids, and other archaeological remains.

Scholars generally distinguish certain clearly marked phases in the rise and decline of Maya civilization: a long formative period from about 1500 BC to 150 AD, followed by a short proto-classical stage leading to the great classical age between 300 and 900 AD. This in turn falls into two stages; the earlier, ending about 600 AD, was based on the lowlands of Petén, once a region of parkland and forest before the latter encroached and finally submerged the abandoned centres of human habitation, when the focus of civilization shifted to the flat highlands of Yucatán. Some time during the early classical period the Maya seem to have undergone, probably as the result of invasion, the powerful influence of Teotihuacán (see page 9). A further wave of invasions from the north, this time by the aggressive Toltecs (see page 10), who brought with them new gods and culture styles, ended the classical period of Maya civilization in Yucatán. For a while (under the 'New Empire'), a synthesis of Maya and Toltec culture bloomed at Chichen Itzá, famous for its great temple pyramid dedicated to Kukulcan (Queztalcóatl), the Temple of the Warriors, the vast court where the ceremonial Ball Game was played, and the sacred pool or *cenote*, the dredging of which continues to yield up its treasure of artifacts and sacrificial human remains. By the beginning of the thirteenth century, the Toltecs seem to have passed from the scene, the vestiges of Maya greatness disappear in inter-tribal and dynastic strife, until the coming of the Spaniards finally extinguishes their independence together with that of the Quiché, Cakchiquel, and other tribes of Maya descent who had established small kingdoms to the south, in the valleys of highland Guatemala.

An aura of mystery still envelops this most remarkable of stone-age civilizations. How are we to account for the artistic and mathematical genius of the Maya, which expressed itself in the erection of impressive temple-pyramids, with their superb sculpture and wall-paintings, in the life-like perfection of their exquisitely carved figurines, in the accuracy of their astronomical observations and the complexities of their calendar? And why, in the ninth century of our era, should magnificent 'cities' or ceremonial centres like Tikal, in the heart of the Petén lowlands, Copán, with its glyph-embellished ceremonial stairway and its great ball-court, Palenque, with its corbel-vaulted aqueduct, its lovely temples and observatory watch-tower, have been deserted by their inhabitants and abandoned to the tropical forest? Many different hypotheses have been advanced: natural calamities such as plague, floods, or earthquake, enemy invasion or the revolt of a peasantry determined to shake off the oppressive yoke of their astronomer-priests, soil exhaustion and the inexorable encroachment of a tropical jungle which stone tools could not keep at bay. All these are but conjecture. Nor is the secret known to their few surviving descendants such as the Lacandón tribesmen, who still steal from their huts in remote jungle clearings to burn copal incense before figures whom they worship in the ruined temples. Sometimes they lead a white man to their secret place, and a Bonampak, with its astounding wall-paintings, stands revealed. Hardly a year goes by without some corner of the jungle canopy being lifted to add a further chapter to the still unfolding story of the Maya.

Teotihuacán and the Toltecs

Roughly contemporaneous with the early period of the Maya's classical age, another high culture was developing in Central Mexico. Teotihuacán, some thirty miles north-east of Mexico City, was both a great religious and cultural centre and a true metropolis, with a large urban population whose dwellings, once the enveloping layer of maize and cactus plantation has been cleared from them, are found to have ranged from splendidly decorated palaces to single-storeyed buildings made up of numerous chambers or cells built round patios after the fashion of monasteries or university colleges. The dominant features of the site are a huge pyramid, the Temple of the Sun, now strikingly but inaccurately restored, the smaller Temple of the Moon, the misnamed Citadel comprising palaces and temples adorned with splendidly carved emblems of serpent-heads and rain-gods and once brilliant with facings of red and white stucco, and the broad ceremonial Avenue of the Dead. Who were the inhabitants of Teotihuacán and whence did they come? Skilled carvers like the Olmecs, from whom they may have derived their jaguar motifs, they constructed their stupendous pyramids with a more consciously architectural sense and a keener eye to astronomical siting. Their beautifully encrusted stone masks, and their myriads of figurines, some of them with movable limbs like toys, suggest a ritual use of a nature unknown to us. But already, in Teotihuacán, we find the chief deities which, in different guises, all the ancient peoples of Mexico came to worship. Tlaloc, the rain-god, was particularly venerated in this parched land, and gay murals depict his worshippers happily disporting themselves in his watery paradise. Quetzalcóatl, the plumed serpent, already has his cult. The very name of the city denotes 'the place where the gods were made' or manifested themselves, and myths relate how one of their number threw himself into the fire and was transformed into the sun, and how his example was followed by the other gods so that the heavenly bodies might be set in motion and light and life brought to the earth. From this myth there was in time to follow a grim corollary; if the gods had sacrificed themselves for mankind, then they should be repaid and nourished by human lives. But in this golden age of Teotihuacán war and human sacrifice appear to have played but little part. The city was unfortified, the warrior-figure rarely portrayed, and the pantheon beneficent.

During the six centuries or so of its existence, Teotihuacán spread its influence far and wide throughout Middle America. Its sway may have extended over an area wider than that of the Aztec empire. The great pyramid of Cholula, the largest man-made structure of ancient America, was begun under Teotihuacán influence and dedicated to Quetzalcóatl. The architecture and frescoes of Monte Albán show the same influence, and the Izapan-Maya culture of Kaminaljuyú too was so strongly affected by it early in the fifth century AD that the city seems to have been altogether rebuilt in the style of Teotihuacán. But of the latter's own history we know very little, for its inhabitants did not share the Maya's passion for recording dates and inscriptions. We cannot even be sure that it was governed, as is generally assumed, by priest-rulers. Nor do we know the events which led to its destruction and abandonment. All we can say is that soon after 600 AD Teotihuacán suddenly ceased to exert influence. Into the vacuum created by its downfall came the Toltecs, semi-civilized warriors from the border zone between the cultivated lands and the deserts of northern Mexico. The harsher, warlike spirit of these newcomers is apparent from the new motifs which distinguish the ruined monuments of their chief city, Tula (Tollán), some 50 miles north-west of the modern Mexican capital, in the state of Hidalgo: jaguars, coyotes, and eagles tearing at human hearts, snakes devouring skeletons, square stone columns decorated with bas-reliefs of warriors, the enigmatic Chac-Mool, reclining figures with their faces boldly turned towards the onlooker and their hands clasping an open bowl as if in readiness to receive their offering of human hearts. Yet these warlike people were so quick to acquire the culture of the people they conquered, that the very name Toltec became in time synonymous with 'craftsman'. Tula passed into legend as a place of magical plenty and perfection, and when fate at length swept this people from the scene, fresh dynasties of Mexican rulers would seek to enhance their status by claiming Toltec descent.

Inseparable from the history of the Toltecs is the mysterious figure of Quetzalcóatl, whom we have seen worshipped as a beneficent deity at Teotihuacán. The name, confusingly, is also used to denote not only their chief god but the Toltecs' high priest and ruler. 'The priest and guardian of the god was also called Quetzalcóatl', an old poem relates. 'They stood in such awe of him that they obediently did whatsoever he commanded them. He taught them saying: "He is the one true god, and Quetzalcóatl is his name. He demands nothing of you in sacrifice, save only butterflies and snakes; these only you may give him." ' How can the cult of this peace-loving god be reconciled with the martial practices of the Toltecs? The cult, it seems, was challenged by Tezcatlipoca ('Smoking Mirror'), the patron god of the knightly orders who were the spear-head of Toltec military expansion. Tula was rent by civil war. Its ruler at the time was a historic personage, Quetzalcóatl Topíltzin, who was ousted and forced into exile. His fate gave rise to a famous cycle of poetry and legend; how Tezcatlipoca's magic caused Quetzalcóatl to succumb to temptation and weakness, his grief on bidding farewell to his city, the sufferings of himself and those who remained faithful to him as he journeyed towards the coast. There, one legend relates, he immolated himself in the flames of the setting sun and was re-born as the Morning Star. Another version has it that Quetzalcóatl embarked on a raft and disappeared over the waves. Here legend may merge with the historical fact that, towards the end of the tenth century, a Toltec expedition is known to have set sail across the Gulf, under a leader called Quetzalcóatl, to land in Yucatán where a new Mexican–Maya dynasty was founded at Chichen Itzá (see page 7). But legend also foretold that one day Quetzalcóatl would return to resume his sway over Mexico. It was this belief that lived on to inspire the Aztec ruler Montezuma II with the superstitious dread that the bearded Spaniard leading the band of desperadoes who were determined to wrest his empire from him was none other than the god himself.

The Aztecs

The eclipse of the military power of Tula was followed by a period of anarchy. Bands of Toltec warriors under local leaders carved out principalities for themselves, no less than five of them in the valley of Mexico alone. Other predatory groups drove down from the northern deserts. These were the barbarous Chichimec, 'descendants of the dog', who established themselves by conquest or by alliance with the Toltecs and gradually came in turn under the influence of the culturally more advanced sedentary population. One tribe, known as the Aztecs or Colhua Mexica, after wandering for years under the protection of their god Huitzilopochtli, a form of the Toltec warriors' fierce war-god Tezcatlipoca, established themselves on some marshy islets in the great Lake of Mexico. Legend relates that the sight of an eagle perched on a cactus and grasping a snake in its beak was the sign indicating that they had reached the place foreordained as the seat of their future empire. There was little at first to suggest that the savage newcomers were destined for higher things. The Aztecs had at this time little to distinguish them save a zest for fighting and an already obsessive concern with human sacrifice. It was not long before they showed their mettle. It is recorded that, in the year 1323, the lord of Colhuacán sought to seal a pact with them by the gift of his daughter. She was promptly sacrificed and the father invited to attend a ceremony in honour of Huitzilopochtli, where the high priest appeared clad in the flayed skin of the girl.

By serving first as mercenaries, then as allies, of neighbouring states, and finally turning against the latter when they had grown strong enough, the Aztecs steadily extended their power basis from their lacustrine capital at Tenochtitlán. Under the guidance of Tlacaélel, kinsman and chief adviser to three successive rulers and reformer of the army, administration, and judicial system, the records were rewritten to present the Aztecs as the only legitimate heirs of the Toltecs and the bearers of a divine mission. Their tribal deity Huitzilopochtli was identified with the god who, according to legend, had thrown himself into the fire at Teotihuacán and so brought into being the life-giving sun. To sustain the sun-god in his daily course across the heavens, human lives had constantly to be sacrificed in return. Should this life-giving nourishment fail, the demons of the night would descend upon the earth and make an end of all human existence. It was the divine mission of the Aztec warrior race to ward off this doom by procuring, through force of arms, an unending supply of captives whose hearts were then torn out upon the sacrificial stone. We have seen, in our own age of miraculous scientific advance, that a man may indeed live on with the heart of another; that the gods themselves could be so sustained was an argument of fearsome logic to the primitive mind. The belief also offered a pious rationale for the Aztecs' instinctive blood-lust and provided an effective way of reducing the military manpower of subject or rival peoples. Tezcatlipoca and Huitzilopochtli reigned supreme from the reeking temples. When the great new temple-pyramid of Tenochtitlán was dedicated, twenty thousand victims were sacrificed in its honour. Though his spirit may have lived on in such rare figures as Nezahualcóyotl, the poet-king of Texcoco (later absorbed by the Aztecs), it seemed that the gentle, beneficent Quetzalcóatl, who required of his worshippers only snakes and butterflies, had indeed forsaken Mexico.

For all their institutionalized ferocity, the Aztecs showed a remarkable capacity for assimilating and developing the culture of the peoples whom they came to dominate militarily. If their art lacks the classic refinement of the Maya, it has a harshly dramatic and sometimes terrifying vigour characteristic of the race. The art treasures sent back by Cortés to the Emperor Charles V made a profound impression on Albrecht Dürer, one of the greatest European artists of his day, as Mexican sculpture has deeply influenced Henry Moore in our own. The Aztecs were lovers of flowers, dancing, music, and poetry. They had a large and varied literature ranging from epic, lyric, and elegiac poetry to myth, esoteric religious lore, and historical narrative. This was basically an oral literature, versified so as to be more easily remembered. As a further aid to the memory, folding screen-books were filled with pictographic and rebus script which was the nearest the Mexicans came to true writing. These were studied and committed to memory in schools known as *calmecac*, which the sons of the nobility and those intended for the priesthood were privileged to attend. If they lacked the mathematical genius of the Maya, they kept meticulously to a similar calendrical system which prescribed innumerable and carefully regulated religious observances for the whole community. Respect for the gods and one's parents, self-control, modesty, and good manners, in addition to the essential military virtues of courage, stoical endurance of suffering, and devoted loyalty, were the qualities most esteemed by Aztec society.

By the time the Spaniards arrived, this society had evolved from a simple tribal basis into something like a complex, highly stratified feudal system. At its apex stood the all-powerful 'emperor', elected from the ranks of the nobility and assisted by his Council of Four. He was a semi-divine figure who not only held supreme secular and military authority but was also mediator between his people and the gods. The nobles, distinguished by the splendour of their attire and supported by the labour of serfs who worked their estates, held the chief posts in the administration and the army and had almost evolved into a hereditary caste. They were closely linked to the priesthood by family ties and a common training in the *calmecac*. The priests were responsible not only for the gory business of temple sacrifice but for the elaborate ritual, based on the changing conjunction of the heavenly bodies, by which the daily life of the Aztecs was regulated. The skilled craftsmen working in gold, feathers, obsidian, jade, and other precious stones were exempt from military and agricultural labour and treated as a privileged class. The mass of commoners laboured on the land and on the construction of temples and other public works, paid the taxes, and were liable for service in the army, though the latter was becoming more and more of a professional force. They were divided into *calpulli* or clans which allotted the land required for the support of each family and formed the basic administrative units of the 'empire'. Beneath the commoners came a growing mass of landless peasants and, mostly in the metropolis, the slaves.

The agricultural basis of the Aztec state remained the cultivation of the staple foods of Middle America—beans, squashes, and especially maize. In dry areas, some forms of rudimentary irrigation were practised, and on the Pacific coast farmers had discovered how to increase the fertility of their fields by the use of fish manure. In the heavily populated region round Tenochtitlán an ingenious means had been devised of growing crops on incredibly fertile plots formed by superimposed layers of mud and rotting lake vegetation, the *chinampas* or so-called 'floating gardens'. Food, clothing, pottery, tools, ornaments, the whole produce of the Mexican state, including slaves cooped up in wooden cages—for, by a curious law, if they escaped there they were free and none but their lawful owners could recapture them—were brought into the markets, whose vast size and admirable organization amazed the Spaniards.

Money was unknown, but barter was general, cocoa beans (the *chocolatl* which was later to be found so attractive to the European palate), goose-quills filled with gold dust, thin copper axe-heads, and other objects serving as the media of exchange. Some of these wares had been brought to Tenochtitlán in the caravans of specially authorized traders known as *pochteca*. The latter formed a class apart—they may indeed have been well versed in commerce before the coming of the Aztecs—and performed a useful service to the state by taking advantage of their trading expeditions to collect detailed information of distant lands, with which the Aztec war leaders could then brief themselves in planning their campaigns of conquest. The diligence of trader and peasant was supplemented by other resources of crucial importance for the maintenance of the large parasitic classes of priesthood, state bureaucracy, nobility, and army. This was the tribute drawn from every part of the Aztec domains, a tribute which in the heyday of Tenochtitlán reached the staggering yearly amount of two million cotton cloaks, huge quantities of other clothes, ornaments, and luxury articles, as well as seven thousand tons of maize and other kinds of food in abundance, all borne to the capital on the backs of human carriers.

The 'empire' was thus a mosaic of provinces or small city states bound to Tenochtitlán by the tribute nexus. Their status varied, but in general, so long as they produced their tribute promptly, the Aztec overlords interfered but little in their internal affairs, though they might replace an unco-operative ruler by one of their own officials and would certainly give the local gods a place in the Aztec pantheon. By the time the Spaniards arrived, the number of these states had risen to thirty-eight, and they covered an area straddling Middle America from the Pacific to the Atlantic, and from the northern deserts where the Chichimec roamed to the decayed Mexican cities of Guatemala. But there were gaps in the pattern. Yucatán remained outside the Aztec borders, as did some of the Zapotec and Mixtec principalities with their rich culture, and the powerful Tarascan kingdom of Michoacán, in the south-west. Tlaxcala remained a hostile enclave in the very heart of their territory; if the Aztecs never succeeded in conquering it, at least they forced it to furnish an abundant supply of captives for the ever-hungry gods. The coming of the Spaniards gave the Tlaxcalans and other subject peoples a miraculous opportunity to turn the tables on their enemies. The empire of the Aztecs, for all its brilliance and impressive power structure, was based on nothing more solid than ruthless militarism, tax extortion, and ritual genocide. Whether it might have evolved in time into a more civilized and viable polity we can only speculate. The Aztec warrior élite rose to power and maintained it by the obsidian-bladed sword-club and the barbed darts hurled from the *atlatl*; it went down before the greater power of Toledan steel, the cross-bow and the arquebus, and the pent-up hatred of the peoples they had subjugated.

The Pre-Inca civilizations

The Aztecs can hardly have failed to become aware, through the reports of *pochteca* trading with the Indians of Guatemala, of the existence of other civilized peoples far to the south. During the millennia of prehistoric southward migrations, tribal groups had filtered through the swamps and forests of the isthmus and out to the Colombian and Venezuelan savannas and the vast Amazonian jungle beyond. Some had then followed the valleys leading up from the tropical lowlands through gaps in the stupendous Cordillera on to the bleak Andean plateau. Others had penetrated to the long, narrow arid zone between the Cordillera and the Pacific ocean. In the seemingly inhospitable habitat of *altiplano* and coastal desert there developed a series of high cultures, of which that of the Incas was the latest and most imposing expression. Like the Aztecs then, the Incas were late-comers to the stage of history. Their exit was to be no less sudden and tragic, but the part they played on it, and the civilizations whose rise and fall formed the prelude to their own, were very different.

The first permanent human settlements developed, in all probability, along the water-line where terrestrial desert meets the ocean waste. Here the mighty upsurge of cold mineral-rich water from the submarine depths is rich too in plankton, which nourishes countless shoals of small fish preyed upon both by larger species and by immense numbers of cormorants, pelicans, gannets, and other birds. Man, too, found sustenance from this inexhaustible marine larder, and the deep middens which mark the site of fishermen's encampments indicate the existence of this archaic stage of man's evolution in these regions as early as 3000 BC. Some two thousand years later, there occurred an event of signal importance; to the indigenous food plants, beans and squashes, maize was added—introduced, probably, from Middle America. Men began to cultivate the valleys formed by the few rivers which, fed by the mountain snows, made their way to the sea at intervals across the parched land. Over many parts of the coast and offshore islands, droppings from innumerable sea-birds had formed a canopy of *guano*. This, it was discovered, when spread over the fields of their fluvial oases, enabled farmers to raise two or three crops a year without exhausting the soil. Once they had devised ways of making the most of the precious river-water and attained the degree of social cohesion required for carrying out irrigation works for common use, the stage was set for the flowering of civilization.

Even before this time, elements of settled life had begun to make their appearance elsewhere in Peru. Through excavations carried out at Kotosh, in a valley 5,000 feet up on the eastern slopes of the Cordillera, work has been discovered which dates back, according to the Japanese archaeologists investigating the site, to well before 2000 BC. A maze of small, room-like constructions surrounds a sacred precinct ornamented with the enigmatic emblem of a pair of crossed hands. What did this cult object signify and who were its devotees? We know as little about it as about the origins of the Chavín cult, so named from the site of the temple platforms honeycombed with interconnecting galleries and chambers, at Chavín de Huantar, in another valley of the northern highlands of Peru. Some archaeologists believe that the Chavín cult derives from the distant Olmecs. But instead of the gigantic basalt heads and the were-jaguar myth of those ancient culture-bearers of Middle America, we find stone carvings of labyrinthine complexity; a feline god, either jaguar or the puma more commonly found in South America, at the centre of an intricate web of stylized snakes, mouths, eyes, and geometrical forms. The absence of fortifications suggests that Chavín may not have been a city or administrative-military centre but rather a sanctuary attracting pilgrims, as shrines like Copacabana on Lake Titicaca continue to attract tens of thousands today. Pottery and stone carvings in the Chavín style have been found widely distributed throughout north and central Peru, and appear to have spread quickly over that area between 900 and 800 BC. A series of explorations carried out in the 1960s to the north of this site, in the high jungle round Chachapoyas, in the Department of Amazonas, has revealed an extensive archaeological zone of temple, cliff necropolis, and fortification. Whether this is related to the Chavín cult and may throw light on the latter's origins and extent must await further study. But there seems little doubt that, whether the centre of an empire or only of a religious cult, Chavín appears to have been the first civilization to extend its influence over any large area of Peru.

Technological advances in this period include the beginnings of metallurgy, in the form of gold ornaments bearing Chavín motifs; the development of pottery in the coastal regions at about the same time that maize was introduced; and the use of textiles, starting with the knotting of cotton fibres and culminating in the elaboration of lengths of sophisticated fabrics characterized by workmanship, colouring, and design which rank them amongst the most beautiful in the ancient world. Some of these antedate the beginnings of the Christian era and have survived in perfect condition after being buried for nearly two millennia beneath the dry desert sand. The most spectacular finds were made in the peninsula of Paracas, near Pisco, where the Peruvian archaeologist Tello disinterred four hundred mummies wrapped in their sumptuous shrouds. We can only wonder at the time and effort which went into the creation of these works of art, and the religious significance attached to the designs with which they are so richly embroidered—birds and fish, dancing warriors with trophy heads, bizarre, writhing figures of many kinds ranged in a sequence of probably religious significance and worked in a rich range of harmonious colour. Were their wearers once priests, left in their desert sepulchres to continue interceding for the living with the mysterious deities represented on their gorgeous attire?

South of Paracas, and a little later in date, a culture developed which takes its name from the valley of Nazca and is famous for the brilliance and delicate workmanship of its polychrome pottery. The area covered by this culture was not large, and the absence of military fortifications suggests that the people were uninterested in military conquest—though head-hunting was practised amongst them, to judge from the prevalence of trophy heads as a pottery motif. Their pottery gives us only an occasional glimpse—a mouse nibbling a maize-cob or a delightful one-man band—into the life of this people. The mythical beings of their religion, similar to those on the Paracas textiles, figure more frequently in it, and religion too, or perhaps astronomical observation, must have inspired the pattern of long straight lines and other geometrical figures gouged from the desert which remain one of the archaeological puzzles of the region.

In the more northerly coastal valleys, centring round that of Moche, there developed another culture roughly contemporaneous with that of Nazca. The abundance of pottery and other artifacts which have survived, and the extraordinary realism which Mochica potters brought to their art, have given us an unparalleled insight into the life of this talented people. We are shown how they built their houses, thatched and sometimes several storeys in height, and equipped with air-vents so as to catch the cool off-sea breezes; how they wove their textiles, for their paintings show in detail the weavers sitting at their looms under the eye of factory overseers; how they fought their wars, carried off their captives, and left criminals exposed to the beaks of hungry vultures. We see their lords carried in litters, their hurrying messengers carrying bags of beans painted with dots which may have been coded messages, their doctors examining patients, women giving birth to children, men washing their hair, playing musical instruments, or fishing from their boats of *totora* reeds. Most extraordinary of all is the intimate portrayal of their sexual practices—a veritable *Kama sutra* in ceramics of startling frankness and variety. Birds and animals are portrayed with equal realism—llamas grazing, mating, scratching their ears; ocelots, desert-foxes, guinea-pigs, deer, frogs, owls, pelicans, parrots, birds, and fishes of every description. The range of human types is no less astonishing: ceramic portraits of turbaned warriors and other notables of extraordinary power and beauty; men and women of every age and condition, deformed and diseased persons depicted so faithfully that medical science today has no difficulty in diagnosing the ailments from which they suffered. No people, in short, has left us a more vivid or extensive picture of the way they lived.

And yet, since they had no written records, we know almost nothing of their history and little of their religion. It was natural that a water-cult should have developed in that parched land, and the fish-, animal-, and maize-deities shown on their pots must all have had a place in their pantheon. The two great pyramids of adobe bricks dedicated respectively to the Sun and the Moon also attest the importance of those heavenly bodies in their worship. They attest too the high degree of social organization which Mochica society must have attained. But that society seems to have been shattered around the year 1000 AD under the impact of the invasion from Tiahuanaco, in the Peruvian highlands, which we shall be considering shortly. Nazca, too, was overwhelmed. The Mochica appear to have been driven northwards from the half-dozen valleys where their civilization flourished. But two to three hundred years later, when the power of Tiahuanaco declined, their residual culture still retained enough vigour to influence the states which began to re-emerge on the shore of the Pacific.

The most important of these new states, that of the Chimú, reformed round the nucleus of the Moche valley. The desert kingdoms of Peru, like the empire of the Egyptian Pharaohs, were dependent on the supply and control of river-water; but in Peru this came, not from one Nile, but from many little

Niles separated by wide stretches of desert. The streams were tapped as they descended from the Cordillera and, with the help of dams and aqueducts, were led down to fertilize ever-widening slices of desert. These irrigation works, some of which are still in use, are masterpieces of early engineering. One of the canals (La Cumbre) was seventy miles in length and carried water from a height of 4,000 feet down to sea level. Another, even longer, shows a width of eight feet and a depth of six. Thanks to their irrigation network, their diligent terracing of mountain slopes, and their use of fertilizer, the Chimú were able to grow enough food to support the population of their capital Chan Chan, the largest city of pre-Columbian America. Its ruins, long a happy hunting-ground for *huaqueros*, stand a few miles outside the city of Trujillo. When viewed from the air, the whole huge urban complex is seen to consist of ten or more great rectangular areas, each enclosed by adobe walls sometimes forty or so feet in height and once adorned with friezes, which are thought to have housed different clans. The open spaces between them were covered with market-gardens, reservoirs, cemeteries, and a jumble of small dwellings. The administration of this complex city-state, and the construction and operation of the large-scale irrigation works on which it was based, demanded an advanced degree of social control, and there is evidence that the Kingdom of Chimor was a despotic and highly stratified state. Its pottery, characterized by the stereotyped and monochrome imitation of Mochica models and mass-produced for local use and for trade with the highlands and, by balsa-raft, with Ecuador, reflects the nature of this society. At its apex, the Grand Chimú ruled in a luxury and ceremonial splendour which the Incas were later to emulate. His sway extended over eighteen coastal valleys stretching from Tumbez in the north to the fortress of Paramonga in the south, more than six hundred miles away. It was buttressed, too, by an alliance with the vigorous Andean kingdom of Cajamarca. Nevertheless, the Chimor-Cajamarca alliance was defeated and the rule of the Grand Chimú brought to an end when the armies of a still mightier empire, that of the Incas, swept down from the Cordillera in the 1460s.

We must now turn to consider those cultures whose impact on the coastal kingdoms had been shaped by the very different environment of the Peruvian highlands. The desolate *altiplano*, standing two miles or so above sea level and swept by the winds blowing down from the snow-capped peaks of the Cordillera, seems at first sight as unfavourable a setting for civilized life as the deserts of the coast. Yet primitive man had not found it so. Maize had even grown there in sheltered places. But the great staple of life in the Andes is the potato. Stones have been found crudely carved in the shape of potatoes with human heads, suggesting that primitive farmers identified Pachamama, the life-giving earth-spirit, with that protean tuber of which some 300 varieties were developed through its age-long cultivation, before the Spaniards introduced it to Europe with far-reaching results on the social and political life of countries like Ireland and Poland. The Indian's animals were his flocks of llamas and alpacas; their wool provided him with clothing, their stringy flesh with his rare meat dishes, and their dung with his fuel. The basic unit of society was the *ayllu*, or kinship group, which still survives in attenuated form today. The *ayllu* held the land worked by its members, directed their communal efforts, and traced descent from a common totemic ancestor—condor or puma, strangely-shaped rock, cave, or mountain stream. Such things were regarded as *huaca*, sacred objects associated with nature spirits and looked upon by the Indians with superstitious awe, as they still are today. In addition to these primitive animistic beliefs, the Andean Indians developed in time a more sophisticated cult, the nature of which we can only surmise through the enigmatic carvings and motifs of their pottery and textiles, and through the ruins of abandoned ceremonial sites. Of the latter, the most famous stands on a bleak plain a few miles from the shores of Lake Titicaca and takes its name from the nearby village of Tiahuanaco.

Tiahuanaco has suffered sorely from the depredations of local inhabitants who have taken its stone-work for the construction of their churches and houses, and even for the embankment of the local railway. Yet what remains is still impressive: a series of large, roughly carved statues and other monoliths, the most striking of which is a gateway hewn from a single block of lava bearing the elaborately carved figure of what appears to be the weeping sun-god or the creator Viracocha, set amidst the ruins of a stone-faced stepped pyramid and adjacent structures. Other partially excavated mounds suggest that this was not only a great religious centre but a city which had known a long period of human habitation. Who built Tiahuanaco and dwelt there remains a mystery. Indian legend has it that it was raised in a single night by a race of giants. Modern speculation has been scarcely less fantastic. Some have claimed for Tiahuanaco a fabulous antiquity and hailed it as the cradle of all American civilization; its destruction has been attributed, on scanty evidence, to floods or volcanic eruption. All we can say with confidence is that its chief monuments seem to have been built sometime before 600 AD and that it appears to have been abandoned before all the ceremonial buildings were completed, following a phase of rapid military expansion which, in association with Huari, a probable off-shoot of Tiahuanacan influence in the north, reached Nazca and other kingdoms on the Peruvian coast and penetrated deep into Chile in the south. Perhaps population pressure on the limited food resources of the *altiplano* gave the impulse for conquest, and the imperial power, over-expanded and lacking the organization and communications necessary for retaining its conquests, weakened at the base and collapsed. Some assert that the dour Aymará Indians who today inhabit much of that part of the *altiplano* were the destroyers of Tiahuanaco; others, on the contrary, maintain that Tiahuanaco with its empire was their creation. Whatever the truth may be, many centuries were to elapse before the *altiplano* became the seat of a new unifying culture and imperial dynasty, this time with the concourse of the Quechua-speaking Indians.

The Incas

The Incas started as one of the small Indian clans who lived and fought on the *altiplano* after the downfall of Tiahuanaco. They begin to emerge through the mists of legend after defending Cuzco, the valley to the north of Lake Titicaca where they had established themselves, from the fierce Chancas. It seems likely that they were themselves an *ayllu* of Aymará origin—the name Inca, commonly used to denote both their supreme ruler, the Sapa Inca, and his people at large, really means 'noble'—whom the Quechua Indians, the nucleus of their future empire, came to accept as their ruling caste. Tradition has preserved the names of some thirteen Sapa Incas, from Manco Capac, the reputed founder of the dynasty, down to Atahualpa, who was killed by the Spaniards. Their extraordinary military expansion, and the no less remarkable political consolidation of their empire, was the work of two rulers of genius, Cusi Yupanqui, better known by his title of Pachacuti, the Transformer, and his son Topa Yupanqui. Invested with supreme authority after his spirited defence of Cuzco against the Chancas, Pachacuti went on to subdue all the tribes of the southern highlands. He then sent his armies northwards into Ecuador, and, in a vast encircling movement, against the great coastal king-dom of Chimor, whilst he turned his attention to organizing his rapidly ex-panding domains and converting Cuzco into a splendid imperial capital. Topa Yupanqui, in campaigns of extraordinary boldness and imagination, then conquered all highland Bolivia and north-west Argentina and drove deep into Chile before being forced by the warlike Araucanians to fix the frontiers of his empire on the banks of the river Maule. His successor, Huayna Capac, devoted his energies mainly to the newly won region of Quito. At his death in 1527, the Inca empire had completed its maximum expansion and encom-passed a mighty area reaching from the present Ecuadorean-Colombian border in the north to the line of the Maule in the south.

The extraordinary success of the Incas in subduing and administering this huge region—a success all the more astonishing considering the topographical obstacles to be overcome and the still rudimentary level of their technology—was due to their genius for organization. The Incas were the great administra-tors, systematizers, and statisticians of pre-Columbian America. Many of the features which we think of as characteristic of Inca rule were in fact derived from earlier civilizations: their techniques of road-building and their use of *quipus*; their elaborate court ceremonial, modelled probably on that of the Chimú; the cult of Viracocha, the creator-god venerated at Tiahuanaco. But where they borrowed they also transformed, deftly welding disparate elements into one interlocking system of political and economic control firmly directed, no matter how far the frontiers of empire were pushed, from the co-ordinating centre of Cuzco, 'navel of the world'. Under the system which they imposed, every tribe, city, and village had its prescribed place and was made to contri-bute its due, every member of every *ayllu* was allotted his rights and his duties. The latter, it is true, seem to have outweighed the former. The Incas' subjects were obliged to devote a given portion of their labours to the upkeep of the state apparatus and its religion. They were liable for spells of forced labour and military service. They were confined permanently to their native soil unless forcibly uprooted and settled elsewhere. They were given no education, no choice of livelihood, hardly even a choice of mate. Each youth was obliged to marry at a certain age and if he was slow in finding a bride an official would allot one to him. He had to till the plot of land, and even to wear the clothes laid down for him. He was allowed almost no personal possessions beyond a couple of llamas, whose wool and dung he could make use of though he might not kill them for their meat. To steal, to produce less than the tribute of food and labour required of him, even just to be lazy, were crimes scarcely less heinous than rebellion and were punished almost as severely. But in return for diligence and obedience, the Indian could count on an assured place, albeit the lowliest, in society, and on enough to wear and to eat, even in times of natural disaster, when rations would be issued to him by the state. His life might be hard, but at least he could live without fear of robbery or oppression by local tyrants, and its monotony was relieved by prescribed festivals of song, dance, and religious rites. The Inca empire, in short, had elements both of the welfare and the totalitarian state. Whether its beneficent or its repressive features are stressed, there can be no doubt that it represented an original and remarkably efficient way of organizing society at an early stage of civilization and in an unusually difficult natural environment.

It was a society divided into two sharply differentiated strata, the rulers and the ruled. The Inca nobility formed something between a caste and a class. The little nucleus which had assisted the first Inca chieftain to establish his sway over the Quechua-speaking tribes round Cuzco had increased sufficiently in numbers to be able to officer the imperial armies and staff the hierarchy of the proliferating bureaucracy. Since unrestrained polygamy was both the privilege and the policy of the Sapa Inca, each reigning monarch fathered enough offspring to constitute a separate *ayllu*. It was also the practice to ensure the loyalty of local chieftains who submitted to Inca rule by presenting them with brides of the blood royal and having their children brought up in Cuzco where they merged with the nobles of pure lineage. In addition, individuals who had shown exceptional worth on the battlefield or in other ways, and young men who had been schooled by the *amautas* or wise men in *quipu*-reading, the religious and historical traditions of their race, and Quechua, the lingua franca of the empire, and had passed a series of ordeals designed to test their courage, endurance, and intelligence, were accepted into the élite. Their initiation was marked by the ceremonial piercing of their ears by the Sapa Inca, and the wearing of the ear-plugs which were the prerogative of the Inca nobility; hence the Spaniards' disrespectful description of them as *orejones* or 'big-ears'. The most important officials after the Sapa Inca were the high priest, generally a brother or uncle of the sovereign, and the governors of the four great territorial divisions which comprised Tahuantin-suyu, the 'four quarters' as the empire was officially called. Outstanding service by an *orejón* was rewarded by special privileges and gifts which could be transmitted to his heirs. The ruling caste thus appeared to be moving in the direction of property-owning hereditary nobility whilst the common people were confined to a strictly communal and anonymous existence.

The Sapa Inca, though of the same blood as the *orejones*, was removed far above them by the power and dignity of his supreme office. Even the mightiest might not raise their eyes to his face or enter his presence without bearing some burden on their backs to symbolize their inferiority. Instead of a crown, he wore the *llautu*, a red fringe surmounted by a feathered headdress, and golden ear-discs of enormous size. He dined off dishes of gold and silver and wore clothes spun from the finest *vicuña* wool. Much of his reign was spent in military campaigns or administrative visitations, when he was borne through his domains in a ceremonial litter along carefully swept and levelled roads. The Sapa Inca's power was absolute. He owned all the herds, forests, waters, and mines, and had vast private estates of his own. He was the master of a large harem and of a hierarchy of officials, attendants, and servants, and he could dispose of the land and lives of his subjects as he deemed fit. It was not unknown for an incompetent ruler to be deposed, but to ensure that only men of proved ability and energy should wear the *llautu* it had become customary for the ruling Inca to choose his heir from amongst his numerous progeny, and to test him out by taking him as co-ruler. If the son failed to live up to his father's expectations, he would be dropped in favour of another candidate. This happened on several occasions. Pachacuti himself had ousted a less competent brother and in turn rejected his own originally chosen heir Amaru in favour of Topa Yupanqui. But the system also had its dangers, for it promoted intrigues and power-struggles, and created uncertainty over the succession should the Sapa Inca die before his heir had been definitely selected and acknowledged. This was the flaw which fatally weakened the empire before the Spaniards arrived to complete its destruction.

Beneath the military and administrative élite presided over by the Sapa Inca, the mass of the people continued to follow very much their traditional way of life, subject only to such modifications as were required to integrate it within the general framework of the empire. Many tribes still lived under the rule of their local chiefs or *curacas*, whose authority was now supplemented and supervised by imperial officials, and who were required to present themselves regularly at Cuzco, where their sons were held as hostages and educated in Inca ways. A uniform and rational threefold system of economic production was maintained throughout the empire. One portion of the land was held by the *ayllus*, who allotted to each household a plot sufficient for its subsistence. Another portion was set aside and worked in common 'for the Sun', i.e., for the upkeep of the priesthood and the maintenance of the religious cults, whilst the third portion was that of the royal demesne, cultivated on behalf of the Inca and the needs of the army and state. In addition, the Indians were liable for communal labour on public works such as roads, irrigation projects, palaces, and fortresses. The first action of the Incas on taking over a new province was to carry out a census and prepare a detailed statistical survey of all its resources. The threefold division of the land was then carried out and the amount of tribute expected from it clearly defined. To facilitate organization and control, the population was assessed in units of tens, hundreds, thousands, and tens of thousands, under a corresponding hierarchy of officials, and the numerical strength of the *ayllus* was adjusted as far as possible to this mathematical pattern. Substantial shifts of population, known as *mitimaes*, were consequently needed. Where population outstripped local food supply, a section was hived off and sent to less intensively cultivated areas. Where it was thought advisable to keep the population under supervision or to set an example of better methods of cultivation, colonies of trustworthy subjects were established amongst them in permanent enclaves. In cases of rebellion, and as an alternative to punishment by extermination or enslavement (which produced the lowest caste of Indian society, the *yanacunas*, lacking even the limited rights of the common people) recalcitrant communities could be uprooted and resettled elsewhere. These transfers of population were ruthlessly carried out and the harshest penalties imposed on any who attempted to return to their place of origin, but care was also taken to see that the settlers were assigned as far as possible to regions of similar climate where they would have a good chance of adapting themselves. These *mitimaes* promoted the homogeneity of the empire and have left their mark on the demographic pattern of the area to this day.

The equilibrium between the widely scattered rural communities and the imperial centre was maintained by a system of communications and record-keeping in which the Incas displayed their full genius. Fine roads had already been built in the coastal kingdoms, marked off from the encroaching desert by low walls, wooden stakes, rows of trees, and ditches. These the Incas linked with the roads which they constructed in the Cordillera—smoothly paved highways which followed the contours of the mountains or scaled them in flights of carefully graduated steps, even at times piercing the rock face in short tunnels. A network of cross-tracks linked the two great parallel arteries, each running in a north-south direction for the full length of the Inca domains—the 2,500 mile-long coastal road, and the Cordillera road, running through what is now Ecuador, Peru, and Bolivia into Argentina. Gorges were spanned by fibre suspension bridges. At intervals along the roads stood a chain of *tambos*, serving both as caravanserais and storehouses, where the Inca and his officials would find shelter, fuel, and food when on their journeys, and where reserves of grain and clothes were kept for issue to the local population in times of scarcity. Teams of relay runners known as *chasquis* maintained a messenger service by which news of risings, natural disasters or other events could be conveyed to and from the capital at a speed of up to 200 miles a day. Messages were delivered orally or by means of *quipus*, knotted cords recording category and number by means of the colour of the string and the position of the knots. The *quipu* was the technical device which made possible the elaborate statistics on which depended the Inca system of tribute, call-up for service in the army and labour battalions, and emergency relief. Every community included men who knew how to record basic information relating to local births and deaths and food supplies, and sent on the appropriate *quipus* to the officials interpreting and collating this information in the capital. Some scholars maintain that the *quipus* also served to record genealogies, historical events, and even legends and poems and thus almost amounted to a form of writing, and that an Inca ruler who had ousted a rival from power could erase

* *

his name from the *quipu* records as easily as a totalitarian regime today can order the re-writing of history.

The cohesion of the empire was strengthened by the practice of the state religion. When they conquered a province, the Incas did not destroy its gods; they simply required that they should be subordinated to the official cult of the Sun, in much the same way as the *curacas* were subordinated to the suzerainty of the Sapa Inca. The common people continued—as they still do today—to venerate their *huacas* whose spirits needed to be propitiated by offerings and holy awe. But above the multitude of local deities shone Inti, the sun-god, whose supremacy in the heavens was the counterpart of that of the Sapa Inca upon earth. The Incas, indeed, claimed to be descended from the sun and to derive their authority from him. To question their authority was to defy the source from which all men received life and light and the earth its fertility. The numerous religious festivals, and especially those held in the great temple of Coricancha in Cuzco, were designed to demonstrate the oneness of this sun-worship with respect for the sun-king. In the temple-gardens of Coricancha, the Sapa Inca ceremonially tended a golden maize-plant in the presence of two great discs of gold and silver, metals sacred to the sun and moon, and when he at length was called 'to join his father the Sun', his mummy was preserved in the temple and periodically brought out to witness the sacred ceremonies. The high priest of the sun enjoyed a status second only to that of the Sapa Inca himself, whilst the 'Virgins of the Sun' who were dedicated to a life of celibacy spent in the duties of the temple, the weaving of garments for the use of the Inca, and the preparation of the vast quantities of *chicha* consumed in the festivals, were held in as much honour as the royal concubines. A portion of the people's food and animals was set aside for the gods; human sacrifice, particularly of girls and young children, was also practised, though never on the horrific scale characteristic of the Aztecs. In addition to the official sun-worship, with its political overtones, there existed amongst the ruling Inca caste the cult of the creator-god Viracocha, 'root of all being, power over all that exists'. From the hymns and prayers to Viracocha which survive, his cult seems to have attained a degree of spirituality which the Christian missionaries were later to channel into a new faith when the material structure of the great empire had been shattered.

The technological advances made under the Incas did not match their great achievements in social and political organization. Agriculture benefited from the practice of terracing and from irrigation techniques probably modelled on those of the coastal kingdoms, and from the introduction of the foot-plough or *taclla*, a bronze-tipped pole fitted with handle and foot-rest which proved a more efficient implement than the traditional digging stick and is still in use today. The use of bronze for tools and weapons was generalized throughout the empire. In stone-work, the masons attained a mastery which has seldom been surpassed. Constructed sometimes from polygonal blocks which fitted together like a three-dimensional jig-saw puzzle, or laid in courses of finely shaped rectangular blocks, interspersed with trapezoidal openings for doors and windows, their work remains a tribute to the patient skill of the

Indians and the organizing might of the Inca empire. Their most impressive monuments are perhaps the fortress of Sacsahuamán, above Cuzco, with its walls of enormous interlocking monoliths, and the superb masonry which once enclosed the sacred precinct of Coricancha. On that foundation the Spaniards superimposed a Dominican monastery—symbol of the racial and cultural amalgam which lies at the basis of modern Latin America.

No other pre-Columbian peoples of South America approached the cultural level of the Incas and their predecessors. Those who came nearest to them were perhaps the Chibchas of Colombia, who lived in organized communities in the uplands round Bogotá and were known for their skill as artificers in gold and precious stones. The Araucanians, who inhabited the land of lakes and monkey-puzzles to the south of the Central Valley of Chile, were at least a match for the Incas in ferocity and military skill. The Guaranís of Arcadian Paraguay were numerous and organized enough to retain their melodious language and much of their racial identity down to the present day. But all of indigenous America, whatever its degree of sophistication or backwardness, was to meet the shock of a totally alien and technologically more advanced civilization which would disrupt its organic evolution and force upon it a new destiny.

The Iberian Imprint

The first discoveries and conquests

On the morning of 12 October 1492, Christopher Columbus, commanding an expedition consisting of three caravels and ninety men, cast anchor off a small island in the Bahamas. They were not the first Europeans to have reached the shores of what came to be known, somewhat oddly, as America, probably after a later Florentine navigator, Amerigo Vespucci, who wrote eagerly of the new discoveries and the part he claimed to have played in them. The Norsemen had long ago founded settlements in the north, on the Atlantic coast, but the doors they half opened into the great continent had blown to again and their colonies had been extinguished. It was left to Columbus to re-open a lasting gateway through which poured the soldiers, missionaries, and settlers of Spain, overthrowing the empires of indigenous America and ransacking its treasures, but implanting as well their own civilization, faith, and order of government, and bringing the animals, crops, and technical skills of the old world which were to transform the face of the new.

The origins of Columbus himself remain something of a mystery. Probably the son of a Genoese weaver, he had previously solicited assistance from Portugal, France, and England, but, after repeated rebuffs, he turned to Spain, where he was finally commissioned by Queen Isabella of Castile for his great voyage. That Spain rather than another nation should have undertaken the conquest of America and reaped the rewards of empire might thus appear in a sense fortuitous. But destiny had clearly poised her for such an enterprise. The royal consent had been given for what was to become the Conquest at the very moment when the fall of Granada, the last Moorish kingdom surviving in Spain, closed the century-long process of the reconquest of the peninsula from Islam. Spain thus found herself with the men and resources, and with the driving spirit of the crusader-conqueror, to embark on this new epic chapter.

After reconnoitring the northern coasts of Cuba and Hispaniola (Haiti), where the *Santa María* foundered and its crew was left as a garrison, Columbus returned to Spain to report that he had found 'many islands peopled by countless inhabitants, and I have taken possession of them all for Their Highnesses'. Though he had seen no signs of the teeming cities and golden-roofed palaces which his reading of Marco Polo's travels had led him to expect, nor found any suitable recipient for the letter to the Great Khan with which his sovereigns had entrusted him, he believed that he had reached the coasts of

China or Japan on the westerly route to India. The golden trinkets worn by the islanders—the simple, unwarlike Arawaks—raised the hopes of the great discoverer and his royal sponsors, who gave him a magnificent reception, confirmed him in his honours as Admiral and Governor of the newly discovered lands, and financed a larger expedition for his second voyage (1493–6). But on returning to Hispaniola, Columbus found that the Spaniards he had left behind had been killed and their fort destroyed. The Indians, goaded by ill treatment, had turned against them. Despite this inauspicious beginning, the Admiral founded a settlement which he left under the stern rule of his brother Bartolomé whilst he sailed on to discover Jamaica and explore the coast of Cuba. During his absence, dissensions broke out in the settlement. The Indians were driven to revolt and fled to the interior. Five hundred of them were caught and shipped off to Spain as slaves. The Queen's displeasure was a significant indication of what was to be the royal policy in the Indies. However grievously conquerors and colonists might maltreat them, the Indians were to be regarded by the Crown as its subjects, not its slaves, and a great body of legislation was to be built up for their protection.

On his third voyage (1498–1500) Columbus reached South America, discovered Trinidad, and realized from the huge volume of fresh water poured into the sea by the Orinoco River that he was on the edge of a great land-mass. But back in Hispaniola the colonists had rebelled against his brother and the complaints of misrule with which they bombarded the Court led the Queen to send out a high official, Francisco de Bobadilla, to investigate. He clapped Columbus, his brother, and his son Diego into chains and sent them back to Spain. Though the Admiral was released and allowed to make a fourth and last voyage (1502–4), his glory remained dimmed and his rights disregarded. Another Governor of Hispaniola was nominated in his place, and Columbus was forbidden to put into the harbour of Santo Domingo, whither the settlement had been moved from its earlier site. He sailed on to explore the coast of Central America from Honduras to Panama. Worn out by forays with the Indians, storms, and shipwreck which kept him marooned on Jamaica for over a year, Columbus returned to Spain broken in health and died there.

After the Admiral's death, the thrust of exploration continued to radiate from the island bases which the Spaniards had established in the Caribbean. The belief that they had reached the approaches to China and India died hard, and to the quest for cities of the Great Khan was added a still more chimerical search for fabulous islands such as Antillia, with its seven cities said to have been founded by seven Spanish bishops fleeing from the Moors, and Bimini with its springs of eternal youth. In pursuit of this latter will-o'-the-wisp, Ponce de León discovered Florida in 1512. Later expeditions attempted to strike into North America from the northern shores of the gulf of Mexico. Others strove meanwhile to penetrate Central America and the north coasts of Venezuela (the 'Little Venice' as one explorer had dubbed it) and Colombia. Most fell victims to hunger, disease, and the savages' poisoned arrows. One of the survivors, Vasco Núñez de Balboa, who had joined an expedition as a stowaway hiding in a barrel to escape his creditors, established ascendancy over the Spaniards and the Indians of Darien and wrote to the King of Spain in 1513 that he had 'discovered the great secrets which lie concealed in this country. . . . On the far side of the mountains some level vales stretch away towards the south. The Indians say that the other Sea lies yonder, three days' journey away.' A few months later, Balboa pushed on to discover this sea, wading in sword in hand and 'taking possession of it' in the name of the King. He had reached the Pacific. It was gradually realized that the terrestrial globe was far greater than had been supposed, that the New World was a separate continent, and that a mighty unknown ocean lay between it and the lands of the Far East. Explorers began to search for the straits which would lead through the land-mass to link the Atlantic with the Pacific.

This passage was discovered seven years later by a Portuguese in the service of Spain, Ferdinand Magellan. After reconnoitring the great estuary of the River Plate only to find that it contained nothing but fresh water, and probing every other likely opening as he sailed on southwards down the coast, his expedition at length found and put into the mouth of the straits. Thinned by shipwreck, mutiny, and desertion, his expedition emerged at the end of November 1520 from its hazards and out into the ocean which, since he had come upon it at a moment of unwonted calm, Magellan christened the Pacific. For nearly a hundred days they sailed on over the immense sea, reduced by hunger to devouring sawdust, rats, and the leather covering off the main-yard, and coming at last to the islands later called the Philippines in honour of the future King Philip II of Spain. There Magellan lost his life in an Indian skirmish. Only one of the five ships which had set out under his command returned to Spain. But its eighteen survivors were living proof that the earth was round and that, as Columbus had believed, men could reach the Far East by sailing west from Europe.

The conquest of Mexico

Whilst Magellan had been making preparations in Seville for the start of his great voyage, a young Spanish *hidalgo* called Hernán Cortés was beginning his fantastic march from the Mexican coast into the heart of the Aztec empire. The core of his expedition consisted of some 400 foot-soldiers, fifteen horse and half a dozen cannon. Sent by Velásquez, Governor of Cuba, with limited instructions, his first move was the formal establishment of a Spanish 'municipality' at Vera Cruz which in turn vested him with supreme authority for the campaign. He then destroyed his ships to prevent any possibility of retreat and, accompanied by a contingent of Indians won over by a mixture of fear and cajolery, he began the three months' march to Tenochtitlán. He next broke the resistance of the warlike Tlaxcalans who, since they were hereditary foes of the Aztecs, thereafter served him as staunch allies. Montezuma (Moctezuma), the Aztec emperor, had been kept informed of these dire events through the picture-messages brought back by his spies. They convinced him that Cortés could be none other than the god Quetzalcóatl come to reclaim his kingdom, and he was paralysed by superstitious dread. A half-hearted attempt to halt the invaders by staging a treacherous attack on them at the great religious centre of Cholula was forestalled, thanks to the quick wits of Malinche ('Doña Marina'), the Indian interpreter and mistress of Cortés, who struck first with a massacre which demonstrated the Spaniards' devastating superiority of fire-power and tactics. Montezuma made no further attempt to check the invaders and himself came out to welcome them as they advanced over the great causeway to Tenochtitlán. 'We were all struck with amazement,' recalled Bernal Díaz del Castillo, a veteran of the campaign, 'and we exclaimed that the towers, temples and lakes seemed like the enchantments we read of in *Amadis*. Some of our soldiers kept asking themselves whether what they saw was not all a dream.'

After entering Tenochtitlán, Cortés conceived the daring plan of seizing the person of the emperor and holding him hostage whilst the whole country was brought peacefully under Spanish suzerainty. Montezuma was made captive, but the rest of the grand design was frustrated by news that a fresh expedition had landed near Vera Cruz under Pánfilo Narváez, a lieutenant of Governor Velásquez, with orders to supplant Cortés. The latter, leaving a strong garrison in the capital, hastened to the coast and by a characteristic display of audacity and craft neutralized Narváez and won over his men. He then marched back at the head of a combined force of 1,300 infantry, nearly 100 horse and his Tlaxcalan auxiliaries. But during his absence the situation in Tenochtitlán had deteriorated. The Indians now no longer concealed their hostility and hatred of the Spaniards, and when Montezuma attempted to calm them from the roof of the palace-fortress where he was kept lodged, a stone hurled by his infuriated subjects struck and killed him. With their royal hostage dead, the Spaniards now faced a general onslaught. Cortés decided to fight his way out before his food and powder ran short. The Aztecs had breached the causeway and they assailed the retreating Spaniards from their canoes and housetops. This was the *Noche Triste*, the Night of Sorrows, when the Spaniards succeeded in escaping from the death-trap by dint of desperate valour and at the cost of fearful carnage.

Cortés had broken out of Tenochtitlán only in order to fight his way back from a secure base and utterly subdue it. To expect a warrior race, whose state and creed were based on military conquest, to subordinate themselves voluntarily to alien usurpers was clearly an illusion. They had to be outfought, subjugated, and the seat of their power destroyed. At Otumba, outside Tlaxcala, the exhausted Spaniards turned to fight off their pursuers. It then took them more than a year to recapture the city, demolishing it house by house, overturning the temples, filling up the breaches in the causeway with rubble, and launching amphibious operations with a fleet of specially built brigantines. Above the battle, Díaz tells us, sounded the dread booming of Huitzilopochtli's war-drum, and 'when we looked up to the lofty temple whence it came we saw that our comrades whom they had captured when they defeated Cortés were being pulled and pushed up the steps, as they dragged them to be sacrificed.' But the Aztecs had to face a weapon more deadly still than the Spaniards' cavalry and cannon. The Narváez expedition had brought with it the smallpox virus which soon ravaged the Indian armies and population, striking down the chief who had been chosen to replace Montezuma. The Tlaxcalans gave valuable help to the Spaniards by providing manpower, warriors, and a friendly base for their operations. As the fortunes of war turned in favour of the Spaniards, other Indian tribes and cities came over to their side. The fall of the Aztec empire can be seen indeed as a revolt of subject peoples spear-headed by a foreign and technologically superior military élite. By mid-August 1521, Cuatémoc, the Aztec leader, was a prisoner and all resistance in the ruined city was at an end.

Cortés, who was confirmed in authority as Governor and Captain-General of New Spain fourteen months later, set about pacifying and reorganizing the country with the same energy and resourcefulness that he had brought to its conquest. Any hint of rebellion was ruthlessly crushed, the Tlaxcalans were rewarded with exemptions from tribute and the Spanish conquerors with grants of land and Indians to work them. Expeditions were despatched to Central America, and when the captain of one of these repudiated the authority of the Captain-General, the latter led a fantastic march through the jungles of Honduras to bring him to book. Cortés also sent an expedition across the Pacific to the Spice Islands, and four by land northwards up the Pacific coast. On one expedition, under his personal command, there was discovered a peninsula which he took to be 'an island very close to the terrestrial paradise' and christened California after a personage in one of those romances of chivalry whose adventures were scarcely more extraordinary than his own. Gradually the plants and animals of the old world were introduced and acclimatized in the new, and the language, faith, and institutions of Spain grafted on to the body of America. The arrival in 1535 of Antonio de Mendoza, the first Viceroy, marked the establishment of the full apparatus of imperial government which was to endure for nearly three centuries.

Others carried on the work of exploration and conquest, though none with the foresight and statesmanship shown by Cortés. His impetuous and ambitious captain Pedro de Alvarado subdued the Maya tribes inhabiting Guatemala, reducing their strongly fortified cities and carrying off much of the population as slaves before hastening south to seize a share of the plunder from the rumoured destruction of the Inca empire. When at last he reached the highlands round Quito (1534), Alvarado found that others had forestalled him, and he was bought off by the gift of a thousand pesos of gold. The conquerors of Peru could afford to be liberal; they had discovered, overthrown and ransacked an empire even mightier and richer than that of the Aztecs.

The conquest of Peru

The prize had gone to a rough and illiterate soldier of fortune, Francisco Pizarro. After serving in Central America, where he had fought under and eventually turned against Balboa, Pizarro entered into a partnership with another veteran, Diego de Almagro, and with a priest who helped finance the venture. It took eight years of arduous preparation and probing of the wild Pacific coast, in the course of which many of his companions lost their lives or turned back, before Pizarro gained possession of the stronghold of Túmbez and prepared to strike inland (1532). He could not have arrived at a more propitious moment. Atahualpa, who had inherited from his father Huayna Capac the northern kingdom of Quito, had defeated his half-brother Huascar and seized Cuzco from him. After destroying Huáscar's armies and massacring his kinsmen, the victor was taking his ease at the hot springs outside Cajamarca, halfway between Quito and Cuzco in the Andean uplands. The empire, though subjugated by the usurper and outwardly tranquil, had been deeply shaken.

Pizarro resolved to repeat the daring plan which had given Cortés victory in Mexico. At the head of his tiny force, he marched into the heart of the unknown land with the intention of seizing Atahualpa. The paved highways scaling the Cordillera, broad enough in places for half a dozen horsemen to ride abreast, and the *tambos* at which the Spaniards were able to draw supplies, were evidence that they had entered a great and well organized empire. Cajamarca they found deserted. Concealing his men in buildings round the main square, Pizarro waited to receive the Inca. Atahualpa approached in great state, surrounded by a throng of nobles and attendants. Valverde, the Spaniards' chaplain, came forward to exhort him to embrace the Christian faith and acknowledge the suzerainty of the King of Spain. Atahualpa, offended at this half-comprehended harangue, knocked the chaplain's proffered breviary to the ground. The Spaniards then rushed out from their ambush, struck down his attendants, and secured the person of the Inca. A great number of his cortège were slaughtered, and many others killed by a falling wall as they rushed in panic to escape from the square. The resistance which a few of Atahualpa's generals tried to organize in different parts of Peru was crushed without difficulty. With the Inca in their power, the whole autocratic structure of this seemingly formidable empire, already weakened by the effects of civil war, was paralysed.

Pizarro's strategy had succeeded brilliantly, but his limitations as a man and leader soon became apparent. All Spaniards, as Cortés had once ironically put it, suffered from a malady which only gold could cure. But Pizarro and his comrades sought this cure with such passionate rapacity that they came to blows amongst themselves and all but lost the empire they had won. In a dramatic gesture, Atahualpa had raised his arm above his head and promised that he would fill the room that high with gold if they would spare his life. Carriers bearing loads of the precious metal were soon converging on Cajamarca from all parts of the empire. Coricancha was stripped of its great sun-disc and sheets of gold, and the nobles of Cuzco were put to the torture in the Spaniards' eagerness to discover still further hoards. The treasure-chamber at Cajamarca was filled until it at length topped Atahualpa's line. The gold was then melted down into bars and shared out amongst the Spaniards. The ransom paid, Pizarro next trumped up the charge that Atahualpa was secretly plotting rebellion and had him put to death. The judicial murder was condemned by many, even amongst Pizarro's own followers. 'Experience has shown,' wrote Oviedo, the official chronicler of the Indies, 'how ill advised and worse done was the taking of Atahualpa's life'; had the Indians not been so mercilessly plundered and their Inca put to death, 'none of his vassals would have moved or risen'. Many Spaniards, too, were discontented with their share of the plunder. Pizarro's partner Almagro, who played the less spectacular but indispensable role of keeping the expedition provided with men and supplies from Panama, already nursed a grievance against Pizarro for securing the chief offices and honours for himself and his brothers. Almagro's men were now allotted a lesser share of the gold. When news was brought from the King that Almagro had been given an independent command south of the loosely defined territory over which Pizarro was to be governor, Almagro claimed that his share included Cuzco and made to assert his claim by force. The quarrel was patched up and Almagro departed on an expedition to discover and conquer Chile. When he returned two years later, he found that the Indians had risen in arms and the Spanish garrison at Cuzco, commanded by Hernando Pizarro, the Governor's brother, were fighting for their lives.

Though the many Indians who had supported Huáscar had no reason to lament the fate of Atahualpa, the Spaniards did little to ensure their loyalty. Manco, one of Huayna Capac's sons, was allowed to wear the *llautu* and was kept in Cuzco as a puppet Inca. From there he at length escaped on the pretext that he was going to fetch some hidden treasure for his captors, raised an army, and laid siege to Cuzco (1536). The city was half burned down and cut off for more than a year from the Spaniards living in Lima, the new capital which Pizarro had founded near the coast. When Almagro returned from Chile, Manco's forces were dispersed and the Inca later killed. Almagro seized Cuzco for himself from its weakened garrison. Before long a full-scale civil war was raging which ended with the defeat of Almagro and his execution on the orders of Hernando Pizarro. Francisco Pizarro was himself struck down three years later (1541) by vengeful Almagrists, and Hernando imprisoned in Spain. Another brother, Gonzalo, claimed the governorship of Peru for himself, refused to acknowledge the Viceroy sent out from Spain, and had him beheaded (1546). The turbulence of the conquistadores was only quelled after Gonzalo Pizarro had himself been executed and the royal authority established (1549).

Spanish and Portuguese expansion

Whilst the heartland of the old Inca empire was suffering these convulsions, new Spanish settlements were developing on what had been its periphery. Almagro's march southwards across the *altiplano* before emerging into what is now the Argentine province of Salta, his recrossing of the icy Cordillera, where many men and horses froze to death, and his descent into the fertile central valley of Chile are epic feats of Spanish endurance. His return to Peru was hastened by failure to find gold and by news of Manco's rebellion. He led his men back across the equally forbidding Atacama desert. Pedro de Valdivia, the veteran whom Pizarro next appointed to carry out the definite conquest and colonization of the lands discovered by Almagro, also took the sun-scorched coastal route and marched on to found the city of Santiago (1541). 'There is no better land in which to live and settle,' he reported to the Emperor Charles V. 'It has but four months of winter, and the summer is so temperate, with such delightful breezes, that a man can be out in the sun all the day long without annoyance. It abounds in pastures and fields, fit for raising every imaginable kind of plant and livestock.' But in the land of lakes and forests south of the central valley, there also abounded the exceptionally warlike Araucanians. Throughout their two and a half centuries of domination, the Spaniards never succeeded in pacifying this frontier, and the conqueror of Chile himself met his end at the hands of an Araucanian brave (1553).

Other expeditions had been despatched to the north and east whilst Francisco Pizarro was still tightening his grip on Peru. Belalcázar, one of his ambitious lieutenants, secured Quito for himself after defeating the Inca general Rumiñavi and—as we have noted—buying off Pedro de Alvarado. He had then founded Guayaquil, destined to become Ecuador's chief port, and Popayán, in southern Colombia, before pushing on over the savannas in the hope of gaining the gold and emeralds of the Chibchas. But here he in turn found himself forestalled. An expedition under Jiménez de Quesada had forced its way up the Magdalena valley from the Caribbean coast and had then been joined by Spaniards under the German captain Federmann, who had spent three years wandering over the *llanos* of Venezuela. By Quesada's newly founded settlement of Santa Fe de Bogotá, today the capital of Colombia, the three conquistadores met and decided that there should be peace, not war, between them. Belalcázar was succeeded as Governor of Quito by Francisco Pizarro's brother Gonzalo, who promptly plunged into the eastern lowlands in a foolhardy quest for the fabled land of El Dorado which he believed to be rich in gold and spices. After unspeakable hardships in a wilderness of swamp and jungle, Gonzalo Pizarro sent on two canoes under the command of one of his captains, Orellana, and having waited in vain for him to return, led the ragged and famished survivors of his expedition back to Quito. Some weeks later, Orellana and his companions reached the Atlantic. They had sailed for two thousand miles down the mighty river which, from the tribe of female warriors they claimed to have encountered on its banks, they christened the Amazon (1542).

The other great river of South America, whose estuary Magellan had reconnoitred in his search for the straits to the South Sea, was the River Plate. Four years before him, Juan de Solís had landed on its shores and been seized and devoured in full sight of his ship's company. Then came Sebastian Cabot (1526), who had christened the river Río de la Plata, or Silver River, from a few metal objects obtained from the natives. These had in reality come from Peru and were the first specimens of Inca treasure to reach Europe. But Cabot's men believed they had struck a rich land, and their tales prompted the fitting out of a large expedition under Pedro de Mendoza who founded the settlement of Santa María de Buenos Aires (1535) before abandoning the country in disgust. Its wealth was to lie only in the grain and cattle raised by future generations. One of Mendoza's captains was sent on up the river Paraguay in search of the rich country in the west and founded Asunción. After some clashes, the Spaniards settled down to live and interbreed in relative peace with the Guaraní people. For nearly eighty years their city, lying in the heart of the continent almost a thousand miles from the sea, was to be the chief centre of Spanish power in the River Plate area, for Buenos Aires had soon been destroyed by the Indians and was only refounded by settlers from Asunción in 1580. Other Spaniards, crossing the Andes from Peru and Chile, linked up with the populated fringe along the River Plate and gradually planted their settlements over the north and north-west of the vast pampa. By the last two decades of the sixteenth century, less than a century after Columbus's first landfall, the gigantic arc of the Spanish conquest had been firmly traced from California to the Magellan Straits over the whole face of the New World. Only one great sector had been reserved for the colonizing energies of another people—the Portuguese territory of Brazil.

Papal rulings had divided up the uncharted world between Spain and Portugal: the former to receive all lands discovered west of an imaginary line fixed first at 100 leagues west of the Azores and Cape Verde Islands, then extended by the Treaty of Tordesillas (1494) to 370 leagues west, Portugal to get any discoveries east of that line. When, therefore, the coast of Brazil was sighted by a Portuguese fleet bound for India under Cabral in 1500 (it may indeed have been already discovered by earlier Portuguese navigators and the secret kept until their title could be made good) the new land was claimed for the Portuguese Crown. Its value at first seemed slight. Here were no teeming cities to win or trade with, as in the Far East, or great empires to be overthrown, as in Mexico and Peru. The only product of immediate value was the red brazilwood from which the country derived its name. A piecemeal hold on the vast coastline was secured, despite the encroachment of Dutch and French interlopers, through a system of fiefs or *capitanias* donated to Portuguese nobles who were authorized to colonize, defend, and exploit them on their own account. By the middle of the sixteenth century a Captain-General had been appointed and a capital established at Bahia to provide some measure of overall control, whilst a small band of dedicated Jesuits laboured to convert and civilize the savage tribes. Though Portugal came under the Spanish crown for sixty years (1580–1640) Brazil was never brought under the influence of Spain and was left to develop under her own institutions and in her own way. The colonization of the huge country took longer than that of the lands conquered by the Spaniards, and it is with the latter that we shall be here mainly concerned.

Strategy and tactics

The bare outline given above of the successive phases of discovery, conquest, and colonization marks the Spanish Conquista as a turning-point in history and one of the most stupendous outpourings of human energies on record. The conquistadores themselves were conscious of playing their part in this great drama, even where their concern was primarily with personal enrichment, against the grandiose backdrop of history. Their very gestures have the ring of myth: Cortés burning his boats, Pizarro tracing a line on the sand of the island where his followers had been marooned and bidding those still prepared to face the dangers and hardships awaiting them in Peru to step across it, the Spaniards of Quito coming out to escort to their city the naked survivors of Gonzalo Pizarro's disastrous expedition to the Amazon, and stripping off their own clothes so as to share in the glory of the wanderers' shame. Everything about the conquistadores is on the grand scale; their valour, endurance, rapacity and cruelty. The very memory of their deeds moves the prosaic Jérez, Francisco Pizarro's secretary, to eloquence: 'For when, either in ancient or modern times, have such great exploits been wrought by so few against so many, under so many climes, across such distant seas and lands, for the conquest of the unseen and the unknown? Who can vie with the men of Spain? Our Spaniards were but few in number, never more than two or three hundred altogether, and sometimes only a hundred or less. And those who took part in the various campaigns were neither pressed nor paid, but went of their own free will, and at their own expense. And thus, in our own days, they have conquered more territory than that which all the princes, either Christian or infidel, were hitherto known to possess, subsisting on the savage food of men who knew neither bread nor wine, making do with herbs and roots and fruits for food, and yet they have conquered what all the world knows!'

What was the secret of this extraordinary Spanish expansion? Can we explain it purely in terms of the technological superiority of iron-age fighting-men over warriors who, in many cases, had scarcely emerged from the bronze age? Obsidian-studded clubs were certainly no match for Toledan blades, nor the spear-thrower for the crossbow, nor feather headdresses for helmets of steel. The Spanish arquebus and small cannon, though the most primitive of firearms, could nevertheless wreak great havoc amongst the serried ranks of a numerically superior enemy. The Indians were hampered by their traditional tactics of trying to capture, rather than kill, their enemies so as to be able to offer them up in sacrifice. Above all, the Spaniards had the enormous tactical advantage of cavalry. The Indians were at first awestruck by those monsters which they took for some sort of martial centaur until they found that rider and horse could surprisingly come apart. But even when they had got over their initial fear, the Indian armies could seldom stand against a cavalry charge. The Spaniards would pass through them, like tanks through unprotected infantry, reform and ride back again, striking the enemy down with their lances without ever coming to the close quarters in which Indian numbers and fighting methods could score advantage. 'After God, our hope was in our horses,' writes Díaz del Castillo, and lists with loving care the names, colours, and qualities of each of the horses which took part in the conquest of Mexico. Of Gonzalo Pizarro another chronicler tells us that he had two horses called

Villano and Zainillo, and that when he was mounted 'he paid as little attention to the squadrons of Indians as if they had been flies'. Fearful, too, to the Indians were the fierce dogs trained to track down fugitives, leading them back gently by the hand if they submitted, but tearing them to pieces when they tried to resist. Balboa's dog Leoncillo, and the latter's father Becerillo, were much prized by their masters for such exploits and earned them a bowman's share of the spoils at each division of booty.

Operating over immense distances and through terrain comprising some of the highest mountain ranges, most impenetrable water-logged jungle, and most arid prairie and desert in the world, the Spaniards were faced with formidable problems of logistics and transport. Sea-communication was, of course, basic, and Spanish expeditions were amphibious affairs, the General commanding also at sea, subject to the professional advice of his *piloto mayor*, and the sailors often lending a hand with operations on land. When forced to it, the soldiers would build their own ships, as Cortés did to such good effect at the siege of Tenochtitlán or Orellana in his navigation of the Amazon, and Hernán de Soto with less success in his wanderings in the Mississippi basin. On land, it was a question of foot-slogging, though Indians were pressed into service wherever possible as carriers or auxiliaries. We have noted the outstanding services rendered in this respect to Cortés by the Tlaxcalans. In Peru, the Spaniards had the advantage of the Inca roads and the stores of food, fuel, and supplies accumulated in the *tambos*, by means of which the Incas involuntarily facilitated their own destruction. For their great expeditions of exploration, the Spaniards mobilized whole armies of Indians. Few of the latter had the endurance of their masters, which suggests that the latter's superiority was not merely one of technology but a matter of stronger willpower and physique as well. Only a handful of those Indians who accompanied Almagro in the terrible crossing of the Andes reached Chile alive, and of the 4,000 who set out with Gonzalo Pizarro in the quest for El Dorado it is recounted that not a single one returned with the Spanish survivors to Quito. The early expeditions from Peru were attended by herds of llamas, poor pack-animals and a source of indifferent meat. Later, when hogs had been introduced from Spain, great numbers of those animals were driven along with the slowly advancing Spanish expeditions and provided more palatable rations.

But the advantages were not always on the side of the Spaniards. Sometimes they campaigned under conditions which neutralized their technical superiority, as in the swamps of Florida and the upper Amazon basin, where their armour simply rusted away and their powder became damp and useless. The Indians, conditioned by millennia of existence in an environment strange to the Spaniards, had learned to exploit its resources for purposes of war as well as peace. Their knowledge of poisonous berries and juices was turned to particularly deadly effect against the Spaniards, who learned to fear their venomed barbs above all things and sometimes discarded their metal breast-plates in favour of the better protection afforded by thickly quilted cotton coats. Garcilaso relates how the Spaniards at last discovered an antidote for Indian poison by shooting a captive Indian with one of his own arrows and then releasing him and noting which herbs he gathered in order to treat his wounds. But if the Spaniards learned from the Indians, the latter learned also from them. They not only dug pits studded with sharp stakes as horse-traps, but some even dared to mount horses captured from the white man or later bred in the country and became much feared for their equestrian skill and ferocity along the Araucanian frontier and over the broad Argentine pampa.

Social, legal, and religious features of the Conquest

The men who volunteered for the expeditions came from all sections of society and many parts of the peninsula, especially from the poor southern provinces of Andalusia and Estremadura. They included a high proportion of *segundones*, younger sons from good families with few career prospects in Spain, but even illiterates like Francisco Pizarro or men of the meanest birth like Almagro might hope for the highest commands. The armies were not based on social class; many *hidalgos* were content to serve as simple soldiers. Where the prospects seemed particularly dazzling, even members of the higher nobility might be tempted to join an expedition. Each man enrolled by personal contract with his captain and had to provide his own arms and equipment. He was entitled to an agreed share of the booty in proportion to his military contribution, the horsemen receiving the largest share, then the arquebusiers and crossbowmen, down to the foot-soldiers. Nor were the expeditions open only to Spaniards. The Emperor's German subjects took part in them, particularly in Venezuela, and contemporary narratives indicate the presence also of Portuguese, Italians, and Greeks. In de Soto's expedition to the Mississippi an Englishman is singled out for mention as being able to outshoot the Indians with his long-bow.

In addition to the Captain-General, the Crown appointed to each expedition a number of royal officers charged with special duties for seeing that the Royal Fifth was duly set aside and shipped back and that the Captain-General kept to his instructions. If he infringed the latter, they could depose him. Mutual suspicion and quarrels between the Captain-General and the royal officers were consequently frequent. The Captain-General maintained his authority not only by virtue of his commission as commander-in-chief, but by displaying a greater degree of daring, endurance, and ruthlessness than his own men. Columbus, Magellan, Cortés, and their successors all had to face plots and revolts from their own ranks and suppressed them with the same severity as they showed towards the Indians. Few of the great captains had a record unstained by a cruelty which we would qualify today as barbarous. Jiménez de Quesada, the founder of Colombia, who was content to live on as a simple *regidor* in the country he had conquered, is an exception. So is Cabeza de Vaca, an officer in the ill-fated Narváez expedition to Florida, who owed his survival to the extraordinary personal ascendancy he established over the natives amongst whom he was first kept as a slave. He made the long trek from one side of the continent to the other, healing their sick and quelling their rivalries, until he was at last able to rejoin his own people. Later he was appointed Governor of Paraguay and achieved the no less remarkable feat of leading his two hundred men from the coast of Brazil overland to Asunción without a single clash with the Indians and the loss of a single soldier through drowning, only to be overpowered and shipped back to Spain by the partisans of a rival captain who ruled by the standard methods of violence and rapine. But even the harshest of the great conquistadores were more than formidable fighters and stern disciplinarians. Pedro de Valdivia summed up his responsibilities towards his men in a letter to the King: 'A Captain to encourage them in war, and to be the first in danger; a father to help them as I could and to grieve for their toils, aiding them like sons to endure, and a friend to speak with them; a land-surveyor to trace out and colonize; an overseer to make channels and to share out water; a tiller and worker at the sowings; a head-shepherd for the breeding of flocks; in short, settler, breeder, defender, conqueror and discoverer.'

Authority for discovery, conquest, and colonization emanated from the Crown. In the annals of the Conquista there can scarcely be found a case of any adventurer throwing off allegiance to the King and setting up openly on his own. Such a course was indeed urged upon the triumphant Gonzalo Pizarro by Carbajal, whose cruelties had won for him the nickname of Demon of the Andes, after the defeat and beheading of the Viceroy, but Gonzalo refused. In the civil war between Pizarrists and Almagrists, each side claimed to be acting for the Crown and joined battle to shouts of 'Almagro and the King!', 'Pizarro and the King!' Great store was set by obtaining the royal licence before the start of any expedition, or if discoveries and conquests had already been unofficially achieved, by securing endorsement for them. A Governor appointed by the Crown could authorize an officer to undertake a given campaign on his behalf, as Velásquez sent Cortés to conquer Mexico, and Francisco Pizarro Valdivia to conquer Chile. Spanish settlers were also empowered to found municipalities with their traditional *regidores* and *alcaldes* who might, in case of need, elect a Governor provisionally pending royal instructions. Thus Cortés, determined to undertake the conquest of Mexico in his own right and not on behalf of another, contrived the founding of Vera Cruz, whose freshly appointed officers then elected him Governor.

But if legitimacy stemmed in theory from the Crown, the practical work of exploration, conquest, and settlement was left to licensed private enterprise. The privileges and responsibilities attending the latter were embodied in an agreement (known as a Capitulation from the chapters or clauses comprising it) between the Crown and the Conquistador. These Capitulations were of different types and for different purposes, although all had certain features in common. The privileges granted by the Crown could vary from a licence for the exploration of a general or specified area, to authorization for definitive conquest and settlement, or for a more limited objective such as the dragging of a lake for gold or the exploration of a volcano's crater. The Crown made sure that it had little to lose from a Capitulation, for everything hinged on the other party finding anything worth winning, and it was only then that the

Crown's obligations to invest him with the agreed rank, privileges, and emoluments came into force. It was unusual for the Crown to invest directly in the venture, though it would sometimes contribute a share of the funds, ships, human and material resources, and take a corresponding share in any profits. The Conquistador was more commonly required to cover the full expenses of the expedition, raise the armed forces required, provide and victual the ships, and where permitted, enlist colonists, introduce crops and livestock, and found settlements. Failure to keep to his side of the contract within a specified time laid him open to penalties. He had also to abide by instructions attached to the Capitulation regulating such matters as navigation and the formalities to be observed on 'taking possession', the evangelization and good treatment of the natives, and abstention from vices such as blasphemy, gambling, and concubinage. These moral precepts were, of course, often blandly ignored, but the strict observance of them insisted upon by some captains could be of benefit to an expedition. Jiménez de Quesada, for instance, had a soldier hanged for stealing an Indian's cloak, and his conquest of Colombia was achieved with the minimum of violence. Gambling, to which the Spaniards were passionately addicted, was a fertile source of quarrels and bloodshed. Some of Francisco Pizarro's soldiers are said to have played away their share of Atahualpa's fabulous booty in a single night, and when the men on de Soto's expedition to Florida found themselves deprived of cards they made them out of deer-skins, which they painted.

Conquest was a matter of 'big business', success leading sometimes to stupendous profits and failure to bankruptcy. Columbus had secured from the Crown the right to one-tenth of the trade and produce of any territories discovered by him. Peru was secured for Spain thanks to a partnership formed by Pizarro, Almagro, and a financially-minded priest called Fernando de Luque which, after conducting profitable operations in mining, agriculture, and Indian labour in Central America, financed nothing less than the discovery and conquest, subject to the Capitulation which Francisco Pizarro solicited for this purpose from the Crown, of the Inca Empire. Another ambitious but less successful piece of capitalist enterprise was the concession for the conquest of Venezuela granted to the Welsers, the German merchant-bankers to whom Charles V was indebted for his election expenses as Holy Roman Emperor. The Crown levied a 20 per cent commission on all gains derived from each expedition through the institution of the 'Royal Fifth', which was set aside under the supervision of officers appointed for the purpose before the Conquistadores proceeded to divide up the booty amongst themselves.

How did this peculiar system of officially-licensed, privately-financed imperialism come about? It stemmed in part from the Renaissance urge for mercantile expansion and the current concern with the lucrative spice trade. Columbus had made his great discoveries whilst seeking a western route for the Far Eastern trade and had no initial intention of founding settlements. Gonzalo Pizarro's quest was for the 'Province of Cinnamon' no less than for El Dorado. But the Spaniards' overseas conquests were also conditioned by their special historical development. An immediate precedent was their conquest of the Canary Islands in 1482. But for centuries before this, ever since the slow struggle to regain the peninsula overrun by the Moslems in the early eighth century, distinctive practices had been evolved by which, in return for certain privileges, the work of the *Reconquista* was carried forward by individuals acting from warlike inclination, religious conviction, the desire for personal gain, or a blend of all these motives. The Crown had encouraged them by entering into agreements with military commanders and had then vested those who won and held the unsettled frontier zones with the privileges of an Adelantado—a rank later conferred for similar services in America. The Crown too had exacted its Royal Fifth—a custom in fact derived from the Moslems—on all captured booty. Christian captains were rewarded with *repartimientos*, or allocations of land worked by a subject Moorish population, and new towns were established under royal charter, in the same way as the lands won later in the New World were incorporated in the Spanish dominions. In continuity of institutions, as in the mental attitudes inspiring them, Reconquista and Conquista can thus be seen as two phases of the same process.

This is particularly true of the religious urge animating both Reconquista and Conquista. That men who threw defenceless savages to their dogs, sent whole tribes to slave labour in mines or plantations, and committed every imaginable crime could yet hold themselves to be pious Christians might seem the sheerest hypocrisy. Yet this was not the case. Though they could sin grievously against its teaching, the Spaniards were ardently attached to their faith. In the centuries of the Reconquista, Christian virtue had become equated with military prowess. A militant Christianity had developed in response to the militancy of Islam. St. James, the apostle of love, had been transformed into Santiago Matamoros, St. James the Moorslayer, patron saint of Spain, who would appear at moments of crisis with flaming sword and mounted on his white charger to give the Christians victory. He had even been rumoured to intervene in the Spaniards' battles against the Aztecs, as Gómara recorded in his *History*. Bernal Díaz refers to the story with a touch of irony but without venturing to dismiss it altogether: 'It may be as Gómara says, but if so, all I can say is that I, poor sinner, was not worthy to see it; what I did see was Francisco de Morla who came riding up on his chestnut horse with Cortés . . .' What Díaz also failed to see was any basic incompatibility between winning fame and fortune for oneself by force of arms and the propagation of the gospel. 'We came here to serve God and also to get rich,' he declares simply. Such had ever been the creed of Spain's heroes; of the Cid, who had done service to God and the King by winning back land from the Moors, of Ferdinand, King and canonized saint, who had recaptured Seville for the Cross. The acquisition of land and wealth was not seen merely as an end in itself but as a service to the King and highly acceptable to God. 'Gold is most excellent,' wrote that hard-bargaining visionary, Columbus. 'The possessor of it does all that he desires in the world and may even send souls to paradise.'

But together with this dominant tradition of St. James the Moorslayer, there had also developed in medieval Spain a purer current of spirituality and apostolic charity represented by such saintly figures as Ramón Lull, the Majorcan mystic and missionary, and Talavera, the first Archbishop of Granada. They had sought to convert the Moslems not by force but by persuasion, love, and a sympathetic study of their beliefs. The discovery of America opened up to men of this stamp a limitless new field for apostolic labour and the call to restrain the excesses of their cruder contemporaries. A few months after the return of Columbus from his historic voyage the Queen appointed the first friar to accompany him on his next expedition and to see that 'the said Admiral treats the Indians well and lovingly, and does them no harm'. Soon the Court was receiving reports of woeful maltreatment of the natives, and at Christmas-tide 1511, before a congregation of all the notables of Santo Domingo, another Dominican friar, Antonio de Montesinos, publicly reproached the settlers for their inhuman exploitation of the Indians: 'By what right do you keep the Indians in such cruel and horrible servitude? On what authority do you wage such detestable wars against these people who were living quietly and peaceably in their own homes? Are they not men? Do they not have rational souls? Are you not obliged to love them as yourselves?' The friar's admonitions stirred the conscience of some, provoked the fury of many more, and started a controversy which was to agitate settlers, theologians, jurists, and the Crown itself, and to have a profound effect on Spanish policies in the New World.

The first attempt at an answer to the friar's questions was a royal instruction of 1513 that a proclamation known as the *Requerimiento* or Summons should be formally read out to the Indians by every Captain before he used force against them. Starting with an account of the creation of the world, the Incarnation, and the divine authority vested in St. Peter, this curious document went on to explain that the Pope had commissioned the King of Spain to take the inhabitants of the New World under his protection for the good of their souls. If they refused to submit voluntarily, they must be regarded as 'rebels' and incur the direst penalties. It is hardly surprising that the Conquistadores treated the reading of the *Requerimiento* as a huge joke, and that such Indians as stayed to listen failed to make head or tail of it. Nevertheless, the Crown insisted on its observance, and as the reformist party gained influence at court, modified it by a less peremptory Ordinance on Discoveries and Good Treatment of the Indians (1526), insisting that each expedition should be accompanied by two friars who were to see that the Indians were well treated and to give their written permission before force was used against them. Adverse reports by the friars could result in the cancellation of the Captain's commission. These and later well-meaning measures were characteristic of the hispanic propensity to expect that complex human problems could be solved simply by finding the correct legal formula—an assumption that was later to father the countless exemplary but impracticable constitutions bestowed on the Latin American republics, and in our own day, perhaps, the no less utopian blueprints of their economic planners.

The good intentions of the Crown were too often nullified by the attitudes of the adventurers who had the practical shaping of the New World. When Francisco Pizarro was reproached by a priest for failing to promote the evangelization of the Indians, he is reported to have answered bluntly: 'That is not what I came for. I came to take their gold from them.' And when there was no more gold to be had, there was always the labour of the Indians themselves. The Spaniard did not aspire to become an agricultural pioneer, clearing the forest and tilling the land with his own hands, but a conqueror and lord of vassals. Such had been the tradition of Castile, whose masters, owners of herds and flocks, would lead incursions into Moorish territory to seize fiefs in which they might rule over a subject and diligent Moorish peasantry. 'He who owns a *moro*, owns *oro*', ran the proverb. In place of the Moors there were now Indians. But the primitive savages of the Caribbean, whether the ferocious Caribs or the gentle Arawaks, though the latter might at first take the newcomers for gods and bring them offerings, were incapable of sustained labour in their service. Columbus had sought to discipline them by making *repartimientos* ('distributions') of Indians among the Spaniards, and had even shipped back some of them to Spain as slaves. The Crown insisted on regarding them as vassals rather than slaves; the *repartimientos* were endorsed and regularized into a system stemming from Reconquista practice and known as *encomienda* under which the beneficiary was 'entrusted' (*encomendado*) with a certain number of Indians who, 'since they are by nature inclined to sloth and evil vices', should be made to work in return for instruction in the Christian faith and civilized ways. The *encomendero's* privileges and duties were laid down in the Laws of Burgos (1512) which prescribed for the Indians a code of working conditions, including adequate food and housing, a maximum workload, and some measure of education. This *encomienda* system, which the Crown fought hard and on the whole unsuccessfully to keep the settlers from abusing, became the chief socio-economic basis of Spanish rule in the New World.

A handful of humane men, mostly friars, had been shocked by the abuses they had witnessed into denouncing the *encomienda* system and striving for its replacement with some form of colonization by Spanish agricultural labourers and Indian communities. Prominent amongst them was Bartolomé de las Casas, one of the *encomenderos* who had listened to Montesinos' reproaches and became converted to the belief that only pacific means should be used to win over and christianize the Indians. In 1520 he obtained permission from the Crown to put his ideas into practice along a stretch of the Venezuelan and Colombian coast where Indian co-operatives were to be established under the guidance of Franciscan and Dominican friars, with the co-operation of fifty 'Knights of the Golden Spur' whose white habit and red cross insignia were to denote their pacific nature and distinguish them from the rapacious conquistadores. Las Casas went to Spain and recruited his colonists, despite the opposition of the powerful landowners who were loath to lose their skilled labourers. They were given free passages to America and other inducements in the shape of supplies of seed, tools, livestock, and land, and granted tax exemption for twenty years. According to the detailed budget which Las

Casas had worked out, the colony was not only to become quickly self-supporting, but should bring in a handsome revenue to the Crown. But enlightened as it was, and far in advance of its times, the scheme proved a complete failure. Some of the Knights, lured by tales of Peruvian treasure, deserted. The Indians remained hostile, and neighbouring *encomenderos* did their utmost to see that the project failed. Bitterly disappointed, Las Casas withdrew to a monastery for nearly ten years before making his second attempt to put his beliefs to the test. This time he achieved some success. With the help of Dominican friars the savage tribes of the Guatemalan province of Tuzutlán were pacified so effectively (1535–7) that it earned the name of Tierra de la Vera Paz—the Land of True Peace. But some years later this venture too came to grief. Friars and settlers fell out, the Indians reverted to their ancient ways, rose against the missionaries and massacred them. The 'Land of True Peace' was only pacified once more by the standard methods of fire and sword.

Mexico, too, was the scene of heroic missionary endeavour. The first friars had come at the express desire of Cortés in order to give a spiritual dimension to the military conquest. They were men whose medieval fervour was enriched by the new currents then stirring the Spanish church. Zumárraga, who became the first Bishop of Mexico and prepared catechisms for Indian use, was deeply influenced by Erasmus. In its finer concepts the friars' religion lay beyond the grasp of the native mind. But it included many practices and beliefs which seemed near enough to their own to make the Indians seize eagerly on the new faith offered them in place of their fallen gods. They had known rites akin to the Catholic sacraments of baptism and confession, had practised fasts and penances and gone on pilgrimages, offered copal incense and prayers after their fashion, and had partaken of their idols in the form of cakes sprinkled with sacrificial blood. They had venerated the wise and beneficent Quetzalcóatl, whose Christ-like attributes led some friars to identify him with St. Thomas. In Peru, the cult of Viracocha was later found to offer still more striking analogies with the true faith. It thus seemed to the friars that the darkness of the Indians' idolatry had been illumined by some sparks of foreknowledge of Christianity. The Indians now only needed to be led, by charity, example, and instruction, into the full Christian revelation. To this end the friars gathered the Indians into settlements around large and splendid churches, built under their direction for defence as well as worship, where colourful Catholic ritual would take the place of the constant round of cult practices formerly lavished on idols. This policy brought the friars into continuous clashes with the *encomenderos*, who took their christianizing duties lightly and coveted the 'free' Indians for their diminishing labour force. The *encomenderos*, after the days of Cortés, found support amongst the more conservative secular clergy and officials who were beginning to set the tone of colonial society.

Not all high officials however favoured the *encomenderos*. Many strove to enforce compliance with the growing body of legislation—and some helped to shape it by their own reports and memoranda—designed by the Crown for the protection of its Indian vassals. Vasco de Quiroga, a judge of the royal *Audiencia* and later Bishop of Michoacán, founded a number of 'hospital-villages' where the Indians led a communal life and held property in common, on lines sketched out in More's *Utopia*. They included many novel features such as the combining of agricultural work with specialized crafts like wood-carving, lacquer-work, and shoe-making, the provision of communal hospitals, granaries and other services, a six-hour working day, an elected judiciary, and regular hours devoted to worship and religious instruction. Quiroga's 'hospital-villages' were to outlive their founder and influence social experiments in other parts of America, such as the famous Jesuit settlements in Paraguay, whilst Quiroga himself is claimed today as a forerunner by both Marxists and Christian Socialists.

It was one thing to devise pilot schemes as an alternative to the *encomienda* system, but could Spain's dominion in the New World be maintained without that system? Should the *encomiendas* themselves be abolished? The pro-Indian radicals, headed by Las Casas, believed that they could and should. They argued their case at court with such persistence that in 1542 the New Laws for the Indies were issued containing not only far-reaching provisions for the further protection of the Indians but a reversal of the whole policy on *encomiendas*. Any further grants of the latter were forbidden and existing *encomiendas* were to lapse on the death of their present holders. Prelates and Crown officials were debarred from possessing *encomiendas*; all grants of Indians acquired illegally, and a part of all excessively large *encomiendas*, to-gether with those held by all who had been involved in the recent disturbances in Peru, were to be given up. These drastic measures cut at the base of the economic power and social position of the Conquistadores, especially those in Peru, who saw themselves defrauded of the just fruit of all their labours. The proclamation of the New Laws fanned the flames of Gonzalo Pizarro's rebel-lion and led to the killing of the Viceroy sent out to enforce them. In Mexico, the outcry was so great that no serious attempt was made to impose observance of them. Three years later the Crown saw itself obliged to revoke at least the most unpopular of the provisions regarding the *encomiendas*. But it never yielded to the demands of the *encomendero* pressure group that their grants should be made permanent and hereditary; the Crown feared that this would lead to the emergence of too strong and independent an aristocracy in its colonies. Nor was the law against the holding of *encomiendas* by royal officials rescinded.

The reformers did not lose heart. A stream of letters, memoranda, and books continued to flow from Las Casas' indefatigable pen, including his *Destruction of the Indies* which was seized upon by Spain's enemies abroad as confirmation of the 'Black Legend' of Spanish cruelty and misrule. Accepted assumptions were coming under challenge too from another quarter. In Salamanca, the famous jurist Francisco de Vitoria was teaching that papal donations provided no legal basis for Spain's dominion in the New World, and laying the founda-tions of international law by advancing as a sounder justification such prin-ciples as the voluntary acceptance of Spanish suzerainty by the Indians, the pursuit of trade and missionary work, alliance with other Indian rulers or the defence of Indians who accepted Christianity. So deeply was the nation stirred by these questions of conscience and policy that in 1550 the Emperor actually decreed that all further conquest should be halted until the most eminent jurists and theologians had expressed their opinion on the Crown's title. In the great debate which followed, Las Casas faced the renowned Ginés de Sepúlveda who argued that the Indians were what Aristotle called 'natural slaves', whose innate racial inferiority justified their reduction by force of arms before they could hope to be turned into Christians and civilized beings. Las Casas presented the more enlightened view that 'the savage peoples of the earth may be compared to uncultivated soil that readily brings forth weeds and useless thorns, but has within itself such natural virtues that by labour and cultivation it may be made to yield sound and beneficial fruits.' Such divergent stands could not be reconciled, and the scholars never gave an agreed verdict; indeed the debate on the nature of the undeveloped world and the policies to be followed by those nations which claim to be more civilized continues into our own times. From the mid-1560s the ban on further conquests was relaxed, though we may perhaps see the influence of the Las Casas party in the comparatively bloodless nature of the annexation of the Philippines in the 'seventies. In 1573 the Crown issued new regulations formally superseding the crude argumentation of the *Requerimiento* and stressing 'pacification' as the guiding principle instead of 'conquest'—a term which Las Casas had denounced with characteristic vehemence as 'tyrannical, Mahometan, abusive, inappropriate and infernal'.

The fusion of races

But time, rather than a new turn of phrase, was beginning to blunt the edge of the problem. The era of great conquests had given way to the era of colonial consolidation. New factors were at work reshaping the human material of Spain's empire. By the end of the sixteenth century, three trends were particularly evident: a drastic decline in the indigenous population, the introduction into certain areas of growing numbers of negro slaves, and the emergence of a mixed or *mestizo* population formed by the interbreeding of white and coloured. It was this latter process which was to give Latin America its distinctive character and produce in time what Simón Bolívar described as 'a world in microcosm . . . neither Indians nor Europeans, but something intermediate between the rightful owners of the land and the Spanish usurpers.'

It is difficult to find reliable figures for the native population before and after the Spanish conquest. Estimates as high as from twelve to fifteen million for pre-Columbian Middle America have been given, and some six millions for the Inca empire. The Caribbean islands were the first to suffer depopulation. In Middle America, as much as six-sevenths of the native population is believed to have been wiped out by the middle of the seventeenth century. The former Inca empire lost about half its inhabitants in the thirty years following the conquest. How are we to account for these catastrophic declines? The cruelty of the conquistador and the callousness of the colonist provide only part of the explanation. More serious were the ravages of epidemics to which the Indians had developed no resistance: smallpox, introduced with the Narváez expedition, typhoid, which decimated the besieged inhabitants of Tenochtitlán when they were forced to drink the contaminated lake waters, and the scourges of the tropical lowlands, yellow fever and malaria. Infection spread the more readily when the Indians were herded together for forced labour in the mines or grouped into settlements round the friars' churches. The disruption of traditional agricultural techniques and of the precarious balance between man and land also hastened the decline. It is true that the Spaniards increased the continent's economic resources by introducing new breeds of animals and improved farming techniques. The ox-drawn plough could break up land which had resisted the Indian hoe. But if more land was thus brought under cultivation, it was also farmed less intensively than under the hoe. Stock-raising, too, claimed more and more land at the expense of the Indians' plots, whilst the Spaniards' need of water for their beasts and mills meant less for the natives' crops. In some areas, such as coastal Peru, the breakdown of traditional irrigation systems led to the reversion of once thickly populated regions to desert.

The shrinking of the native labour force stimulated the introduction of slave-labour from Africa. This course was even advocated by the humanitarian Las Casas in his single-minded zeal to shield the Indians from the crippling demands made on them by the *encomenderos*. By the second decade of the sixteenth century, Governor Velásquez of Cuba was importing negroes to work in the cane-fields. In 1518, the royal permission was given for 4,000 negro slaves to be shipped out to the Caribbean, and before long a yearly average of up to 10,000, rising in the course of the following two centuries to 75,000, was being regularly sent out to the Americas. The Portuguese controlled the African sources of this lucrative trade and could ship their merchandise direct to their plantations in Brazil, or else dispose of it, under a system known as the *asiento*, for re-sale in the Spanish colonies. To this steady influx Haiti owes its almost wholly African character today, and Cuba and Brazil the strong African elements in their ethnical and cultural make-up.

The Iberian conquest of the New World was biological as well as military. Few of their own women accompanied the conquistadores from Europe. From the time of Columbus's return to Hispaniola on his second voyage the unceasing threnody was to be heard: 'They have taken our wives from us.' Native women were as much part of the booty as gold and pearls. On the amazing advent of the bearded white men, many gave themselves freely, not only as to the victorious fighting male, but as offerings to beings who were manifestly gods. Chiefs sought to placate the invaders, or to cement alliances with them, by gifts of women which the Spaniards saw no reason to refuse. Montezuma gave Cortés one of his daughters, and Atahualpa one of his sisters to Francisco Pizarro, who fathered two sons by her before marrying off the princess to one of his pages. Even the common soldiers, if fortune favoured, could accumulate a veritable harem by means of gifts or rapine. The narrative of Ulrich Schmidl, a German serving under Pedro de Mendoza in Paraguay, reads like an inventory of Don Juan at large in Arcadia: 'The women are very beautiful and go as naked as their mothers brought them into the world. . . . They are painted very beautifully from their breasts to their privy parts; a painter from Europe could scarcely have made a finer job of it. They are handsome after their fashion and go stark naked; they fall to temptation on occasion. . . . Here I conquered for myself as booty nineteen persons, young men and women. I had no use for the old, but preferred the young.' The attraction of the Indian woman could sometimes be strong enough to make the Spaniard turn native. On landing in Mexico, Cortés encountered two such cases. One of them, although he had forgotten all but a few words of Spanish and would squat on his haunches in native fashion, rejoined his countrymen and did useful service as an interpreter. The other sent word that he had married an Indian and fathered three fine sons; besides, the Spaniards would laugh to see his face painted and his ears pierced in Indian fashion. He persisted in his refusal despite Cortés's stern admonition to 'remember he was a Christian, and not to lose his soul on account of an Indian woman'.

The Indian woman was capable of remarkable devotion to her white mate and an identification with his cause which greatly facilitated the process of the Conquista. The most famous case is that of Malinche or Malintzín, who served Cortés as interpreter, adviser, and mistress, and is execrated today in Mexico as a symbol of native collaboration with the alien intruder. The Crown's attitude towards such alliances was ambivalent. Concubinage was formally forbidden under the terms of the conquistadores' Capitulations, but the prohibition was clearly unenforceable. Marriage with native women was at first also forbidden, but after 1514 permitted. For how could conqueror and conquered be more effectively integrated than through miscegenation? There was, besides, a chronic shortage of Spanish women in the young colonies. The early records tell of a few adventurous spirits such as Inés Suárez, Valdivia's companion, who once stoutly defended Santiago against Indian attack, and the wife of Alvarado, who succeeded her husband in the governorship of Guatemala and lost her life in a volcanic eruption. But between 1509 and 1533 only 470 women sailed from Spain for the Indies—an average of less than twenty a year. Some were fortune-hunters like their menfolk. The Crown granted *encomiendas* for 'two lives', so a young woman might be prepared to marry an elderly, battered conquistador in expectation of an early and affluent widowhood and a second husband more to her taste. Garcilaso describes the indignation of some veteran *encomenderos* in Peru on overhearing the uncomplimentary remarks about their appearance made by a party of marriageable ladies recently arrived from Spain, which made them decide they would do better to take an Indian to wife. But for most Indian concubines, from Cortés's Malintzín to Pizarro's Inca mistress, the appearance of a bride from Spain meant the eclipse of themselves and their families, with disturbing social, economic, and psychological consequences on the rising *mestizo* generation. Some of the latter nevertheless took pride in the lustre of their names and strove to add to it. Almagro's son, Diego the Younger, succeeded to the leadership of the Almagrist faction and met the same fate as his father. Malintzin's son, Martín Cortés, cut a splendid figure in New Spain. Garcilaso de la Vega wrote his *Royal Commentaries of the Incas* 'since I felt myself under obligation to two races, as I am the son of a Spanish father and an Indian mother . . . not only for the honour and renown of the Spanish nation which has accomplished such great things in the New World, but no less for that of the Indians.'

The reason for the rapid growth of a *mestizo* population is clear from contemporary reports. One friar tells us that every conquistador, in addition to his lawful wife, would take an average of three concubines. Paraguay, a happy hunting ground for Schmidl and his like, was a particularly fertile breeding ground. 'Here some men have as many as 70 women, and the very poorest does not have less than five or six,' wrote the chaplain González Paniagua to the King. No wonder that Asunción became known as 'Mahomet's Paradise'. Within ten years of its foundation in 1537 the little settlement contained 500 *mestizo* children; by 1575 its population consisted of some 5,000 *mestizos* and only 280 Spaniards. Today Paraguay is one of the most homogeneous and fully *mestizo* countries of Latin America, with a bilingual population proud of the strong Guaraní element in its make-up.

Elsewhere the process of miscegenation proceeded more unevenly. Of the population of New Spain, which had sunk to its lowest ebb by 1650, some 1,270,000 were described as Indians, 120,000 as white, and 130,000 as *mestizos*. By the end of the eighteenth century, the latter had increased by more than seventeen times, to reach some 2,270,000, whereas the number of Indians had quadrupled to give a figure of 5,200,000. Since then, the strength of the Indian population has remained at about the same level, whilst the number of *mestizos* has steadily increased to form the overwhelming bulk of the Mexican nation of today. In Bolivia, Peru, and Ecuador, heirs to the old Inca Empire, the process of racial integration was less intensive; at least half their total population can still be reckoned as Indian, most of the remainder as *mestizos*.

In Brazil and the Caribbean islands, where the Indian population was either scanty or in rapid decline, miscegenation developed mainly between whites and negroes. By 1585, the population of Brazil was estimated to be still only 57,000, of whom nearly one quarter were African slaves. By the close of the eighteenth century, before the flood of European immigrants increased the white element, the Africans formed the majority. The stark confrontation of the two races, European and Amerindian, thus gradually evolved, as Conquista merged into colonization, into the emergence of the following categories: a smaller dominant group of European-born Spaniards and Portuguese, their white descendants born in America (generally referred to as Creoles), the subject Amerindians and negroes, and the population of mixed blood (known as *castas* or *mestizos*) formed by the interbreeding of white and coloured, or hybrids between the different groups of coloured. These racial categories corresponded broadly to social divisions, the master-class formed by European and American-born whites, the base of the pyramid by the negro slaves and by Indians who, although nominally free citizens, were in practice generally condemned to servile status, and the intermediate *mestizos* who identified themselves individually as far as they could with the white élite, but more often became a restless, rootless, disinherited fringe-group. The borders between the categories were fluid, social and economic factors being more of a determinant than the purely racial. Thus Indians who learned Spanish, acquired money or possessed estates—and not a few members of the old Aztec and Inca nobility made the transition in this way—could be reckoned amongst the *gente de razón* or 'civilized people'; whatever their racial origins, they would no longer rank as Indians. They might even obtain from the authorities a document formally confirming that they should be 'considered white'. 'Poor whites' on the other hand—and the number of these soon multiplied, for not all conquistadores were rewarded with *encomiendas* and a stream of hungry fortune-hunters kept arriving from Spain—could quickly sink to the level of *mestizos* and produce offspring belonging to that group. European-born Spaniards who married and settled in America would father children who were technically Creoles. The latter, though priding themselves on their Spanish blood, came in time almost invariably to include some non-white strains in their ancestry.

Few of the men who conquered America for Spain lived on there as its rulers. Many perished, like Almagro and Pizarro, in the civil wars which followed conquest, or were killed, like Valdivia, before they had completed pacification. The powers and privileges originally wrung by Columbus from the Crown were soon whittled away, and his son Diego spent much of his life in the struggle to vindicate his hereditary rights. Cortés was first rewarded with lands and honours and then edged out of authority in Mexico. Though the Crown might be obliged, under the terms of the Capitulations entered into with individual captains, to grant them the governorship of the land they conquered, its aim was in fact to replace them as far as possible by its own nominees. The high-born courtier, the European-trained administrator, and the *letrado* or cleric replaced the conquistador. It could be argued that the freebooting qualities which had enabled the latter to win the new lands did not make him the most fitted to administer it. But the Crown's basic interest was to avoid the emergence of a hereditary élite who might come to believe that, since it had won and continued to rule Spain's distant possessions, it should by rights be their legal masters. The royal policy was at least successful in delaying the demand for independence for three centuries.

Patterns of Spanish colonial life

Examples of the differing fortunes with which the conquistadores met in soliciting office from the Crown are provided by the case of the three captains who returned to Spain to press their suit for the governorship of Colombia (see page 34). Belalcázar managed to obtain the lesser governorship of Popayán, Federman got nothing, whilst Jiménez de Quesada, the real conqueror of the country, was awarded the honorific title of Marshal and appointed as *regidor* for life. This office fulfilled an important function in the early days of colonization. It was usual for a captain, on discovering a new land which he deemed fit for settlement, to go through a formal ceremony, in the presence of the notary and Crown officers, of 'taking possession' in the name of the King of Spain. He might then proceed, if the site was suitably situated with regard to access, defence, water supplies and so on, to lay out a 'municipality'. The future roads were traced according to a standard grid-iron plan, which divided the ground into rectangular plots from which the *cuadras* or blocks of the modern Latin American city derive. A central plot would be left blank to form the main square or *plaza de armas*. Here the gallows would be set up to remind the citizens that law would be strictly enforced. Round the *plaza* there would in time arise the chief public buildings —church, governor's palace, arsenal, prison. The plots were allocated to individual Spaniards who thus became *vecinos* or householders. Their homes might at first be no more than wooden cabins or wattle-and-daub shacks, but these in time would be replaced, thanks to Indian labour, by commodious stone buildings, many of which would bear their owners' carved escutcheons over the gateway. Soon the primitive settlements would take on the aspect of towns, some of them magnificent, and all characterized by a certain dignity as enjoined by the Laws of the Indies which laid down that 'every city in Spanish America should evoke wonder in the Indians when they saw it, so that they would thereby understand that the Spaniards were permanently settled there and should accordingly be feared and respected, their friendship sought, and no offence given.'

Though his wealth might be based on land and the Indians who worked it, the Spanish colonist was essentially a city-dweller. As a *vecino* he was eligible for election as *regidor* or *alcalde* to the *cabildo* or town council. These offices were generally unsalaried, but they carried with them valuable privileges and powers of patronage and offered a peaceful outlet for the energies of the conquistador. Municipal life had deep roots in medieval Spain and began to flourish vigorously when transplanted to the New World. The *cabildos* were a useful means of stimulating and consolidating the process of colonization and at first enjoyed considerable powers. They might on occasion elect a Governor—a right which, as we have noted, Cortés turned to his advantage. They could send reports, petitions and even their own delegates or *procuradores*, to the King. They had within themselves, in short, the seeds of self-government. This the Crown was quick to perceive and to prevent. The rebellion of the *Comuneros* in Spain during the 1520s was a warning of what might follow if the independence of the municipalities in the distant colonies grew unchecked. Laws were accordingly issued to prevent any form of consultation or association between the separate *cabildos*, to which the Crown increasingly appointed its own nominees. Offices ceased to be filled by election and were put up for sale. Eventually they became little more than sinecures which were often held in Spain and delegated to hirelings or simply allowed to lapse. Only in the remoter areas well away from the centres of colonial administration did the *cabildos* continue to attract some degree of popular participation. This was to be a factor of some importance in the gestation of the independence movement, though democratic aspirations found expression more often through the informal assemblies known as *cabildos abiertos* rather than through the moribund *cabildos*.

The royal power was exercised primarily through the Viceroy, an office which had also evolved in the course of Spain's own historical process. The peninsula had been unified under the hegemony of Castile. In theory, the component kingdoms remained separate entities linked together in loyalty to the same monarch. As the latter could not be in more than one kingdom at the same time, he was regarded as being present by proxy in the others in the person of a Viceroy. Viceroyalties thus developed in Aragón, Catalonia, Valencia, and Navarre, and as Spanish power spread through the Mediterranean, in Sardinia, Sicily, and Naples as well. It followed logically that they should be set up in New Spain in 1535, in New Castile (Peru) in 1542, in New Granada in 1717 and finally in the River Plate in 1776. Spain's possessions in the New World thus theoretically remained individual 'kingdoms' rather than colonies. This did not imply however that they were allowed any autonomous powers; the system of government remained highly centralized, first in the Council of Castile, which Queen Isabella entrusted with special responsibilities for the newly discovered lands, and then through the Council of the Indies, set up for that purpose in 1524. That body, acting for and reporting to the Crown, attempted to direct all the administrative, financial, and military affairs of the distant possessions in meticulous detail.

The Viceroys, generally chosen from the Castilian nobility and sometimes men of proven administrative ability, like Francisco de Toledo in Peru, wielded enormous but by no means unlimited powers. Another institution, the *audiencia*, was at hand to assist and, if necessary, to check them. *Audiencias* were vested with judicial, consultative, and certain administrative powers, and might take over those of the Viceroy in the event of his death or incapacity. Their members, the *oidores*, formed the top layer of the imperial bureaucracy. Beneath the Viceroy and his *audiencia* came the hierarchy of Governors of provinces (sometimes called captaincies-general or presidencies) with their respective *audiencias*, and the *corregidores* who presided over small administrative sub-divisions. In its judicial capacity, an *audiencia* might challenge a Governor's or Viceroy's conduct of public affairs. The Crown could also exercise supervision by means of *visitas*, enquiries by inspectors specially sent out from Spain, and by the *juicio de residencia*, a formal hearing held at the conclusion of every official's tenure of office, where grievances could be aired and the official called to account for any alleged abuse of office. The Viceroy, for his part, could modify or even invalidate the instructions sent to him from Spain. It was recognized that, in view of the slowness of communications over the vast distances involved, circumstances could arise which rendered the application of measures drafted by the Council of the Indies undesirable or impossible. The Viceroy's discretionary powers might thus be tantamount to a veto, which he could reconcile with submission to the royal will by pronouncing the famous formula: *Obedezco pero no cumplo*, 'I obey but do not carry out.'

The Crown also exercised a strict control over all trade with the New World through a body created in 1503 for this purpose, the Casa de Contratación. Its many-sided activities included the drafting of commercial regulations, the training and licensing of pilots, the keeping of a master map recording new discoveries, the collection of maritime taxes, and the receipt of royal funds. It worked closely with the merchant guild (*consulado*) of Seville which, for more than a century and a half, enjoyed a monopoly of all trade with corresponding *consulados* in Mexico, Lima and a few other privileged centres in the New World. It organized the despatch, twice a year, of two great convoys bearing the Spanish goods essential to the colonists such as iron, arms, mercury (for mining operations), cloth, olive oil, wine, paper, and soap, and returning with the raw materials produced in the colonies—sugar, cacao, leather, tallow, indigo and above all, the precious gold and silver. The great fleets from Spain sailed alternately to Vera Cruz, whence all Mexico was supplied, and to Portobello and Cartagena, the focal points for the Isthmus of Panama and the Spanish Main. From there, goods were transported overland and reshipped to Lima and other parts of the Pacific coast. Even the growing settlements round the River Plate, so inviting for Atlantic shipping, were kept supplied by the incredibly circuitous route via Panama, the Pacific coast, and over the Andes. This closed economic system excluded trade amongst the colonies themselves and legal interchange between the colonies and other European powers. As the colonies' wealth and demand for European goods grew, and the mother country's ability to supply such goods herself diminished, smuggling increased apace until, by the time the monopolistic system began to be officially relaxed in the second half of the eighteenth century, a large proportion of all goods reaching Spanish America consisted of contraband.

Portuguese colonization

Portugal, like Spain, favoured a monopolistic trade system and, from the middle of the seventeenth century, sought to defend it by means of armed convoys. But her policies were less rigid than those of Spain. Many of the goods reaching Brazil were of English origin, since Portugal could not supply enough of them herself, and were carried in English or Dutch bottoms. Foreign merchants, especially Jews, were allowed to settle and trade in Brazil, and the great chartered company formed in the sixteenth century with the monopoly rights of supplying the colony's imports was financed largely by Jewish capital. So long as her trade with the newly discovered lands of the Far East continued to boom, Portugal had little reason to show much interest in Brazil, whose dye-woods found a market in Europe's expanding textile industries. Profits from this source, however, were soon swollen and then surpassed by those from the plantations which, thanks to the labour of imported African slaves, began to produce valuable crops of cotton and sugar; of the latter commodity Brazil became the world's chief exporter by the end of the sixteenth century, and of the former for most of the eighteenth. Trade followed a triangular pattern between Lisbon, Angola, where the valuable cargoes of 'black ivory' were taken on, and Brazil. Since the Portuguese settlements on the immensely long Brazilian coastline depended almost entirely on sea communications, a considerable coastwise traffic was allowed to develop. But the isolation of the settlements also offered temptations to other maritime powers who saw no reason to consider themselves excluded from the riches of the New World by any papal ruling. Except during the sixty years when Portugal was under the Spanish Crown (1580–1640), when several raids were made on Brazilian settlements, Portugal had little to fear from England, her traditional ally. But the French and Dutch proved more serious rivals. The former gained footholds at several points on the coast, and some of them, such as Villegagnon's colony in the Bay of Rio de Janeiro, proved difficult to dislodge. The Dutch posed even more of a threat. They established an admirably run agricultural colony in Pernambuco, based on their capital of Recife, and even seized the Portuguese capital at Bahia for a time. The mother country proved too weak or indifferent to offer effective help to the Portuguese colonists who had to depend on their own exertions before the Dutch were forced to evacuate Pernambuco (1654). This struggle against the foreign interlopers gave the settlers their first awareness of awakening Brazilian nationhood.

Only gradually did the Portuguese settlers begin to penetrate into the vast, unexplored hinterland of Brazil. Their aim was primarily the capture and enslavement of the Indians, though the latter's primitive, stone-age way of life made them ill-suited to the hard labour of the plantations. The slavers organized themselves into para-military bands, sometimes hundreds strong. These *bandeirantes* ranged the interior, often for years on end, mating freely with the native women, subsisting by hunting and by clearing patches of forest for the growing of manioc and maize, and founding settlements, some of which grew into great cities like São Paulo, the centre of all this restless pioneering. At the end of the seventeenth century they discovered rich deposits of alluvial gold and then diamonds. A frenzied gold-rush set in for the 'General Mines'—the plateau which is now the state of Minas Gerais—where in due course there arose the splendid colonial city of Villa Rica de Ouro Preto, the Rich Town of Black Gold. This sudden wealth proved both bane and blessing. It stimulated the settlement and development of the interior. But it also provoked a fierce civil war between the men of São Paulo and other fortune hunters, and led to the enrichment of profiteers, many of whom squandered their gains in ostentatious luxury in Portugal. The country's more solid sources of wealth, the coastal plantations, found themselves suddenly denuded of men and resources.

Mining and agriculture

The search for mineral wealth also had enormous importance and mixed consequences for Spain's American colonies. The gold seized in such spectacular fashion by the conquistadores in Mexico, Peru, and Colombia had been slowly accumulated by generations of Indian labour; the mines themselves proved disappointingly meagre in their yields. Silver was found in greater abundance and efficiently produced with the use of mercury thanks to a new amalgamation process developed by the Spaniard Bartolomé de Medina. In the middle of the sixteenth century the rich mines of Zacatecas and Guanajuato were discovered in Mexico, and the still more fabulous mines of Potosí. At the foot of this great cone-shaped silver hill on the bleak and remote plateau of what is now Bolivia, a boom town, adorned with splendid baroque churches and palaces, a theatre and royal mint, thronged with a quarrelsome multitude of fortune-seekers, officials, slaves, and Indian labourers and provisioned by vast trains of pack-mules and llamas, grew rapidly into the largest urban conglomeration in the New World. The treasure of the mines made many private fortunes, built cities, nourished the ostentatious, pleasure-loving colonial society and sent back a stream of bullion to fill Spain's empty exchequer, finance her wars, and pay for the products her declining agriculture and industry could no longer themselves supply. It set in motion the great price revolution of sixteenth-century Spain which saw a fourfold increase in the cost of living and ultimately brought many to destitution and misery. It was Northern Europe, rather than Spain, a mere channel for the mainstream of this flow of bullion, that profited from the increased liquidity which was to make possible the ensuing phase of capitalist expansion.

To operate the mines the Spaniards had recourse to forced labour. This ran counter to the principle which the Crown had always striven to uphold against the callous rapacity of conquistadores and colonists—that the Indians were vassals, not slaves, and should be treated as free men. Well-meaning attempts to induce the Indians to offer their labour voluntarily foundered on the refusal of the colonists to pay for something they believed should be theirs by right and on the Indians' natural instinct to escape what was virtually a sentence of death. So, unless the whole economic value of the colonies was to be lost, the Indians had to be compelled to work. An instrument lay ready to hand in the pre-Columbian traditions of stints of forced labour which the Incas had enforced on a wide scale under the name of *mita*; a similar system was developed in Mexico under a system which the Spaniards called *repartimiento*. The Crown could do no more than try to mitigate what it regarded as an unavoidable evil by issuing meticulous instructions limiting the duration of labour, restricting its application to a given proportion of able-bodied males, and by prescribing minimum standards of food, wages, and working conditions. The regulations drawn up along these lines by the great Peruvian Viceroy Francisco de Toledo constituted a labour code for which it would be hard to find a parallel in the Europe of his day. But in practice, such safeguards were all too often ignored, with tragic results for the Indians. Toribio de Benavente, the Franciscan friar whom the Mexicans affectionately called Motolinía, 'the little poor man', tells us that Indians were rounded up for work in the mines over a distance of seventy leagues or more and were forced to bring their own food with them. Some died of hunger before ever reaching the mines; still more, from starvation and exhaustion on their way home. Many perished in the inferno of the mines themselves from which 'such a great stench arose that it caused pestilence and could be smelled half a league away, and for much of the way you could only stumble on corpses and bones, whilst the light of the sun was darkened by the vultures and other birds which flocked to feed on them, for which cause many villages were abandoned and the countryside was depopulated, whilst other Indians fled to the mountains and forsook their homes and plots of land.'

The Indians were liable for *mita* service not only in the mines, but in the no less notorious *obrajes* or textile workshops and in agriculture. In the latter they also gradually became victims of a new and more insidious form of exploitation—peonage, or debt servitude. The landowner would 'advance' food and wages to destitute Indians who would then find themselves compelled to spend the rest of their lives working for him to pay off the debts, and often left their children saddled with the same liability. In this way the *patrón* was assured of a permanent supply of labour, and the *peón* of a limited measure of economic security. Though denied any education or hope of bettering himself, he could at least subsist on the plot of land allocated him by the *patrón*, and perhaps be allowed the use of a chapel or other favours, provided he remained duly deferential, hardworking, and obedient. The old system of *encomiendas*, granted and withdrawn at the pleasure of the Crown, gradually gave way to the institution of the *hacienda* or large estate, generally entailed, based on *peón* labour, and built up by the purchase of Crown or private lands and at the expense of the common lands traditionally in use by the free Indian communities. This *hacienda* system was to remain the basis of Latin America's social structure down to our own times (see pages 228–32).

Civil and ecclesiastical administration

The decay of Spain's power in the seventeenth century was reflected in the declining quality of the officials sent out to administer her colonies. Originally forbidden to own *encomiendas*, they now acquired estates of their own and too often took a hand in exploiting the Indians they were supposed to protect. The *corregidores*, whose function it was to collect tribute from the Indians and enforce the *mita* in the districts under their control, were particularly prone to abuse their powers. The celebrated secret report which two Spanish officers, Jorge Juan and Antonio de Ulloa, prepared for the Crown after their visit to the colonies in the middle of the eighteenth century, contains many horrifying examples of such maladministration. The *corregidores* also enjoyed the monopoly of selling European goods to the Indians who were obliged to pay inflated prices for articles which they did not want but which the merchants had been unable to dispose of in the towns; books on theology were palmed off on illiterate Indians, and silk stockings on barefoot labourers. Native *curacas* or *caciques* acted as overseers and intermediaries in such transactions, and generally identified themselves with Spanish interests. But occasionally, when oppression and exploitation drove them beyond endurance, the Indians rebelled. The most serious rising occurred in 1780, when José Gabriel Condorcanqui, a *curaca* in the Peruvian sierra, assumed the style of Tupac Amaru II, seized and executed the local *corregidor*, led his Indian levies against Cuzco, and demanded an end to forced labour, forced sales, and the institution of *corregidores* and a general redress of native grievances. Protests against exorbitant taxation and other abuses led to a simultaneous rising in New Granada (Colombia). These movements were suppressed and their leaders brought to justice, but the Crown did make serious attempts in the second half of the eighteenth century to improve colonial administration by introducing a number of reforms.

The reforms were reflections of the 'Enlightenment' which had reached Spain after the advent of the Bourbon dynasty and achieved its full brilliance in the reign of Charles III (1759–88). That monarch's able ministers, with the confident rationalism of the French Encyclopaedists, set out to make the administration of the colonies more efficient, their economy more productive, and their trade structure more flexible. Though the basic institutions of vice-royalties and *audiencias* were retained, the office of *corregidor* was discarded in favour of larger territorial units administered by *intendentes* after the centralized French system. The languishing mining industry was revitalized, the trading monopoly enjoyed by Seville and Cadiz abolished, and trade with the colonies thrown open to all Spanish ports. Scientific enquiry and technical progress were stimulated by a series of expeditions undertaken by distinguished foreigners—Frézier (1713), La Condamine (1738), Bougainville (1767), Vancouver (1795)—and by the monumental scientific and sociological labours of the great Alexander von Humboldt (1769–1821). Spain, so long a laggard in Europe's technical advance, took notable strides forward. Mutis, the distinguished Cadiz-born botanist, settled in Bogotá and embarked on the herculean task of collecting and cataloguing specimens of the flora of all South America north of the Equator, whilst the pioneering medical expedition brilliantly conceived and organized by Francisco Javier Balmis (1803) brought Jenner's recently discovered vaccines to protect the population against the ravages of smallpox which had cost the colonies so many lives.

In one direction the reforming zeal of the Enlightenment proved counter-productive and resulted in the ultimate weakening of the royal power. The Spanish conquest, we have noted, was not only military but spiritual. With the conquistadores, or close on their heels, had come the friars. They had learned the languages of the vanquished and sought to incorporate their charges spiritually, as the soldiers, *encomenderos* and administrators incorporated them physically, into the King of Spain's domains. Nor did they relax their labours after the initial impetus of the conquest had spent itself. During the three centuries of colonial rule, the missionaries steadily pushed forward the frontiers of Christian society, converting and pacifying the savage tribes on the disturbed periphery of the empire from the deserts of Northern Mexico to the Araucanian forest of Southern Chile and the pampas of Argentina. To protect their converts against the rapacity of slavers and *encomenderos* the missionaries organized them into 'reductions' or mission settlements. Following the interesting pilot-projects of Vasco de Quiroga in Mexico (see page 45), the Jesuits and Franciscans showed themselves particularly adept at this work. In California, on the Peruvian *altiplano* and in the vast basin of the Amazon they organized flourishing Indian communities. But it was in Paraguay, along the upper Paraná and Uruguay rivers, that the Jesuits' most remarkable and sustained achievement was to be found. Here some dozens of Indian *pueblos*, devoted to the raising of cattle and the cultivation of cotton, tobacco, and *yerba mate*, each largely self-supporting but carrying on a lively trade amongst themselves and selling their surplus for the benefit of the communities and the Jesuit Order which ran them, formed a theocratic, Guaraní-speaking polity segregated as far as possible from contact with Creoles and Spanish officials. Though Indians held the rank of *alcaldes*, *regidores*, and the other standard offices of Spanish administration, every detail of *pueblo* life was in fact organized by the Fathers according to a strictly paternalistic routine of communal agricultural work, religious duties, handicrafts, and *fiestas*. The Indians proved apt and docile pupils—the remarkable series of books written in Guaraní and set up and printed in the settlements by Indian craftsmen showed that they were far from being regarded as mere mindless rural labourers—but hardly more than pupils. It could be objected that, instead of gradually leading them to adulthood and participation in the life of the wider community, the Jesuits condemned them to a state of permanent if humanely administered apartheid. The *hacendados* and *bandeirantes* objected on cruder grounds, for the settlements formed reserves of Indian labour which they coveted for themselves. In four years alone, Brazilian slavers are reported to have raided and carried away 60,000 Indians from the settlements into captivity.

The Crown had its own reasons for regarding the Jesuits with hostility. Though their settlements represented a valuable economic asset and were prompt in payment of the tribute due from the Indians, they constituted virtually a state within a state. This was intolerable both to the absolutist doctrines of the Spanish Bourbons and to the anti-clerical zeal of the Marquis of Pombal, the King of Portugal's all-powerful minister. Nor was their control of the mission settlements the only aspect of the Jesuits' predominance which aroused the royal displeasure. The Society had long exercised a commanding influence over all forms of higher education, particularly in Brazil. Its economic power was formidable; the Society owned huge plantations and managed business and agricultural enterprises, the profits of which went to finance its seminaries and missions. These valuable assets were confiscated and the Jesuits expelled from the territories of Portugal (1759) and Spain (1767). The Indian settlements, bereft of the guidance of the Fathers, were rapidly despoiled and abandoned. With one blow the apostles of Enlightenment had knocked away one of the chief props of Church power and Crown influence, deprived the colonies of some of their most devoted missionaries, administrators, and scholars, and aroused a resentment which was in time to feed the flames of colonial revolt.

The Spanish Crown was able to strike against the Jesuits with such assurance because of the unique control it had so long exercised over the Catholic Church. The latter furnished the State with officials, governors, and even Viceroys, and functioned virtually as a branch of the administration and the

chief instrument of the royal will. By virtue of the *Patronato Real*, the Crown
had the right to nominate all ecclesiastical appointments in its American
colonies. It disposed of church tithes, received the emoluments of vacant
benefices, and exercised a general supervision over the whole life of the
Church. The Pope had no more than a nominal authority over what was in
effect a national church, and could not even promulgate rules or regulations
without prior permission from the Crown. In return, the Church was accorded
unprecedented powers and privileges and accumulated wealth which in time,
through donations and pious bequests, amounted to perhaps half the total
land comprising the Spanish colonies. Monasteries, convents, and lavishly
ornamented churches multiplied, and so many persons sought their livelihood
in the Church that, by the beginning of the seventeenth century, well over
ten per cent of the population of Lima consisted of nuns, friars, and priests.
The price paid for this power and opulence was a decline in the quality of
many of those who served the Church and the increasing identification of its
hierarchy with the wealthy ruling élite. Nor did its numerical strength make
for increased unity. The history of the Church in the colonial period is largely
a succession of rivalries and disputes; disputes between civil and ecclesiastical
authorities, prelates, and lower clergy, missionary friars and secular priests;
disputes between one order and another, and between Creoles and Spaniards
within the same order. Absorbed by these petty rivalries, the Church lost
much of its zeal for the great task of evangelizing, instructing, and protecting
its native charges, and its internal tensions prefigured the rifts which were to
appear during the struggle for independence and after.

Despite the corruption and abuses which came to abound, as we know from
such candid revelations as Juan and Ulloa's *Noticias Secretas*, there is no gain-
saying the great historical achievement of the Church. It substituted, however
imperfectly, the Christian faith for the multiplicity of often barbarous pagan
practices prevailing over a gigantic area which would otherwise have felt only
the edge of the conqueror's sword. If it included worldly prelates and loose-
living monks, it also comprised countless heroic missionaries and not a few
canonized saints; St. Rose of Lima and St. Mariana of Quito, Martín de
Porres, the mulatto lay-brother who devoted his life to the poor and sick of
Lima, and St. Peter Claver, who devoted his to the African slaves. To the
Church the colonies owed the greater part of their sculpture, paintings, and
splendid baroque architecture, their social services and their charitable
institutions—hospitals, orphanages, and poor-houses, their schools and their
universities. To the industry and intellectual curiosity of priests and friars,
particularly the Jesuits, Latin America is indebted for the innumerable works
of research into her botany, zoology, geography, history, and languages of her
indigenous peoples which first started to reveal the nature of the great continent to herself and to the world. The Church produced figures as outstanding
in their diverse fields as Bernardino de Sahagún, whose monumental work on
pre-Columbian Mexico became the cornerstone of the new science of ethno-
logy, tireless missionaries and protectors of the Brazilian natives like the
Jesuits Nóbrega, Anchieta and the great statesman-diplomat Antônio Vieira,

and Sor Inés de la Cruz, the Mexican nun whose learning, poetic genius, and winning virtues were the wonder of her contemporaries. The Inquisition, it is true, cast its shadow over colonial life. But it never operated with the thoroughness and ferocity habitual in the mother country. Indians were totally excluded from its jurisdiction, heretics few and mostly confined to the handful of luckless Protestant privateers who fell into its clutches, and its attentions were mainly directed to the less objectionable pursuits of suppressing witchcraft, disciplining dissolute clerics, and censoring books which smacked of heresy or political subversion. But if it discouraged intellectual speculation and restricted access to new currents of thought from abroad, it never completely succeeded in eliminating the influence of 'dangerous' books. The latter could often be obtained through contraband channels, whilst European travel brought some Creoles into direct contact with the disturbing writings of men like Voltaire, Montesquieu, Rousseau, and Raynal, whose *Histoire des Indes* was the most impassioned and widely read indictment of Spain's record in the New World.

Prelude to emancipation

By the close of the eighteenth century, the Spanish and Portuguese colonies appeared to be more prosperous and better organized than at any time before. Mexico, Havana, and Lima compared with the great cities of Europe in size and opulence. Buenos Aires, the long-neglected gateway to the cattle-rich pampa, had grown as large as New York. The genius of O Aleijadinho, the crippled mulatto sculptor, was endowing the cities of Minas Gerais, where the Portuguese had ruthlessly silenced the first clamourings for political independence (1788), with their incomparable baroque masterpieces.

And as the colonies grew, they inevitably became more different—different both from the mother country and also from each other. The Habsburgs had in principle recognized their individuality by referring to them as 'kingdoms'. The Count of Aranda, Charles III's far-sighted minister, had urged his master to set up princes as the heads of these kingdoms in Mexico, Lima, and Bogotá, whilst retaining the overall imperial suzerainty. Such a devolution of authority would have run counter to the Bourbons' absolutist policies. It was therefore left to time, distance, and poor communications, to the influence of varied climates, altitudes, and physical environments, and to miscegenation with a wide range of native peoples to give rise to the process of differentiation which was to lead first to emancipation from Spain and then to strife amongst the nascent nation-states.

There had been friction between Spaniards and Creoles since the earliest times. The conquistadores and their American-born offspring had resented the pretensions of newcomers from Spain who had appropriated all the senior Crown offices. Of the sixty Viceroys and more than six hundred Captains-General appointed during the colonial period, not more than four of the former and fourteen of the latter had been Creoles. 'The most miserable European,' Humboldt observed, 'without education or intellectual cultivation, deems himself superior to the white born in the new continent.' As the Creoles grew in wealth and sophistication and the mother country sank into decay, such an assumption of superiority became increasingly intolerable. Juan and Ulloa had already noted that 'this ill will reaches such a pitch that in some ways it surpasses the rabid hatred which two countries openly at war feel for one another.' The Bourbons' attempts to set their house in order only made matters worse. What the Creoles wanted was not better government, which meant stronger, more effective, and highly centralized control by the metropolis, but a greater say in running things themselves.

In particular, they wanted more freedom in ordering their economic affairs. The Bourbons, as we have noted, relaxed the old monopolistic system to the extent of permitting Spanish ports other than Seville and Cadiz to trade with the colonies, and the latter to trade more freely amongst themselves. This liberalization gave a welcome stimulus to commerce, but it was not enough. Spain could not herself meet the demands of the colonies' expanding economies, and her ports served largely as mere entrepôts for goods produced or required by her commercial rivals. The latter were becoming increasingly interested in her overseas possessions as a source of the raw materials needed for their growing industries and for the bullion to assure liquidity for their increasing world trade. They were looking too for new markets for the goods which the industrial revolution was enabling them to produce in abundance. Britain, who was already providing Portugal with most of the goods needed for supplying Brazil, was also determined to force a way into Spain's preserves through large-scale illicit operations organized from such well-placed bases as her West Indian free ports and Trinidad, which she had seized from Spain in 1797. The colonists could buy those contraband goods at a fraction of the cost—swollen by high freight rates, duties, and commissions—charged for articles reaching them through the authorized channels. The latter, moreover, were liable to dry up altogether in the frequent periods when Spain and Britain found themselves at war. In such times of stress, Spain had no alternative but to open the Spanish American ports to neutral shipping (1797). Though she subsequently attempted to revoke the concession, or at least to control it by a system of licensing, the old monopolistic trading structure could never be fully restored. In this the Creoles, once they had begun to taste the benefits of free trade, would no longer acquiesce. 'Is it just,' the Argentine Mariano Moreno asked the Viceroy of Buenos Aires in 1809, 'when the subjects of a generous and friendly nation present themselves in our port and offer us, at a cheap rate, the merchandise of which we are in want and which Spain cannot supply, that we should reject the proposal? . . . Is it just that, when we are entreated to sell our accumulated agricultural produce, we should refuse to do so and thereby spell the ruin of our landowners, our country, and society in general?' The immediate beneficiaries of Spain's grudging relaxation of her monopoly were the North Americans. Even when the old restrictions remained in force, twenty-six North American ships had made their appearance in Chilean ports between 1788 and 1796; in the following thirteen years the number rose to 226. A similar expansion of trade could be observed between the United States and other Latin American ports, notably Montevideo and Buenos Aires.

These North Americans came as traders rather than apostles of liberty— not a few made fortunes in the slave trade—but the example of their recent and successful struggle for political freedom was certainly not lost on the Creoles. Some traders were active propagandists, as we learn from Richard Cleveland's *Narratives of Voyages and Commercial Enterprises* which relates how he lectured his Mexican and Chilean clients on the commercial benefits to be expected from political emancipation and distributed Spanish translations of the Declaration of Independence amongst them. The Count of Aranda had rightly foreseen that Spain was likely to pay dearly for her encouragement of the Thirteen Colonies in the war against their mother country. The example of that other mighty upheaval—the French Revolution —was still more to be feared. The Spanish and Portuguese authorities strove to prevent the spread of the contagion by banning the import of dangerous books, pamphlets, and broadsheets—even the fans or watches ornamented with the subversive figure of Marianne. Only the tiniest handful of Creole radicals would have wished to see the French Revolution extended to Spain's colonies. But many noted the speed and completeness with which the old order in Europe was falling and asked themselves, in hope or alarm, what this might mean for their own destinies. The dramatic chain of political events which followed in Europe was soon to give the answer.

On one corner of the western hemisphere—that part of Hispaniola which the French had acquired from Spain in the seventeenth century and ruled as a prosperous sugar-producing colony under the name of Saint-Domingue—the French Revolution was to have an immediate and violent impact. The original Amerindian inhabitants and their Spanish conquerors had been replaced by a population consisting of negro slaves, wealthy white plantation-owners, and an intermediate mulatto stratum. The proclamation by the revolutionaries in France that slavery had been abolished gave the signal for the collapse of the colonial social and economic structure. After ten years of savage and confused fighting, the negro and mulatto rebels, under their indomitable and noble-hearted leader, the ex-slave Toussaint L'Ouverture, controlled not only the French but the larger Spanish part of Hispaniola as well (1801). Napoleon, who cherished dreams of empire in the new world as well as in the old, had no intention of tolerating the loss of this rich colony and sent an army under his brother-in-law General Leclerc to restore French authority. Though Toussaint L'Ouverture was seized and died in one of the Emperor's prisons (1803), his no less intrepid but more brutal successor Dessalines succeeded in driving out the French, who had been decimated by yellow fever. The whites were either expelled or butchered, and Saint-Domingue became Haiti, an independent republic of negroes and mulattoes, and the first country of Latin America to cut free from the old world.

Very different was the impact which events in France were to have on Portugal and her vast, sprawling colony. Locked in his death-struggle with England, Napoleon determined to put teeth into his Continental System by occupying Portugal and closing the ports of her traditional ally and trading partner. But before a French army could enter Lisbon, the regent João and the whole Portuguese court were on their way to Brazil under the protection of the British navy (1807). An extraordinary reversal now occurred in the roles of colony and mother country. For Portugal, the French occupation spelt political impotence and commercial ruin. For Brazil, despite the burden of supporting an extravagant parasitic court, there dawned a new era of political importance and economic expansion. The monopoly which had routed all commercial transactions through Portugal was abolished and Brazil's ports were thrown open to free trade. Her products were sold for higher prices and goods were imported more cheaply from abroad, particularly from Britain, whose protection was rewarded with valuable tariff concessions which guaranteed her trading pre-eminence in Brazil for many years to come.

If Brazil was not yet independent she had at least ceased to be a colony. Under the well-meaning, easy-going regent (who became King João VI the following year) her equality with the European territory of the Portuguese Crown was formally proclaimed in 1815. The ex-colony's enhanced status was demonstrated by the founding of a national bank, a mint, a printing press, a medical school, and a military college. New schools and factories were opened and foreign immigrants welcomed. Rio de Janeiro took on the appearance of an opulent capital with fine mansions and well laid out avenues. Wealthy Creoles were flattered by the lavish grant of titles and honours. Not all, however, even of Brazil's small privileged minority (for slaves still made up two-thirds of the population) shared in the benefits dispensed by the Court or were content with this half-way house to autonomy whilst the Spanish colonies were well on the way to becoming sovereign republics. In Pernambuco, regional resentment of Rio, animosity between Creoles and Portuguese, and the republican sympathies of a small group of radicals led to a rising which was repressed by royalist troops (1817). But full independence was soon to follow as the result of a further shift of the European scene. In 1820, the regency which had ruled Portugal in the absence of the king was overthrown and demands for the monarch's return grew more and more insistent. Though it professed liberal sentiments at home, the new governing junta seemed clearly resolved to reimpose the old metropolitan hegemony and reduce Brazil to its former colonial status. After much vacillation, João VI sailed back to Europe leaving his son and heir Dom Pedro as regent in Brazil. Summoned in turn to Lisbon, Dom Pedro, urged on by his resolute and sagacious Creole adviser, José Bonifácio de Andrada e Silva, venerated as 'Father of Modern Brazil', refused. In a dramatic scene on the banks of the River Ypiranga, where the despatches demanding his return reached him, the impetuous prince trampled the summons underfoot and proclaimed that the hour of Brazil's independence had struck (7 September 1822). A royalist garrison at Bahia stood firm for Portugal and had to be driven out with the help of a squadron of cosmopolitan volunteers commanded by Lord Cochrane, fresh from his naval exploits in the patriot cause in the Pacific. Within three months

of the 'Grito de Ypiranga', Dom Pedro had been crowned in Rio as constitutional Emperor of Brazil.

Britain and the independence movement

The role of Britain, as the greatest naval and commercial power of the day, had
been of crucial importance in the establishment of Brazil's independence, and
was to remain so in the formative years of the Empire (see pages 338–9).
Britain's attitude to the Spanish colonies was more ambivalent. Trade was
her overriding interest; preferably regular, legal trade, or failing that, 'the
silent and imperceptible operation of our illicit commercial intercourse'—
Castlereagh's euphemism for contraband. But did she wish to see these
desirable trading partners still a part of the Spanish Empire, or as sovereign
states, or even as dependencies of her own? The answer varied according to
the shifting European scene. In times of war, open or undeclared, against
Spain, her sailors had raided Spanish American ports and preyed on their
commerce since the days of Drake and the buccaneers of the Caribbean. But
conquest and permanent settlement, at least on the mainland in Spanish
America, had not been her policy. A few footholds had been almost casually
acquired; British Guiana, from the Dutch, at the end of the eighteenth century; British Honduras, on the coast of Central America, where buccaneers
had cut logwood and found secure anchorages; the Mosquito coast of Nicaragua, where Amerindians had bred with white and negro interlopers and been
taken under a British Protectorate founded in the 1830s but given up in 1860;
the Falkland Islands, also occupied in the 'thirties, despite Argentine protests,
and retained for strategic reasons. But none of these outposts did the British
Government take much interest in or try to use as bases for further territorial
expansion. It was only when Spain had allied herself with Napoleonic France
and her colonies threatened to fall under French influence that Britain gave
serious thought to detaching them. Wellesley was authorized to raise an army
which was to land in Mexico and then turn south to strike against Venezuela;
it was diverted to Spain at short notice when the Spaniards rose against the
French in 1808 and changed overnight from Britain's enemies into her allies.
Thereafter, the mounting revolt of Spain's colonies presented Britain with
something of a dilemma. She wanted to trade with them (and Spain was loath
to grant this concession even to an ally) but clearly could not encourage
rebellion. Their reconciliation with the mother country seemed rather to her
advantage, and she offered her good service to this end. As the struggle gained
in intensity she did no more than remain neutral. But neutrality itself worked
to the advantage of the patriot cause. Britain made it clear that, if Spain was to
re-establish her authority in America it must be through Spain's own efforts;
she refused to allow other countries (who might be rewarded to her disadvantage) to help in this task, and declined to lease or lend the ships and resources
which might have enabled Spain to transport reinforcements strong enough
to crush the Creole armies. Nor did she put an effective stop to the volun-
teering or the sale of British ships which made such a useful contribution

to the patriots' ultimate victory. And when the latter was achieved, British sea-power was the young republics' firmest guarantee against reconquest by Spain or fresh subjugation from another quarter. 'All America combined', Bolívar realistically observed, 'is not worth as much as a British fleet.'

Before the Creoles' struggle for independence began, and when England was still at war with Spain, one fumbling attempt had been made to substitute British for Spanish sovereignty over part of Spain's Empire. The venture started as a piece of unauthorized private enterprise; its apparent success prompted official backing and its ultimate failure an ignominious retreat. In June 1806, a British squadron, fresh from the capture of the Cape of Good Hope, appeared off Buenos Aires. Its commander, Sir Home Popham, put ashore an expeditionary force under General Beresford which caught the Spaniards unawares, scared off the Viceroy, and captured the city with the loss of one British soldier killed. Popham's unauthorized coup led to his reprimand and recall, but the arrival of more than a million pounds' worth of captured specie, which was deposited in the vaults of the Bank of England with much triumphant publicity, led the Government to despatch reinforcements and enterprising merchants to fit out a hundred or so ships for the new South American trade. The cargoes included—according to contemporary accounts—unsuitable goods like warming-pans, skates and coffins, and 'the old rubbish that had been lying up for years in the warehouses', much in the same way as useless surplus stock had been palmed off on the Indians by the Spaniards under the *repartimiento* system. But a new act in the drama soon followed. The population of Buenos Aires, under the leadership of Santiago Liniers, a French officer in the Spanish service, turned on the occupying forces and forced their surrender. When British reinforcements arrived, they attacked Montevideo, attempted to recapture Buenos Aires, and were again defeated and compelled to withdraw from both cities. The British merchants, incredulous at the rout of a seasoned British army and defrauded of their commercial expectations, denounced the British commander, General Whitelocke, for treachery or gross incompetence—charges which he had to face in a court martial at home—and were forced to auction off their stock and leave. Some nevertheless stayed on to swell the growing foreign merchant community in the River Plate.

The consequences of this abortive military and mercantile incursion were nevertheless important. Britain, having burned her fingers, learned that the Creoles, however discontented they might be, had no mind to exchange Spanish for British rule. Whitelocke admitted that had General Beresford and the Admiral, on their first arrival, and before any blood was shed or property confiscated, declared South America an independent state, we should now have her as an ally.' The Creoles themselves had perceived not only Spain's incapacity to defend them, but their own strength. Their raw levies had twice defeated seasoned European troops; what more would they not be capable of achieving? Their appetite for higher material standards too had been whetted. Despite the skates and the warming-pans, the sudden liberalization of trade had given them a taste of unprecedented prosperity. But the episode had also revealed some of the pitfalls which were to attend the struggle for independence and the subsequent history of the liberated republics. Montevideo and Buenos Aires, though they had faced a common foe, soon gave vent to a mutual antipathy which revealed the strength regional rivalries were to assume. There was to be no unified, co-ordinated emancipation movement culminating in the emergence of one great united independent Spanish-speaking state. The provinces of Spain's Empire were to pursue their individual paths to independence, in their own time and in their own way, with only fitful and limited attempts at co-ordination. The outline of these differing endeavours must thus be traced separately.

Miranda the Precursor

A few weeks before the appearance of a British squadron off Buenos Aires, three ships filled with 200 ill-armed men and fitted out with the help of well-wishers in North America were foiled by the Spaniards in an attempt to disembark near Puerto Cabello, on the Venezuelan coast. Three months later, a fresh attempt was made by a larger expedition which seized Coro, where local feeling against Caracas, the Venezuelan capital, ran high and a revolutionary outburst demanding the establishment of a republic, freedom for slaves, and lower taxes had been suppressed less than a dozen years before. But the rebels found little response from the population and were forced to withdraw. Both incursions were led by Francisco Miranda (1750–1816), a Caracas-born adventurer who had served in the Spanish forces against the British, held a command in the French revolutionary armies and travelled widely through North America, Europe, and Russia canvassing support for his visionary schemes for an independent Spanish America ruled by an 'Inca' sovereign and a democratically elected parliament. Pitt had listened and kept him on the British pay-roll. Wellesley had conferred with him whilst planning his expedition against the Spaniards in Mexico and Venezuela. But the events of 1808 dashed Miranda's hopes that Britain would be the midwife of Spanish American independence and left the Creoles themselves to handle the difficult birth.

When Napoleon decided on the invasion of Portugal, Charles IV and his minister Godoy, the real ruler of Spain, had consented to the passage of French troops through their country. But in 1807, Godoy was forced from office under popular pressure and Charles himself compelled to abdicate in favour of his son Ferdinand. These events were little to the liking of Napoleon, who summoned father and son to Bayonne and forced both to renounce the throne in favour of his own brother Joseph. In the following May, the Spanish people rose against the French forces of occupation, set up *juntas* which claimed to exercise popular sovereignty in the name of Ferdinand VII, declared war on France and sought alliance with England. News of these events caused consternation in Venezuela and other parts of the Spanish Empire. The commissioners sent by Napoleon to demand loyalty to Joseph were indignantly rebuffed. But if the people of Spain had set up their *juntas* recognizing Ferdinand as the rightful sovereign, why should not the king's subjects in Venezuela and other parts of the empire, which were theoretically attached to the Crown as separate 'kingdoms', be entitled to do likewise? The Creoles would not accept Joseph's representatives; nor did they see any reason to submit themselves to those of the Seville *junta*, which had established its authority over the other *juntas* springing up throughout Spain, nor yet the Council of Regency and Cortes in Cadiz which succeeded it. On 19 April 1810, a popular *junta* formed by a *cabildo abierto* in Caracas deposed the Spanish Governor-General and assumed full authority for Venezuela in the name of Ferdinand VII. Other *juntas* were set up in Buenos Aires and Bogotá (May), Asunción (July) and Santiago (September). By the end of the year, the chief cities of Spanish America, with the exceptions of Lima and Guatemala City, had embarked on a course of self-government which was to lead, after more than a dozen years of strife, to complete political emancipation.

One of the first acts of the Caracas *junta* was to send a mission to London. This included the fiery young Creole, Simón Bolívar, and his friend and mentor Andrés Bello, who was to become the leading South American scholar and educationalist of his day. Having failed to secure from the British Government anything more than polite expressions of sympathy, the mission returned to Caracas, followed soon after by Miranda. The hour for which the latter had laboured so long seemed to have struck. The Spanish Regency, alarmed at the return of the arch-conspirator and under pressure from the Cadiz merchants who wanted a return to their old commercial monopoly, declared Venezuela to be in a state of rebellion and attempted to blockade its coasts. The *junta* summoned a Congress, adopted a republican constitution, and proclaimed a Declaration of Independence (5 July 1811). Miranda, who had been appointed Commander-in-Chief and virtually dictator of Venezuela, found to his chagrin that pro-Spanish sentiment amongst his countrymen was stronger than he had expected and that the royalist commanders were rallying more and more support. Providence itself seemed to frown on the patriot cause. On 26 March 1812, the country was struck by one of the worst earthquakes in its history. The capital was devastated. An eye-witness who saw Bolívar feverishly organizing relief work and silencing the reactionaries who were declaring that this was God's judgement on the rebels, heard him exclaim: 'If Nature is against us, we will fight against her too and bend her to our will!' The Commander-in-Chief did not show the same indomitable and passionate spirit. Long years of exile and diplomatic intrigue had alienated him from the mood of his countrymen. His military thinking was in terms of the ordered movements of disciplined troops on the battlefield; he lacked the flexibility necessary to direct the sort of irregular warfare which was now developing. Reverses too easily discouraged him. Bolívar was forced to surrender the fortress of Puerto Cabello but escaped capture. On 25 July 1812 Miranda himself suddenly capitulated to the royalists. Before a British ship could carry him to exile and safety, Bolívar and a group of fellow officers had seized their Commander-in-Chief and turned him over to the Spaniards, who sent him back to his death in a Cadiz dungeon. Bolívar, who was himself permitted to go into exile after this coup, maintained that his action was justified on the grounds of the older man's cowardice and betrayal of the patriot cause. Miranda had played out his role of Precursor; it was now for the Liberator to move to the centre of the stage.

Bolívar the Liberator

By the end of 1812 Venezuela had reverted to the condition of a subject colony. But in neighbouring New Granada (Colombia) the *junta* set up in Bogotá still remained in control. At the head of a mainly Colombian force, Bolívar invaded Venezuela and recaptured Caracas after a brilliant campaign of less than three months. The savage reprisals which Monteverde, the royalist commander, was taking against the Creoles, caused Bolívar to proclaim a 'War to the Death' in which no Spaniard who opposed the patriot cause could expect mercy. Terror was used by both sides as a deliberate weapon. Eight hundred Spanish prisoners in the port of La Guaira were put to death on Bolívar's orders. Boves, the brutal Spanish leader of the fierce lancers from the *llanos*, exterminated soldiers and civilians alike. As he advanced upon Caracas, where a grateful *junta* had acclaimed Bolívar Captain-General and *Libertador* (October 1813), the patriots were forced to evacuate the city. By the end of 1814, except for a few guerrilla bands holding out in the interior and a contingent occupying the island of Margarita, the patriots had been driven from Venezuela.

Bolívar's spirit was not broken by these reverses. He had the strategic insight to realize that the Spaniards, now reinforced with seasoned troops released by the ending of the Peninsular War, could be destroyed only through a vast outflanking movement thrusting across the great plains and over the Andes to join forces with the patriots in Colombia. After obtaining supplies in the friendly republic of Haiti, Bolívar re-entered Venezuela and set up his headquarters at Angostura (later renamed Ciudad Bolívar) in the Orinoco valley. The base was well chosen. The plains were an inexhaustible reservoir of horses and cattle, and the *llaneros* found in their leader Páez a champion still more formidable in the patriot cause than the bloodthirsty Boves had been in that of the royalists. Volunteers were now beginning to arrive from Europe, mainly from Britain, and were to provide Bolívar's army with an invaluable stiffening of veterans. After summoning a Congress to reaffirm the political ideals of the enterprise, Bolívar began his march. It took a month's hard going to cross the flooded plains and weeks of still more arduous battling against cold, hunger, and fatigue to climb the formidable Cordillera. The army lost most of its supplies, all its horses, and a hundred men, half of them British, from exhaustion and exposure. But it still had enough fighting spirit left to defeat the royalist forces who tried to bar the way to Bogotá in the great battle of Boyacá (7 August 1819). Bolívar then returned to Angostura and proclaimed the union of what are now Venezuela, Colombia, and Ecuador in the independent republic of Gran Colombia. In Spain, the Liberals had won temporary ascendancy over Ferdinand VII and hoped that it would still be possible to reach some compromise with the Creoles. Morillo, the royalist commander, was instructed to conclude an armistice and open negotiations with Bolívar. But the patriots would now not settle for anything less than the recognition of full independence, and hostilities were resumed. The decisive battle of Carabobo (24 June 1821), at which the volunteer British Legion did sterling service at the cost of two-thirds of its men, marked the virtual end of Spanish power in Venezuela. An expeditionary force commanded by Bolívar's most brilliant general Sucre similarly cleared the Spaniards out of Quito at the victory of Pichincha (24 May 1822). Bolívar then led the bulk of his Colombian and Venezuelan forces to link up with the prong of the emancipation movement thrusting up from Argentina and Chile under the command of the other great father of South American independence, San Martín. On 25 July 1822, the two men came face to face in Guayaquil.

San Martín and the campaigns in Argentina and Chile

We must now turn to consider the train of events which had brought the Argentine leader from the distant pampas to this torrid tropical port. The repulse of the British incursions of 1806 and 1807 had been followed by a period of confusion and frustration. The Creoles declared their support for the captive Ferdinand VII but would accept neither Viceroy nor Council of Regency; yet they hesitated to cut all ties with Spain, and it was only in 1816, at a Congress summoned in Tucumán, that independence was formally proclaimed. Whether the new state was to be a republic or a monarchy, whether it should be a federation or run on centralist lines from Buenos Aires, even how much territory it should comprise, were alike uncertain. Regional patriotism was quick to assert itself. The Paraguayans had proclaimed their independence and signed an alliance with Buenos Aires in 1811, but they defeated an army sent to assert Argentine authority over them and their strong-willed leader Dr. Francia made it clear that Paraguay would remain a separate state under his personal dictatorship (see pages 191-2). The future of the Banda Oriental—the region lying to the east of the Uruguay river—was longer in doubt. The area had been an old bone of contention between Portugal and Spain. In the rough *gaucho* leader Artigas it now produced a *caudillo* who was determined not only to free it from Spain, but to keep it from falling under the domination of either Argentina or Brazil. An army sent from Buenos Aires captured Montevideo but was driven out. A stronger force from Brazil then overran the country and clashed with the Argentines. Finally, after British mediation, rival claims were renounced and regional loyalties satisfied by the creation of the independent republic of Uruguay (1828).

Amongst the Argentine Creoles were men of integrity and talent—Moreno, who had argued so eloquently in favour of free trade, Belgrano, a conscientious administrator turned soldier, the versatile Rivadavia and the fair-minded Pueyrredón—but none with the personal authority and military flair needed if the only nominally United Provinces were to be made secure against Spanish reconquest and welded into a viable state. Upper Peru, commanding the old trade route and the strategic lines of communication with Lima, was still in the hands of the royalists. The Spaniards had stifled attempts to set up independent *juntas* there at La Paz and Chuquisaca in 1809. Troops sent under Belgrano failed to dislodge them, nor were they any more successful when the command was given to San Martín, an Argentine-born officer who had made a brilliant career in the Spanish army and thrown up his commission in order to return to America and offer his services to the patriots. But a grand strategic design was soon forming in San Martín's mind. If the way to Lima through Upper Peru was barred, why should he not strike further south across the Andes, liberate Chile and attack up the Pacific coast? As the base for this grandiose enterprise he chose Mendoza, capital of Argentine's prosperous wine-growing province of Cuyo, little more than a hundred miles from Santiago as the crow flies, but separated from the Chilean capital by the towering bulk of the Cordillera. Here he set about methodically training a new army and gathering supplies and equipment.

West of the Andes the independence movement, after a promising start, had suffered a grave reverse. Taking advantage of Chile's immensely long and unprotected coastline, the Viceroy of Peru had sent an expeditionary force to the south which had gradually reconquered the whole country. The bulk of the patriot army attempting to bar its advance on Santiago had been trapped and all but annihilated at Rancagua (1814). The survivors had fought their way out under Bernardo O'Higgins, the natural son of an Irishman who had ended a remarkable career in the Spanish service as Viceroy of Peru. A bitter feud now divided the followers of O'Higgins from those of the dashing young *caudillo* José Miguel Carrera, whose incompetence and overweening ambition they blamed for Chile's misfortunes. Both Carrera and O'Higgins, together with a pitiful train of civilian refugees and the remnants of their army, fled across the Andes to escape the royalists' vengeance. San Martín at once saw that the coming of Carrera and his no less turbulent brothers would only add to the factions which were already weakening the patriot cause in Argentina. But he welcomed O'Higgins and his brother officers into his Army of the Andes. The trust and friendship which developed between the two men became the corner-stone of the Chilean-Argentine alliance that was to lead to the liberation of Chile and the carrying of the war into Peru.

By the end of 1816, San Martín's army numbered some four thousand men and was superior in training, discipline, morale, and equipment to any force hitherto seen in South America. In the following January it began the difficult march across the Cordillera, the main body by the pass of Los Patos, the most direct route to Santiago, and another column over the Uspallata. Thanks to San Martín's meticulous preparations and organization not a single gun was lost, though the horses and pack-mules suffered heavy toll. The royalists attempted to block their passage at Chacabuco, on a hilly ridge linking the western slopes of the Andes with the coastal range, and were defeated. The victorious Army of the Andes entered Santiago and O'Higgins was proclaimed Director Supremo of Chile (February 1817).

The task now facing O'Higgins and San Martín was threefold; to clear all the royalist forces from Chile, to lift the country out of the anarchy and economic prostration into which it had fallen, and to build up a navy capable of wresting command of the sea from the royalists and landing an expeditionary force in Peru. The Viceroy continued to send reinforcements to the south of Chile, and their advance was only halted at the approaches to Santiago on the plains of Maipú (April 1818). Rejoicing at this victory, which removed for good the threat of any royalist reconquest of Chile, was soon however clouded by popular resentment at the increasingly autocratic measures of the O'Higgins administration and its domination by Argentine officers, particularly by members of the Logia Lautarina, the masonic lodge whose 'brothers' had pledged themselves to the emancipation of America and were suspected of being the real masters of Chile. The Carreras fanned the flames of these suspicions from abroad and plotted to return to Chile and seize power from San Martín and O'Higgins; their eventual arrest and execution by the Argentine authorities removed this danger but increased the implacable resentment of their followers in Chile. The country, too, was feeling the burden of equipping the expeditionary force and creating a navy. The latter was officered mainly by foreign volunteers, most of them British, and commanded by Lord Cochrane, who displayed his brilliance and audacity in such exploits as the cutting-out of the Spaniards' crack warship *Esmeralda* under the Callao shore-batteries, and the capture of the reputedly impregnable fortress of Valdivia which had been holding out for the Spaniards in the south of Chile. By August 1820 the expeditionary force was ready. 'Four small ships once gave Spain the dominion of America,' O'Higgins is reported to have exclaimed as he watched the flotilla sail out of the Bay of Valparaíso. 'These will wrest it from her!'

The end of Spanish rule in South America

The liberation of Peru was not a purely military problem. 'I am certain,' San Martín reported soon after disembarking his troops north of Lima, 'that our army will not have to fire a single shot. Everything indicates that the liberty of America will be won without further bloodshed.' But the population did not rise spontaneously to welcome their liberators. Traditional loyalty to the Crown, the economic privileges enjoyed by the merchants under the old commercial monopoly, and the passivity of the Indians were all factors which prompted an ambivalent attitude towards the idea of independence. After prolonged negotiations in secret with its leading citizens, San Martín was invited to enter the viceregal capital and there proclaimed the independence of Peru on 28 July 1821. The Marquis of Torre Tagle, a vacillating Creole aristocrat, who was later to defect to the royalists, headed a congress which was soon torn by factions. But the royalists were still undefeated. The Viceroy had withdrawn to the sierra where he began reforming and reinforcing his army. San Martín, who had been proclaimed Protector of Peru, was now in a precarious position. The impetuous Cochrane, angered by the Commander-in-Chief's dilatoriness and his reluctance to pay the crews their due, left

Chile with part of the navy. The Protector, whose strength had lain in his singleness of purpose, organizing genius, and shrewdness of judgement, now seemed to have fallen victim to ill health and indecision. Military victory, he came increasingly to believe, could be achieved only with the help of Bolívar's armies, after which some European prince should be invited to rule over an independent Peru. These, it seems, may have been the views which San Martín put to Bolívar at Guayaquil. What exactly transpired there between the two men will never be known with certainty. It seems likely that San Martín must quickly have realized that his monarchical views were incompatible with the republicanism of the Liberator, and that only the latter could provide the leadership necessary to crown the work of liberation. Returning to Lima, the Protector resigned his office (September 1822) and then left via Chile and Argentina for Europe, where he spent the rest of his long life in retirement. O'Higgins was also forced out of office and into exile (1823).

The royalists were defeated after a hard-fought campaign in the *sierra* culminating in Bolívar's successful cavalry engagement at Junín (August 1824) and Sucre's brilliant and decisive victory at Ayacucho (December 1824). The Viceroy was captured with many of his senior officers. Though Callao held out for another year, Spain's cause in America was lost.

Bolívar now had pressing problems of political organization to face. An irresistible process of fragmentation seemed already to be setting in. The Creoles of Upper Peru declared their independence not only from Spain but from Lima, named their new state Bolivia in honour of the Liberator and took Sucre as its first President. For a few months Bolívar enjoyed a hero's prestige in Lima but had to return to face his own troubles in Colombia without succeeding in establishing a stable government in Peru. During his five years' absence from Colombia, his deputy Santander had ruled in Bogotá and the *llanero* leader Páez in Caracas. Behind the dissensions which had arisen between the two men lay the deeper divisions between the territorial components of the Colombian union. A convention was convened at Ocaña (April 1828) and tried in vain to decide whether the state should have a centralized or federal constitution. Disintegration was prevented only by Bolívar's assumption of autocratic powers which led to mounting opposition and an assassination attempt which almost proved fatal. Frustration and failing health caused Bolívar's resignation in March 1830, and his death nine months later. Caracas and Quito had already repudiated the union with Bogotá, and within a year of the Liberator's death the formal dissolution of Gran Colombia was complete.

Mexico's struggle for independence

We must now consider the development of the emancipation movement in Mexico where its course had taken many unexpected twists and turns. Its starting point, as in South America, had been the French invasion of Spain which had forced Creoles and Spaniards—*gachupines*, as they were derisively termed in Mexico—to choose where their allegiance lay, Iturrígaray, the Viceroy, seemed to favour the Creoles and was seized and shipped back to Spain by the *gachupines* who, after two years of confusion, managed to re-establish their control over the country. Some Creoles, nevertheless, continued plotting. One group, in the prosperous mining area of Guanajuato, was denounced to the authorities and spurred into a premature rising. Its leading spirit was Miguel Hidalgo, the parish priest of Dolores, whose advanced views had brought him into trouble with the Inquisition but who was beloved by the Indians for the pains he had taken, in the tradition of the humanitarian Vasco de Quiroga, to better their lot by teaching them improved methods of farming and new handicrafts. Hidalgo gave an unexpected turn to the Creole conspiracy by addressing an impassioned appeal to the Indians—famous in Mexican history as the Grito de Dolores—to rise against their traditional oppressors. Invoking the protection of the Virgin of Guadalupe, the little dark-hued image long revered by the natives, the Indians began to arm themselves with machetes and whatever weapons came to hand. A few regular troops under a young landowner, Miguel de Allende, also joined them. The rebels marched on Guanajuato and overwhelmed the royalist garrison. The rising spread through all Central Mexico, where *gachupines* were slaughtered and their property plundered. Hidalgo proclaimed the abolition of Indian tribute and the restoration of lands wrongfully seized from the natives. More than an army fighting for Mexico's political independence, this was a peasant revolt, a rising of the down-trodden Indians against the whites after the fashion of Tupac Amaru's rebellion in Peru. Alarm spread not only among the Spaniards but among the richer Creoles, who hastily armed their peons, whilst the Church exhorted the faithful to loyalty to the Crown and devotion to the rival Señora de los Remedios. Within a few weeks, Hidalgo's followers had swollen to a host of eighty thousand and were at the approaches to the capital. But the priest, appalled perhaps at the violence of the forces he had unleashed, never gave the order to assault. The rising began to lose momentum. Dissension broke out amongst the leaders and the royalist general Calleja routed the rebels near Guadalajara. The Indians began to disperse and Hidalgo, Allende, and other ringleaders were caught and executed.

But the fire had not been extinguished; its sparks had been scattered far and wide and flared up again into guerrilla warfare under men who were often little more than bandit chiefs but sometimes leaders whose very names— Bravo, Guerrero, Guadalupe Victoria—had the ring of heroism. But the greatest figure to follow in Hidalgo's footsteps was a middle-aged *mestizo* priest, José María Morelos, who had once been his pupil and now revealed military and organizing gifts of the highest order. Soon all southern Mexico, except for Puebla, Vera Cruz and the capital itself, were held and administered by Morelos who summoned delegates to a congress at Chilpancingo (November 1813) which proclaimed that the country had become the independent republic of Anáhuac, that the great estates were to be broken up and given to the peasants, the clergy and military deprived of their unjust privileges, and a new democratic constitution drafted. The congress pointed the way to the reforms which Mexico was eventually, after much turmoil and bloodshed, to achieve. But its immediate results were negative. By the end of the year the rebels began to suffer serious reverses at the hands of Calleja, now appointed Viceroy, and an ambitious young officer called Agustín de Iturbide. Morelos, his army decimated, was deprived of his command by Congress, loyally accepted their decision, and was caught by the royalists and shot (December 1815).

Following the execution of Morelos and the elimination of most of the guerrilla nuclei, Mexico seemed to have reverted to Spanish rule. But in Spain itself events were occurring which were to cause a curious shift in the Mexican scene. The Cortes, meeting at Cadiz, passed a liberal Constitution and enacted reforms abolishing the Inquisition, limiting clerical and military privilege and proclaiming freedom of the press. Mexico was invited to send seven delegates to the Cortes and the Viceroy was instructed to apply its decisions to Mexico. He soon realized, however, that to do so would only weaken still further the existing social order which was already reeling under the blows dealt it by Hidalgo and Morelos. The liberal Constitution was therefore suspended in Mexico and revoked altogether when Ferdinand returned from captivity in 1815 resolved to re-introduce absolutist rule. One militant Spanish liberal, Francisco Javier Mina, after an unsuccessful attempt to take up arms against Ferdinand in Spain, transferred his activities to Mexico, where he was eventually captured and executed on the Viceroy's orders. In 1820, the Liberals in Spain succeeded for a time in obliging Ferdinand to restore the liberal Constitution. The conservative Creoles were now thoroughly alarmed. Hidalgo's Indian hordes had frightened most of them into siding with the *gachupines*. But if Spain herself was now to go liberal and enact reforms which undermined their privileged social and economic position, it would be better to cut loose from the mother country and remain masters in their own house. The new mood was quickly sensed by the astute and resourceful Iturbide. Renouncing his allegiance to the Crown and making a deal with Vicente Guerrero, the only remaining guerrilla chief of any consequence, Iturbide propounded his three-point 'Plan of Iguala'; independence under a monarch, preferably Ferdinand VII, equality between Creoles and Spaniards, and fidelity to the Catholic faith. Here was a formula to which Creoles, *gachupines* and the church hierarchy could all subscribe; even O'Donojú, the new Viceroy sent out from Spain by the liberal government, thought it prudent to accept. Only the disquieting aspirations of the Indian and *mestizo* masses were ignored. Even so, given the exhausted and divided state of the country, the Plan of Iguala might have passed for a statesmanlike compromise had not Iturbide soon revealed his own self-seeking designs and administrative incompetence. The proposal that a European prince should be found for the throne was quietly dropped, and Iturbide himself was proclaimed Emperor of Mexico under the name of Agustín I (May 1822).

Prospects and problems of nationhood

By the end of 1824, all of Spain's American colonies, except for her Caribbean possessions, had virtually broken away from their mother country. The independence of Mexico, Colombia, and Argentina was recognized by Washington in 1822 and by London three years later. Politically, the ex-colonies were free; but were they not in danger of domination of another sort? By 1825, they were beginning to feel the effect of the flow of British trade and investment, the latter already to the value of some £25 million. Marxist historians were later to see in this 'economic imperialism', and still more in that subsequently attributed to the United States, a curb on the republics' real independence. But radical thinkers of the day were more concerned with the need for 'mental emancipation'. Whilst conservatives stressed the importance of preserving what was best in the Spanish tradition, the radicals called for a clean break with the past and blamed all their ills on the colonial legacy (see pages 312–13). The Conservatives allied themselves with the Church in defence of the established social order and the privileged economic position they had hitherto shared with the Spaniards, whilst the Liberals were anti-clerical and believed in the perfectibility of society by well-phrased constitutions and enlightened legislation. Conservatives and Liberals bore little resemblance to the well-organized parties of those names in Europe, but were rather the personal followers of some *caudillo* who happened to be of conservative or liberal temper (see page 289).

But whether conservative or liberal—even when championing parliamentary democracy against Spanish absolutism—the *caudillo* was essentially an autocrat. 'No one loved liberty more sincerely than General Bolívar,' wrote his old friend and tutor Andrés Bello, 'but he, like everybody else, was caught up in the nature of things. Independence was necessary for Liberty and the champion of Liberty was, and had to be, a Dictator.' Independence only sharpened the dilemma. Spain had allowed the Creoles no training in self-government, no experience of the give-and-take necessary if democracy was to work, and political freedom readily degenerated into anarchy. Men's loyalty was to some chosen *caudillo* and to the *patria chica*, the region or city which was their home. The republics emerged for the most part from the larger administrative units—viceroyalties or captaincies-general—into which the empire had been divided. They had not yet coalesced into nation-states, and only a dictator—a *caudillo* on a national scale—could impose his will on lesser chiefs and give some unity and sense of wider community. His strength alone could stem the fissiparous tendencies of factions and local loyalties. Hence another recurrent theme of the post-independence period: the struggle between those who supported a centralized or a federal structure for the state. Sometimes the centrifugal forces proved too strong for the centripetal authority of the dictator and the wider union—Bolívar's Gran Colombia or the short-lived Central American Confederation—disintegrated. In other cases, as in Argentina, there followed a bitter civil war between the capital and the provinces.

Could this fragmentation of Spain's Empire have been averted? Could independence have brought into existence a United States of Latin America, or at least some loose federation of sister states instead of twenty wholly

separate republics? With that unique blend of vision and realism which constituted his genius, Bolívar had written: 'I cannot persuade myself that the
New World can, at the moment, be organized as a great republic,' but he fully
realized the need for the greatest possible degree of co-operation between the
recently liberated states. In 1826 their representatives were invited to a congress in Panama. Colombia, Central America, Mexico, and Peru sent delegates,
and Britain an observer. Argentina, Brazil, and Chile were not represented,
and the delegates of the United States only arrived when it was all over.
Among the proposals which Bolívar wished the conference to consider was the
settlement of mutual disputes by arbitration, defence of national sovereignty,
and non-intervention in each others' affairs. The conference broke up without
any practical achievements. Many years were to pass before the first steps
were taken towards effective inter-American co-operation (see page 322). The
sense of wider community stemming from the colonial past which the young
republics now repudiated was never, however, wholly lost, and has re-emerged
with new vigour in our own times. But in the century and a half which has
elapsed since the colonies began their struggle for independence, the history
of Latin America has been mainly that of its twenty component states. It is
thus to the history of the individual republics that we must now turn our
attention.

The Twenty Republics

1 Mexico

No part of Latin America has a stronger, more distinctive or more enigmatic national personality than Mexico. The presence of her pre-Columbian past emanates not only from the superb works of art preserved in her museums and innumerable archaeological sites, and from the clamant murals of the revolutionary period, but from the very ways of life and thought of her still large Indian population. Yet Mexico lives intensely in the present. With her booming, bustling cities and expanding industries, she is a modern nation, and one of the three most important, in population and economic strength, of Latin America. She has also become one of the most stable. Once a byword for revolutionary turmoil, she has evolved a framework of ordered government which has made possible an impressive record of steady economic growth. There are those who chafe under the system and call for change; the sense of violence is never far below the surface of Mexican life. But for the majority of her citizens, the system of strong government based on one dominant official party seems to correspond to the country's needs. It is Mexico's answer to the Latin American dilemma of either anarchy or dictatorship.

Mexico has had ample experience of both of these extremes. In the first fifty years of her existence, the Republic knew as many Presidents—only two of whom completed their full term of office—an endless succession of military coups, *pronunciamientos* and revolts, the feud between 'Conservatives' and 'Liberals', centralists and federalists, the tyranny of local *caciques* and the depredations of endemic banditry. The country, ravaged by civil war and distracted by foreign invasions, was stripped of half its territory. The mass of the people, whether the *léperos* or the neglected inhabitants of Indian villages, lived in ignorance and starvation. In this unpromising soil, the seeds of national maturity were nevertheless slowly germinating; so too was a proliferation of problems which could in time only be cleared by the revolutionary's knife.

Iturbide's reign as 'emperor' (see page 74) lasted less than one year. Forced to abdicate, he made a bid to regain power but was caught and shot. Mexico was to be a republic. But was it to be organized as a centralized unitary state or on a federal pattern? Was it to be ruled by the Conservatives, who wanted few changes in the traditional structure but to see themselves instead of Spaniards in power, or by the Liberals, themselves split into moderates and *puros*, but all equally incapable of adapting to Mexican realities those liberal sentiments which they borrowed from Europe and the United States? The Conservatives had two main props: the Church (or at least the official hierarchy) and the Army. The latter was sometimes a dubious asset, as the rank and file consisted largely of Indians, ill-trained and ill-equipped, often in rags and accompanied by their womenfolk, and prone to wander off to their villages or desert to some rival *caudillo*. After the murder of Guerrero, a hero of the independence who had briefly held the presidency (1829), the Liberals had no leader of commanding stature until the emergence of Juárez in the 'fifties. The outstanding Conservative leader was Lucas Alamán (1792–1853), an engineer by training and a scholar by inclination, who strove to grapple with the country's plight by encouraging foreign capital and technicians to rehabilitate the mining industry, and by promoting new industries such as textiles. But above the competing alternation of Conservative and Liberal *caudillos*, manipulating them to suit his own interests and embracing their respective causes with nonchalant opportunism, towered the flamboyant figure, hailed repeatedly as the saviour of his country despite the disasters he had brought upon it, of Antonio López de Santa Anna.

Santa Anna and the loss of Texas

Santa Anna had served in the royalist army, passed over to Iturbide, and then led the garrison of Vera Cruz against him. His chance came in 1829 when a Spanish force which had reconquered the fortress of Tampico was stricken with yellow fever there and forced to surrender to him. The victor rode in triumph to Mexico City, where he dominated the scene, whether under the Liberal or Conservative banner, for most of the next two and a half decades. In his love of the theatrical gesture and personal display, his extravagance, his amorous escapades, and his rhetorical exuberance, Santa Anna epitomizes the irresponsible *caudillo*. Indifferent to the real problems of his country and unconcerned even to seek out those who could deal with them, Santa Anna was at length faced with an issue which was to leave a profound mark on his country's fortunes and prepare the way for his own undoing: the problem of Texas.

This remote, sparsely populated province, covering an area the size of France, had attracted some settlers from the United States when Mexico was still a Spanish colony. After Independence, Stephen Austin of Connecticut and other American entrepreneurs had secured concessions from the Mexican Government authorizing further immigration, and by 1830, some 25,000 white settlers, with their negro slaves working the cotton plantations, were established in Texas. By the time the Mexican government—which had hopefully believed that this influx would prove a useful accession of manpower and seal off the territory against United States expansion—had recognized the danger to the country's territorial integrity, it was too late. Measures were hastily enacted to halt the process; slavery was declared illegal throughout the territory of the Republic (little was in fact to be found outside Texas) and further immigration prohibited. But still the settlers poured in. When, in 1835, the federal system was abolished and the central government tried to assert full control, the Texans revolted. Santa Anna set out to settle matters by force. After the Mexican army had scored some initial successes, including the annihilation of the entire Texan force defending the old mission station of Alamo in San Antonio, it met its nemesis at the hands of Sam Houston's men on the banks of the Jacinto River in April 1836. Santa Anna himself was captured, but released after promising that he would recognize the independence of the Lone Star Republic. Though he at once went back on his word and the Mexican government refused to acquiesce in the loss of Texas, all hope of recovering it had vanished.

Still heavier blows were in store for the Republic, which now faced the threat of virtual dismemberment. In Yucatán, a rising of the Mayan tribes resulted in heavy bloodshed and the concession of autonomy, until the central government managed to re-incorporate the province. In the meantime, after an unsuccessful attempt by President Polk's expansionist administration to persuade Mexico to sell California and the tracts of desert linking it to Texas, and the latter's formal adhesion to the United States in 1845, war broke out between Mexico and the United States. Ill-equipped, disorganized and badly led by Santa Anna (who had regained some prestige, at the cost of losing one leg, by expelling a French expeditionary force from Vera Cruz), the Mexican forces stood little chance against the American armies, which soon overran the north and pushed up into Central Mexico from Vera Cruz. Despite valiant resistance at certain points and the defiant hostility of the population, American troops entered the capital and imposed a settlement (1848). In return for an indemnity of fifteen million dollars, and the settlement of some minor claims, Mexico was obliged to acknowledge the cession to the United States of Texas, New Mexico, and Upper California. Though never effectively incorporated into the Republic, these provinces had constituted more than half of Mexico's national territory. Santa Anna survived the disgrace, to which he subsequently made a personal contribution by selling off a further slice of land (the Mesilla Valley), which the United States needed to round off its acquisitions, for ten million dollars. With these funds he staved off national bankruptcy and maintained himself in lavish and despotic state until 1855, when he took his final exit from public life.

The reforms of Juárez and the empire of Maximilian

Mexico's misfortunes were in part the cause, and in part the result, of her social and economic plight. The wars of independence and internal strife had swallowed up most of her resources. It was not until after the middle of the nineteenth century that the production of her once famous mines regained the level reached at the end of the colonial era. To rehabilitate the mines and develop other resources, the government turned to foreign experts and entrepreneurs, at first mainly British, then also French, German, and North American, and to foreign capital; Mexico herself possessed not a single private banking house. Loans were raised abroad, chiefly in London, and the country found herself saddled with a mounting burden of debt repayment. Government revenue, drawn mostly from heavy customs dues imposed at Vera Cruz, was totally insufficient and went largely on frivolities, graft, and the demands of the armed forces. The latter accounted in 1825 for no less than 90 per cent of the entire national budget. The sums available for essential purposes such as roads and schools were thus pitifully meagre. In 1844, less than 5 per cent of the children of school age were attending school, and thirty years later the proportion had only risen to 16 per cent. Such conditions made it clear that the illiterate mass of the population, particularly the Indians, were still far from integrated into the national life and had known little improvement in their lot. The Liberals blamed this backwardness, and most of their country's other ills, on one institution—the Catholic Church.

Scores of village priests, like Hidalgo and Morelos, had thrown themselves into the cause of Independence. But the hierarchy as a whole had been fervent in support of the royalists and, once Independence had become a fact, of the Conservatives who wanted to preserve as much as possible of the traditional values and structures. The Church held a heavy stake in the old order. It formed a state within a state, with its *fueros*, its own courts, and above all, its vast financial resources which were estimated to yield an annual revenue at least five times that of the Government, and to comprise, in land and buildings, about half the property of the entire nation. In the mid-'fifties, with the enactment of the Ley Juárez abolishing ecclesiastical courts, the Ley Lerdo expropriating church estates against compensation, and the proclamation of the 1857 Liberal Constitution, the Liberals intensified their campaign against the Church. Most of the clerical party refused to accept these restrictions and plotted revolt. There followed three years of civil war (1857–60) in which churches were gutted and priests shot by the one side, and Liberal prisoners executed and their properties seized by the other. The triumph of the Liberals resulted in the Laws of Reform which decreed the suppression of the monasteries, the outright confiscation of all ecclesiastical property, except the church buildings themselves, not already sold under the Ley Lerdo, and the disestablishment of the Church.

The chief architect of the Reform, and the greatest national leader to be thrown up by the turmoil of the Republic, was Benito Juárez. His origins and character were in themselves a portent of the new Mexico which was painfully taking shape. A pure-blooded Zapotec Indian who had made his way first as a small-town lawyer, then as an enlightened governor of Oaxaca State, he had nothing of the irresponsible flamboyance of the Creole and *mestizo caudillos* who had hitherto dominated the country. A man of simple tastes and unshakable integrity, he could be tenacious to the point of ruthlessness in defence of the national interests and the liberal principles in which he believed. Not all his reforms had the beneficial effect expected of them. The sale of church lands, for example, did not produce a new class of Indian smallholders, but a set of parvenu landowners who bought up the estates for themselves. Even the *ejidos*, or common lands attached to the towns and village communities, sometimes suffered the same fate. But Juárez never lost his concern for the exploited Indian masses and strove to better their lot by building more schools and roads and encouraging good government and economic development. If these goals were less likely to be achieved through democratic processes than through a paternalistic rule which looked back to the Enlightened Despotism of the eighteenth century and forward to Mexico's strongly presidentialist system of the twentieth, the reason was inherent in the backwardness and turmoil of the country, with its illiterate and poverty-stricken masses and lack of any educated, industrious middle class. Nor was Mexico left in peace to overcome these difficulties in her own way. She had first to face the threat of conservative reaction and the ordeal of foreign intervention.

By the middle of 1861, the country's economic plight had become so desperate that Juárez decided to suspend all service on the foreign debt. Britain, Spain, and France, Mexico's chief creditors, thereupon decided to exert pressure by means of a joint expeditionary force which landed at Vera Cruz early the following year. The first two powers soon recalled their contingents, but France had more ambitious plans than the mere recovery of a debt. Napoleon III, lured by the prospect of a new colonial empire, lent a willing ear to the Mexican exiles who solicited French aid for the restoration of a conservative regime and prevailed upon the romantic, well-intentioned Habsburg prince, Maximilian, brother of the Austrian Emperor Franz Joseph, to accept the Mexican throne. The moment seemed propitious, for the United States was too embroiled with its own civil war to attempt to deter foreign intervention by invoking the Monroe Doctrine. Though suffering a defeat at Puebla, the French expeditionary force pushed on to Mexico City and occupied it (June 1863) after Juárez and his adherents had fled to continue resistance in the North. Maximilian and his imperious young Queen Carlota set up court, to the plaudits of the clergy and the expectant delight of the Conservatives. But the latter soon saw that they had chosen badly. The Emperor refused to restore to the Church the lands confiscated from it, and filled the statute book with laws abolishing peonage and other advanced legislation which, if they had only stood the slightest chance of being carried into effect, would have moulded Mexico in the Liberal rather than the Conservative spirit. Maximilian's utopian dreams of 'regenerating' Mexico, no less than his incompetence, extravagance, and fatuity—he lavished money on court banquets and buildings and spent much of his spare time botanizing or composing a manual of court etiquette—alienated his Conservative backers without winning over the Liberals, for Juárez stoutly rejected his overtures. When Napoleon went back on his pledges and recalled the French troops from Mexico in order to face the menace of Bismarck's Prussia, Maximilian found himself without support. After a courageous but hopeless last stand at Querétaro, he was captured and executed by a firing squad (1867). The capital capitulated to one of Juárez's able young generals who, when the President had concluded his five remaining years of rule, was to emerge as Mexico's new master—Porfirio Díaz.

The age of Porfirio Díaz

For the next three and a half decades, except for a four-year interlude when the presidency was entrusted to his nominee and old comrade-in-arms General Manuel González, Mexico remained in the grip of the Díaz dictatorship. By the end of this period, the whole aspect of the country, like that of its master, had changed. The rough, half-educated *mestizo* soldier had become a dignified old gentleman. Yet for all his distinguished mien and courtly manners, Don Porfirio never mastered the elements of Spanish spelling; nor did the country he ruled, for all its air of progress, master its basic problems. These, for the dictator, were no more than a matter of enforcing law and order and promoting economic development. That the benefits of the latter seldom percolated down to the masses of the people was of little account. To the competent but cynical ministers in the service of the dictatorship, the Indian masses were culturally and racially too inferior to be given the opportunity of bettering themselves or participating in running the country. Mexico's salvation would come from the skills and capital investments of foreigners. That the latter, together with their privileged Mexican associates and pillars of the *porfiriato*, should be adequately rewarded was only just. By the beginning of the twentieth century it could thus rightly be said that 'the North American and the foreigner have prospered in Mexico, but not her own sons'. The latter had to rest content with the greatest boon the dictator could give them: three decades of peace after more than half a century of wars and lawlessness.

The maintenance of peace was identified with the perpetuation of the dictator's personal power. His formula was an effective blend of inducement and coercion—*pan y palo*, bread and stick. The main wielders of the stick were the army and a newly created police force known as *rurales* who either hunted down bandits or simply enrolled them into their own ranks. The army was kept loyal by the fat salaries, perquisites, honours, and opportunities for graft (often at the expense of their own rank and file) lavished on the generals, by frequently switching them from one command to another to prevent them winning a dangerous ascendancy over their units, and by playing off their ambitions against those of rival officers, state governors, and *caciques*. The latter were either won over or, if recalcitrant, liquidated, many of them according to the *ley fuga*. The stick was also ruthlessly applied to workers in the country's incipient industries who tried to stand up for their rights, to the still rebellious Maya tribesmen whose labour was needed for the cultivation of henequen in Yucatán, and to the primitive Yaquis whose crime was to inhabit lands in the north-west coveted by the Creoles for their rice and cotton-fields. Most of the intellectuals, including Mexico's outstanding writer and restorer of the national university Justo Sierra, came to terms with the dictator. The regime even adopted an ideology of its own—the Positivism of Comte and Herbert Spencer—with its creed of scientific progress. Its apostles, the *científicos* or technocrats on whom Díaz relied for the economic development of the country, believed in the innate superiority of the whites over the Indians, conveniently excusing their master's dusky skin on the plea that 'he had the soul of a white man'. The politicians too were obliged to work within the framework of the dictatorship. No true political parties existed, though one was occasionally allowed to function so as to return the dictator to a fresh term of office through rigged elections. The courts were no less subservient; their bias in favour of the political boss, the landowner, and the foreign capitalist became proverbial. Even from the Church—though he was nominally a Liberal—Díaz knew how to secure backing. The Laws of the Reform still remained on the statute book, but Díaz secretly let it be known that the clergy had nothing to fear on this score so long as they used their influence in support of his regime.

Buttressing the whole structure of the dictatorship was the country's economic revival and the financial power which went with it. By the mid-'nineties, the government achieved something unprecedented in the history of the Republic: a balanced budget. Mexico's international credit stood high, its foreign reserves increased, and there were ample funds to buy off any opposition at home. The *científicos* aimed to transform Mexico into a capitalist state. To attract foreign investment, the legislation by which mineral wealth had traditionally remained the inalienable property of the state was amended (1884) so as to vest these rights in the owners of the land surface. This resulted in a great influx of foreign capital, the quadrupling of gold and silver production, and the creation of copper and petroleum extracting industries which brought rich profits to their promoters, but little enough to the state or people of Mexico. By 1910 foreign capital, much of it North American, accounted for probably more than two thirds of all investments in Mexico. The dictator found scope for his talents by playing off one group of foreign capitalists against another. Though the United States steadily outgrew Britain in economic influence, some British entrepreneurs such as Weetman Pearson (later Lord Cowdray) were able to build up remarkable commercial empires thanks to the dictator's favour. The new north-south network of railways, however, linked the country increasingly to her dynamic neighbour who now took the bulk of Mexico's raw materials and furnished more than half her imports. The coming of the railways also sharpened the appetites of Mexican and foreign investors for the growing of crops for export. The scramble for land increased apace, the government disposing of state and allegedly 'unoccupied' land to the extent of almost one fifth of the whole national territory and acquiescing in the absorption of lands hitherto held by the Indian communities and small-holders by privately owned estates—an absorption which sometimes reached gigantic proportions. The result was a polarization of the population into a handful of immensely powerful landowners on the one side and the landless masses on the other. The latter accounted for more than 99·5 per cent of the population of the states of Morelos, Oaxaca and Mexico. At the other end of the scale, a single individual acquired nearly twelve million acres in Baja California and other northern states, one family owned an area greater than the whole state of Oaxaca, whilst another possessed more than four million acres in Durango and Chihuahua.

Supporters of the dictatorship could cite economic statistics to prove that it had been a brilliant success. They could point, for example, to the phenomenal ninefold growth in the country's foreign trade. But other figures, if less readily adduced, showed a dark side to the picture. The growth in foreign trade meant that more crops were being produced for export, and less for home consumption; between 1877 and 1910, the annual production of maize, the peasants' staple food, declined from two and a half million tons to two million, whilst that of beans also dropped by about 25 per cent, although there were many more mouths to feed. Nor was the drop made good by an increase of imported foodstuffs. The peasant simply had less food to eat, and less money with which to buy it, for in real terms his wages steadily declined. When the harvest was bad, as in 1909, many died of starvation. Only one item of diet showed a marked increase in consumption—this was tequila and other rough alcoholic drinks made from the maguey plant, so that if Mexico City, by the turn of the century, had no more than thirty-four bakeries, it could at least boast 1,300 bars. The resulting conditions were reflected in the mortality and illiteracy rates. By the end of the century, 44 per cent of all live-born infants died before reaching their first birthday—a rate nearly four times that of contemporary London—whilst the average life expectancy by the end of the *porfiriato* was hardly more than thirty years, as compared with fifty in the United States. Half the population, according to the census of 1910, was classified as living in *chozas*, little better than hovels. Though the regime claimed that it had more than doubled the number of primary schools, less than one in every three children of school age was even enrolled for school attendance, whilst 80 per cent of the population over the age of ten could neither read nor write. Elementary school-teachers were paid no more than domestic servants, and the state's annual expenditure on education worked out at not much more than one peso for every citizen.

The Mexican Revolution

Desperate social and economic pressures were thus building up below the brash surface of Porfirian prosperity. They burst forth at length in a series of explosions which lasted for a decade, causing perhaps two million deaths and untold damage, and destroying not only the dictatorship itself but the whole fabric of society. The Mexican Revolution cannot simply be explained as the product of the three causes considered by Lenin as essential to every revolution: the demands of a rising new class, the breakdown of the state apparatus, and the guiding hand of a revolutionary party. In Mexico, revolution was less the expression of any coherent programme than that of general protest. There was a deep hatred for everything Díaz stood for, and a determination to replace it by its opposite. The dictatorship was based on rigged elections and the perpetuation in power of one man; hence the watchword 'effective suffrage and no re-election'. The latifundia had been swallowing up small-holdings, *ejidos*, and state lands; so the cry of 'land and liberty' was raised and agrarian reform demanded. The workers were exploited and forbidden to organize; they must therefore be protected by the state and their rights guaranteed. The Church had allied itself to the dictatorship; so the attack must be renewed on its power and wealth. Under Díaz, national interests had been subordinated to those of foreign capital, the Indians had been despised, their customs and history denigrated; the Revolution would destroy the foreigners' privileged position, reassert control over the nation's natural resources, regenerate the Indian, exalt the pre-Columbian past and glory in the cult of *mexicanidad*. Such were the ingredients thrown pell-mell into the melting-pot. At times the flames of revolution burned low, and the fumes which arose from the brew had the familiar tang of *caudillismo*, graft, senseless violence, and empty rhetoric. But when at last the dish was done, though some might wonder at the lack of recipe or find it bitter to their taste, it had at least to be admitted that here was something new. There was no mistaking its authentically Mexican flavour.

When, in 1910, a company of distinguished and applauding guests gathered in Mexico City to celebrate the centenary of Mexican independence and toast their host in the dictator's champagne, bands of embattled peóns under Emiliano Zapata had already begun to attack the foundations of his system by invading and burning down the *haciendas* in Morelos, to the south of the capital. Two months later, an exiled politician slipped back into the country from the United States and raised the standard of revolt in the north. It would be hard to imagine anyone less likely to lead a successful revolution, or less fitted to embody the Mexican ideal of *machismo*, than this unimpressive little man with the big head and squeaky voice, with his addiction to teetotalism, spiritualism and sentimental tears. Francisco Madero was a landowner whose eccentricity had extended to the point of treating his peons well. Though his Plan de San Luis Potosí (5 October 1910) proclaimed his intention of restoring lands wrongfully seized from their rightful owners, Madero himself was against any general programme of land reform, and did not even admit the existence of an agrarian problem in Mexico. He had first come to public attention as the author of a little book on the 1910 elections in which he had respectfully suggested that, if Don Porfirio insisted on standing again for the Presidency, at least the Vice-President should be freely elected. The solutions he envisaged for his country's ills were purely political, and scarcely radical at that. He maintained, with his gaze fixed on the Reform of half a century before rather than on any revolutionary future, that what was wanted was not new ideas but the honest application of those which had already been put forward. Liberty was the people's greatest need, for with liberty they would be able to pass the laws they needed and earn a decent livelihood. Unfortunately, for many of Madero's countrymen liberty meant something very different. For Pancho Villa, the illiterate bandit chief who headed the insurgents in Chihuahua, it meant liberty to pillage the rich and to shoot his enemies—and indeed sometimes his comrades of an hour before—or at best to carve up the great estates or distribute wads of worthless paper money bearing his signature amongst his penniless supporters in an impulse of rough justice. Under the impact of such anarchical forces the corrupt apparatus of the dictatorship cracked and finally collapsed. Don Porfirio himself was forced into exile, exclaiming as he left: 'Madero has unleashed a tiger; let us see if he can control him.'

For fifteen months Madero occupied the presidential palace whilst the popular enthusiasm which had carried him there evaporated in the face of his manifest inability to curb the mounting turmoil and give coherence to the nation's confused aspirations. The tiger which finally destroyed him was not the popular fury unleashed by the Revolution, but a new *caudillo* of the old school, Victoriano Huerta, who, like other opportunists, sought to exploit the Revolution for his own ambitions. A general notorious for his cruel repression of the Maya insurgents in Yucatán, and then of Zapata's agrarian revolutionaries, Huerta was called in to quell a rising against Madero, which he did by bombarding the rebels into submission in the capital and then turning against Madero, who was murdered according to the *ley fuga*. But Huerta failed to impose his rule on the whole country. Zapata still warred against the *hacendados* in Morelos. In the north, a new figure emerged: Carranza, a landowner and former senator under Díaz, uneasily allied with the untamable Villa and with the coolly competent Alvaro Obregón from Sonora. By mid-1914, thanks largely to Obregón's military talents, Carranza had driven Huerta out of the country and assumed the Presidency. But Villa refused to recognize his authority. Carranza was forced to flee to Vera Cruz. There followed a period of chaos, with the capital alternately in the hands of Villa and Zapata, and the rest of the country tyrannized by local *caudillos*. Obregón finally drove Villa back to the north where he led forays across the United States border and eluded the efforts of General Pershing's punitive expedition to run him to earth.

Beneath this confusion and bloodshed, which seemed a reversion to the conditions Mexico had known before Díaz imposed his iron rule, something new was nevertheless beginning to stir. Carranza had served his political apprenticeship under the dictator; his dignified appearance concealed an overbearing nature and his grandiloquent monologues extolling the Revolution a contempt for the workers. But he was realist enough to recognize the demand for reform and to convene a Constituent Congress which, after much passionate debate, promulgated a new Constitution in February 1917. This document was both a restoration and an innovation. It looked back to the Reform of 1857 and forward to the still unformulated aspirations of the twentieth century. The old liberalism was now laced with a strong admixture of nationalism, social justice, and state *dirigisme*. New ingredients were added to the traditional anticlericalism. Not only church lands, but the church buildings themselves were now declared to be the property of the state. Priests were required to register with the civil authorities, who had the right to determine their numbers in each state, and they were forbidden to play any part in public education or political life. The workers, on the other hand, were guaranteed a series of new rights: freedom to organize in trade-unions and to strike, an eight-hour day and protection against industrial accidents, child labour, and other forms of exploitation on the part of their employers (Article 123). Most far-reaching of all were the provisions relating to the use and ownership of land, and specifically of subsoil wealth such as minerals and petroleum, which the Constitution declared to be vested in the nation (Article 27). Concessions for the exploitation of subsoil rights were to be strictly regulated by Mexican law, and since private property was made subordinate to the public interest, land could be expropriated (against compensation) from its owners and made over to inalienable *ejidos* for use of the peasants.

The 1917 Constitution, like other Latin American constitutions, was a declaration of principles rather than a codification of existing realities. It still remained not only to introduce appropriate practical legislation, but for the country to attain certain levels of political and economic maturity before it could be effectively implemented. The new labour code, for instance, was practicable only when Mexico had reached higher levels of industrialization and productivity. Nor was the agrarian reform introduced overnight. Carranza vigorously reasserted national ownership over some thirty million acres which had passed into private hands under the Díaz regime but he showed no hurry to give land to the peasants. Only Zapata's agrarian revolutionaries—though their leader was treacherously slain in 1919—were confirmed in possession of the lands they had seized from the *hacendados* of Morelos. A start was thus made with carrying into effect some at least of the revolutionary principles which the 1917 Constitution had written into the law of the land. As attempts were made to implement other controversial provisions, so Mexico travelled on towards the goal it had set itself, and so too came the inevitable clash with the powerful foreign interests which found themselves affected by these revolutionary changes.

'Poor Mexico; so far from God, and so near to the United States!' History has not always justified the gibe; for if her northern neighbour had been to blame for the loss of half Mexico's territory in the nineteenth century, some of the greatest Mexican leaders—Juárez in his struggle against Maximilian, and Madero, though warring against a dictatorship which had shown itself complaisant to American business interests—found safety for themselves and resources for their cause north of the Río Grande. The American Ambassador, it is true, later turned his influence against Madero and in favour of the monstrous Huerta, but President Wilson sharply reversed the trend by sending in marines to occupy Vera Cruz (1914)—an episode which nearly led to outright war between Mexico and the United States—and by extending American arms and recognition to Carranza. The latter was no friend of the United States. His sympathies lay with Germany, and though he was prudent enough to reject the Germans' offer to assist Mexico to regain her 'lost provinces' from the United States, he aroused the latter's alarm and resentment by threatening to invoke retroactively the provisions of Article 27 of the Constitution to the detriment of American business interests. But the confrontation with foreign capital was not yet to be. Carranza was overthrown and murdered (May 1920) and Mexico emerged into a period of firm and relatively settled rule under his successor Obregón.

The Revolution institutionalized

Obregón brought to bear on the problems of government the same cool efficiency which had given him victory on the battlefield and was later to win him a fortune in private business. His zeal for reform was tempered by a bent towards conciliation, an instinctive realization of what was economically desirable and politically feasible, and a certain geniality in his handling of men which marks him as one of the more sympathetic figures of the Revolution. Calles, his successor in the Presidency (1924–8) and old comrade-in-arms, took office as a more uncompromising radical and evolved into something not far short of a reactionary despot who was to rule, after Obregón had been assassinated following re-election to the Presidency in 1928, for another half-dozen years through a succession of puppet presidents—Portes Gil (1928–30), Ortiz Rubio (1930–3) and Abelardo Rodríguez (1933–4). Under Obregón and Calles the country seemed to be reverting to the old formula of dictatorship as the only alternative to disorder. But in 1928 Calles took a step which was to prove Mexico's answer to the dilemma. The party which he then founded differed in essentials from those personalist groupings which had hitherto been dignified by that name. The National Revolutionary Party aimed at bringing together, in broad support of the regime, the chief sectors in the nation's political and economic life: labour, organized at first in the officially sponsored Confederación Regional Obrera Mexicana (CROM) under its powerful trade-union boss Morones; the agrarian sector, represented by the more loosely organized National Confederation of Peasants; the army, which had furnished the Revolution with its sinews and its leaders, but now threatened to become a factor for instability unless it could be assured a suitable place in the regime; the 'popular' sector comprising organizations of government employees, professional men, craftsmen, traders—in short, the representatives of the growing middle classes. The financial basis for the party was assured by requiring every state employee to pay a fixed quota of his salary into its funds. As the country's internal consolidation proceeded and military expenditure dropped from one third of the national budget in 1929 to one fourteenth in 1950 and one thirtieth in 1964, the military was absorbed into the 'popular' sector which was becoming the dominant element in the party. Though the latter steadily extended its grip over all branches of the nation's life, it stopped short of becoming a totalitarian organization. Opposition groups—the Party of National Action (PAN) on the right, the Communists and People's Socialist Party (PPS) on the left—were tolerated, though never permitted to become a serious challenge. And within the government party itself, the differing sectional interests and opposing leftist or rightist trends could compete for power in determining the party line and choosing the candidate who would inevitably become the next President of Mexico. The party, in short, was an instrument for combining flexibility with stability. In 1946 it significantly changed its name to that of the *Institutional* Revolutionary Party (PRI). The Mexican Revolution had acquired its 'establishment'.

The stability of the revolutionary establishment did not however depend solely on its efficient power structure. Even before it received the underpinning of the economic expansion of the 'fifties which followed the nationalization of the oil industry, progress had been made on the no less important 'nationalization of ideas'. Octavio Paz, the Mexican thinker and poet, has described the Revolution as primarily 'a discovery of our own selves, a return to our origins'. Hence the new interest and pride in Mexico's pre-Spanish past, the emphasis on the Indian element in the nation's racial and cultural heritage, the resolve to incorporate the Indian fully into the life of the nation and bring him into the modern world. Teachers journeyed to remote parts of the country with missionary zeal to build schools and to serve, as President Cárdenas was later to put it, 'as a social leader, an adviser, an orientator . . . not only to teach how to read and write, but also to show the proletariat the manner of living together better, of creating a more human and just existence.' In José Vasconcelos, a writer and thinker of exuberant temperament, Obregón found a Minister of Education who threw himself into his work with energy and vision. But few revolutionary leaders shared Vasconcelos's paradoxical devotion to Spanish culture and Catholicism. For them, the unholy trinity of conquistador, cleric, and capitalist was to blame for all their country's ills. Such was the message vividly proclaimed in the great series of murals which burst forth from the walls of Mexico's public buildings in an astonishing explosion of revolutionary art. Here, in Orozco's moving, stylized Indians and sublime symbolic figures, in Rivera's sensitivity to natural forms and peasant faces, in the raised fists, foreshortened limbs and shouting mouths which crowd the frescoes of Siqueiros, is the visual creed of revolutionary Mexico; the struggle of an oppressed people to burst their bonds and build a juster, more prosperous, and more truly Mexican society.

Not all Mexicans, however, shared this Utopian vision. Some were simply out to line their own pockets, and found revolutionary licence an excellent means to this end. Others, including the Indian peasantry of some regions where the influence of the village priest and attachment to the traditional cult remained strong, could be readily incited against the 'godless' government. Both Obregón (1924) and Calles (1928) had faced and suppressed revolts led by ambitious generals. Both too faced more serious and widespread dis-affection under church leadership. Obregón had shown little sign of wishing to enforce the anti-clerical clauses of the Constitution and the trouble had been mainly confined to Jalisco, where guerrilla bands of *cristeros* took up arms to the war-cry of 'Christ the King!' The more inflexible Calles reacted to the hierarchy's formal denunciation of the anti-clerical clauses of the Constitution by rigorously applying the same. Church schools were closed and priests hounded. The hierarchy replied with a weapon which had been used to some effect locally in Jalisco: the suspension of all church services. From the beginning of August 1926—for the first time since Cortés had landed more than four hundred years before—no Sunday mass was publicly said in Mexico, though services continued to be celebrated in secret and the churches themselves remained open. In Jalisco and neighbouring states, bands of *cristeros* reappeared, schools were burned down, teachers, labour leaders, and officials murdered. Savagery increased on either side, and crimes of sensational enormity were committed. The train between Mexico City and Guadalajara, in the heart of the *cristero* country, was dynamited and scores of passengers done to death. Calles replied by exiling all the bishops and archbishops, whilst local zealots hanged priests and cynical generals deported the populations of entire regions and enriched themselves with the spoils. After three years, the church leaders called off the 'strike'. Neither side would admit defeat. The clergy, reduced to about one twentieth of their former number and still hampered by many disabilities, continued to find the means of harassing the government. It was not until the 'thirties, under the presidency of Cárdenas, that a move was made to reach a *modus vivendi*. The government did not need to sacrifice the basic principles of the Revolution; it needed only to recall the wisdom of colonial days—*Obedezco, pero no cumplo*. So efficacious did the formula still prove that, in 1938, the Archbishop of Mexico was able to declare publicly that the Church was fully behind the government in its efforts to resolve the crisis which now threatened its existence and the whole programme of the Revolution: the question of the expropriation of the foreign oil companies.

Cárdenas and his successors

Rather more than half of Mexico's oil industry was in British, and the rest in American, hands. The concessions liberally granted to the foreign companies under the Díaz regime had been exploited energetically—ruthlessly and recklessly, according to their enemies—so that by 1921, despite the disorders of the revolutionary decade, Mexican oilfields accounted for nearly one quarter of total world production. But the provisions of the 1917 Constitution made a clash with the companies ultimately inevitable. Carranza had hinted that Clause 27, declaring the Mexican subsoil to be the inalienable property of the nation, would necessitate a revision of existing concessions; Obregón had given assurances that these provisions would not be retroactive. Under the presidency of Lázaro Cárdenas (1934–40), who was resolved to give a more radical and nationalistic impetus to the government's programme, the issue came rapidly to a head. It was to be fought out not on Article 27, but on Article 123, with its advanced charter of workers' rights. Labour was now no longer organized in CROM, under its corrupt boss Morones, but in a new body, the Confederación de Trabajo Mexicano (CTM) led by Lombardo Toledano, a doctrinaire Marxist and enemy of 'capitalist imperialism'. It could count on the unreserved backing of the government, the President, and the courts. The latter rejected the companies' pleas that the workers were demanding exorbitant wage increases and privileges which would amount to a stranglehold over management, and that the government's policies towards the companies were discriminatory and unconstitutional. On 18 March 1938 Cárdenas signed the expropriation decree. The companies fought back by organizing an international press campaign against the Mexican government and by taking what steps they could to deny the Mexicans technical, transport, and marketing facilities. They also appealed for backing to their respective governments. President Franklin D. Roosevelt, conscious of the need to cement hemispheric solidarity in the face of the growing threat from the Axis powers, was reluctant to take up the cudgels on behalf of the American oil companies and the latter reached an agreement with the Mexican government over compensation in 1941. The Foreign Office, on the other hand, protested so forcefully that President Cárdenas decided on a break in diplomatic relations with Britain which were not renewed until October 1941. It was only in 1962 that the last compensation payments were made and the dispute was finally settled. Mexico had recovered full control over the important natural resources which were basic for her industrial expansion. She had vindicated her 'economic independence' and boosted national morale by demonstrating that her people were fully capable of running a complex and sophisticated business without alien tutelage.

President Cárdenas also gave a new impetus to agrarian reform. Born and bred in a Michoacán village, he had an instinctive sympathy for the needs of the peasants and spent much of his time travelling in the country districts listening to their problems and dispensing sometimes rough and ready solutions. During his presidency more land was distributed than under all his predecessors in office taken together. By 1941, almost half the country's cropland had passed into the possession of nearly 15,000 villages. The process of redistribution continued, with variations of tempo, under his successors, so that today between one third and one half of Mexico's population depend for their living on the *ejido*. The latter has become the very symbol, the most distinctive creation, of Mexico's Revolution. Originally common lands attached to Indian villages, the recovery of which from the encroaching *haciendas* had been the aim of Zapata's agrarian revolutionaries, the *ejidos* were declared inalienable communal property and generally divided up into plots for the individual use of their members. As the reform developed, *ejidos* were also formed to enable peons to take over the *haciendas* themselves or to farm commercially valuable crops, such as the rich cottonfields of the Laguna area, on a co-operative basis. The *ejido* system has not, however, proved to be, as Conservatives predicted, the thin end of the wedge of 'collectivization'. It has remained one communal feature in the nation's overall capitalist pattern and tended rather to promote amongst its members that sense of security and personal dignity which stems from the small-holder's attachment to his soil.

Nor has the *ejido* led, as its advocates expected, to greatly improved farming efficiency. For many years, yields continued to be disappointingly low: the 1930 maize harvest was the smallest for more than a hundred years. Even after Cárdenas had improved the credit and technical facilities available to the *ejidos*, it was chiefly the commercial crops and stock-raising of the small-holdings and larger privately owned estates, which were allowed to co-exist with the *ejidos*, that began to raise the level of production. From the 'fifties this process gathered such momentum, thanks to the use of improved strains of hybrid maize and the bringing of new areas under cultivation through dam-building and irrigation, that Mexico's agricultural production more than trebled in some twenty-five years. This remarkable expansion has called in question the economic, as distinct from the social and political, value of the *ejido* system. The *ejidos* are already being made to support many more than the immediate families of their members. A great number of peasants—

perhaps as many as two million—still wait to receive land, for the state has exhausted its reserves of 'vacant' lands and is loath to add to the *ejidos* at the expense of the more productive private sectors of agriculture. Rural living standards, though higher than before the Revolution, remain low, and some parts of Mexico still suffer from hunger and backwardness. The safety-valve of seasonal *bracero* labour in the United States has now been closed, though some 'wet-backs' still manage to find their way across the border. To relieve the growing pressure on the land—for Mexico's population is still increasing at an annual rate of more than 3 per cent—a vast new investment in the country's industrial and agricultural infrastructure is required. The *ejido* has proved its worth as an institution adapting traditional agrarian concepts to the needs of a new age. But the latter change as the nation develops; time will tell whether the *ejido* system will in turn prove flexible enough to evolve the new forms and usages which the future may require.

Since the era of accelerated reform under Cárdenas, the political pendulum has continued to oscillate between Right and Left. His more conservative successor Avila Camacho (1940–6), assured of sufficient support from the Left after the German invasion of Russia, improved relations with the United States and brought Mexico into the war on the side of the allies. Under Miguel Alemán (1946–52) Mexico moved to the Right in a phase of rapid industrial expansion and large-scale public works which brought fortunes to the entrepreneurs and political bosses who were becoming the ruling class of the revolutionary establishment. The administration of Ruiz Cortínez (1952–8) proved less corrupt and showed more concern for the avowed social aims of the Revolution, whilst that of López Mateos (1958–64) seemed to promise something of a return to the days of Cárdenas. López Mateos announced that his government would be 'of the extreme Left Wing'; then, under the pressure of alarmed business interests and mounting labour ferment, prudently added —'within the limits of the Constitution'. His successor, President Díaz Ordaz (1964–70), steered Mexico firmly along a middle course, demonstrating its revolutionary sympathies by maintaining relations with Castro's Cuba, but drastically suppressing his own extremist agitators in the student demonstrations preceding the 1968 Olympic Games. Luis Echeverría Alvarez, who began his six-year presidential term in December 1970, launched an energetic drive to overhaul the nation's administrative and tax systems and to tackle the two problems of widespread corruption and rural poverty.

The steady rise in prosperity since World War II had indeed been impressive. The war brought high prices for Mexico's raw materials and stimulated her import-substitution industries. Investment capital, mostly channelled into manufacturing, and a rising tide of tourist dollars continued to flow in from the United States. Though the traditionally dominant mining sector declined in relative importance, the nation now controlled its own petroleum resources and its electric power industry, which had increased sixfold in twenty-five years. The dynamic expansion of this mixed economy resulted in a steady yearly growth rate of 6 per cent and, in the view of some economists, was lifting Mexico out of the ranks of the developing countries and bringing her to the point of 'economic take-off'. Few other countries of Latin America could claim as much.

Yet a closer look at the 'Mexican miracle' reveals that all is not well. It shows that there are really two Mexicos, and that the gap between them is widening. There are many who still have little or no share in the nation's growing prosperity—the inhabitants of the remote, unchanging Indian villages and of the urban slums, descendants of the *léperos* of the last century, whose continuing 'culture of poverty' has been movingly revealed to us by the researches of Oscar Lewis and other social anthropologists. Statistics show an encouraging improvement in health standards, literacy, and mortality rates and *per capita* income, yet there still remains this enormous marginal population— some observers put it at as much as between 50 and 70 per cent of the whole— whom these benefits seem somehow to have passed by, whose real wages have risen little or not at all, and who still live with pitifully low standards of housing, education, and nutrition, and at times in real hunger. There has been growth but no balanced development. Too large a slice of the national cake is enjoyed by too few of its citizens. Those with a right to a higher share cannot make their voice heard adequately through the one-party system whose 'labour sector' represents primarily privileged groups of workers (in the oil, railway, and electrical industries, etc.) and where the financial, commercial, and professional interests now grouped together in the 'popular sector' are becoming more and more dominant. Elections do not allow for any real swing of popular opinion, nor does Congress exercise an adequate check on the executive, for the power of the PRI, reaching down through loyal governors and political bosses at the local level, guarantees the party against any serious challenge. The President, selected by party caucus before general elections are held to formalize the choice, is vested with enormous executive powers, but even he remains to a large degree the prisoner of the political system. He rules by balancing and manipulating the forces which have brought him to the top of the 'establishment'. The system makes it difficult for him to take the fundamental and probably unpopular decisions which may in the long run be required for the political and economic health of the nation.

2 Central America and Panama

For about a thousand miles between the borders of Mexico and Panama stretch the territories which today comprise the five Central American republics and which once constituted, for a brief period, one federal republic—Guatemala, Nicaragua, Honduras, El Salvador, and Costa Rica. The aspiration for reunification has by no means died, and economic, if not political, forces seem to be tending again towards that eventual goal. These small states are what foreigners have dubbed 'banana republics'; more exactly, coffee-and-banana republics, for their economies, despite some progress towards agricultural diversification and industrialization, are still dominated by those two crops, the former grown in the valleys of the Cordillera which run not far inland from the Pacific coast, whilst much of the broad Atlantic plain is given over to the banana plantations developed by the American-owned United Fruit Company, traditional target of Leftist and nationalist abuse. The five republics appear at first sight to have much in common: economic and social structure, language, race, culture, and religion, and nearly three centuries of colonial history under the Captaincy-General of Guatemala. But these general similarities conceal important differences. Ethnically, the republics are less homogeneous than is often assumed, and range from 80 per cent white in Costa Rica to 70 per cent almost pure Indian in Guatemala and mixed Indian and Negro on the Atlantic coast of Nicaragua. Spanish remains the official language, but in Guatemala alone there are many Indian communities who speak only one or other of the country's numerous indigenous tongues. Catholicism is the prescribed religion, though there are large areas virtually untouched by the Christian faith or the influence of the Church. Nor has living under the same Captaincy-General proved a bond of much significance, for the Central American's real loyalty has traditionally been to his local city and his local *caudillo*. These regional loyalties crystallized in time into separate identities and produced national histories calling for individual treatment in the pages which follow. But first, a brief account must be given of the attempts made by the five republics to live together in one state.

Representatives of the different regions of Central America declared their independence from Spain in 1821 and attached themselves to Iturbide's ephemeral Mexican empire (see page 74). On the latter's collapse, they were thrown back on their own resources and declared a Federal Republic under the name of the United Provinces of Central America (1823). Though admirable in theory, the Republic's Constitution was based on a hodge-podge of ideas, some of them unsuited to Central American conditions, and soon foundered on regional rivalries, the politicians' lack of experience, and the feud between anti-clerical Liberals and Catholic, centralizing Conservatives. Manuel José Arce, the well-meaning Liberal President of the Republic, failed to establish a consensus, and revolts, civil war, and secession movements led to the collapse of the republic (1838). The major figure and champion of the federal ideal was the liberal leader, General Francisco Morazán, who was born in Honduras, served as President in Guatemala and El Salvador, and died before a firing squad in Costa Rica (1842). The opposing faction found its leader in Rafael Carrera, who rallied his wild Indian hordes under the battle-cry of 'Long live religion and death to foreigners!', destroyed the Confederation, and massacred as many Liberals as he could lay hands on.

In the course of the following century, more than two dozen attempts of one sort or another were made towards reunification. Most foundered on the feuds between Conservatives and Liberals, fear of Guatemalan hegemony, or Costa Rican 'isolationism'. The pattern generally followed was to call a conference of delegates from the five republics in order to work out some acceptable constitution. In 1885, an unsuccessful bid to unite the republics by force, on the lines of Italy and Germany, was made by Justo Rufino Barrios of Guatemala. Ten years later, President Zelaya of Nicaragua took up his task, but his union of Honduras, Nicaragua, and El Salvador lasted only three years. A different approach to the problem was made at the end of the century by the Central American Unionist Society, a student group led by Salvador Mendieta, who believed that reunification must be preceded by a campaign of political education through public meetings and propaganda. The Unionists advocated the elimination of existing national frontiers and the restructuring of a Republic from provinces centring round the chief towns of Central America and based on natural economic and geographical affinity (e.g., much of the coastal plain of Honduras and Nicaragua would form one unit). Though this project had some logical justification and might have removed the stumbling-block of Guatemala's preponderant size and influence, national sentiment and vested interests had progressed too far to make it practical politics. The founding of the Central American Court in 1908 attempted to provide legal machinery for adjudicating the perennial disputes between the republics but lasted only ten years. More than three decades were to elapse before some modest progress could be made towards reviving 'the ideal of Morazán' by the establishment of the Organization of Central American States and the first moves towards economic integration and the setting up of a Common Market (see page 327).

The issue of Central American union was complicated by the attitude of other powers, notably Britain and the United States. The Confederation hoped to strengthen its position by seeking from Britain diplomatic recognition, a commercial treaty and a loan. But news of civil strife in Central America shook the confidence of British investors, and though a Consul was sent, diplomatic recognition was withheld. Britain had already established a foothold in Belize (British Honduras) and for a time retained a protectorate over Mosquitia (a stretch of Caribbean coast bordering the Honduran and

Nicaraguan hinterland) and a colony on the off-shore Bay Islands. But Britain's interests in the area were commercial rather than territorial and in the face of Central American alarm and the displeasure of the United States, the Bay Islands and Mosquitia were abandoned. After the conclusion of the Clayton–Bulwer Treaty (1850), under which the two powers renounced any territorial ambitions in Central America or exclusive rights over any canal which might be constructed there, Britain's influence in the area began to wane before that of the United States. The latter had recognized the Confederation and looked with sympathy on the Central Americans' aspirations for union; the Central Americans had reciprocated these friendly feelings and El Salvador had even sought annexation by the United States. In the late 1880s the area began to assume a new importance for the latter as the easiest highway to California and its newly discovered wealth. The sensational career of William Walker, an American adventurer who seized control of Nicaragua and threatened to dominate all Central America, was a warning that growing 'Yankee' interest might become more of a danger than a blessing. The disunity of the small and weak republics was a constant invitation to foreign intervention. It was to prove part of the high price they were to pay for choosing to go their own separate ways.

Guatemala

The largest in population of the Central American republics, and the second largest in area, is Guatemala. Much of its territory, however, including the huge northern province of Petén lying between Mexico and British Honduras, is virtually undeveloped, whilst the Indian subsistence farmers and seasonal labourers who make up more than two thirds of the population keep as much as possible to themselves and can scarcely be said to be integrated into the life of the nation. The heritage of *conquistadores* and *encomenderos* lives on in the line of military despots and powerful landowners who continue to dominate the country. Though the intermediate *ladino* caste is growing in numbers and influence, Guatemala's experience of democratic rule has been limited to a troubled decade following World War II and a few years in the second half of the 'sixties. A climate of violence still hangs over the land and has bred the rural guerrillas, the counter-revolutionary bands and the urban terrorists who can number amongst their exploits the 'execution' of a foreign Ambassador, the kidnapping of an Archbishop and a Foreign Minister, and the murder of an unrecorded number of victims from every walk of life. Democracy has failed to take root, whilst the traditional forms of political and social authority are coming under increasing challenge.

In the succession of dictators who held power during the century following the break-up of the Central American Confederation, four names stand out: Rafael Carrera (1838–65), who imposed a Conservative, clerical despotism and pursued his feuds against the Liberals in other parts of Central America; Justo Rufino Barrios (1873–85), the ablest of the Liberal leaders, who curbed the power of the Church and turned over much of its confiscated land to promote the new export industry of coffee growing; Manuel Estrada Cabrera (1898–1920), whose regime was marked by corruption, harsh repression, and the increasing grip on the country of United States economic interests; Jorge Ubico (1931–44), who came to power in the wake of the world economic crisis and proved a no less ruthless but more efficient ruler in his management of state affairs and promotion of public works.

Ubico was swept from office in the upsurge of democratic euphoria in the closing stages of World War II. In 1945 Juan José Arévalo, a teacher whose left-wing views had earned him ten years' exile in Argentina, took office as Guatemala's first democratically elected President. The general hope was that Guatemala might develop along much the same lines as Mexico, integrate the Indians in the life of the community, encourage the growth of labour and peasant organizations, introduce some measures of agrarian reform, enact social legislation and generally set the country on the path of democracy and modernization. There was also strong nationalist feeling against powerful United States interests such as the United Fruit Company and the International Railways of Central America, who feared for their privileged position and found it difficult to modify their traditional proprietary attitudes in dealing with the new Guatemalan authorities and the emergent labour organizations. Arévalo was handicapped by his countrymen's lack of political experience, the shortage of trained staff and the need to build up basic institutions such as political parties and trade unions from scratch. The government's programme was one of Social Democrat reforms, but such was the political backwardness of the country that even moderate measures of social legislation appeared as revolutionary innovations. No organized movement existed to provide a clear ideology or to translate the vague aspirations of *arevalismo* into a concrete programme. Attempts to do so soon aroused the hostility of the landowners and a powerful section of the military headed by the chief of the armed forces, Francisco Javier Arana. Another section of the army, however, including Jácobo Arbenz, the Minister of Defence, favoured reform and was prepared to collaborate with the left-wing intellectuals and the trade-union organizers, some of them Communists, who formed the core of Arévalo's support. Arana's assassination in 1949 removed the main curb to the increasing ascendancy of the Left and ensured the succession of Arbenz to the Presidency when Arévalo completed his term in March 1951.

During the three years of the Arbenz administration, the Guatemalan Communists, who had been driven underground under the preceding dictatorships, re-emerged as a legally recognized party, consolidated their hold over organized labour, and exercised growing influence in the schools, the state bureaucracy and in the formulation of government policies. The latter included plans to develop new road and port facilities which would offset the concessions granted to the large United States firms, and an Agrarian Reform aiming at the expropriation of uncultivated land against compensation in government bonds. In the two years during which the Reform was in operation, a million and a half acres were expropriated and some 100,000 peasants allotted land, either in individual plots or co-operatives. Though moderate in its basic conception and widely admitted to be desirable in principle, the Land Reform aroused increasing alarm amongst Guatemala's middle and upper classes as the Communists proceeded to penetrate the organization set up to administer it, incited the *campesinos* to seize land for themselves and began to indoctrinate and organize the traditionally apathetic peasantry. The prospect of an armed and organized peasant militia seemed to foreshadow the neutralization of the regular army. The arrival of a shipload of arms from Eastern Europe confirmed these fears and indicated the new international alignment of the Arbenz administration.

Developments in Guatemala were watched with growing concern by the government of the United States and the neighbouring right-wing regimes in Nicaragua and Honduras. The Tenth Inter-American Conference held in Caracas in March 1954 passed, on Washington's initiative and with the Guatemalan situation clearly in mind, a Declaration denouncing the 'domination or control of the political institutions of any American State by the International Communist movement'. The Guatemalan delegation, in voting against the Declaration, asserted that it foreshadowed 'the tendency to intervene sooner or later in the internal affairs of the American States on the pretext of combating Communism'. Anti-Arbenz exiles in Nicaragua and Honduras were already rumoured to be receiving active CIA support for their plans to return to Guatemala and overthrow the Arbenz regime. In June, the expected invasion was launched under the command of Carlos Castillo Armas, a colonel who had been implicated in previous revolts against the Guatemalan government. The latter appealed to the Security Council, where the Soviet Union attempted in vain to secure the intervention of the United Nations. After some desultory fighting, the Guatemalan army leaders decided to come to terms with Castillo Armas, presented President Arbenz with an ultimatum urging him to purge the Communists who were now feverishly attempting to raise armed units of workers and peasants, and on his refusal, forced him to resign.

From the fall of Arbenz the most widely differing conclusions were drawn. Placed in the context of the cold war, it was hailed as a notable victory for the free world, a unique case of a country which had struggled free from the embrace of Communism in the nick of time. Throughout much of Latin America it was seen as yet another case of United States intervention, a manoeuvre engineered by the ubiquitous CIA. What was demonstrated beyond doubt was the difficulty facing any Latin American state seeking to emerge from a long tradition of despotic rule and lacking any experience of democratic government or institutions proof against rapid Communist infiltration. The reformists' middle road, if indeed they honestly sought to tread it, had led them nowhere. Guatemala's experience seemed to indicate that the choice must lie starkly between a Communist-dominated revolution and a military dictatorship. It also strongly suggested that Washington would not permit any likelihood of the first alternative where the country in question lay in strategic proximity to the United States and contained important American commercial interests. A further conclusion might be drawn by radicals who sought to bring about fundamental social changes in Central America and the Caribbean. The one hope of doing so would seem to lie in turning decisively, as Arbenz had failed to do, towards the only other power which might have the means and the will to counter a threatened American intervention. Such was the deduction which, half a dozen years later, Fidel Castro was to put to the test in Cuba.

On taking over the government of the country, Castillo Armas rapidly reversed the major measures introduced by his predecessor. The Agrarian Reform was brought to a standstill and much of the land restored to its original owners. Existing political parties were dissolved and labour organizations curbed. Supporters of the former regime were arrested, harried or forced into exile. Castillo Armas himself was assassinated in 1957 and the government then passed into the hands of General Ydígoras Fuentes, under whose less repressive but corrupt and idiosyncratic rule the country stumbled into a four-year economic recession, despite large injections of American aid and private investment. Ydígoras was in turn ousted by his Minister of Defence, Colonel Peralta Azurdia, on the eve of elections which might have restored Arévalo to the presidency (1963). Three more years of military rule followed. When elections were at last held (1966), victory went, somewhat unexpectedly, to Julio César Méndez Montenegro, candidate of the moderate reformist Partido Revolucionario. He was permitted to assume office on the understanding that his Minister of Defence should be appointed by, and remain answerable to, the armed forces. Being thus entirely dependent on the latter's good will, Méndez Montenegro achieved little during his three years' administration. Promises to reactivate the Agrarian Reform and to introduce a new tax structure came to nothing, though higher coffee prices and some progress in promoting industrialization and improving the infrastructure brought the country a measure of prosperity.

The most pressing problem during the Peralta and Méndez Montenegro administrations was that of political polarization around the extreme Right and the extreme Left and the increasingly bitter duel between them. The radical Left, frustrated and persecuted after its heyday under Arbenz, joined forces with some dissident army officers in a guerrilla movement which made a considerable impact in the 'sixties, despite its later division into a pro-Cuban and a pro-Chinese faction. The violence of the guerrillas was matched by the ruthless repression carried out by the army and the terrorism of para-military right-wing groups. The guerrillas carried their attacks into the towns, where pro-government supporters and foreign diplomats were murdered or abducted. Left-wingers suspected of organizing or even of sympathizing with these terrorist attacks were themselves liable to be shot or to disappear. The well-meaning government of Méndez Montenegro was powerless to check this violent confrontation and on one occasion found itself obliged to barter the release of an arrested terrorist leader for the life of the kidnapped Foreign Minister. Its manifest weakness led to the defeat of the government candidate in the presidential elections of March 1970 and to the victory of Colonel Carlos Arana, the favourite of the Right, who had made a name for himself for his success in suppressing the guerrillas of Zacapa province through military ruthlessness, coupled with a civic action campaign which had gained the co-operation of the local population. Guatemala's next President thus assumed office with the reputation of a man who would combine the stern qualities expected of a military ruler with some concern for bettering the lot of the country's neglected peasantry. Though the cycle of violence continued with the kidnapping and murder of the German Ambassador (April 1970) by guerrillas, and the slaying of prominent left-wing intellectuals and politicians by right-wing terrorists, the new President showed himself unexpectedly aware of the need to find basic solutions to the nation's ills. His Five Year Development Plan—the first in Guatemala's history—envisaged important advances in public health, education, and the rural sector. The continuing climate of political violence promised, however, that its implementation would not prove easy.

Nicaragua

Nicaragua, the largest in area of the Central American republics, straddles the isthmus where a break in the Cordillera affords the easiest overland route between Atlantic and Pacific. From the days of the Californian gold-rush and the hunt for the best site for an inter-oceanic canal, down to the recent discovery of oil in Alaska and the carrying out of feasibility studies for the construction of an oil-pipe across the isthmus, Nicaragua has been of special strategic interest to the United States and the scene of its most protracted intervention. For the last three decades and more Nicaragua has evolved its own unusual formula for maintaining political stability. The trappings of a republican constitution are preserved, but the reality is that of a hereditary monarchy, with controlled elections taking the place of coronations. Three members of the ruling dynasty have sat in turn upon the presidential throne and given their country peace, autocratic rule, and some measure of prosperity.

When Nicaragua started life as an independent republic following the break-up of the Central American Confederation in 1838, the usual Latin American rivalry between anti-clerical Liberals and Conservative landowners became merged with the feud between Granada, seat of the leading Creole families, and the old capital of León, centre of a region of small farmers. The León Liberals secured the services of William Walker, an American soldier of fortune who captured Granada from the Conservatives and had himself elected President of Nicaragua (1856). Walker had the backing of powerful interests in the United States, particularly in the South, where the possible accession of another slave-owning state (for he had rescinded the legislation abolishing slavery and the slave trade) was welcomed. Walker's ambitions, however, clashed with other foreign interests, notably those of Commodore Vanderbilt's Transit Company which had secured the concession for conveying travellers up the San Juan River and over Lake Nicaragua en route for California. Control of these communications and the operations of an expeditionary force from Costa Rica helped to frustrate the adventurer's plans to make himself the master of all Central America. Forced to surrender, he returned to the United States, and on making further attempts to regain his influence in Nicaragua he was captured and shot. There followed a decade of rule by the Conservative general Tomás Martínez (1857–67) and a succession of presidents from Granada who gave the country peace and some slight economic growth. Their ascendancy was ended by the dictatorship of José Santos Zelaya (1893–1909), whose ambitions brought him into conflict with his Central American neighbours and with widespread American interests in the isthmus. His forced resignation ushered in nearly three decades of weak presidential rule and direct intervention by the United States.

The mismanagement of Zelaya's dictatorship and the disorders following his fall brought financial chaos to the country. A Conservative government headed by President Adolfo Díaz (1911–17) accepted United States plans for re-organization and a loan, while American interests acquired a stake in Nicaragua's railway, central bank, and customs revenue which reduced the country almost to the level of a financial dependency of the United States. A Liberal revolt, launched under the slogan of 'Down with Yankee imperialism!' was suppressed with the help of marines landed from American warships. Díaz was succeeded by another Conservative President, Emiliano Chamorro (1917–21), already in Washington's good books through negotiating the Bryan-Chamorro Treaty (1914—terminated 1970) which gave the United States an exclusive option on the construction of a trans-isthmian canal via the San Juan River and Lake Nicaragua. By 1925 the country seemed sufficiently settled to allow the withdrawal of the marines, but they soon returned in force when civil war broke out again. After an attempt to impose Adolfo Díaz for a second term, supervised elections were held and the Liberals returned to office (President Moncada, 1929–33; President Sacasa, 1933–6). Not all Nicaraguans, however, were prepared to accept the humiliation of an American presence as the alternative to chaos. A dissident general, Augusto César Sandino, refused to lay down his arms. Though dismissed by his enemies as a mere bandit, Sandino won fame throughout Latin America as the symbol of resistance to 'Yankee imperialism'. He continued to maintain a stubborn guerrilla resistance until 1934, when, on accepting a peace offer from President Sacasa, he was treacherously shot.

When the marines pulled out of Nicaragua, they left behind them a well-trained force which was to give political stability to the country and furnish its effective rulers. The commander of the National Guard, Anastasio ('Tacho') Somoza García, was a quick-witted, energetic, debonair officer who soon forced his way to the presidency, which he either held himself or manipulated until his assassination eighteen years later (1937–55). Somoza's rule was based on a formula which has held good down to the present day: the rigorous maintenance of law and order through control of the National Guard, reliance on the material assistance of the United States, good relations with the Church, and the promotion of public works and of a wide range of economic enterprises likely to yield the ruling dynasty and its supporters a generous share of the profits. Gifted with considerable flair as an entrepreneur, 'Tacho'

Somoza was able to lay the foundations of an extensive commercial empire in real estate, sugar and banana plantations, cattle ranches, shipping, lumber, textiles, distilleries, cement, and many other flourishing businesses. The two sons who succeeded him in the presidency, Luis and later Anastasio ('Tachito') extended this empire still further, until Nicaragua became not only the political fief, but to a large extent the private economic preserve, of a single dynasty.

No regime has been more avowedly anti-Communist than that of the Somozas; nor has any other party probably gone so far as the ruling Liberal Nationalists in equating 'Conservative=Communist' and using this as an electioneering slogan. Opponents of the regime, whether Social Democrats like President Figueres of Costa Rica, with whom 'Tacho' Somoza carried on a bitter feud, bourgeois adherents of the old Conservative Party, or pro-Castro guerrillas, have all been indifferently dubbed Communist and dealt with accordingly. The government nevertheless takes pains to cultivate the image of a benevolent autocracy. Luis Somoza (President 1955–63) gave the country a labour and social security code, founded a Housing Institute, and even had an Agrarian Reform Law placed on the statute book. His successor René Schick (1963–6), who proved to be less of a puppet president than had been expected, took some steps to curb corruption and liberalize the regime. But the National Guard's repression of an opposition rally in the centre of Managua (January 1967), in which some 100 people lost their lives, showed that the regime would brook no challenge to its authority. The following month, General 'Tachito' Somoza, like his father before him, stepped from the command of the National Guard into the presidential palace to begin a five-year term of office.

Honduras

Honduras, a country half the size of England with a population little more than a third that of London, is the poorest and least industrialized of the Central American republics. Agriculture is still the backbone of the economy, and bananas, grown chiefly in the Caribbean coastal zone by the United Fruit Company, are its main export. Unlike most Latin American countries, Honduras has no class of all-powerful, well-to-do landowners to affront the poverty of the people and sharpen social tensions by its ostentatious wealth. Nor, though it has suffered from the usual Latin American heritage of dictatorship, has the country been wholly without experience of democratic rule. For most of the last decade, however, Honduras has been governed by a Conservative military regime.

The collapse of the Central American Confederation, in which Francisco Morazán of Honduras had played a leading role, was followed by a time of turbulence in which unionist and anti-unionist presidents struggled for control of the young republic. It was only under the presidencies of Marco Aurelio Soto (1876–83), Luis Bográn (1883–91) and Policarpo Bonilla (1893–9) that some progress was made towards giving the country a modest system of education, roads, and banking. During the first third of the present century the country showed signs of developing a fairly steady democratic rhythm, 'Liberals' and 'Nationalists' competing in elections and succeeding each other in power. But the sixteen years' rule of another dictator, Tiburcio Carías (1933–49), marked a resumption of the authoritarian tradition. Apart from the growth of banana cultivation on the Atlantic coast, which brought Honduras the distinction of becoming the world's largest producer of bananas, there was little economic progress under the Carías dictatorship. Though the pace quickened under his successor, Juan Manuel Gálvez (1949–54), Honduras was still a weak and backward state in 1957 when it ventured to match its strength against Nicaragua in a brief war over a boundary dispute.

The administration of the left-of-centre President Villeda Morales (1957–63) was a time of promise for Honduras. The dispute with Nicaragua was settled, after reference to the Hague Court, on favourable terms. Overdue reforms were introduced into many branches of the nation's life. An enlightened social security and labour code opened the way for the development of a sound trade-union movement. Many new schools were built and measures taken to improve public health standards (the President being himself a doctor). An Agrarian Reform Law, somewhat hastily drafted and modified in the light of objections by the powerful United Fruit Company, began to be put into effect. The country's trading prospects were improved as the movement for Central American economic integration, of which Villeda Morales was a keen advocate, gathered momentum. But there remained uncertainty as to how far the armed forces would be prepared to accept these innovations. The war with Nicaragua and their intervention in the disputes between Liberals and Nationalists had strengthened their hand. A new Constitution (the twelfth in the country's history) permitted the Chief of the armed forces to challenge the President's authority if he saw fit and refer the dispute to Congress (Article 319). Villeda Morales had founded a Civil Guard which, though placed under the control of the army, might be seen by the latter as an eventual challenge. As the 1963 elections approached and the Liberal Party's candidate made no secret of his intention to clip the military's wings, the army decided to act. Villeda Morales was deposed and Colonel López Arellano, the Commander-in-Chief, installed himself in power through a pre-emptive coup. Nearly a year and a half later fresh elections were held and confirmed López in the presidential office for a further six-year period.

President López ruled with the collaboration of the Nationalist Party, the support of the army, and the provision of generous aid from the United States. Private investment rather than state initiative was expected to furnish the chief stimulus to the country's economic development. Freed from the threat of expropriation, the United Fruit Company launched a five-year development plan and increased its stake in the country. Some social progress took place, though with little official encouragement, at the grass-root level of trade-union and co-operative organization. But the pace of the country's development, particularly in the manufacturing sector, still lagged behind that of its neighbours. Specially marked was the contrast with thickly populated

El Salvador, some two to three hundred thousand of whose subjects had settled in Honduras. The increasing numbers of these immigrants and their propensity to appropriate good land and jobs aroused Honduran resentment and eventually precipitated a brief war between the two countries in July 1969 (see below, page 107). The quarrel with El Salvador resulted in the disruption of the Honduran economy, through the flight of many thousands of industrious immigrants, and a general set-back to the process of Central American integration, and made it probable that the armed forces would continue to play a leading role, either overtly or behind the scenes, in the national life. López did in fact retain control of the army, even when he was succeeded in the presidency in 1971 by a civilian, Dr. Ramón Cruz, the seats in Congress being divided equally between Liberals and Nationalists.

El Salvador

El Salvador is the smallest and most densely populated country in Central America. An independent republic since 1841, it survived repeated attacks from its larger neighbours and the feuding of its own nominally 'Conservative' or 'Liberal' *caudillos* to achieve, by the end of the century, a strongly developed sense of national identity and a certain degree of prosperity, thanks largely to the crop which still today brings in nearly half its export earnings—coffee. In its social structure the country showed in microcosm the characteristic Latin American pattern—a small and wealthy oligarchy, often referred to as the 'Fourteen Families', superimposed upon a rural and mainly landless population of *mestizos* with a high proportion of Indian blood. With the help of foreign capital, mostly from Britain and the United States, the country developed a number of light industries, the output of which doubled during the course of the 1960s and turned El Salvador into the most highly industrialized of the Central American republics. Though handicapped by lack of raw materials and the small size of her domestic market, the country's economy has been powerfully stimulated by the Central American Common Market with its prospect of access to a market of thirteen million in place of El Salvador's current three million. But the war with Honduras in 1969 virtually paralysed the Central American Common Market, leaving El Salvador with the problem of finding fresh markets for its exports and intensifying the country's already acute social problems.

A previous economic crisis, caused by the world depression of the late 1920s, led to a rising of the peasants, nine tenths of whom are still without land of their own today. It was suppressed, after several thousands of the rebels had been executed, by General Hernández Martínez, who seized power in 1931 and retained it until his overthrow in 1944. Soon after the end of World War II some steps were taken to modernize the country's social structure by such measures as the legalization of trade-unions and programmes of social security and cheap housing. Military coups continued to alternate with elections. The setting up in 1960 of a short-lived *junta* composed of left-wing officers and intellectuals who appeared to be opening the door to Communist agitation and propaganda showed that new currents were stirring the traditionally Conservative ranks of the military (see page 241). Although this *junta* was soon overthrown by another military group, the Directorio which the latter set up proceeded itself to carry through a number of radical measures such as the nationalization of the Central Bank and the influential Coffee Company, and alarmed the wealthy by attempting to enforce legislation for a minimum wage and higher income tax. The election in 1962 of Colonel Julio Adalberto Rivera for a five-year term of constitutional rule marked an attempt to reassure the traditional forces and to steer a middle course between Left and Right. The more favourable investment climate thus created attracted foreign loans and made possible a strengthening of the country's economic infrastructure and an upsurge of industrial production. Colonel Sánchez Hernández, who succeeded Rivera in 1967, continued broadly the same policies.

A safety valve for the social pressures which the modest reforms of the 'sixties did little to relieve, had long been afforded by illicit emigration into Honduras, a country possessing more than five times as much land as El Salvador but with a far smaller population. The settlers were hard-working folk who made a valuable addition to the human resources of the neighbouring republic but often aroused the resentment of the local inhabitants by their success in farming and commerce. Resentment reached boiling point through a series of incidents which occurred when the national teams of the two countries met in competition to decide which should represent Central America for the World Soccer Cup. Honduran ire vented itself in the expulsion of some Salvadorean settlers from Honduras and the alleged persecution of others, and led to the outbreak of armed hostilities between the two countries in July 1969. Though patched up with the help of the Organization of American States, the conflict left a legacy of bitterness and economic dislocation and faced El Salvador with the grave problem of housing and reintegrating into her economy between a third and a quarter of the 300,000 Salvadoreans estimated to have emigrated to Honduras. It is a measure of this small country's resilience and resourcefulness that she has been able to cope with these difficulties and take up the interrupted and still formidable task of social reform.

Costa Rica

Costa Rica has been independent since 1821; independent not merely in a formal sense, but standing apart from her Central American neighbours in many important aspects of her national life and institutions. The distinctive character of the country has its roots deep in the colonial period. With no native population numerous enough to serve as a labour-force for the Spanish conquerors, there developed neither Latin America's characteristic *hacienda* system nor the contrast of white élite and coloured substratum. The optimistically named 'rich coast' was found to contain no precious minerals, and constant pirate raids hampered the development of the colony's cocoa plantations and forced the settlers further inland. There thus grew up an unusually homogeneous white population (now about 2 per cent negro and 1 per cent Indian), largely of Gallego and Basque stock, a community of small-holders predisposed to a democratic way of life and relatively free from the social tensions resulting from glaring inequalities of wealth. Though the landscape is dominated by volcanoes whose eruptions periodically cause human and economic devastation, Costa Rica continues her even and cheerful tenor of life, proud of her democratic traditions (she was, characteristically, the first country in the world to ratify the United Nations' Convention of Human Rights), high literacy rate and moderately advanced living standards and gingerly feels her way towards closer integration with Central American neighbours to whom she tends to feel superior.

In the century following independence Costa Rica nevertheless had her taste of autocratic rule, particularly under Tomás Guardia (president, or power behind presidents, from 1870 to 1882). By the time another serious bid to impose dictatorship was made by General Tinoco in 1917, democratic traditions had taken firm enough root for the dictator to be forced from office within two years. A modern economy was, in the meantime, taking shape. With the help of British traders, coffee quickly established itself as the country's chief export crop and remains so to the present day. Following the completion in 1890 of the British-owned Northern Railway, a profitable banana industry was also able to develop, the firms engaged in it being later consolidated into the powerful United Fruit Company. Though the Costa Ricans fought to repel a Nicaraguan invasion in 1836, and in turn helped to overthrow the regime established in Nicaragua by the American adventurer William Walker a score of years later, they showed little taste for military aggression and their 1848 Constitution provided for the abolition of the regular army, though more than a century was to elapse before this was actually carried out and the present Civil Guard established as the republic's sole means of defence.

Following the presidencies of Calderón Guardia (1940–4) and Picado (1944–8), when an advanced labour code and other radical measures were introduced, though at the price of growing corruption, inefficiency, and Communist influence, the Conservative Ulate (1949–54) was elected but was able to take over the presidency only after the attempt by the Picado–Calderón Guardia faction to block him had been defeated in a short civil war. The chief organizer of victory, who himself succeeded to the presidency in 1953 (and was re-elected for a second term in 1970) was José ('Pepe') Figueres, an energetic reformist politician who created a nationalized banking insurance and social security system, built up an efficient party (Partido de Liberación Nacional—PLN), settled a long-standing dispute with the United Fruit Company on favourable terms, and attempted to turn the tables on the Central American dictators who had been meddling in Costa Rican politics by forming a 'Caribbean Legion' dedicated to their overthrow. In this he had little success (for he had also abolished his country's army), but in Costa Rica itself elections, since 1949, have been fair and orderly, and governments have succeeded one another constitutionally.

Though more stable and democratically structured than her neighbours, Costa Rica's troubles are not yet behind her. According to President Figueres, 'one third of the population still live in conditions which are unacceptable in the world of 1970'. A factious parliamentary opposition sometimes hinders the passage of essential legislation, particularly in the matter of taxes. Left-wing agitation against 'Yankee imperialism' has held up the development of the country's valuable bauxite deposits. The Communist Party, though it may only operate for electoral purposes under a cover organization, is vigorous, and is believed to draw its funds through the commissions on coffee deals with the Soviet Union. Dictatorships in neighbouring countries, irritated that political exiles should find asylum on Costa Rican soil, sometimes harass her. Costa Rica's own population is increasing exceptionally fast (at nearly 4 per cent per annum) and the supply of land under cultivation is growing scarce and squatting more frequent.

Although fairly prosperous and enjoying an exceptionally good growth rate (8 per cent in 1968), Costa Rica is aware of the need to broaden the basis of her economy by increased diversification, industrialization, and new markets. More of her resources need to go into improving port facilities, communications, and other essential services and less into the import of consumer goods. Additional revenue has to be raised to make up for the falling-off of receipts from customs dues as tariff barriers are lowered to Costa Rica's partners in the Central American Common Market. To the latter concept she has never been more than lukewarm. Though it may offer her greater scope for her own exports, the import of more cheaply produced foodstuffs (e.g. Salvadorean rice) presents a sharp challenge to her own agriculture. Some useful steps have been taken to meet the new situation. In addition to the coffee and banana exports, Costa Rica is building up a promising meat-exporting sector, whilst the fishing and lumber industries also show promising prospects for development. The first modern sugar refinery is now in production and other projects are under construction or consideration. But the urgent problem of closing the trade gap remains. In 1968, Costa Rica's exports totalled 173 million dollars, her imports 212 million (the United States accounting for 80 million of each). Until she can bring these more nearly into balance, Costa Rica's economic expansion will not match the soundness of her political institutions.

Panama

Panama is not, strictly speaking, a part of Central America, nor has it shared the historical development of the five republics we have been considering, though its future may well lie more with theirs. The youngest and smallest in population of all the Latin American countries, Panama owes its independent existence to the Canal, and it is the Canal, owned and operated by the United States, that has dominated its economic and political life. The present Canal is now approaching obsolescence and in little more than a decade may have ceased altogether to be a valuable asset. Momentous decisions have now to be taken as to what new waterway will take its place—and where. In the less than seven decades of independence, this nondescript and backward ex-province of Colombia has been moving towards a national identity of her own. With this has come a sharpening of the strains and stresses within her still far from homogeneous population and a society marked by striking disparities in wealth, education, and influence. The country has thus now to find both a new social and political equilibrium and a new role to play in the world.

Ever since Balboa first gazed upon the Southern Sea in 1513, men had dreamed of finding, or of themselves constructing, some waterway linking the two great oceans. The Californian gold-rush of the 1840s gave fresh urgency to the need for a quick passage across the isthmus. Panama was then a province of New Granada (Colombia), and a treaty negotiated in 1846 between that country and the United States guaranteed to the latter's citizens the right of transit, 'and over any canal or railroad which may be constructed to unite the two seas'. Within ten years an American-financed railroad was in operation. The concession for the construction of a canal was first obtained by a French company, but the difficulties of the terrain and climate, and the terrible toll exacted by malaria and yellow fever, frustrated the attempts of Ferdinand de Lesseps to repeat his Suez Canal triumph in the western hemisphere. A second company was formed from the ruins of Lesseps's venture but lacked the vast resources needed to complete the work. The United States government was meanwhile growing convinced of the need for an oceanic canal on strategic grounds—for the Spanish–American War of 1898 had demonstrated how essential it was to be able to transfer warships quickly between the Pacific and Atlantic—and was now moreover determined to secure exclusive control over any such canal. The Clayton–Bulwer Treaty (see page 98) was accordingly abrogated, and Britain induced to abandon her claim to an equal share in the zone of the proposed canal (Hay–Pauncefote Treaty of 1901). Washington first favoured the construction of the new canal through Nicaragua, but switched preference to the Panama route thanks to the persuasions of Bunau-Varilla, formerly de Lesseps's chief engineer, and other lobbyists of the canal company. An agreement was negotiated between the United States and New Granada and ratified by the United States senate. But Bogotá, playing for time in anticipation of the expiry of the company's concession and the reversion of its valuable assets, refused ratification. The American President, the ebullient Theodore Roosevelt, resolved to break the deadlock by going over the heads of the Bogotá politicians and doing a deal with the separatist faction in Panama which had long been chafing under the authority of the distant Andean capital.

This faction rightly anticipated that American warships would be sent to neutralize any attempt by the Colombian authorities to reassert control. Panama's independence was proclaimed and at once recognized by Washington, where Bunau-Varilla was accredited as the new republic's representative (1903). Within a fortnight a treaty had been signed providing for a ten-mile wide canal zone running through Panamanian territory, and the United States government then bought up the company's assets. In return for a down payment of ten million dollars and a further quarter of a million in annual rent, the United States undertook to guarantee and 'maintain the independence' of Panama (Article 1) and was given the right to police Panama City and Colón. In his haste to clinch the deal, Bunau-Varilla had redrafted Clause 3 of the Treaty to give the United States all the rights and authority in the canal zone 'which it would possess if it were sovereign'. Clause 2, however, merely granted the United States 'in perpetuity the use, occupation and control' of the zone. The contradictions inherent in the Hay–Bunau-Varilla Treaty were to prove a fertile source of conflict between the United States and Panama. The latter found itself cut in half by an immensely richer and more powerful alien enclave controlling the waterway which provided the republic with its *raison d'être*. The United States exercised effective 'sovereign rights' over territory in which Panama was theoretically 'sovereign'.

As these 'sovereign rights' were vigorously asserted, the Americanization of the zone proceeded apace and intensified the differentiation between American personnel and Panamanians. The latter, paid 'in silver' whereas the Americans were paid 'in gold', became resentful of the widening economic and social gap. The 'Zonians', proud of their role as guardians of a strategic key to their country's defence and operators of a superb technological achievement, developed an arrogant colonialist mentality. Treaty rights to intervene in Panama's internal affairs outside the zone were exercised with scant regard to national susceptibilities.

The canal brought prosperity to Panama but the privileged American presence was bitterly resented. To secure a larger share of the economic benefits and make effective Panama's claim to sovereignty over the zone became the aims of the republic's policy. The United States made some concessions in this direction. In 1936, and again in 1955, Washington agreed to raise the annuity payable in respect of the zone and to give up certain rights both within it and outside, but surrendered none of her basic 'sovereign rights'. The symbolic 'flag issue' assumed a crucial importance and twice led to major crises between the two countries—in 1959, provoked by Panamanian attempts to fly the republic's colours in the zone, and in 1964, when Zonian high-school students insisted on hoisting the Stars and Stripes in defiance of the Governor's orders. The latter incident sparked off Panamanian counter-demonstrations and riots leading to serious loss of life and a rupture in diplomatic relations. The outburst underlined the gravity of this continuing dispute and induced the Johnson administration to begin negotiations for an entirely new treaty.

By 1967 the draft of a basic treaty replacing the 1903 Hay–Bunau-Varilla Treaty had been worked out. It was to be of limited duration instead of 'in perpetuity', recognizing Panamanian sovereignty over a reduced 'Canal area', where there would no longer be job discrimination between Panamanians and Americans, and providing for a Joint Administration to operate the canal and set the tolls, an agreed proportion of which would go to Panama in place of an annual rent. Linked with this were the drafts of two further treaties, one dealing with the construction of a proposed new sea-level canal, the other with defence —an issue of vital concern to the United States not only in respect of the canal itself, but on account of the location there of the Southern Command head-quarters, with its counter-insurgency training facilities for use by the armed forces of all Latin America. These treaties, if implemented, would put Panama's relations with the United States on an entirely new footing. But emotions on the canal issue ran high in both countries, and ratification—or a fresh attempt to renegotiate the Canal Treaty—still waits upon the troubled course of Panamanian politics.

This course has hitherto been set by a small number of leading families who have also dominated the country's economy. The native rural population, scattered, backward and impoverished, has not yet become a factor in the national life. In the towns, however, a growing middle and working class of nationalistic and often radical temper (particularly amongst the students) is starting to make its voice heard. In the 1930s, the influential Arias family began to rally support also from amongst these popular sectors, and the tempestuous, autocratic Arnulfo Arias was thrice elected to the presidency and thrice unseated by officers of the National Guard. Following their most recent *golpe* of October 1968, power has remained with the latter, General Omar Torrijos being the effective master of the country though its government is formally headed by the civilian President Lakas. Some measures of radical reform have been announced by the regime with a view to improving the lot of the middle and under-privileged sectors, but little has so far been done to implement them. Real change is only likely to follow a settlement of the canal issue which will in turn determine the shape of the country's economic future.

For all her difficulties over the canal, Panama has been growing in pros-perity. Over the last ten years, the economy has been expanding at the rate of about 8 per cent per annum. Output of citrus fruit, bananas, cattle, petroleum derivatives, and other products is growing, and her businessmen are asking themselves whether the country's interests can best be served by closer association with regional groupings such as the Central American Common Market and the Caribbean Free Trade Area, or by developing her free-trade facilities so as to become a sort of Latin American Hong Kong. The recent discovery of gigantic deposits of high-grade copper in difficult terrain in Colón province may in time revolutionize her economy and eliminate its dependence on the canal. Until then, however, Panama's traditional pre-occupations remain, and are heightened by questions of growing urgency: will a new status for the Zone be enough? What about the new canal which must surely be built? Will it lie in Panamanian territory, and if so, where? And what consequences is it likely to have for the republic?

The present canal is finding increasing difficulty in handling the expanding volume of shipping, and by 1985, or earlier, it is expected to reach saturation point. Many warships, merchant vessels, and tankers are already too large for its locks. A far deeper and broader sea-level canal is needed, for both com-mercial and strategic reasons. Detailed surveys have been carried out to ascertain the most suitable route, and four or five main possibilities present themselves. Two of them lie within Panamanian territory. One would pass through Darien, some 110 miles south-east of the present canal, in wild and sparsely inhabited country, where relatively economical nuclear-powered excavation techniques could be used. The other possibility would be to enlarge or duplicate the course of the present canal, using more expensive conventional methods of construction, since nuclear blast might endanger life and property in the built-up areas. This is the alternative favoured by the Interoceanic Canal Commission, which has advised President Nixon that a sea-level canal running some fourteen miles west of the present lock-canal would take around fifteen years to build and cost 2·88 billion dollars. The Darien route, on the other hand, would open up a neglected area of the republic but would also lead to the obsolescence of the present canal and the decline of Panama City, Colón, and the Zone. In any case, wherever it may be constructed, a sea-water canal would require only a fraction of the present labour force for its maintenance and could lead to serious unemployment. These and other problems would become still more acute should the decision be taken to build the canal outside Panama. The route along the San Juan River and Lake Nicaragua (see page 102), being considerably nearer to the United States, still has its advocates. An alternative route along Colombia's Atrato and Truando Rivers, though longer and more remote, is favoured by others. Colombia is considering an alternative scheme of her own in that region for the construction of a great hydro-electric complex designed to develop her neglected north-west territory and at the same time to link the Atlantic and Pacific by an inter-oceanic waterway. These ambitious and competing projects are bound to raise a question-mark over the long-term prospects of Panama, whose possession of the sole oceanic canal has been the bane and blessing of the republic's existence.

3 Haiti and the Dominican Republic

Haiti

Haiti, the small and beautiful country occupying the western third of the island of Hispaniola, has a national identity and history unlike those of the other Latin American republics. An ex-colony of France, it still retains French as the official language, while Creole, the local French-derived dialect, is the mother tongue of almost the entire population. The latter is composed of negroes and a small minority of mulattos, the wealthier, better educated, and often sophisticated traditional élite. Racial and social tension between this minority and the black majority has been a recurrent theme in Haiti's politics; another is the hatred felt for their lighter-skinned, Spanish-speaking Dominican neighbours. Other features of the Haitian scene are the explosive growth which has led to over-population, giving rise to the progressive fragmentation of already diminutive holdings; the haphazard cultivation of coffee as the country's main cash crop, the implacable march of erosion, the primitive agricultural techniques and the general underdevelopment from which the country seems powerless to escape, the widespread illiteracy, and the diseases resulting largely from malnutrition, the fecklessness and fatalism of the people —but also their joyous exuberance, the generosity and patience under a government which has seldom been anything other than tyrannical, corrupt, and inept. Some pages in the Haitians' history are amongst the most glorious and spectacular of the western hemisphere. Theirs was the first country in Latin America to win its political independence, and the only one to carry through a social revolution as well. It was the first, and for long remained the only, independent black republic anywhere in the world. These glories lie far in the past. The present is sombre, and the long years which lie between tell mostly of frustrated hopes and continuing misery.

Haiti's independence was formally proclaimed at the beginning of 1804 (see page 62). Tearing the white from the French Tricolour and leaving only red and blue as the colours of the new republic, Dessalines declared all slavery abolished and forbade any white man to own land. The ex-slaves, no longer compelled to toil for a master, abandoned the sugar estates and the ruined irrigation works and let the coffee bushes grow wild on the hillside. The merciless Dessalines, who had stopped at no violence to achieve his country's independence, believed that only force could restore its prosperity. Seizing for the state the lands formerly held by French planters and mulattos, he set the population to work under the bayonets of his army. Order and prosperity were to be assured at the cost of a new tyranny. But the Emperor Jacques I—for such was the style now assumed by the ex-slave—was not himself to exercise his despotic power for long. His own soldiers rose against him and another revolutionary general—Christophe, whose name recalls his origins as the son of free negro parents from the English island of St. Christopher—took his place as master of northern Haiti, whilst its southern part passed under the rule of the mulatto leader Alexandre Pétion.

Christophe (in power 1808–20) continued Dessalines's stern regime. The peasants were kept working in the fields to the sound of bugle and drum, their free time was carefully regulated, their conduct and even their dress strictly controlled. A measure of prosperity returned to the island and solvency to the treasury. Christophe had none of Dessalines's obsessive hatred of whites and mulattos, and foreign traders were encouraged to return. Though illiterate himself, he had great respect for learning and established a system of compulsory schooling. He believed that the black republic could become as civilized and enlightened as any nation on earth and he was determined to make it so after his own lights. He created a hierarchy of nobles, headed by himself as 'King Henri I', and squandered lives and money on the construction of two great monuments—the palace of Sans-Souci and the fantastic and useless mountain-top Citadelle. Christophe's once popular rule grew more and more arbitrary and oppressive until, incapacitated by a stroke and deserted by his army and most of his court, Haiti's negro monarch put an end to his own life.

In the southern part of the island, under Pétion's milder rule (1808–18), things took a different course. His French education had given Pétion a sincere regard for democratic and liberal principles which he attempted, with mixed results, to apply to Haiti. Though he gave his people more liberty than they had ever known before, and did his best to heal the divisions between negro and mulatto, the economic consequences of his liberalism were little short of disastrous. The large estates were broken up and parcelled out, and the minimum size wisely prescribed by Toussaint L'Ouverture for individual plots was abolished. The course was set for the progressive fragmentation of smallholdings which afflicts Haiti today. Sugar production stopped, state revenue dwindled, and the peasants, left to their own devices, contented themselves with subsistence farming and some desultory coffee-growing. The choice seemed to lie between liberty with impoverishment, on the one hand, or despotism with some degree of economic efficiency on the other. Pétion opted for the first, Christophe for the second. Too many of Haiti's later rulers were to give their country the worst of both worlds—both tyranny and poverty.

Pétion's successor Boyer (1818–43) not only reunited Christophe's kingdom with the south, but extended Haitian rule over the entire island; it was only in the confusion following his fall that Santo Domingo was able to regain its independence (see below, page 118). Boyer, too, was a mulatto, and during his long rule the social structure solidified into its characteristic pattern of a small light-skinned élite, better educated and generally dominant economically though seldom politically, and the illiterate Creole-speaking negro

masses, never living far above the starvation line, but attached to their colourful folk customs and the Voodoo cult in which African animistic beliefs were
strangely blended with elements from the Catholic religion and their own
Haitian history. The whole aspect of the landscape was now changing; the
French-built cities and plantations were utterly decayed, whilst the thatched
roofs of African-style mud and wattle huts rose amongst the untended coffee-
bushes. The parcelling out of the land continued, despite an unavailing attempt by Boyer to halt the decline in production by introducing a Code
Rural binding the peasant to his land and requiring a given output from him.
Boyer desperately needed revenue, for France had recognized Haiti's independence in return for a large indemnity payable in yearly instalments which
the state was quite unable to raise. But the negro peasantry would have none
of Boyer's code or his tax-collectors and all attempts to coerce them were in
vain. The President was finally unseated by a conspiracy of urban mulattos
who were in turn obliged to yield power to a long line of mainly negro rulers.

In the dark decades that followed, Haiti's presidents are mostly remembered
—if at all—for their crimes and follies, rather than for any services rendered
to their country. The fantastic and ferocious Soulouque (1847–59) attempted
in vain the re-conquest of Santo Domingo, massacred all mulattos suspected
of conspiracy against him, crowned himself Emperor and created four princes,
fifty-nine dukes, ninety counts, and two hundred barons. His successor
Geffrard (1859–67) happily preferred to establish a number of schools and
public works, encouraged cotton growing and concluded a concordat with the
Vatican. Salomon (1879–88) introduced a number of useful financial reforms
but perpetuated the negroes' vendetta against the mulattos. Hyppolite
(1889–96) gave promise of becoming a Liberal reformer but soon succumbed
to the tradition of despotism. In the first decade and a half of the twentieth
century, the rhythm of repression and revolt quickened, bankruptcy loomed
as the debts contracted to France, Germany, and the United States mounted,
and total anarchy threatened. One president was blown up in the national
palace, another was poisoned, and finally, in 1915, the incumbent President
Sam was dragged from asylum in the French embassy and lynched. At this
point a force of marines landed from an American warship anchored in the
harbour, restored order and occupied strategic points in the capital. They
remained in Haiti for nineteen years.

Some gains could no doubt be claimed from the American occupation; an
end was made to mob violence and financial chaos, the unruly Haitian army
was disbanded and a disciplined constabulary trained, and a public health
campaign was launched against the prevalence of malaria, hook-worm, and
syphilis. But the cost in national humiliation was high. The first independent
black republic was now virtually a protectorate of the whites, who often
behaved with arrogance and brutality. The fundamental law which forbade
any whites to hold Haitian land was changed on the grounds that foreign
ownership was the only way to raise agricultural standards and bring waste
land into cultivation. The ruined roads were repaired—but with the use of
forced labour. This apparent restoration of the hated *corvée* system fanned the

flames of anti-American resentment which led to a rising by the *Cacos*, the primitive highlanders, half peasants, half bandits, who had traditionally made and unmade Haiti's presidents. The rising was put down at the cost of many lives.

The mulatto élite was now in power again after more than half a century of negro dominance, and retained it, after President Roosevelt had ordered the evacuation of the marines in 1934, during the presidencies of Sténio Vincent (1930–41) and Élie Lescot (1941–6). Although Vincent claimed credit for negotiating the American withdrawal and thus achieving the 'second liberation' of Haiti, and Lescot completed it by ending American supervision of the country's finances seven years later, the mulattos had become discredited by their generally pro-American stance and by Vincent's kow-towing to Trujillo after the massacre of thousands of Haitian peasants in the Dominican Republic (see below, page 121). In contrast to the mulattos' attachment to French language and culture, the negro majority was now growing increasingly conscious of its heritage of *négritude*; Creole was coming into use as a literary language, an astonishing outburst of creative activity in painting was taking place, and increasing stress was being laid on Voodoo as an expression of the national spirit. The post-occupation period saw the emergence of new political groups—Liberal, Marxist, or nationalistic. It also saw the re-emergence of the army, now modernized and reorganized, as a key political factor. In 1946 Lescot was unseated by a general strike and replaced by a military *junta* composed of Colonel Magloire, the commander of the Palace Guard, and two other officers. Contrary to tradition, the military did not retain office but handed over to Dumarsais Estimé, a negro schoolmaster, whose administration (1946–50) marked the resurgence of negro power with a new programme of democratic rule and economic and social reform. But Estimé's government was marred by peculation, incompetence, and demagogic anti-mulatto agitation. The army struck again, and this time Magloire retained power. His rule profited at first from the boom of the Korean War and an inflow of foreign capital but ended (1956) in financial scandal, falling coffee prices and mounting labour opposition. The following year, Dr. François Duvalier, an opponent of the Magloire dictatorship, secured election to the presidency.

Duvalier's rule began with high hopes. As a doctor specializing in public health questions and a negro intellectual known for his study of Voodoo and his understanding of the Haitian peasants, he seemed well equipped to tackle their basic problems of poverty, ignorance, and over-population. These hopes were quickly disappointed. Duvalier's chief preoccupation was to extend and perpetuate his power. Rigged elections first prolonged his presidency (1961) and then confirmed him in it 'for life' (1964). Ruling first with the backing of the army, he gradually reduced its power by raising his personal militia, the dreaded army of lawless thugs known as *tonton-macoutes* who terrorized the population, extorted money from rich and poor, and mercilessly put down periodic revolts and incursions by exiled opponents. A practitioner of Voodoo himself, 'Papa Doc' was credited by the ignorant peasants with magic powers. He whipped up the racial hatred of the negro masses for the lighter-skinned and better-educated mulattos, many of whom fled the country, thus reducing still further any prospect of lifting the people out of their backwardness. The misery of the land and the clamant iniquities of its government posed a problem for the United States. Washington would have liked to see the tyrant's fall; but might it not be followed by something worse? Duvalier astutely played on fears of the Communist threat. He also denounced any coolness towards his regime as racial prejudice against a small and weak black republic. He knew, moreover, that Washington needed Haiti's support in the OAS for the ostracism of Cuba (see page 325) and his vote was only given in return for a pledge of increased aid. For a short time in 1963 this aid was cut, then resumed; there was already trouble enough in the Caribbean without Washington forcing a fresh showdown.

In April 1971 'Papa Doc' died, after presenting his son Jean-Claude to the nation as the heir apparent. The youthful President announced his determination to continue his father's 'mission' but also, with an eye to attracting more United States aid and investment, held out some hope that the regime would be liberalized. But the country's problems remain daunting. Haiti's annual *per capita* income stands at seventy-five dollars—by far the lowest in Latin America and well below that of the next poorest country (Bolivia, with 210 dollars). The already tiny dwarf-holdings are being further subdivided as population remorselessly grows, so that the average is now only one hectare, though seven are reckoned the minimum necessary to support one family. Coffee, the country's chief export crop, is grown by some 300,000 peasant producers, but the area under cultivation is declining for lack of irrigation and fertilizers as erosion proceeds apace. Unlike some other dictators, Duvalier did not seek to justify his tyranny by spectacular public works. A few, like the Péligre barrage built a dozen years ago but long left without hydro-electric plant, have been carried out in spite of corruption and inefficiency. The few industries which exist are foreign-owned and profits go abroad. The lure of cheap labour may perhaps attract others despite the country's lack of infrastructure and political stability. A few promising co-operative enterprises, for which the government can claim no credit, and the beginnings of a tourist industry point to what might be developed under happier circumstances. In the meantime, unemployment and illiteracy hold the country back. Nearly four fifths of the adult population are illiterate and more than three quarters of the children grow up without going to school. Expectation of life is no higher than fifty years. That Jean-Claude would himself survive in office and effect any radical improvement in his countrymen's lot was thought likely by few other than those who believed that Papa Doc could still wield his magic from the grave.

The Dominican Republic

The Dominican Republic, which shares the island of Hispaniola with Haiti, has a smaller population than the latter but nearly twice its land area. Fear of the black republic's demographic pressure and the memory of occupation by its negro armies still remain important factors in the Dominicans' national psychology, though their country is now far richer and stronger. Another factor is the looming presence of the United States, vitally important to their economy as a market and source of aid and investment, but traditionally prompt to intervene in their domestic affairs. A third factor is the proximity of Cuba, similar to their own land in its history, culture, and ethnic composition, but so different in its espousal of the Communism which the majority of Dominicans fear but a few would like to see installed in their own country. A fourth factor in the national psychology is the trauma of their own past—the long experience of despotic rule interspersed with periods of anarchy, the thirty-one deadening years of the Trujillo dictatorship and the ensuing troubled decade with its civil war, foreign intervention, and continuing factional strife, through which the Dominican people is still groping to find the path to democracy and development.

Until the middle of the last century, the history of the Spanish-speaking part of the island remained inseparable from that of Haiti. Santo Domingo had lost its power and splendour as Spain's first metropolis in the New World long before Toussaint L'Ouverture entered at the head of his black troops. The experience of this subjection, and the still harsher Haitian occupation of 1822-44, left an indelible impact on the national consciousness. Once the Haitians had been driven out by the idealistic Juan Pablo Duarte and his fellow patriots, power alternated between two rival *caudillos*, the bold and uncouth mulatto Santana and the more cultured but no less despotic Báez. To perpetuate himself in office and prevent the danger of a renewed Haitian occupation, Santana applied for Santo Domingo's re-admission to the Spanish empire. Between 1861 and 1865 the country was a Spanish colony once more, but the misgovernment and arrogance of the Spaniards provoked constant revolts and the enfeebled mother country was no longer able or particularly eager to prolong her rule. Báez, despairing of leading the country to a viable independence, next sought annexation by the United States. A treaty to this effect was negotiated in 1869 but rejected by the United States senate. After a brief interlude of honest government by President Espaillat, the country sank ever deeper into confusion until the Haitian-born general Ulises Heureux imposed his corrupt and brutal rule (1882-99). Assassinated at last, the dictator left a bankrupt country, its customs revenue mortgaged, and foreign creditors clamouring for their due. In 1905, the United States secured treaty rights for appointing a receiver of customs who allocated the lion's share of the national revenue to the country's creditors and what was left to its government. Notwithstanding its humiliating dependence, the republic achieved some financial stability by this arrangement and there was a brief spell of good administration under Ramón Cáceres (1908-11). When assassination removed this enlightened President, the country relapsed into anarchy and civil war. In 1916 Washington sent in the marines. American military rule was well intentioned but high-handed and deeply offensive to Dominican patriotism. When it ended eight years later, financial and civic order had been established and some material advances achieved, but no progress had been made towards endowing the country with healthy democratic institutions of its own. The chief legacy of the American occupation was the formation of a well-armed National Constabulary for the maintenance of law and order. After half a dozen years of political floundering, the government of the day was overthrown by the commander of the Constabulary, General Rafael Leónidas Trujillo.

The subsequent dictatorship (1930–61), exercised either directly by the *caudillo* himself or through kinsmen or puppets, was one of the longest and most ruthless of modern times. The country is still suffering the disastrous effects of the 'era of Trujillo'. A chorus of paid sycophants lauded its alleged achievements, and apart from the caucus which profited directly from the organized plunder of the national patrimony, there were many, especially among the simple peasantry, who honestly believed that the beribboned Generalissimo was indeed the Benefactor of the Fatherland. A hurricane devastated the capital and gave its master a chance to show his mettle. After his rapid and grandiose rebuilding of it, Santo Domingo was renamed Ciudad Trujillo. The dictator pressed ahead with the public health programmes begun by the Americans and with the construction of a network of new roads which extended his grip throughout the island. Many small mixed farms were taken over to swell the more remunerative sugar plantations, and their owners forced into the shanty towns springing up around the capital. The urban sector of the population rose from about 17 per cent at the beginning of the 'Trujillo era' to 30 per cent at its close, while sugar production was doubled in the course of the 'fifties. The dictator saw to it that a large slice, perhaps as much as 80 per cent, of the sugar business, as of every sort of commercial and financial enterprise, was acquired by the Trujillo interests, who were further favoured by tax exemptions and other privileges. Increased revenue from exports and heavy indirect taxation permitted the government to pay off the national debt and invest heavily in public works and new industries. United States capital, both public and private, hastened to take advantage of these conditions. The attitude of the island's old ruling class was more ambivalent; the upstart had imposed a near-monopoly on the whole economic life of the country, on organized graft, on political power, even on crime. Some threw in their lot with the regime, others remained aloof and resentful. A new power élite was being carefully nurtured from the ranks of the Constabulary—the army, whose inflated and privileged officer caste was to remain a baneful legacy of Trujillo's rule. His bitterest foes were to arise from the middle and working classes, which steadily increased with the growth of urbanization and became more and more restive in the late 'fifties as economic boom declined into unemployment and crisis, the result of the government's extravagant schemes, increased expenditure on arms, accumulated graft and the cynical transferring abroad of the huge fortunes accumulated over the years by Trujillo's family and associates as the end of the long bonanza loomed near.

Dominican political life atrophied during the three decades of Trujillo's rule. His official Dominican Party was the only party tolerated, but was not allowed to develop any independent power of its own. Rigorous police control made any opposition within the country impossible, and even abroad the dictator's henchmen had been known to hunt down their quarry. Haiti, ever a convenient base for anti-government exiles, was intimidated by a massacre of Haitian immigrant labourers in 1937. The Communists never succeeded in organizing any effective anti-Trujillo action, and a mixed Cuban–Dominican expeditionary force infiltrated, in the euphoria following Castro's rise to power, with the aim of launching a similar guerrilla revolt, was quickly decimated. In seeking to carry the war into the enemy's camp Trujillo was less successful. The attempted assassination of President Betancourt of Venezuela by the dictator's gunmen in 1960 led to the regime's arraignment before the OAS and the imposition against it of strong diplomatic and commercial sanctions. These increased Trujillo's economic difficulties and put fresh heart into those who were suffering from his tyranny or felt themselves to be excluded from its fruits. The Benefactor's sham democracy could manifestly not be reconciled with the good intentions of the Alliance for Progress, and Washington made it clear that dictators were no longer in favour. At the end of May 1961, Trujillo was struck down by conspirators. Two of them, one a former provincial governor, the other an ex-mayor of the capital, survived; the others were killed by Trujillo's police.

The tyranny was now headless, but its corpse still bestrode the Dominican scene. For a time it seemed likely that Trujillo's brothers and son might succeed in perpetuating the dictatorship, or that another general might seize power; under pressure from Washington, however, the Trujillos were induced to leave the island and prevented from returning. In default of any political parties, a loosely organized National Civic Union, backed mainly by relatively uncompromised middle-class business and professional men, was set up and gingerly took the first steps towards dismantling the huge apparatus of police power and corrupt commercial interests and prepared the way for free elections. The Civic Union was set up as an apolitical body, but though the Communists did their best to infiltrate it, it soon tended to develop into a Conservative party. The chief electoral challenge to the Civic Union came from Juan Bosch, a self-educated mulatto intellectual who had spent many years in exile and was known for his books of fiction and his frequent denunciations of dictatorship. For middle-class liberals, particularly the young, for urban workers impatient for more radical improvements in their living conditions than the Civic Union could be expected to give them, for the *campesino* masses attracted by the promise of land reform, Juan Bosch became the hope of a new and democratic republic. His small *émigré* following, the Partido Revolucionario Dominicano (PRD), rapidly grew into a large party which completely overshadowed the small Communist and pro-Castro cliques of the extreme Left and returned Bosch to the presidency with a comfortable majority over the Civic Union in the 1962 elections. Democracy, so long paralysed by the fear and corruption of the dictatorship, seemed at last to be recovering the use of its limbs.

Bosch remained President for only seven months (February–September 1963). Dedicated and intelligent, imbued with a messianic sense of his own mission and righteous wrath not only against the discredited partisans of

Trujillo but against all members of the old 'oligarchy' whom a more flexible politician might have tried to win over, he could also be both capricious and obstinate. The economy, disrupted by the collapse of the Trujillist system and the loss of assets salted abroad, was slow to pick up, despite the boost given to it by an enlarged sugar quota and numerous Alliance for Progress loans. The country was still too unstable, and the government's policy towards foreign investment too ambivalent, for private capital to be readily attracted. There were neither the funds, nor the time nor the expertise needed to redeem the pledges of speedy improvement in the lot of the worker and peasants, whose enthusiasm for the new regime soon began to wane. The political immaturity of the people and the administrative inexperience of the government offered scope for a Communist penetration which the President was accused of doing nothing to prevent. An ultimatum gratuitously launched against President Duvalier and a massing of Dominican troops on the Haitian border demonstrated the irresponsibility of the government also in the field of foreign affairs. Though the invasion was called off, the United States government, loath to see any further disturbances in the Caribbean, grew alarmed. When a group of Dominican officers took it upon themselves to overthrow the President and replace him by a puppet civilian triumvirate, alarm deepened to consternation. For all his unpredictability and touchiness, Bosch had been the prototype of the reformist leader of integrity and impeccable democratic credentials which the Kennedy administration believed would be Latin America's staunchest bulwark against both Rightist dictatorship and Communism. For nearly three months Washington withheld recognition from the triumvirate and hesitated to resume the aid which had been brusquely suspended.

The next eighteen months saw an uneasy lull, whilst the economy deteriorated as a result of falling sugar prices. A Cuban-type guerrilla rising was put down with customary ferocity. The triumvirate, now controlled by Dr. Reid Cabral, a businessman of Scottish extraction, remained in being but heavily dependent on the military, who defied all attempts to curb the generals' more flagrant peculation and abuse of privileges. In April 1965, the most influential commander, General Wessin y Wessin, decided to withdraw his support and precipitated the fall of the government. But the armed forces were not united. Moreover, the middle and popular classes now constituted, at least in the capital, a politically conscious force which refused passively to follow the dictates of the military. Stiffened by a number of units commanded by Colonel Francisco Caamaño, the 'Constitutionalists', as they styled themselves, clamoured for the return, not of Reid Cabral's shadowy triumvirate, but of the exiled President Bosch. General Wessin, from an Air Force base outside the city, sent in tanks in an attempt to crush the 'rebels'. The republic was torn by civil war. The United States government feared for the lives and properties of its citizens in Santo Domingo; it feared still more that the rising, which ominously recalled the collapse of the Batista regime in Cuba, might mark the start of another Communist take-over. The decision was taken to send in the marines.

The American military intervention, despite the mantle of legality given it by retrospective OAS endorsement (see pages 325-6), fed the flames of nationalist indignation throughout Latin America. In Santo Domingo, after unsuccessful attempts to dislodge the 'Constitutionalists' from their stronghold in the centre of the city, an uneasy truce dragged on whilst a provisional government under the apolitical diplomat Dr. García Godoy attempted the difficult task of reconciliation. Caamaño, Wessin, and other prominent figures on both sides were eventually induced to leave the country, the 'Constitutionalists' were offered theoretical re-integration into the Dominican armed forces, and general elections were scheduled for June 1966. These resulted in the defeat of ex-President Bosch and the victory of Dr. Joaquín Balaguer, who had lived down his reputation as a former Trujillo protégé and seemed the most promising rallying point for such moderate opinion as yet remained in the bitterly divided country.

Balaguer's administration (1966–70) was faced with the twofold task of economic recovery and political reconciliation. By mid-September the Inter-American Peace Force had been withdrawn, but the civil war had left commercial life almost at a standstill, disrupted production and exports, and frightened off foreign investors. Whilst more than a third of the labour force remained unemployed, the national budget was burdened by the payments made to an inflated bureaucracy and overprivileged military caste. To touch the latter was still dangerous, as Balaguer depended as heavily on the army for his survival as had his predecessors. But he cut down the government's payroll and made other savings, whilst a liberal sugar quota and United States aid permitted some revitalization of the shattered economy. Confidence gradually returned and some important foreign investments (e.g., for a large oil refinery) were made. But the goal of political reconciliation proved more elusive. The PRD still remained the most representative expression of progressive middle and working-class opinion, despite the apparent disavowal by a disillusioned ex-President Bosch of his democratic faith in favour of a new formula of 'dictatorship with popular support'. The extremist groups to the Left of the PRD, though bitterly divided, were increasing in numbers and militancy. The army chiefs and the traditional oligarchy, now no longer cowed by Trujillo's rancour, constituted a scarcely less aggressive Right. Balaguer astutely held the balance between these opposing factions but offered no lead towards any real reconciliation. Disregarding charges of *continuismo* and the boycotting of the elections by the PRD, he was re-elected in 1970 for a further term in the presidency.

4 Cuba

Cuba, the Pearl of the Caribbean whose beauty enchanted Columbus and whose fertility was to turn it into the world's sugar-bowl, has another special claim to our attention today. The last territory of Latin America to break away from Spain, it has also been the first to break economically and politically with the United States. To Fidel Castro, the creator and master of this Latin American Communist state, the process is the culmination of a natural and consistent national evolution, liberation from the Spanish colonial power leading to liberation from 'Yankee imperialism'. To his admirers it is a hopeful and fascinating experiment which other Latin American countries will sooner or later emulate; to his critics, an alien intrusion into the American community of nations, a salient of the Soviet bloc projecting into the western hemisphere to within ninety miles of the United States, and a sinister aberration from whose contagion the Latin American countries must be shielded until the unhappy island comes again to its senses.

Cuba before Castro

Spain's Caribbean possessions of Cuba and Puerto Rico were not caught up in the general movement for political emancipation but remained under her control (apart from a British occupation of Havana in 1762–3) until the end of the nineteenth century. There were several factors which enabled Spain to maintain a hold for so long over this residue of her American empire. Cuba, an important military base which she could keep supplied by sea with men and arms, was beyond the reach of Bolívar's armies, though the Liberator had contemplated sending an expeditionary force to the island in 1826. Although there existed the usual causes of friction between Spaniard and Creole, the wealthy plantation owners, whether Spanish or Cuban, shared broadly the same economic interests of maintaining a thriving slave-based sugar industry, and the island continued to prosper under Spanish rule until impoverished later in the century by revolt and war and by restrictions on trade with the United States. Negro slaves accounted for more than one third of the island's population, and the massacre of the whites in Haiti was a dreadful warning of the social upheaval which a relaxation of traditional authority might mean. The influential Creole families were thus uncertain and divided. Some believed that the aim should be autonomy under the Spanish crown. A few, impressed by the economic vigour of the northern republic and sharing much the same outlook as its slave-owning South, would have welcomed annexation by the United States. But as the century wore on, the number of those who yearned for full national independence and were prepared to fight for it steadily increased.

The emancipation movement took the form of invasion attempts, mostly launched by Cuban exiles operating from the United States, and popular risings of ever-increasing scope within the island itself. Foreign volunteers often played an important part. The Venezuelan soldier of fortune Narciso López, for example, led three such expeditions (1849–51), whilst the Dominican Máximo Gómez became famous in the Ten Years' War. The latter, launched with a proclamation known as the *grito de Yara* in 1868 and led by the Liberal Creole landowner Carlos Manuel de Céspedes, developed into prolonged guerrilla warfare between Cuban *mambises* and Spanish regulars which is estimated to have cost some 200,000 lives. The fighting was suspended at the Pact of Zanjón (1878) but flared up again the following year in the Guerra Chiquita ('Little War'), primarily a rising of negro slaves. The Spaniards promised reforms; the abolition of slavery was decreed in 1880 and made effective six years later, but the country's economy received a new blow through ill-advised Spanish restrictions (1894) on Cuba's vital exports of sugar and tobacco to the United States. Old resentments were aroused and hostilities resumed. The heroes of the Ten Years' War—Gómez, Calixto García, and the mulatto general Antonio Maceo—though sometimes quarrelling amongst themselves, took the field once more. Prominent amongst them was the noble-hearted José Martí, Cuba's foremost writer (see page 316), who returned from exile and fell on the battle-field. After some initial success, the insurgents were pushed back to the east of the island. The Spanish commander, General Weyler, determined to deprive them of popular support by herding the civilian population into concentration camps where thousands died of disease and starvation. *Mambi* terrorism provoked harsh counter-measures which in turn aroused a wave of sympathy for the Cuban cause abroad and helped to convince the United States that the time had come to intervene. When the American warship *Maine*, which was lying in Havana harbour for the protection of United States citizens, mysteriously blew up with heavy loss of life, the government could no longer hold back. Washington declared war on Spain (April 1898), quickly routed the antiquated Spanish navy, and landed forces in Cuba, Puerto Rico, and the Philippines. Spain had lost the last of her American colonies; but who was to enter upon the inheritance?

There had always been those who, like John Quincey Adams, believed that once Cuba had cut loose from Spain it must gravitate towards the United States as inevitably as an apple falls to the ground. In the 1850s, Washington had offered to buy the island outright from Spain for 130 million dollars. So long as slavery existed in Cuba, the slave-owning Southern states had favoured annexation as a means of strengthening their cause. But the weight of opinion in the United States had been against annexation. The Congressional Resolution of 1898 authorizing the President to use armed force in support of the Cuban insurgents had promised 'to leave the government and control of the island to its people' (the Teller Amendment). The first task of the American occupying forces, after the Spanish defeat, was to help get the ravaged country back on to its feet and then to work for a political settlement. Headway was quickly made towards the first objective. One notable achievement in Cuban–American co-operation was the eradication of yellow fever, thanks to the identification of the disease-carrying mosquito by the Cuban Dr. Carlos Finlay. But the reconciling of Cuban aspirations for political independence with the United States' desire to perpetuate its influence over the island proved a far more difficult matter. The solution attempted was to incorporate in Cuba's new Constitution (1901) an amendment by Senator Platt recognizing the United States' 'right to intervene for the preservation of Cuban independence, the maintenance of a government adequate for the protection of life, property and individual liberty'. The Platt Amendment also limited the republic's freedom to conclude treaties and contract debts, gave the United States the right to establish naval stations (hence the American base of Guantánamo Bay) and left undefined the status of the Isle of Pines, strategically placed off the south-western tip of the island. It was argued in justification of the Platt Amendment that, given Cuba's weakness and the appetite of other imperial powers, some form of client status was desirable in Cuba's own interest, no less than that of the United States. But such a view could hardly be accepted by a proud people who had suffered greatly to gain their independence, and now saw themselves given little credit for it and another power, more alien than Spain in race and culture and far more formidable, re-imposing the yoke from which they had struggled to be free.

The United States' interest in Cuba was not only political and strategic but economic. A flourishing trade had developed between the two countries, and Cuba's sugar, for the production of which her soil and climate were ideally suited, found an expanding market in the north. In the struggle against Spain, two thirds of the island's agricultural wealth had been destroyed and the annual sugar crop reduced from over a million tons to less than a quarter of a million. Production had been largely in Spanish and Creole hands, but after the 1895–8 war the ruined economy was built up with the help mainly of American technology and capital, whilst more and more land was turned over to sugar cane and bought up cheaply by foreigners, so that by the mid-'twenties about one third of all Cuba's land, and two thirds of her sugar output, were in foreign hands. The reciprocal commercial treaty of 1903 allowed low-tariff American goods into Cuba in exchange for a preference granted to Cuban sugar, so that Cuba came to draw four fifths of her total imports from the United States. The island became a commercial colony, but a very flourishing one, of the northern republic. Until the early 'twenties, the sugar industry showed spectacular growth; the decline, from the mid-'twenties, as the world slid towards the Great Depression, was no less dramatic. In the 'thirties, when the economy began to pick up to a slow and erratic growth, the foreign banks and corporations started selling their sugar-mills and plantations. In 1940, 55 per cent of Cuba's production was still in American hands, but by the late 'fifties this share had sunk to 37 per cent whilst the Cuban-owned share had risen to 62 per cent. But the United States nevertheless remained Cuba's chief market, access to which was by a unilaterally fixed sugar quota, and the owner of nearly a billion dollars' worth of investments in the island. Though some progress had been made towards diversification—the island possessed more than five and a half million head of cattle and was developing chemicals, cement, textiles, sugar derivatives, and other industries—Cuba's economy was still lopsided, dangerously dependent on sugar, and closely geared to that of the United States.

Monoculture and foreign economic penetration gave a special character to Cuban society and politics. The stable nineteenth-century society of medium and small landowners had been broken up in the struggle against Spain. The large plantation, often company-owned and operated, was now the distinguishing feature. A large labour force was required for the cutting and milling of the *zafra* but remained under-employed during the rest of the year. In the two decades of rapid expansion at the beginning of the century, there was a shortage of labour and recourse was had to large contingents of negro immigrants from Jamaica and Haiti, some of whom stayed on and only slowly merged with Cuba's rural proletariat, much of which was no more than a generation or so removed from slavery. Such conditions precluded the development of the master-man relationship which to some extent humanized the *latifundio* system in other parts of Latin America, and prepared the ground for the strong and militant labour unions which grew up in the years of depression.

The upper and middle classes—if the latter could properly be said to exist, for they had nothing about them of a stable and confident bourgeoisie—were conditioned by the all-pervading American presence and the fluctuations in world sugar prices. Fortunes were quickly made and could be as quickly lost. The operations of the great corporations brought power and wealth to the few who successfully integrated with them; but the many suffered the frustration of finding their way to the top in business and commerce blocked. The foreigner was everywhere; in banking and insurance, in control of the great companies and the world markets whose prices meant slump or prosperity for Cuba, in the streets of the capital as businessmen, advisers, soldiers, or free-spending tourists. Politics, the one 'industry' which the Cubans had made their own, was a struggle between personal factions for the spoils of office. As the economy stagnated and frustration increased, this struggle became more violent; terrorism and gang-warfare became commonplace, especially amongst the radical-minded students of Havana University who saw violence as their only recourse against the repressive brutality of the government. There were no institutions to give the country effective stability. The army, reduced to the role of rural guard during the American occupation and reconstituted in 1917, became a mere instrument in the power struggle. The Church, staffed mainly by Spanish priests and associated with the period of colonial domination, commanded the loyalty of few. The nearest most Cubans came to finding common ground was in their mounting resentment of the United States. If there was not yet a fully integrated nation, nationalism—most vociferously expressed by the frustrated middle sectors of society—was rapidly becoming the dominating force.

The country's official representatives, however, were at first ambivalent in their attitude towards the Americans, on whom they knew they depended for their political survival. The first President of the republic, Estrada Palma (1902–6), attempted to perpetuate himself in power and turned to the Americans for help when his opponents rose in arms. There followed a fresh period of American intervention and administration (1906–9). The presidencies of José Miguel Gómez (1909–13) and Mario García Menocal (1913–21) were a time of increasing corruption and administrative and political confusion, punctuated by intermittent American involvement. Under Alfredo Zayas (1921–5), American tutelage became more marked, and though aiming at greater honesty and efficiency of government, fanned the flames of nationalist resentment. Gerardo Machado (1925–33), a former general in the war against Spain, launched a programme of public works, encouraged some economic diversification, and in some respects favoured more nationalistic policies. But as the world economic crisis intensified and sugar prices fell, his regime became more repressive and its corruption more scandalous, labour and the radical Left being its special victims. Though business circles regarded his regime as a bulwark against chaos, Washington attempted, through the discreet diplomacy of Sumner Wells, to induce Machado to mend his ways. The dictator turned a deaf ear, until the mounting chorus of student protest and labour defiance, together with the militant action of a group of dissident army sergeants, obliged him to take flight.

There followed an interlude of provisional government by the moderate Carlos Manuel de Céspedes, who enjoyed Washington's confidence but was soon forced from office. A bewildering change now came over the Cuban scene. In Havana, the students carried to the presidency one of their professors, Ramón Grau San Martín, who issued a number of nationalistic and revolutionary laws but failed to impose his authority. Disorder spread to the countryside, where workers took over sugar plantations and mills and even set up a number of 'soviets'. But the Cuban Communist Party failed to turn this now patently revolutionary situation to account. Established eight years previously, it had lost its most dynamic figure, the charismatic student leader Julio Antonio Mella, who had been exiled to Mexico and murdered there. His successors had made the tactical blunder of attempting to do a deal with Machado by trying to call off the general strike in return for a promise of a free hand in the labour movement. This had lost the Communists the confidence of the anti-Machado masses, which they then sought to regain by agitating against Grau. The latter faced a still more serious threat from the army, which had played an important part in unseating Machado and now, four months later, turned against his successor. This too, in its way, was another manifestation of the prevailing revolutionary temper, for the successful conspirators were mainly NCOs, whose ringleader, a mulatto sergeant called Fulgencio Batista, was to become Cuba's strong man. Under pressure from Batista, Grau was replaced by the more moderate Carlos Mendieta (January 1934–December 1935). The repeal (1934) of the Platt Amendment marked the United States' approval of the regime, and the ruthless suppression of another general strike in 1935, followed by the murder of Antonio Guiteras, who had been the most dynamic figure in the Grau administration, signified the end of this phase of Cuba's revolutionary movement.

Batista cherished two ultimately incompatible ambitions. A man of the people, he saw himself as a democratic leader who would do for Cuba what Abraham Lincoln and Franklin D. Roosevelt had done for the United States. But as a thrusting parvenu in the Latin American *caudillo* tradition, he was also determined to secure the maximum of power and wealth for himself. In the first phase of the regime, his democratic aspirations were in the ascendant. He presided over the passage of the utopian and impeccably democratic Constitution of 1940, easily won the presidential elections of the same year, and passed a number of laws favourable to the workers. The Communists made with Batista the bargain they had wanted to strike with Machado— backing for the government in return for control of the labour movement. Batista took two of their representatives into his government—the first time in Latin America that Communist leaders had been given cabinet rank. But he also had powerful enemies. Grau rallied his supporters into a new party— the *Auténticos*—and succeeded unexpectedly in defeating Batista's candidate in the relatively free 1944 elections. For the next eight years, the *Auténticos*, first under Grau San Martín (1944–8) then under Prío Socarrás (1948–52), ruled the country. They produced some progressive legislation, limitless graft, and an unprecedented degree of political liberty which soon degenerated into the licence of warring factions but which also allowed the government to be openly criticized and its corruption freely denounced. A new party, the *Ortodoxos*, was launched with a programme of reform and clean government. Its candidate seemed well set for winning the 1952 elections when Batista, returning from exile and mobilizing his supporters in the army, seized power by a coup. During the next six years, as opposition to Batista assumed increasingly violent forms, the dictator's rule grew more arbitrary and repressive until it finally rivalled the horror of Machado's brutal police tyranny. Breaking his former alliance with the Communist Party and keeping the ex-Communist Eusebio Mujal in charge of the labour unions, Batista made a few gestures towards the workers and kept them passive until all but the end of his regime. Opposition to his rule came mainly from the *Auténticos* and *Ortodoxos*, and particularly from a number of revolutionary but often rival groups in the University of Havana. It was as leader of one of the smaller and more militant groups, on the Left of the *Ortodoxo* party, that Fidel Castro, a law student and son of a poor Spanish immigrant who had made good, first came to notice. Outside Havana, hostility to the dictator was reinforced by the resentment of the provinces against the capital, and Castro thought that if he could manage to secure a foothold there, the revolt might spread throughout the country. On 26 July 1953, a band of his followers attempted to storm the Moncada barracks in Santiago. The revolt failed; a number of rebels—mostly students —were shot or killed in cold blood, and Castro himself went into hiding and gave himself up only after the Archbishop of Santiago had intervened to secure a pledge that his life would be spared. Brought to trial, he conducted his own defence in a speech subsequently published under the title of *History will Absolve Me*, in which he outlined a programme of radical but democratic reform. Castro received a fifteen-year prison sentence but was given amnesty in 1955, after which he left Cuba vowing that he would soon return to carry on the struggle against Batista. His group now called themselves the 26 July Movement after their ill-fated attempt against the Moncada barracks.

Castro armed and trained his men in Mexico, where they were joined by the Argentine Ernesto 'Che' Guevara and other revolutionary adventurers, and finally disembarked with them on the swampy east coast of Cuba on 2 December 1956. Most were soon killed or captured, but a handful, including Castro, his brother Raúl and Guevara, escaped to the hills of the nearby Sierra Maestra. The landing was to have coincided with risings planned by the 26 July Movement's clandestine organization elsewhere in Oriente province. One of his lieutenants, Frank Pais, managed to capture and hold Santiago for a couple of days, but the rising had been stamped out before Castro set foot on the Sierra Maestra. There he succeeded in destroying a few weak military outposts and gradually won the confidence of the peasants who were suffering from the tyranny of Batista's soldiers and officials and gladly accepted the promise of a land reform which would give them the ownership of their own plots. News of this growing pocket of resistance in the mountains put fresh heart into the anti-Batista movement in the towns. Sabotage and propaganda against the regime were stepped up and supplies and recruits collected for the guerrillas. Not all the opposition recognized Castro's leadership. The Communist Party held aloof, regarding his tactics as 'adventurism' until it became evident that they were going to succeed. Many of the Havana students, organized under a revolutionary *Directorio*, fought their own war against Batista and made a desperate bid to kill him in the presidential palace (13 March 1957). Another group was sent by the *Directorio* to establish a base of their own in the Escambray mountains halfway between the Sierra Maestra and the capital. Castro sent Guevara to bring these guerrillas under his command whilst his brother Raúl extended the front to the north of the province. Batista's army of 40,000 had little stomach for this sort of fighting and gradually melted away before Castro's *barbudos*, who never numbered more than 2,000. There were few full-scale engagements, but many feats of individual heroism. Batista finally took flight, a group of his officers attempting to seize power was swept aside, and the rebels found themselves the masters of Cuba.

The Cuban Revolution

Castro entered Havana on 8 January 1959 amidst almost universal acclamation. The rank and file of his army were mostly peasants, its leaders mainly students and other young men of middle-class origin and predominantly white stock; the poorest coloured strata of the population, who were to benefit most from his revolution, were slow to rally to it and had few representatives amongst its leading cadres. Labour too played little part in Castro's triumph. An attempt of the previous April to overthrow Batista by means of a general strike failed through lack of response on the part of the workers, who remained under the influence of Mujal or that of a Communist Party wary of the guerillas' 'adventurism'. Though Cuba's economic development during the 1950s had been patchy and uneven, and little headway had been made, for all the 'progressive' legislation of recent years, towards curing seasonal unemployment and the workers' other problems, conditions were by no means bad by Latin American standards. In general social and economic development, Cuba ranked fourth amongst the republics with a *per capita* income of some 554 dollars—almost double that of the Latin American average and four times that of India. In terms of life expectancy, literacy, energy consumption, communications, and public health, Cuba had already reached a higher standard than have many Latin American countries today. But the way to further development, political no less than economic, seemed barred. For Castro's middle-class supporters—and they were at first many—his victory promised a return to the individual liberties, democratic processes and social justice proclaimed by the 1940 Constitution but violated by Batista's tyranny. The youth and idealism of the guerrillas promised an end to the cynical corruption of previous governments. Few foresaw the threefold process—the consolidation of the *líder máximo*'s personal power, the defiance of the United States, and the increasing radicalization of his reforms—which was to give Castro's revolution its alarmingly novel character and wrench the country into the economic and political orbit of the Soviet Union.

The first year and a half of the new regime saw a drastic redistribution of the national income. Labour's share of the latter rose from 60 to 75 per cent or more, whilst that of the property-owners and entrepreneurs showed a corresponding drop from 40 to 25 per cent or less. In the cities, house rents were halved and their ultimate abolition promised; in the country, small tenant-farmers were given full property rights and relieved of amortization payments. Wages and salaries were raised, in real terms, between 25 and 30 per cent while prices were kept down by entrepreneurs afraid of being denounced as 'counter-revolutionaries' and able to increase production by taking up the slack in industry's unused capacity and cutting down on investment. This all led to a marked and rapid rise in living standards for the poorer sections of the population, enormously increasing Castro's popularity amongst them and shifting the basis of his support from the wealthier middle class at whose expense the reforms were introduced. It also increased the appeal of the Revolution and prepared the way for its further radicalization. In the course of 1959, starting with businesses 'illegally acquired' or owned by members of the Batista regime, almost all major private firms and industries, together with the country's foreign trade and banking system, were taken over by the state.

An increase was also achieved in agricultural production during the first two years of the new regime. An Agrarian Reform Law was promulgated on 17 May 1959, and although the full effect was not felt until the following year when large-scale expropriations were carried out, most landowners believed (mistakenly, as it turned out) that they were more likely to retain their estates if they stepped up production. The Reform Law, though radical, hardly appeared 'Socialist'. Its purpose was officially described as promoting diversification in agriculture and assisting industrialization by increasing the purchasing power of the rural population. It abolished the *latifundio* and limited the size of privately-owned farms. Expropriated owners were to receive compensation in state bonds. No company or foreigner was permitted to hold land, but tenant-farmers would become owners and holdings be made available to the landless. Co-operatives for farming and profit-sharing were to be encouraged and a state agency, INRA, set up with wide powers to carry through the reform. The revolutionary nature of the Law became apparent from the manner of its implementation. No bonds were ever issued in compensation, INRA took over property where and when it liked, and the co-operatives proved to be virtually indistinguishable from the state farms which were soon set up and eventually (1962) absorbed them. The reform was defended on the grounds that, in Cuban circumstances where wage-earning labourers were more numerous than peasant-farmers, some form of collective organization was needed if production was to be maintained and fragmentation into *minifundios* avoided. INRA, too, could point to the schools, houses, clinics, etc., which it was building for the improvement of rural living standards. By the end of 1961, agriculture was probably already more collectivized than in Eastern Europe. A Second Agrarian Reform Law of October 1963 eliminated the class of independent medium farmers by reducing the permitted maximum for privately owned farms. The 200,000 or so remaining smallholders were formed into an organization (ANAP) and placed under the control of INRA, which bought up their produce at fixed prices. A further momentous change followed in 1964/5. The policy of agricultural diversification was officially reversed and Cuba turned back to monoculture. Though his subjects might now be revolutionaries, Sugar was king again.

The rapid transformation of Cuba's economic and social structure was the work of an increasingly totalitarian government over which its *líder máximo* exercised the absolute control of a *caudillo*. All the reins of power were quickly gathered into Castro's hands: the army, secret police, and militia; the press, the judiciary, and a nation-wide network of vigilante bodies known as Committees for the Defence of the Revolution. Respected figures nominated to serve as Prime Minister and President of the Republic were soon discarded, the former office being retained by Castro himself, the other given to a trustworthy but little known associate, Dr. Osvaldo Dorticós. Instead of taking steps to institutionalize his amorphous 26 July Movement, Castro turned more and more to the Communist Party (Partido Socialista Popular—PSP) whose collaboration now appeared to be essential for the radicalization of the revolution. The new course became apparent in November 1959 when Castro personally ejected his old comrades of the 26 July Movement from the leadership of the trade-unions and replaced them by PSP members. The Communists' penetration of the rapidly expanding army, the state administration and INRA caused many veterans of the Sierra Maestra days to break with the revolution. Hubert Matos, a senior officer who wished to resign in protest against this trend, was sentenced to twenty years' imprisonment. Major Díaz Lanz, the head of the air force, went into exile, as did Manuel Artime, Manolo Ray, and other officials concerned with the Agrarian Reform, whilst Sorí Marín, the Minister who had drafted the Law, took up arms and was executed as a counter-revolutionary. But the Communists too had to be taught their place, which was to help carry out the policies decreed by Castro, not to determine them. When, in March 1962, an influential group within the PSP appeared to be gaining too much influence, Castro struck against them and exiled their leader, Aníbal Escalante. To strengthen his political control, Castro progressively merged the PSP with the remnants of his old 26 July Movement and the smaller student *Directorio*, first in the loose framework of the Integrated Revolutionary Organization (ORI, 1961), then in the United Party of the Socialist Revolution (PURS, 1962), and finally (1965) in a reconstructed Cuban Communist Party which now recognized his credentials as an authentic Marxist–Leninist as well as his authority as the architect of Cuba's Revolution.

Cuba's leftward course was watched with growing concern in the United States. Although American officials and businessmen had often shown a partiality for Batista, sympathy and supplies had also been forthcoming for Castro in the United States. Pressure of public opinion led the United States government to cease supplying Batista with arms in March 1958, and though it might have preferred to see the fighting end in some compromise rather than in Castro's total victory, it showed no hostility towards his regime in the latter's initial, reformist phase. Castro himself visited the United States in April 1959 and had talks with American officials. He showed no interest in securing American aid; he was more concerned, it seems, at this time with obtaining arms for the re-equipment of his expanding army and the expeditionary forces which he believed would succeed in carrying the revolution to other Latin American countries. Failure to secure such arms from the United States probably sharpened his resentment and strengthened his resolve to turn to the Soviet bloc. The progressive nationalization of Cuba's economy was also bound to exacerbate relations with the United States. American-owned sugar estates and mills, public utilities, banks, and refineries (which refused to refine the oil which Castro decided to import from the Soviet Union instead of Venezuela) were taken over and led to counter-measures by the Eisenhower administration: Cuba's sugar quota was cancelled, a trade embargo imposed, and diplomatic relations finally broken off (January 1961). Denunciation of 'Yankee imperialism', ever a popular rallying-cry in Cuba, became the constant refrain which kept revolutionary and nationalist fervour at white heat. It appeared only too justified when a force of anti-Castro rebels, armed and trained in the United States, landed at the Bay of Pigs in April 1961. Their speedy defeat greatly enhanced Castro's prestige and caused Washington a corresponding loss of face.

Defiance of the United States had as its corollary a rapprochement with the Soviet Union. Cuba's history offered many instances of armed intervention by the United States. Though such open intervention was no longer in vogue,

Guatemala's experience in 1954 showed the sort of covert action which was likely to be taken if a government showed signs of steering a pro-Communist course. The only power able and perhaps willing to provide military protection, and also to supply the economic resources now denied by the United States, was the Soviet Union. The latter had done nothing to bring about Castro's victory. Though the Cuban Communists were now helping to radicalize his revolution, its establishment, within a hundred miles of the United States and in defiance of the laws of 'geographic fatalism' implicit in the Monroe Doctrine, was a windfall for Moscow. Diplomatic relations were not restored until Castro had been in power for nearly a year and a half, but a commercial agreement of the previous February pledged the Soviet Union to purchase nearly five million tons of sugar over a five-year period, and this amount was later increased to compensate Cuba for the cancelled American sugar quota. A hundred-million-dollar credit was also opened to allow Cuba to acquire Soviet industrial and agricultural equipment. The drastic reorientation of Cuba's foreign trade from the United States to the Soviet Union was begun. Personal contacts between Cuban and Soviet leaders multiplied, and in July 1960 Khrushchev declared ominously that 'in case of need, Soviet artillerymen can support the Cuban people with their rocket-fire'. Just over two years later, President Kennedy informed the startled American people that Soviet rockets were in fact being installed in Cuba. Castro's alliance with the Russians had precipitated the missile crisis of October 1962 and brought the world to the brink of nuclear war.

The settlement of the crisis between Moscow and Washington over his head left Castro humiliated and resentful, but by no means deterred from pressing on with his own revolutionary designs. He was convinced of Cuba's special hemispheric mission and saw himself as its latter-day Bolívar. Castro's call to youthful revolutionaries elsewhere to 'turn the Andes into the Sierra Maestra of Latin America' (26 July 1960) did not fall on deaf ears, and in the euphoria of the first months of his regime, he believed that Cuban guerrilla tactics might quickly topple other reactionary governments. Nearer home, armed raids were sponsored against Haiti, the Dominican Republic, Nicaragua, Guatemala, and Panama. Though none succeeded, Castro continued to support revolutionary action where and when he could: through the provision of training facilities in guerrilla warfare and sabotage, through subsidies, and sometimes through despatching Cuban 'volunteers'. The Second Declaration of Havana, issued shortly after Cuba's expulsion from the OAS (February 1962), openly asserted Cuba's claim to lead the Latin American revolution and called for the overthrow of governments that stood in its way. There was scarcely a country which did not at some time have to cope with some Cuban-sponsored attempt at subversion. The main targets were Peru (1963–4), Venezuela (1962–6) and Bolivia (1967). The dramatic failure of the guerrilla venture in the latter country, ending with the death of Che Guevara and other veterans of the Sierra Maestra, led to a shift of emphasis away from guerrilla warfare to the tactics of urban terrorism. But Cuba continued to provide some facilities for Latin American guerrilla fighters, whilst becoming the Mecca for hijackers and the exponents or beneficiaries of political kidnappings. The sponsoring of a Tricontinental Conference (January 1966) and the formation of a Latin American Solidarity Organization (August 1967) were moves to stimulate and co-ordinate international revolutionary action under Castro's aegis.

Attempts to export Cuba's revolution abroad went hand in hand with the drive to intensify it at home. The economic results soon made themselves felt. The spurt of the first two years, culminating in the exceptional sugar harvest of 1961, gave way to agricultural stagnation, diminishing food supplies, and a decline in productivity and living standards. One cause was the over-ambitious programme of industrialization, launched under Guevara's guidance in 1961, which was abandoned three years later (possibly on Russian insistence) in favour of concentration on sugar production. Another was the emigration of many managerial and professional staff—nearly half a million Cubans were to choose exile in the first decade of Castro's rule—and the inexperience of the cadres who took over the running of the whole national economy. Despite the efforts of the dedicated but diminishing core of Castro supporters and the injection of large contingents of volunteers for the *zafra*, labour indiscipline and absenteeism created serious problems. In combating them, Castro pinned his faith on 'moral' rather than 'material' incentives, partly to preserve the purity of Cuba's revolutionary spirit, and partly perhaps to make a virtue of necessity—for there were scarcely any material goods to be had. Rationing of some meat and fats was introduced in 1961, extended the following year to the staple foodstuffs rice and beans, and later to fish, eggs, and milk, then to bread and most remaining foods (even including sugar), to clothing, tobacco, and petrol. From March 1968, when Castro decreed the expropriation of thousands of small businesses, shops, and bars in a new 'revolutionary offensive', all trade and production was in the domain of the state, with the exception of the peasant small-holdings, which still accounted for nearly one third of the land and kept food production from foundering altogether. A number of ambitious new ventures were launched on Castro's initiative with the ultimate purpose of diversifying and increasing Cuban agriculture: cattle-raising, rice production, citrus and coffee plantations in a new green belt round Havana, a greatly expanded fishing industry. It was hoped that such schemes would account by the mid-'seventies for more than half the total agricultural production. But the 1970 sugar harvest, though the largest in the country's history, fell one and a half million tons short of the much-publicized target of ten millions. The whole economy showed signs of falling productivity; the revolution seemed to be running out of steam. To give it fresh impetus, Castro promulgated a law against absenteeism and vagrancy, disciplined free-wheeling intellectuals and writers, accepted a greater measure of Soviet control over economic planning and administration, and generally tightened the screws.

For all the revolutionary changes of the 'sixties, some features of the Cuban scene remained in the familiar Latin American tradition. Its government, headed by the man carried to power by his army and with army officers in control of its key-posts and its regimented economic and educational life, could be seen as a form of military regime (see page 242). It was also government by *caudillo*. All decisions stemmed from the *líder máximo*, for whose will government and party served as mere transmission belts. The attempt made by a 'microfaction' of the Communist Party, headed once more by Aníbal Escalante, to substitute orthodox party control for Castro's personalist rule was crushed (1968). An undisclosed number of liberal, anti-Communist critics of the regime continued to languish in prison. Of the elections and new Constitution once promised by Castro no more was heard. Contact between leader and led was maintained by Castro's tireless travels throughout the island and his often electrifying harangues at mass rallies. After ten years of absolute rule, his popularity with many still remained great. He could claim to have abolished unemployment and class privilege. Illiteracy had been greatly reduced and educational opportunities, at least in the vocational and technical sphere, opened to all. Medical services had been extended and more doctors trained. Many things—sport, cinemas, telephones, most housing—had been made free, and Cuba set on the course towards an ultimately moneyless society. If the once gay capital now looked down-at-heel, the vice and scandalous corruption of the old days had disappeared. Castro's followers believed that the 'new man', bred by the revolution and responding to 'moral incentives', was leading to a juster, egalitarian society, and one which—when the heavy annual investment of 25–30 per cent of the national income began at last to pay off—would bring greater prosperity. To many of his countrymen, Castro had given a new sense of *dignidad* and pride. Some still fervently believed in Cuba's messianic mission to extend the benefits of the revolution to other parts of Latin America.

The USSR's attitude to that mission was ambivalent and put some strain on Soviet–Cuban relations. Two visits by Castro to the Soviet Union (April 1963, January 1964), in which he was given a hero's welcome, did something to dispel the bitterness left by the missile crisis. The decision was taken to switch the Cuban economy to maximum sugar production and was underwritten by a new long-term agreement for Soviet purchases of Cuban sugar at stable prices (see page 260). Over 95 per cent of Cuba's vital petroleum supplies came to her in Soviet tankers from Soviet oil-fields. Cuba was now at least as dependent economically on the Soviet Union as she had ever been on the United States. Moscow was believed to be subsidizing the Cuban economy to the tune of over one million dollars a day, quite apart from the value of the arms and military equipment supplied which Castro in early 1970 put at a billion and a half pesos. There seemed little prospect, as Cuba entered the new decade, of any speedy change in the international alignment which she had chosen. Washington's policy of economic denial, which Havava termed a blockade, was still in force, and in neither capital did there appear to be any disposition to seek a *rapprochement*. Nor was there any sign of Cuba's return to the inter-American system, though some Latin American voices had been raised in favour of at least a renewal of economic links. Cuba remained committed to the revolutionary course chosen by her *caudillo* and tied to an ally and trading partner at the other end of the world.

5 Venezuela

After giving a brilliant lead in Latin America's struggle for independence, Venezuela sank back under the narrow despotism of successive *caudillos* and did not emerge as a modern state until our own century. The cue for her re-entry on the stage was the discovery of oil. But sudden wealth brought with it no automatic transformation of the country's archaic social and political life. It was only after a decade of constitutional government and the peaceful transfer to political power in the 1960s that one could begin to speak of a political miracle comparable to the economic miracle which the country had experienced. Democratically elected governments fought off the challenge from old-style military rebels and new-style guerrilla revolutionaries and pursued their task of spreading more broadly the benefits of national prosperity by far-reaching educational, agrarian, fiscal, and administrative reforms. This was the policy known as 'sowing the oil', i.e. using oil revenues to stimulate general economic and social development. From one of the poorest, rawest, most backward, and tyrannically ruled of the Latin American republics, Venezuela began to be known as one of the richest and most dynamic. The spread of education and a growing regard for civilized values and the arts tempered the brash materialism of the parvenu. Political life became less dominated by personalism, factions, and fear of the *golpe*. The task before it in the 1970s was to consolidate and deepen these very real economic, political, and social achievements.

The age of the caudillos

Venezuela came into existence as an independent state following the dissolution of Bolívar's Gran Colombia in 1830. Its first master, and the real founder of the nation, was the *llanero* General Páez. Ruling twice as President (1831–5, 1839–43) or the real power behind the scenes, and later as military dictator (1861–3), he showed honesty and a capacity for hard work, as well as a legendary valour, and gave his country its first orderly administration, opened schools, improved roads, reduced the public debt and even the army. There followed the rule of the Monagas dynasty, two brothers and a son, whose confused misgovernment was redeemed by one liberal measure—the formal ending of slavery. Venezuela's next master was Guzmán Blanco (1870–89), a *caudillo* ruthless and adroit in his handling of men and energetic in promoting the country's economic interests, which he blandly assumed to be identical with his own. He had the advantages of good birth, some education and certain pretensions to liberalism, but he was also corrupt, inordinately vain and ostentatious, self-indulgent, and much given to prolonged visits to Paris, whence his enemies at length prevented him from returning. From the years of anarchy which followed, there first emerged an upright soldier, Joaquín Crespo (1894–8), whose rule was cut short in a skirmish with rebels, and then Cipriano Castro, a *mestizo* landowner and *guerrillero*, as fearless in battle as he was cruel in vengeance against his enemies and truculent in his dealings with foreigners, and unashamedly corrupt and dissolute in his private life. For nearly a decade (1899–1908) Castro ruled with the help of his army, his spies and his astute right-hand man and fellow Andino, Juan Vicente Gómez. With this rough schooling—for he had little other—Gómez at length ousted his chief and ruled with an even more absolute despotism than any of his predecessors until his death twenty-seven years later (1908–35). Despite the six new constitutions promulgated during this time, the regime's efficient machine of repression stifled individual liberties and allowed the people no say in the government of their country. Though he was hailed as the creator of a new nation, the contribution of the dictator to this achievement amounted to little more than order harshly maintained. The rest flowed from the newly discovered wells, now operated by the international oil companies, which brought unrecorded wealth to Gómez, his progeny and henchmen, furnishing funds for the liquidation of the national debt, the accumulation of reserves, the encouragement of commerce, the building of roads, and even a few schools.

The rule of the *caudillos* was based on control of the army and tacit alliance with the landowners who, provided their estates, wealth, social status, and local influence were left untouched, seldom aspired to a role on the national stage. The Church too had come to accept this order of things. Páez, an indifferent Catholic himself, had favoured religious toleration and had allowed an English church to be built in Caracas. Guzmán Blanco, a virulent anticlerical, had closed monasteries and convents and done all he could to strip the Church of its power and privileges. Federalism or Centralism had been inscribed on the banners raised by rival *caudillos* but the issue was little more than a power-struggle between national *caudillo* and local *caciques*. It has its echo today in the readiness of the Andean states which, together with the *llanos*, have furnished so many of the nation's fighting men, to challenge the authority of the capital.

Two further incidents from the age of the *caudillos* have left their legacy— the dispute over the frontier with British Guiana and the attempt at coercion by European naval powers. The border with the British colony, running through wild and almost unpopulated country, had been left undemarcated until the explorer Robert Schomburgk was commissioned to survey it in the 1830s. Venezuela refused to accept the 'Schomburgk line' and, after prolonged wrangling, invoked the Monroe Doctrine and appealed to President Cleveland of the United States, who forced Britain to submit the dispute to arbitration. The arbitral award of 1899 assigned most of the disputed area to Britain but satisfied Venezuela's chief aspiration by giving her dominion over the mouth of the Orinoco. The award, recognized by both parties as a 'full, perfect, and final settlement', appeared to have concluded the matter for good, until the dispute was reopened by Venezuela sixty years later (see page 339). There next followed a crisis provoked by the damage suffered to the person and property of foreign subjects during the civil wars and by President Castro's high-handed refusal to pay compensation or fulfil other government obligations. In 1902, British and German naval forces (later joined by Italian) blockaded the Venezuelan coast and bombarded a couple of forts. The United States had her own claims against Venezuela and pressed them with greater moderation, but made no move to invoke the Monroe Doctrine and deter this coercion. The dispute—the last of many cases of European intervention in Latin America to enforce financial claims—was finally referred to the Hague Court, and its settlement marked the passing of the era of 'gunboat diplomacy'.

With the death of Gómez it seemed that Venezuela might go the way of Mexico after the fall of Díaz. Crowds rampaged through the capital sacking the dictator's houses and taking vengeance on some of his more notorious satraps. Foreign oilmen feared for their lives as well as their installations. But the Gómez system, though shaken, survived. The new forces—the growing middle and working classes, and the modern-minded younger officers—were finding their voice but had not yet learned to sing in concert. A rising spear-headed by university students had been suppressed in 1928, its leaders driven into exile, the university closed, and the students put to work on the roads. Despite the overwhelmingly hostile mood of the country, the administration could still control a Congress elected by municipal councils and state legis-latures packed by Gómez supporters which in turn 'elected' the President of the Republic. The two men thus successively chosen to follow Gómez were Eleázar López Contreras (1936–41) and Isaías Medina (1941–5), both *Andino* officers holding the office of War Minister in their predecessor's government. These transitional dictatorships attempted the difficult task of permitting a limited degree of democratization within the framework of the old regime. A progressive labour law was passed and embryo trade unions and political parties began to emerge. But an attempted general strike (1936) was crushed, opposition leaders exiled, and the Trade Union Congress dissolved. The government of López Contreras, whom his supporters had hailed as *El Presidente Humanizador*, turned away from the dangerous experiment in political liberalization to a vigorous programme of economic expansion. A new oil law (1938), which gave the government a larger share of the profits from this booming industry, financed a broad programme of public works, school building, and the expansion of the country's lopsided industry and neglected agriculture. The Medina administration continued along the same lines, and after surmounting a crisis caused by war-time difficulties in transporting the country's oil exports, obtained for the government a still larger share in the profits from petroleum production which, as World War II drew to its close, reached a pitch that stimulated the economy of the whole country.

From dictatorship to democracy

With the end of World War II, President Medina had been obliged to surrender his emergency powers and make further concessions to the mounting demands for democratization. The country's conservative interests, thoroughly alarmed, were rumoured to be preparing a coup to reinstate his predecessor. But before they could act, Medina had been unseated (October 1945) by action from an unexpected quarter—a seven-man *junta* formed jointly by young army officers, dissatisfied with poor service conditions and the discredit they believed their seniors were bringing upon the armed forces and the country, and the strongest of the recently founded political parties, Acción Democrática (AD), under its energetic leader Rómulo Betancourt. The coup was unlike the many which the country had experienced before, since it carried to power for the first time a political party representing wide sections of the population, particularly organized labour and liberal-minded members of the middle and professional classes. A programme of thorough constitutional, social, and economic reform was rapidly put into effect. A Constituent Assembly framed a new constitution (the twenty-second in Venezuela's history) providing for a strong presidency and a congress elected by direct, universal, and secret suffrage. The ensuing elections returned AD to power with a crushing majority under the presidency of the country's most distinguished writer, Rómulo Gallegos (1947). Leading figures in the previous regime were brought to trial on charges of peculation and their fortunes confiscated. The oil companies were forced to revise their contracts on terms more favourable to the government and the latter embarked on a determined programme for the progressive 'Venezuelization' of the country's basic industry. A drive to improve housing, labour conditions, and wage levels, education, public health, and the social services was launched. The state, through the newly established Venezuelan Development Corporation (CVF), began to play an increasingly active part in directing the development of industry and agriculture. The latter had been allowed to stagnate, since the country's income from oil allowed the unrestricted import of food and other necessities. But the attempt to modernize agriculture brought the government up against the archaic *latifundio* system and necessitated the introduction of an Agricultural Reform Law. This the small but still influential landowning class saw as a threat to its vital interests. Business and manufacturing circles too had grown alarmed at what they regarded as the government's undue partiality towards labour. Persuaded that, in alienating these important interests, the reformers had over-reached themselves, the armed forces withdrew their support and decided to seize power themselves (November 1948).

For the next ten years, the country reverted to authoritarian military rule, first under a triumvirate, and then (1952), after government pressure appeared unlikely to prevent an electoral victory by the civilian URD, under the dictatorship of the dominant member of the *junta*, Colonel Marcos Pérez Jiménez. The clock seemed to have been put back to the days of Gómez. The AD was banned, most of the labour unions it had controlled were dismantled, and the bulk of its legislation was repealed or nullified. Opposition was quelled by means of vigorous press censorship and police repression. Petroleum production soared as the result of this enforced 'stability', pegged wages and reductions in the labour force, and the new concessions liberally granted to the oil companies. The government used its huge oil revenues to line its own pockets, endow the capital with spectacular roads and buildings, including the world's most ostentatious military club, and also to build up some useful though often wastefully executed public works and new industries, notably in iron and steel. After initially allowing some freedom to AD's rivals, the Christian Socialists (COPEI), URD, and the Communists, Pérez Jiménez clamped down on all political activity other than that of his own supporters. Common persecution in time drew erstwhile rivals together into a clandestine opposition organization, the Junta Patriótica. This finally succeeded, with the help of dissident groups in the armed forces, in replacing the dictator by a *junta* of officers and civilians headed by Admiral Wolfgang Larrazábal (January 1958). Within a year elections had been held and AD returned to power under Rómulo Betancourt.

For the first time in its history, Venezuela embarked on a decade of demo-cratic, representative government, initially under President Betancourt (1959–64) and then under another veteran AD leader, Raúl Leoni (1964–9). To have broken the long tradition of dictatorship (though his enemies declared that Betancourt himself ruled as a *caudillo*) and to survive at all was in itself a major achievement. The challenge was keenest, and the government's response most dynamic, during Betancourt's presidency. The administration had to contend with grave economic difficulties, since fear of the regime's radical policies prompted a flight of capital, and it was not until 1962, when business confidence had begun to revive and foreign capital to flow back again, that industrial output rose annually by 9 per cent (still well below the 14 per cent averaged in the 'fifties). Unemployment ran high, though the govern-ment had abandoned the more ostentatious and extravagant schemes of its predecessor and was pressing ahead with its own development plans. These included the setting up of two important new state agencies: the Guayana Corporation (CVG), with responsibility for the integrated development of a giant hydro-electric and industrial complex on the banks of the Caroní and Orinoco rivers, and the Venezuelan Petroleum Corporation (CVP), which aimed to enter the industry on its own account, to see that irreplaceable resources were used with maximum benefit to the exchequer, and to control yet not to frighten off foreign investment and initiative. (See page 264.) If the government's programme seemed to lose momentum during the Leoni administration, the increasing dynamism of the private sector kept most branches of the national economy flourishing. But the high cost and wage levels of this economy kept it apart from the accelerating process of Latin American economic integration; Venezuela only joined LAFTA belatedly and held back altogether from joining the Andean Group (see page 330).

In the social field, the government's aims were defined in the new consti-tution (1961) as 'protecting and uplifting labour . . . achieving an equitable participation by all in the enjoyment of wealth according to the principles of social justice.' The restrictions imposed by Pérez Jiménez on the unions were at once lifted and an invigorated labour movement soon showed itself the administration's firmest basis of support, though unemployment remained a problem and programmes to relieve the urban housing shortage lagged behind the growing influx of uprooted rural labourers pouring into the cities. The government again took up the task of agrarian reform, this time with greater circumspection, distributing state lands first and expropriating only those private estates which were unworked or blatantly neglected and offering compensation on a scale which led critics to complain that land reform was being carried out in the interests of the landowners themselves. By the end of the Betancourt administration, a real though still modest beginning had been made in transforming the traditional agrarian structures. Over 60,000 families had been settled on their own land and some 700,000 hectares of arable land distributed to poor *campesinos*. Progress had also been made, though less quickly than had been hoped, in such fields as public health and education. In spite of a nation-wide campaign against illiteracy, one out of every four adult Venezuelans still remained unable to read or write in 1964, and although the proportion of the budget allotted to education had been raised from 3 to 10 per cent, students from the country's expanding universities were amongst the AD administration's most militant critics.

Acción Democrática had the difficult task of waging a war on two fronts: against the Right which, if interfered with too roughly in its basic interests, would turn to the armed forces, still able, and some sections of them only too willing, to overthrow the government; and against extremists of the Left who held that the government was not going far or fast enough in its reforms. These conflicting pressures led to successive fissures within the party and government themselves. First, a radical group (MIR) split off from AD, and finally, towards the end of President Leoni's administration, an important wing (MEP) which presented its own rival candidate in the presidential elections and thereby made possible the victory of AD's rivals, COPEI. Even at the beginning of his term, President Betancourt lacked the majority for a purely AD government and had to form a coalition with COPEI and URD. The latter withdrew into opposition in 1960, as did a fresh group of AD dissidents, and in the same year the Communist Party and MIR launched a campaign of urban and rural violence in the hope of overthrowing the government as Castro had overthrown that of Batista. The campaign of bomb-throwing, kidnapping, armed robbery, and assassination in the cities and guerrilla action in the country reached its climax at the end of 1963 in a bid to prevent the elections being held. The gamble failed, and thereafter the guerrilla threat gradually receded, the bulk of the Communist Party and a section of MIR finally abandoning violent tactics and leaving only a remnant of competing bands. President Betancourt's government had also to defend itself against attacks from the armed forces; right-wing *cuartelazos* in 1960 and 1961, and more serious attempts at subversion, in which radical elements in the marine corps, acting in concert with Communist and MIR militants, launched risings at Carúpano and Puerto Cabello (1962). As if these challenges were not enough, President Betancourt himself narrowly escaped death at the hands of assassins hired by Trujillo (1960). These foreign-inspired attempts at subversion prompted the government to pursue its policy of ostracizing both the revolutionary regime in Cuba (to which it had been initially sympathetic) and the Dominican dictatorship, and to seek to rally opposition throughout Latin America against dictatorships in general by refusing diplomatic recognition to governments which had come to power as the result of an armed coup (the 'Betancourt Doctrine'). The government also secured the extradition of Pérez Jiménez from the United States and brought him to trial on charges of peculation and abuse of authority.

In 1969 a Christian Democrat administration, the second in Latin America, took over from AD after the latter's decade in office—the first constitutional transfer of power from one political party to another in Venezuela's history. In attempting to pursue a middle-of-the-road policy, President Caldera found himself faced by many of the same problems as his predecessor and without some of the advantages, such as AD's solid backing from labour. He had won only a narrow electoral victory and his hold on Congress remained precarious. AD had learned to live with the armed forces, though they had little liking for the Betancourt Doctrine. The latter had led more to the diplomatic isolation of Venezuela than to the discouragement of military coups elsewhere in Latin America, and President Caldera quickly abandoned it. Though some elements in the armed forces looked with approval on the recent military take-overs in Peru and Bolivia, the army as a whole had shown sympathy for COPEI's more conservative policies, and both army and party had drawn their main strength from the Andean states in the west of the country. Though in no sense a clerical party, COPEI also enjoyed the advantage of good relations with the Church, which had gradually recovered from the anti-clerical blows rained upon it in the nineteenth century and had reached a *modus vivendi* with the previous government in 1964.

President Caldera set the country's course towards consolidation, reconciliation, social advancement, and steady economic growth rather than the goal of further radical reform. One of his first acts was to offer an amnesty, in which the Cardinal Archbishop of Caracas played a leading role, to the remaining guerrilla groups. The latter remained weak and divided, though there was some recrudescence of student unrest. The prevailing mood seemed to be one of growing nationalism, which President Caldera showed skill now in moderating, now in using, to give impetus to an otherwise rather colourless regime. Two potentially explosive frontier issues had to be faced. The quarrel with Guyana (see page 138) was 'frozen' and relations with that country improved. Differences with Colombia over demarcating the common frontier in the Gulf of Venezuela (potentially rich in submarine oil deposits) and the unauthorized presence of several hundred thousand Colombian immigrants caused tensions which the leaders of both countries strove to reduce. By moving away from Venezuela's traditional 'open-door' investment policy and imposing limitations on foreign-owned banks and fresh tax burdens on the oil companies (who were also made to surrender control over their natural gas reserves) President Caldera's administration reflected Venezuela's deepening mood of economic nationalism.

6 Colombia

Colombia is the fifth largest in area of the Latin American republics, and by the end of the present decade will have outstripped Argentina to rank third in population. Until the coming of the steam engine, the motor car, and above all of the aeroplane, her national development was seriously impeded by the formidable mountain barriers separating her widely differing provinces. Here the landowning oligarchy, though the size of their estates was comparatively moderate by Latin American standards, ruled with unchallenged local authority and fierce regional pride. They professed allegiance to one or other of two political creeds, Conservatism or Liberalism, which were not easily differentiated except in terms of clericalism and anti-clericalism, but were nonetheless held with passionate intensity. Latterly, this ruling élite (grudgingly enlarged to include leading figures in industry, commerce, and the professions) has had two main preoccupations: to maintain a *modus vivendi* between the two rival parties and so escape the disaster of unchecked factionalism, and to steer the country along a course of controlled modernization without relaxing its grasp on the essential levers of power. Traditional institutions, such as the army and the Church, now reflect the stresses of change. The 'popular forces'—industrial labour, the middle sectors, and the poorer population of the towns, the largely illiterate and unorganized *campesinos*—still lack sufficient strength and cohesion to impose any alternative process, though their frustration has on occasion broken out into explosions of urban rioting and rural *violencia*.

Liberals versus Conservatives

Following the collapse of Bolívar's Gran Colombia in 1830, the country we now know as the Republic of Colombia (so styled only in 1886) reverted to its earlier name of New Granada and was organized as a state by Bolívar's former Vice-President, the cautious and legalistic Santander (1832–7). Though other *caudillos* from the wars of independence, notably General Obando (President 1853–4) and General Mosquera (thrice President, first in the Conservative interest, 1845–9, then as a Liberal, and finally, 1865–7, as a military dictator) dominated the country from time to time, Colombia suffered less than most of the other Latin American republics from dictatorial rule. Power alternated between Conservatives and Liberals. The former organized their party around 1840 and ruled for nine years, and again from 1857 to 1860. The Liberals, heartened by the revolutionary ferment of 1848 in Europe, took power the following year and held it (with an interlude, 1857–60) until 1880, which ushered in nearly half a century of renewed Conservative rule.

The alternation of power between the two parties was punctuated by frequent revolts and by civil wars of sometimes fanatical ferocity in which the local population took sides in much the same way as retainers rallied to the support of their feudal lords in the Middle Ages. In no country did the Catholic Church command such fervent loyalty or arouse more passionate hatred. In none had an intractable geography segmented the land into such self-contained, mutually hostile regions. Religion and regionalism thus became the most powerful divisive forces. The Conservatives, who generally favoured strong, centralized government, for a time espoused the cause of regional autonomy. During the 1850s, Panama and then other provinces were constituted as semi-independent states, each with their own President or Governor and their own constitution, and were loosely linked together in the Confederación Granadina of 1858. A further constitution, promulgated in 1863, enigmatically declared that 'nine sovereign states unite and confederate . . . and form a sovereign nation'. This unworkable formula only deepened the anarchy, in which Conservatives and Liberals continued to struggle for local power, and increased the country's administrative impotence and economic exhaustion.

The election to the presidency of Rafael Núñez, a thoughtful, widely travelled man who began as a Liberal and ended as a Conservative, marked the gradual strengthening of centralized government and an attempt to find a middle way between the extreme partisans of Conservatism and Liberalism. From his accession in 1880 until his death in 1894, Núñez was the dominant influence, both in and out of office, in the country's political life. A Conservative reformer, he promulgated a constitution (1886) introducing unitary government for the 'Republic of Colombia' whilst permitting a measure of administrative autonomy for the regions, which had however to content themselves with the status of departments rather than that of nominally 'sovereign states'. Núñez also concluded a Concordat with the Vatican and restored much of the power of the Church. The price paid for this return to stability and the moderate degree of economic progress which it promoted was the harassment of all opposition and the suppression of individual liberties. Old animosities were neutralized, not healed. Núñez had had to suppress numerous revolts, some of them (such as that of 1885) serious. Once his strong hand had been removed, passions flared up again to plunge the country into the War of the Thousand Days (1899–1902). This sanguinary and disastrous conflict left the nation too weak and divided to prevent a further humiliating disaster in the following year—the loss of Panama. (See page 110.)

The Conservatives nevertheless remained in power for nearly three decades. They found an energetic and autocratic leader in Rafael Reyes (1904–9), who aspired to emulate the Mexican example of Porfirio Díaz and develop the country through ambitious public works financed by foreign capital. Reyes finally misjudged the national temper by seeking to perpetuate himself in office and to conclude a *rapprochement* with the United States, whose recent encouragement of Panama's secession was fresh in the nation's memory. The Conservatives who succeeded Reyes in the presidency were more conciliatory, conducted elections relatively fairly, and allowed the Liberals to play some part in public life. Improved communications began to draw the country more closely together, while injections of foreign capital, mostly from the United States, stimulated industrialization and population growth. Economic and political power, however, remained firmly in the hands of the traditional ruling élite. Population pressure on land led to *campesino* invasions of private estates which were met by forcible evictions, whilst attempts by workers in the oil-fields and the banana plantations to strike for better conditions were broken, at times (as in 1928) with heavy bloodshed. Coffee had become the country's chief export, but the boom in coffee prices which continued during the 'twenties collapsed with the onset of the world economic depression and the long hegemony of the Conservatives, now discredited and divided, was brought to an end.

The Liberal administration of Olaya Herrera (1930–4) bore the brunt of the depression and was also distracted by a dispute with Peru, when Letitia, Colombia's outlet on the Amazon, was seized and only evacuated after an appeal to the League of Nations. It was left to his more dynamic successor Alfonso López (1934–8) to come to grips with the country's pressing need for modernization. The old battle-cries of anti-clericalism and regional rights had by now lost much of their resonance. The examples of the Mexican and Russian revolutions had injected a new radicalism into Liberal thinking which found expression in the changes made by López in the Constitution (1936). The latter broadened the franchise and defined the state's role in economic development, the social function of private property, and the rights of labour, including freedom to organize in unions and to strike. Laws were introduced to improve labour conditions and enforce taxes on income, profits, and property, and to expropriate uncultivated land and limit the landowners' powers to evict squatters. Other measures were taken to curtail the powers of the Church and the privileges accorded to foreigners and to expand education. Some of these reforms got little further than the statute book, but even so they appeared dangerously radical innovations to most sectors of the ruling élite. The industrial and commercial interests which had backed the Liberals' first moves towards modernization grew alarmed at the concessions made to labour. López was succeeded by Eduardo Santos (1938–42), a representative of the party's moderate wing. When López was recalled to the presidency (1942–5) a dangerous polarization of political forces had taken place. The extremists of his own party and a broad popular following outside it had found a charismatic leader in Jorge Eliécer Gaitán, whom they trusted to launch the revolution from which López held back. The Conservatives had their champion in Laureano Gómez, an uncompromising clerical and Axis admirer, who became Foreign Minister in the administration of Mariano Ospina Pérez which took over from the Liberals in 1946.

In the next two years events moved to a crisis. Nominally, Conservatives and Liberals continued a measure of collaboration, for López had handed over office to the conciliatory Liberal leader Lleras Camargo, who had briefly taken three Conservatives into his cabinet before their party gained the presidency in the 1946 elections; even under Ospina, the Liberals retained a majority in Congress and had some representation in the cabinet. But the voice which now dominated the Liberal Party, and still more, the popular masses beyond it, was that of Gaitán. A man of the people himself whose talents had won him an exceptional place amongst the élite, he did not scruple to denounce the oligarchs, Liberals no less than Conservatives, and aroused the masses to the need for direct political action. Gaitán was neither specific nor particularly radical in the changes he so eloquently advocated. It was in appealing direct to the people over the heads of those who had traditionally claimed to act in their name that he appeared such a dangerous demagogue. When, in April 1948, Gaitán was struck down by an unidentified assassin in the streets of Bogotá, the urban masses, suddenly deprived of their idol, vented their fury in the worst riots ever seen in Latin America. Whole areas of the city were given over to burning and looting and thousands of lives were lost. Gaitán left neither political organization nor authentic heirs. His visions of a better life and juster social order vanished in the smoke of the *bogotazo* and the *violencia* which now became the scourge of rural Colombia.

The mixture of political and personal vendettas, endemic guerrilla warfare, rural anarchy, genocide, and banditry which goes by the name of *la violencia* was a uniquely horrible phenomenon in Latin America. It cannot be explained as a 'war of national liberation'. It was not primarily a class struggle or even a spontaneous *jacquerie*, although it contained elements of both. Though the Liberals and later the Communists (who called a conference of guerrilla leaders in 1952) attempted to give it political orientation and coherence, the violence remained largely unco-ordinated, purposeless, and localized. The number of victims claimed between 1948 and 1964, including often sadistically massacred women and children, has been variously estimated at between 100,000 and 300,000. The causes of *la violencia* were complex and no doubt stemmed in part from the dormant regional rivalries and political feuds between local Conservative and Liberal bosses in the nineteenth century, which the polarization of political attitudes in the 1940s had revived. Following the murder of Gaitán and the *bogotazo*, each side became convinced that the other was bent on its destruction. Liberal partisans throughout the country resorted to arms and were met by an 'official' counter-terror from the Conservatives, marshalled by the intransigent Gómez (President 1950–3), who proclaimed as his mission the re-establishment of order and the traditional hierarchical structure. But the social organism had been irremediably crippled and could not struggle back to health. The population was increasing fast, and landless *campesinos* invaded the landowners' estates or flocked to the towns, from which they often drifted back still more desperate and rootless. In *la violencia* many sought an outlet for their frustrated urge to assert themselves and display their *machismo*. Others turned to it for economic advantage. To terrorize a farmer and take over his land, particularly in time to reap the coffee crop, or else to impose a protection racket, could be a profitable game, and those who played it often claimed the justification that their own property and livelihood had already been unjustly taken from them. *La violencia* thus became a way of life. Children who had seen their fathers murdered and their mothers raped grew up to become in turn the leaders of a lawless generation which knew no other existence.

Gómez failed in his drive to restore order. His restrictions on labour and the freedom of the press and his moves to amend the Constitution so as to concentrate more power in his own hands soon eroded support even within his own party. In June 1953, after nearly half a century of political abstention, the army intervened to depose the President. General Rojas Pinilla, the Commander-in-Chief who replaced him, was welcomed by the bulk of both Liberals and Conservatives as likely to heal the wounds of the country by giving it a national, non-sectarian administration, together with a controlled measure of development in the social and economic spheres. The amnesty and rehabilitation schemes sponsored by the new government did succeed in damping down rural unrest, though it was to flare up again before long. Public works and social welfare programmes were launched and measures taken to stimulate agriculture and trade. A regional development plan was prepared for the Cauca valley along the lines of the Tennessee Valley Authority and national agencies for petroleum and aviation were set up. But the regime began to assume authoritarian and Peronist overtones, especially when Rojas Pinilla attempted to build up his own labour and political organizations on populist lines. When, in 1957, he attempted to manoeuvre for another term, he was forced from office. Though the dictatorship had been relatively mild, it had lost its initial backing from the two traditional parties, from the Church, even from the army itself, and had failed to build up a solid basis of popular support with which to counter this loss.

The National Front

Liberals and Conservatives had sunk their differences in order to bring about the fall of a dictator; it now remained, if further bloodshed was to be avoided, to find some more permanent and institutionalized form for this co-operation. The 'National Front' in which their leaders finally agreed to unite went further than the occasional coalition of the past. It was a formal agreement, to be binding for sixteen years, for a complete sharing of power; it envisaged the rotation of the Presidency between the two parties, parity in Congress, the administration, and all key offices, and a bi-partisan basis, expressed in a two-thirds majority, for all legislation. By this arrangement it was hoped that old passions would have time to cool, the last of the *violencia* die down, and the country grow accustomed to constitutional transfers of power from one party to another. It was also aimed to ensure sufficient national unity for a process of modernization carefully controlled and directed by the traditional élite. The old rivalries were to be subordinated, so that, as Alfonso Lleras Camargo, the first National Front President, candidly put it, 'the national governing class might dedicate itself for sixteen years to realizing a gigantic effort of progress and justice, without tearing itself to pieces'. The formula seemed to work. The Liberal Lleras Camargo (1958–62) was succeeded by the Conservative León Valencia (1962–6), who in turn handed over to the Liberal Lleras Restrepo (1966–70), leaving another Conservative, Misael Pastrana Borrero, to complete the final term envisaged under the bi-partisan system. But if the latter gave the country relative tranquillity (for the *violencia* was reduced though not entirely eliminated) it also produced anomalies and draw-backs of its own. One was the promotion of factionalism within each of the two authorized parties. The 'official' Liberals were weakened by the emer-gence of a radical wing led by Alfonso López Michelsen, son of the old Liberal reformer; the Conservatives by still more serious schisms between the fol-lowers of Ospina and Gómez, and later by further factions which presented rival Conservative candidates for the 1970 elections. Even Rojas Pinilla campaigned at the head of his own organization (ANAPO) in nominal adhesion to the Conservative cause and was all but voted back into office. The support still commanded by the ageing ex-dictator was a measure of the disenchantment or indifference of the electorate, half of which abstained alto-gether from voting. The Colombian people, who had identified themselves so long and so passionately with Liberal or Conservative interests often in reality having little relevance to their own, had yet to find a cause which could arouse their enthusiastic participation.

Nor did a decade of government by the National Front see more than a modest beginning in 'the gigantic effort of progress and justice'. Lleras Camargo and his cousin Lleras Restrepo, a competent administrator and economist, had made resolute efforts to get to grips with the country's econo-mic problems. The former prepared a Ten Year Plan—the first such national plan to win approval under the Alliance for Progress—which attracted a wel-come flow of foreign development funds and caused Colombia to be regarded for a time as something of a show-case for the Alliance. In spite of the oppo-sition of the Church, the government pressed ahead with plans to encourage family planning as a means of slowing the rapid rate of population increase which was eating away the slow increase in economic growth. An Agrarian Reform Institute was set up with the aim of buying out some of the larger estates, attenuating the problem of the *minifundio* and converting 60,000 rural labourers and tenants into free-holders. Steps were taken towards the difficult goal of diversifying the country's economy by lessening its dependence on coffee, which continued to provide employment for about a quarter of the agricultural workers and accounted for two thirds of the country's export earnings. Fluctuations in the price of this commodity on the world market, though moderated by the International Coffee Agreement, caused constant balance of payments difficulties, inflation, and a serious recession and flight of capital in the mid-'sixties. By 1970, President Lleras Restrepo had succeeded in restoring a measure of economic stability and renewed confidence in the future. Industrial growth, in which the enterprising inhabitants of the Medellín region had long taken the lead, was well under way, with prospects of the wider markets offered by Colombia's participation in the Andean

Group (see page 330). But there remained a grave problem of unemployment, for the rate of economic expansion was still not high enough to absorb the increasing numbers of young people coming onto the labour market. This has deepened unrest amongst students and workers. In economics as in politics the question remained essentially the same: could Colombia's ruling élite achieve the wider participation of the large and under-privileged sectors of the population and make good its claim to lead the nation along the path of modernization?

7 Ecuador

Ecuador is the smallest of the Andean republics. It is also one of the poorest and, many would add, the furthest from achieving any real sense of national identity and purpose. Between a third and a half of her population consists of unassimilated Indians; not a homogeneous minority, but a congeries of tribes and communities speaking different dialects and varying widely in their levels of culture and material well-being. The Indians live mostly in the temperate valleys of the sierra; the population of the steaming coastal lowlands is more mixed. Guayaquil, the country's chief port and commercial centre, and Quito, the pre-Inca and colonial city in the sierra, are two different worlds and the tension between them has done much to shape Ecuador's history. Guayaquil prides itself on standing open to the world's commerce and ideas, on the enterprise of its merchants, bankers, and export-minded plantation-owners, and on devotion to a Liberalism which it identifies with its own local interests. Quito represents those of the traditional landowners of the sierra, deeply Conservative for the most part, and convinced of their right to govern the country but seldom powerful enough to impose absolute acceptance of their will. Economically, it is the coast that calls the tune, one form of monoculture succeeding another and making millionaires of a few fortunate families— cacao, until the 'thirties, then cotton, and today bananas. Tomorrow— although almost any type of crop will flourish in the range of climate from sea-level to 12,000 feet above—Ecuador's wealth may come less from agriculture than from oil. But oil, far from calming the troubled waters of politics, tends to stir them up, and Ecuador still seems a long way from finding the solution for her problems.

Ecuador emerged into uneasy statehood, on the dissolution of Bolívar's Gran Colombia, under the Venezuelan-born General Flores (1830–5 and 1839–45) who set about organizing the country on Conservative and autocratic lines. Worsted in a clash with New Granada (Colombia) for the possession of the Cauca valley and facing stiffening opposition from the Liberals, Flores reached an understanding with the latter by which their leader should alternate with him in the presidency. Rocafuerte (1835–9), a man of aristocratic birth and good education, who had travelled widely in Europe and professed the enlightened views of the age, attempted with resolution and some degree of success to apply them before handing the presidency back to Flores. Ecuador acquired the rudiments of an administrative, legal, fiscal, and educational system, some discipline in the army, some money in the treasury, and a measure of public order and tranquillity. The Indian peasantry, however, remained little touched by these advances or by the formal abolition of slavery (1852), and it was only with the ending of their liability to forced labour under the traditional *mita* system (1857) that they experienced a slight alleviation of their servile lot.

Flores devoted much of his second administration to a futile expedition against New Granada and an attempt, by changing the constitution, to perpetuate himself in power. This unashamed *continuismo* provoked a general rising, in which Rocafuerte played a leading part, and obliged Flores to retire into exile. There followed a decade and a half of disturbed and ineffectual Liberal rule, culminating in an attempt by a *caudillo* in Guayaquil, General Franco, to cede that city and its adjacent province to Peru. This led to a general rising to which the returning Flores lent his military skill and the new star of the Conservative faction, Gabriel García Moreno, his indomitable energies.

For the next fifteen years (1860–75), either as President or power behind the scenes, García Moreno proved himself to be the most forceful and competent ruler in Ecuador's history and one of the most remarkable personalities which Latin America has produced. As fearless, dynamic, and ruthless as any military man, he was also an intellectual who composed verse in the neoclassical style and was driven by passionate scientific curiosity to explore the craters of volcanoes. He opened schools and founded an observatory, introduced the telegraph and the railway to his backward country, and strove to break down their isolation and mutual distrust by building a new wagon-road connecting Quito with Guayaquil. He stimulated agriculture, trade, and banking, reformed the currency and tax systems, founded a mint, and paid his own salary as President into the exchequer. But not for these services is García Moreno chiefly remembered today. A man of intense personal piety, he was resolved to make the Church supreme in the land and to transform Ecuador into a theocratic state. Though driven physically into the modern age, its spirit was to remain that of the Middle Ages, or at least of the Counter-Reformation. A Concordat was concluded with the Vatican renouncing the state's right to the *patronato real* and according the Church many privileges, including those of censorship of all books and the enjoyment of special tithes. The Jesuits were recalled from exile and given a leading role in education. The Church itself was thoroughly purged and reformed, for religion was not exempt from the dictator's obsession with efficiency. The army was reorganized, the regiments receiving titles such as Soldiers of the Infant Jesus, Volunteers of the Cross, and Guardians of the Virgin. The whole country was finally dedicated to the Sacred Heart of Jesus. Opponents of the regime were treated as heretics and punished as criminals. The Liberals were cowed or driven into exile, where the celebrated writer Juan Montalvo continued to fulminate against the tyrant. When, in 1875, the 'Regenerator of the Fatherland and Martyr of Christian Civilization' was struck down by assassins, Montalvo is said to have boasted: 'My pen slew him!' Under García Moreno's lesser successors the country rapidly lapsed into turmoil, and the disenchanted Liberal wrote: 'When I see what has befallen Ecuador after the death of García Moreno, I wish I had let the Dictator live!'

With the advent to power of their *caudillo* Eloy Alfaro (President 1897–1901 and 1906–11) and the more staid Leónidas Plaza (President 1901–4 and 1912–16) the Liberals took their turn at the helm of state. What remained of the theocratic structure was dismantled; Church and State were separated and education secularized. Restraints on civil liberties were relaxed but little serious effort was made to tackle the land problem or other basic issues. Ecuador's exports of cacao beans found a good market abroad and brought fortunes to a few families until disease blighted the crop. World War I gave a not unwholesome jolt to traditional patterns of trade and a mild stimulus to local manufacturing. A small oil-field was discovered and developed with the help of British capital. Attempts by the nascent working class to assert its rights were sternly suppressed (1922). Such economic prosperity as the country began to experience benefited mainly the merchants, bankers, and landowners of Guayaquil, against whose prolonged domination a rising, spearheaded by army officers from the sierra, was at length successfully launched (1925). Whatever aspirations for genuine reform the *golpistas* may have had soon evaporated in the confusion of the next eight years, during which time six presidents made their rapid entries and exits, and the army itself was torn by factional strife (1932).

Whether the creed invoked was Liberalism or Conservatism, *personalismo* remained Ecuador's real system of government. Presidents continued to imprint their varied personalities on the country's fortunes even if their positive achievements were slight. Arroyo del Río (1940–4), a wealthy company lawyer from Guayaquil, aligned Ecuador with the victorious allies in World War II but could not prevent the loss of most of his country's eastern lowlands to Peru (see page 321). Under Galo Plaza (1945–52), a genial and businesslike gentleman farmer, a number of sensible schemes for agricultural improvement were launched but were largely nullified by administrative incompetence, bad harvests, and a terrible earthquake (1949); more popular in the United States than among his own people, the President managed to make history by completing his term but then found fresh scope for his talents abroad as the UN mediator in Cyprus and Secretary-General of the OAS. Ponce Enríquez (1956–60) steered a course somewhat to the right but gave the country relative stability. Carlos Julio Arosemena (1961–3), with his drinking bouts and his political oscillations, at least gave it drama, until replaced by a *junta* of reform-minded officers (1963–6) who made some attempt to reorganize the chaotic fiscal system and enact a mild Agrarian Reform. They were succeeded by Clemente Yeroví, and then by Otto Arosemena (1966–8), both interim presidents. But outshining all these successive stars of the political firmament, fitfully obscured by storm-clouds of his own making, then reappearing with still brighter promise, there moved the meteor of Ecuadorean politics, five times called to the presidency of the republic and four times deposed—José María Velasco Ibarra (1934–5, 1944–7, 1952–6, 1960–1, 1968–72). Constant only in his passionately proclaimed nationalism and desire to better the lot of the common man, Velasco Ibarra has followed policies which smack at different times of Conservatism, Liberalism, *justicialismo,* and moderate reformism. Hardworking and personally honest, though too often surrounded by corrupt collaborators, the septuagenarian spell-binder has been too mercurial and autocratic to achieve more than a few gains in his five terms of office. In June 1970 he assumed dictatorial powers and dissolved Congress, after the latter had opposed his proposals for tax reforms and exchange controls which Guayaquil business circles feared would harm their interests. He was deposed by General Rodríguez Lara in 1972 after suppressing student dissidence and an army revolt and exiling Assad Bucaram, Guayaquil's leading *politico*, and was thus prevented from completing his fifth term of office.

Ecuador's needs are clear enough: more schools, particularly in the country districts, to raise the calibre of her labour force and reduce illiteracy; better farming techniques and more crop diversification to break the precarious dependence on monoculture; new markets abroad (which may include the Communist countries, for, as Velasco Ibarra has put it, 'bananas have no ideology'); a land reform which will help to integrate the Indians, who now have transistor radios even if they are still without the vote; more industrialization, though as a late-comer Ecuador will find it hard to make goods which are produced better and more cheaply elsewhere; a mitigation of the old rivalry between coast and sierra and a reorganization of the fragmented tax and administrative system so as to permit the application of coherent national development policies. No government has yet had the strength or the funds to make much progress along these lines. High hopes are now being pinned on the exploitation of recently discovered copper deposits in Azuay province and the development of new oil-fields in the Oriente, as the source of the increased revenue which may not only solve current budgetary difficulties but also finance most of the cost of the basic structural reforms required. The new oil boom comes too at a time when the future of the current source of the country's export earnings—bananas—seems in jeopardy from the growing competition of Central American producers (see page 258). But even if oil comes to Ecuador's financial rescue, the political difficulties in the way of radical reform still remain formidable—backward and apathetic masses, a weak middle class, a feudal aristocracy entrenched in the sierra and a financial and commercial oligarchy supreme on the coast which, if they are often at daggers drawn amongst themselves, know how to unite in the defence of their common privileges.

8 Peru

No Latin American country has a name more evocative of wealth and romance than Peru. *Vale un Perú!*—'It is worth a Peru!'—the Spaniards would exclaim to describe something incomparably rare and costly. Such riches as the country possesses today are not the Incas' gold and silver mines in the sierra, but more prosaic products, mostly from the coast, like sugar and cotton, copper and fish-meal. *Sierra, costa, selva*—the Amazonian lowlands east of the Andes, which comprise nearly two thirds of Peru's territory and may one day furnish new sources of wealth—these are the country's basic topographical divisions. Its social divisions have been scarcely less marked—the 'oligarchy' of landowners, industrialists, bankers, businessmen; the Indians and *cholos* of the sierra and the marginal population of the shanty-towns; and the intermediate urban middle sectors. But this human landscape, unlike the geographical, now seems to be in flux. New political and social forces are at work which may reshape Peru as drastically as Mexico was reshaped by her revolution of fifty years ago, or Cuba by hers in the 'sixties. What face the new Peru will bear, if its present military rulers, revolutionary yet authoritarian, pursue their course, it is too early to say. But it is likely to be very different from the Peru we have known.

The post-independence period

The republic which succeeded a century and a half ago to the old Viceroyalty of Peru was far inferior to the latter in territorial extent, population, and political importance. Though it secured the disputed coastal areas of Tumbes, Jaén, and Maynas, the key port of Guayaquil was lost to its northern neighbour. More serious still was the amputation of all Upper Peru to form the new state of Bolivia. These boundaries left Peru with more than enough room for her own development, but the uncertainties and alleged injustices attending their demarcation were to furnish much cause for future strife. The population of the republic amounted (1826) to 1,200,000, more than half of whom were Indians and some 50,000 negro slaves; despite the founding fathers' humanitarian ideals, neither the Indian tribute nor the institution of slavery were abolished until the middle of the century. Until that time, too, when steamships began to replace sail, Peruvian ports suffered greatly from the competition of such rapidly growing ports as Buenos Aires, Montevideo and Valparaiso, which were less remote from European markets. But truncated and impoverished as Peru now found herself, the Creole landowners were at least masters in their own house. Their already extensive estates were enlarged at the expense of Indian communal lands and properties previously owned by Spanish royalists. They had, however, to share their power with men of the rising merchant class who had the flexibility and energy to adapt themselves to the new commercial conditions, and with the constitution-making lawyers in congress. Above all, they had to come to terms with the soldiers who had fought and won the wars of independence— men whose blood was generally more mixed and birth humbler than their own, and who had something of the thrusting, ruthless energy of the old conquistadores. For most of the rest of the century, the country was to be ruled by a succession of military *caudillos* of this stamp.

Peru had first to face the challenge of being forced into union with Bolivia under the latter's crafty and ambitious ruler, General Santa Cruz. After defeating the armies of the Peruvian *caudillos* Gamarra and Salaverry, Santa Cruz assumed the style of Protector of a Peruvian–Bolivian Confederation which was to consist of three component parts centred respectively round La Paz, Lima, and Arequipa. Chile watched with alarm the emergence of this powerful new state from its power base in the Andean sierra and resolved to take the offensive. An expeditionary force under the Chilean general Manuel Bulnes landed in Peru and, with the support of the anti-Santa Cruz faction in that country, brought the Protector to battle and defeated him. The Confederation was dissolved, and Bolivia and Peru went their respective ways.

Under the firm rule of her *caudillos*, notably that of General Ramón Castilla (1845–51 and 1855–62) and of Manuel Pardo, the founder of the *Civilista* party and the first civilian to become President of Peru (1872–6), the foundations of a more modern economy were laid. Improved irrigation of the coastal valleys was yielding a valuable sugar crop, and some cotton, for export. A railway—the first to be built in South America—connected the capital with its port of Callao, and the mining areas of the interior were soon to be linked to the coast by the spectacular railways built by the indomitable American engineer, Henry Meiggs. Above all, a new asset had been discovered—or rediscovered, for the Incas and their predecessors had put it to good use—the *guano* deposits now in brisk demand for raising the fertility of Europe's fields. In one year alone (1860), no fewer than 433 vessels took on cargoes of *guano* from a single group of islands, the Chinchas, in the Gulf of Pisco. The state, as well as a handful of profiteers, benefited dramatically from the bonanza. By 1859, it was drawing nearly four fifths of its national revenue from *guano* sales. But the men who ruled Peru had little notion of sound finance, and the *guano* revenue was squandered and irreplaceable deposits depleted. By the 'seventies, revenue from *guano* had dwindled until it was only enough to cover the servicing of the country's mounting foreign debts. Nature, it is true, had obligingly concealed other valuable resources beneath the forbidding crust of the coastal desert—nitrate of soda, borax, and silver—which were also now being exploited and profitably marketed. But the utilization of these new sources of wealth brought fresh dangers in its train. The nitrate fields were primarily to be found in Atacama, a border province which no one had bothered to demarcate so long as the desert was deemed to be sterile and worthless but which had been theoretically assigned to Bolivia, and in the neighbouring Peruvian provinces of Tarapacá, Arica, and Tacna. But it was Chilean capital and manpower which was taking the lead in developing the hidden riches of Atacama.

The War of the Pacific and after

To stiffen Bolivia's resistance to Chilean penetration of the Atacama, Peru had signed a secret treaty with Bolivia in 1871, and found herself drawn into the War of the Pacific which broke out between La Paz and Santiago two years later. After rapidly crushing Bolivian resistance, Chilean forces pushed on into Peruvian territory and occupied Arica and Tacna. Peru's few warships were no match for the Chilean navy. Her flag-ship, the monitor *Huascar*, was captured after a gallant resistance. The way was clear for the landing of a Chilean expeditionary force, which captured Lima (1881) after breaking the desperate defence organized by Nicolás Piérola, the fiery leader of the Democrat Party which he had founded in rivalry to Pardo's *Civilistas*. The Peruvians carried on the war from Arequipa and from guerrilla bases in the sierra, but two years later were compelled to agree to the Peace of Ancón by which Tarapacá was ceded outright to Chile, whilst Tacna and Arica were made over to her for an initial period of ten years, after which their future was to be decided by plebiscite.

The shock of Peru's defeat in the War of the Pacific roused the country to the need for finding a more solid foundation for its economy than the bonanzas from *guano* and nitrate, and a broader social and political basis for her political life. There was heart-searching by intellectuals anxious to discover the cause of Peru's backwardness and seeking ways of 'redeeming' the unassimilated Indian masses through Positivist prescriptions for modernizing the country. The latter still suffered from the feud between *Civilistas* and Democrats, and though the generals continued to rule, it was clear that they were ill fitted to find solutions for its problems. When General Cáceres, a hero of the war against Chile who had already held the Presidency from 1886 to 1890, tried to manipulate the elections so as to secure his return to power, he was thwarted by a popular movement which Piérola once again hurried from exile to lead. A phase of rule by civilian presidents now set in. The oligarchy had at last asserted itself over the military and governed the country through two political parties: the now increasingly reactionary *Civilistas*, and the more radical Democrat Party of Piérola. Under the latter's presidency (1895–9), fiscal and educational reforms were introduced and the country began to enjoy a period of political stability and economic progress which was continued during the two administrations (1904–8 and 1915–19) of José Pardo, son of the *Civilista* founder.

A new figure now emerged from the ranks of the *Civilistas*. A dynamic, self-made businessman, Augusto B. Leguía never felt at his ease with the Conservative oligarchy whose control of Congress hampered the schemes for economic expansion and public works which he wished to introduce during his first term of office (1905–12). Returned for a second term (1919), he replaced the elected Congress by a hand-picked Assembly and embarked on eleven years of autocratic rule. Leguía used his dictatorial powers to force through ambitious programmes of road and railway construction, irrigation, urban re-planning, and industrialization. To finance them, massive injections of foreign investment were sought, mostly from the United States, and left the country heavily in debt. The onset of the world depression in the late 'twenties caused this vital flow of funds to dry up and led to mounting unemployment and discontent. The material benefits which Leguía had given Peru—and which he had even tried to extend to the emerging industrial proletariat through a paternalistic system of social services and trade unions—were no longer substantial enough to make up for the lack of political liberties. Nor had nationalist opinion been mollified by the compromise reached in 1929, with United States arbitration, which resulted in Chile retaining Arica and only Tacna being returned to Peru. In August 1930 Leguía was forced by a military rising to leave office and was denounced for subordinating his country to the interests of foreign capitalists.

Army, oligarchy and APRA

The organizer of the rising was a rough *mestizo* officer, Sánchez Cerro, who legitimized his coup by winning victory in the subsequent presidential elections (1931). His opponents claimed that the elections were rigged and plunged the country into near civil war. The chief challenge to Sánchez Cerro came from the Alianza Popular Revolucionaria Americana (APRA) which had emerged in the mid-'twenties under the dynamic student leader Víctor Raúl Haya de la Torre. Born of a well-to-do family in Trujillo, Haya de la Torre had introduced into Peru the ideas of the University Reform Movement (see page 247) and organized university extension courses which won him a following amongst the workers. Many lower-middle-class and professional people, who either hated the oligarchy or had little prospect of winning acceptance into it, supported his programme. This was framed in nationalistic and radical terms and comprised resistance to 'Yankee imperialism', the internationalization of the Panama canal, the nationalization of land and industry, the political union of Latin America and international solidarity with all oppressed classes. Though it gained little effective support in the sierra, it also claimed to stand for the revindication of Indian rights. This programme was close enough to that of Peru's embryonic Communist groups, with whom the *apristas* at first worked in harmony, to arouse the alarm of the oligarchy and the hostility of the army. Though the Communists possessed in the brilliant Mariátegui (1895–1930) a Marxist thinker of power and originality and a leader of great personal integrity, they soon broke with the autocratic Haya and never matched the powerful organization and demagogic appeal of APRA. The latter, under the charismatic spell of its *caudillo* and influenced by the militancy of the Mexican revolutionaries and contemporary

Fascist techniques in Europe, felt strong enough to challenge simultaneously the Communists, the oligarchy, and the military. When a naval mutiny broke out at Callao and was followed two months later by a serious rising in the APRA stronghold of Trujillo, which was only suppressed with the loss of between one and two thousand lives, and when Sánchez Cerro himself finally fell to an assassin (1933), these acts of violence were laid to the charge of APRA.

Another military strong man, Marshal Benavides (1933–9), seized the succession. A moderate, middle-of-the-road professional soldier, Benavides steered the country back to a steady economic recovery and started work for political reconciliation. But a bitter feud still raged between APRA and the oligarchy, outraged by the sensational murder (1935) of two of its notable figures, Antonio Miró Quesada, proprietor of the influential newspaper *El Comercio*, and his wife. It was not until the time of his civilian successor Manuel Prado (1939–45) that appeasement seemed possible. The President's hand was strengthened by the successful outcome of a war with Ecuador (1941) which left Peru in virtual control of the upper basin of the Amazon, and by the brisk demand for the country's products during the Second World War into which Peru followed the United States on the side of the western powers. APRA too had been quietly toning down the strident note of its anti-imperialist programme. Foreign capital ceased to draw APRA's denunciations as an unmitigated evil, and was now welcomed provided it could be controlled in the national interest. The government's grant (1948) of an important concession to the International Petroleum Company (IPC), a subsidiary of Standard Oil, thus paradoxically received APRA's backing against the opposition of many right-wing business circles. But if its revolutionary wings had been clipped, APRA could still show its claws in the power struggle. When Dr. Bustamante, a respected judge from Arequipa, was elected to the presidency (1945–8) with a programme of reconciliation and national consensus, APRA attempted to use its dominant influence over Congress and the trade unions to impose its own will on the executive. Bustamante's difficulties were increased by the slump which had now followed the wartime boom. Once again the military moved to resolve the deadlock, and the President was ousted by his former Minister of the Interior, General Odría (October 1948). For the next eight years Peru experienced another period of dictatorial rule, social calm—the lot of the urban proletariat was improved by a programme of public works and new social services, whilst the Indians remained quiescent in their traditional neglect—and *laissez-faire* economic growth. The Korean war gave another boost to Peru's exports, but its end caused corresponding hardship and discontent.

The election of Manuel Prado for a second term of presidential office (1956–62) suggested that the oligarchy was again in full exercise of political power. But victory had only been achieved at the cost of the unlikeliest concession—an alliance with APRA. The reason for this *rapprochement* was the emergence of Acción Popular, a new movement of the democratic Left which was attracting support from disillusioned *apristas* and some tactical backing from Christian Democrats, Communists, and other extremist groups. At the next Presidential elections (1962) Haya de la Torre and Fernando Belaúnde, the Acción Popular leader, headed the polls with 33 and 32 per cent respectively of the votes cast. The army leaders, who had never made their peace with APRA, stepped in to prevent Haya de la Torre from assuming the presidency and ruled the country through a military *junta* until fresh elections (1963) gave victory to Belaúnde with 39 per cent of the votes as against 34 per cent for Haya de la Torre. The vast increase in the size of the electorate from less than half a million in the mid-'thirties to over two million in 1963 had done much to erode APRA's former dominance. Belaúnde was allowed to assume the presidency, but Congress remained controlled by the APRA-led opposition.

Belaúnde, an architect from Arequipa, was in the line of descent from those reforming Presidents who sought the salvation of their country in ambitious programmes of modernization and public works. He promoted irrigation and hydro-electric schemes and set great store by improving communications, particularly through the building of the grandiose *Carretera Marginal* (see page 271). As a patriot with an unrivalled personal knowledge of his own country and a thinker of the democratic Left, he also believed that modern Peru should draw inspiration from its Inca past and rediscover its genius for state planning and communal action. By encouraging local initiative for such matters as the building of feeder roads, irrigation channels, schools, and clinics, he believed that the Indians could be gradually reincorporated into the life of the nation and 'The conquest of Peru by the Peruvians'—to quote the title of the book in which he developed his ideas—be brought about. The task of the Central Government was to provide the large-scale infrastructure and assist local initiative with funds and technical advice. This idealistic programme was enthusiastically taken up by Belaúnde's supporters, but met with hostility from their Conservative and APRA opponents in Congress, who blocked the new taxes required for financing it and forced the resignation of his successive ministers. The Indians themselves responded in some degree to the President's obvious interest in their welfare but caused alarm by invading a number of *haciendas* in the La Convención valley and other parts of the sierra. An abortive guerrilla rising under Cuban-trained extremists (1965) shook confidence, especially among the military, still further. Financial scandals, an attempt to settle the old dispute with the International Petroleum Company on terms considered humiliating to nationalist sentiment, and the mounting burden of foreign debt continued to erode public support for the government. On 3 October 1968 President Belaúnde was deposed and the armed forces once again took power.

Revolution by military fiat

Military intervention has been a familiar, indeed an inevitable, feature of Peruvian politics. But the 1968 *golpe* quickly revealed novel characteristics. Firstly, it marked the resolve of the armed forces acting as an institution, and not just as the tool of some uniformed *caudillo*, to take over power and continue exercising it for an indefinite duration and specific purposes. Secondly, its uncompromisingly nationalistic inspiration ranged it in frank hostility to the United States, hitherto accustomed to look with favourable eyes on Latin American military governments. Thirdly, far from depending on an alliance, or at least an accommodation, with the traditional oligarchy, the new military leaders proceeded to denounce it and to enact a series of measures aimed against its vital interests. Radical changes, they declared, were overdue in the nation's political, social, and economic structure and the armed forces intended to carry them out. Yet to do so, they chose the authoritarian methods traditional to the military. Within eighteen months of seizing power, the old political parties had been reduced to impotence, Congress suspended, the judiciary purged, newspapers muzzled and some of them expropriated. Elected municipal administrations were replaced by government nominees, labour unions regimented, peasant squatters evicted, and turbulent students disciplined. The people, on whose behalf the military reformers claimed to be acting, were not consulted as to the nature of the reforms and were debarred from organizing politically in their support. Only in the form of 'co-operatives' generally set up to break the power of unions still controlled by APRA, and of Cuban-style Committees for the Defence of the Revolution was some opportunity for popular participation allowed. But what precisely was the nature of this Revolution which the people were permitted to defend, if not to take a hand in making?

The first action taken by General Velasco Alvarado, the Commander-in-Chief now installed in the presidential palace, was clear and decisive. The unpopular agreement negotiated with the IPC by Belaúnde was abrogated, the company's refinery at Talara nationalized and the oil-field at La Brea-Pariñas taken over. To avoid Washington's Hickenlooper Amendment automatically coming into force—a clause which envisaged the cancellation of US aid and the sugar quota in the event of confiscation of American assets without an offer of reasonable compensation—the government paid a cheque into the company's account and then immediately froze it pending a settlement of a claim for a sum, nearly ten times that amount, in respect of profits said to have accrued to the company as a result of its 'illegal operations'. A further strain on relations with Washington followed from the arrest and fining of United States vessels which had been fishing in the 200-mile zone of territorial waters unilaterally claimed by Peru. In June 1969 the government moved on to enact a measure of far-reaching domestic reform: an Agrarian Reform Law (coupled with a law relating to water rights) providing for the expropriation of all estates of more than moderate size, against compensation mostly payable in government bonds, and their operation as profit-sharing co-operatives. Unlike previous programmes of agrarian reform, the Act was initially applied not against some anachronistic *haciendas* in the sierra, but against the profitable, efficiently run, and often company-owned plantations of the coast. By the end of 1969, the government was claiming that it had expropriated more than 2½ million acres, and that agricultural production had actually risen as a result of these changes. The government's five-year plan aimed to increase output still further and to give land to half a million Peruvians. The Agrarian Reform looked, in short, as if it was beginning to justify the regime's declared intention 'to achieve a realignment of Peruvian society and to change the structure of economic, political, and social power in our country'.

Were the military also leading Peru towards a revolution which would inevitably become 'Socialist'? They lost little time in establishing diplomatic relations with the Soviet Union and other Communist states, but these moves had already been set in train under the previous administration. Fidel Castro, scarcely noted for partiality towards Latin American military regimes, spoke in surprisingly warm tones of Peru's new masters. The attitude of Peru's own Left was more ambiguous. The Communist Party applauded the government's anti-American stance, approved of the Agrarian Reform, did its best to infiltrate the Committees for the Defence of the Revolution, and looked for official encouragement in attempting to strengthen its influence in the labour movement at the expense of APRA. But the imprisoned pro-Castro and Trotskyist leaders of the abortive guerrilla movement of a few years before still awaited release, and official spokesmen affirmed that, though the government was against the oligarchy, it was not for Communism. A series of new laws nationalizing foreign banks and asserting the State's exclusive rights to refine, and eventually to market, all minerals, nevertheless suggested that the country was moving towards a managed economy. By May 1970, when energies had to be temporarily diverted for urgent relief and reconstruction work following an earthquake disaster which cost the nation some 50,000 lives, the pattern of the sort of society envisaged by the revolutionary government seemed to be taking shape: a society under firm military tutelage and intermediate between free enterprise and state socialism, which would promote national development with the help of domestic capital and the carefully controlled support of foreign investment.

But the government was faced with a dilemma. Its economic and social policies called for large-scale investment, yet the nature of these policies might well frighten off the foreign investor. The government argued that the case of the IPC was *sui generis*; yet other American interests, such as the extensive grazing lands owned by the Cerro de Pasco Mining Corporation, several sugar plantations on the coast and Lima's telephone company, had also been nationalized. At the end of 1969, the government dismayed its left-wing supporters by signing an important new contract with the Southern Peru Copper Corporation for the exploitation of the valuable Cuajone copper deposits. Would not this deal, which envisaged an investment of some 300–400 million dollars—more than half the value of existing United States investments in Peru—forge anew the bonds of economic dependence which the revolutionary government claimed to be breaking? The government replied that this contract was necessary for the development of the country, and that its terms were such that the foreign investor would be given a fair deal without any detriment to Peruvian sovereignty. But the foreign investor still had his doubts. According to the new General Industrial Law (July 1970), foreign firms might still go on operating in Peru, but under contract and partnership with the State, which would acquire a majority shareholding in them once they had recouped their initial investment and made a 'reasonable' profit. The same law also provided for state ownership of basic industry and, in the private sector, for the creation of 'Industrial Communities' based on profit-sharing and the progressive participation of the workers in ownership and management up to a level of 50 per cent. Novel as such requirements might seem, few could doubt the good intentions behind the government's proclaimed aim of modernizing and restructuring the economy so as to produce a classless society governed by social justice. But doubt remained as to whether the government could adhere to a programme along those lines, carry its citizens with it, and at the same time secure the necessary financial backing from foreign investors and the international financial agencies.

9 Bolivia

'A beggar sitting on a chair of gold'—the famous phrase could aptly be applied to Bolivia, except that her chair was once of silver and is now of tin. Eighteen years ago a popular rising resulted in the nationalization of the mines and the breaking up of the great estates in a movement which seemed more truly revolutionary than any since Mexico's. Yet Bolivia remained poor; her *per capita* income is still the lowest in South America. Though the revolution gave her people a new sense of dignity and independence, and the Indians their first sense of being a real part of the nation, it failed to bring any substantial improvement in living standards or much prospect of escape from under-development. And when, in 1969, it seemed to have gathered fresh momentum, nationalizing the leading American oil company and proclaiming anew its radical intentions, it was the army which was at the helm and which was setting a course that none could predict. Would it keep to an intransigent economic nationalism, rejecting the foreign capital and technology hitherto assumed to be essential to the country's development? Would it turn into a Cuban-style revolution and seek alignment with the Soviet bloc? Would the military forge closer links with their like-minded colleagues in Peru? Would they veer round to a right-wing authoritarianism, or might they be manoeuvred out of office altogether by some civilian coup? Whichever direction she might take, Bolivia seemed set for momentous changes in the 'seventies.

Caudillos *and tin barons*

Bolivia's existence as an independent state dates back to 1825 (see page 72). Her first President, Bolívar's brilliant lieutenant Sucre, was succeeded by Andrés Santa Cruz (1829–39), who established a triple Confederation briefly uniting Bolivia with Southern and Northern Peru. Though vain and ambitious, Santa Cruz was able, energetic, and honest, and he gave Bolivia the best administration it was to know for most of the troubled century. His Confederation was recognized by Britain and the United States but aroused Chilean and Argentine fears and did not survive the defeat of its founder at the battle of Yungay (see page 156). After Santa Cruz, a rapid succession of *caudillos* rose and fell: Ballivián (1841–7), an autocrat of more aristocratic stamp, who foiled a Peruvian attempt at annexation; Belzú (1845–55), a crude military demagogue who exhorted the mob to 'do away with the property-owners and the inheriting of property'; Linares (1857–61), fanatical in his resolve to crush all opposition and impose his absolute authority; Melgarejo (1864–71), the most spectacular of all these violent men for his daring and brute strength, his debauches, his grotesque vanity and ignorance, the plundering of his subjects, despoliation of the Indians' communal lands, and mortgaging of the nation's resources to foreigners; Daza (1876–9), who was vanquished in war against the Chileans and paid for his venal incompetence with the loss of Bolivia's maritime provinces.

The history of Bolivia in the nineteenth and early twentieth century is not to be found solely in the bloody feuds of the *caudillos*, the reprisals, riots, and savage restorations of order, or in the fitful stirring of the illiterate Indian masses. Its course was also marked by successive amputations of national territory and the interplay of new economic factors. In colonial times Bolivia's mines had yielded fabulous wealth but they were stagnating by the time the wars of independence and the ensuing anarchy completed their ruin. In the second half of the century silver production somewhat revived. Most of the deposits were complex, and it was now the other minerals, particularly tin, hitherto discarded with the refuse, which came into demand for industrial use. Lead, zinc, copper, antimony, wolfram, bismuth, sulphur, iron—these and many others, some still hardly exploited, Bolivia was found to possess in abundance. The new food-canning techniques helped to create a brisk demand for tin, the production of which rose from 1,000 tons in 1890 to fifteen times that amount in as many years; it still remains the mainstay of her national economy (see page 268). But though possessing all this potential wealth, Bolivia's backwardness and inaccessibility made production heavily dependent on foreign capital and technology. Massive investments were needed in roads, railways, and plant for extraction and concentration of the metal. The final smelting could only be done abroad, for Bolivia lacked the power and fuel resources needed to undertake this; nevertheless, the possession of a tin smelter of her own remained a cherished national aspiration.

Whilst the *altiplano* was experiencing this revival of mining, the discovery of new economic resources was bringing less fortunate results to outlying parts of the national territory. The rubber boom was beginning in the Amazonian forests, and Melgarejo sought to raise money by selling off tracts of land on the undemarcated border with Brazil. This led to the steady infiltration of Brazilian interlopers and, at the turn of the century, to open hostilities which resulted, despite the stout resistance organized locally by Nicolás Suárez, chief of Bolivia's own rubber barons, in the cession of the district of Acre. In return, the Brazilians undertook to construct a railway which would link the valley of the Mamoré in Bolivia with that of the Madeira in Brazil, and so give Bolivia an outlet for her trade onto the Amazon system. In Bolivia's Pacific province, Melgarejo also sold concessions to enterprising Chileans eager to exploit the *guano* and nitrate deposits there, and the discovery in the same area of a rich silver mine speeded the transformation of what had until recently been a worthless desert into a valuable zone which the Chileans resolved should not pass from their grasp. In 1879, when the Chilean Government refused to evacuate the coastal zone, Bolivia with her ally Peru declared war on Chile. The War of the Pacific (see page 157) brought speedy defeat to Bolivia, and although a Treaty of Peace (1904) guaranteed her free-port facilities in Antofagasta and Arica, and the construction by Chile of a railway linking the latter city to La Paz, Bolivia never reconciled herself to the loss of her maritime province.

By the end of the nineteenth century, the country experienced rather more settled and responsible government and some economic progress was made. Under 'Conservative' Presidents such as Pacheco (1884–8) and Arce (1888–92), and 'Liberals' like Pando (1899–1904) and Montes (1904–9 and 1913–17), politicians began to concern themselves not merely with the struggle for power but with issues of general public interest, such as centralized government versus regional autonomy and the relationship between Church and State. The military too discovered a new role for themselves in holding the ring and ensuring a rotation of office between rival parties rather than merely seizing power for themselves. Though the despised and illiterate Indian masses remained well outside the political arena, some at least of the urbanized *cholos* began to gain admittance to it. Dissident Liberals formed a new Republican Party (1915) which, though soon splitting into rival factions under Juan Bautista Saavedra (President 1921–5) and Daniel Salamanca (President 1931–4), showed itself open to progressive ideas from Europe and built up a considerable popular following. In the ferment following the world economic crisis, falling tin exports and closed mines, Salamanca was elected President on a platform of reform and respect for the constitution. But one of his first acts was to declare war on Paraguay and subject his country to the disastrous haemorrhage of the Chaco War (1932–5).

Bolivia's interest in the remote tract of wild country lying on her undemarcated frontier with Paraguay had been stimulated by the loss of her Pacific province and the urge to find some compensating outlet to the Atlantic through the River Plate basin. The Chaco was known to be rich in quebracho wood and pasture land and rumoured to conceal valuable oil deposits. Though nothing has subsequently been discovered to justify such expectations, several small wells were already in production in south-eastern Bolivia by the early 'twenties, when Standard Oil of New York acquired the concessions and began more intensive operations (see page 265). By the end of the decade, border clashes were becoming more frequent. The Bolivian government made some conciliatory moves, but when these failed, felt confident that its army, with its Prussian commanding officer, its aeroplanes and artillery, and its far greater manpower, would soon settle matters. But the rank and file of the Bolivian army consisted largely of Indians who had little rapport with their white or *mestizo* officers, lacked any experience of the jungle lowlands, and had little stomach for the fight. The Paraguayans, on the other hand, were adept at guerrilla tactics well suited to a familiar terrain, and constituted a homogeneous, resolute fighting force backed by short lines of communication. When, in 1932, a serious border incident grew into full-scale war, the Bolivian army, soon decimated by disease and heavy casualties, was driven back to the Andean foothills where the Paraguayan forces, extended too far from their base, were unable to clinch their advance with a decisive victory. The stalemate ended in 1935 with an armistice, followed in 1938 by a peace settlement which awarded Paraguay the greater part of the disputed territory but promised Bolivia a corridor to the Paraguay River and the right to build a port there.

Nationalism and Revolution

The trauma of the Chaco disaster set Bolivia on a fresh and troubled course. Many of the demobilized Indians, whose experience of war had given them a new militancy and sense of nationhood and deepened their distrust of the incompetent traditional leading caste, drifted to the mines and towns to swell the ranks of the growing proletariat. The revolutionary mood of the country was voiced by the younger army officers, strongly nationalist and more Fascist than Socialist in outlook, and by the National Revolutionary Movement (MNR) led by a left-wing intellectual, Dr. Víctor Paz Estenssoro. Popular fury was vented against the tin barons, who were blamed for the low wages and inhuman conditions endured by the miners, the foreign firms, particularly the Americans, associated with them, the landowners and the *rosca* in general. In 1936 power was seized by a military *junta* headed by Colonel Toro, who proclaimed a 'Socialist' state and expropriated the Standard Oil Company before being shouldered aside by a brother officer, Germán Busch (1937–9). Elected 'Constitutional President' and then assuming dictatorial powers, Busch enacted a number of radical measures designed to promote labour organization and curb the power of the landowners and tin barons. That the latter still remained the real masters of the country seemed only too apparent when Busch committed suicide (or was murdered, as many suspected). He was succeeded by General Peñaranda (1940–3), an old-style military *caudillo* who shot down the striking miners of Catavi (1942), stepped up the production of tin needed for the allied war effort, and cemented good relations by paying compensation for the expropriated property of Standard Oil, receiving in return loans from the United States. But Peñaranda was swept from office in a wave of popular discontent and Bolivia's leftward course was resumed by a government formed from MNR supporters and a military group headed by Major Gualberto Villaroel (1943–6), whose erratic rule was brought to an end by the lynching of the President in front of his own palace. There ensued a six-year (1946–51) reversion to rule by politicians of the old Liberal and Radical Parties, followed by elections which gave a mandate to the MNR, but a *junta* intervened to prevent their accession to power. Within a year (April 1952) the *junta* was in turn overthrown, largely with the help of squads of armed miners, and Paz Estenssoro, who had served briefly as Villaroel's Minister of Finance before being exiled, was summoned to assume the Presidency.

In the next twelve years, under Paz Estenssoro (1952–6 and 1960–4) and Siles Zuazo (1956–60), the country's social, political, and economic structure underwent a transformation radical enough to justify the claim that, of all the Latin American republics, only Bolivia, Mexico, and Cuba can be said to have

had authentic revolutions. Three fundamental measures were quickly undertaken: the extension of the franchise to the illiterate Indian peasantry (hence-
forth to be known as *campesinos*), the nationalization of the three tin empires,
and the breaking up of the great estates by means of an Agrarian Reform. The
first ensured that politics ceased to be the preserve of the better educated
minority, drew the despised Indian masses increasingly into the national life,
and gave the regime a solid basis of rural support. The second, inevitable in
the prevailing nationalist mood, brought at first more difficulties than benefits.
The boom of World War II and the temporary fillip given to tin production
by the Korean war were over. The Bolivian mines, unable to compete with
the more easily worked placer mines of Africa and Asia, found themselves in
danger of being priced out of the world market (see page 268) and were only
kept in operation by heavy purchases from the United States, who wished to
see neither the take-over of a bankrupt industry by Peronist Argentina nor a
Communist regime ousting a discredited MNR. In 1961 a scheme for the
rehabilitation of the nationalized industry ('Operation Triangle') was launched
with technical assistance and massive injections of capital provided by the
United States, West Germany, and the Inter-American Development Bank.
But the political cost was high. The inflated labour force had to be
reduced and wages cut. Galloping inflation fanned the discontent of the
workers, particularly of the miners, the most militant section of the recently
organized Labour Confederation (COB). In seizing power, the MNR had
armed peasant and miner militias against the regular army; the latter had
been dissolved but was now reconstructed and used to put down the miners.
The viability of the mines was with difficulty restored and production raised,
but the price paid was the alienation of an important sector of MNR's old
supporters.

Agrarian Reform was the outcome both of government action and the pressure of the Indian peasantry itself. This pressure expressed itself mainly
through the rural *sindicatos* which began to be formed in the mood of militant
discontent following the Chaco War. They first appeared in the Cochabamba
area, largely through the efforts of José Rojas, a peasant leader from the
village of Ucureña, from where, after being at first suppressed by local landowners, they gradually spread to other parts of the country. The *sindicatos*
played little part in the 1952 revolution which brought the MNR to power,
but the weakening of the old social order made it easier for them to take over
many of the large estates. The MNR, whose leaders were mostly middle class
intellectuals, had expressed hardly more than a theoretical advocacy of land
reform, but quickly sent party organizers into the countryside to win over the
peasants and gain the support of the *sindicatos*. The following year, the Agrarian Reform Law abolishing the *latifundio* was solemnly and symbolically
proclaimed by the Government at Ucureña (2 August 1953). Somewhat
hastily drawn up, with little regard for the role of the *comunidad* or the necessity for preserving units of co-operative production like Mexico's *ejidos*, the
reform aimed primarily at giving maximum satisfaction to the Indian's craving
to own his own land. By 1965, 4 million hectares of arable and nearly 2

million of grazing land had been distributed to more than 173,000 families—a substantial proportion of the rural population. But the immediate result of a reform carried out on these lines was to promote subsistence farming and lead to a proliferation of *minifundios*. To counter these effects, the government also sponsored resettlement schemes from the crowded *altiplano* to the tropical lowlands. Despite the difficulties of adaptation for a peasantry psychologically conditioned by centuries of dependence on an all-powerful *patrón*, and physically adjusted to the peculiar habitat of the *altiplano*, these schemes met with some success. But it was only in the 'sixties that agricultural production began to recover its pre-1953 levels.

To stimulate its lagging agriculture, no less than its mining, the MNR became increasingly dependent on large injections of foreign aid. The campaign to open up the eastern provinces of Beni and Santa Cruz and settle them with peasants from the *altiplano* required huge investments in roads and other infrastructure. In the 'fifties Bolivia became the chief Latin American recipient of United States aid. Large sums were dispensed both in direct budgetary support and in underwriting the government's whole development policy. Private foreign capital was called in too to promote the plans for diversifying the economy and easing its dependence on tin. A new Petroleum Code (1956) permitted foreign oil companies to resume prospecting and production—an opportunity which the American-owned Bolivian Gulf Oil Company was to turn to good account (see page 266). The MNR, which had come to power with a nationalist, 'anti-imperialist' programme, thus ironically found itself a leading client of the world's chief capitalist power. This undoubtedly contributed to the revulsion of popular feeling against party and government, which its enemies accused of having rescued the country from domination by the Patiño interests only to deliver it up to a still more oppressive domination by United States interests. By the time the 1964 elections came round—Paz had amended the Constitution so that he could stand for a further term—the MNR had lost most of its middle-class support. Lechín, Siles Zuazo, and other once prominent figures had left the party. The miners were in sullen opposition. Even among the *campesinos*, some local bosses had arisen who preferred to hitch their fortunes to other rising stars, notably to that of the dashing, Quechua-speaking young air-force general, Rene Barrientos, who was popular in the Cochabamba area. As its backing dwindled, the MNR came to rely increasingly on graft, totalitarian methods of control, and close association with the armed forces. Paz was returned in the elections of May 1964—the opposition parties abstained—but was forced to take Barrientos as his running mate. Five months later he was deposed by a military coup and the twelve-year hegemony of the MNR was brought to an end.

For nearly five years, until the death of Barrientos in a helicopter accident (April 1969), Bolivia was under the control of a military *caudillo* whose rule was also a sort of rural populism based on peasant support. This he used both to reinforce and to balance the other pillar of his regime—the army, under its astute and enigmatic Commander-in-Chief, General Ovando. Barrientos did not attempt to dismantle the basic reforms of the MNR—universal franchise, nationalization of the large tin mines, and agrarian reform—and indeed he continued much of his predecessor's basic policy. But the spirit and emphasis of political life had changed. Instead of the consensus of labour, peasantry and middle class which had made possible the early MNR reforms, there was now a plethora of ephemeral groups, some supporting and others opposing the Government, which was thus given a façade of democracy, to which the formal accession of Barrientos to the Presidency (1966) also contributed. The strong, if confused, revolutionary nationalism of the MNR had been replaced by a *laissez-faire* attitude which left the initiative for the country's economic development increasingly to foreign private enterprise. Despite a sharp fall in tin prices in 1968, most sectors of the economy maintained a steady upward trend, particularly in the production of oil and natural gas, for which new concessions were negotiated by the Bolivian Gulf Oil Company (1968). Army men continued to hold key positions in the economy and administration, but beneath this military carapace the government's critics averred that a new take-over of the country by foreign interests was proceeding apace. Some substance seemed to be lent to these charges when the *caudillo*'s own Minister of the Interior, Antonio Arguedas, revealed that he had been both secretly in the service of the CIA and in sympathy with Havana, to which he had sent a copy of the famous diary kept by Che Guevara in the ill-conceived Cuban attempt to stir up a guerrilla revolt in eastern Bolivia (1967). General Barrientos certainly relied heavily on United States help in equipping and training the army which he used ruthlessly to break strikes in the mines and to destroy the guerrillas. Nevertheless, it was from the ranks of the army that a fresh wave of nationalist, left-wing, 'anti-imperialist' fervour was shortly to arise.

The constitutional successor to Barrientos was Vice-President Siles Salinas who held office (April–September 1969) until deposed by General Ovando. The reserved and inscrutable personality of the new ruler was in marked contrast to the panache and demagogy of Barrientos, and the colour of his government soon showed itself to be no less different. Its first act was to decree the nationalization of the Bolivian Gulf Oil Company, as the military government in Peru had decreed that of the IPC (see page 161). This move aroused much popular enthusiasm but caused interruption of production, considerable unemployment, and loss of foreign exchange until arrangements were eventually made for resuming the operation and the marketing of Bolivia's oil and new finance was found to allow work to continue on the pipeline which was to supply Argentina with Bolivian gas. Other measures, such as the setting up of a state monopoly to handle all mineral exports and the activization of diplomatic and commercial relations with the Soviet Union, strengthened the impression that Bolivia had embarked on a nationalist, left-wing course similar to that of Peru. But Ovando's power base seemed uncertain and his policies ambiguous. With labour his government had to temporize. Lechín, back from exile, was again at the head of the miners' union. COB, once more a force to be reckoned with, could not forget the rough treatment received a few years before at the hands of the army, which was now itself torn between factions of the Left and of the Right. The latter proved strong enough to force Ovando's resignation (October 1970) but the new regime which emerged, after a series of coups and counter-coups, appeared pledged to left-wing and nationalist policies.

Bolivia, under its new President, General Juan José Torres, a soldier of humble origins and an earlier supporter of Villaroel and the MNR, now embarked on a course of extreme political instability and continued economic decline. Its general trend seemed leftward; several challenges from the right-wing army sectors were beaten off and the US-owned Matilde zinc mines nationalized. But the government also moved against the extremists of the Left (weakened but not discouraged by the failure of their attempt to launch a new guerrilla rising in the Teoponte area in July 1970) and rejected the claims of an 'Assembly of the People', held in the buildings of the National Congress, to dictate more radical policies. The Torres government had no firm power base for its manoeuvres. It could count on no support from the MNR, which probably remained the strongest political force in the country despite its divisions, and faced unrest in Santa Cruz, where separatist sentiment was latent and the economic pull of Brazil and Argentina strong. The long-expected right-wing reaction occurred in August 1971 and General Torres was ousted by Colonel Hugo Bánzer Suárez. Bolivia, nevertheless, remains one of the most unstable of the South American republics.

10 Chile

'Chile', prophesied Bolívar, 'is destined by her natural situation, by the simple and virtuous character of her people, by the example of her neighbours—the proud republicans of Araucania—to enjoy the blessings which flow from the just and gentle laws of a republic. If any republic is to have long life in America, I am inclined to believe it will be Chile. There the spirit of liberty has never been extinguished; the vices of Europe and of Asia will reach her too late or not at all to corrupt the customs of that uttermost part of the earth. Her territory is limited and will always remain beyond the contagion of the rest of mankind. She will not change her laws, ways, and practices; she will preserve the uniformity of her political and religious opinions. In a word, Chile can be free.' How far has the Liberator's confidence proved justified? Compared with most Latin American countries, Chile achieved considerable success in the nineteenth century in evolving strong and stable institutions, orderly government, and a fair measure of economic development. But today she is no longer 'beyond the contagion of the rest of mankind'. As elsewhere in the hemisphere, the traditional social order is under attack and her citizens are demanding a quickening in the pace of their country's economic and political development. Whether the 'building of Socialism' embarked upon by the present coalition government of Communists and Socialists follows the familiar totalitarian pattern or retains some at least of the country's traditional democratic features, Chile is now no longer the model Conservative republic which Bolívar foresaw.

The nineteenth-century republic

The young republic had to overcome many initial difficulties. With more than 3,000 miles of territory, much of it desert or wooded mountain, stretched in a long ribbon between Andes and Pacific, the country was something of a geographical extravaganza. In the south, the unruly Araucanians continued to give trouble until contained at length by European immigration and improved communications; in the north, the deserts separating Chile from Peru had not yet begun to yield up the wealth which was to precipitate war with her neighbouring republics. The country itself was prostrate after the exertions of the war of independence. The resignation of O'Higgins (see page 72) was followed by the short-lived dictatorship of a brother officer, Ramón Freire, and growing anarchy. From 1830 the task of reorganizing the state was taken in hand by the Conservative President Prieto and his remarkable minister Diego Portales. Though he eschewed supreme office himself, Portales did more than any other statesman to establish orderly government, respect for law, financial probity, and efficient administration, and to encourage a sense of Chilean nationhood in place of the cult of the *caudillo* which he saw to be the curse of Latin American political life. Portales admired the pragmatic spirit of the English and believed that the Chileans, like them, should become a commercial and seafaring nation. But far from imitating foreign models, he held that every country must work out for itself the institutions best adapted to its own needs. He distrusted the Latin Americans' propensity for theorizing, rhetoric, and constitution-mongering, and believed that the democratic liberalism professed by many of the founding fathers of Independence led only to anarchy and factionalism. 'The democracy which so many of its deluded supporters advocate here,' he wrote, 'is absurd in countries like these.' He held that Chile needed a 'strong centralized government, whose men are veritable models of virtue and patriotism'. Government moreover should be in the hands of civilians, not soldiers. Though he laid the foundation of the tradition of strong civilian government which has kept Chile largely immune from the plague of military intervention, it was the ironic fate of Portales to lose his own life at the hands of a group of mutinous officers (1837).

After suppressing an attempted coup by Freire, who had been exiled to Peru, Portales became convinced that the threat from that country must first be neutralized if Chile was to develop into a secure and prosperous nation. Peru had recently united with Bolivia under the ambitious General Santa Cruz (see page 156), and although Chile was far inferior to the Confederation in population and resources, Portales set about preparing for war. After his death an expeditionary force was despatched to Peru and demonstrated the progress that Chile had already made towards becoming an efficient modern state by capturing Lima and defeating Santa Cruz at the battle of Yungay (1839). General Manuel Bulnes, the Commander of the expeditionary army, returned in triumph to Chile and was soon afterwards elected to the Presidency. His administration (1841–51) was a time of peace, reconciliation, and prosperity. The nitrate deposits in Northern Chile were beginning to yield revenue which the government ploughed back into the construction of new roads, shipping, schools, and other essentials. A Chilean settlement was founded on the Straits of Magellan and immigrants were brought over from Europe, whilst steps were taken to improve relations with Spain, Bolivia, and Peru. But towards the end of the Bulnes administration, largely because of the prevalence of nepotism, its popularity began to decline. Opposition intensified between the extreme Conservatives and the Liberals who, heartened by news of the revolutionary movements then sweeping Europe, clamoured for reforms which would secure a wider franchise and more press freedom and reduce clerical influence and the powers of the Executive. Bulnes himself was a moderate Conservative, but when he decided to back his able but more inflexible minister Manuel Montt, for the succession, the Liberals took up arms. It was only after Bulnes had defeated them at the battle of Loncomilla (1851) that Montt was able to begin his government.

Montt proved to be one of the ablest and most active of Chilean presidents and the spiritual heir to Portales. Thanks to his autocratic drive, reforms were carried out in almost every branch of the national life; the civil service and taxation system were overhauled, railways and other public works built, commerce, agriculture, and education expanded, and colonies of European immigrants settled in the south. Though the last phase of Montt's administration (1851–61) was troubled by an Araucanian rising and the onset of an economic crisis, the country's growth was continued under his Liberal successors. Economic advance was now matched by an increasing democratization of political life, and a new Radical Party began to emerge onto the stage hitherto monopolized by Conservatives and Liberals. Once again, Chile decided to pit her new strength against her larger but less advanced neighbours Peru and Bolivia. The War of the Pacific (1879–83) was fought primarily for the possession of the nitrate fields which her enterprising businessmen were active in exploiting in the coastal provinces under nominal Bolivian or Peruvian sovereignty (see page 157). Its outcome demonstrated the superior efficiency of the Chilean state, whose territory was expanded by the inclusion of the coveted provinces. But the war left her with a frontier problem which, though formally regularized by the 1929 settlement confirming her in possession of Arica and assigning Tacna to Peru, still tends to sour her relations with Peru, and even more with Bolivia, to this day.

Chile's victory led to a grave dispute as to who was to have the last word—Congress or President—in deciding how the revenues from the nitrate fields were to be used. The gifted and dynamic President José Manuel Balmaceda had begun his career as a Liberal reformer but had become impressed by the need for centralized government planning and was prepared to ride roughshod over a Congress which believed with equal fervour in the virtues of *laissez-faire*. When his opponents made use of their parliamentary majority to withhold funds and tried to impose a cabinet of their own choice, Balmaceda dissolved Congress and assumed openly dictatorial powers. Congress retaliated by attempting to depose him and prepared for civil war. The army backed Balmaceda, but the Congress leaders, with naval support, set up a *junta* at Iquique and raised forces in northern Chile which they financed from the nitrate revenues. After his troops had been defeated in the battles of Concón and Placilla, the President was forced to resign and seek asylum in the Argentine embassy, where he committed suicide (1891). Balmaceda has gone down in Chilean history as one of its most tragic and controversial figures. His opponents regarded his defeat as vindicating the ultimate supremacy of Congress over the Presidency and a triumph of democracy over dictatorship. His admirers claim that it represented only a success for the wealthy oligarchy and the foreign business interests who felt themselves threatened by the President's nationalist policies and his concern for social justice.

Chile since 1891

For nearly three decades following the death of Balmaceda, Chile was ruled by a succession of weak presidents and dominant but unstable parliamentary governments. There were few external complications during this period, apart from frontier disputes with Argentina which were settled largely through the arbitration of the United States (1899) and Britain (1902). Commerce and industry continued to expand, leading to a rapid growth of the towns and the gradual transformation of a rural into a predominantly urban population. Chile's political institutions, though more flexible than those of most other Latin American countries, could only adapt themselves with difficulty to the new social forces which were emerging. The landed oligarchy opened its doors to those who had made their mark in business and industry; the heterogeneous but growing middle class rallied chiefly to the reformist Radical Party; the new proletariat, spear-headed by the militant nitrate workers and numbering nearly one million by 1907, began to organize in a Workers' Federation under Luis Emilio Recabarren. A succession of strikes and workers' protests in Santiago, Valparaíso, and Iquique (1907), savagely repressed with the loss of hundreds of lives, shook the country and continued well into the 'twenties. Recabarren took his seat in Congress in defiance of his opponents' efforts to get his mandate annulled. He also affiliated his political following to the Third International and visited the Soviet Union. His tragic and mysterious suicide, soon after returning to Chile in 1924, plunged the nascent Communist Party into a disarray from which it took more than a decade to re-emerge as a major force in the country's political life.

The bulk of the middle class and a large section of the workers found a champion in Arturo Alessandri, a dynamic *caudillo* of the type which often appeared in other Latin American republics but seldom in Chile. Brought up in the Conservative tradition, he had espoused the cause of the workers and been elected Senator for Tarapacá and then President of the Republic (1920). After four years of battling against determined clerical and Conservative interests Alessandri was driven into exile by a military coup, but returned amidst popular acclaim six months later to introduce a new Constitution (1925) which effected the separation of Church and State and restored the powers of the Presidency. Alessandri also sponsored a great body of social legislation and provisions for universal primary education and a graduated income tax before being forced out of office by his Minister of War, Carlos Ibáñez. Four years of mildly dictatorial rule (1927–31), in the course of which Ibáñez carried through a lavish programme of public works and encouraged massive United States investment, petered out in the misery and confusion brought about by the world economic depression. In less than a year and a half, Chile experienced a kaleidoscopic succession of cabinets, two general strikes, a naval mutiny, and a short-lived 'Socialist republic'. The election of Alessandri for a second presidential term (1932–8) marked Chile's return to constitutional rule. But the ageing Lion of Tarapacá had lost his reformist fervour, and now embodied the desire of the country's middle and Conservative classes—the 'gilded *canaille*' he had once so eloquently denounced—for political stability and economic recovery.

By the elections of 1938 the country was ready for a change and returned a Popular Front government of Radicals, Socialists, and Communists. This opportunist alliance of the moderate and extreme Left bore little resemblance to the 'anti-Fascist' Popular Front regimes then in vogue in Europe, for it had been supported at the polls by the followers of Ibáñez and the small Chilean Nazi Party, and offered neither sympathy nor help to the western democracies then grappling with the Axis powers. Weakened by the defection of the Socialists and the parliamentary blocking tactics of the Right, the Popular Front soon gave way to a coalition dominated by the Radicals, whose leader, President González Videla, turned on his Communist partners and banned their party in 1948. Harassed by mounting inflation and other economic and social ills, the electorate recalled Ibáñez for a second term of office (1952–8), but the strong man of former years had lost his dynamism and could offer the country little more than a dexterous reshuffling of cabinets and a pale brand of Peronism which made little appeal to the great majority of Chileans. He was succeeded (1958) by Jorge Alessandri, son of the *caudillo*, whose Liberal and Conservative supporters triumphed by a narrow margin over the Communist–Socialist alliance which had been reconstituted without Radical participation under the banner of the Frente de Acción Popular (FRAP). Though a popular and incorruptible figure, whose Conservative policies had the support of Chile's commercial and industrial sectors, Alessandri made little headway in solving the pressing problems of inflation and economic stagnation.

The Christian Democrat experiment

The country was now in the mood for a more radical onslaught against its ills. The choice offered at the 1964 elections lay between FRAP's revolutionary programme and the alternative of a 'Revolution in Liberty' put forward by the Christian Democrats (see page 300). The latter's candidate, Eduardo Frei, won the presidency with 56 per cent of the poll, and subsequent congressional elections strengthened the position of the party in Congress, though lack of a majority there was seriously to hamper the passage of their reform legislation. The Christian Democrats had an impressive leader, a coherent programme, and a well-organized, confident party. But six years in office were to demonstrate the dilemma facing any regime which claimed to offer the democratic alternative to Marxist revolution. The industrial, business, and landed interests which had voted for them as the lesser of two evils, and whose support or at least acquiescence was still needed if a consensus for peaceful reform was to be preserved, soon found themselves hurt. For these sectors, and for the middle classes pressed by the higher taxes needed to finance the reforms and by the rise in prices which the government managed for a time to slow down but could not arrest, the pace was too fast and too painful. For the left wing of the party, and particularly for its youth organizations, it was too slow and half-hearted. An important left-wing section split off in 1969 to form an independent group which had more in common with the Christian Democrats' FRAP rivals. In the field of labour, the Christian Democrat Party failed to shake FRAP's control of the trade unions but looked for compensating support from the rural labourers who had benefited from the Agrarian Reform and were now permitted for the first time to organize on a national scale. Opposition to the government also began to take forms alien to the country's orderly traditions: sporadic rural and urban terrorist activity, mostly by student extremists, and a military mutiny (October 1969) in the interest of improved pay and service conditions.

If the 'Revolution in Liberty' was slow to yield its fruits—inflation had only been slowed up, not halted, by the end of President Frei's administration—some radical and probably irreversible changes had nevertheless been set in train. Under the policy of 'chileanization' (see page 267) the government had acquired a controlling interest in the vital copper industry, whilst production had been nearly doubled and the world price of copper remained high. The Agrarian Reform, despite the sometimes violent opposition of the landowners and attempts by extremists to give a revolutionary twist to the process, had resulted in the expropriation of some 12,000 rural properties and the start of a reshaping of Chile's traditional social structure. Moreover—so the Government claimed—the reform had been accompanied by a rise, rather than a loss, in agricultural production. A notable expansion had been achieved in the housing programme and, above all, in most branches of education, from primary to university level. On the international stage, Chile had taken a lead in promoting economic integration (see page 300) and gaining a wider hearing for Latin America's case vis-à-vis the United States and other developed countries (see page 326).

Popular Unity in power

In the elections of September 1970, however, the Christian Democrat Radomiro Tomic came third, with less than 28 per cent of the votes, whilst ex-President Alessandri received nearly 35 per cent and Dr. Allende over 36 per cent. Since there was no absolute majority, Congress had now to decide which of the two leading candidates should ascend the presidency. The Christian Democrats, who retained their majority in Congress, opted for Allende provided he confirmed and made explicit his intention to respect the individual liberties enshrined in the Constitution. These guarantees given, Congress endorsed his victory, and Allende became the first avowed Marxist Socialist to be democratically elected to the presidential office.

President Allende's Popular Unity government, successor to the FRAP, comprised the Socialist and Communist Parties, most of the Radicals, the left-wing Christian Democrat splinter group (MAPU), and some other small parties of the Left. The Communists, the strongest and best-organized component of the coalition, received three posts in the new cabinet. Popular Unity's electoral programme appeared little more extreme than that of the Christian Democrats, who had chosen a candidate more to the Left than ex-President Frei and now also declared themselves in favour of what promised to be one of the main planks in the Popular Unity programme—the outright nationalization of the big US-owned copper firms. But the presence of Communists in key positions in the administration, President Allende's known sympathy for Cuba and the extremism of his Socialist Party, together with the government's avowed resolve—albeit within the framework of 'bourgeois legality'—to 'finish with the domination of imperialist monopolies and land-owners and to build a Socialist society', aroused consternation amongst Chile's conservative middle class and raised fears that the country's democratic traditions must succumb to Marxist totalitarianism. There ensued a temporary business paralysis and the exodus of a number of well-to-do families, but confidence was somewhat restored after Allende had been installed as President (3 November 1970) and displayed moderation as well as skill in the implementation of his promised reforms. But the assassination of the Commander-in-Chief of the Army and the ex-Minister of the Interior by extremists respectively of the Right and of the Left, indicated the continuing trend towards political polarization and violence.

The results of the municipal elections in the following April showed increased support for Popular Unity, which gained just under 50 per cent of the votes cast, and in particular for the 'Comrade President' and his party (Socialists, over 22 per cent; Communists, nearly 17 per cent; Christian Democrats—still Chile's biggest single party—over 25 per cent). The government had won popularity through the uncontroversial benefits of some of its social measures, such as the provision of free milk for schoolchildren and the standardization of the quality of bread. Its policy of freezing prices while authorizing wage increases to compensate for rises in the cost of living was also welcome, whatever its long-term economic effects might prove to be. The government had pushed ahead with the intensification and radicalization of the Agrarian Reform and had nationalized important textile plants and major sectors of the steel and coal industries. Legislation to take over the copper giants was affirmed, though crucial battles no doubt still lay ahead over compensation. The government had also made headway in controlling the supply of credit through buying up shares in private banks, and though the opposition press was still vocal, had increased its hold over the news media. In foreign affairs it had taken the popular step of resuming relations with Cuba, had established them with China and East Germany, and had drawn nearer in general to the Communist camp, whilst taking care to retain correct, if chilly, relations with Washington.

But the Popular Front had also run into difficulties. In the first place, there was the problem of preserving harmony between Socialists and Communists, traditional rivals as much as allies. There was the challenge, too, from impatient extremists, notably the pro-Cuban, Tupamaro-style MIR, who claimed to be 'watch-dogs of the Revolution' and were intent on forcing its pace by encouraging land-invasions by the peasants, especially in the old home-land of the Araucanians, and, in the towns, squatting operations by militant shanty-dwellers. Some of the government's measures, such as the bill to set up 'Neighbourhood Courts' on the lines of the People's Courts in Cuba, smacked too strongly of revolution and had to be withdrawn in the face of congressional opposition. The economic hurdles to be overcome were particularly daunting. The private sector remained unconvinced by assurances that it would be allowed a worthwhile role despite the tightening grip of state control. The government urgently needed large injections of capital, if the rising tide of unemployment was to be halted and its ambitious development plans carried through, but foreign investment had virtually dried up. Even the scheduled expansion in copper production suffered a set-back owing to labour indiscipline, the flight of technicians, and a decline in copper prices. Nor could anyone foresee whether the threatened confrontation with the United States, fraught with dire economic consequences, could be indefinitely postponed. President Allende hinted that he might have recourse to a referendum which could result in the replacement of Congress by a single-chamber 'Assembly of the People' and mark a new stage in the process of 'building Socialism'. What sort of Socialism this might prove to be, whether specifically 'Chilean' as claimed, respectful of human rights and adapted to a pluralistic society, or patterned on the familiar totalitarian model, remains in doubt. Whatever the outcome—whether President Allende proves a 'Chilean Kerensky' or the pioneer of a genuinely new venture in democratic Socialism—his administration seems likely to rank as one of the most momentous in Chilean history and the most important current political experiment in Latin America.

11 Argentina

Argentina, the largest of the Spanish-speaking republics, is a promised land which has yet to fulfil its promise. Half a century ago, following decades of spectacular growth, the country seemed to be heading for an expansion and rising standard of living as assured as those of Canada or Australia. The vast triangle of her territory encompassed more than a million square miles, unsurpassed agricultural resources, and a vigorous, educated, and homogeneous population of European stock. With the world depression and the political upheavals of the 'thirties, the nation's development faltered. After a false start under Perón, the country has lurched uneasily from civilian to military government in a search for the solution to her political and economic problems. The prosperity, national unity, and continental greatness to which she seems destined still elude her.

The age of Rosas

Of all the republics brought to birth at the collapse of the Spanish empire, none seemed marked out for more rapid development than Argentina. Independence had been won with relative ease. The land possessed a temperate climate, a flourishing capital, markedly European in character and situated at the mouth of the great river system which seemed to invite European commerce and influence into the very heart of the continent, the vast agricultural potential of the great *pampa* roamed by herds of cattle and fiercely independent *gauchos*, and cities like Córdoba, Mendoza, and Tucumán, nourished by the varied resources of the inland provinces and the old trade routes leading to Chile and Peru. Yet the very vastness and diversity of the land precluded the rapid attainment of the pre-condition for its greatness—national unity. San Martín, the greatest Argentinian of his age, saw it as his mission to bring liberation to America as a whole rather than unity to his lesser *patria*. By 1830, the designation of 'United Provinces of the River Plate' had come to sound tragically ironical, and its use was officially discontinued. Argentina saw herself defrauded—and not for the last time in her history—of her promised birthright. Some problems—those, for instance, caused by the physical isolation and underpopulation of the inland provinces and the incursions of nomadic Indians—were in time to yield to advancing technology or energetic government action. Others have survived, under some form or other, to frustrate the full attainment of the nation's potential down to our own times.

The gravest of these problems was the dichotomy between metropolis and hinterland. The *porteños*, inhabitants of the port and province of Buenos Aires, which accounted for one third of the country's population and at least half of its wealth, differed in economic interest, outlook, and ethos from their neighbours of the Littoral Provinces (Santa Fé, Corrientes, and Entre Ríos), and still more from those of the interior. They owed their prosperity to the export of hides and the salted meat required for food for the slave populations of Brazil and Cuba and the import of a wide variety of manufactured goods from Europe. These displaced the more expensive and primitive products of the inland provinces which thus found themselves condemned to economic decay. The Littoral Provinces, also well placed geographically for the overseas trade, were denied their share in it by the riparian monopoly claimed by Buenos Aires and the latter's control of the customs house, the state's chief source of revenue. The prolonged struggle between Federals, advocates of provincial autonomy, and *Unitarios*, supporters of centralized government, thus stemmed from the divergence of economic interests between capital and provinces, and was heightened by conflicting political and cultural attitudes. The *porteños* were progressives who believed in education, immigration, theories of constitutional government and human rights, and scientific progress; the provinces, particularly those of the interior, tended to be Conservative, clerical, suspicious of the foreigner and his innovations. Most intractable and anarchic of all were the *gauchos* who were averse to all urban ways, all government, all law, and all institutions, and prepared to give their loyalty only to some *caudillo* tougher and more ruthless than themselves. The confrontation between the 'civilized' and the 'barbarous' world, vividly described in a contemporary classic (see page 313), was to be a dominant theme of Argentina's history.

The *porteños* had attempted to get their own way in 1819 by imposing a centralized constitution on the nation. The provinces replied by sending their *gaucho* hordes against the capital, dissolving Congress and the national government, and reducing Buenos Aires to the status of a mere province. But under the enlightened administration of Bernardino Rivadavia, who raised a million-pound loan in London, founded a discount bank and a university, curbed Church privileges, improved the port facilities, and reorganized the army, the city's trade and influence rapidly revived. It was to Buenos Aires that all Argentines naturally turned again for leadership in their struggle with Brazil for control of the Banda Oriental (see page 69). Though Argentine arms proved victorious, Rivadavia himself was discredited by the terms of the peace settlement and also by attempts to reimpose another centralized constitution on the country. His successor was murdered by a rival general, and the country overwhelmed by a fresh wave of anarchy. Buenos Aires aligned itself with the Littoral Provinces against the interior, where Facundo Quiroga's *gaucho* bands were imposing a reign of terror under the slogan of 'Religion or Death'. With the assassination of that *caudillo* in 1835, the balance of power shifted again to Buenos Aires, whose governor, Juan Manuel de Rosas, had established himself as the commanding personality.

For the next seventeen years (1835–52) Rosas was the virtual dictator of all

Argentina and gave that country its first rough taste of national unity. It was a paradoxical situation, for Rosas stood in theory for the Federalist principle and was all too ready to apply his battle-cry of 'Death to the vile savage *Unitarios!*' But though the country had no institutionalized basis for unity, and the provinces were each left to the mercy of local *caudillos*, the latter recognized the personal supremacy of Rosas, entrusted him with the conduct of foreign affairs and were unable—despite frequent revolts—to shake the disguised hegemony of Buenos Aires or its commercial monopoly. A landowner and consummate horseman himself, Rosas seemed to embody the fierce spirit of the *gauchos*, and took pains to cultivate their loyalty, together with that of the rabble of Buenos Aires whom he incited against his political enemies. A successful campaign against the *pampa* Indians had enabled him to divide their lands amongst his supporters and himself, and he had then gone on to make a further fortune in the salted meat business. The domination of the country by *estanciero* and *saladero* interests left no room for the encouragement of small-holdings, crop-farming, or even improved animal husbandry. Rivadavia's schemes to promote immigration, education, and scientific progress were all abandoned and the country condemned to economic and intellectual stagnation and political impotence. An attempt by Rosas to bring the former Banda Oriental within his orbit led to a prolonged siege of Montevideo (where many anti-Rosas exiles had taken refuge) and conflicts with France and Britain. The latter countries blockaded Buenos Aires and diverted their trade to other ports. Though the blockade was later lifted, it gave Entre Ríos and other riparian provinces a taste of the prosperity stemming from direct trade with Europe and made the reimposition of the old Buenos Aires monopoly intolerable. Urquiza, the Governor of Entre Ríos, decided that the moment had come to challenge the tyrant. Allying himself with *porteño* exiles and Brazilian and Uruguayan forces, he defeated Rosas at the battle of Monte Caseros (1852) and drove him into exile.

The forging of the nation

Another ten turbulent years passed before a balance was struck between Buenos Aires and the other provinces and national unity could be consolidated. In 1853 a Constitution was promulgated based on the federal, democratic, and republican principles laid down by Juan Bautista Alberdi, a distinguished political thinker exiled by Rosas. This provided for freedom of navigation and trade over the country's inland waterways and the proportional allocation of customs revenue. It also established a strong executive empowered to 'intervene' (take over) dissident provinces. Buenos Aires chafed under these restrictions to its privileges and for seven years two rival governments opposed each other in Argentina, first by economic warfare and then by arms. After an initial defeat at the battle of Cepeda (1859), followed by an attempt of the other provinces to 'intervene' Buenos Aires, the latter regained the upper hand and its commander, the distinguished historian, statesman, and general Bartolomé Mitre, was elected President of the Argentine Confederation

(1862–8). The metropolis thus regained its primacy, but at the cost of accepting the principles embodied in the 1853 Constitution which, with a few modifications, remained in force down to our own times. The old feud nevertheless persisted, breaking out from time to time into armed clashes, during the presidencies of Sarmiento⁻(1868–74) and Avellaneda (1874–80), who sought to settle matters by detaching Buenos Aires from its province and making it the federal capital, the provincial capital being transferred to the city of La Plata. The national territory as a whole had been enlarged by the incorporation of a substantial part of the Gran Chaco and Misiones area, which was seized in a war against Paraguay (1865–70).

Whilst the long struggle between metropolis and hinterland was being fought out, far-reaching economic and social changes were transforming the country. The progress of the industrial revolution in Europe was creating an expanding demand for wool and for cheap meat more palatable than the slave-fare produced by the *saladeros*. Sheep production was now the profitable thing, and the flocks in Argentina's coastal zone increased from a quarter of a million in 1810 to some five million in 1850. The replacement of sail by larger and faster steamships made it possible to export animals on the hoof or frozen carcases. Other technological innovations had important results. The use of wire fencing—first applied to enclose an entire ranch by an enterprising British *estanciero* in 1844—made real improvements in animal husbandry feasible, and the new network of railways, which provided an alternative to transport by bullock-cart or drove, facilitated the flow of resources from hinterland to port. The effective area of this hinterland too had been increased by some 150,000 square miles cleared of marauding Indians, thanks largely to the superiority of the modern rifle over Indian lance and *boleadoras*, in General Roca's ruthless 'conquest of the desert' (1879–80). These years also saw the first trickle of that golden flood of grain shipments which were to provide Argentina with 50 per cent of her exports by the turn of the century.

These changes brought with them a demographic as well as an agricultural revolution. Sheep-raising and crop-farming called for more manpower than cattle. The progressive, Europe-orientated men now in power did everything they could to foster the immigration they believed to be needed for the economic, political, and cultural health of the nation in conformity with Alberdi's dictum that 'to govern is to populate'; 'a minister of state', he added, 'who does not double the population every ten years is wasting his time in trifles.' Many of the immigrants were agricultural labourers who returned to Spain or Italy after the season's work. Others stayed on, to give an influx of 76,000 immigrants from 1860 to 1870, 85,000 in the following decade, 100,000 in the next, to reach a peak of 800,000 in the last decade of the century and 1,200,000 in the five years before 1910. By 1914, the population of the country had reached 7,885,000, as compared with less than four million in 1895. Some newcomers settled in agricultural colonies, where they long retained their own language and customs—the Welsh colony of Chubut remains an interesting example. The fortunate few managed to save up enough to buy their own flocks or small-holdings, particularly along the route of the new railways with

7—LA * *

their promising marketing facilities, and in the Littoral Provinces where land was cheaper. But the mass of immigrants remained landless rural workers or tenant farmers, or found jobs in metropolitan Buenos Aires, which grew in population from 230,000 in 1869 to 783,000 in 1895 and to over two million in 1914. Argentina was still a country of great *estancias*, whose owners increased in power and wealth as they realized the advantages to be derived from improved methods of stock-breeding and from the new techniques of meat processing brought into use in the 'eighties by the *frigoríficos*, and later still, by the superior quality of chilled meat (32°F) rather than frozen (−22°F). The publication in 1872 of the famous poem *Martín Fierro* was a lament for the passing of the *gaucho*, who was now no longer free to roam a *pampa* tamed by the forces of law and order, wire fencing, and telegraph. Foreigners, according to the 1895 census, comprised one quarter of the nation's population; by 1914, they accounted for nearly one third. Three out of every four of the adult citizens of Buenos Aires had been born outside Argentina. The problem was how to absorb these valuable but culturally disparate elements into the national community. The great system of primary schools built up by Sarmiento (President, 1868–74) served as a solid foundation for this process, though the more wealthy and compact communities, such as the Germans and British, tenaciously adhered to their own language and cultural identity.

More difficult still was the task of integrating this expanding and heterogeneous population into the political life of the nation. Between 1880 and 1916 power remained in the hands of the traditional 'oligarchy', secure in their possession of land and the wealth derived from cattle, sheep, and cereals, and firm believers in the Positivist creed of progress and the civilizing influence of European culture and commerce. The newcomers from Europe itself, apart from the few who made rapid fortunes and gained admission into the ruling élite, swelled the ranks of the growing middle and working classes. The financial crisis of 1890, brought on by over-expansion of the economy and harvest failures, sharpened social tensions and accelerated the formation of two new groupings: the Unión Cívica, supported by the bulk of the middle class, and organized labour. The latter, though torn by feuds between Socialists and Anarchists, was strong enough by 1902 to paralyse the city of Buenos Aires in a general strike. The radical wing of the Unión Cívica attempted an abortive coup three years later and was returned to power in 1916, after the passage of a new electoral law providing for secret and compulsory suffrage.

Hipólito Irigoyen, the sixty-four-year-old leader of the Radicals, was carried to the presidency with fervent popular acclaim. Idolized by the poor for whom he showed a genuine concern and hated by the oligarchy whom he despised, an upright man and astute politician, Irigoyen was the most powerful President since Rosas and expected by friend and foe alike to introduce sweeping reforms. Yet once in office he showed little notion of how to apply his powers beyond securing the enactment of some modest social welfare measures and dislodging, by means of frequent 'interventions' in the provinces, the local

representatives of the oligarchy, whom he then replaced by new-style demagogic *caudillos* loyal to himself. His rule was arbitrary, personalist, and uncertain, lacking any clear objectives for reform and leaving the traditional social
structure intact, despite a token agrarian reform law, upon its twin pillars of
estancia and *frigorífico*. Expectations of far-reaching change were frustrated
not only by the personal limitations of their chief but by the Radicals' tendency to show less concern with securing basic changes in the social order than
with those benefits which they were themselves beginning to derive from it.
The middle classes were content to enjoy their share of the prosperity in which
the ruling élite, despite their loss of political influence, continued to bask.

Irigoyen's policy was to keep Argentina neutral in the First World War.
Though the *estanciero* and manufacturing interests benefited from good markets and high prices for the country's agricultural products, and from the
stimulation of some export substitution industries, this brought no advantage
to the poorer classes. Attempts to improve their lot by direct action, as in the
strike of Patagonian farm-workers and the labour disturbances of the 'tragic
week' in Buenos Aires in 1919, were brutally suppressed. Irigoyen's government, as many others after it, began to see that it was easier to rally support by
appealing to national sentiment rather than by initiating constructive reforms.
By remaining neutral during the war, he had made a gesture of independence
from the United States, whose influence was beginning to be of more account
than the country's traditional British connection. No less flattering to
nationalist pride was his setting up of a state petroleum corporation (YPF) and
the refusal to grant any further oil concessions to private firms.

The next Radical President, Alvear (1922–8), tried to give the country a
more Conservative and less personalist administration. His presidency was
followed by the re-election of Irigoyen for a second term of office, but the old
Radical leader soon proved too manifestly senile to cope with the nation's
problems, which were now aggravated by the onset of the world depression.
In 1930 he was overthrown in a coup by Uriburu, a general attracted by the
corporativist ideas then fashionable in Europe. Though Uriburu was replaced
the following year in rigged elections by General Justo, an officer of more
traditional type, it was clear that the period of frustrated democratic reformism
had now ended and that the country had embarked on a stage in its evolution
from which it has not yet emerged today—the stage of the military's increasing
involvement in politics.

There followed thirteen years (1930–43) of Conservative rule. The workers,
though increasing in numbers and organized since 1930 in the CGT, were hard
hit by the unemployment and depressed living standards resulting from the
world depression and were not as yet a major political factor. The Radicals,
divided and discredited, were nevertheless strong enough to deny a genuine
majority basis to the governing coalition or *Concordia*; the latter was therefore
obliged to maintain itself in power by the fraudulent manipulation of elections,
which did little to restore the credit of genuine democratic institutions now
increasingly under attack by pro-Fascist ultra-nationalist groups. The oligarchy was intent on restoring its former political and economic ascendancy.

But times, and the nature of the oligarchy itself, had changed. The world depression had forced the country to cut imports and develop its own manufactures. The restriction of traditional sources of supply during the Second World War gave further impulse to the trend towards import substitution. The industrial sector steadily increased in importance, and the neo-oligarchy took on more and more the aspect of a plutocracy. By 1941, industrialists outnumbered *estancieros* by more than three to one in the highest tax group, and by 1943 manufacturers began to contribute more than agriculture to the gross national product—a trend which has persisted down to the present. But the need to protect exports of grain and meat still determined economic policy, though to do so it was now necessary to abandon the customary reliance on *laissez-faire* and to substitute measures of state control, such as the establishment of a Grain Board which bought grain from the producers and exported it at prices fixed so as to be competitive in the depressed world market. As a further protection to these exporting interests, which saw their markets in Britain threatened by the introduction of Imperial Preferences in 1932, an agreement known as the Roca–Runciman Pact was concluded. This guaranteed the position of Argentine exports in return for preferential imports of British manufactures and the operation of British-owned enterprises in Argentina, notably the monopoly of public transport in Buenos Aires—a concession which the nationalists resented as an affront to the country's sovereignty.

The neo-oligarchy thus found itself divided in its interests and loyalties. One section, with the majority of the middle classes, still looked to their traditional trading partners and sympathized with the allies against the Axis powers, whilst the latter commanded the sympathies of the increasingly restive and vocal right-wing extremists. President Justo (1932–8) was succeeded by Roberto Ortiz (1938–40), whose pro-Allied leanings and attempts to restore some measure of genuine democracy (he took the bold step of 'intervening' the province of Buenos Aires in order to remove its autocratic and frankly pro-Fascist governor) were frustrated by ill health. He was succeeded by President Ramón Castillo, who favoured the Axis powers and resisted Allied pressure to break with them.

The Perón regime

In 1943 the Conservatives' rule was ended by a military coup similar to that which had brought it into being. It was characteristic of the time-lag which often operates between Latin America and Europe that the officers now in power (first General Rawson, then General Ramírez and finally General Farrell) should have held authoritarian, pro-Axis sympathies, and only reluctantly aligned their country with the democracies by an eleventh-hour declaration of war (27 March 1945), when it was already clear that their European prototypes were doomed. But though at first unperceived, the military regime contained within itself a catalyst capable of releasing new forces which were soon to transform the political scene. The uncoveted office of Secretary for Labour and Welfare had been solicited by Juan Perón, a colonel aged 48 who had kept his eyes open during a term of duty in Europe and realized the political potential of the growing masses of Argentine workers whom previous governments had ignored, the Radicals neglected, and Socialists and Communists failed to win over. Some were the sons or grandsons of European immigrants, still more were workers who had migrated from the stagnating interior to Buenos Aires and other coastal cities. These were the *descamisados* who were to grow in number from half a million in 1935 to one and three-quarter million in 1947. Gifted with an easy, commanding manner and manly presence, a flair for oratory spiced with appeals to nationalist pride and scorn for the oligarchy, Perón set out to win the loyalty of the workers by voicing their hitherto inarticulate aspirations and securing for them wage increases, bonuses, and improved welfare benefits. New life was breathed into the CGT, which was gradually transformed into a formidable political instrument in his hands. His ally in this task was his mistress and later his wife, Eva Duarte, who rose by her wits, good looks, and ruthless drive to be the First Lady of the land and the darling of the *descamisados*, detesting and detested by the aristocratic wives and daughters of the oligarchy. Alarmed at Perón's rising influence—he had also built up a following amongst the NCOs and officer corps and had added to his powers those of Minister for War and Vice-President of the Republic—the Conservatives in the army, with upper- and some middle-class backing, managed to secure his dismissal and imprisonment (October 1945). Eva and the *peronista* labour leaders thereupon threatened a general strike and brought the embattled workers into the centre of Buenos Aires. The Farrell government capitulated to this unwonted pressure and announced new elections which Perón was able to win with 55 per cent of the votes.

The Second World War had left Argentina in a favourable economic position which made it possible for Perón's programme to get off to a flying start. Large credit balances had accumulated, mostly in blocked sterling, as a result of Allied purchases of Argentine foodstuffs. These Perón was now able to use for buying out the British railways and other foreign-owned utilities. Moreover, an exhausted Europe still needed Argentine beef and grain. Perón sold them to her at exorbitant prices through his state trading monopoly, which purchased them at low cost from the producers and used the differential to finance his pet schemes. The result in the long run was disastrous. It forced Britain to cut down her purchases to about a third of what they had been ten years before, discouraged Argentine farmers and caused an eventual drop in agricultural production from 90 million tons of grain in the period 1939–44 to 33 million in 1950–5. By 1952 the Argentine public was being urged to reduce home consumption of beef by the amazing expedient of observing 'meatless days'. The immediate profits from this short-sighted policy Perón had used to increase his popularity with the workers by boosting wages and social benefits to unprecedented heights—the Eva Perón Foundation, vested with the monopoly of all charitable and welfare activities, mushroomed into a veritable financial empire under the personal control of the President's wife—and to promote the heavy industrialization envisaged under the first Five Year Plan (1947–51) and the lavish re-equipment of the armed forces. The latter aspect of Perón's policy aroused particular concern amongst Argentina's neighbours who noted with alarm the boast of his militaristic supporters that Argentina's destiny was to secure hegemony over all South America by first dominating Paraguay, Chile, and Uruguay and then challenging Brazil.

The Constitution had been amended in 1949 to allow Perón to continue in office for a further term. But from 1952—the year of Eva Perón's death from cancer, which caused the grief-stricken *descamisados* to petition the Pope to have their benefactress canonized as the *madona de América*—his troubles increased. The Second Five Year Plan (1953–7) attempted too late to reverse the country's agricultural decline and secure greater productivity from the workers. The latter were now finding their wage increases eroded by galloping inflation, for the cost of living increased sixfold between 1945 and 1955, and the size of the bureaucracy nearly fivefold. Though the government claimed a fivefold increase in industrial production between 1943 and 1947, the foundations for the country's economic expansion, and particularly for the increased power resources she needed, had not been soundly laid. It was the realization of this failure which prompted Perón in 1954 to negotiate extensive concessions with an American oil company—a surprising reversal of his nationalist policy quickly seized upon by his enemies. The latter now included the oligarchy, whom he had excluded from political power, roundly abused, and occasionally intimidated by acts of brutality such as setting mobs to burn down the Jockey Club, their sanctum in Buenos Aires, but had never seriously attacked by any radical measures of land reform or heavy taxation; middle-class Liberals and Democrats, including a few independent labour leaders, whom he cowed by police repression and an increasingly totalitarian grip of all public media of expression; some sections of the armed forces, particularly the navy, who had grown resentful of his demagogic pretensions and the damage he was doing to Argentina's good name; and, from 1954 onwards, church leaders alienated by provocative legislation legalizing divorce and prostitution and threatening punitive taxation on the property of the Church and an end to her teaching activities, and by the incitement of *peronista* mobs to burn down churches. By September 1955, opposition from these quarters, together with the decline of the Argentine economy in the face of severe droughts, falling world prices for agricultural products, and the competition of more efficient suppliers, had made Perón's position untenable. Despite—or perhaps to some degree because of—threats that he would arm and rally the workers to his defence, Perón was overthrown by a coup and forced into exile.

The search for a new role

The dictator had gone, but there remained the problem of his supporters. How could the country be restored to democratic and constitutional ways whilst not less than one third of the electorate continued to hanker after the dictator's return, or at least after some form of 'Peronism without Perón'? General Lonardi, the organizer of the coup, declared that there should be 'neither vanquished nor vanquishers', and seemed disposed to introduce a Conservative Catholic regime. But the divisions within the country were now deep and bitter. Lonardi was replaced by the more uncompromising General Aramburu (November 1955–8) who banned the Peronist Party, vigorously purged its supporters from the administration and trade unions, and had some thirty ringleaders of an abortive revolt executed. There followed a succession of experiments in civilian government punctuated by innumerable abortive revolts and several major military interventions, an administration formed by one section of the old Radical Party, the Intransigents, led by President Frondizi (1958–62), an interlude of disguised military rule under President Guido (March 1962–3), a minority government of the People's Radicals under President Illia (1963–6), a further military take-over by General Onganía (1966–70). None of these governments found a solution to the problem of securing the effective participation of a working class which still looked back with nostalgia to the benefits, real or illusory, it had enjoyed under Perón, and the country seemed condemned to a process of irremediable fragmentation; the once mighty Radical Party, Perón's own political following, the labour movement, the armed forces—now themselves split into the hard line 'Red' faction and the more conciliatory 'Blues'—all were rent by divisions. Argentina was without unified leadership or national consensus, and until these could be re-established there could be neither political stability nor economic advance.

Frondizi, an adroit politician and economist, did an electoral deal with the Peronists and believed he could incorporate them into the national life. Though reputedly an advocate of economic nationalism and state intervention, his manipulation of the economy led to a neo-liberal stabilization and development programme which granted far-reaching concessions to foreign oil interests and saddled the country with 3,000 million dollars' worth of foreign debt. Continuing political unrest sapped the initial confidence of foreign investors and led eventually to a net outflow of funds, a drop in agricultural exports despite the devaluation introduced to boost them, rising unemployment, and a threefold increase in the cost of living in four years. The gross national product (1962) amounted to less than it had been in the heyday of Peronism (1948). The army had always distrusted Frondizi's gyrations and his overtures to the Peronists, and when the latter showed signs of sweeping the board in the gubernatorial and congressional elections of March 1962 it stepped in to depose him. Illia's administration and personal style were in complete contrast to those of the dynamic but volatile Frondizi. An elderly country doctor, almost unknown to the nation at large, he prescribed a convalescence of caution and conciliation. Apart from a dubious concession to nationalist sentiment in cancelling Frondizi's oil concessions, he seemed to believe that the best cure was to let nature take her course. Good harvests and the effects of some of his predecessor's wiser investments promised for a time that the cure might work. But what had first been praised as a 'gradualist' was at length discredited as a 'do-nothing' administration from which only the Peronists were really profiting. When they showed signs of gaining control of Congress under the nose of an apathetic government, the military struck once more and General Juan Carlos Onganía assumed power.

General Onganía's government announced that its policies would fall into three successive stages: the economic, the social, and the political. In the first, it achieved considerable success. Firm stabilization measures led to a return of confidence on the part of foreign investors, an inflow of capital and a favourable balance of payments, and an annual growth rate of nearly 7 per cent by the end of 1969. But the cost of the anti-inflationary programme was borne mainly by the workers, who were hard hit by wage freezes and growing unemployment. The government was strong enough to hold industrial discontent in check but failed to rally the divided labour movement behind its policies before passing on to the avowed 'social phase'. The prospect for any progress towards normal democratic processes, which was what most Argentines would understand by a 'political phase', seemed even more remote. The regime appeared rather to favour some form of corporativist organization. It attempted a crude purge of the universities, clamped down on the activities of the old political parties and showed no disposition to mitigate its authoritarian rule. At the end of May 1969, popular discontent suddenly vented itself in an outburst of riots and strikes, particularly at Córdoba, where students, workers, and some 'progressive' priests made common cause against the government. The latter survived this crisis for a year, though with diminished prestige and at the cost of some concessions to the unions. The armed forces, alarmed at the government's mishandling of a situation in which they had found themselves cast in the unpopular role of police force, and dissatisfied with the authoritarian style of government of General Onganía, deposed the latter by a coup and replaced him by a little-known general, Roberto Levingston, in June 1970. The new President, soon abandoning attempts to find a formula which would reactivate the political life of the country and turning instead to a populist-nationalist line in economics in the hope of bolstering his personal position, fell foul of the chiefs of the armed forces and was replaced by the army commander-in-chief, General Lanusse, in March 1971.

12 Paraguay

Paraguay lies deep in the heart of the continent, a land-locked, riverside nation linked to the Atlantic seaboard by 1,000 miles of waterway, most of it in Argentine territory, and now by a road running overland through Brazil. The competing pressures of these two far larger neighbours have done much to form the virile, homogeneous character of her people. Nowhere in Latin America has the fusion between Spaniard and Indian been more complete. The Paraguayans are proud of their Guaraní blood and of the melodious Guaraní tongue which most of them speak as well as Spanish. From the native race they have inherited martial qualities as well as their love of music and primitive, bucolic way of life. There is still an Arcadian quality about the land where Jesuit fathers once ruled their submissive Indian flocks and Voltaire's Candide learned the virtues of simple living. Yet Paraguay's history has been tragic and violent. Twice in the course of one century the country has been bled by devastating wars, once almost to the point of national annihilation. It has known little else than the rule of ruthless tyrants. Even today, as her sister republics move restlessly along the path of industrialization, social ferment, and political experimentation, Paraguay still nods beneath the longest surviving despotism in South America, which—as is the way with such despotisms—has given her peace and order at the cost of restricted personal liberties and a slow rate of material progress. Something like one third of her population, either through choice or necessity, have turned their backs on their native land and now live outside its borders.

Paraguay's independence dates from 1811, when the Governor was replaced by a *junta* in which Dr. José Gaspar Rodríguez de Francia became the dominant figure (see page 69). Three years later he made himself dictator and remained the country's absolute master until his death in 1840. Under the stern rule of the frugal, hard-working, intolerant, and implacable 'El Supremo' Paraguay became a closed world from which the foreigner, with his skills, his capital, his intrigues, and his unsettling liberal ideas, was excluded. Foreign trade came virtually to a standstill and the country learned to rely on its own simple resources. Francia's dictatorship also inculcated a spirit of blind obedience to the leader which was to become the nation's chief source both of weakness and of strength. So long as El Supremo lived, he at least kept Paraguay free from the internal anarchy and foreign feuding which was the lot of most of the other republics.

His successor, Carlos Antonio López (1841–62), continued to rule despotically, if somewhat less repressively. He abandoned Francia's isolationism for a more aggressive and nationalistic defiance of Argentina's designs to extend her political and economic hegemony. Francisco Solano López (1862–70), who inherited from his father an efficient army and a well-stocked treasury, had the folly to imagine himself the Napoleon of Latin America. Believing Paraguay's independence to be threatened by Brazil's increasing influence in Uruguay, he not only prepared for war against those two countries, but by marching his troops through the territory of Argentina, provoked hostilities with that country too. It took the combined armies of the Triple Alliance four years to prevail against the desperate valour of the Paraguayans and to destroy the cruel, capricious but indomitably resourceful megalomaniac who had drawn them into his suicidal venture. The war left Paraguay with a shattered economy, a population reduced by about a half, including the loss of most males of military age, and a territory from which Argentina and Brazil had amputated substantial slices.

The war against the Triple Alliance might well have meant the extinction of a nation less tough and resilient than the Paraguayan. Slowly the devastated country revived, and the population, replenished with immigrants from Europe, began to build up again. Presidents succeeded each other in Asunción, but the country still lacked the strength to provide a power base for any autocrat as ruthless as its first three rulers. Whilst Europe was heading towards World War I, Paraguay began to brace itself to face another challenge. The frontier with Bolivia, a wilderness of forest, swamp, and scrub-land north-west of the Paraguay River, had never been demarcated. The Bolivians claimed the whole of the Gran Chaco on the grounds that it had formed part of the *audiencia* of Upper Peru; the Paraguayans asserted that it was theirs by right of exploration and settlement. Rumours of rich oil deposits in the disputed region whetted the appetites of the contestants, tension increased during the 'twenties, and in 1932 frontier skirmishes developed into full-scale hostilities (see page 166-7). The Chaco War, Paraguay's second great ordeal, imposed new sacrifices on the nation but at least brought the compensation of victory and possession of the territory under dispute.

It did not however bring peace at home. President Ayala, a competent ruler but too moderate for the passions kindled by the war, was ousted by Colonel Rafael Franco, a war hero who voiced the mood of radical discontent (February 1936). Franco had been exiled a few months before on the charge of Communist activities, but his ideas seem to have been nearer to those of contemporary European Fascism. He proclaimed the establishment of a totalitarian state and issued decrees nationalizing industry and introducing labour legislation, and others banning non-official parties and extending state control over the press and all political and social activities, together with an Agrarian Reform expropriating four million acres of idle land. But the Conservative elements in the army and country were still strong enough to force Franco's resignation and rescind these reforms. There followed the reactionary autocracy of General Morínigo (1940–8) and the more progressive but little less autocratic administration of Dr. Federico Chávez (1949–54). Several unsuccessful coups and risings occurred during this time, including an attempt in 1947 by Franco and his *Febreristas* to regain power, which plunged the country into five months of civil war. In 1954 the civilian politicians of the dominant but divided *Colorado* party were pushed aside by the army's commander-in-chief and General Alfredo Stroessner inaugurated his long rule.

The eighteen years of General Stroessner's regime have been outwardly uneventful. The forms of democracy have been preserved, elections being held at regular intervals (1954, 1958, 1963, and 1968) to confirm the General in the presidency, and the *Colorados*, now an increasingly Conservative party, in their control of Congress. Token Liberal and *Febrerista* opposition in that body has also been permitted. Occasional exile incursions and some guerrilla activity in the early 'thirties posed little real threat to the regime, and a state of siege has been periodically imposed to justify repressive measures. Since 1969 criticism has been mainly voiced by the Church on the grounds of the government's maltreatment of political prisoners and general disregard for individual rights.

The regime's preoccupation with the maintenance of stability has also been extended to the economic field. Stress has been placed on keeping prices steady and maintaining a stable currency; there has been little inflation and no devaluation since 1960. But the persistence of what can perhaps be described as the country's major industry—smuggling—and the stagnation of agricultural production, particularly the important cattle-raising sector, has widened the trade gap and led to short-term borrowing. The government has attempted to save foreign exchange by launching a campaign to become self-sufficient in wheat and has promoted some measure of industrialization, mostly on an import substitution basis. A national petrol refinery has been built and the first hydro-electric project launched. The Guairá falls of the Alto Paraná provide a vast energy potential which Paraguay is anxious to share with Brazil. Despite a dispute as to the demarcation of their common border, the Stroessner regime has managed to maintain good relations with that country, as with its other powerful neighbour, Argentina. Real economic progress seems unlikely to come to Paraguay, however, until the large-scale development of the whole River Plate basin is undertaken by the joint efforts of all the riparian states and with the investment of capital which she herself can never hope to furnish from her own modest resources.

13 Uruguay

Uruguay is the smallest country in South America: a model land, its citizens have been proud to claim, in the double sense of being both diminutive and exemplary. Whilst other Latin American states continued too often to suffer dictatorship and military coups, Uruguay evolved democratic institutions, a tradition of respect for individual rights, and a system of social services as comprehensive and generous as anywhere in the world. Half a century ago, its flourishing agriculture and foreign trade produced a gross national product and standard of living which put Uruguay into the same class as Denmark, Holland, and New Zealand. Now, though her people still retain many admirable and amiable qualities, she lags far behind such countries. The agriculture which provides her chief exports of wool, meat, and hides, is badly in need of modernization. The head—Montevideo—has grown too big for the body. The traditional political institutions seem unable to cope with the crisis through which the nation is passing. There has been violence in the streets and unwonted curtailment of civil rights by the government. The lustre of Latin America's first welfare state has grown dim and the struggle to achieve a new balance between ordered government, personal liberties, and national prosperity is likely to be long and hard.

Uruguay has known great changes in the century and a half which has elapsed since Artigas led his people in their fight for freedom (see page 69). For the inhabitants of the Banda Oriental, emancipation from Spain did not automatically bring national independence; they had also to free themselves from their more powerful neighbours. There followed annexation by Brazil, then a war between that country and Argentina, before a peace treaty of 1828, concluded largely as a result of British mediation, brought the República Oriental del Uruguay into being. The new state was blessed with an equable climate and a fertile soil, where today some eight million head of cattle and more than twenty million sheep provide the economic basis for a human population of less than three millions.

The early history of the republic was a time of extreme turbulence. The feuds of its *caudillos* led to the emergence of two factions known as the *Blancos* and the *Colorados*, distinguished chiefly by the violent hatred of each for the other, though the Blancos could be said to represent very broadly the Conservative, clerical, and rural interests, whilst the *Colorados* drew most of their support from the towns and invoked Liberal principles. From the mid-1860s, the *Colorados* managed to exclude their rivals from power for almost nine decades.

The unsettled state of the country kept it from progressing as rapidly as neighbouring Argentina. There was less in Uruguay to attract foreign capital or immigrants, and little incentive to develop its still pastoral economy. Nevertheless, the urban middle class gradually increased in strength, and at the turn of the century there emerged a powerful figure, very different from the *caudillos* of the old school, who was eloquently to express its new, progressive aspirations. This was José Batlle y Ordóñez, one of the great formative influences of Latin America and a man who left a more durable stamp on his country than any dictator. As President (1903–7 and 1911–15), newspaper editor, and tireless architect of social reform, he carried through or prepared the ground for a series of measures which were to win for Uruguay her reputation as the most democratic, progressive, and enlightened republic of South America: the right of workers to organize in their own trade unions and to strike; compensation for industrial accidents and dismissal; a minimum wage, holidays with pay, an eight-hour day, and old-age pensions; the extension of free schooling, both elementary and secondary, to the rural areas, and an end to clerical influence over education (and also over other aspects of public life). Full freedom of press, speech, and suffrage was assured. The state was given an increasing role in running public services and participating in the sources of the nation's wealth. The foreign-owned utilities, and ultimately the British-owned railways, passed into Uruguayan hands, and state management was tried out in activities as diverse as banking and insurance, meat-packing, oil-refining, cement and alcohol production, and the hotel business. To prevent the greatly extended power of the state from becoming the instrument of one man, a nine-member National Council was set up to assist, and ultimately to replace, the presidential office. This collegiate system of government modelled on Swiss constitutional practice, which Batlle had come to admire during a period of exile in Europe, proved the most original and controversial of the innovations which transformed the once turbulent Uruguay into an enlightened and progressive welfare democracy.

These changes did not pass unchallenged. The *Blancos* fought a brief civil war against Batlle in 1904. Nor was his own party united behind him. Some held his reforms to be too radical, others not radical enough, and sub-groups began to form within each of the two traditional parties. The onset of the Great Depression of 1929, when prices for Uruguay's wool and meat fell disastrously, put her economy and state services under great strain and led to a period of mildly authoritarian rule under General Terra (1931–8). But by the Second World War, which stimulated the demand for her products, Uruguay was set again on her democratic course and, despite the pro-Axis leanings of one group of *Blancos*, made no secret of her sympathy for the Allied cause.

The post-war period has, however, proved a time of deepening malaise. Uruguay's problem has been how to sustain her role as a political democracy and model welfare state on the basis of an economy which, despite a modest degree of import substitution industrialization effected during the depression and the 1939–45 war, remains essentially pastoral. Though such events as the Korean war may provide temporary stimuli, her exports remain vulnerable to the deterioration in the terms of world trade. Yet the cost of her social services mounts and the state payroll, on which some 40 per cent of the active population now figures, continues to lengthen. The result has been a growing burden of foreign debt, galloping inflation bringing with it a decline in the value of the Uruguayan peso as against the dollar from 2 to 80 in the course of ten years, a drop in the gross national product, and a fall in living standards. That a worker may retire before reaching the age of fifty is of little benefit if a devalued pension forces him back again onto the labour market.

The 'sixties witnessed mounting social unrest, strikes, and militant action by extremist groups. The fragmentation of the two traditional parties into numerous sub-groups made it difficult to pass essential legislation through Congress. The executive found its hands tied by the requirement that one third of the seats on the National Council should be held by the Opposition. The latter succeeded in defeating the *Colorados* in the 1958 elections but proved no more successful than their rivals in providing an effective government. The times clearly called for an end to the collegiate system and a return to stronger presidential rule. The electorate voted in 1966 for the Constitution to be changed in this sense, returned the *Colorados* to power, and entrusted the presidential mandate to a retired general, Oscar Gestido. The latter died of a heart attack in the following year, and the succession passed to the Vice-President, Jorge Pacheco Areto, who proceeded to implement a tough deflationary policy and to suppress labour and student unrest with unexpected vigour. In the teeth of parliamentary obstruction, the opposition of the Communist-dominated trade unions, and some spectacular terrorist coups by the Tupamaros (see page 305)—including the kidnapping and nine-month captivity of the British Ambassador, Geoffrey Jackson—the government had made some headway by mid-1970 towards the goal of restoring economic and political stability within the framework of constitutional democracy. A five-year 'Strategy for Development Plan' was launched which envisaged a 5 per cent annual increase in GNP and a 10 per cent annual rise in exports—targets which had, in fact, been more than achieved in 1969.

Uruguay nevertheless still faces formidable problems: how to expand and modernize the national economy and thus halt inflation and ease the burden of the social services; how to check the imbalance between the swollen metropolis and its rural hinterland, which Batlle's reforms had left largely untouched and where some sections of the population, such as the cane-sugar workers, still live in poverty and backwardness; how to ensure that a small republic, weakened by social unrest and economic difficulties, would continue to resist the gravitational pull of its stronger neighbours, Argentina and Brazil. Some pin their hopes for a brighter future on the exploitation of new mineral wealth in the interior of the country; others look to Montevideo as the future mercantile and banking centre of an invigorated Latin American Free Trade Association or a new grouping of the River Plate countries. The Communists favour popular front tactics but failed to realise their hopes that General Liber Seregni, the candidate of their *Frente Amplio*, would win the 1971 presidential elections and launch Uruguay along the path blazed by Chile. The

Tupamaro gunmen hold that the country's corrupt democracy must be swept away by force. In the first half of this century Uruguay demonstrated to her Latin American neighbours that a small country could build up a flourishing economy on the basis of democratic institutions, social justice, and civic liberty; the challenge now is to restate the message in the different and more complex circumstances of today.

14 Brazil

Brazil is not just another Latin American republic; it is a world of its own. Roughly equal in size (over three million square miles) and in population (now around 100 million) to all the Spanish-speaking countries of South America combined, Brazil escaped the fragmentation which befell the latter on shaking off the colonial yoke and remained one united, though regionally diversified, state. In language, racial composition, and many aspects of her culture, history, and national ethos, Brazil differs profoundly from her neighbours. Her very size and the richness of her natural resources mark her out for a special future. If any Latin American country is destined to achieve great power status, it will—so most Brazilians confidently believe—be theirs. Brazil, without a shadow of doubt, is the land of tomorrow; cynics hasten to add that it always will be. The gulf between dream and reality, between Brazil's promise and its fulfilment, is manifest. Her rulers and people today face the challenge of bridging it.

'Order and Progress' was the motto chosen by the founders of the Republic. Translated into the current terms of 'Development with Stability', this remains very much the goal which the nation's present rulers have set themselves. But no simple slogan can do justice to the complexities of a great country, and Brazil's condition can more properly be described as one of lopsided development than of mere under-development. The sophisticated inhabitants of São Paulo, probably the fastest growing city in the world, or of the whole prosperous and industrialized zone contained by the Rio–São Paulo–Belo Horizonte triangle, seem to be living not only at a different level of development but at an entirely separate phase of human evolution from the stone-age Indians of the Amazonian jungle or the twenty million peasants who eke out a living in the disaster-prone north-eastern 'bulge' of Brazil. Racially and culturally, the nation has fused its diverse Indo-American, African, and European elements to a remarkable degree. Socially and politically, the process is far less advanced. The country's untapped natural resources have their counterpart in the human realm. Less than ninety years ago, Brazil was still a slave-owning society. Her huge and rapidly growing population of today, in large part the descendants of slaves and poor European immigrants, still lacks the educational facilities, the institutions, and the means of political participation which are necessary if its potential is to be realized. 'Order and Progress' is a valid formula for a great nation only when Order means more than repression and Progress an authentic widening of the scope of social justice, economic opportunity, and democratic rights.

The Empire (1822–89)

Brazil's path to independence, as we have already seen (pages 62–4), took a different course from that followed by Spain's former colonies. The Portuguese court found refuge in Rio from Napoleon's armies, but after King João had returned to Europe, his son Pedro refused to follow and stayed on as the ruler of an independent Brazil (1822). For the next sixty-seven years, that country remained a hereditary monarchy. This preserved it from the *caudillismo* rampant in the nominally more democratic Spanish-speaking republics and made for peace and stability. Even more important, it helped to keep the sprawling, under-populated sub-continent together under the unifying symbol of the Crown.

Pedro I's romantic Brazilian patriotism proved ephemeral, his liberalism skin-deep, and his rule capricious. He summoned a Constituent Assembly and exhorted it, somewhat ominously, to draft a Constitution 'worthy of my imperial sanction'. Its efforts failed to pass this test, the Assembly was dissolved and several of its leaders, including Bonifácio and his brothers, were sent into exile, and a Committee appointed by Dom Pedro produced a fresh draft. This was then circulated for the inspection of a number of municipalities and promulgated in 1824; with some modifications granting greater autonomy to the provinces (1834) it was to remain in force until the abolition of the monarchy. The Constitution established a Parliament consisting of two houses, the lower to be elected on a restricted suffrage, the upper composed of members nominated for life by the Emperor, who retained the right to convoke and dissolve it and, within prescribed limits, to veto its measures. Much would clearly depend on the way the Emperor chose to use his powers. When he appointed more and more Portuguese to high office, treated his Brazilian ministers like lackeys and followed the whims of his ambitious mistress in matters of state, vied with his courtiers in rifling the treasury and allowed the army to be worsted by Argentina in the struggle over the Banda Oriental (see page 69), Dom Pedro's popularity slumped and he was forced to abdicate (1831). Government passed to a Regency until such time as his five-year-old heir could mount the throne.

The next nine years proved a testing time for Brazil. The authority exercised first by a three-man Council of Regency, then by a single Regent (Father Feijó, 1835–7, Araújo Lima, 1837–40) was challenged by factions ranging from the ultra-Conservatives who favoured the recall of Pedro I, to the few Liberal extremists who were already pinning their hopes on the establishment of a republic. The country was shaken by army mutinies (Pará, 1832–6), slave rebellions (Bahia, 1835) and widespread regional discontent. The latter assumed its most serious form in Rio Grande do Sul, where the rebels set up their own government and fought for their independence for ten years (1835–45). This time of troubles marked a necessary stage in the nation's development. Brazilians were now, for the first time, in full control of their own affairs; counsels of moderation, a growing experience in handling the country's still rudimentary political institutions, and a deepening sense of nationhood brought them through.

The teenage prince whom the politicians, impatient to be rid of the Regency, hastened to declare of age was to rule Brazil for nearly half a century. He had been given a careful and disciplined education and brought to his unique office a painstaking devotion to duty, an exceptional probity of mind and morals, and a lively interest in the arts and sciences, coupled with a humane and liberal outlook and modest personal tastes. If he had not been an emperor, as he himself once observed, Dom Pedro II would have liked to be a teacher. But Emperor he was, and he exercised the wide powers which the Constitution vested in him firmly, often arbitrarily, and perhaps even—so his enemies averred—dictatorially. By nominating to the Senate, appointing governors and ministers, and controlling the official pyramid of patronage, and by his power to summon and dissolve Parliament, he wielded the authority of a benevolent and enlightened despot. As the linchpin of an essentially Conservative monarchical system he could seldom give rein to his own progressive inclinations; he made no secret, for example, of his abhorrence of slavery, but could do little to hasten the end of that institution. He was the prisoner as much as the master of the situation. He might go through the motions of a constitutional monarch, but there was no enlightened, liberal electorate to which he could turn for support. When, at length, economic change and new currents of Positivist thought had begun to reshape the traditional structures and make the rudiments of such an electorate possible, the monarchy and the man who had so long been its embodiment were swept away as anachronisms.

The plainest mark of Brazil's backwardness was the persistence of slavery. Old assumptions still held sway: the African was by nature a slave, and his incorporation into civilized society and the Christian faith was more than enough to compensate the savage for any loss of liberty. His labour, moreover, was essential to the nation's prosperity; without the slaves, the sugar plantations would go to ruin. In Europe, and particularly in Britain, to whom Brazil was bound by treaty and trade (see page 338), the public had come round to the contrary view: slavery was morally indefensible and economically undesirable. Trafficking in human lives was felt to be particularly abhorrent, and the British Navy assumed the task of suppressing the slave trade. Brazil had been obliged to pass a law (1831) forbidding the trade, but had neither the means nor the will to enforce it. Her armed forces were fully engaged in suppressing internal revolts, and her government was swayed by those who had a vested interest in maintaining the trade. Contraband shiploads of slaves continued to pour into Brazil. Britain sent her warships into Brazilian ports to seize or sink the vessels and try the slavers under English law. Such high-handedness provoked a storm of national indignation and diplomatic relations with Britain were temporarily broken off. But Brazil could not afford to court the enmity of the world's leading sea-power. There were other arguments too to suggest that the time had come to end the slave trade. By mid-century, probably three millions out of Brazil's total population of seven millions were slaves. If still more were imported, the African element in the population would be strengthened, the danger of slave rebellions increased, and the immigration from Europe which the government was anxious to encourage would be inhibited. In 1850 a new law was passed prohibiting the trade in slaves and this time serious efforts were made to implement it. Some 23,000 negroes were imported into Brazil in that year, but between 1853 and 1856 the figure had shrunk to little more than 500 and thereafter the trade dried up altogether.

Nearly four decades were still to elapse, however, before slavery itself was abolished. The goal was reached gradually, and with neither the bloodshed nor the disruption to the national economy prophesied by the traditionalists. Milestones on the road were the banning of public slave auctions (1869), the Law of Free Birth (1871) guaranteeing the freedom of all children born to slave mothers (a law containing many loop-holes and widely disregarded by slave-owners), and the manumission of all slaves decreed in the 'eighties by Ceará and some other states. An active campaign for abolition was organized by leading politicians and publicists such as Joaquim Nabuco, Ruy Barbosa, and the negro José de Patrocínio. Their arguments found a ready hearing with the growing populations of the towns, who felt little inclination to defend an institution mainly of benefit to wealthy plantation-owners, and amongst the more modern-minded coffee-growers, who had economic grounds for preferring free labour to slave labour. Nor did the army wish to see itself obliged to organize large-scale manhunts to round up the slaves who were now escaping from the northern plantations in growing numbers and seeking a new life in factory, coffee-farm, and city. Many plantation-owners voluntarily freed their slaves as a means of stemming the exodus and inducing the negroes to stay on as hired workers. The 'Golden Law' of 1888, which freed the three quarters of a million or so slaves remaining in the country without compensation to their owners, thus set the seal on a process of emancipation which was already far advanced.

From 1850, when the country embarked on a decade and a half of political stability, important changes began to take place beneath the seemingly stagnant surface of Brazilian society. The ending of the slave trade meant that the large sums of money hitherto invested in human merchandise could be put to other uses. The first railways began to be built, and a steamship service to ply regularly between Brazilian and British ports. Sugar ceased to dominate the economy, for the *fazendas* of the north had to face growing competition from the cane-fields of Cuba and the British West Indies. Coffee exports shot up and a new class of *entrepreneur* began to make its mark, either in that remunerative field or in a surge of banking and industrial enterprises. An unfamiliar phenomenon began to appear in the hierarchical society of imperial Brazil—the self-made man professing the almost sacrilegious creed of hard work and technological progress. Prototype of this first generation of Brazilian capitalists was the Baron de Mauá (1813–39) who, starting his business career in a British firm, had been inspired by a visit to a Bristol iron foundry with the vision of his backward country as a great industrial power. Though Mauá's multifarious activities in banking, company-promoting, railway and port building, and industrial pioneering ended in his bankruptcy, modern Brazil has been fashioned largely after his vision.

Like other empires, that of Brazil grew at the expense of its neighbours. The attempt to consolidate her southern frontiers by the inclusion of the Banda Oriental, claimed also by Argentina, resulted in her defeat at the hands of the latter and the establishment (1828) of an independent Uruguay (see page 69). Neither Argentina nor Brazil reconciled themselves easily to the existence of this buffer state, and when the Argentine dictator Rosas laid siege to Montevideo and threatened to take over the whole country, Brazil allied herself with the anti-Rosas forces, invaded Uruguay, and helped to raise the siege. Uruguay paid for this intervention by transferring a zone of disputed border territory to Brazil (1851). Four years later another Brazilian force was sent to Uruguay to support the pro-Brazilian *Colorados*, and further unofficial incursions followed in support of Brazil's growing business interests in the country. When the *Blanco* faction countered by appealing for help to Paraguay, a Brazilian expeditionary force crossed the Uruguayan frontier in 1864 and precipitated war against Paraguay (see page 192). Over the following decades Brazil gained successive accessions of territory: from Paraguay (1872), from Bolivia (1867 and 1903), from Argentina (arbitral award of 1895), from Ecuador (1904), from Colombia (1907), and from Venezuela (1859 and 1905).

One important effect of the war against Paraguay was to shake the army's confidence in the government and monarchy. In order to crush the poorest and weakest state in South America Brazil had needed five years and the co-operation of the Argentines and Uruguayans. The army blamed the apathy and backwardness of the country, the incompetence of the bureaucracy, and the personal indifference of the Emperor. Many disgruntled officers lent a ready ear to Auguste Comte's Positivism with its belief in scientific progress and its vague religion of humanity. The creed had its enthusiastic adherents too in laymen like Benjamin Constant and Ruy Barbosa, who believed that Brazil could only make real progress as a republic. The war had also stimulated a certain amount of manufacturing which strengthened the trend towards modernization, and increased general impatience with the *fazendeiros* of the north who were fighting a stubborn rearguard action to maintain their slave-owning privileges. When abolition came at last—the decree was signed by the Emperor's daughter while her father was travelling abroad —the *fazendeiros* saw no reason to go on supporting a monarchy which they felt had betrayed them. The Church had also been alienated by a dispute over freemasonry in which Dom Pedro contrived to offend the bishops without pleasing the freemasons. In the face of a disgruntled and progressively more radicalized officer corps, a resentful Church and landowning oligarchy, an expanding urban middle class and a growing number of thrusting *entrepreneurs*, the ageing emperor found his support impossibly eroded. He offered

no resistance when a group of officers headed by Marshal Deodoro da Fonseca and Benjamin Constant demanded his abdication and packed him off to
Europe.

The Republic (1889–1930)

Brazil was now a republic. Its new Constitution (1891) separated Church and
State and allowed a good deal of autonomy to the twenty federal units comprising the 'United States of Brazil', but also conferred extensive reserve
powers on the President. Deodoro, the first holder of that office, soon fell out
with Congress and dissolved it. Under the still more high-handed rule of his
successor Marshal Floriano Peixoto and the stress caused by financial mismanagement, there were revolts within the army and clashes between land
and naval forces. The ignorant and conservative peasantry, particularly in the
remote north-east, had little interest in a republic and fell easily under the
spell of local leaders like the fanatical and half-crazed 'Antonio the Counsellor', who organized a desperate rebellion in the backlands which lasted for
four years and was immortalized in Euclides da Cunha's classic. (See page
314.) With the election of the first civilian president, Morais Barros, in 1894,
the country gradually settled into a political rhythm which was to last for
three decades. The centre of gravity had now shifted away from the decaying
sugar zones of the north to the coffee-growing regions whose most dynamic
centres were the states of São Paulo and Minas Gerais. The economic interests
of *paulistas* and *mineiros* came to dominate the nation's policies, their state
militias were built up into veritable armies, and their nominees alternated in
the Presidency. The republic had achieved the first of its twin goals of Order
and Progress; this order, only fitfully challenged by the stirrings of an incipient labour movement and the vague aspirations for social reform of the 'lieutenants' revolt' of the early 'twenties, gave the country stability until the onset
of economic crisis and political turmoil at the end of that decade.

'Progress' too was undoubtedly achieved, though it was uneven and lopsided, leaving whole regions and large sections of the population untouched
and on a scale quite insufficient to bring modernity to the whole vast country.
Symbols of this progress were the railways, the new ports, the cities either
rebuilt (like Rio) or newly founded (like Belo Horizonte), but all growing at a
dizzy pace after the fashion of São Paulo, which mushroomed from a town of
65,000 in 1890 to become Latin America's largest metropolis. The country's
growth owed much to the capital which poured in from abroad, chiefly from
Britain, to the foreigners' skills in engineering and manufacturing and to their
enterprise in banking, insurance, utilities, and the profitable import-export
business. (See page 217.) But most of all was owed to the flood of immigrants
—nearly five million of them between 1884 and 1963—many of whom settled
in the rapidly expanding cities, swelling the ranks of the middle and working
classes and adding a fresh infusion of European blood to Brazil's population.
Most, particularly the largest contingents from Portugal, Italy, and Spain,
merged readily with their neighbours. The Germans, and still more the

Japanese, proved less willing to integrate, though they set valuable examples of industrious and intelligent labour in a society where work still too often bore the stigma of slavery. Between 1870 and 1920, more than half the immigrants from Europe went under contract to the coffee plantations of São Paulo. The Germans established their colonies mostly in the south. In the north, an erratic population movement was stimulated by the great rubber boom of the late nineteenth century, when ruthless promoters dragooned defenceless Indians and desperate labourers from the drought-stricken northeast into gathering rubber in the Amazonian jungle. By the First World War, the latter area had ceased to be a field for spectacular fortunes and large-scale exploitation of human misery. The rubber seeds collected years before by an English scientist, carefully nurtured at Kew, and then transplanted to Ceylon and Malaya, had started rival industries which equalled and then surpassed the Amazon's production. Coffee was left as Brazil's chief source of wealth, and by 1900 she was producing some three quarters of the world's supply. But the very lavishness of the returns from this profitable crop was to bring disaster. The period between the world wars saw recurrent cycles of over-production, fluctuating prices, and the burning of surplus stocks (see page 258).

The Vargas period, 1930–54

By 1930, discontent caused by the economic crisis and a growing impatience with the alternation of political power between *mineiro* and *paulista* interests came to a head when the outgoing President Washington Luiz broke the gentlemen's agreement by trying to pass the presidential succession to a fellow *paulista*. Getúlio Vargas, Governor of the *gaúcho* state of Rio Grande do Sul, marched on the capital, seized the presidency, and began to fill key posts throughout the country with men loyal to himself. This was not at all what his allies intended, and the powerful state of São Paulo declared itself in rebellion and was only subdued by the Central Government after three months of fighting. Though he was to face subsequent revolts, the most serious of which was the Communist-inspired rising of 1935 headed by Luiz Carlos Prestes, a former leader of the 'lieutenants' revolt', and an abortive coup by the Fascist *integralistas* in 1938, Vargas remained the master of Brazil for fifteen years. A hybrid Constitution combining liberal principles with some of the aims for state-directed socio-economic reforms which the 'lieutenants' had stood for, was introduced in 1934 but was soon eclipsed by a system of increasingly personalist and authoritarian rule formalized at the end of 1937 by the proclamation of the Estado Nôvo (New State).

Brazil had known no dictator like Getúlio Vargas. His enemies dubbed him a Fascist, though he had smashed the green-shirted *integralistas*, and his Estado Nôvo was undoubtedly coloured by the Fascist and National Socialist creeds then current in Europe. But this was a brand of Fascism made milder by passing through the filter of *brasildade*. Vargas controlled the press, banished and imprisoned opponents, disregarded parliamentary institutions and civil rights, and destroyed much of the traditional autonomy of the states. But his system, though autocratic, was not totalitarian. He never attempted to bolster his power by forming one monolithic government party. He wished to be regarded—and to a large extent was so regarded—as 'the father of the people'. The underprivileged urban masses, many of them migrants from the countryside where the tutelage of the land-owning 'colonels' was taken for granted, looked up to him as a benevolent and all powerful *patrão*. Vargas repaid their confidence by enacting legislation in respect of working conditions, a minimum wage, pensions, and medical benefits which was in theory amongst the most advanced of the time, however inadequately administered. In return, he expected docility from a labour movement organized in government-controlled trade unions. The rural masses remained largely beyond the scope of these changes. Such was the compromise at the base of *getulismo*: a labour code to match the modern rhythm of the great cities, but in the vast acres beyond, the traditional structures virtually intact.

World War II brought new dilemmas and new opportunities. The dictator's ideological sympathies lay with the Axis, but the country's strategic position and his own economic policies pointed to co-operation with the democracies. The collapse of coffee prices in the world economic depression had already demonstrated how vulnerable was a prosperity based on the export of commodities and indicated the desirability of widening Brazil's industrial scope. The war at sea, which interrupted her normal supply of imported manufactures, reinforced the same lesson and stimulated the process of import substitution which was to give such impulse to Brazil's industrialization. This process was also fully in line with the economic nationalism implicit in the Estado Nôvo. Conditions thus favoured the launching of Vargas's programme of state-financed and directed industrialization, based on ambitious projects such as the great Volta Redonda steel mills 90 miles from Rio. When, after Pearl Harbour, Brazil decided to declare war on the Axis, Vargas could count on the financial backing of the United States who, since she needed an economically strong ally, assumed the novel role of aiding an under-developed country's state-directed industrialization. Washington also gave valuable assistance in the form of arms and war material, whilst Brazil lent the Allies the use of Atlantic bases and also despatched an expeditionary force which gave a good account of itself on the battlefields of Europe. Brazil was thus able at the end of the war to share honourably in the prestige of the victorious Allies. Not so the dictator himself. His Estado Nôvo was too manifestly tarred with the Fascist brush. In October 1945 the army compelled Vargas to resign, and his Minister of Defence, Marshal Dutra, was elected President.

The Dutra administration (1945–50) went some way towards restoring democratic processes and introduced a new constitution, based largely on that of 1891 but retaining some of the Estado Nôvo's labour code. *Laissez-faire* liberalism became the order of the day, and resulted in an orgy of unwise investment and extravagant spending which finally obliged the government to impose painful and unpopular controls. Vargas, meanwhile, had been trimming his sails to the winds of democratic change and sailed home at the next elections for a further term (1950–4). His followers now filled the ranks of two parties, the Brazilian Labour Party (PTB) designed to catch the growing working-class vote, and the ill-named Social Democrat Party (PSD), which marshalled his more conservative rural supporters. In economics, as in politics, Vargas was adept at riding two horses. Whilst his Finance Minister Oswaldo Aranha applied orthodox measures to halt inflation and improve the country's credit standing, Vargas refurbished the weapons of economic nationalism. A state agency, Petrobras, was set up to keep the country's petroleum resources in Brazilian hands even if they lacked the financial and technical means of developing them. Restrictions were imposed on the remittance of dividends abroad, and the exploitative designs of foreign capital came under increasing fire in the President's speeches. The United States incurred additional odium for cutting down her purchases of Brazilian coffee just when prices were at their highest, and for offering a large loan to Brazil's rival, Argentina. Labour was courted and João Goulart, a politician with a reputation for opportunist collaborating with the Communists, was appointed Minister for Labour. When Goulart showed signs of trying to emulate Perón by establishing a demagogic control over the labour movement, Vargas dropped him but continued courting labour by decreeing a 100 per cent increase in the minimum wage, despite the damaging effect this would have on his government's campaign to combat inflation. Important sections of the middle classes and of the military grew more and more alarmed. Alarm deepened to outrage when a *getulista* gunman attempted to shoot down Carlos Lacerda, a political journalist and critic of the President, and killed an air force officer who was with him. Once again, Vargas faced an ultimatum from the military. But this time he chose suicide instead of resignation. An unsigned typewritten note allegedly left behind by the President declared that he had been hounded to his death by unnamed foreign financial interests. Whether genuine or not, this note contributed to arouse a wave of popular sympathy for Vargas and the populist policies he stood for.

The post-Vargas decade (1954–64)

Following a short interlude of caretaker government, the *getulistas* again triumphed at the elections. Their candidate was Juscelino Kubitschek, whose dynamism as Governor of Minas Gerais won him the PSD nomination; Goulart, of the PTB, was returned again to the Vice-Presidency. The anti-*getulista* forces were disposed at first to contest the verdict of the polls, but a preventive coup by Marshal Lott, who had been Vargas's Minister of Defence, ensured that the succession passed to Kubitschek (January 1956). The ebullient President, promising 'fifty years' progress in five', launched the country on a course of breakneck expansion. Between 1957 and 1961, the economy expanded at an annual rate of 7 per cent, *per capita* income at nearly 4 per cent. The early stages of the import substitution process had now been passed, and emphasis shifted to the production of capital goods. This was to be achieved by the joint efforts of private and public investment. Kubitschek took pains to create favourable conditions for foreign investors and also succeeded in attracting numerous loans from the United States government and international lending agencies, the whole development programme being loosely co-ordinated according to a series of 'production targets' rather than specific plans. Pride and symbol of the country's febrile growth was the spectacular new capital, Brasília, hewn from the wilderness 600 miles from Rio and designed to open up new areas of Brazil's vast interior.

A high price was paid for this rapid expansion, which was financed largely by recourse to the printing press, with the result that the rate of inflation averaged 50 per cent a year during Kubitschek's administration and rose still higher under that of his successors. The priority given to industry deepened the gulf between 'developed' and 'undeveloped' Brazil, whilst important sectors such as agriculture and education suffered neglect. Rapid industrialization, it was assumed, would bring with it a solution of the country's ills, and would provide a cause in which political differences could be sunk and a programme offering something for everyone. Internally, the President relied primarily on the two offspring of *getulismo*, the PTB and his own PSD. Externally, his ambitious developmental schemes depended heavily on financial support from the United States and the international lending agencies. Kubitschek had attempted to induce Washington to back a grandiose programme for the long-term economic and social development of the whole of Latin America, but his initiative met with little response until some years later, when the advent of Castro imparted a new urgency to the situation and his 'Operation Pan-America' was taken up as the basis for the Alliance for Progress (see page 325). As his administration drew to a close, Kubitschek's balancing act grew more difficult. International pressure increased for the brakes to be applied to Brazil's runaway economy, whilst counter-pressure from the ultra-nationalists and the Left likewise increased. Goulart renewed his demagogic charges against the excessive profits of the foreign capitalists, and any moves to heed the pleas of the international agencies for monetary restraint were denounced as *entreguismo*. Kubitschek finally gave in to this clamour, and left the problems of runaway inflation, foreign indebtedness, and the overdue need for stabilization to his successor.

The brief presidency (January–August 1961) of Jânio Quadros marks a strange interlude in Brazil's history, and the personality and intentions of its protagonist remain an enigma. The rise of Quadros from schoolteacher to mayor, and then governor, of São Paulo had been meteoric. He was voted into the presidency largely by the anti-Vargas UDN, but the Vice-Presidency went again to Goulart of the PTB. Neither *getulista* nor anti-*getulista* himself, Quadros stood as an amateur against the professional politicians; his platform of honesty and efficiency in administration was little short of revolutionary. Quadros chose the broom as his electoral symbol; he promised to sweep away both the corruption of the Kubitschek era and the deeper social injustices of 'the system'. His actual programme was vague. Public health, education, and agriculture—all neglected by his predecessor—were to get more attention. The breakneck speed of development was to be curbed by a return to the more sober policies of a balanced budget, wage and price restraints, tighter credit, and a rephasing of the repayment of the nation's huge foreign debt. But if his economic policies were orthodox, the innovations introduced by the President into foreign policy seemed disturbing. Quadros displayed sympathy for the new regime in Cuba, presented Che Guevara with the country's highest decoration, and prepared to re-establish relations with the USSR which had been broken off at the height of the Cold War. Brazil seemed set on a neutralist course. This alarmed both the military and the more conservative sectors of the middle class who were already feeling the pinch of the stabilization policy and the promised shake-up of the bureaucracy. Lacerda, the formidable journalist-politician who could now speak with authority as Governor of Guanabara (greater Rio de Janeiro) again led the anti-presidential attack. On 25 August Quadros submitted his resignation to Congress. The latter, dominated by politicians who had always regarded him as a tempestuous outsider even when lending him their support, quickly accepted it. Whether Quadros was daunted by the superhuman task of cleaning up 'the system', or whether he had miscalculated that he could be reaffirmed in the presidency by demonstrations of mass support remains a mystery. The man with the broom swept himself out of office and was never to regain it.

The country was stunned by the President's resignation. It was also deeply agitated over the succession. According to the Constitution, it should devolve on the Vice-President, and the 'legalists', together with others such as Goulart's pugnacious brother-in-law Brizola, Governor of Rio Grande do Sul, demanded that he should be proclaimed President at once. Others distrusted Goulart, who was out of the country at the time touring the Communist states, as a shifty opportunist. The officer corps, some of whom foresaw that Goulart might try to challenge their power by manipulating labour and courting popularity amongst other ranks of the services, was itself divided on the issue. For a time there loomed the danger of civil war. A compromise was then found; Goulart might become President, but some of his powers would pass to a Prime Minister. The Constitution was amended in this sense and Goulart assumed office (September 1961). Lack of experience or the will to operate the new parliamentary practice played into Goulart's hands, and fifteen months later (January 1963) the country reverted to the presidential system.

The way now seemed clear for Goulart to implement the Three Year Plan drawn up by his able young Minister of Planning, Celso Furtado. This had the ambitious aim of regaining Brazil's previously high rate of growth whilst simultaneously fighting inflation and introducing a series of basic reforms in such fields as education, land ownership, and fiscal policy designed to remove those structural obstacles believed to be impeding the country's development. To his middle-class opponents, such reforms seemed rather to aim at a dangerous shift of political power. A government-backed campaign to reduce illiteracy, for instance—still more, a proposal that illiterates should be given the vote—might create a landslide in Goulart's favour at the next elections. The effectiveness of the whole plan, and a resumption of the foreign aid needed to help finance it, hinged on the government's ability to slow down inflation. But the President proved unwilling or unable to pay the political price. Yielding to pressure, he authorized a 70 per cent increase in salaries for the civil service and the armed forces. Rather than the desired development without inflation, Brazil continued to suffer inflation without development. By mid-1963 the vacillating President had turned from the Three Year Plan and was beginning to lend an ever more willing ear to the counsels of the vociferous but fragmented radical Left.

The spectrum presented by the Left ranged through the Moscow-oriented Communist Party, still under Prestes who had learned caution from the failure of his 1935 bid for power; a more militant, but far smaller pro-Chinese Communist Party; Acção Popular, a radical student organization of originally Catholic inspiration; the personal following of men like Brizola and Miguel Arrães, the Governor of Pernambuco; and the Peasant Leagues which had grown strong under an assortment of Marxist and 'progressive' clerical leaders, especially in the north-east, where they had been invading the large estates and clashing with the private armies raised by the 'colonels'. Disturbing to the established order as the mobilization of these left-wing forces was, the military might not have been provoked to action had it not been for attempts to win over two further sectors of society: organized labour and the NCOs and other ranks of the armed forces. President Goulart seemed unmoved when a handful of sergeants seized the President of the Chamber of Deputies in Brasília and tried to take over the Government (September 1963). When, the following March, a naval mutiny occurred and was suppressed, Goulart appointed a new Minister for the Navy who gave amnesty to the ringleaders. The President's apparent endorsement of subversion in the armed forces came a few days after he had addressed a mass rally of trade unionists in Rio at which he had ostentatiously signed decrees promulgating new measures of land reform and the expropriation of privately owned oil refineries, proclaimed his intention of revising the Constitution which 'legalizes an economic structure that is already obsolete, unjust, and inhuman', and inveighed against the 'reactionary forces' opposing him. It seemed clear, as many had warned, that Goulart was casting himself in the role of Brazil's Perón.

The 'reactionary forces' now pitted against the President comprised the bulk of the deputies to Congress, over whose heads the chief executive had decided to appeal to the people, the majority of the officer corps including moderates like the Chief of Staff, Castelo Branco, and the mass of middle-class opinion which brought out half a million protesters, most of them women bearing Catholic slogans, into the streets of São Paulo as a counter-demonstration to Goulart's Rio rally. By the end of March, the governors of all the major states together with the military commanders of São Paulo and Minas Gerais had come out against the central government 'for the restoration of the constitutional order'. After some vacillation the commander of the First Army in Rio followed suit. President Goulart fled to his home state of Rio Grande do Sul, rejected his brother-in-law's pleas to make a stand, and crossed the Uruguayan border into exile (4 April 1964).

Brazil under military rule (1964–70)

The intervention of the military marked a turning point in Brazil's history, as it had in 1889 and 1945. The troubled democratic course on which the country had been set for nearly two decades was abruptly halted, the old political system and its operators swept aside as corrupt and discredited. The military believed that only they could succeed where the politicians had manifestly failed. They had moved to arrest what they took to be the process of social dissolution, the infiltration of subversive Leftist forces which the President seemed to have been encouraging. These forces quickly melted away and offered surprisingly little resistance to the military take-over. But grave problems remained. The needs recognized in the Three Year Plan and so half-heartedly tackled by Goulart still called for urgent attention: to restore momentum to Brazil's economic development, curb inflation, and remove the structural bottlenecks impeding growth. The last of these carried implications of 'basic reforms' to the established order which the military government, though claiming to be 'revolutionary', preferred to shelve. Attention was concentrated on the pressing economic and monetary situation. Where previous governments had stressed the role of the state in Brazil's mixed economy, the military government now stressed that of the private sector. To attract the foreign capital necessary to stimulate this sector and to persuade Brazil's creditors to reschedule the huge debt which was draining away the country's foreign exchange and impeding her capacity to import, stabilization measures had to be urgently implemented. No democratic government had been prepared to face the unpopularity which would inevitably follow from stern anti-inflationary policies. But the new government was not democratic. It did not fear electoral defeat, since it had no intention of calling elections. It was not to be deterred by opposition, for though the opposition might grumble, it had no means of overthrowing the government, which could, when it wished, muzzle a hostile press and suppress labour unrest. It was free, in short, to impose unpopular policies. Could this, then, be the way out of Brazil's dilemma? An authoritarian government administering the bitter medicine prescribed for stabilization, followed by a revived inflow of foreign investment, a resumption of economic growth, and only then the degree and type of basic reform and popular participation in political life which the nation's military mentors might deem good for her?

The military's choice for the new head of state was Marshal Castelo Branco, a former director of the Higher War College, and advocate of a strategy of 'national security' embracing a wide range of economic and social measures beyond the mere repression of 'Communist subversion' with which the military hard-liners were obsessed. Castelo Branco wished to preserve the framework of the existing Constitution, modifying it by a succession of 'Institutional Acts' under which the political and administrative machine could be purged and brought under firmer control by the executive. The gubernatorial elections of October 1965 showed, however, that the old regime was still firmly entrenched and that more drastic measures were called for. Congress was suspended and later induced to approve a new Constitution (1967) greatly increasing the powers of the President and the Federal Government. Key posts were filled with government nominees, the old parties dissolved, and two artificial creations set up: a government party (ARENA) and another (MDB) destined for permanent and ineffectual opposition. Three years later, fresh congressional elections were called and ARENA enabled to consolidate its control of an emasculated Congress.

Marshal Costa e Silva, elected (no longer by direct vote, but by Congress) to be successor to the austere Castelo Branco, took office in March 1967 amidst expectations that the regime would soon be 'humanized'. The stage, it seemed, might now have been reached when restraints could be lifted and the people given more say in ordering their own affairs. But by the end of 1968, under pressure from the 'hard-liners', a new series of Institutional Acts led to a fresh curtailment of the powers of Congress, which had proved less pliant than expected, and of individual liberties. Active opposition to the regime continued to be shown by small dissident student groups and some Liberal elements in the Catholic Church which now, for the first time in Brazil's history, was beginning to speak up in criticism of the established order and the repressive practices of government. (See page 236.) Protest took more violent form in the increasingly spectacular coups of the urban terrorists, which extended to the kidnapping of the ambassadors of the United States (1969), Germany and Switzerland (1970). The retaliatory 'law enforcement' of the authorities, involving the alleged torturing of political prisoners by the police and the elimination of undesirables by officially tolerated Death Squads, did considerable damage to the Government's image at home and abroad.

The Government nevertheless remained in firm control of the country and showed no disposition to modify its policies. When President Costa e Silva was incapacitated by a heart attack in 1969 he was succeeded not by the Vice-President, as the Constitution required, but by a fresh nominee of the armed forces, General Garrastazú Médici. There seemed little prospect of Brazil being allowed to return to a democratic course until the expiry of the new President's term in 1974.

In the economic field, the Government could point to more solid achievements. The stabilization plan had reduced inflation from the runaway levels of the early 'sixties to an annual rate, tolerable by Brazilian standards, of 20–25 per cent. Coffee prices were good, exports increased by 50 per cent between 1964 and 1968, foreign exchange reserves rose, and private investment, both foreign and domestic, flowed again into the economy. This flow was supplemented by heavy government spending in such fields as petroleum processing, steel production, hydro-electric works, and road construction, designed as far as possible to benefit the less developed regions of the country. By 1968, the State thus found itself accounting for well over half the investment in the national economy, though the government's intention had been to let the private sector have its head. The general economic recovery was reflected in the rate of increase of the gross national product which, in the early 'sixties, had been eroded by the annual population increase, but which rose through the 'sixties to levels approaching those of the boom years of the previous decade and seemed likely to sustain its momentum in the 'seventies (9 per cent in 1969, 9·5 per cent in 1970). The cost of this economic progress, however, had been largely borne by the working class, whose minimum wage level did not keep pace with the rising cost of living. With no autonomous trade unions or effective channels of political participation, many Brazilians still lacked the means of pressing their claim to share in the country's growing prosperity.

The Government had promised a series of unexceptionable reforms in education, housing, public health, and the like. Plans had been announced for a national cadastral survey, with the help of computer techniques, as a preliminary for agrarian reform. But implementation of basic reforms hung fire. Would they not upset the equilibrium of the traditional political and social forces in the nation? Would they not prove incompatible, as the critics of the Left maintained, with the military government's strategy of 'national security' as the essential framework within which all economic and social development must take place? The keystone of this national security was held to be the maintenance of the relationship with the United States, both as the chief source of development capital and as the leading power in the confronta-tion with international Communism. The Marxist Left, the 'progressive' wing of the Catholic Church, and some ultra-nationalists held that it was precisely this dependence on a great capitalist foreign power, and on the Conservative sectors inside the country whose interests were bound up with it, which was perpetuating Brazil's chronic under-development and stood between the nation and her destiny as a great power. But the optimists might counter—and most Brazilians are optimists—that Brazil was now entering upon her heritage and that, in the words of the slogan current in the mood of national euphoria after Brazil's outright winning of the World Football Championship Cup in 1970—'No one can hold this country back!'

The Latin American Scene

1 The Social Structure

The ruling élite

The commanding figure in the social, political, and economic life of Latin America has traditionally been the great landowner. The *conquistador* was quickly transformed into an *encomendero*, beneficiary of the Indians' labour and lands. The *encomendero* in turn became the *hacendado*, owner of the ranch or large farm. The many terms by which he has been known denote the varied facets of his power and privilege. He was a *latifundista*, lord of vast estates or *latifundia*. In the Brazilian backlands, he was a *poderoso do sertão* and also a *coronel* or 'colonel' commanding military forces raised on and for the protection of his domains. In his political capacity he was a *cacique*, heir to the native chieftain, or a *caudillo*, boss of a district or even of a whole nation. For the quasi-serfs who worked his lands and served his house he was simply the *patrón*. In the Peruvian sierra he was the *gamonal*, a term which conveyed his alliance with lawyer, local official, and parish priest to dominate and despoil the Indians of their communal land. The name might vary but the reality it expressed remained the same—ownership of land and power over those who worked it.

At the local level, this power was absolute. The labourer, bound to his *patrón* by a system of share-cropping or debt peonage, was generally permitted a plot of land sufficient, or nearly so, for the support of his family, and required in return to give so many days' labour in the fields or the house of his master. The *encomendero* had been expected to christianize and civilize his Indians. The *hacendado* let them attend service in his chapel—for they were now nominally Christian—and occasionally even had a school for them attached to his *hacienda*. But the view of the *patrón* was commonly that it was both superfluous and dangerous to offer his peons any schooling: superfluous because they were congenitally incapable of profiting from it, and dangerous, because the attempt would only give them ideas above their station. But if the *patrón* exploited his peons, he also extended his protection to them. He provided them with a means of subsistence, however minimal, and help in times of sickness or other need. They came to him with their problems and petitions and he graciously gave them advice, defended them against the pretensions of other *caciques*, and intervened on their behalf with the local authorities. He was their intermediary with the outside world, to which his wealth, wisdom, and family connections gave him access, and from which he could secure favours for his clients and dependants. The *patrón*, in short, was the master of his family, household, *hacienda*, and district, from whom were due loyalty, submission, and support. His rule might be either benevolent or tyrannical, like that of those harsh landowners in the novels of Alcides Arguedas, Ciro Alegría, Jorge Icaza, and José María Arguedas. But whatever the nature of his rule, within the radius of his influence it was absolute and unquestioned.

On the national scale, power was exercised in the same fashion. The President would rule the republic as a *patrón* his estate. He might be ousted by some general or *caudillo* more ruthless than himself, but the dominant social stratum to which he belonged, the landowning 'oligarchy', would remain. The envious upstart might clip its wings but would end by feathering his own nest from the clippings. Perón fulminated against the oligarchy in front of his *descamisados* but never struck at the basis of its power. Trujillo persecuted the Dominican notables and reared the fortunes of his family on the ruins of theirs, but the system itself survived three decades of his tyranny. The oligarchy was less concerned with the direct exercise of political power than with protecting its fundamental interests. In the face of any serious threat, such as an Indian rising or radical reforms in vital matters of tax structure or land tenure, it would show a common front. But the oligarchy was less a monolithic power-group than a congeries of influential families coalescing into cliques or pressure groups according to kinship, personal friendship, and political or regional loyalties, and normally competing with one another for status and economic advantage. It was these manoeuvrings which gave to political life a certain tincture of democracy.

Such had been the character of Latin America's ruling élite. But even at its heyday in the nineteenth century, new forces were beginning to limit its range and modify the composition of the oligarchy itself. Population increased, creating new sources of wealth, new social sectors, and a new relationship between town and country. Of the immigrants arriving from Italy, England, France, Germany, Spain, Yugoslavia, and the Near East some would make their fortunes in the towns, marry into the old landowning families, and acquire estates and social status. The more enterprising members of the old families would themselves build up new fortunes in mining, commerce, banking, and financial speculation. Some would turn to producing profitable crops for export, leaving their poorly farmed, patriarchally administered self-sufficient *haciendas* in the remoter areas to develop modern, efficiently run plantations where soil and climate were more favourable and markets more accessible. The old-style *hacendados* still enjoyed social prestige and political influence locally, and could bring pressure to bear on national policies through their representative organizations such as the Sociedad Rural in Buenos Aires and the Sociedad Nacional Agraria in Lima. But in fast-growing cities like São Paulo and Rio de Janeiro, and even in the old viceregal capitals of Lima and Mexico City, the pace was increasingly set by the plutocracy rather than the oligarchy. Many made the transition from one to the other, for inherited wealth and social status eased the way. Even where, as in Mexico and Bolivia, the expropriation of the great estates destroyed the economic basis of the old oligarchy, not a few of its members entered the ranks of the new ruling class which replaced it.

Latin America's ruling élite thus comprises today the residual landowning 'oligarchy', the leading figures in business, finance, and the export trade who are generally closely linked to it, and industrial *entrepreneurs*, often of recent immigrant stock. Though a few localities, such as Antioquia in Colombia and Monterrey in Mexico, have produced a vigorous native breed of *entrepreneurs*, industrial pioneering finds in general little place in the hispanic tradition. Mexico, the country which has gone furthest in officially repudiating this tradition, is also today the most development-minded. Argentina and Brazil owe the origins of their industrial expansion largely to immigrants or sons of immigrants whose recently acquired wealth and influence enabled them to take their place with the great families. When the latter themselves ventured into business, they tended to carry over into it their traditional paternalistic attitudes and to regard their firms as family concerns which provided openings for sons, nephews, dependants, and protégés and constituted a useful means of extending the family's influence and resources. Though the increasing size and complexity of modern commercial operations and the influence of the more impersonally run foreign-owned subsidiaries are tending to modify these characteristics, family businesses remain a feature of the Latin American scene. Even a great industrial complex like that founded in Brazil by the Italian immigrant Matarazzo, and now presided over by his son, still bears the stamp of this patriarchal pattern. Personal relationships, not only with the enterprise concerned but with other business interests and with the state agencies involved in granting export and import licences, in placing contracts and concessions, or in operating a wide range of economic activities, are of key importance. Family connections, political influence, the interchange of favours between patron and client, the *mordida* offered in the right quarters at the right moment—these, rather than technical expertise and efficiency, provide the quickest path to success.

The middle sectors

The traditional two-tiered structure of Latin American society left little scope for the emergence of an independent middle class. But the influx of immigrants in the nineteenth century, and the growth of towns, commerce, and manufacturing gradually produced an intermediate sector of society which was more than the lower fringe of the traditional élite or the summit of the submerged majority. It could still scarcely be termed a middle class proper, since it lacked that homogeneity and common outlook which distinguished the middle class in older societies. It comprised rather a cross-section of the population ranging from professional men and 'intelligentsia'—doctors, lawyers, journalists, schoolmasters, university teachers, and students—a growing host of civil servants, clerks, and shopkeepers, the medium and small businessmen, the engineers, technicians and small farmers, and the army officers whose special role we shall be examining later. The numerical strength of these 'middle sectors' is now hard to assess; it may perhaps amount to one fifth of the population of Latin America as a whole, and more than half that of a highly urbanized country such as Uruguay. From these strata of the population the political parties draw their members, the state most of its presidents and cabinet ministers, and the churches their congregations. Though impatient to increase their share of material goods, improve their social position, and secure a better education for their children, they are also keenly concerned with the role which their countries and Latin America as a whole should play in the world and are the most responsive to the appeal of nationalism. Their abilities and drive might also be expected to furnish the motive power for their countries' economic development. Yet it is doubtful whether this is so. Uruguay, Argentina, and Chile, where the middle sectors are relatively strongest, are also countries whose economies have latterly proved disappointingly stagnant. The explanation may perhaps be that Latin America's middle sectors, though including a predominantly left-wing intelligentsia and numerous militants pledged to a revolutionary restructuring of society, are nevertheless more interested on the whole in gaining access to the higher living standards and social status of the privileged élite than in securing their more egalitarian redistribution.

The urban working class

The rising strength of the middle sectors is one result of the phenomenal growth of Latin America's cities; another is the emergence of an urban working class. In recent years, the population of the towns has been increasing about three times faster than that of the countryside, and the great cities are growing more rapidly than the smaller and medium-sized towns. There are now (1972) some eighteen cities in Latin America with populations of over one million each; by 1980 there will probably be more than two dozen. Mexico City now has some six million inhabitants, São Paulo (reputedly the fastest growing city in the world) five and a half, Rio four. Montevideo contains nearly half the nation's population, Buenos Aires, which expanded from over 4,500,000 in 1950 to over 6,500,000 in 1960, over one third. But this rapid urbanization does not reflect a correspondingly rapid rate of industrialization. Only between 5 and 6 per cent of the urban population in fact work in industry; the other urban workers find employment, or part employment, in the tertiary sectors. Industry tends to concentrate in relatively small areas; half Brazil's, for instance, is in the São Paulo area and a quarter around Rio. Skilled workers, though their ranks are growing, remain only a fragment of Latin America's labour force and constitute privileged industrial élites, such as Chile's copper workers or Venezuela's oil workers, organized into unions whose functions we shall be looking at more closely later. Only in Perón's Argentina, when nearly six out of every seven workers belonged to a trade union, have the urban workers ever attained any high degree of unionization.

Many unskilled workers live in the vast shanty-towns which ring the great cities. Though their names vary, the *favelas* of Rio de Janeiro, the *callampas* of Santiago, the *barriadas* of Lima (now euphemistically referred to as 'young towns'), or the *barrios* of Caracas present a uniformly squalid jumble of insanitary huts thrown together from boards and pieces of corrugated iron. Yet these are not slums proper, nor do their inhabitants have the mentality of slum-dwellers. The shanty-town population is mostly composed of immigrants who have poured in from the countryside in search of jobs and a better chance in life for themselves and their children, or of families from the overcrowded city tenements who, often in well-organized quasi-military operations, move out to the outskirts to squat on some pre-selected vacant plot. Sometimes the owner of the lands calls in the police and the squatters are evicted. But often they are left in possession of the site where, if the men are lucky enough to find paid employment, brick walls in time replace the wooden boards of their huts, proper roofs are fitted with the help of neighbours, and basic services such as water, lighting, and drainage laid on with the assistance of a housing organization or of a local politician in search of votes. A 1963 United Nations estimate put the number of new houses which were needed in Latin America each year at 1,140,000; they are being constructed at only a fifth of this rate. A million people already live in the *favelas* of Rio and 400,000 in Lima's *barriadas*. The problem of providing jobs, schooling, and services for this proliferating marginal population is indeed a formidable one.

The campesinos

Wretched as conditions may be in the shanty-towns, they are, however, often better than those from which the rural immigrant has escaped. Many millions of *campesino* families live in a chronic state of hunger, with a food intake of little more than half that considered adequate by nutritionists, and scarcely ever taste meat, eggs, milk, fresh vegetables, fruit, or fats. Periodic failure of their scanty crops set in motion a mass exodus from the afflicted areas, as from the drought-prone north-east of Brazil. Or it may be news of the jobs to be had on some new industrial complex or hydro-electric works which acts as a magnet. Provided the uprooted *campesinos* can be constructively employed elsewhere—which, as we have noted, is at present by no means always the case—this movement from the countryside to the towns is to be welcomed. Between 1945 and 1960, the proportion of Latin America's labour force employed in agriculture fell from 56 to 47 per cent of the total; but despite this relative decline, the number of people who try to gain a living from the land is still, in *absolute* terms, increasing. Their status and occupation vary widely. They work in the cane-fields and coffee-plantations, as cowboys on the *pampas* or rubber-gatherers in the Amazonian forest. They may be subsistence farmers, *minifundio* owners, or tied labourers on a *hacienda*. But except in a few areas, such as the south of Brazil, the *campesino* bears little resemblance to the prosperous peasant smallholder of Europe. He is frequently unable to subsist on his own land, and has to offer his services for wages elsewhere for part of the year. Most wretched of all are the many who have no land at all of their own, even as tolerated squatters, and follow the precarious calling of itinerant labourers. Some become absorbed by the large commercial plantations or the shanty-towns. Within a number of years, necessity may have converted the uprooted *campesino*, or at any rate his children, into members of the urban proletariat.

The Indian problem

One section of the rural population, however, has shown itself remarkably resistant to change. Inscrutable to the white man and indifferent to his creed of 'progress', which they suspect is only the covert form of some new exploitation, the remnants of the pre-Columbian native races remain tenaciously attached to their ancestral ways and largely unassimilated by the modern states of which they are nominally citizens. Many speak only their native dialects or at best a few phrases of debased Spanish. Those who live on in their traditional communities remain outside, or on the fringes of, the money economy. If they earn anything in cash, they prefer to lavish it on a fiesta where alcohol gives them ritual release and liberal spending wins the respect of their fellows. To many non-Indians it still seems, as the Bolivian racist writer Rene Moreno put it, that 'the Indian is useless . . . a passive, inert mass, a stone blocking the viscera of the social organism'. In the Andean *altiplano*, where the indigenous population is most thickly concentrated, the Aymará are generally accounted to be still less adaptable, and when once aroused, more implacably hostile to the non-Indians, than the more numerous Quechua. Though pilot projects such as the work of the Andean Mission in Ecuador and the 'Vicos experiment', which has transformed the ex-peons of a Peruvian *hacienda* into a prosperous Indian co-operative, have achieved some success, the Indians have so far stubbornly defied attempts to lure or force them into the modern world.

It is difficult to find reliable figures for Latin America's Indian population. In Peru and Ecuador, the Indians make up nearly half, and in Bolivia considerably more than half the nation. Mexico has at least one to two million Indians, and there are large unintegrated communities in Guatemala and other parts of Central America. Nor is it easy to say whether the Indian portion of a nation's population is growing more or less rapidly than the non-Indian; whether, in short, 'Latin' America is becoming 'Indo'-America. In general it would seem that the Indians, though they may be increasing in absolute terms in certain countries, constitute a declining element in the population as a whole. Bolivia, in the view of some observers, might prove the exceptional case of a nation which is in process of becoming more 'Indian', at least in its culture and values. Nor is Bolivia the only Andean country where there has been something of a recent revival in the use of the Quechua language. But not all Indians are agreed that they wish to have their children taught Quechua in school. So ingrained is the distrust of the white man and all his doings that when he offers education for them in their own tongue, the Indians sometimes look upon it as a stratagem to prolong their inferior status. A Quechua cultural renaissance, which might in time foster a stirring of racial or pan-Quechua sentiment in much the same way as the submerged Slav peoples of Central and South-East Europe were aroused to a national revival in the last century, thus hardly seems likely. Native loyalty is still primarily to the clan and the locality. The Indians do not easily speak with one voice, and where they are most numerous, cannot even agree amongst themselves whether it should be a Quechua or a Spanish voice. If they speak and act as Indians, what place will they find in the modern world? But if they speak and act as the white man, will they not cease to be Indians?

This brings us to the question of determining just what is meant by the term 'Indian'. Its connotation is certainly as much economic and social as it is racial. It is generally used in a pejorative sense to describe anyone whom the speaker regards as culturally or socially inferior to himself, and the use of the word *indio* is itself now often officially discouraged in favour of the anodyne term *campesino*. (In Brazil, however, it has long been socially respectable to claim a tincture of Indian blood, and in Mexico today the cult of the Indian is official.) An Indian is, in reality, one who lives in a native community and clings to ancestral values and traits. Once he discards these, learns to read and write, acquires money and assumes the dress and habits of a white man, he ceases to be considered or to consider himself an Indian. In colonial times, an Indian who had fulfilled these requirements could even obtain a certificate declaring that he should be 'considered white'. Should he wish, after living in the white man's world, to re-enter his native community, the process of acculturation has to be put into reverse; the anthropologist Ricardo Pozas, in his *Juan Pérez Jolote*, relates the experiences of a Tzotzil Indian who took this course after the Mexican Revolution.

Assimilation into the white man's world has thus traditionally been assumed to be the only solution to the Indian problem. But cannot the Indians' basic culture traits and institutions still be preserved and yet adapted to the needs of modern life? Mariátegui (1895–1930) argued that *gamonalismo* was so strong in Peru that any improvement in the Indian's lot was impossible without a radical rebuilding of society on the basis of the *ayllu* or native community, for even where this seemed to have disappeared, 'there still persist robust and tenacious habits of co-operation and solidarity which are the empirical expression of a communist spirit'. Mariátegui, though a Marxist, was not so naïve as to equate the primitive agrarian communism of the Incas with the Communism of Marx and Engels, or to urge that the great estates should be converted into Russian-style state farms; he held rather that the Indians' instinct for communal action should be turned to account in planning the modernization of the country on socialist lines. During Belaúnde's presidency, something of the same belief inspired the movement known as Cooperación Popular, which stressed the Indians' tradition of voluntary communal work as a means of promoting, with government guidance and aid, the construction of roads, schools, clinics, local irrigation schemes, and the like. Others have sought to direct the Indians' instinct for communal action towards more specifically political objectives. Native risings have occurred in this as in previous centuries. One of the most serious was that of 1923, when a frustrated *mestizo* official, Major Teodomiro Gutiérrez, appointed by a reformist president to investigate native grievances, sought to redress them himself by assuming the name of Ruminavi, Atahualpa's famous general, and calling on the Indians to take the law into their own hands. In the 1930s, the Peruvian Communists proclaimed that 'the Indians have the clearest right to self-determination and to set up the government they see fit, and to establish their own independent republics', but the Indians showed singularly little interest in any Quechua or Aymará republic. The young Trotskyist leader Hugo Blanco had more success in the 'sixties when he initiated the Indians of the La Convention valley in the Peruvian *altiplano*, into the techniques of the agricultural strike, the occupation en masse of *hacienda* land and the setting up of revolutionary *sindicatos* (see page 253).

In two countries—Mexico and Bolivia—the Indians' social status, though not their economic condition, has been significantly improved. The redemption of the Indian was one of the proclaimed ideals of the Mexican Revolution. The heroic virtues of the subject race were exalted in the work of the great muralists, and a President of the Republic took pride in naming his son after the last Aztec chief, Cuauhtémoc. When, in 1949, it was announced that the bones of that hero himself had been discovered, there followed an outburst of patriotic fervour which refused to accept the findings of the Commission of experts which subsequently pronounced them to be unauthentic. Yet despite the cult of their forbears, the Indians of Mexico still form the lowest economic stratum of the nation. The same may be said of Bolivia. Following the 1952 take-over of power in La Paz by the radical intelligentsia of the MNR, the Indians, organized into revolutionary *sindicatos*, began to occupy the *haciendas* and to drive out the landowners. Their action, legalized the following year by the government's land reform programme, together with important reforms such as the granting of the vote to the Indian and the introduction of universal education, marked a great step forward towards incorporating the native population in the life of the nation. The Indians' new status was symbolized by the removal of the restrictions which have prevented them from entering the centre of La Paz. Yet ten years later, the bulk of Bolivia's predominantly Indian population was still living little above the starvation line, and the death rate from undernourishment was almost twice as high amongst them as in any other Latin American country.

The negro elements

Brazil can be said to have no serious Indian problem. Cynics may add that this is because the native races have now been virtually exterminated. Brazil has never had a compact indigenous population comparable to that of Mexico or Peru. The base of the social and economic pyramid has been formed by imported African slaves and their offspring, who have interbred freely with both whites and Amerindians to produce the complex racial mosaic of today. From the earliest times, there began to develop, thanks to this miscegenation and the patriarchal character of the great plantations, what Gilberto Freyre has described as 'zones of fraternization between conquerors and conquered, between masters and slaves'. Brazilian society is thus singularly free from race discrimination. Amongst a population showing every gradation of colour and combination of racial characteristics anything resembling the white–black dichotomy of North America is unthinkable. Brazil boasts of being the true melting-pot of the New World, where no man is handicapped because of his race or colour. The country has had a negro president, great artists like the mulatto sculptor O Aleijadinho and the novelist Machado de Assis, and popular heroes like the negro football star Pelé.

But if Brazil is free of racial prejudice, it is far from free of class distinctions in which race is a basic ingredient. 'The darker the skin, the lower the class', the Brazilian saying has it; or, put the other way round, since social and financial positions are so bound up with each other, 'Money whitens the skin'. The descendants of negro slaves still broadly form the lowest social and economic classes, less because of racial prejudice on the part of their fellow citizens than through the weight of inherited poverty and lack of opportunity. Research carried out in 1940 indicates that though those who are classified as white make up 64 per cent of Brazil's population, they account for 90 per cent of the professional men, 81 per cent of the employers, 79 per cent of those in commercial and financial positions, and 76 per cent of the civil servants. The racial problem has been largely merged with Brazil's social problem, which calls for a bridging of the abyss separating the very rich from the intolerably poor, the sophisticated from the illiterate, the booming cities from the backward countryside.

European and Asian immigration

Many countries have left their imprint on Latin America's ethnic fabric. Italy's is most manifest in Argentina, whose population and *mores* bear at least as strong an Italian as a Spanish stamp. Southern Brazil has been chiefly developed by colonies of Italians, Slavs, and Germans who have kept tenaciously to their own ways of life and their industrious methods of mixed farming and have extended their influence into many branches of industrial development. The Germans have also formed flourishing communities in Argentina, Chile and Guatemala, and the Slavs—Poles, Russians, Ukrainians, and Yugoslavs—chiefly in the River Plate countries, though flourishing Yugoslav outposts may be found as far afield as Punta Arenas and Antofagasta in Chile. Japanese agricultural communities have made good in Brazil, Paraguay, Bolivia, and Peru, and Chinese traders in Havana, Lima, and Panama City. Jews and *turcos*—merchants hailing mostly from Syria and Lebanon—have established themselves everywhere in commerce and industry. The British too are to be found mostly in business, for the few schemes to introduce colonies of small-holders met with little success, though the Welsh of Chubut in Argentina still constitute a flourishing community which cherishes its language, traditions, and love of music. These and many other immigrant groups have added their distinctive skills and colours to the Latin American scene. The great sub-continent still has its empty spaces, but it seems doubtful whether these will ever be filled by any fresh surge of immigration. Latin America has now generated its own dynamic of demographic expansion and set in motion new formative trends to which we must turn our attention.

The population explosion

The first trend which we cannot fail to note is that Latin America's population is growing very fast; faster, indeed, than that of any other part of the world. From 1920 to 1950, it increased by 73 per cent as against the average world increase of 35 per cent. Its growth has been most rapid in Central America and in some countries with relatively large populations, such as Venezuela, Mexico, Brazil, and Colombia. Only in two countries—Argentina and Uruguay—has the annual rate of increase fallen below 2 per cent. In Venezuela and Costa Rica it has respectively approached and exceeded 4 per cent. The average rate for Latin America as a whole is 2·8, as compared with 2 for Africa, 1·9 for Asia, and 0·8 per cent for Europe during the same period (1950–60). In 1955 Latin America's population was 175 million; by 1975 it is expected to reach nearly 293 million, and by the end of the century to total anything between 514 and 756 million.

There are several reasons for Latin America's abnormally high population growth rate. Firstly, the area has benefited from modern medical technology sooner than other parts of the Third World; public health programmes began to produce a decline in the mortality rate during the 1920s, some two decades earlier than in either Africa or Asia. The average Latin American may already expect to live nearly sixty years, and by 1975 his expectation of life may have risen to seventy. But the slowing-up of the death rate has not been balanced by any decline in the birth rate. It is still usual for families to be large and for women to marry, or to enter into physical relationships, at an early age. In a needy family, more children soon mean more breadwinners. Numerous offspring, moreover, are evidence of a man's *machismo*, and he is trammelled by no legal obligation to support those of them that are born out of wedlock; not surprisingly, Latin America's illegitimacy rate is the highest in the world. Furthermore, to multiply and people an empty land has traditionally been regarded as a patriotic and socially desirable task. The belief that more population is the precondition of sound and prosperous nationhood —Alberdi's slogan *gobernar es poblar*, 'to govern is to populate'—dies hard. For these reasons, and on the political and religious grounds considered below, the gospel of family planning has found little favour.

But rapid population growth creates more problems than it solves. It threatens to outstrip the rate of economic expansion and eat up the resources of countries still struggling to develop. It imperils a country's political and social stability. Industry cannot absorb the stream of migrants flocking to the towns, nor can public services expand quickly enough to keep pace with their needs. Schools can scarcely be built, or teachers trained, soon enough to educate the rising generation. Less populated countries like Honduras and the Dominican Republic wonder apprehensively how long they will be able to prevent their more densely populated neighbours, El Salvador and Haiti, from spilling across their respective frontiers.

Latin America appears, at first sight, to be a still relatively empty land waiting only for more population to open up its almost limitless resources; this is the light in which many of its own peoples like to see it. It covers one sixth of the world's land surface and has only one fourteenth of its population. Yet much of this land is uncultivated and will remain unsuited for cultivation; in its cultivated areas, density is much the same as—and if we exclude the three largest countries, Argentina, Brazil, and Mexico, higher than—the world average. This would present little problem provided crop yields were substantially increased; but in Latin America—Mexico is here an encouraging exception—yields remain disappointingly low. Total agricultural output for the whole region has indeed increased—largely by bringing fresh land under cultivation—since the pre-war period, but population has increased still more, so that, on a *per capita* basis, there has actually been an 8 per cent decline (see page 256). As a United Nations survey for 1966 puts it: 'In the last ten years, agricultural output has lagged behind population growth in ten out of the twenty Latin American countries, exceeding it in five countries by a margin of less than 1 per cent.'

Declining *per capita* agricultural output is not being balanced by booming industrial expansion. In countries which, like Britain, had their industrial revolution at an earlier stage of technological development, spare hands were absorbed in labour-intensive factories. But today, with the increasing spread of automation, small numbers of skilled workers rather than Latin America's large numbers of unskilled workers are required for industrial expansion. Between 1950 and 1960, industry was able to take only 10 per cent of the increment of the labour force, and by 1965 the percentage had fallen to 7½. Governments are tempted to absorb what they can of this excess labour force into the top-heavy public services and state enterprises, at the cost of swelling the budgetary deficit and spurring inflation. Unemployment, under-employment, feather-bedding, and a swollen tertiary sector are consequences of the unchecked rate of population increase.

Another consequence is that Latin America has an unusually 'young' population; over 40 per cent are estimated to be under fifteen years of age (as compared with 31 per cent in the United States and 25 per cent in Europe). It follows that a relatively small proportion of the nation—the 55 per cent between the ages of fifteen and sixty-five who rank as theoretically 'economically active'—have to feed, clothe, and educate the 40 per cent under fifteen as well as provide for the elderly 5 per cent. This contrasts with the population of Britain, 65 per cent of whom are 'economically active' and who perform a similar function in their wealthier society. The burden on the budgets of the Latin American governments, particularly for the basic educational needs of their people and the provision of the technical training on which their economic future largely depends, is consequently very heavy. The demand for improved facilities in all branches of education is becoming more insistent, and governments have shown varying degrees of success in trying to meet it.

Between 1956 and 1965, the percentage of Latin America's total population enrolled in schools of some kind rose from 13·3 to 17·1 per cent, at more than twice the rate of population increase. This expansion occurred however mainly at the middle and higher educational levels, whilst primary school enrolments hardly kept pace with the growing number of children of school age. Some fourteen million of the latter were estimated to be still without any school facilities in Latin America in 1965. Some countries have made laudable efforts to remedy this state of affairs. Cuba claims to have nearly doubled the number of primary school places in a decade, and Chile to have stepped up general educational enrolment by nearly 40 per cent, compared with a population increase of only 10 per cent, between 1964 and 1968. Vocational and technical education is also making rapid strides in some countries such as Cuba and Venezuela; in the latter, enrolments of this type trebled in six years. Yet much still remains to be done and student frustration, spreading down from the universities to the secondary schools, constitutes a disturbing problem in almost every country (see page 248).

Can the problems resulting from a too rapid population growth be solved, or at least alleviated, by introducing some degree of birth control? The traditional attitude in Latin America has been to deny that such problems exist, or if their existence is admitted, to reject birth control as a solution. Catholic teaching is against it, and Latin American governments are reluctant to provoke a clash with the Church by sponsoring birth control campaigns. But though the hierarchy may still disapprove, young priests have been known to send poor parishioners to family planning centres for treatment and advice, and more thought is now being given to population problems in progressive Catholic circles. Nationalist opinion tends to see birth control, in the words of one Latin American spokesman, as 'a lever for the international egotism of the rich nations in allowing them to evade their duties of assistance and solidarity with the developing nations'. President Johnson's statement of June 1965 to the effect that 5 dollars invested in population control would be better than 100 dollars invested in economic growth was taken as evidence that the United States was trying to slide out of its moral obligation to provide economic aid. Brazil's hypersensitivity to suspected attempts by the United States to prevent her from reaching Great Power status has led to hysterical charges that the contraception advice offered by Protestant missionaries in Amazonia was tantamount to the 'foreign sterilization of Brazilian women' and even the Brazilian Medical Association saw fit to declare that 'Brazil cannot permit the genocide that is carried out with rings or other substitutes for the gas chamber used by the Nazis to exterminate the Jews'. The Left, ironically, is at one with Nationalist and Catholic Right in opposing birth control. Latin America's under-development, it is argued, is the outcome of domination by the United States and the ruling oligarchies; to advocate birth control is to obscure the need for revolutionary action and to inhibit social change. 'Let the population grow fast', one left-wing Christian Democrat spokesman has declared, 'so that pressures on the *status quo* are increased and change comes about.'

Nevertheless, in spite of opposition from these varied quarters, many governments, with Chile, Costa Rica, and Colombia to the fore, are becoming increasingly alive to the consequences of unchecked population growth and have been taking discreet measures to promote a knowledge of family planning techniques. In a 1962 motion in the United Nations 'to give technical assistance as requested by Governments for national projects and programmes dealing with problems of population', only Chile and Costa Rica voted in favour, two thirds of the Latin American delegates were in opposition, and one quarter abstained. By 1966, however, a more strongly worded resolution of the General Assembly on this topic was adopted unanimously. One factor making for change has been the growing realization by women of the extent to which birth control might alleviate their lot. The figures for induced abortion are very high in Latin America: for example, one for every two live births in Chile, and one for every three in Uruguay. As the general level of education rises and women become better able to make their voice heard in a society where the cult of *machismo* is still strong, the old prejudices against family planning may gradually be overcome and Latin America's runaway population growth brought under control.

2 Institutions

The hacienda *system*

Latin America's most characteristic, durable, and basic institution has been the large estate or *latifundium* known variously as the *hacienda, estancia, finca, fundo, rancho,* and (in Brazil) *engenho* or *fazenda*. We have noted the rise of the landowning oligarchy through the grant of *encomiendas* to conquistadores and early colonists (see page 43) and the growth of the great estates in the nineteenth century (see page 215). Although the *hacienda* is now, except in a few countries such as Paraguay and Ecuador, to be found only in attenuated, transitional, or residual form, whilst in others (e.g. Cuba, Costa Rica, and Haiti) it has been altogether superseded, it still deserves our attention for the profound social, economic, and political impact it has had and the difficulty now often encountered in altogether destroying its vestigial influence or finding suitable new forms to fill the gap which its passing may leave in the life of the community. As one leading Latin American sociologist has put it: 'For a long time every facet of the social structure of Latin American bore traces of the formative influence of one fundamental institution: the *hacienda*. All the economic, social, and political history of Latin American is largely the history of the consolidation and transformation of that particular unit. And consequently the story of the gradual downfall of the traditional structure is interwoven with that of the slow decline of this ancient institution.'

The *hacienda*, in its heyday, was far more than a large estate or mere system of land-holding. It has been described as a society under private auspices, an instrument for establishing order and social cohesion in sparsely populated lands. Economically and socially, each *hacienda* was a largely self-sufficient unit. It produced not only sugar, cereals, cattle, or fruit according to the natural resources of the locality, but often much of the furniture, tools, clothes, and other necessities of the community. It tended to remain outside the money economy and seldom had much surplus produce to bring in income, except when turning to cattle-raising, sugar, coffee, and other commodities for export, which then tended to transform its traditional way of life into that of a modern-style capitalist enterprise. Militarily, the *hacienda* played an important role in providing nuclei of men who could be armed to beat off foreign intruders in undefended frontier zones, raise levies in times of civil commotion (as in the wars of independence), or simply to keep order within the owner's fief or to defend it against a rival landowner. Generally, however, the *hacendado* was linked to his neighbour, and indeed to other landowning families through the whole country, by ties of kinship and common interest which gave a certain cohesion to a land often fragmented by vast distances and formidable natural obstacles. In those isolated, largely self-contained communities to which they were bound by economic necessity, tradition, habits of psychological dependence, and often by debt and legal obligations, the quasi-serfs spent their lives. Their world was more than the lowly hut of the subsistence farmer; it was formed by the great house which they served, with its ancillary buildings—store, granaries, carpenter's and blacksmith's shops, sometimes a church and a school—which took the place of independent village or township.

The *hacienda*, for all the social inequalities which it manifestly perpetuated, fulfilled a need during a long stage in Latin America's evolution. It continued to dominate many rural areas whilst other forms of social organization—the mining centres, the cities, the commercially-run plantations, and the incipient industries—gradually established themselves. Some *haciendas*, under the stimulus of technological innovation or their owners' interest in profitability, adapted themselves to the new conditions. On the Argentine *pampa*, a powerful initial impetus was given to this process by the introduction of refrigeration techniques in the 1870s; in Northern Brazil, by the abolition of slavery in 1888, and the use of steam-powered sugar-mills. Where this occurred, the *patrón* became the capitalist *entrepreneur* or was superseded by a limited company, the state labour code replaced such paternalistic security as the *hacienda* had provided, and the peons or ex-slaves became wage-earners who often looked to the trade-union leader or demagogic politician as a substitute *patrón*.

But elsewhere the *hacienda* lived on. According to a 1951 United Nations estimate, as much as one half of all the agricultural land in Latin America was composed of large estates of more than 15,000 acres, some of them many times that size, and a great number of them old-style *haciendas*. The latter had been altogether swept away from one country—Mexico—and though some large estates survived or were later reconstituted, these were run on modern, commercial lines. Mexico evolved, or rather revived and adapted, its own institution to take the place of the *hacienda*, though the *ejido* could never match the latter in prevalence and dominance of the national life. Bolivia followed suit with its revolutionary land reform of 1953, which effectively broke up the old *haciendas* of the *altiplano* in favour of small-holdings. Cuba's land reform of the early 'sixties was the most radical of all, though the transitory co-operatives and huge permanent state farms which it brought into being were mainly created, not at the expense of traditional *haciendas*, but of large, often foreign-owned, commercially operated sugar plantations. The radical Agrarian Reform promulgated in 1969 by the military government in Peru (see page 161) has likewise been initially applied to the large and efficient agro-industrial plantations on the coast; should it be extended to the sierra, as its promoters promise, the old-style *hacienda* will vanish from Peru as it has vanished from Bolivia.

Even where there is no desire to go as far as the Mexican, Bolivian, Cuban, or Peruvian models, the need for some changes in Latin America's traditional pattern of land ownership has won increasing recognition during the last decade. In his 1961 Message to Congress recommending aid to Latin America under his new Alliance for Progress programme, President Kennedy referred to the unequal distribution of land as 'one of the greatest social problems' and made it clear that any Latin American government determined to launch a thorough-going but constitutional programme of land reform could count on United States assistance. In the same decade almost every other country of Latin America, except for highly urbanized Uruguay and Argentina, enacted some type of land reform programme (Venezuela in 1960, Haiti, Panama, the Dominican Republic, Chile, and Colombia in 1962, Honduras, El Salvador, Costa Rica, Nicaragua, and Paraguay in 1963, Brazil and Ecuador in 1964, Peru in 1964 and 1969, and Cuba again in 1967). Some of these were no more than paper reforms or localized colonization projects; but Venezuela's is a serious and extensive scheme, and Chile's one that is beginning to change the face of her traditional society.

What is the case against the *hacienda* system today? That it has outlived its usefulness as an institution and has become a drag on economic development and an obstacle to a juster social order and a more genuine democracy. Where soil and climate favour extensive farming or large-scale production of cash crops there is much to be said for the large estate; but little for the seigneurial master-and-man relationship, the opting-out of the wider life of the nation, and the gross under-utilization of natural resources inherent in the *hacienda* system. Though centuries of dependence on the *patrón* may condition them to an apparently resigned acceptance of their lot, the quasi-servile status of the *hacienda*-workers no longer seems tolerable in a state aiming at modernization and development. Even in a country such as Ecuador, where the old order has been slowest to change, the *huasipungero* is at least no longer legally subject to the degrading burden of personal service, though in practice his lot may scarcely have changed for the better.

On economic grounds, the retention of the old *hacienda* system is equally hard to defend. Though greedy to grab fresh land, it fails to make use of more than a fraction of what it has. Landowners have generally preferred to seek quicker returns on their capital than they could expect from long-term invest-ments in improving their land, unless the prospect of a profitable cash crop tempts them to move the *hacienda* altogether into the plantation economy. Most *hacendados* are therefore simply content to acquire land and leave it largely unimproved as a hedge against inflation. Though much of the land in a country as bleak and mountainous as Bolivia will of course never be made productive, the percentage of only 1·2 cultivated on its pre-reform *haciendas* seems absurdly low; for Latin America as a whole, the cultivated proportion of all *hacienda* land is between 10 and 15 per cent. By monopolizing but failing to utilize so much of the land, the *hacienda* system has thus paradoxically created a virtual land shortage in a continent still full of empty spaces. It neither makes proper use of natural resources itself nor permits others to do so. Latin America has consequently never known, apart from certain exceptional regions, the 'moving frontier' which played such a part in the development of the United States, where pioneers were welcome to push back the wilderness by hacking out their farms and so win ownership of their own holdings. In those countries where there is virgin land for the taking (e.g. Brazil, Venezuela, Bolivia) it lies so far from the occupied areas, owing to the interposition of enormous idle private estates, that the individual pioneer has often lacked the means to get or maintain himself there, colonization schemes have succumbed through remoteness and marketing difficulties, and those now sponsored by governments burden the country with the enormous cost of road construction and other infrastructure expenses. Successful cases do nevertheless exist to show that problems of integrated reform and development, though formidable, can be overcome. The most striking of these is the scheme in Brazil's North Paraná where an entire region has been developed into what is generally accounted the largest and most prosperous pioneer zone of small independent farmers to be found in all Latin America. Not the least interesting feature of the scheme is that it was launched in the mid-'twenties by a British company, as its nostalgically named and now flourishing regional capital Londrina may serve to recall.

How much longer will the remains of the old system survive, which methods will be used to accelerate its passing, and what is likely to take its place? The *hacienda* has proved remarkably durable. It is now likely to be defended less by legal sanctions (though landowners have proved adept at using the machinery of the appeal tribunals to delay expropriation) or by force (though police and army units may still be called in to prevent the unauthorized take-over of private property). The *hacendados*' most telling weapons are the influence they still wield in Congress and government administration and over their own peóns. One effective way of compelling landowners either to put their idle lands to use or to sell up is to introduce a scale of graded taxation on inefficient or inadequately exploited farms; *hacendados* have often succeeded in blocking legislation of this nature through the influence they exert in government circles, particularly in local state legislatures where, as in Brazil, these have been the responsible organs. In many countries, however, appropriate legislation is now at least on the statute book. The *hacienda*-workers too can sometimes be manipulated by the *patrón* to oppose changes which would in reality be in their own interests. The powerful father-figure who has long provided them with work and whatever security they have known may persuade them that they have nothing to gain from the break-up of the great estate and his own disappearance.

Can an institution so deeply rooted as the *hacienda* system be simply voted out of existence by the enactment of a well-drafted Agrarian Reform Law (and by no means all such laws in Latin America have been clearly and comprehensively drafted)? The experience of the militant *sindicatos* of Bolivia and of Zapata's agrarian revolutionaries in Mexico (though their leader was killed and the triumph of their cause long delayed) suggests that some degree of *campesino* militancy is essential if an Agrarian Reform programme is to gain real momentum. But the sponsoring government, unless it is itself professedly revolutionary, is liable to grow alarmed by such pressures lest the floodgates of violent revolution be opened, and to falter and compromise accordingly. Reformist regimes thus often seem insincere or incapable of implementing an effective land reform.

Whether by violent or relatively peaceful means, the last of the old *haciendas* will in time disappear, but what will then take their place is by no means clear. It is often assumed that it must be some form of collective organization. Cuba points in this direction; but the political regimentation and indifferent production record of its state farms scarcely entitle them to qualify as universal models. Mexico can show its collectively-run *ejidos*, but they form only a small portion of all *ejido* lands and their performance is no better than that of many private farms. The Bolivian *campesinos* used their *sindicatos* to destroy the *haciendas* but have shown little interest in adapting them for the communal running of the expropriated lands. Chile's *inquilinos* were first given the choice, after an initial period under specialist guidance, of choosing whether to farm the land allotted them in individual plots or collectively; they now have to join 'agrarian reform centres' which seem to be camouflaged collectives. The plantations in Peru have passed under the nominal control of worker co-operatives. Elsewhere in the Andean countries there are a few instances—a very few, and then only as a result of careful fostering by international agencies or foreign universities—of traditional Indian communities or groups of ex-peons working former *hacienda* land more or less on the lines of modern co-operatives, a form of association for which Latin Americans have in general shown little enthusiasm. Yet unless some co-operative or collectivist ventures emerge from the ruins of the *hacienda* it looks as if the latter will simply be fragmented into small and generally inefficient small-holdings. The *latifundio* problem includes within itself a *minifundio* problem, since the plots traditionally allotted to *hacienda* workers rarely suffice for more than mere subsistence. Strip away the *latifundio*, and *minifundio* conditions are laid bare. Mexican experience shows that even when the large estates are subdivided, there may still not be enough land to go round, since much of it may be of too poor a quality to be cultivated with the beneficiaries' existing skills and resources. Credit, tools, seeds, fertilizers, marketing facilities, and agricultural training and advice—and often costly infrastructure investment in irrigation and access roads—are thus called for on a scale beyond the present means of most Latin American governments. The dividing up of the large estates is thus clearly not in itself the panacea its advocates sometimes assume. It does not automatically set in motion a country's development, as we know from Haiti's experience, though it may be a pre-condition for long-term development. Reform may well be accompanied at first by social ferment, economic dislocation, and a drop in agricultural output—though Chile's reformers claim that it has already had the effect of increasing production. The days of the old *hacienda* are numbered. The countries of Latin America are now faced with the task of evolving in its place those new institutions, whether co-operatives, individual ownership, or some form of mixed structure, which best suit their own conditions and aspirations.

The Church

If the *hacienda* system has become irremediably anachronistic, the other institution which has done so much to shape Latin American society shows signs of belatedly and painfully striving to adapt itself to the needs of a changing world. The role of the Catholic Church has been more varied and vital than its now ossified structure might suggest. America was conquered spiritually as well as militarily and incorporated by the Church, however imperfectly, into western civilization. The Franciscans in Mexico, Las Casas at the Spanish court, the Jesuits in Paraguay and Brazil, and a host of other devoted priests and missionaries stood as the protectors of the Indians against the cruelty of conquistadores and the exploitation of colonists. Even after the Church had grown wealthy and increasingly identified with the Spanish power structure, men like St. Martín de Porres laboured for the poor of Lima and St. Peter Claver for the slaves of Cartagena, and village priests like Hidalgo and Morelos raised the cry for freedom and justice in Mexico. In the nineteenth and early twentieth centuries, when Catholicism seemed to have become wholly identified with clericalism and reaction, the Church could still sometimes raise its voice against the tyranny of a Perón, a Rojas Pinilla, or a Pérez Jiménez and help bring about the dictator's fall. But it is only in the last decade, and particularly after the stimulus of the Second Vatican Council, that the Church in Latin America has begun to stir with something of its old apostolic fervour and the ferment of new ideas.

The resources which the Church can claim to muster are still formidable. Latin America now accounts for about one third of the world's Catholic population, and by the end of the century the proportion may have risen to nearly one half. Brazil is the largest Catholic country in the world. Yet behind this impressive façade grave weaknesses lie concealed. According to an estimate by one Jesuit writer, 70 per cent of Latin Americans lack any proper knowledge of the Catholic faith. The Indian population has been imperfectly Christianized and the worship of the ancient gods is inextricably blended with that of the Catholic saints. African cults such as *macumba* in Brazil and Voodoo in Haiti continue to flourish. Protestantism, though commanding the loyalty of little more than 2 per cent of Latin America's population, has been growing fast in certain areas and exercises an influence far beyond its numerical strength. In the great cities, with their proliferating shanty-towns, the masses live largely outside the orbit of any organized religion. The number of parishes in Brazil is about the same as that in tiny Portugal. For its total population of some 260 million, Latin America has less than 40,000 priests—a ratio of one priest to every 6,500, compared with one to 1,500 in Portugal, one to 1,200 in Spain, and one to every 800 of the Catholic community in the United States. Still more serious is the fact that of this inadequate body of priests, nearly one half are of foreign birth. Spain still supplies the largest contingent (and France most of those for Haiti); the United States has between two and three thousand priests and nuns working in the Latin American field. In countries where distrust of the foreigner often runs high, this reliance on foreign priests (and also on the financial help sent by wealthier Catholic communities) can be a grave drawback. When Castro came to power in Cuba, some four fifths of the priests there were Spaniards and many were deported as undesirable aliens and potential counter-revolutionaries; in other countries, conservative hierarchies have been able to secure the deportation of foreign priests whose progressive outlook they consider subversive.

Not only for manpower and resources has the Church in Latin America been heavily dependent on outside help, but for its ideas and spiritual guidance as well. New currents often take long to cross the Atlantic. It was not until the first decades of this century that the influence of Pope Leo XIII's *Rerum Novarum* encyclical of 1891, which sought to attune the traditional views of the Church on political and social issues more closely to popular aspirations, and the thinking of progressive Catholic writers such as Maritain stimulated a small élite of Latin American priests and laymen to lay the foundations of a native Christian Democrat movement. Prominent amongst them was a group of Jesuits in Santiago (Fathers Fernando Vives, Fernández Pradel, and Alberto Hurtado) which influenced the young Catholics who broke with the Conservative Party to form the Falange Nacional, forerunner of the Chilean Christian Democrat Party (see page 299). Father Hurtado formed a confederation of labour unions which was later to assume continental scope. He also prepared the ground for the Centro Bellarmino, dedicated to the study of social questions, which was joined in the 'fifties by a number of young Jesuits such as Father Roger Vekemans, whose energy and influence were to win him the reputation of being the *éminence grise* behind President Frei. The Centro Belarmino thus helped to form a generation of intellectuals who were to play leading roles in the Christian Democrat Party and government, and also acted as a brains trust and ginger-group stimulating the thinking of the Catholic Church, then sharply divided into Left and Right wings, along new lines. Today the Church in Chile is reckoned to be one of the most progressive in Latin America.

In 1955 the Vatican set up a body which was to play an important role in the process of *aggiornamento*. The Episcopal Council for Latin America (CELAM), composed of bishops from each of the countries of Latin America, was designed to study problems of common concern and to suggest ways of solving them, to co-ordinate church activities in the interests of greater efficiency, and to act generally as a link between the Vatican and the Latin American Church. Thanks largely to the influence of two liberal-minded vice-chairmen, Bishop Larraín of Chile and Dom Helder Câmara of Brazil, CELAM came to concern itself not only with matters of administrative, pastoral, and liturgical reform but also with social issues such as the gulf between rich and poor, the need for better health services, housing and education, and land reform. The Church— to the discomfiture of its Conservative supporters whose ears were more attuned to such watchwords as anti-Communism and the defence of the family—was urged to understand and participate more actively in the processes of social change and economic development. As a token of the awakening of the Catholic conscience, Bishop Larraín undertook the distribution of Church lands in his diocese.

Papal encyclicals such as John XXIII's *Mater et Magistra* (1961), with its plea for a juster distribution of the product of men's labours, and Paul VI's *Populorum Progressio* (1967), with its appeal to end the poverty and hunger of the Third World, gave added impetus to the new trend of social thinking and a fresh urgency to the task of applying it to the conditions of Latin America. But the ferment which the reforming Bishops hoped would revitalize the Church soon seemed to be leading to a dangerous polarization between Conservatives and Radicals. Demands for measures far more drastic than anything put forward by CELAM were voiced from all sides: by left-wing Catholic students, by clergy from working-class parishes, and by *avant-garde* priests from France, Belgium, and even from Spain, where the Church was also beginning to feel the winds of change. Dialogue was demanded between the lower clergy and their bishops, between Catholics and Communists; priests began to campaign for the right to marry, to elect their own bishops, to help in the formation of trade unions or peasant leagues; manifestos were issued deploring the Church's indifference to ancient wrongs and advocating revolutionary action as the only means of righting them. Some priests helped or even joined guerrilla groups. Catholic laymen and priests staged a sit-in in Santiago Cathedral. If a split in the Church was to be averted, guidance from the highest quarter was clearly needed as to how far the Church was to go, and which methods it was to use, in urging social and economic reform.

It was in the hope of restraining impatient Radicals and moving Conservative hierarchies and governments to a fuller acceptance of their responsibilities within a disciplined Catholic consensus that Pope Paul decided to pay a visit to Latin America in 1968 to celebrate the Thirty-Ninth Eucharistic Congress in Bogotá. The issuing, three weeks before, of his encyclical *Humanae Vitae*, restating the Vatican's rejection of birth control, was a discouragement to Liberal Catholic opinion, though less so in Latin America where views were coloured by the left-wing suspicion of population limitations as an imperialist device to perpetuate under-development (see page 226). In his address at Bogotá, and subsequently at Medellín, where the bishops met in the second general assembly of CELAM to attempt to apply Vatican thinking to the specific conditions of Latin America, the Pope put most stress on the need of the Church to rediscover its mission to the poor and to promote social and economic change, though by peaceful rather than violent means. The bishops themselves went further in issuing a statement denouncing 'repressive regimes', against which violence might be justified in cases of 'evident and prolonged tyranny or the maintenance of obviously unjust and tenaciously defended structures'. They also attacked the selfishness of the traditional oligarchies and the domination of Latin America's economic life by foreign interests and called on the Church to give up its privileges, defend the rights of the workers, encourage the development of trade-unions and co-operatives, and allow laymen more scope in her own activities. If the Pope had hoped by his visit to close the ranks of the Church round a programme of moderate reform, the bishops seemed resolved to steer it more decisively to the Left and, in the words of one of their spokesmen, 'to identify the Church with the change of social structures and the recognition of the need for her own internal change'.

The speed and degree of this change has varied from country to country. In Mexico, scene of fierce anti-clericalism and religious fanaticism of a few decades ago, Church and State have come to terms and the former has regained much of its influence but has learned to exercise it in a new way. It is still debarred from participation in political life and is not recognized as a legal entity. But the bulk of the population remain attached to their ancient faith and are free to enjoy the ministrations of the Church which are now tacitly permitted by the authorities. Some 5,000 priests are again active in the country, Catholic schools and universities flourish, and church organizations such as Catholic Action operate both on their own account and also in co-operation with the Government. Though the village priest may still rule paternally over his flock in remote and backward villages, the old image of the Church as a reactionary organization has largely disappeared with the traditional peon-exploiting *hacienda*. In Bolivia, the Church weathered the revolutionary storms of the 'fifties, and later championed the rights of the tin-miners against the harsh measures imposed by General Barrientos. In Paraguay, the Church has been moving away from its previous identification with the Stroessner regime and raising its voice against the maltreatment of prisoners and the denial of political liberties. In the Dominican Republic, where the Church had long turned a blind eye to the enormities of the Trujillo regime, priests are now beginning to speak out in favour of land reform and a juster social order. In Argentina, the traditionally Conservative bishops saw no reason to deplore the seizure of power in 1966 by a general of known Catholic sympathies, but within three years, Catholic priests were adding their voices to the clamour of students and workers in the anti-government riots at Córdoba.

Nowhere has the struggle for *aggiornamento* been more acute than in Colombia and Brazil. In the former country, despite the pioneering social work among the peasantry by means of a remarkable network of Catholic radio-schools, the hierarchy has long been reputed a pillar of Conservative society. In 1966, Camilo Torres, a young professor of sociology and university chaplain, left the priesthood to fight with the guerrillas and was killed soon afterwards in a skirmish; his name has been taken as a banner by the small number of extremists who claim that in Latin America Christians should commit themselves to armed struggle in order to achieve social justice. The Colombian hierarchy, now conscious of the danger of reform-minded Catholics being driven from the fold, has been steadily moving away from its traditionally Conservative positions and now includes a 'progressive' wing which is loud in its condemnation of the capitalist system.

Most significant of all, perhaps, are the changes which have been taking place in Brazil, with its large ecclesiastical establishment, headed by nearly 250 archbishops and bishops, and its still vigorous influence in that vast country's welfare, charitable, and educational institutions. Apart from the Catholic students of Acção Popular, who even outshone the Marxists in their revolutionary fervour, and a few radical priests, such as those who organized the Peasant Leagues of the north-east, the Brazilian Church followed a generally conservative or middle-of-the-road course. It nominally showed little concern with politics, except at election-time when it might publish lists of those candidates whose moral principles were deemed such as to justify good Catholics voting for them. It was only in 1964, when the country's apparent drift towards Communism under the Goulart administration alarmed the Church into mobilizing middle-class opinion in defence of the family and traditional values, that it played an important political role by preparing the ground for the military take-over. But the Church nevertheless kept its distance from the new regime, for its own internal evolution was moving it towards the Left, and it was soon openly voicing its criticism of the government's disregard of individual rights and its concern for the urgent social problems which still awaited solution. Tension between Church and State grew particularly acute in the poverty-stricken north-east, where Dom Helder Câmara, the best-known but by no means the most extreme spokesman of the progressives, held the archiepiscopal see of Recife.

Changes—some of them radical—in her own traditional structure and attitudes may well be called for if the Church is to play a significant role in the future. A greater participation of laymen in the life of the Church, and a reform of the out-of-date parochial system, which at present leaves vast sectors of the population without pastoral care, and a drastic overhaul of church machinery in general are needed. More scope must be allowed to initiative from below—from dedicated laymen and from the *padres populares* who live as worker-priests and labour in conditions of apostolic poverty in slums and shanty-towns. Collegiate bodies such as CELAM and the episcopal councils of individual Latin American countries will probably come to assume executive powers well beyond the merely consultative functions they at present exercise, in place of the old vertical chain of command from nuncio and head of the hierarchy. Fuller use is already being made of deacons, but a married clergy is probably unavoidable if the pressing problem of the lack of native vocations is to be overcome and an end made to the traditional reliance on foreign manpower and guidance. If many of the faithful remain ignorant of her dogmas and ignore her precepts, the Church nevertheless still possesses considerable moral authority. A renewed and invigorated Church can use it to give a spiritual dimension to the new forces which are shaping the Latin America of tomorrow.

The military

The armed forces rank amongst the most important of Latin America's institutions, and intervention by the military has long been a familiar feature of the political scene. Armed coups, barrack-room revolutions, the ousting of civilian presidents by ambitious generals, rule by *junta* or uniformed dictator—all these are common enough in the contemporary world, particularly in emergent nations, but it was in Latin America that the pattern was first set. By the beginning of the 1970s, well over half Latin America's population was still living under military rule. The armed forces were in power, though they may have donned civilian trappings, in Brazil, Argentina, Peru, Panama, Bolivia, Cuba, Paraguay, Nicaragua, El Salvador, and Honduras. In others, the military wait menacingly in the wings whilst civilians rule precariously by their grace. Of the major republics, only Mexico has succeeded in bringing the soldiers firmly to heel. Costa Rica alone has found that she can get on very well without any army at all, whilst Chile and Uruguay, proud of their tradition of civilian rule, can no longer be quite sure that the military will not some day force a return to the stage. The list of instances of military intervention in the course of the last four decades is long and may well have lengthened by the time these words appear in print.

Major Military Interventions, 1930–1971

Country	1930–59		1960–71		
	Number	Date	Number	Date	Description
Argentina	4	1930	3	1962	Pres. Frondizi deposed
		1943		1966	Pres. Illia deposed
		1955		1970	Pres. Onganía deposed
				1971	Pres. Levingston deposed
Bolivia	5	1936	4	1964	Pres. Paz Estenssoro deposed
		1937			
		1943		1969	Pres. Siles Salinas deposed
		1946		1970	Pres. Ovando deposed
		1951		1971	Pres. Torres deposed
Brazil	3	1930	2	1964	Pres. Goulart deposed
		1945		1969	Gen. Garrastazú Médici succeeds incapacitated President in place of constitutional successor
		1954			
Chile	1	1932	0	—	
Colombia	2	1953	0	—	
		1957			
Costa Rica	0	—	0	—	
Cuba	3	1933	—		(Fidel Castro in power since 1959)
		1952	0		
		1959			
Dominican Republic	1	1930	3	1961	Generalissimo Trujillo murdered by military plotters
				1963	Pres. Bosch deposed

| Country | 1930–59 | | 1960–71 | | |
---	Number	Date	Number	Date	Description
				1965	Military revolt precipitates civil war
Ecuador	2	1944 1947	1	1963	Pres. Arosemena deposed
El Salvador	2	1944 1948	2	1960 1961	Government ousted by military *junta* which is itself overthrown by new *junta*
Guatemala	3	1930 1944 1954	1	1963	Pres. Ydígoras deposed
Haiti	2	1946 1950	0	—	(Pres. Duvalier ruling dictatorially 1957–71)
Honduras	1	1956	1	1963	Pres. Villeda Morales deposed
Mexico	0	—	0	—	
Nicaragua	1	1933	0	—	(Somoza dynasty in power since 1933)
Panama	1	1951	1	1968	Pres. Arias deposed
Paraguay	2	1936 1954	0	—	(Pres. Stroessner ruling dictatorially since 1954)
Peru	1	1948	2	1962 1968	Pres. Prado deposed Pres. Belaúnde deposed
Uruguay	0	—	0	—	
Venezuela	3	1945 1948 1958	0	—	

The military regimes now in power differ widely in their origins, nature, and aims. A few, like Stroessner's in Paraguay and Somoza's in Nicaragua, remain essentially old-style military dictatorships, though they may take pains to cultivate a modern 'developmental' image. Others have followed rather the reverse process and come to rely more and more on their military machines. Thus Duvalier, the country doctor elected to the presidency with high hopes, became a tyrant perpetuating himself in office through control of the army and the para-military *tonton-macoutes*. Fidel Castro, whose improvised forces swept away Batista's decadent military establishment and who proclaimed the abolition of conscription amongst his aims, is today the master of probably the most efficient fighting force in Latin America and of a country where militarization has been increasingly extended to education and agricultural production.

The character and orientation of today's military regimes have also changed and no longer follow the simple pattern of earlier days. The republics won their independence by force of arms; it was natural that victorious generals should find themselves at the head of the new states and that their successors should seek to take over the government in the national interest (which they seldom distinguished from their own personal interest). The choice seemed to lie between anarchy and tyranny. Freedom rapidly degenerated into licence and the army—or whoever commanded its key units—stepped in to 'restore order'. Throughout much of the nineteenth century, and even well into the twentieth, the military thus generally tended to be a conservative, often a reactionary, force. Though not unconditionally at the service of the ruling oligarchies, their intervention, more often than not, would be aimed to protect or restore the status quo. The army, together with the Church (with which it was frequently allied), was often the only institution capable of representing the nation's wider needs and aspirations which sectional, local, or *cacique* interests threatened to disrupt. The army was also, to a certain degree, a democratic institution, since it was by no means the preserve of the landed élite; men of outstanding ability or ruthlessness could rise to the top, and from there might control the destinies of the nation. It also provided a mechanism by which power could change hands, the processes laid down in the constitution being generally disregarded by rulers who could only be dislodged by force. The leaders of the armed forces wore the mantle of the heroes of the wars of emancipation and often themselves embodied the qualities of *machismo* so prized by their people. That soldiers who forced out presidents at bayonet point, dissolved parliament, and ruled very much at their own whim could claim to be acting in defence of legality might seem cynical or merely absurd. Yet this often was, and still is, their contention. The *pronunciamiento* of rebellious generals invariably declared that the army had been compelled to intervene in order to put an end to the corruption and misgovernment of the *políticos* or their betrayal of national interests, and in order to preserve the constitution. In Brazil, the tradition has been somewhat different but still remains a powerful factor. There the Emperor exercised a moderating influence, but when he was forced from office in 1889, it was by officers inspired by the Positivist creed which they believed would lead to the modernization of Brazil, and the Republic's first two presidents were generals. Today, when a general is again Brazil's head of state, the armed forces still see their role as the upholders of order, the promoters of progress and guardians of the nation's constitution, even if they feel themselves obliged to suspend or amend those parts of it which they find inconvenient.

Civilian governments have seldom managed to protect themselves effectively against the threat of military intervention. Bolivia's army was disbanded after 1952, but within a dozen years it had been reconstituted and was able to overthrow the government. Strong police forces or people's militias are sometimes built up as a counterpoise. The 'Red Battalions' of workers helped to foil the last major attempt by the army in Mexico to impose its will on the government (1924). But more often the armed forces have been able to nip this danger in the bud. The attempt by President Chávez of Paraguay to militarize his police force (1954) and that by President Villeda Morales of Honduras to strengthen his National Guard (1963) led directly to their respective falls. Politicians may also try to strengthen their hand by playing off one force against another, and there have been cases in Latin America of armies coming to blows with navies (as in Argentina) or with air forces (as in the 1965 civil war in the Dominican Republic). More sophisticated ways of neutralizing military trouble-makers include the rapid rotation of commands, secondment to lucrative civilian posts in the administration or nationalized industries (the practice known as *agregacão* in Brazil) or posting to honorific diplomatic posts abroad. Mexico disciplined its army by institutionalizing it for a time as the ruling party's 'military sector' (balanced by other sectors representing the workers, the peasants, and the professions, business and bureaucracy), whilst Castro ensures loyalty through the *instructores revolucionarios* and other party organs under his personal control. Attempts to clip the wings of the military by curtailing their power and privileges, or by reducing their share of the national budget, are almost always counter-productive and likely to lead to a pre-emptive coup. For a marked tendency of recent years has been for the armed forces to act less as an instrument for the personal use of some powerful military chief than as an institution with its own interests, its own rights, and a growing corporate sense of its social and political mission.

This mission was traditionally conceived, as has already been mentioned, as primarily that of preserving 'order', and tended to inhibit democratic development and social change. With the growth of a militant labour movement and the dissemination of dangerously 'subversive' ideas by an intelligentsia much given to Marxist phraseology, military intervention came to wear an increasingly anti-Communist face. 'Communist' became a convenient label for any civilian politician whom the military had a mind to remove, and the pressures of the Cold War made unsavoury military dictatorships appear too often as Washington's most trusty allies. But two other forces were at work which were radically to change the picture. The first was the growth of nationalist sentiment, the second—with which it was increasingly coupled—the conviction that fundamental changes in the social, economic, and political structures were in fact called for and that the army, rather than the *políticos*, should bring them about.

An early manifestation of this awakening social concern was the revolt of the Brazilian *tenentes* in the early 'twenties; from this generation of restless young officers sprang many figures later prominent in the pro-Vargas, Integralist, Communist, or post-1964 movements. This diversity reflects the lack of precision in the aims of the military's emergent Left. There is no clear-cut 'Young Turk' or 'Nasserite' movement, but rather a number of roughly similar currents which, though they may be temporarily dammed up, diverted, or fragmented according to the circumstances of each country, appear to be flowing in the direction of radical reform. It may well be that these same currents are to be found beneath the more Conservative surface of the military regimes of Presidents Lanusse and Garrastazú Médici and that they will one day carry those important countries in the same direction. Here it may be enough to outline the course which the military regimes seem to be taking in four other countries: El Salvador, Cuba, Peru, and Bolivia.

On the miniature stage of El Salvador, the military set itself the difficult task of carrying through radical social reforms against the extremes of both Right and Left. The setting up of a *junta* of officers and left-wing intellectuals in 1960 led to a rapid infiltration by Castroite sympathizers and its ousting (1961) by another *junta*. The latter was set up and controlled by the 450-officer corps acting as a body, which continued to replace members of the *junta* who appeared either too reluctant or too zealous in implementing the prescribed course of middle-of-the-road reforms, and finally nominated one of its members (Colonel, later President, Rivera) as candidate in the presidential elections. The regime subsequently, however, lost much of its early impetus, the promised structural reforms lagged, and the government let itself become absorbed in the sterile conflict with Honduras and its aftermath of economic and resettlement problems.

The Revolutionary Government of Cuba does not like to think of itself as a military regime. Its Communist nature and the charismatic aura of its leader should nevertheless not obscure the fact that it is one, though of a markedly original type. Fidel Castro's amateur guerrilla bands, in the line of descent from the *mambises* which waged irregular warfare against the Spanish colonial authorities, have grown into a well-trained and well-equipped army which is the bastion of the regime against external attack and domestic subversion. Fidel Castro remains its Commander-in-Chief and his brother Raúl its Minister of Defence. Frequent interchange of top personnel and a common ideological indoctrination ensure close co-ordination with police and security forces. Army officers hold key positions in the administration and economy and fill two thirds of the places on the Central Committee of the Communist Party. Persons who are considered socially undesirable or politically unreliable (e.g. members of certain religious sects) find themselves called up for compulsory military service and swell the supply of cheap labour, whilst important economic activities, such as the clearing of land for agricultural work and the organization of the *zafra*, are carried out largely as military operations and with the assistance of specially created military commandos. Girls are also drawn into the military and para-military organizations on a scale unparalleled elsewhere in Latin America, whilst the militarization of the educational system, from the training given to the infant 'Pioneers' to the reorganization of secondary education on lines which are designed to combine academic, manual, and military instruction, proceeds apace. The armed forces, stiffened by cadres of Soviet advisers, instructors, and technicians, provide in short an institutional framework for the revolutionary regime which appears much more solid than its cumbrous bureaucratic apparatus and Communist Party.

The nature of the military regimes in power in Peru and Bolivia is harder to assess. After deposing the civilian President by a *golpe* in familiar fashion in 1968, the Peruvian armed forces quickly began to reveal a style of their own.

By taking over the IPC and then other American interests they demonstrated their extreme nationalism. But in establishing relations with the Communist countries, passing a drastic Agrarian Reform Law, and thundering against the oligarchy, they showed an unexpectedly radical, perhaps even revolutionary, streak. By muzzling the press and political parties, purging the judiciary, and keeping a firm hand on labour and students, they displayed the authoritarianism characteristic of the military in power. The formula of *peruanismo*, compounded of these three elements of heady nationalism, social radicalism, and traditional authoritarianism, aroused a quick response in Latin America. It was a spur to General Ovando's take-over in Bolivia, his speedy nationalization of Gulf Oil, exchange of diplomatic missions with the Russians, and a good deal of strong left-wing talk. In Cuba, where the advent of yet another government of *gorillas* was normally quickly denounced, the Peruvian experiment was followed with sympathetic interest. Castro was a political revolutionary who had become a soldier and so seized power; the Peruvian *junta* was composed of professional soldiers who seemed bent on using their power for social revolution. Whether they would achieve a genuine transformation of their country, or merely, as other *juntas* before them, merge again in time into the changeless Peruvian landscape is a question which may be answered in the 'seventies. Their Bolivian counterparts have already veered to the Right.

The changing mood of the military reflects the change in the nature of their functions. The armed forces are seldom called upon for operations overseas (though Colombia's expeditionary force to Korea and Brazil's to Europe in World War II acquitted themselves well). Nor are they expected to make much serious contribution to the defence of the continent; the Monroe Doctrine postulates that they may count on the United States' mighty shield against extra-hemispheric aggression. Their role is now primarily that of countering internal subversion, particularly from Cuban-inspired guerrillas. To this end they have not only become increasingly effective in counter-insurgency techniques, but have grown more aware of the whole complex of problems for which the guerrillas claim to offer the solution. The guerrilla can only operate with the goodwill of the peasantry; counter-guerrilla action must therefore be directed to winning over the rural population by methods of psychological warfare and practical measures such as the building of roads, schools, clinics, etc. The soldier thus gains personal knowledge of the problems of long-neglected areas and of the need to find solutions, such as land reform, for them. In some countries, the army already has an honourable tradition of civic action. Where there are large, unassimilated Indian communities (Mexico, Guatemala, the Andean countries) it has done useful work by teaching conscripts to read and write and by drawing them generally into the national life. In Bolivia, the army has played an important role in helping to colonize the Oriente, whilst in Brazil, since the days of General Rondón, army engineers, educationists, and medical teams have done valuable pioneering service amongst the primitive tribes. Such work has helped to deepen the army's awareness of its social and political role.

At the same time, the officer corps has become more professionally and technically minded. Bright young officers are trained at institutions like Brazil's War College, where French influence helped to form the 'Sorbonne group' which worked out the national policies applied after the 1964 military take-over, or Peru's Centre for Advanced Military Studies (CAEM), where the men who were to form General Velasco's government came under the influence of 'progressive' ideas. The ambitious graduate from such schools is no longer likely to be content with the prospect of merely gaining 'the presidency of the bayonets'; if he wants power, it will be in order to use it to speed the modernization of the nation-state, with a developed industry and agriculture, and an efficient and honest administration. His outlook is nearer to the technocrat's than to that of the sergeant-major, though he may still tend to assume that enlightened reforms can be commanded into existence, and that no real dialogue with the citizens he claims to represent, and genuinely aspires to benefit, is really necessary. Hence two dangers—that of a widening gap between a government contemptuous of civilians with their ill-applied democratic processes of parties and parliaments, and a people denied any effective political participation or expression of opinion; and that of suspicion and growing estrangement between the non-military governments of Latin America and the military regimes, with the latter's tendency to exacerbate rival nationalisms which, as in the case of the 'football war' between El Salvador and Honduras, may easily flare into armed conflict.

Military regimes, or governments where military pressure behind the scenes is strong, have also sometimes been blamed for encouraging an 'arms race' in Latin America. The memory of old grievances, such as those harboured by Peru and Bolivia against Chile, dies hard. There is also the spur of traditional rivalry, particularly that between Argentina and Brazil, each of whom aspires to be the dominant military power in South America. Thus, when Argentina ordered an aircraft carrier from Britain in 1958, Brazil at once felt obliged to follow suit. Competition now tends to concentrate more on the purchase of modern aircraft. But it is doubtful whether this can be said to amount to anything approaching an 'arms race'. Latin America still spends proportionately less on arms than any other developing area of the world apart from Africa south of the Sahara. This proportion, moreover, dropped from more than 23 per cent of total government expenditure in 1947 to less than 13 per cent in 1966. It may indeed be urged that Latin America needs every penny of its money for its own development. After the 1967 Punta del Este Conference, the American presidents issued a declaration pledging themselves, amongst other things, to forego all 'unnecessary' military expenditure. But who is to define what is necessary or unnecessary? An officer corps with a strong sense of national and professional pride is unlikely to rest content with possessing obsolete or obsolescent weapons.

The problem has led to international complications. Since World War II, Latin America has obtained its arms mainly from the United States, which also maintains large military missions in most countries and plays an important part in the training of the armed forces. This has brought the latter important advantages. It has given them arms at bargain prices and helped to raise technical and professional standards. But as national pride and self-confidence increase, the military tend to chafe under a growing sense of dependence. 'Strings' have sometimes been attached which are bitterly resented. Former United States naval vessels made over to the Argentine navy, for example, may only be used for purposes approved by Washington. Specially resented have been the latter's attempts to put pressure on Latin American governments not to acquire sophisticated material such as jets, tanks, and warships on the grounds that these are irrelevant to the main business of combating subversion, divert funds needed for urgent economic and social development, and make bad blood between the sister republics. A major crisis arose in 1968 when Peru made clear its intention of purchasing Mirages from France in defiance of Washington's objections; this did much to foster the anti-American mood of the military who took power with General Velasco. Washington thus finds herself today facing a new and unwelcome situation. Since President Kennedy launched the Alliance for Progress, efforts had been made to encourage democratic reformist governments in Latin America and to be less fulsome in support of ostensibly anti-Communist military dictatorships. But in the course of one decade constitutional governments have been overturned in Argentina, Brazil, Peru, Bolivia, Panama, and elsewhere, and the uniformed men who followed them could no longer be assumed to be pro-American. If not positively hostile, the new brand of national military regime was likely at best to make a most difficult ally.

The universities

There are about 150 universities in Latin America, including the oldest in the western hemisphere (at Santo Domingo, Mexico City, Lima, Sucre, and Bogotá). About half their number have been founded since World War II. Only Brazil, which now possesses more than two dozen, was allowed none in the colonial period and did not receive her first full university until 1920. They range in size from the huge national institutions, like those in Mexico City and Buenos Aires, to modest provincial, Catholic, or private non-denominational foundations which may have less than a thousand students each.

The administrative structure of most universities has changed little in the last hundred years. At the head of each stands the Rector, either nominated by the government or else elected by the university council or professors, generally for a term of office too short to allow him to carry through any effective reorganization. The larger universities tend to be little more than loose associations of faculties, which are left to run their own affairs under their respective deans, and are often scattered widely in different parts of the city. As universities grow and their curricula are extended to cover new fields of study, schools and *institutos* are added in haphazard fashion. Provision is seldom made for post-graduate work and what little research is undertaken is sharply separated from the teaching side.

The universities aim less at offering a liberal education than at turning out men and women with the paper qualifications they require for their professions. Unfortunately, the professions favoured by the majority of Latin America's students are not those which seem most needed for the countries' development. In the colonial period, law, theology, and medicine were most highly esteemed. Law, in particular, continues to attract large numbers of students today, perhaps because it is thought to open the door to a career in politics or the administration and to a good place in society. Science, engineering, and technology find fewer students and carry less prestige than the traditional professions. For every 10,000 of the population Latin America produces less than 3 engineers; the comparative figures are 33 for the United Kingdom, 42 for Germany, 48 for the USSR, and 61 for the USA. Bolivia, which depends on tin-mining, produced 1,261 lawyers but only 210 engineers between 1953 and 1962. Uruguay, whose national economy is based on agriculture and stock-raising, produced in a typical year (1960) 143 graduates in law, 36 in civil engineering, but only 5 in agricultural engineering. Nor do the few who qualify all remain to work in their own countries. Latin America has its problem of the 'brain drain' in an acute form. Between 1958 and 1965 it is estimated to have lost 45,868 professionals and technicians to the United States. Colombia, for example, lost no less than 50 per cent of its new graduates from 1962 to 1964, and 64 per cent from 1959 to 1963.

The inadequacies of the universities reflect the weakness of the general educational foundations on which they rest. Despite a growing realization that there can be no real economic and social development without a drastic raising of educational levels, most Latin American countries devote less than a fifth of their national budgets to education. In the mid-'sixties, more than 14 million children of school age were estimated to be still without any school facilities, 8 million of them (an increase from less than 6 million in 1957) in Brazil. Even in Mexico (where the school building programme has since been stepped up) some 1½ million children had no school places. Between 1955 and 1965, the increase in school enrolments scarcely managed to keep pace with Latin America's rapid growth in the number of children. Those who did attend primary school stayed on for an average of little more than two years, only one fifth completing the whole course and still fewer going on to secondary schools. The number of the latter had indeed been increased, but about half of them were private, fee-paying establishments which only the better-off middle-class families could afford. The curricula and text-books in use in most schools are out of date, teaching methods tend to be old-fashioned and unimaginative, laying excessive stress on memory work and learning by rote, to the neglect of vocational and scientific subjects. There are not enough teachers; and those there are are often ill-trained and ill-qualified, and all are underpaid. Lack of adequate schooling has produced a high rate of illiteracy. In the mid-'sixties, nearly 40 per cent of the population of Latin America over fifteen could neither read nor write. Though some countries have reduced this proportion to creditably low figures (less than 10 per cent in Argentina and Uruguay, whilst Cuba claims to have virtually eliminated the problem altogether) nearly two thirds of Bolivia's population and four fifths of Haiti's still remain illiterate. (See table of basic data.)

Handicapped by such an unfavourable educational background, it is not surprising that a very low proportion of those who enrol as university students (only, in any case, between 3 and 4 per cent of the population of university age, compared with 30–35 per cent in the United States) ever complete their course. Though tuition fees are nominal or non-existent, there are few maintenance grants and the great majority are part-time students who have to earn their own living and therefore take a long time over their studies. This means that, in terms of results, the Latin American countries pay very heavily for their mediocre educational systems. Most of those who teach at a university do so too on a part-time basis. A busy lawyer, for example, may think it worth while to spare the time to give a few lectures for the prestige, rather than the derisory salary, which a university Chair confers. There thus tends to be very little contact between teacher and pupils, and nothing—except in a handful of new, experimental institutions—in the way of seminar work or tutorial supervision.

The first attempts to apply radical remedies to archaic academic structures were made more than half a century ago, when the rising middle classes began to send their sons to the universities in increasing numbers. The University Reform Movement started in the ancient city of Córdoba, spread rapidly throughout Argentina, then on to Uruguay, Chile, and Peru and in time to Mexico, Colombia, Ecuador, Bolivia, Cuba, and Venezuela, until hardly a single republic remained unaffected. The colonial universities had been modelled on the medieval lines of self-governing scholarly communities of teachers and taught, where professors were elected by their students, but they had degenerated into authoritarian institutions catering primarily for the children of the well-to-do. The Reform attempted to revive the earlier concept (Venezuela's University of Law of 1958 defines the university as 'a community of spiritual interests bringing together professors and students') through the two principles of university autonomy and student participation in university administration. *Co-gobierno* was intended to give the students a say in the appointment of professors and the setting of curricula, to ensure that teachers would be kept up to the mark, standards raised, and student grievances settled, whilst autonomy would guarantee the university against interference by reactionary and dictatorial governments. The Reform also demanded that more attention should be given to teaching and research in the sciences, and that the university should be geared to the needs and specific characteristics of its own nation, rather than modelled on formulae taken from Europe or the United States. It should be an institution serving the whole community, the social conscience of the nation. An impulse was also given to the founding of 'People's Universities' and other forms of university extension work designed to bring the advantages of adult education to the under-privileged urban masses. From the outset, the University Reform Movement thus had strong nationalist, social, and political overtones. It not only profoundly affected the educational systems of almost every Latin American country but was to have a strong impact in other spheres as well.

In some countries, militants of the University Reform Movement soon found themselves heading the opposition to authoritarian governments, who showed no disposition to tolerate this challenge to their monopoly of power. In Venezuela, they fought against the long dictatorship of Gómez, and later—with more success—against that of Pérez Jiménez, many of the country's future democratic leaders (such as Betancourt and Leoni) emerging in the struggle. In Peru, they took up labour's demand for an eight-hour day against Leguía, and from this alliance between students and workers Haya de la Torre, himself a gifted student leader, fashioned APRA, which was to dominate the universities and trade unions in his country for many decades. Elsewhere, the Communist parties, which at first scorned the Reform as a bourgeois movement, came to recognize the tactical importance of the student arm, infiltrated into youth organizations and in some cases came to wield a decisive influence over university life. Mella, the most dynamic of the early Cuban Communists, was also the founder of the Federation of University Students; in a later generation, Fidel Castro (not then a Communist) won his first battles on the university campus. Any party seriously intending to gain political power took good care to build up a solid basis of student support, as did the Christian Democrats in Chile in the early 'sixties. Such youth organizations are invariably more extreme than their parent bodies and act on them as pressure groups in favour of more radical policies. All tend to be strongly nationalist and 'anti-imperialist'. Though a few rightist groups exist, such as those of the PAN in Mexico, most student organizations profess allegiance to the Left, which is subject to a constant process of fermentation and fragmentation as fresh groups of Communists, Maoists, Fidelistas, adherents of the Revolutionary Left (MIR), and other radical factions compete in revolutionary fervour.

The twin principles of *co-gobierno* and university autonomy have come to serve political as much as educational ends. Students use their representation on university boards to attack professors of whose political attitude they disapprove and to prevent them from holding administrative office. Measures designed to raise academic standards, such as insistence on adequate entrance attainments or the disqualification of students who persistently fail examinations, may be resisted on the grounds that they discriminate against the underprivileged. Ambitious student leaders realize that the campus can be an excellent jumping-off ground for a political career, and some parties find it worth their while to keep 'professional students' on their payroll to further their interests in the faculties. 'University autonomy' has been invoked, as at the Central University of Caracas, to turn academic premises into a stronghold for the recruiting, indoctrination, and arming of guerrillas and urban terrorists, since authorities are reluctant to incur the odium of 'violating university autonomy' by sending in the police. Universities thus tend to become foci of anti-government activity. Sometimes a student demonstration or strike will serve as a catalyst for the discontent of other sections of the population and shake even the seemingly strongest of regimes, as the ruthlessly suppressed student demonstrations of October 1968 shook Mexico and the *Cordobazo* of May 1969 shook General Onganía's government.

The Latin American university is thus often prevented from playing its full educational role in society both by its inherited structural weaknesses and by attempts to make it serve political ends. The militant sees it primarily as a field for revolutionary action and holds that, until things are radically changed, the university remains a pillar of an unjust and reactionary order, the instrument of 'cultural exploitation', which can never be put right without a prior transformation of the society it is meant to serve. The concept of a university as a centre for the advancement of learning, uncommitted to any one party or pogma, but universalist in outlook and open to ideas and intellectual co-operation from all quarters, including the scientific and financial aid offered by the great universities and foundations of the United States, runs counter to strong Marxist and nationalist currents. But in one field at least—the exercise of Student Power—the Latin American universities have been pioneers and will probably remain second to none.

The trade unions

Trade unions have appeared on the Latin American scene much later than the other institutions we have been considering, and in some countries where the economy still remains predominantly rural (e.g. Paraguay and Ecuador) they play only the most modest of roles. Latin America's relatively small industrial proletariat, the large proportion of the latter who retain the *campesino*'s mentality of dependence on the *patrón*, the predominance of small and medium-sized enterprises, the physical isolation of many of the larger industrial and mining enterprises, the high rates of illiteracy and unemployment are among the factors which have inhibited the growth of a healthy labour movement. Yet, as the older institutions decay or modify their functions, and the proportion of the active population engaged in agriculture falls (by 1975 it is expected to be little more than 36 per cent against nearly 64 per cent in non-agricultural employment), the importance of the trade unions is bound to increase. In some countries they have already established themselves as significant factors, though hardly in the way familiar in Europe and the United States.

The first unions came into being at the end of the last century, chiefly on the initiative of European immigrants, particularly in Argentina, Uruguay, Brazil, Chile, and Cuba. Most of these workers were either anarcho-syndicalists or socialists, whose rival ideologies—challenged in the 'twenties by that of the Communists—at first dominated the labour movement. Their efforts to organize and to assert their rights were violently repressed by employers and authoritarian governments and were attended by strikes and bloodshed. Following the stimulus given to industry in World War I, some governments and political parties began to see advantage in encouraging and controlling these new forces. In Uruguay, labour's rights were assured and the foundation of the welfare state laid by the far-reaching legislation passed by Batlle y Ordóñez between 1911 and 1915. Mexico needed years of bloody revolution before similar rights were written into the new Constitution of 1917. The economic depression of the early 'thirties, the influence of Fascist syndicalist models, the growth of import-substitution industries in World War II, the guidance offered by competing international trade union organizations, and the paternalism of some regimes and the intolerance of others, all contributed in their varied ways to the shaping of Latin America's labour movement. The upshot was a pattern which has varied widely from country to country.

Argentina has the largest and most highly developed trade-union movement, though its strength has been sapped in recent years by divisions and disorientation. Early labour agitation and repression reached a peak in the 'tragic week' of July 1919, with its toll of 700 dead. In the following decade the advance of the labour movement was hampered by rivalry between Socialists, Communists, and anarcho-syndicalists, with the eventual eclipse of the latter and the deportation of a number of Spanish and Italian workers. The foundation in 1930 of the Confederación General de Trabajo (CGT) marked a new stage in working-class unity. When, in 1943, a military regime started to crack down on the CGT, the latter found an unexpected champion in one member of the government, Colonel Perón, who built it up as the power-base for his dictatorship (see page 187). Though inflation eventually eroded the steep salary increases and other material benefits conferred on them, his *descamisados* at least enjoyed the illusion that their voice was being heard and the country governed in their interest. Perón and his nominees dominated the labour movement and ruthlessly crushed any attempt by independent trade-unionists to assert themselves. Yet when the dictator fell in 1955, the CGT failed to rally effectively to his support and the hollowness behind its monolithic façade was revealed. Labour became divided into three main groupings: the *peronista* unions proper (known as the '62' from their number, or as 'Azopardo' from the location of their head office), a group of miscellaneous socialist or independent unions, mainly of white-collar and skilled workers; and the '19' Communist-dominated unions, which later disbanded in order to infiltrate the two other groups. After General Onganía's seizure of power in 1966, the '62', composed principally of the *participacionistas* headed by the metal-workers' leader Augusto Vandor (assassinated in 1969), who were prepared to accept some degree of co-operation with the regime, faced a 'rebel' CGT led by Raimundo Ongaro, who maintained an attitude of intransigent opposition and gained strong support amongst the workers of Córdoba and Tucumán. Confrontation between militants and government reached its peak in the strikes and riots of 1969, which were repeated on a smaller scale in the following year, despite labour's temporary quiescence during the early part of General Levingston's administration. The workers showed that they were still a force to be reckoned with, though any return to the old unified system of labour organization seemed unlikely in view of the greater sophistication and diversification which had taken place in the country's industrial structure. A lasting solution still waited upon the hoped-for upsurge of the national economy and some means of politically reincorporating the *peronista* masses who, in spite of everything, still nostalgically recalled the benefits once received at the hands of the now exiled and ageing demagogue.

Mexico has a strong labour movement, but one which remains firmly under government control. The workers' demands for social justice gave powerful impulse to the Mexican Revolution, though some years elapsed before the newly won rights written into the 1917 Constitution began to be implemented. The anarcho-syndicalism of the early period gave way to the hegemony of the Confederación Regional Obrera Mexicana (CROM) dominated by henchmen of the labour *caudillo* Morones, notorious for their strong-arm methods and ostentatious living, who claimed to have built up their organization from 50,000 in 1920 to $2\frac{1}{4}$ million in 1927. This huge trade union empire was, however, dismantled by the government which it had begun to threaten and was succeeded by the Confederación de Trabajadores de Méjico (CTM), led by the Marxist Lombardo Toledano. To keep its power within bounds, the CTM was then incorporated within the framework of the official party, and a parallel organization, the Confederación Nacional de Campesinos (CNC), officially established for the peasants. Toledano, who had sought to steer the CTM along a Stalinist course, was eased out of its leadership. But neither the dissident union which he founded, nor an attempt to unionize the dissatisfied and still landless rural labourers, have been able to pose an effective challenge to the government's solidly based labour establishment.

In Cuba, the trade unions are a still more disciplined tool of government, though here their organization follows standard Communist lines. For some three decades before Castro, the unions had been highly organized but led by bosses, Communist or anti-Communist, who showed themselves ready, for tactical advantage or personal gain, to support Batista or other corrupt and dictatorial governments. They did little to assist Castro's rise to power, and were quickly purged of the few independent leaders they possessed and placed under the control of Communists. Their function is now to promote productivity, labour discipline, and conformity with the aims of the regime.

Chile has a well developed and highly politicized labour movement, the tradition of militancy being particularly strong amongst the former nitrate workers and the present-day copper-miners of the north. Communists and Socialists dominate the Central Única de Trabajadores de Chile (CUTCH) where they have beaten off the challenge of the more recently founded Christian Democrat trade unions which, however, have managed to build up some following amongst the agrarian workers. In Uruguay, the Communists have also succeeded—despite the enormous services performed for labour by Batlle's Colorado party—in becoming the dominant influence in the country's chief labour organization, the Unión General de Trabajadores (UGT), from which they have been able to launch crippling strikes against the government. In Bolivia, the harsh exploitation of the tin-miners produced some of Latin America's most militant workers, whose armed intervention in 1952 on behalf of the MNR led to the triumph of that revolutionary movement, the nationalization of the mines, and a decade of co-operation between the Confederación Obrera Boliviana (COB), under an MNR leadership strongly challenged by Trotskyist and orthodox Communist groups, and the government, until dissensions within the latter and attempts to play off the more Conservative *campesinos* against radical miners prepared the ground for the 1964 coup by General Barrientos. The latter's government took harsh measures against the unions in an endeavour to restore labour discipline and rehabilitate the mines, but with General Ovando's assumption of power (1969) the unions began to re-emerge as an important political force.

Brazil, with its history of slavery and its belated industrialization, has been slow to develop a labour movement corresponding to the size and importance of the country. Vargas had little difficulty in suppressing the Socialist, anarcho-syndicalist and Communist unions and, in 1937, substituting a unified system of syndicates on corporativist lines and under firm government control. The system was relaxed under his second, more democratic administration, and a still wider measure of independent trade union activity permitted under the presidency of Kubitschek. But the tradition of state control still persisted and was utilized by President Goulart to promote increasing Communist influence in the unions. With the military take-over of 1964, the pro-Communist leaders were replaced and the unions disciplined. But they have still not been permitted to function as an independent labour movement.

The differing nature and stages of development reached by the labour movements described above, and their varying ideologies and degrees of dependence on the state, make their linking together on a continental scale a difficult matter. The Communists have attempted this more than once: for half a dozen years in the early 'thirties through a largely paper organization affiliated to the Red International of Trade Unions, and in the longer lived (1938–64) Confederación de Trabajadores de América Latina (CTAL) which, under Lombardo Toledano's presidency, also included a number of non-Communist unions and did useful work in promoting labour unity and combating Fascist influence during World War II, but lost credit by serving as a tool of Moscow in the Cold War. Attempts to replace CTAL with another Communist-orientated grouping have so far borne little fruit. The field has thus been left open to the Organización Inter-regional Latinoamericana de Trabajadores (ORIT), half of whose members belong to unions in Canada and the United States. ORIT is affiliated to the International Confederation of Free Trade Unions and follows a frankly anti-Communist line. A newcomer to the scene is the Confederación Latino-Americana de Sindicalistas Cristianos (CLASC), founded in 1954 as the labour arm of the Latin American Christian Democrat movement, but more left-wing than the latter and concerned less with opposing its Communist rivals than with denouncing ORIT and the bogey of Yankee imperialism. CLASC claims to be striving 'to gain for the organized forces of labour a decisive and preponderant participation in the social revolution'. Though it lacks the backing of the main Latin American unions, it has gained some influence in a number of smaller countries and commands a following amongst the agrarian workers.

The agrarian workers have scarcely figured so far in our review of Latin American labour. Too down-trodden, dispersed, and parochially-minded to be an attractive target for unionization, and neglected by Marxist agitators in favour of the supposedly more revolutionary urban proletariat, they have in general remained on the fringes of the labour movement. In some countries, the landowners have made sure that the *campesinos* are forbidden by law to organize, or at least to link their organizations together on a national scale. Yet on occasion, though only for a limited time and purpose, the *campesinos* have shown considerable ability to organize in unions and to use the latter for pressing their aims. Agrarian *sindicatos* organized the take-over of the large estates and precipitated the Bolivian land reform of 1953. Prompted by the Trotskyist Hugo Blanco, *sindicatos* carried out agricultural strikes and land invasions on the Peruvian *altiplano* in 1963. The Ligas Camponesas led by Francisco Julião in north-east Brazil threatened revolution in the early 'sixties. In Chile, where rural unions were not fully recognized until 1967, the organized pressure which they are now able to exert is an important factor in the progress of the current agrarian reform. The *campesino*, in short, is unlikely to remain indefinitely on the sidelines as the struggle for social change in Latin America gathers momentum.

Where, in general, does the labour movement stand today on this crucial issue of social change? Is the working class in Latin America really the 'carrier of revolution' posited by Marxist theory, and are the unions its militant vanguard? Originally, the movement was one of protest against intolerably unjust conditions which it sought to change or at least ameliorate; violent strikes, terrorism, counter-terrorism, and harsh repression were the order of the day. But attitudes on both sides gradually changed. Governments, particularly 'populist' regimes like those of Perón and Vargas, and reformist parties such as Acción Democrática in Venezuela and APRA in Peru, found that the trade unions could make valuable political allies; unions discovered that they could gain more in wage increases and fringe benefits by making a deal with those in power than by seeking their overthrow. Latin America offers few cases of unions resisting a dictator's coup or a military take-over; it became their practice rather to come quickly to terms with their new masters. The fixer and the adroit, often corrupt, labour boss, rather than the leader with grass-root support amongst his fellow-workers, too often dominated the unions and secured for themselves and their followers what benefits they could. At worst, the unions have been little more than small cliques of parasitic officials and professional activists. Sometimes governments have bought off the unions at a price the country could not afford, thereby storing up trouble for any successors who attempted to rehabilitate run-down concerns (e.g. the tin-mines of Bolivia or the state-owned *frigorífico* works in Uruguay) by rationalizing labour costs. It cannot be said that the Latin American unions have failed to improve conditions for their members; but these improvements have often depended on political deals (which may be called off when a government changes) with scant regard to the community at large, or even to the less privileged sectors of the working class. Labour has been indifferent to the wider interests of society, as society has shown itself indifferent to those of labour.

Unionized labour has thus tended to become an élite primarily concerned with preserving and increasing its own privileges. The Mexican oil-workers, for instance, have managed to restrict entry to their well-paid employment to their own children. An immense gulf in living standards yawns between the unionized Chilean copper-miners or Venezuelan oil-workers and the mass of unskilled workers in their respective countries. The conditions which have given rise to the influx of migrant labour from the country to the cities, and the latter's rapid growth in contrast to the slow growth of industry, have already been discussed (see pages 218–19). One result of this trend has been to weaken the sense of working-class solidarity and to create a relatively prosperous unionized 'aristocracy' less concerned with changing the social order than with assuring its own place in it. The Latin American unions remain highly politicized, for the political game is the source of such power and well-being as they possess. But the scope allotted them is not unlimited; no Latin American government, for instance, would think of inviting union participation in working out its plans for economic policy. Nor have the unions the financial basis for independent action. The apparently invincible reluctance of Latin American workers to pay voluntary dues means that their unions must remain dependent on the state, which can deduct contributions at source, or on subsidies from foreign unions. The influence of the latter, though it may offer organizational experience and training facilities, is not, in any case, an unmixed blessing. The context in which the United States labour movement operates is entirely different from the Latin American, and the methods appropriate to the former may have little relevance to the latter. In labour questions, as in so many other fields, Latin America has problems and possibilities of its own and must find its own solutions.

3 Economic Problems

Latin America's economy is generally described as 'dependent'. From early colonial times, it has served primarily as a source of valuable minerals and natural commodities and as a market for the goods produced by more advanced countries. Even after her political emancipation, the economy of the area remained dependent on that of Europe and, later, on that of the United States. Industry was slow to develop, and grew up behind high tariff walls and in small, widely separated pockets. Today, as the technological gap between the developed and the developing nations widens, Latin America's industry finds difficulty in expanding and placing its products on the world market. The industrialized countries still need her raw materials, though alternative sources of supply and the invention of synthetic substitutes have lessened demand for them. The prices they fetch have accordingly not kept pace with the rising cost of the manufactures which Latin America needs to import. Development, starved of domestic capital and of foreign aid in the quantity and on the terms required, remains heavily dependent on foreign investment with its attendant political implications. Hence Latin America's mounting burden of debt repayment, her chronic shortage of foreign currency, and her balance of payments difficulties, the resentful awareness that she has not yet escaped from the cycle of under-development and economic dependence.

By the mid-'sixties the annual growth rate had slowed down to about 4·8 per cent—well below that of many industrialized countries, and less than half the rate for Japan. In population, however, Latin America has been growing faster than most other parts of the world (see page 224), tripling in the last half-century whereas that of the world as a whole has scarcely doubled. The result has been the erosion of the modest increase in productivity, to give only a niggardly 1·7 per cent annual increase in real terms of *per capita* income (1960–6). The latter was estimated (early 1969) as around 410 dollars—about one seventh that of the United States, or one fifth that of Western Europe. Low as it is, the average conceals the fact that about half Latin America's population have a yearly income which is nearer to 120 dollars, whilst that of the wealthiest 5 per cent of the population averages 2,600; the same 5 per cent accounts for about three tenths of the region's total consumption, whilst half the population consumes only one fifth. The overall figure for the growth rate in Latin America's *per capita* product likewise conceals wide differences between countries (e.g., Brazil's was 2·1 and Venezuela's 2 per cent from 1955 to 1964, whilst Bolivia's was 0·4 and Haiti's −0·9 per cent). The gap between the

United States and the wealthier Latin American countries is less than that between the latter and their poorer sister republics.

Agriculture

(i) *Stagnation—causes and cures.* From the appearance of the first pre-Columbian maize-based civilizations, down to the modern export-orientated production of coffee, sugar, bananas, wheat, and livestock products, agriculture has been basic to the economy of Latin America. It still provides the livelihood for over 42 per cent of the population (1969) and accounts for a considerable share of the gross domestic product; about one third in the more backward countries (e.g. Haiti, Honduras), and less than one fifth only in Brazil, Peru, Uruguay, Argentina, Chile, Mexico, and Venezuela. Even in Brazil, with its booming industries, it still contributes nearly one third to the gross national product. Many of Latin America's economic ills have been attributed to the relatively slow expansion (3·2 per cent annually) of its agriculture compared with the rapid growth of its population. Surpluses previously available for export have had to be diverted to feed the growing number of mouths at home. The upshot has therefore been that whilst *per capita* output in agriculture has gone up in most regions of the world since the pre-war period it has actually declined in Latin America by some 8 per cent. Only in three of Latin America's twenty republics (Venezuela, Mexico, and Guatemala) has output increased appreciably faster than population. Most marked has been the failure of the livestock sector to keep pace with the growth in human population. Countries which should be able to produce more than enough for their own needs have thus found themselves obliged to spend valuable foreign exchange on importing foodstuffs. Yet, if Latin America is to be able to feed the hundred million or so new mouths which may be expected to appear before the end of the decade, and to raise the subnormal standards of the already large underprivileged sector of its population, ways must be found of overcoming this agricultural stagnation and raising production to a level which the experts put at least at 4·3 per cent a year. To achieve this target is technically possible, though the obstacles are formidable.

What accounts for this stagnation, and how can it be overcome? Excessive pressure of population on limited land resources can hardly lie at the root of the trouble, as in much of overcrowded Asia and Africa. Though Latin America's rapid rate of population increase is now changing it for the worse, the land/man ratio stands at the not unfavourable figure of over four hectares of agricultural land, or about one hectare of land under crops, per head of rural population. About one quarter of the total land surface of the sub-continent is utilized, albeit often only extensively, for agriculture, but only about one twentieth of the total for crops. It has been estimated that this area could be increased perhaps two and a half times, though much would probably remain fit for nothing more than light grazing, and it is doubtful whether the soil which is now covered by vast forests would really support crops.

Such rise in agricultural production as has occurred in parts of Latin

America has generally been due to bringing new land under cultivation, but the limits of this potential source of increase have now in some cases nearly been reached. A more pressing need is to increase yields. This can be done by such measures as introducing higher bearing strains (as in Mexico, where a dramatic trebling in the wheat yield occurred between 1948/52 and 1965), and improving farming techniques. The use of fertilizers, a key factor in expanding productivity, is still very limited; though it has increased fairly rapidly in recent years, it still remains less than one quarter that of the per hectare average in developed countries. In many parts of Latin America the hoe continues to be the basic farm tool. Mechanization is still in its early stages; the number of tractors used per hectare of arable land in Argentina, which has more than any other Latin American country, is still only one fifth that of Canada, or one ninth that of the United States. One reason for this lag is the high cost of agricultural machinery; even where manufactured locally, as in Argentina, a tractor will cost the equivalent of 1,300 quintals of wheat, as compared with only 315 quintals in Britain.

The claim is now often made that there is one infallible formula which will put an end to agricultural stagnation: Land Reform. There is hardly a government in Latin America today which has not its Agrarian Reform Law, in some form or other, on the statute book. The old *hacienda* system, as we have seen (see pages 228–32), has certainly proved oppressive and anachronistic and there is a strong case for its suppression on grounds of social justice. But it cannot be assumed that Land Reform, in its basic sense of the expropriation of large privately owned properties, must automatically lead to increased agricultural production. The lesson of Latin America's three most radical agrarian reforms, those of Mexico, Bolivia, and Cuba, suggests rather that the immediate result will be a *fall* in production, with the *possibility* of a subsequent increase. Mexico had to wait until the 'fifties before reaching a high and sustained agricultural growth rate, Bolivia's production did not pick up until a decade after her Reform, whilst Cuba only managed to surpass her pre-Revolutionary peak through a massive national mobilization for the 1970 harvest. Agrarian Reform, it would seem, may be a pre-requisite for economic growth, but provides no easy short cut to it. It needs to be conceived in the broadest sense; not merely in terms of the redistribution of ownership, which may lead either to the problem of the *minifundio* or, at the other extreme, to inefficient state farms, but as part and parcel of a country's overall development process, in which industrialization has an important part to play and the backward rural population is integrated fully into the life of the nation.

(ii) *Food crops*. The basic crops which sustained the life of pre-Columbian man were maize (Mexico, Central America, and parts of Peru) and tubers (potatoes in the High Andes and manioc in the tropical forest lowlands). Manioc, the root of the cassava plant, is today largely confined to Brazil, where it remains a staple food. Potatoes, America's most lavish gift to man's food supply, are still widely cultivated in their place of origin and in the temperate south, but now make up no more than 2 per cent of world production. Maize remains by far the most important cereal, exceeding wheat in volume by more than two and a half times, and doing particularly well in Central Mexico, Guatemala, south Brazil, and the humid parts of the Argentine *pampa*. Total output has been rising, thanks mainly to an increase in the area under cultivation which expanded from fourteen to twenty million hectares during the 'fifties. Except in certain localities such as Chile, where the introduction of a new hybrid variety more than doubled output in a decade and a half, there has been little improvement in yields, which remain at only about one quarter of the level in the United States. Wheat yields, on the other hand, have shown marked improvement, especially in Argentina, Latin America's main producer, and Mexico, which nearly tripled its output in a decade, and stand at about world average.

Rice, which owes its relatively recent introduction into Latin America to immigrants from Asia, has doubled its production since the last war and yields, though still below world average, are increasing. It is grown mainly in Brazil and the coastal zones of Cuba, Peru, and Ecuador. Following a drop in prices in the 'forties, a new crop began to be cultivated in the latter country on a large scale—bananas. Thanks to their high carbohydrate content, bananas can be a basic food in primitive communities and thrive in tropical lowlands. As a commercial crop, they are less satisfactory, since they are perishable, liable to disease, and easily damaged in transport. Though Ecuador remains the world's chief exporter of bananas it has latterly been losing ground to Honduras, Panama, and Costa Rica, which are better placed to supply the important United States market. In a drive to make their product more competitive, Ecuadorean producers have been reducing the size of their plantations and replacing the traditional Gros Michel plants with the higher yielding, disease-resistant Cavendish variety now popular in Central America. The EEC and Britain have their own preferential arrangements with Ecuador's competitors, and though Ecuadorean exports to the EEC actually did better in the 'sixties than those from the associated Yaoundé territories, the struggle to maintain her position in world markets is hard.

(iii) *Coffee*. If coffee no longer rules as absolute king, it is still dominant in the economies of several Latin American countries. At the turn of the century, Brazil was producing more than three quarters of the world's supply; by the end of the 'sixties, her share had fallen to well under one third. Prosperity built on coffee is precarious. A fall of only one cent in the price of a pound of coffee may cost Brazil or Colombia a 4 per cent drop in their gold and foreign currency reserves and cause a loss of many millions of dollars. A rise in prices results in quick fortunes and a rush to plant new bushes which, when they mature four years later, may lead to over-production and eventual slump. Brazil's coffee production oscillated from a peak of nearly 44 million bags in 1959/60 to little more than 10 million in 1964/5. The need to maintain prices and stabilize production led in 1962 to the conclusion between thirty-eight exporting and twenty-three importing countries of an International Coffee Agreement. This grew out of an arrangement previously reached amongst the Latin American countries themselves, and assigned yearly export quotas for traditional markets to each supplier (18 million bags to Brazil, rather more than 6 million to Colombia, and nearly one million to Costa Rica). The Brazilian Coffee Institute, by means of 'valorization' (stock-piling), large-scale uprooting and replanting with better-yielding plants, and the promotion of crop diversification, has kept the accumulation of surpluses within bounds and so avoided a repetition of the monstrous destruction of some 73 million bags which occurred between 1931 and 1943.

Problems nevertheless remain. Other countries have not made Brazil's strenuous efforts to cut back production, and some have found means of evading their quota restrictions. Brazil, who herself has areas of cheap production (Paraná) and the higher cost, higher quality areas of São Paulo, faces the challenge of the cheaply produced, strongly flavoured *robustas* which are generally preferred for the preparation of soluble coffee. The growing world demand for the latter has brought new opportunities to Brazil, since it offers one way of moving on from the mere production of primary commodities to a manufacturing process based on those commodities. It also led, however, to friction with the United States, whose manufacturers complained that they were handicapped unfairly by having to make their product from green coffee purchased at quota prices, whereas their Brazilian competitors made theirs from beans purchased on the cheaper domestic market. Other changes too have been occurring in the pattern of production and demand. Brazilian growers have seen their crops threatened by the deadly fungus known as coffee rust, which once destroyed Ceylon's coffee industry. For her own needs, Brazil requires some 8 to 9 million bags annually, and more than another 17 million if she is to fulfil her export quota. She has also been vigorously searching for new markets outside the quota area (e.g. in Japan and the Communist countries). With her production down to 20 million bags a year (1969/70) she has been steadily dipping into stocks. In the 'seventies coffee may be in short supply and a new cycle of higher prices leading in turn to increased and perhaps over-production could well be set in train.

(iv) *Sugar*. Sugar is grown for home consumption in every country of Latin America (in the form of cane, except in Chile which has beet). It is dominant in the economy of Cuba, the world's leading producer for export, and important in a number of others (Brazil, Colombia, Peru, Mexico, and the Dominican Republic). Since World War II, world production has grown rapidly. About half the volume destined for export is disposed of under special arrangements such as the Commonwealth Sugar Agreement, the United States quota system, and the Cuban–Soviet Sugar Agreement of 1964. The rest is sold on the free market and, unless controlled by mutual agreement, is subject to wide fluctuations in price. Following the 1961 breakdown of the International Sugar Agreement, which had been relatively successful in achieving equitable and stable prices by the allocation amongst the producing countries of export quotas linked to prices, the latter veered erratically from over twelve to less that two cents per pound. The 1968 Sugar Conference, attended by some seventy countries under United Nations auspices, restored a precarious

equilibrium and negotiated the following quotas (1969–71) for the main Latin
American producers:

	Tons
Cuba	2,150,000
Brazil	500,000
Colombia	164,000
Dominican Republic	75,000
Peru	50,000

The crisis on the world sugar market stemmed largely from the internal and
external policies followed by Cuba. Arguing that the loss of her quota for the
United States market entitled her to a larger share of the free world market,
Cuba sold more than her allotted world quota and waited in confidence for
the resulting price collapse to drive her competitors, who could produce less
cheaply, off the market. The placing of the bulk of her own production was
assured under the 1964 Sugar Agreement with the Soviet Union, who undertook to buy Cuban sugar at the fixed rate of six cents a pound, to the extent of
three million tons in 1966, four millions in 1967, and five millions in 1968,
1969, and 1970. Cuba's need of foreign currency also made her anxious to
retain as large a share as she could of the free world market. Her own lagging
production has not, in fact, enabled her to supply both the quota promised to
the Soviet Union and the quota to which she is entitled on the free market. In
the event of the annual target of ten million tons being reached in the 'seventies,
she might, if she chose, again attempt to flood the market with low-priced
sugar to the detriment of her Latin American and other competitors. Production, however, has so far remained well below the annual targets set:

Cuban sugar production 1959–70 (millions of tons)

Year	Target	Actual production
1959		5·96
1960		5·86
1961		6·76
1962		4·81
1963		3·88
1964		4·47
1965	6	6·15
1966	6·5	4·53
1967	7·5	6·23
1968	8	5·16
1969	9	4·45
1970	10	8·51
1971	7 (reduced to 6·65)	5·9

(v) *Other products.* Cotton is grown in the humid tropics and under irrigation
in drier areas, both for export and for home consumption in the textile mills
which generally form an important part of the first stage of a country's industrialization. Yields have shown a far more satisfactory rate of increase than in

most sectors of Latin America's agriculture. Brazil and Mexico are the leading exporters, followed by Central America, where in the 'fifties cotton grew rapidly to become Nicaragua's major export crop and second only to coffee in El Salvador and Guatemala. Peru's long stapled cotton and the crops grown in northern Mexico have become noted for their quality. Wool is produced mainly in Uruguay, where it provides the chief source of national income, in the drier fringes of the Argentine *pampa*, and further south in Patagonia and Tierra del Fuego. Though Argentina has much the same sheep population as New Zealand, and Uruguay somewhat less than half, wool yields are very much lower, and little has been done to raise them by pasture improvement or feed concentrates.

Latin America's livestock population has increased very little in the last decade (an annual 2·6 per cent) and at a considerably slower rate than her human population. Yet, as living standards rise in the industrialized countries and the need for a more nutritious diet for her own people is recognized, the demand for meat is certain to rise. The market could probably absorb an annual growth rate of 4·6 per cent. The achievement of such a target would mark a turning point in Latin America's development and is technically possible. Large areas, such as the *pampa* of Argentina, Uruguay, and south Brazil, have proved themselves admirably suited to stock-raising and, given the necessary technological and financial resources, important new centres of production may also soon make their appearance. Castro has claimed, for instance, that Cuba could become a major exporter of high quality meat and promising results have already been obtained there through experiments in cross-breeding and new forms of feeding from sugar derivatives. But to build up Latin America's herds to the required levels will take time—perhaps as long as twenty years—and require heavy investment and a determined effort to raise general standards of herd management, to expand and improve the area under pasture, to improve stock, and to eliminate diseases such as brucellosis and foot-and-mouth.

The prevalence of the latter disease has contributed to the decline in the volume of Argentina's meat exports to Britain, which comprised about two thirds of Argentine shipments after World War II, but fell to one third in 1965 and little more than a quarter in 1968. The broad acres of Argentina support more than fifty million head of cattle, which account for 700,000 tons of meat exports a year and a quarter of all her foreign exchange earnings. In the north and west of the country (but not in the south) foot-and-mouth is endemic, and though the healthy climate and a campaign of vaccination keeps it in check, the disease shows no sign of being stamped out. Following the outbreak of a severe epidemic in the United Kingdom in October 1967, suspicion fell on Argentine meat, especially chilled lamb, as the source of infection, and a ban on the import of all further consignments was imposed. Although this was lifted from beef imports four months later, trade was slow to pick up, as Argentine exporters felt aggrieved not only at the slur cast on the quality of their meat, but at the (for them) unsatisfactory practice of auctioning their produce for whatever it would fetch at Smithfield instead of selling at fixed prices before shipment. When Argentine beef exports to Britain were resumed, they took the form of quick-frozen, pre-packed boneless cuts (for bone is the carrier of suspected infection) instead of the traditional sides of chilled beef. After the serious interruption of 1967/8, trade quickly picked up, to the mutual satisfaction of both trading partners, along these new lines. In a world increasingly hungry for meat, beef of Argentina's superb quality can hardly fail to command a market, and the need at present is rather to build up the herds and increase production.

Fishing is an industry which has been making an increasing contribution to Latin America's food supplies and export earnings. The mid-'fifties saw the remarkable development in Peru (to be followed on a much smaller scale by Chile) of a new industry based on the catching of vast shoals of anchovies and their processing into fish-meal (a valuable component in animal foodstuffs) and oil for use in cooking fats and margarine. By 1964, a total catch of nearly nine million tons put Peru ahead of Japan as the world's leading fishing nation. The new industry is not however without its problems. The marine gold-rush led to over-production, price fluctuations, and the bankruptcy of small firms unable to produce the higher levels of technological and managerial efficiency which the industry now demands; many were under-capitalized, expanded rapidly on borrowed money, and proved unable to weather any storm. There is an urgent need to ensure that over-fishing does not upset the delicate ecological balance by depleting the food supplies of the myriad sea-birds on which Peru's still valuable *guano* industry depends. Thought is now also being given to the possibility of adapting fish-meal for human consumption, since its rich protein content would make a welcome addition to the wretchedly inadequate diet of much of Peru's population.

Mining and minerals

Since its discovery, America has always been prized for its minerals. The gold which once dazzled Europe accounts for only about 5 per cent of world production today, and silver (still mined in Mexico and Peru) for some 40 per cent. Latin America's mineral wealth now comes primarily from its petroleum, copper, and tin (which are considered separately below) and from other minerals: nickel (Cuba), platinum and emeralds (Colombia), quartz crystals (of which Brazil is almost the sole source), manganese and phosphates (Brazil and Mexico), sulphur (Mexico), zinc and lead (Mexico, Peru, and Bolivia). Some minerals, such as nitrates, once in great demand, have now either dwindled in volume or been challenged by substitutes. Others, such as coal (found in Colombia, Chile, Mexico, and in Brazil) are poor in quality and limited in quantity. Iron, the sinews of industry, is mined mainly in Brazil and Venezuela, and to a lesser extent in Chile and Peru, whilst Bolivia is believed to have important undeveloped deposits (El Mutún).

(i) *Oil.* Oil is of key importance both in the economies and in the politics of the Latin American countries. It supplies some 75 per cent of all their energy

Latin America's Oil

Country	Year when production began	Crude oil production	Refinery capacity (millions of tons—1968)	Export of crude oil	State corporation	Date of foundation	Chief foreign companies still operating	Major nationalizations
Venezuela	1917	188·4	60·1	118	CVP	1960	Standard Oil of NJ, Shell, Gulf, Texaco, Sun, Mobil	—
Mexico	1901	20	24·8	—	PEMEX	1938	Standard Oil of NJ, Shell	1938
Argentina	1907	17·18	25	—	YPF	1922	Cities Services, Shell, Sinclair, Cities Services	—
Colombia	1921	8·9	6·1	5·07	ECOPETROL	1948	BP, Texaco, Chevron	—
Brazil	1940	7·9	20·5	—	PETROBRAS	1953		
Peru	1896	4·2	4·2	0·27	EPF	1934	Lobitos	1968
Bolivia	1950	2·2	0·7	0·3	YBFP	1936		1937, 1969
Chile	1929	1·7	4·6	—	ENAP	1950	Shell, Esso, Texaco, Gulf	—
Ecuador	1917	0·3	0·9	0·08	CEPE	1970	Anglo-Ecuadorean	—
Cuba	1881	0·1	4·5	—	ICP	1959	—	1960

requirements and is basic to their economic development. That this key should rest in the hands of foreign interests, who siphon off allegedly exorbitant profits, make their own decisions in matters of vital concern to the countries where they operate, and may exert pressure by threatening to withhold fuel supplies or marketing facilities, is intolerable to national self-respect. That the Latin American governments receive from these same international oil companies some 2,000 million dollars of annual revenue and rely on them, to varying degrees, for the production, refining, or distribution of their oil, makes this dependence the more galling. Latin American governments have accordingly mounted against the oil companies a prolonged offensive on several fronts: (*a*) pressure to pay higher royalty rates and generally hand over a larger share of their profits. Venezuela has taken the lead in this, negotiating in 1943 the 'fifty-fifty' basis which became generally adopted by other producing countries, and then raising the proportion in 1958 to a ratio of 60/40 to its own advantage, and finally to the 70/30 which is thought to be the practicable maximum. (*b*) Nationalizing the oil companies, or, if this is not feasible, tightening up control over them and reducing their field of operations. Here Mexico blazed the trail in 1938 with the expropriation of the British and United States oil companies. Peru followed suit belatedly in 1968 with the nationalization of IPC, and Bolivia with that of Gulf Oil in 1969, whilst Cuba took over her foreign oil refineries in 1960. (*c*) The formation of state oil enterprises. All countries, with the sole exception so far of Paraguay, now have entities of this nature, though some may handle only refining and distribution, not production. (*d*) Co-operation between the state enterprises, with the possibility of ultimately forming a Latin American Petroleum Authority, on the pattern of the Coal and Steel Community in Western Europe, which would control and direct all oil production, refining, and intra-Latin American trade. Five years after the foundation of the Organization of Petroleum Exporting Countries (OPEC), formed on Venezuelan initiative in 1960 to strengthen the developing nations' bargaining power, a specifically Latin American association (ARPEC) was set up and has been holding regular meetings with a view to co-ordinating oil policies in the sub-continent.

Venezuela is still the world's main exporter of crude oil, though her share of world exports has fallen from about one third (1956) to less than one fifth (1968). She is now under competitive pressure from such new exporters as Libya and Nigeria, who can produce more cheaply, and she will shortly face the additional challenge of the new Alaskan oil-fields. Though production has now surpassed its 1957 peak, there has been little exploration or fresh development since that year. Venezuela's subsoil may still have new stores of mineral wealth to yield, but her present 'proved reserves' are expected to reach exhaustion in the 'eighties. More than three quarters of Venezuela's production is in the hands of three foreign companies. Nationalist opinion has so far stopped short of demanding the latter's nationalization, but the State has taken over development of the promising young natural gas industry which may one day rival oil as a source of the nation's wealth. The government's immediate preoccupation is to arrest the decline of oil exports to Venezuela's main customer, the United States, which dropped from 60 per cent of the latter's oil imports in 1958 to less than 42 per cent in 1968. Venezuela resents the preferential treatment granted by the United States to her Mexican and Canadian competitors, and does not accept the argument that restrictions have to be imposed in view of the high sulphur content of Venezuelan oil which contravenes United States anti-air pollution legislation.

Mexico, after a period of dislocation and reduced production following the 1938 nationalization of the foreign companies, proved its ability to run its own oil industry and steadily increased output until becoming Latin America's most important producer of oil after Venezuela. PEMEX has become the most successful and sophisticated of the state corporations and—though extreme nationalist opinion may look askance at the association—has gone into partnership with foreign firms as a means of increasing its technological efficiency and building up a flourishing petro-technical industry. Until 1960, PEMEX gave priority to building up Mexico's refining capacity but has latterly invested heavily in exploration and prospecting and the country is now assured of ample resources for its further development.

Argentina remains with the dilemma of either entrusting its state corporation with a monopoly of oil production or accepting the foreign collaboration which results in stepping up production and saving the foreign exchange otherwise spent on petroleum imports, but is liable to provoke outbursts of nationalist resentment. Perón's overthrow in 1955, and that of Frondizi in 1962, and even the ousting of President Illia who had revoked the Frondizi concessions, were in part due to such outbursts. Present legislation (1967) permits foreign companies to operate under carefully prescribed conditions. Production now almost covers domestic needs, and extensive reserves have been discovered, mainly in Mendoza, the chief oil-bearing province.

Oil has also been a lively issue in Brazil. 'The oil is ours' proved an effective slogan in returning Vargas to power in 1950 and his creation of PETROBRÁS three years later gave Brazil the most powerful of its state entities. Though little progress has been made towards making Brazil self-sufficient in oil and production remains a monopoly of PETROBRÁS, private enterprise is now permitted to participate in the refining and petro-chemical industries.

Colombia experienced a decline in oil production during the 'sixties, but expects to restore an upward trend once the new transandine pipe-line provides an outlet for the oil-fields recently discovered in her eastern Putomayo province.

Ecuador, in addition to her small coastal oil-field, is also believed to have extensive reserves in the remote jungles of her Oriente Province bordering on the Colombian oil-fields. The government has recently established a state petroleum corporation, but the exploitation of these new resources rests chiefly in the hands of a Texaco–Gulf consortium which is building a pipe-line from the eastern oil-fields to the Pacific port of Esmeraldas.

The problem for land-locked Bolivia has been to find outlets for the products of the rich oil-fields in her eastern lowlands. Standard Oil, which had carried out extensive exploration and some production in the 'twenties and 'thirties, was denounced by Paraguay for inciting Bolivia against her in the Chaco War, and was in turn later accused by Bolivia, who expropriated the company in 1937 on the charge that it had secretly favoured Paraguay. The Petroleum Code introduced by the MNR government in 1955 permitted foreign companies to operate again in addition to the state corporation. The discovery by the Bolivian Gulf Oil Company of rich new deposits of oil and gas led to the construction of the Sica-Sica pipe-line (completed in 1960 but only opened in 1966), transporting oil across the Andes to Arica in Chile, and to plans for another pipe-line which would bring Bolivian gas to the Argentine border. The expropriation of Bolivian Gulf by General Ovando's government in 1969, though welcome to nationalist opinion, posed new problems for the marketing of Bolivia's oil and the completion of her new pipe-line.

Chile's oil-fields are in the remote south, in Tierra del Fuego, from where the crude makes the long haul to refineries near Concepción and Valparaíso. The state corporation enjoys a monopoly of exploration, production, and refining.

Cuba previously imported its crude oil from Venezuela and processed it in three foreign-owned refineries. These were nationalized in 1960 after refusing to refine the crude oil which Castro determined to import from the Soviet Union. The latter has subsequently supplied virtually all Cuba's fuel requirements, which have risen from little more than three million tons a year before the Revolution to around five million. Cuba's subsoil may be rich in oil, but intensive prospecting has so far met with little success and domestic production probably still falls far short of the quarter-million tons a year target set for 1970.

Since the expropriation of IPC (see page 161), which had been responsible for almost all refining and well over half the country's output of crude oil (British-owned Lobitos accounting for another third), Peru's oil operations are now increasingly in the hands of the state corporation. There is still a considerable gap between domestic production and the country's needs. It remains to be seen whether the nationalist policies of the government will allow them to grant new concessions to foreign companies for the exploitation of the rich deposits which almost certainly exist east of the Andes and possibly also off-shore.

(ii) *Copper*. After petroleum, Latin America's most important mineral, in terms of output and export earnings, is copper. Chile has long been in the lead as a producer and possesses what seem to be the largest reserves in the world, though no one yet knows the full potential of southern Peru (Cuajone) or of the vast deposits recently discovered in Panama's inaccessible rain forests and in Mexico's Sonora province. In the middle of the last century, Chile was the world's foremost producer and accounted for one third of world output. By the First World War, her share had dwindled to a mere 4 per cent. Following the introduction of the new 'flotation' process, production then rose to 20 per cent of world output, but declined again to little more than half that figure in the mid-'fifties. Production is now once more on the up-grade, and Chile competes with Zambia for second place (after the United States) in the non-Communist world. When her current expansion programme is completed in the early 'seventies, she should again be in the lead with an annual output of nearly one and a quarter million tons.

The modern development of Chilean copper mining has been largely the work of two United States parent companies, Anaconda and Kennecott, whose subsidiaries, including the enormous open-cast mine of Chuquicamata (Anaconda) in the northern deserts and the astonishing cone of copper ore at El Teniente (Kennecott) near Rancagua, accounted for more than four fifths of Chilean production. So powerful a stake in the nation's key industry was bound to lead to a clamour for nationalization, much as nationalist sentiment elsewhere demanded the expropriation of foreign oil companies. When, however, President Frei's administration came to power in 1964, it was with a programme of 'chileanization'—partnership, by means of joint enterprises, and a share in profits, investments, management, and policy-making. Agreements in this respect were concluded in 1966 in regard to El Teniente, and in 1969 for Chuquicamata, the Chilean state obtaining a 51 per cent interest in the enterprises, with payments to be spread over twelve years, and with provision for the purchase of the remaining 49 per cent at prices calculated according to a complex formula based on profits. The state also secured a share in joint enterprises set up to operate the promising Río Blanco, Exótica, and other mines and undertook to participate in an ambitious programme of investment and modernization. Another significant initiative of the Christian Democrat administration was the foundation of CIPEC, an international association of copper-producing states (Chile, Peru, Zambia, and the Congo) on the lines of the oil-producers' OPEC, for the exchange of information and co-ordination of policies.

A fateful new chapter for Chilean copper opened in 1970 with the advent of the Popular Front government. The latter was pledged to outright nationalization instead of 'chileanization', and legislation to this effect was passed through Congress in May 1971. Threatening clouds now hung over the industry. The previous high price of copper had led important customers, the car manufacturers, to give fresh thought to the use of substitutes. Then came a fall in copper prices induced by the prospect of an end to the war in Vietnam, rumours of the unloading of America's stock-pile and general uncertainty as to the future of the industry and the nature of American reactions in the event of an inadequate offer of compensation. There ensued a fall in production at the larger mines owing to labour troubles and the exodus of many highly qualified technicians. This led to the State's 'intervention' of the El Teniente mine without waiting for formal nationalization. Further dislocation of the Chilean copper industry seemed likely to occur before popular aspirations for the 'recovery of the nation's natural resources' could be realized and production expanded as planned.

(iii) *Tin*. Bolivia, the world's greatest producer of silver during the colonial period, entered upon a new phase of mining activity at the end of the nineteenth century, when the canning industry stimulated a demand for the tin which had once been regarded as mere dross incidental to the extraction of silver. With the help of English capital, Bolivia was soon producing 10 per cent of the world's tin, the bulk of its output being in the hands of the Patiño, Aramayo, and Hochschild families. Following the 1952 Revolution, these three enterprises were nationalized and merged into the Bolivian Mining Corporation (COMIBOL), smaller companies being left in private hands but subject to some control through the state Mining Bank. Nationalization occurred at a time when tin prices were falling as a result of the end of the war in Korea and the competition of low-cost production in Africa and Asia was making itself felt. The weaknesses of Bolivia's tin industry were soon revealed. The inaccessibility of her mines meant heavy transport and operating costs. The tin content of the ore averaged only 2 per cent and needed to be separated from other minerals by a complex process before the concentrates so formed were despatched, mostly to Britain, for final smelting. The industry was further handicapped by lack of reserves, shortage of managerial talent, and an inflated and excessively politicized labour force, whose support the government was unwilling to forfeit by taking unpopular but necessary measures to make the mines viable. COMIBOL's labour force rose from 24,000 in 1951 to over 36,500 in 1956, whilst *per capita* productivity and exports declined.

In 1961 an attempt was made to put the industry on a sounder footing by a massive injection of capital subscribed under a 'triangular operation' by the United States, West Germany, and the IADB. This resulted in some increased production, but by 1965, tin exports had fallen to a new low level of little more than 17,000 tons, labour accounting for four fifths of the production costs and the latter standing, in one of the largest mines (Siglo Veinte), at about 50 per cent above the quotation on the London tin market. Following the 1964 take-over by General Barrientos, the army attempted to settle matters by occupying the mines, smashing the unions, and enforcing wage cuts and labour discipline. These drastic expedients led to some increase in production and reduction in cost but have brought no lasting solution to the dilemma that Bolivian tin is a high-cost industry which can only remain competitive on the world market if costs, including wages, are kept to levels hardly consonant with social justice and human dignity. National pride insists, furthermore, that Bolivian tin must no longer be smelted by foreign interests but on her own soil. Bolivia now has her first smelter, at Vinto, near Oruro, but its operating costs are high and its capacity is limited to about one quarter of the country's annual output of tin. Further expansion of capacity is planned; in the meantime, the industry is pinning its hopes on a continuation of the high prices now obtaining on the world market and on the interest latterly shown by the Soviet Union in Bolivia's tin.

Transport

Poor communications have been amongst the chief obstacles to Latin America's economic and political development. The astounding network of Inca roads remained the sub-continent's one great achievement in this field until the modern era of railway construction, motor-highways, and air transport. Even today glaring deficiencies remain. Few South American capitals are linked by rail. Only one major road runs between central Chile and neighbouring Argentina, and that is closed for much of the winter. It generally costs more to send a cargo of goods across the continent than to Europe or the United States. Almost all the centres of the extractive and other industries are located within a relatively short distance of sea or waterway: where this is not the case (e.g. with Bolivia's tin mines) industry is hampered by high costs. Lack of good communications accounts to a large extent for the meagre volume of intra-Latin American trade and the differentiation of regional and nationalist loyalties. To improve communications is thus a pre-condition for any closer integration of Latin America (see below, page 328).

Long before Columbus sailed into the Caribbean, sea and river had served as important means of communication in the New World and continue to play this role today. South America possesses three major river-systems: the Amazon, the Paraguay-Paraná, and the Orinoco. Traffic on the Amazon reached its zenith with the rubber-boom of the last century. Ocean-going vessels still ply to Manaus, nearly one thousand miles from the Atlantic. With the introduction of new forms of transport such as the Hovercraft, which was tried out successfully in 1968 in a round trip up the Amazon and the Río Negro and back down the Orinoco, the huge internal maze of waterways, now hazardous through swamps, floods, and rapids, may one day be opened to more regular navigation. Grandiose plans have even been considered for opening up the whole interior of South America through a system of enormous, inter-connected inland lakes formed by building a chain of low dams between the ridges through which the myriad tributaries of the Amazon now flow. Less visionary are Venezuela's plans to make the Orinoco the main artery for her new industrial zone in Guayana and the concerted efforts to develop the River Plate basin (see page 330). Another important waterway, though the volume of traffic carried is not comparable to that of the River Plate, is the Magdalena–Cauca, which has long provided Colombia with her chief axis of communications. That country may in time also come to possess a second important waterway if current plans come to fruition in her Choco province, adjacent to the Panamanian border, for an artificial lake connecting the rivers Atrato and San Juan, which flow respectively into the Atlantic and the Pacific. This would create a new inter-oceanic highway and provide a hydro-electric complex serving the development of this hitherto neglected region.

Sea-borne traffic has also been of great importance, particularly to those countries like Brazil, Argentina, and Chile which have long coastlines. In maritime no less than overland transport Latin America has had to contend with daunting obstacles, such as the almost total lack of natural harbours on her west coast and the dominant position of the great maritime powers in oceanic trade. After World War II, the Latin American countries attempted to increase their share of this trade by writing into their commercial agreements a 'transport clause' recognizing the right of each party to carry in its own ships up to half of the goods traded. Though the lack of shipping space brought little but theoretical advantage to the Latin American countries, the clause was not to the liking of their trading partners and it fell into disuse. Measures subsequently envisaged, either unilaterally or under LAFTA arrangements, to increase the Latin American countries' share of the carrying trade have laid them open to charges of flag discrimination. Nevertheless, an expansion of their maritime capacities—modernization of ports, enlargement of merchant fleets, etc.—seems indispensable for their economic development, and some countries have already taken energetic steps in this direction. Cuba, for instance, multiplied her merchant tonnage sixfold within the first seven years of her revolutionary regime. Brazil, as befits her size, has the most ambitious programme of ship construction, with a target of achieving four million tons—more than all the rest of Latin America's merchant shipping combined—by the mid-'seventies.

Latin America is poorly served by its railways. Though they have twice the length of Canada's track they carry less than half the Canadian railways' volume of freight. Rather than one integrated system, they comprise a number of small, disconnected networks or single lines, operating on several gauges, under different owners, and with varying degrees of efficiency. Argentina possesses most mileage—nearly one third of Latin America's total—the lines chiefly radiating from Buenos Aires like the spokes of a wheel. Brazil comes next, with a concentration of lines in the coffee-producing state of São Paulo and in Minas Gerais, but with recent extensions designed to link the older centres of population with Brasília and to provide outlets for the country's growing iron and steel industry. Mexico City lies at the hub of a local network and of lines linking the capital with the Pacific and Atlantic coasts and with the important markets of North America. Cuba and Central Chile are not inadequately served, the first partly with railways built by the sugar companies, and the second with local services round the capital and with longitudinal lines reaching out north and south into her elongated territory. The builders of the railways had to contend with formidable natural obstacles. The lines linking Chile and Argentina over the towering bulk of the Andes, and those climbing up from Lima, Arica, and Antofagasta onto the *altiplano*, were marvels of engineering in their day but remain costly to operate and maintain.

Despite the great contribution which they have made to Latin America's development, the railways have come under nationalist attack for having primarily served the interests of exporters concerned with conveying their products out of the country and for having neglected their function of helping to integrate the nation by linking the centres of population in the hinterland and promoting local development (see page 315). With few exceptions (until recently, the Bolivia–Antofagasta Railway and Costa Rica's Northern Railway) major lines are now nationally owned, the foreign companies having been bought out with funds accumulated during World War II (see page 187). With their ownership, governments have acquired a number of formidable problems. Much of the equipment and rolling stock is now antiquated and in urgent need of costly rehabilitation. Some stretches of the line are uneconomical and should be closed. In some countries (e.g. Argentina) the labour force employed on the railways is vastly inflated, but its reduction poses grave social and political problems.

In most parts of Latin America, the construction of new roads has been far outstripping that of railways. Impressive modern highways (not always located where they can best serve the country's economic needs) have been sponsored by dictators eager to demonstrate the benefits they confer upon their peoples and by statesmen fired by the dream of continental unification. The most ambitious project of the latter sort is the Pan-American Highway, starting at the Mexican–United States border and designed to link together all the capitals of Latin America, governments being responsible for their own national sectors though able to draw on the financial and technical help of the United States and various international agencies. This network is now more or less complete, except for the 'Darien Gap', some five hundred miles of waterlogged jungle south of Panama City. Another great project, which may prove to have even more far-reaching economic consequences, is the Bolívar Highway of the Jungle's Edge (Carretera Marginal) designed to run for nearly 6,000 miles from Ciudad Bolívar on the Orinoco to Brazil's Atlantic port of Paranaguá, with a spur branching off through Bolivia to the Argentine frontier. Access roads are planned from the capitals of the four Andean countries to join the Carretera Marginal as it threads its way over the eastern slopes of the Andes. If this grandiose piece of infrastructure is ever completed it would not only permit the economic exploitation of the rich but neglected eastern territories of the Andean republics but would link the whole Andean glacis, and the upper reaches of the Amazon and Orinoco–Apure river systems, with the River Plate basin. Brazil too has her own ambitious project, the Trans-Amazonian Highway, designed to open up her vast jungle territories in the Amazon valley.

Aviation has proved a boon to the under-developed regions of the world, and to none more so than Latin America. In the person of Santos Dumont, famous in his native Brazil as the 'Father of Flight', the sub-continent boasts one of the world's greatest pioneers of powered flight, and it was quick to make good its deficiencies in conventional communications by evolving a comprehensive and efficiently run aviation network. By 1930, these otherwise backward lands could show a greater mileage of regularly operated airlines than either the United States or Europe. They remain well served today, both by their domestic lines and by numerous international companies (which are not allowed to compete on the purely internal routes). Brazil, which is now making increasing use of jets for its internal passenger traffic, has also taken the lead in developing the use of freight-carrying aviation. Brasília was built with equipment and material flown into a site which was then without overland communications, and the roads which subsequently linked it were likewise constructed largely by means of a prolonged air-lift.

Industry

It is widely assumed today that the surest way for a country to escape from under-development is through rapid industrialization. This was not always the fashionable view. Alberdi, Argentina's leading nineteenth-century political thinker, believed that 'the very backwardness of South America is an advantage; instead of inheriting a bad industry, she has at her disposal the most advanced European industry.' His country began to acquire its own industries, with little encouragement from a government dominated by landowning and exporting interests, in the period 1870–1914, when Europe was pouring capital and immigrants into the country and providing a ready market for Argentine exports. In Mexico, foreign capital had been welcomed by Díaz and his *cientificos* and channelled mainly into mines and railways, and it was only after it had had its revolution that the country embarked on a deliberate policy of industrialization. Brazil too was a late-comer. The mentality of a patriarchal, and until recent times a slave-owning, society was not propitious for the development of manufacturing, and the latter only quickened the pace of expansion under the stimulus of World War I. Since then, industrial growth, though extremely uneven in time and place, has been rapid, particularly in Argentina, Brazil, and Mexico, and to a considerable extent also in Venezuela, Chile, Colombia, and elsewhere. Though in 1957, industry had accounted for less than one fifth of the region's gross product, by 1964 it was contributing nearly one quarter to that of Brazil and Mexico, and almost one third to Argentina's. In 1936 roughly 60 per cent of Latin America's active population was engaged in agriculture, and 40 per cent in non-agricultural activities; by 1960 the ratio had shifted to 47 per cent for agriculture and 53 per cent for the non-agricultural sectors. Though the situation varied widely from country to country, Latin America seemed to have entered decisively on the path of industrialization.

The earliest forms of manufacturing had been the processing of the region's mineral and agricultural resources (the melting down of gold and silver, sugar-milling, etc.), and simple techniques for the preparation of such locally needed items as foodstuffs, building materials, and textiles. Other manufactured goods were imported in exchange for primary commodities. But when the 'international division of labour' became disrupted through two world wars and the great economic depression, the Latin American countries found themselves obliged to manufacture locally as many as they could of those goods which, since the demand for their own exports had fallen off, they could no longer afford to import. This encouraged local manufactures based on 'import substitution' to fill the economic vacuum created by the suspension of traditional imports. The goods produced in this way were generally relatively costly to produce and could only establish themselves behind tariff walls which in some cases might be as high as 500 per cent or more. Once the limited domestic market had been satisfied, these industries could not expand into the export market because of their high costs and the similarly protective policies of their neighbours. Much of their capacity remained under-utilized, and modernization was handicapped by the financial weakness (especially in inflation-ridden countries) and traditional family management of many enterprises. Though import substitution provided a powerful stimulus to Latin America's industrialization it thus also saddled it with disabilities from which it is still struggling to escape today.

The relatively advanced countries such as Argentina, Brazil, Mexico, Colombia, Venezuela, and Chile are today virtually self-sufficient in consumer goods for current consumption produced by the simpler forms of import substitution and have gone on to the more difficult task of producing durable consumer and capital goods, for which the import of raw materials or machine tools is often needed, more complex manufacturing techniques are required, and larger markets have to be found. The practical considerations which gave the initial impulse to the process of import substitution have been reinforced by motives of national self-respect and prestige. These demand, as we have seen, that a country's chief source of power, its oil, should be nationalized or at least brought under strict governmental control. They also call for the expansion of other forms of power, particularly the hydro-electric resources with which the region is well endowed and which are seen as essential infrastructure for its economic development. Some of the schemes now under construction are on a spectacular scale. Argentina's El Chocón–Cerros Colorados scheme is designed to harness two rivers flowing down from the Andes in order to open up northern Patagonia as well as to provide more power for Buenos Aires and increase Argentina's electric capacity by some 30 per cent. The country's first nuclear power station is also now under construction. Brazil is building the vast Urubupungá complex on the Paraná, which will add more than 4,000 mw. to her installed capacity and dwarf Egypt's Aswan dam. Each of the major countries too has set store by building up its own iron and steel works. Brazil, which began production in the mid-'twenties with a modest annual output of 8,000 tons, now has its giant works at Volta Redonda, near Rio, and by 1970 was producing more than five million tons of ingots. Argentina's target is four million tons by 1971/2. Venezuela has its ambitious Guayana development programme comprising a steel plant at Puerto Ordaz on the Orinoco with associated aluminium, chemical, and other industries powered by a hydro-electrical works on the Caroní River, which its promoters dream will open up the whole of eastern Venezuela and one day become the Ruhr of Latin America. Chile has her own steel-mills at Huachipato, Mexico hers at Monterrey and Monclova, Colombia hers at Paz del Río, Peru hers at Chimbote. Thanks to these and the region's semi-integrated mills, Latin America was already producing more than three quarters of her requirements of steel, and was even exporting a little, by the mid-'sixties. But expansion has been uneven, and some years have seen a contraction of output. High tariff walls are still needed to protect this high-cost heavy industry from competition by the more efficient producers of the developed countries.

Though the import substitution process started off virtually as a by-product of forces external to Latin America and developed along the lines of least resistance, governments have increasingly taken a hand in guiding and stimulating its course. This they may do through state agencies, such as CORFO in Chile, vested with general powers to initiate a wide range of projects, or specialized bodies such as PEMEX and PETROBRAS concerned with key sectors of the economy, or regional development corporations like Venezuela's CVG or Brazil's SUDENE. This *dirigisme* has sometimes met with coolness in countries where *laissez-faire* has its convinced, though not always very dynamic, partisans, and there is still widespread belief that, as the Brazilian saying goes, 'our country grows by night—when the politicians are asleep'. But the necessity for some degree of planning and control is now generally accepted, and Latin America's slow and lopsided growth is sometimes blamed on the lack of adequately conceived or implemented developmental planning. Governments, it can be argued, are still too dominated by traditional interests, and respond neither to the drive of any dynamic entrepreneurial sector nor to the pressure of organized industrial labour. The latter is growing only slowly as a consequence of industrialization. In Brazil's decade of rapid economic advance (1950–60) the number of industrial workers increased at the annual rate of 2·8 per cent—slower than the general rate of population increase. The consequent failure of industry to absorb its expected share of Latin America's surplus manpower is one result of the adoption, at current levels of techno-logical sophistication, of capital-intensive rather than labour-intensive pro-cesses. The developed countries passed through their industrial revolution when mills and factories had an insatiable appetite for workers; today's highly mechanized plant needs only a few skilled operators, not the unskilled rural immigrants who crowd the *barriadas* and wait expectantly at factory gates.

Though conditioned by these same general factors, Latin America's three most industrialized countries have followed differing patterns of development. In Brazil, manufacturing output grew at the annual rate of nearly 9 per cent between 1947 and 1956, accelerating in the following five years to almost 13 per cent, to constitute over one third of gross national product by 1961. These were the boom years of President Kubitschek's unrestrained and some-times undiscriminating industrialization, accomplished despite the decline of coffee prices from their peak in the mid-'fifties; years which saw the rise of Brasília from the wilderness but also the rise of uncontrolled inflation. Decline followed in the early 'sixties, the industrial growth rate shrinking almost to nothing in the muddled lurch to the Left which preceded Goulart's ouster by the military in 1964, to pick up again to a 12 per cent rise in the annual level of industrial production by 1968.

In Argentina, the prospects for attaining economic take-off had seemed amongst the most promising in Latin America. The country had emerged from World War II with large credit balances of foreign exchange. These were used by Perón to buy out foreign-owned utilities and launch an ambitious Five Year Plan (1947–51) aiming at maximum self-sufficiency through rapid industrialization and economic controls. Manufacturing output rose by 50 per cent from 1943 to 1948, but after the latter year—the peak of Argentina's post-war prosperity—declined almost to stagnation in the mid-'fifties. A second Five Year Plan attempted to set the nation's development along more realistic lines, and in 1953 the government reversed its policy of excluding foreign capital in a desperate effort to stimulate development. These concessions— especially those granted to foreign oil companies—offended nationalist senti-ment, whilst attempts to check excessive labour costs eroded Perón's support amongst the workers and led to his fall in 1955. Much of the machinery of state control over banking, exports, and other sectors of economic life was dismantled, but recovery was slow. Foreign investment was switching to specialized capital-intensive rather than labour-intensive enterprises; this could only make the task of the political and economic absorption of the *descamisados* more difficult, though it was later to bear fruit in the greater capacity for industrial productivity which, despite the vicissitudes of the post-Perón era, led to an annual growth in the industrial sector of nearly 8 per cent in 1968.

Mexico's industrial development has differed from that of Brazil and Argentina in that it has remained, since the Revolution, at a more constant level (an average of 7·7 per cent annually between 1940 and 1964) and has allowed greater scope to private enterprise. Though the State operates the oil-fields, basic petro-chemical production, and electric power, promotes some sectors of industrial expansion through its development bank (Nacional Financiera) and guides overall policy through its industrial incentive legislation, it owns and controls less than 500 of the country's more than 100,000 enterprises and employs less than a tenth of the total industrial labour force.

To transcend the limitations of its import-substitution origins, Latin American industry is now looking for progress in a number of different directions. First comes the need for each country to expand its own domestic market by reforms in such fields as tax structure, land tenure, and wage levels which should transfer more purchasing power to the under-privileged strata of the population, mostly in the rural areas, which still remain virtually outside the money economy. Even in Mexico, which some economists see as having already passed the threshold of economic take-off, this remains an urgent necessity. Secondly, the market must be expanded beyond national frontiers and development be planned for the whole region; hence the trends towards Latin America's economic integration (see page 327). Thirdly, markets must be found outside the sub-continent, not only for Latin America's traditional commodities but for more of her manufactures (see page 384). Finally, both the quantity and the quality of her industrial output need to be increased by injections of more advanced technology and investment capital.

The role of foreign capital

About nine tenths of the capital which Latin America needs for its development is found from its own resources; the remaining tenth—the 'savings gap' —is provided by foreign investment. Though this may seem a small proportion, its importance is great. In the last few decades the flow of foreign capital has changed greatly in respect of its origins, function, and application. Its traditional role had been to enable the Latin American economies to produce and export the food and raw materials required of them and to help build up an infrastructure of ports, railways, and public utilities necessary for this purpose. The latter function was financed in many cases by investments in fixed yield securities, the former by share investment. The world economic depression, when all the Latin American countries (except Argentina) found themselves obliged to default on their bonds, virtually put an end to investment by fixed yield securities, and most foreign-owned utilities were bought out after World War II. The financing of Latin America's new requirements in infrastructure is now performed mainly by public capital operating through national institutions of the industrialized countries and through international agencies such as IBRD and IADB. Private investment has switched from utilities and primary activities (apart from petroleum and some minerals) to the manufactures which have developed on the basis of import substitution. The United States has taken the place of Britain as the chief source of new technological skills and capital. Before World War I the nominal value of foreign investments in Latin America amounted to about 8,500 million US dollars, of which the United Kingdom accounted for 3,700 millions and the United States for 1,700 millions. By 1968, the United States' share had risen to about 70 per cent of all private foreign investment and had reached the huge figure of over 17,000 million dollars, about four tenths of it in petroleum and mining. Over 70 per cent of these investments was in four countries—Venezuela, Mexico, Brazil, and Argentina—whilst European investment was mainly confined to those South American countries with which historic ties had been closest.

Foreign private and public capital, on this and even a more massive scale, is generally assumed to be required if Latin America is to attain the growth rate necessary for full economic development. The inflow of funds is also expected to bring access to new technologies and managerial skills and to provide the foreign exchange which Latin America would otherwise lack for her essential imports. The boost thus given to the national economy should be more than enough to repay the cost of the imported capital. Mexico's booming economy, nourished by ever larger but strictly disciplined injections of foreign capital, is cited as a shining example. But over Latin America as a whole the picture is less encouraging. Amortization, interest, and profit remittances may grow so heavy that inflows of funds are actually converted into outflows, and a country's shortage of foreign exchange becomes cumulatively more acute. By the mid-'sixties, debt repayments were eating up, on an average, more than one third of the income earned by the Latin American countries through the export of their goods, and in some cases considerably more. For the twelve-year period 1950–61 as a whole Latin America repatriated more, in capital, interest payments, and dividends, than it received, the outflow of funds exceeding inflow by an average of 170 million dollars a year. The region's external debt more than doubled during the period 1960–8 to reach a total estimated at certainly not less than 20,000 million dollars.

To staunch the financial haemorrhage of servicing this huge and still mounting debt is a most pressing need. Allied to it is the problem of stemming the flight of Latin America's domestic capital. Fiscal controls have so far had little success, especially where inflation is rampant, in preventing the wealthy from salting away their savings in such safe and profitable havens as New York, London, Paris, and Zurich. A twofold process of foreign inflow and domestic outflow has thus set in, injections of external capital investment substituting paucity of domestic savings. It can even be argued that the foreign enterprise, with its superior financial resources and managerial and technological skills, pre-empts the most profitable growth industries and so inhibits domestic initiative and reinforces the tendency of local capital to look elsewhere for easier returns. Once, however, a sufficiently high rate of economic growth is generated—provided that it is accompanied by a climate of political security—domestic capital is no longer driven abroad and may be channelled into local investment as has occurred in Mexico and Venezuela. This trend is encouraged by a form of business enterprise which has latterly been gaining ground in Latin America—the joint venture.

The joint venture or mixed enterprise is a form of partnership between the Latin American investor and *entrepreneur* (who may also be, as was the case with the copper companies in Chile, a state corporation) with foreign capital, know-how, and management, in which the latter may, or may not, retain a controlling interest. There are many advantages in such arrangements: they reduce the foreign exchange costs of a new investment, facilitate the transfer of technology and management skills to domestic groups, link the foreign investor with partners likely to have more intimate knowledge of local conditions and readier access to official circles and sources of credit, and associate the foreign concern more closely with the country in which it operates. The latter aspect is of special importance given the intensifying climate of economic nationalism. Foreign enterprise has traditionally controlled key sectors of the economy, particularly the extractive industries, which have been developed for their export potential. It has generally operated through subsidiaries with head offices abroad where important decisions regarding development strategy, cost and price structure, new processes, and export targets, etc., are taken with an eye to the company's world interests rather than those affecting the country which happens to be the host to the subsidiary. The latter has thus tended to be regarded with odium as a foreign enclave. Hence the stiffening resolve—particularly, as we have noted, in the sensitive field of petroleum production—to nationalize, or at least to 'venezuelanize', to 'chileanize', to 'peruvianize'. When nationals of the country concerned take their place on the governing bodies of mixed enterprises, a greater correlation can at least be expected between its policy decisions and the country's development needs.

Some governments seek to safeguard the national interest by limiting foreign participation to certain sectors. Mexico has gone furthest in this direction by excluding foreign investment altogether from the oil and petrochemical industries, electrical power, telecommunications, and other fields, and by restricting it in a number of others, such as transport, mining, banking, and insurance. Though a number of additional requirements are laid down in such matters as the proportion of foreigners on the staff and the renunciation of any recourse to foreign intervention in the event of litigation, Mexico has not sought to limit the repatriation of foreign capital or dividends. Brazil's attempt to introduce legislation to this effect in 1962 resulted in the drying up of foreign capital inflows and a major economic and political crisis. Governments have, however, sought to relieve the pressure on their foreign exchange holdings by inducing companies to reinvest some portion of their profits inside the country. By spreading and diversifying its interests in this way, and through the growth of joint ventures and the involvement of the overseas investor in the Latin American manufacturing industries, foreign capital has been finding that, if it has been forced to give up some of the commanding heights, it can nevertheless entrench itself in the broader reaches of the domestic economy.

A foreign subsidiary which ceases to control a key sector on the national scale does not necessarily lose influence in the region as a whole. As economic integration gathers pace, the foreign subsidiary remains well placed, by virtue of its superior resources and managerial flexibility, to seize the new opportunities. Governments which have been successful in opposing the domination of the 'foreign monopolies' within their own frontiers may find that the key positions within the wider Latin American market are already passing into the same alien hands. To guard against this danger, the Andean Group countries, influenced by the nationalist tone of the legislation recently enacted in Peru, pledged themselves to follow a common policy with regard to foreign investment. This laid down that foreign enterprises set up from 1971 onwards must transfer 51 per cent of their shares to local shareholders within a period of fifteen years (twenty, in the case of Ecuador and Bolivia); foreign firms already operating in the area were given the choice of similarly transforming themselves into mixed enterprises or foregoing the prospect of regional expansion. A process of 'fade-out' is, in short, envisaged, by which foreign-owned projects are allowed to operate for a limited period during which they may draw a 'reasonable' return on their investment (up to 14 per cent a year under the Andean Pact Investment Law) before passing under the control of local interests. Time will tell whether foreign investors will in fact regard such requirements as 'reasonable' and be prepared to make new investments on these terms.

If foreign private investment has proved to be a development tool with a cutting edge which Latin America needs to handle with care, what of the public capital received from abroad—that transfer of skills and financial resources loosely designated under the term of aid? Up to the Great Depression and World War II, infrastructure activities—ports, railways, utilities, etc.—were generally financed, as we have noted, by foreign-owned fixed-interest securities; this role has been increasingly taken over by public capital, operating on either a bilateral or a multilateral basis. The chief source of both types of funds (as for the supply of private capital) remains the United States, which provides more than 75 per cent of all aid to Latin America. This reaches the region through a variety of channels: the Agency for International Development, the State Department body charged with planning, directing, and co-ordinating United States aid operations, the 'Food for Peace' programme for the supply of surplus agricultural commodities, and the Eximbank which makes long-term loans to promote the export of United States goods and services. The principal multilateral agencies are the World Bank and its affiliates, and the Inter-American Development Bank, to which the United States is by far the largest contributor (see page 332). Aid sometimes takes the form of grants or loans designed to bolster a government whose survival is considered vital on political or security grounds; Bolivia and the Dominican Republic have been beneficiaries of such 'supporting assistance'. More often, aid consists of 'development loans' ear-marked for approved projects and tied to goods which have to be procured in the United States. Latin American recipients of aid would like to see a loosening of these ties, which have meant higher prices for the goods they need, and more say in the selection and formulation of development projects. They have also been eager to lessen their dependence on the United States by securing an increase in the very modest amounts of aid offered to Latin America by the European countries. United States aid has latterly been channelled mainly to Brazil, Bolivia, Colombia, Chile, and the Dominican Republic and has declined in volume with the loss of momentum of the Alliance for Progress (see page 337).

The inflation problem

A problem which greatly complicates the operations of foreign private investment and public aid is the high rate of inflation which has persisted in many Latin American countries. Private investors may be discouraged from placing their capital where galloping inflation erodes it and makes earnings uncertain, and aid may be withheld until governments undertake to implement measures of orthodox monetary stabilization. The inflation upsurge began in the late 'thirties and worsened in the 'fifties, particularly in Brazil, Argentina, Chile, Uruguay, and Bolivia, after the end of the Korean War. In Chile, the cost of living increased fourfold in 1953–5, and in Bolivia, twenty-five times in 1953–8. The annual rise in the cost of living index between 1961 and 1966 averaged 60 per cent for Brazil, 40 per cent for Uruguay, and 27 per cent for Chile. Attempts to bring the problem under control have met with varying and in general only partial success. Bolivia managed to bring down her hyperinflation to a manageable 6 per cent during that period. The military governments in Brazil and Argentina slowed their respective rates from 86·6 in 1964 to 20 per cent (1969) and from 38·2 in 1965 to 6·7 per cent (1969). Chile's Christian Democrat administration reduced the rate of inflation to 25·9 per cent in 1965 and 17 per cent in 1966, but by 1969 it had risen again to around 30 per cent.

The inflationary process—price–wage–cost spiral, strikes, and other forms of labour unrest, the tendency towards increased consumption instead of saving, the stimulation of imports bringing with it balance of payments crises, foreign exchange controls, and currency devaluation—is one which many countries have experienced. But the Latin Americans have to some extent resigned themselves to living with it, often preferring the disease to the bitter medicine prescribed for its cure. Some indeed maintain that it is less a disease than the growing pains of a developing society. No sure assessment of the relationship between inflation and development can be made from an examination of the Latin American scene. Some countries (Venezuela, Mexico) have had development and little inflation. Others (Bolivia, Uruguay) have had inflation and little development. For limited periods at least, some (e.g. Brazil in the 'fifties) have known both high inflation and rapid development, whilst others (e.g. some Central American countries) have had little inflation but little development.

This has given rise to a vigorous debate on the real causes of inflation in Latin America and the remedial measures called for. There are two broadly differing schools of thought. The 'monetarists' hold that inflation is essentially a monetary phenomenon which can be put right by monetary and fiscal means. Too much money must cease chasing too few goods, and governments must stop having recourse to the printing press to close the gap between revenue and expenditure. Credit should be restricted, budgets balanced, and government controls lifted from domestic price levels and access to foreign exchange. Business confidence will thereby be restored, a good investment climate created, and market forces be given a chance to generate sound economic growth. The citadel of this doctrinal orthodoxy has been the International Monetary Fund (IMF), to which governments have had to turn for help in solving their foreign exchange difficulties. The latter have been intensified by inflation, and it has been the practice of the Fund to make drawings conditional upon borrowers agreeing to adopt orthodox stabilization measures; financial aid from Western Europe and the United States has also generally depended on acceptance of the Fund's terms.

The 'structuralists', on the other hand, without going so far as to advocate inflation, or even deficit financing, argue that inflation stems from the prevailing deformations in Latin America's unjust and inefficient socio-economic structures and its persistence must be expected at the present stage of development. It will only disappear as a result of radical structural changes. In the agricultural sector, it is the anachronistic *latifundium* system which prevents output from expanding in response to the rising demand created by industrialization and rapid urbanization. The fiscal system, too, fails to provide governments with adequate revenue through fair and efficient taxation. Latin America's inflation is not so much due to a general excess of demand over supply as to excess demand in certain sectors. The structure of supply has failed to match the change and growth in the structure of demand, as Latin America's expanding population clamours for better living conditions. To attempt to curb inflation by monetary restrictions is merely to attack symptoms rather than root causes and is not only misguided but positively harmful. A restriction of bank credit is likely to lead to industrial contraction, bankruptcies, rising unemployment, and shortages of supplies and funds for the payment of taxes, wages, and normal business transactions, as happened in the severe recession provoked in Argentina in 1962/3. Instead of promoting a country's development, the structuralists maintain, the restrictive policies imposed by the monetarists actually slow it down.

The structuralists favour a high degree of government control over prices, foreign trade, and investment. Some are prepared to work within the existing social and political establishment to effect the transformation they believe to be necessary; others, sceptical of the capacity of Latin America's ruling élites to countenance measures which must cut at the root of their privileged positions, hold frankly that a social revolution is an essential pre-condition. Cuba has had a social revolution and is free of inflation; but can it be said to be enjoying economic development? Mexico has development and no inflation problem, though opinions differ as to how far-reaching its social revolution has been. Both structuralists and monetarists cite the Mexican experience as a vindication of their respective theses, the former attributing its high growth rate primarily to the results of its agrarian revolution and the firm state controls exercised over its natural resources, whilst the monetarists ascribe it to prudent monetary policies and the dynamism of the market forces. Despite the difference in their basic positions, structuralists and monetarists are not entirely without common ground. Failure of conventional measures to cure inflation once and for all has made the monetarists more ready to concede the importance of some non-monetary aspects of the problem in Latin America. The structuralists, not being themselves in power and thus unable to test their theories against reality, have influenced the thinking of many Latin American governments, even where the latter have been obliged to follow the lines prescribed by the IMF. The structuralist case has been put forward with special effect by the economists of the United Nations' Economic Commission for Latin America (ECLA) in Chile, where long experience of inflation offers a fruitful field for research. Particularly influential have been the arguments formulated by ECLA's former head, Dr. Raúl Prebisch, on one aspect of the problem which we have not yet considered—Latin America's traditional exports and foreign trading position.

Foreign trade

Foreign trade is of great importance to the Latin American countries. They export an exceptionally large proportion of their output and depend on their export earnings for the import of goods essential to their development. The growth of their import-substitution industries has not in fact lessened their dependence on imports; it has merely changed the type of goods imported. The Latin American countries nevertheless still need to import some durables, as well as the more sophisticated capital goods. But if the composition of their imports has changed considerably, that of their exports has changed far less. These still primarily consist of traditional commodities, which account for about nine tenths of their export earnings. Mexico, Argentina, and Peru have gone furthest in diversifying their exports, but nearly half the Latin American countries still look to a single product for more than 50 per cent of their export earnings. Chile, Colombia, and Venezuela, for instance, depended respectively on copper, coffee, and oil for 65, 67, and 90 per cent of their total exports over the period 1964–6.

The basic pattern of trade has thus changed little from colonial times; the Latin American countries continue to supply food and raw materials and to receive manufactured goods in exchange. More than three quarters of their exports are sold to the western industrial nations, rather more than one tenth to Asia, Africa, and the Communist countries, and rather less than that percentage in markets inside the Latin American area. Not only is Latin America failing to find new markets, but her share of existing markets is falling and her exports are increasing at a slower rate than the world average. Thus her share of the all-important United States market dropped from 21 per cent in 1960 to 13 per cent in 1968. In the same period, the value of Latin America's total exports grew at the rate of 4·7 per cent a year, compared with an 8·2 per cent rate for world exports, so that the increase in the latter was 75 per cent greater than that for Latin America. It is thus clear that Latin America is not exporting enough and that her relative importance in world trade is declining; in 1950 her exports had accounted for 11 per cent of world exports, but by 1967 the proportion had dropped to less than 6 per cent.

Latin Americans attribute many of their difficulties to two economic factors: the trend of prices of primary products to fluctuate more violently than those of finished goods, and in the long run to fall in relation to the latter. Fluctuations in export prices mean variations in foreign exchange receipts and the capacity to import, and make orderly growth extremely difficult. The downward price trend means that the developing countries find the burden of servicing their foreign debt growing heavier and the cost of modernizing their economies higher. President Lleras Restrepo of Colombia once cited an example of what this meant for his own country. In 1954, when the wholesale price of coffee was eighty cents a pound, a foreign-built jeep could be purchased for fourteen sacks of coffee; by the end of 1969 the price of coffee had dropped to forty cents a pound, the jeep had risen in cost, and to purchase one took the equivalent of forty-three sacks of coffee.

Latin America is thus suffering the consequences of a deterioration in her terms of trade (the ratio of export to import price indices). The explanation given of how this has come about, generally known as the 'Prebisch Effect' after the Argentine economist who has been so influential in formulating it, has won wide acceptance in Latin America, though not all economists elsewhere accept the validity of its premises or conclusions. The demand of the industrial countries for the primary commodities supplied by the developing countries, according to the Prebisch thesis, increases more slowly than the latter's demand for industrial goods. These become more expensive as living standards and wages rise in the developed countries. Growing prosperity however does not lead to a proportionate increase in the demand for more food and raw materials, but rather for more manufactured goods. When, on the other hand, cyclical depressions occur or when primary commodities rise substantially in price, the industrial countries, with their superior technology, tend to economize in their use or to switch to cheaper substitutes. Latin America, moreover, is placed at an additional disadvantage on account of the preferences extended by some industrialized countries, such as the United Kingdom and the EEC, to their own associated colonial or ex-colonial territories. There is thus a strong tendency for the industrialized 'centre' to grow richer in relation to—at the expense of, many would add—the less developed 'periphery' of world trade.

The widespread acceptance of this thesis has hardly tended to improve Latin America's export performance. Why, after all, work to increase the volume of exports if demand is so inelastic that the result can only be to lower prices? This assumption tended to increase the emphasis placed on import substitution in the 'fifties and to neglect of, or even discrimination against, exports. The latter, it was commonly held, were 'exportable surpluses'—that which was left over for disposal abroad once the domestic market had been satisfied. Not every Latin American country, indeed, took that line. Peru, for instance, followed policies of export promotion—and in the 'sixties the general attitude began to change. The remarkable results which could be achieved once a government chose to remove obstacles to exports and set about actively encouraging them were demonstrated by the rapid growth in a wide range of Brazilian exports.

One line of approach favoured by the primary producing countries in order to strengthen their position *vis-à-vis* the industrialized countries has been to press for commodity agreements which would adjust production more closely to world demand and thus secure higher and more stable prices for their basic exports. Agreements of this nature are now in force for coffee and sugar, and (without United States participation) for tin and olive oil. The underlying principle is that producers undertake to limit their annual exports to traditional markets according to an agreed scale of quotas. Governments buy from their domestic producers and re-sell on the world market, using their buffer stocks to even up supplies and utilizing price differentials to diversify the national economy by financing alternative sources of production. Brazil has done most along these lines and has devoted sizeable resources to cutting back output of coffee. Commodity agreements have helped to iron out price fluctuations but cannot be said to have made much impact on basic problems. They can only prove effective where consumer countries are prepared to co-operate and producers able and willing to control production, and where the commodity itself is not subject to competition from substitutes; the latter factor would make copper, for instance, a difficult object of commodity agreement.

The Latin American countries have also been making efforts both to find new outlets for their exports and to enlarge their share of traditional markets. They have been attracted at times by the prospect of substantial sales to the Communist countries, but the latter have so far been unable to show a sustained interest in their chief products or to offer them the range of manufactured goods needed in return, and Cuba stands as a warning of the high political price likely to be exacted for any close trading relationship. To enlarge Latin America's share of traditional markets is only possible if the developed countries agree to relax the preferences granted to the primary producers with which they are formally associated (e.g. the EEC's African suppliers) and reduce the protection enjoyed by their own domestic producers (e.g. the oil and sugar interests in the United States). Recognition of Latin America's aspirations in this direction has been voiced by the General Agreement on Tariffs and Trade (GATT), which is pledged to the principles of non-discrimination and trade liberalization by means of reciprocal tariff concessions, and by the United Nations Conference on Trade and Development (UNCTAD), but few steps have so far been taken to give practical expression to these views. In his 'Action for Progress' speech at the end of 1969, President Nixon promised that his government would use its good offices to secure a reduction in the discriminations imposed by the developed countries against Latin American exports and that if these failed, the possibility would be examined of allowing them more favourable access to the United States market.

Other lines of approach towards improving Latin America's trading position are the development of intra-zonal trade and the expansion of exports of non-traditional, manufactured goods. We have noted that the policy of import substitution has now reached the stage where expansion depends on access to markets larger than the tariff-protected domestic market. The creation of LAFTA and regional groupings such as the Central American Common Market and the Andean Group (see pages 329–30) has already increased the flow of intra-zonal trade and opened up fresh prospects for the goods produced by Latin America's own industries. As the latter become more efficient through serving the wider regional market, their competitive position in world trade will correspondingly improve. But though the developing countries may have the advantage of lower labour costs, they remain handicapped by the great and growing technological gap separating them from the developed countries. The latter have consequently been urged to grant tariff preferences for manufactures and semi-manufactures from Latin America and other developing countries, who hope thereby to offset the slow rate of increase in their exports of commodities by a more rapid growth in their exports of manufactured goods. If 'infant industries' need protection before they can establish themselves in their own domestic markets, Dr. Prebisch has argued, they clearly need even more protection, in the form of preferential non-reciprocal treatment, in the foreign market. Proposals to this effect, voiced particularly in the UNCTAD conferences of 1964 and 1968, raise issues of great complexity and met initially with a cool response from the developed countries. The latter nevertheless agreed to 'refrain from taking any measures which would adversely affect the expansion of exports from developing countries' and promised that their imports from the developing countries would 'constitute a proportion of growing importance in their total imports'. Though there is now perhaps more awareness of Latin America's foreign trade difficulties and more thought is being given to ways and means of surmounting them, the developed countries have still to translate their promises into deeds.

Development prospects

The 1970s are likely to be a time of crucial importance for the countries of Latin America. 'Development' is now the watchword, as 'progress' was once that of an earlier generation. The creed proclaimed by Benjamin Constant and his fellow positivists in Brazil, and by Porfirio Díaz and the *científicos* of Mexico, may seem naïve today; it certainly tended to ignore the need for material progress to be matched by radical political and social transformation, as the outbreak of the Mexican Revolution was to demonstrate. 'Development' assumes the necessity for qualitative and not merely quantitative change.

Opinions differ as to whether this can be brought about by constitutional processes (e.g. the Christian Democrats' 'Revolution in Liberty'), by military fiat, or only by violent upheaval (the Communists' class-struggle or the 'instant revolution' of the guerrillas). Opinions differ too as to what role, if any, foreign capital and assistance should play in Latin America's development.

The conclusions reached in 1969 by the Commission on International Development set up under Mr. Lester Pearson by the World Bank were that the developed countries should increase the transfer of resources to developing countries to at least one per cent of their own gross national product, and that this level should be reached not later than 1975. In a report presented to the Inter-American Development Bank in 1970, Dr. Prebisch argued that an inflow of foreign capital on this scale, provided it is strictly controlled and applied and offered on suitable terms, should be enough to meet Latin America's needs. But the main development effort must come from the Latin American countries themselves. He urged that they should increase their investment coefficient from its present level of 18·3 to over 26 a year in order to reach an annual growth rate of 8 per cent by 1980—a considerably higher target than the 6 per cent set (and rarely achieved) by the Alliance for Progress. Most of this growth, moreover, should be in the industrial sector, so that more jobs could be created for the under-employed and steadily increasing labour force which would have grown to some 120 millions from 77 millions in 1965. The projected 8 per cent growth rate would produce an annual increase in *per capita* income of 3·6 per cent over the next decade, rising to 5 per cent thereafter, so that Latin America's average *per capita* income would stand at 570 dollars by 1980 and 900 by 1990. Parallel with this increase in production, Dr. Prebisch urged, measures should be taken to limit the growth in consumption by all but the poorest sections of the population, whose growing income and purchasing power would provide a stimulus to industry by pushing up demand.

The sort of development strategy outlined by the distinguished Latin American economist has implications which clearly transcend the strictly economic field. Would the wealthier classes be prepared to accept the restrictions proposed on their levels of consumption in the interests of a more equitable distribution of national income, or would their opposition lead to a deterioration in the investment climate and to a fresh flight of capital? Would the present governments and political parties be capable of achieving a degree of national consensus and enforcing 'the discipline of development' required for the achievement of these goals? To throw light on these questions, we must look more closely at the present political structures and machinery of government of the Latin American countries.

4 Political Forces

In earlier chapters we have given some account of the history of the Latin American countries and of the social, institutional, and economic factors which have shaped them. But when we turn to describe their political characteristics we at once become aware that the realities of political power do not correspond —or correspond only in approximate and imperfect fashion—to the theoretical patterns from which they are supposed to derive. The blueprint is one thing, the actual mechanism another. We must not conclude from this that the Latin Americans are necessarily more hypocritical or cynical than other folk. The divorce between practice and theory stems rather from the nature of their historical development and from the legalistic cast of mind which tends to assume that one needs only to formulate just and enlightened laws in order to conjure up a just and enlightened society. It is the same spirit which sought to legitimize the Conquista through the formal proclamation of the *Requerimiento* and to ensure good government through the vast corpus of the Laws of the Indies, and which today sees in planning the way to Utopia.

Constitutions

The device for ensuring good government to which well-intentioned men of the last century chiefly pinned their hopes was the Constitution. The rejection of the Spanish Crown, from which all power had emanated, left the ex-colonies with the problem of a 'legitimacy vacuum'. To fill it, a body of principles had to be formulated which would provide the juridical justification for the new states and define the lines on which they were to operate. A pattern was already to hand in the Constitution of the United States, and this, modified by certain features from French revolutionary and Napoleonic theory, was taken as the general model for the various constitutions adopted by the republics of Latin America.

The more disturbed a country's history, the more frequent have been its attempts to improve matters by changing the constitution. Sometimes the existing one would be scrapped altogether and a brand new one introduced; at others, the old one might be amended so as to legitimize a forcible change of government or remove the restraints upon an autocrat's exercise of power. Or the return, with or without modifications, to an earlier constitution might be invoked. Such tinkerings make it difficult to say what can rightly be described as a new constitution, but according to one calculation, Bolivia, Haiti, and Venezuela each had well over twenty different constitutions before the 1970s, and El Salvador, Ecuador, the Dominican Republic, Peru, and Nicaragua not far short of that number. Sometimes the constitution would be changed merely to allow the dictator to continue legally in office. For Porfirio Díaz the beginning of the end was the issue of 'no re-election', when Madero's mild slogan triggered off the vast social upheaval of the Mexican Revolution. Nowadays the principle that no chief executive may succeed himself after the lapse of his prescribed term of office has won wider acceptance and is written into most constitutions. It cannot so easily be flouted, except in the more backward countries such as Haiti where the Head of State blandly caused a new clause to be enacted in 1964 to the effect that 'Dr. François Duvalier, the elected President of the Republic, will exercise his high functions for life' (Article 197).

Most of the Latin American constitutions have certain features in common. Apart from early monarchical experiments in Mexico and Haiti, and the persistence of the titular emperor in Brazil down to 1889, there has been general adhesion to the republican form of government and the principle of the separation of powers; how far the latter exists in practice we shall be examining shortly. In the early years of their existence, federalism was often a burning issue, but the degree of regional autonomy enjoyed by those republics which today have a federal constitution is more apparent than real. In Venezuela, provincial governors are nominated by the central government. In Mexico, with very rare exceptions, they belong to the same ruling party and accept its centralized discipline, whilst in Argentina, any signs of untoward local independence lead to the province being 'intervened' by a government nominee. Only in Brazil, by virtue of its immense size, is regional diversity likely to raise major issues. The country has lived for long periods under a federal constitution, but authoritarian governments such as that of Vargas and the post-1964 military regime have imposed more highly centralized control.

The constitution not only lays down the form of government for the state but defines the rights which its citizens shall enjoy: freedom from arbitrary arrest, freedom of speech and assembly, universal education, etc. That a large proportion of Latin America's population has never in effect enjoyed any such rights must not lead us to attribute cynicism to its law-makers. Many clauses of the constitution must be seen as aspirations rather than statements of fact. Citizens can only be expected to enjoy the rights 'guaranteed' to them when the state reaches a stage of greater political maturity and social justice and finds the economic resources to provide, say, the schools and teachers required for any system of universal education. Yet the mere defining of such goals, if nothing more is feasible at the time, may increase the chance of their ultimate attainment. When the revolutionary leaders drew up the new Mexican Constitution in 1917 they included clauses foreshadowing an entirely new form of labour code, though it was not until many years later that the country achieved the political and economic stability which made possible the relevant legislation in such matters as the right to unionize, and to receive unemployment and sickness benefit, pensions, accident insurance, holidays with pay, compensation for dismissal, and so on. Between 1930 and 1960 almost all the Latin

American countries followed Mexico's example and incorporated some form of labour charter into their constitutions, and in many cases appropriate legislation has by now also been introduced which at least benefits the relatively privileged sectors of labour, though for the great mass of Latin America's urban and rural poor, the achievement of such conditions still lies in the future.

In the matter of constitutions, as in so much else, Castro's Cuba marks a sharp break with tradition. In 1940 the country adopted a new constitution containing an advanced labour charter as well as the customary guarantees of civil liberties which Batista, who had sponsored it, later outrageously violated. The restoration of the 1940 constitution was one of the declared objectives of Fidel Castro's revolt. On gaining power, however, Castro set about the radical restructuring of society on lines totally unforeseen by the constitution, and with even less regard than Batista for its guarantees of individual liberties, freedom of the press and association, and the independence of the judiciary. The goal he had set for Cuba was not the 1940 constitution, 'progressive in its day, but based on the defence of private capitalist property and the protection of the bourgeois system', as his party mouthpiece put it, but a Socialist society which was pragmatically building up its own institutions and would one day be given a formal Socialist constitution.

Caudillos

The case of Cuba, where profound political and social change has occurred outside any constitutional framework, shows that it is not to the latter that we must look for the substance of political power. It is to be found rather in the tradition of personal authority which has always characterized Latin American society. This tradition stems from a double source, indigenous and hispanic. In pre-Columbian times, power was wielded by tribal chiefs or *caciques*, whose authority was generally allowed to persist even under their Aztec and Inca overlords. The conquistadores, adventurous individualists and soldiers of fortune, made themselves lords of Indian vassals, and their descendants and successors became the owners of great *haciendas* where, provided they showed nominal respect for Crown and royal officials, their word was law. When Crown and royal officials at length disappeared, the power of these Creole landowners became even greater and could make itself felt on a national scale. The native chieftains had long since died out or been absorbed, but the term *cacique* came, appropriately enough, to denote the boss of the locality. In Brazil he was more often known as *coronel* or colonel, on account of his powers as a militia commander. When his operations reached a larger scale he was generally denoted by the term *caudillo*, and the power system of which he was the centre as *caudillismo*.

The *caudillo* was often, but by no means invariably, a soldier whose military command could frequently be—as we have noted earlier—a stepping stone towards the seizure of political power. But he could also be simply a landowner, a bandit, a lawyer, or one who combined all these and perhaps other callings as well. He might seize power by a coup or be voted into office where he could then reign supreme. He might choose to isolate his country from contact with the outside world, as Francia did in Paraguay, or he might throw open its doors, as did Leguía in Peru and Díaz in Mexico, to foreign *entrepreneurs* and capitalists. Sometimes the *caudillo* would deem it prudent to step aside and let a puppet president hold the stage for a time. Occasionally he might succeed in transmitting power to one of his own family and found a dynasty like that of the López in Paraguay or Somoza in Nicaragua. It was rare for a *caudillo* to die in his bed—though Venezuela's Gómez was amongst those who surprisingly achieved the feat—for other aspiring *caudillos* would be impatiently waiting to strike down the ageing autocrat as soon as he showed signs of losing his grasp of power. Often the *caudillo* was a *mestizo*, sometimes a full-blooded Indian like Carrera in Guatemala and Juárez in Mexico, and not infrequently he had fought his way up from the humblest origins. In this way *caudillismo* introduced a certain fluidity into the traditionally hierarchical power structures, but the rise of a man of the people was far from meaning that power was used to effect reforms in the social structure for the benefit of the poor. Juárez is one of the few *caudillos* of note whose memory is still held in honour for achievements of this sort. Though the *caudillo* might court and win the acclaim of the common people by demagogic gestures and the rough treatment he meted out to their superiors, his primary aim was to seize the levers of wealth and power for himself. Under the tyranny of a Perón or a Trujillo, the oligarchy might suffer from his spite and his cupidity, but—at least until the advent of a revolutionary *caudillo* like Castro—they had little reason to fear any onslaught on their basic class privileges.

The qualities which all *caudillos* had to some extent in common may best be described by the expression *don de mando*, the 'gift of commanding'. Thanks to his greater energy and ruthlessness, to his keener insight into human nature and skill in playing off other men's weaknesses and ambitions, sometimes by virtue of his spell-binding oratory or charismatic appeal, the *caudillo* dominated the lesser *caciques* and compelled respect for the law—not the abstract law of the constitution and the statute book, but the concrete, arbitrary law of his own will. Though the chronic disorders of his country generally gave him the opportunities for his own rise, the *caudillo* was himself essentially a man of order. Once free, Spain's ex-colonies tended to lapse into anarchy, from which men turned at length in desperation to the man with authority whom they believed capable, if not of putting an end to all violence, at least of monopolizing and institutionalizing it in such a way that, provided they gave him their obedience and the spoils of office, they would be allowed to go about their own affairs in peace. From his followers and dependants, who were essential for the attainment and exercise of his personal authority, the *caudillo* expected devoted loyalty; in return, he gave them his protection, his prestige, a free hand with their enemies, good jobs, valuable concessions, and a generous share of the spoils; this nexus between the *caudillo* and his partisans is still, as we shall see below, a feature of Latin American political parties. To the country as a whole, the *caudillo* might give roads, railways, ports, and other needed public works. Occasionally, for García Moreno of Ecuador was a scientist as well as a religious fanatic, and Argentina's Sarmiento was a great educationist as well as a *caudillo* in his own way, he might even give it schools. There have been *caudillos* who have saved their countries from disruption and given them the stern rule essential to them at that particular stage of their development and who still have their admirers today. There have been many others of whom the best that can be said is that their name has a place in the chronology, if scarcely in the history, of their countries.

President, Government, and Parliament

If the constitution has been the *de jure* and *caudillismo* the *de facto* form of political power in Latin America, the Presidency of the Republic is generally the chief point of interaction between the two. The *caudillo* needs presidential office in order to legitimize his authority, keep the opposition disarmed, and build up a more favourable image at home and abroad. Constitutional formulae, if they are to have any validity at all, need to be stiffened by the realities of personal power. The constitutions provide in theory for the separation of powers between the executive, the legislative, and the judiciary. They are in fact weighted in favour of the former, so that the system of government might be more accurately described as one of presidential dominance. The *caudillo* thus becomes President, and the President, whilst scarcely needing to violate the letter of the constitution, can rule very much as a dictator. When the Nobel prize-winner Asturias wrote his novel on the horrors of dictatorship he appropriately entitled it *El Señor Presidente*.

Alternatives to the presidential system of government have been rare in Latin America. In 1919 Uruguay instituted a collegiate system, based on that of Switzerland, over which the majority members of a nine-man National Council (the opposition being represented by a minority of three) took turns to preside; but economic and political pressures impelled a return to the stronger form of presidential government for eight years following the world depression in 1930 and again in 1967 (see page 196). Cuba is exceptional in having an all-powerful Prime Minister who forced the resignation and replacement of a President whom he had himself selected and who combines in his person the powers of commander-in-chief, first secretary of the only permitted political party, and those of his most appropriate designation, *líder máximo* of the Revolution. Other countries have at times known authoritative prime ministers (e.g. Pedro Beltrán during Manuel Prado's presidency in Peru) but such derogations of power have been limited, exceptional, and temporary. There have also been ineffective Presidents, stop-gaps, or puppets acting for a *caudillo* behind the scenes. But the general rule has been that a President should rule, and is expected to rule, as a strong man; weakness will almost certainly signal his overthrow.

The first weapon which lies to hand is the provision generally made in the constitution for its own suspension. The President has only to declare a 'state of siege' which authorizes him to ban public meetings, impose press censorship, abrogate the guarantees against arrest, and give legal sanction to other measures of autocratic rule. The proclamation of a state of siege should have prior congressional approval and last only for a limited period, but the resourceful President is not likely to be troubled by such niceties. He is often only too happy to find legal cover for prolonged arbitrary rule. The intention of the constitution-makers was to strengthen the hand of the President in any emergency arising from a challenge to his legitimate authority. The practical effect of the state of siege clause is more often to mark a concession to the realities of political power.

Even without having recourse to suspending the constitution, the President holds many trumps in his hand. He may issue decrees which have the force of law, and often initiates more legislation than parliament. He appoints to key posts, and may 'intervene' not only provincial governments but bodies such as trade unions which challenge his authority. Through his control of police and army he can be ruthless in quelling labour unrest and breaking strikes, sometimes by the device of calling up the strikers for military service. His vast powers of patronage allow him to reward loyal followers and buy off opposition. As chief architect of his country's economic development, he can make sure that lucrative contracts for new factories, mines, and public works reach the right hands, that loans are granted or withheld, that roads and irrigation works benefit certain areas and certain private properties rather than others. By deciding to expropriate a foreign oil company he may precipitate an international crisis or unleash a wave of nationalist fervour; by granting a fresh contract to a mining corporation he may alter the credit-worthiness of his country and its economic prospects with a stroke of the pen. Nothing is too great or too small for his personal attention. He may fly to a remote village, as did President Galo Plaza of Ecuador, to dispel the peasants' distrust of a census, or to appeal to them, as did President Belaúnde of Peru, to call off their land invasions until his land reform programme could take effect. The delegations of *barriada*-dwellers or dispossessed Indians who throng his anterooms are convinced, for their part, that once they come face to face with Don Víctor, the Benefactor, or Papa Doc, he will listen to their troubles and personally put them to rights. The President remains the *patrón*, and all the nation his *hacienda*.

An important field for the exercise of presidential patronage is the public service. To find posts—real or nominal, exalted or humble, according to the status of his partisans—is an obligation which a new President can hardly avoid. If the senior posts rotate with major changes in government, the lower ranks of the bureaucracy tend to be augmented rather than purged. Large-scale dismissals would only arouse animosity and increase the number of the workless. The result is an inflated bureaucracy of under-employed, ill-trained civil servants, most of them obliged to supplement their low salaries by graft or outside jobs, which is increasing more rapidly than the sector engaged in productive employment and gives to Latin America a higher ratio of administrators than is found necessary to meet the needs of more complex, sophisticated societies. In Uruguay, one fifth of the whole population is estimated to be drawing benefits from public funds, and retirement on full pension before the age of fifty is common there and in some other countries. The President must not, however, overplay his hand with this army of bureaucrats. When Pérez Jiménez made it known in Venezuela that government employers must present concrete proof that they had not voted against him in the 1957 plebiscite he aroused feelings of revulsion that prepared the way for the coup which unseated him. Outside the chief urban centres, presidential influence may pale before that of the local *cacique* or *coronel*. The degree of formal independence enjoyed by province or municipality has varied greatly from country to country. In pre-Castro Cuba, each of the six provinces elected its own governor and its own assembly, and every municipality its mayor and council. Though the proud traditions of the *cabildo* have not been entirely forgotten, the independence of local institutions has in general been whittled away by *caciques* on the one hand and, on the other, by the centralizing appetite of the state. The most stubborn defence of local rights and institutions has come from the Indian communities which often preserve their own structure of authority parallel to that imposed on them from outside.

One source from which a check on the President's autocratic rule might be expected is the judiciary. Latin America has produced many excellent jurists and made notable contributions to international law. It has also evolved some characteristic legal concepts of its own. One of these is the right of asylum which recognizes that a regime's political opponents may seek refuge in a friendly Latin American embassy whence they will in time (though Haya de la Torre was made to wait for six years in the Colombian Embassy in Lima) be granted a safe-conduct allowing them to go into exile. Another cherished privilege is that of university autonomy—a privilege sometimes disregarded by both sides, as when anti-government students turned the Central University at Caracas into an arsenal and guerrilla recruiting ground and the government sent the armed forces into the campus. Some countries have evolved a procedure, known as the *amparo* in Mexico and as *mandato de segurança* in Brazil, by which the individual can seek redress of wrongs received at official hands. Citizens have not been slow to have recourse to such protection; no less than 35,000 cases of this sort were before the Mexican Supreme Court in 1956. But on matters of principle, the judiciary has been more chary of challenging the executive. Modelled as they are on the Supreme Court of the United States and entitled to do so under the constitution, the supreme courts have hesitated to pronounce on the constitutionality of the government's measures and tend to take the line that these are political issues which lie outside their province. On occasion, however, rulings may be handed down which are little to the liking of the executive. After the 1964 coup in Brazil, the judges had the courage to declare that the detention of Governor Miguel Arrães, whose left-wing stance had made him a particular object of dislike, was illegal, and the new executive had the civic sense to comply with this ruling and release him. But in general, the law can offer only a fragile defence against tyranny. When a government is intent on carrying through drastic reforms the judiciary itself is likely to come under the axe. Perón made a clean sweep of the judges, as did Castro, together with the whole apparatus of 'bourgeois justice'.

Parliament has seldom proved strong enough to assert itself effectively against a Latin American President. Chile managed to do so for some three decades following the defeat and suicide of President Balmaceda in 1891 and Honduras for a few years at the end of the 1920s, whilst Uruguay's National Council was held in check by Parliament under the 1919 Constitution and Argentina's Presidents were forced to pay heed to a strong congress for more than half a century after 1860. But elsewhere, though it may have proved victorious in individual battles, Parliament has seldom fought a successful campaign against a President. The latter holds too many cards in his hands: the right to initiate legislation, to declare a state of siege, to suspend Parliament or simply to decline to summon it. Often he is able to avoid trouble by making sure that it is packed with his own partisans. Even without going so far as to falsify the returns, the government in power can influence an election by such means as monopolizing the use of publicity and transport, by depriving opposition leaders of their political rights, or by banning entire parties (the Communists frequently suffer this fate), by simple intimidation or the promise of the spoils of office. Most countries now follow a system of proportional representation and some (e.g. Mexico and Paraguay) allot a certain number of seats to a tolerated minority party, thereby preserving the façade of parliamentary democracy through a display of token opposition.

The President has a free hand in the appointment of his cabinet, which acts more as a body of technical and administrative aides than as the source of collective policy-making. In the event of the President's death or resignation, the constitution generally provides for the succession to pass to the Vice-President, where that office exists, though a stronger contender may shoulder the rightful heir aside (e.g. when General Garrastazú Médici stepped into Marshal Costa e Silva's shoes in 1969). The most important members of the cabinet are generally the Minister of Defence, whose control of the armed forces leaves him well placed to oust the President if the latter relaxes his grasp of power, and the Minister of the Interior or *Gobernación*, who controls the police force, is responsible for the maintenance of law and order, the supervision of the elections, and the functioning of the government machine, and is thus also a likely candidate for presidential office. The cabinet is not responsible to Parliament, but in some countries the latter has the right to summon ministers before it and may force their resignation, thus putting the President to the embarrassment of finding a replacement, though not compelling him to change his policies.

Except in the smaller countries (Haiti, Paraguay, and all the Central American republics but Nicaragua) Parliament is bi-cameral. The Upper House or Senate is formed from representatives of the constituent provinces or states, sometimes of certain national institutions together with a number of distinguished public figures. It tends to be a more conservative body than the House of Representatives, in which urban reformist parties may be more influential. Where there is a genuine multi-party House, the President may be handicapped by being able to rely only on the support of a small party of his own. Parliament may then come nearest to offering a serious challenge to his policies, as in Peru under President Belaúnde, Colombia under Lleras Restrepo, and Chile under Frei, where radical programmes in such fields as tax and agrarian reform encountered strong resistance from vested interests, or when the fight against inflation calls for policies of wage restraint which anger the representatives of labour. Though parliaments originally represented little more than different sections of the oligarchy, the growth of a middle class, an industrial sector comprising *entrepreneurs* and organized labour, and the extension of the franchise to wider sections of the population have been giving them a more genuinely representative character. The delegates elected to Parliament are now no longer just landowners or lawyers, but include trade union leaders, representatives of business and industrial interests, and of course the professional *políticos*. Parliaments are battle-grounds between competing group and party interests where wider national issues tend to be lost sight of. It is thus sometimes claimed that the President, whether constitutionally elected or not, is likely to represent the people's will more faithfully than their spokesmen in Parliament. The truth is that a large portion of the population is denied any say in choosing its rulers, whether presidential or parliamentary. President Kubitschek, probably one of Brazil's most popular and democratic presidents, was elected by only 12 per cent of the population over eighteen years old, though voting is supposed to be compulsory in Brazil. In that country, as in some others, illiterates have no vote, the argument being that this prevents the *cacique* or demagogue from manipulating the ignorant peasant masses under a democratic veneer. But the result is that a considerable proportion of the population remains altogether disenfranchised. Nevertheless, the rapid population increase, and the extension of the franchise in some countries to women (an important factor in Frei's presidential victory of 1964) is broadening the basis of popular participation in government. It is tending too, as we shall see below, to modify the nature of Latin America's political parties.

Political parties

Latin American political parties still bear the unmistakable mark of *caudillismo*. The party tends to be first and foremost a loosely knit organization bringing together the partisans of a political leader. Programmes are less important than personalities. Parties thus appear fluid, ephemeral, and opportunistic. They split easily into sub-groups as new leaders come to the fore. Personal rivalries give an edge to party differences. Stable alliances on common doctrinal ground are rare, but remarkable *rapprochements* may result between opposite extremes (e.g. ultra-Conservatives and Communists) if their bosses see advantage in burying the hatchet. Where attempts are made to formulate the leader's ideas in a systematic creed, it still tends to bear his name; thus *justicialismo* could never catch on in Argentina in place of *peronismo*, or *trabalhismo* in place of *getulismo* in Brazil. Contemporary Cuba provides the most recent example of this phenomenon. A henchman of Fidel Castro would start out as a member of his 26 July Movement (a name which does not indicate the nature of the movement but a heroic feat on the part of its leader), and would find himself successively a member of the 'Integrated Revolutionary Organizations', then of the 'United Party of the Socialist Revolution', and finally of the 'Cuban Communist Party', the reconstruction of a political grouping to which he had once in all probability been opposed. Though he will have to profess a belief in Marxism–Leninism, since this is now the creed proclaimed by the Maximum Leader, his real and constant loyalty has been to *Fidelismo*.

(i) *Traditional parties*. For much of the century following Independence, the only effective check on *caudillismo* was the limited democracy of government by oligarchy. This was practised most successfully in Chile after the reforms of the great minister Portales. The landowners called the tune, the dependent labourers followed their respective *patrón*, whilst the middle class was as yet too weak to provide any alternative focus of leadership. The oligarchs might style themselves Conservative or Liberal, and though these labels indicated only the most superficial resemblance to their European models, they did generally imply something more than loyalty to a particular chief. Liberals tended to be more receptive to 'progressive' ideas, were often bitterly anti-clerical and favoured liberty even at the risk of anarchy. The Conservatives put their emphasis on order, which they equated with defence of the Church and the nearest possible approximation to the colonial status quo. Generally (though not in Argentina) the Liberals stood for greater regional autonomy, whilst a strong central authority was championed by the Conservatives. The latter claimed the loyalty of most of the larger landowners, whilst the professional men of the towns were more attracted to the Liberal banner. The struggle between Liberals and Conservatives was prolonged and bitter in some countries. In Ecuador, it reached its most dramatic form in the duel between President García Moreno, who strove to combine modern technical progress with a return to the values of a theocratic medieval order, and the Liberals who finally killed him. In Colombia it has persisted down to our own times and has now reached the compromise by which Conservatives and Liberals peacefully alternate in power. (See page 148.)

The second half of the nineteenth century, and the first quarter of the twentieth, saw the rise of the Radicals, either as independent parties or as wings of the Liberal Parties, whose anti-clericalism they inherited. They drew strength from the rising middle classes and sought to promote their influence by introducing appropriate modifications into constitution and electoral procedures. Under such leaders as Irigoyen in Argentina and Arturo Alessandri in Chile they did much to break the oligarchy's traditional monopoly of political power and laid a basis of useful social and labour legislation. In Uruguay, they wore the familiar mantle of the *Colorados* (Liberals) and left their traditional *Blanco* (Conservative) rivals very much to their own devices in rural areas whilst endowing the urban population of Montevideo with the benefits of Latin America's first welfare state. Their great days now seem to be past, and many of the issues on which they took their stand, such as anti-clericalism, to have lost their relevance.

(ii) *Populist parties*. From about 1930, following the impact of the world economic depression and the influence, to varying degrees, of the rise of Fascism and National Socialism in Europe, there began to develop in Latin America movements of a new type which, for want of a better word, have sometimes been described as Populist. Under this heading can be grouped Perón's movement in Argentina and that of Vargas in Brazil, APRA in Peru, the MNR in Bolivia, Acción Democrática in Venezuela, and a variety of similar if less durable phenomena elsewhere. No two examples are quite alike, for each claimed to reflect a heightened awareness of the national environment in which it evolved. Many show features which to some extent are already familiar. Their advent nevertheless signals something new in Latin America's development, for though none now holds the centre of the stage, their role has profoundly affected the course of the action.

'Populism', in its connotation of Russian *Narodnichestvo*, has generally implied a certain 'return to the people', particularly to the peasantry, as the source of national values; an attempt on the part of an urban-based intelligentsia to rediscover the true nature of their people by means of personal sojourns amongst them and a study of their ways and beliefs, and to adapt political programmes to take these indigenous characteristics into account and incorporate those who hold them more fully into the organized life of the nation. This has occurred only to a very limited extent in Latin America, principally perhaps in Mexico and Peru. In the former, the Revolution inspired its devotees on the one hand to go out into the country areas to help the Indian peasant build schools and clinics, and on the other, to adopt at least the symbols and cult figures of the Indian heritage as a part of their revolutionary ideology. This in time became the accepted orthodoxy of a one-party system which has largely lost its original populist inspiration. In Peru, Mariátegui combined his Marxist convictions with a belief that pre-Columbian forms of social organization, notably the *ayllu*, could be made the basis for a programme of radical political reform; his views were, not surprisingly, later denounced by Soviet ideologists as populist, and the Communist Party which he founded has never attempted to apply them. APRA subsequently gave support, though it was chiefly verbal, to Indian aspirations and it was left to the young followers of Belaúnde's Acción Popular to live and organize practical work amongst the Indians and *cholos* to give substance to their leader's populist ideas. Only in Bolivia did the land reform, extension of the franchise, and other measures to incorporate the Indian peasantry into the life of the nation have a lasting effect in this direction, though the MNR which sponsored them has ceased to be a dominant political force.

The section of rural population to which the Latin American populist leader addresses his appeal is rather to the uprooted mass of migrants who leave their villages and flock to the vast shanty-towns ringing Latin America's capital cities, and who bring with them their traditional need of a *patrón*. To the latter they may turn for titles to the land on which they have squatted, for schools for their children, for jobs for themselves and for all other needs. On the national scale, they are quite ready to accept him as the father figure who will know what is best for the country. Long after the dictator's fall, there were more shacks in the *barriadas* of Lima to be seen daubed with slogans in support of Odría, reputedly a military and Conservative dictator, than for the Communists who claimed to represent the proletariat. Perón addressed his appeal primarily to the *descamisados*, whilst Vargas in Brazil and Betancourt in Venezuela built up a solid following amongst the working classes of their respective countries.

The populist parties are thus based on a partnership between a demagogic *caudillo*-type leader and an under-privileged, generally urban, mass following, with the addition of certain other elements which we shall be describing later. This has also been the basic formula, as we have noted, for other movements such as Irigoyen's Radical Party. But whereas the latter type of movement is, or holds itself to be, a democratic organization, the populist leader is frequently—though he may think it prudent to pay lip-service to democracy—anti-democratic. Vargas, in his early phase, had clear affinities with Fascism, and Perón with National Socialism. The group of Bolivian officers who brought Villaroel to power in 1937 considered themselves Nazis, though Paz Estenssoro later gave a democratic colouring to the movement they had set in train. As heir to the *caudillo* tradition, the populist leader tends to dispense favours to the underdog whose cause he has espoused rather than to enact the reforms which they themselves may have elected him to carry through. Hence the ephemeral and demagogic nature of his measures in the social field; largesse is irresponsibly lavished rather than a difficult and sometimes unpopular change effected in the underlying structures which will alone transform transitory benefits into viable reforms. Hence the practice of feather-bedding in industry, the creation of superfluous jobs in the bureaucracy, and the pervasiveness of graft. Hence the irresponsible readiness to grant wage increases, regardless of their inflationary effect. Hence too the failure of leaders like Vargas and Perón to attempt real structural reforms, despite the great popular backing they enjoyed, for fear of alienating the other sectors of the population upon whose support, or at least tolerance, they also depended.

For all his apparent power and popularity, the populist leader's position is often precarious. His party is generally little more than a network of personal contacts held together by patronage and personal loyalties. If he can sway the votes of the marginal population of the cities, those of the rural masses are still likely to be under the control of *caciques* who need to be placated and if possible won over. Accommodations are thus often reached (as we have seen in the case of the *Colorados* and *Blancos* of Uruguay) between those who control the urbanized modern sectors of the population and those who control the rural areas. The latter are tacitly left to their own devices, whilst benefits and reforms fall to the lot of the urban areas. Thus the gap between town and country is perpetuated, and the division between the two branches of Latin America's society intensified. In Brazil, this dichotomy was actually formalized by the creation of two distinct political parties which became the twin pillars of the Vargas regime: the PTB, the progressive labour party of the cities, and the Social Democrat Party (PSD) supported by the rural landowners. This helps to explain why President Goulart, whose fall was brought about by his concessions to left-wing extremists, was at the same time personally one of the largest landowners of the country. Only when the populist movement develops an integrated and efficient party structure, as happened in Mexico and to some extent in Venezuela, where the urban-based Acción Democrática managed also to build up strong peasant syndicates, is this trend likely to be reversed.

Populism also makes its appeal to the urban middle classes, particularly the white-collar workers and poorer wage-earners who may themselves have emerged from the city's marginal population and depend largely on ill-paid jobs in the tertiary sector fostered by the populist leader. To these, and also to the politically more articulate students and intellectuals, populism has offered a creed to which every section of its heterogeneous following can in some measure subscribe—nationalism. Its organization and ideology claim, however spuriously, to reflect the true spirit of the nation, in contrast to the cosmopolitan outlook and frank admiration for European models of the traditional parties. The nationalization of foreign-owned assets, particularly the oil companies and utilities, evokes the warmest response even amongst sections of the population who are far from regarding themselves as Socialists. Coming to power following the Great Depression and in World War II, populist leaders have been largely responsible for the policy of import substitution which, for all its shortcomings, has given the Latin American countries most of whatever level of economic development they have yet attained.

The heyday of the populist parties seems to have passed, though some of their features still distinguish the newer types of party which have taken their place. In Argentina and Brazil, Peru and Bolivia, the military are in power and seem to manage quite happily with only a loose backing of insignificant parties, the façade of parliamentary support such as Brazil's ARENA, or without any political parties at all. In Mexico, populism has been disciplined in the virtually one-party system of the PRI whose *modus operandi* has already been described (see page 90). Its divergence from the populist model may perhaps be traced back to President Calles's creation of the party machine and President Cardenas's decision to hand over to a successor selected by party caucus rather than continue in power as a popular but unconstitutional *caudillo*. Castro's 26 July Movement had once all the hallmarks of populism before it was forced into a Marxist straight-jacket, and some elements, such as its fervid nationalism and the Maximum Leader's mystic communing with the people by means of the mass rally and informal mingling, still remain. Certain populist elements can also be recognized (e.g. in Chile's Promoción Popular, which aims to incorporate the marginal population, both materially and socially, into the national life) in the movement to which we may now turn—Christian Democracy.

(iii) *Christian Democracy*. The Christian Democrats emerged as an important political factor in the course of the 1960s, particularly in Chile and Venezuela where they won the presidential elections respectively in 1964 and 1968. In Chile they began as an offshoot of the Conservative Party, taking the name of

Falange Nacional in 1938 but making little headway until the 'fifties when they merged with the bulk of the Partido Conservador Social Cristiano to become the Partido Demócrata Cristiano. In 1958 they polled a quarter of the votes cast, and their candidate Eduardo Frei came third in the presidential elections. Six years later he scored a victory over the FRAP candidate and set up the first Christian Democrat government in Latin America. In Venezuela the Christian Socialist Party (generally known as COPEI) traces its origins back to 1948, following the fusion of two Catholic groups a couple of years before. During the first AD administration, and the subsequent dictatorship of Pérez Jiménez, the Party was in opposition, but it joined the AD coalition under President Betancourt's second administration, gained a fifth of the votes cast in the 1963 elections, and won the next (1968) by a narrow margin. In the other larger Latin American countries such as Brazil, Argentina, Mexico, and Colombia, Christian Democracy has failed to take root, but there are Christian Democrat parties, some of them vigorous, in a number of others. In Peru, they became an important element in the coalition supporting President Belaúnde, and in El Salvador, though founded only in 1960, the party appeared to have become a serious contender for political power by the end of the decade.

The Christian Democrats profess allegiance to an ideology which claims to give concrete expression to the Christian concern for social and economic justice as expressed in Leo XIII's *Rerum Novarum* and subsequent papal encyclicals (see page 234). Their thinking has also been influenced by the Marxist analysis of economic factors and the attempts of previous Christian thinkers to reconcile this analysis with Christian principles. In its early days, Christian Democracy in Latin America owed much to European writers like Jacques Maritain and to the programmes and principles—and perhaps at times to the financial resources—of the Christian Democrat parties in Italy, Germany, and France. But though they look to a common source of inspiration and hold the same general assumptions, the Christian Democrat parties of Latin America differ considerably amongst themselves and from their European prototypes. Ranging from the relatively Conservative COPEI and the left-of-centre Chileans to the impatient extremists of the youth organizations and some of the smaller parties, they are in general well to the Left of their counterparts elsewhere. 'In Western Europe,' Radomiro Tomic, the Christian Democrat candidate in the 1970 Chilean presidential elections, has explained, 'it is logical that the Christian Democrats should see themselves primarily as the champions of Christian values against the menace from Soviet Communism; these values have produced a basically just social order which deserves to be defended. This is not the case in Latin America, where the Christian and democratic values are little more than phrases, and the reality is a privileged minority living at the expense of the neglected poverty-stricken masses.' Hence it follows that 'the Christian Democrats of Western Europe would do wrong to destroy the social order in which they live, and are right to defend and perfect it; but we Christian Democrats in Latin America would do wrong to defend the social and moral *disorder* in which *we* live, and are right to strive to transform and replace it.' The Christian Democrats thus consider themselves a revolutionary force and may be prepared on occasion, particularly when both find themselves in opposition to a dictatorship, to co-operate with the Communists. But 'we have no illusions', as President Frei has written; 'we know that, in reality, we are their worst enemies.'

Christian Democracy claims to present a democratic and Catholic alternative to both Communism and unrestrained capitalism. Whilst standing for the right to private property, it believes that this should be brought within reach of those hitherto deprived of it; hence its concern for the 'marginal' population of the shanty-towns and for the rural labourers. Hence its stress on the need for 'participation' by such means as workers' co-ownership and co-management, vigorous local government, the programme of 'popular promotion' to raise the social and cultural level of the under-privileged, and the rather vague ideal known as 'communitarianism'. To close the glaring gap between rich and poor, the gradual redistribution of wealth is advocated by means of agrarian reform, a graduated income tax and a tax on inadequately exploited land—measures which can hardly be described as revolutionary in themselves but which may indeed be regarded as such within the context of Latin America's traditional social order. Christian Democracy rejects the Socialist demand for the control of the means of production, but recognizes the need for national planning and for direction of private investment into fields of high social priority. The 'chileanization' or 'venezuelanization' of the nation's basic resources are preferred to outright nationalization. In external affairs, stress is placed on the need to promote the closer integration of Latin America and the cultivation of relations with all countries, including those which are 'Socialist'; the 'third position' thus aimed at is not, however, 'neutralist', as Latin America is regarded as falling within the orbit of Western civilization, but has been defined rather as 'a position of independence and integrity'.

Christian Democracy is not linked institutionally to the Catholic Church; whatever its name may imply, it has hardly more to do with organized religion than has Christian Science with the Royal Society. No national hierarchy has come out in support of a Christian Democrat party or instructed the faithful to vote for it. The Chilean Christian Democrats encountered strong opposition from some Church quarters in their early days and still number ardent Catholics amongst their opponents. Nevertheless, the thinking of the men who were later to form the first Christian Democrat government in Latin America was deeply influenced by a small élite of dedicated and politically articulate priests, especially the European-trained Jesuits associated with the Centro Bellarmino in Santiago, whose work still influences the climate of opinion, both of the Church and the public at large. (See page 234.) The new progressive 'Vatican II' outlook which has been stirring the Church in a number of other Latin American countries is likely to be of at least initial and indirect benefit to the Christian Democrat groups there. But once the Christian Democrats become established as major political parties, their specifically Christian inspiration tends to be dimmed and the proportion in their ranks of militant Catholics to diminish. 'Whereas our party was once a Catholic Party which did not exclude non-believers,' a young Chilean Christian Democrat has observed, 'it is now a secular party which does not exclude Catholics.'

(iv) *Communists and Socialists*. Communist parties exist, either legally or clandestinely, in all the countries of Latin America. In one—Cuba—the Communist Party is the sole and governing party; in a few others, notably in Chile, it is well led and organized and a major political force. Elsewhere, especially where the party is banned or operates through cover organizations, particularly for electoral purposes, its strength is difficult to assess and varies from potentially great (Uruguay, Venezuela) to negligible (Mexico). The principal parties came into existence during the 'twenties and developed under the control and guidance of the Comintern, which maintained for this purpose a special agency known as the South American Secretariat based in the River Plate countries. Though there is now a number of small pro-Chinese parties or splinter groups, these have failed to make much headway, and the parties as a whole keep obediently to the Moscow line. In a few cases (e.g. Bolivia, Paraguay) the Communists have split into two parties, the pro-Chinese and the pro-Soviet. Only one Communist party, the Mexican, openly criticized the Soviet Union for invading Czechoslovakia in 1968, though this issue also helped to cause a later split in the Venezuelan party. Castro supported the Soviet move against Czechoslovakia and has since kept more closely than before to the Moscow line, though his Cuban Communist Party remains *sui generis*.

For all its tensions and manifest social injustices, Latin America has not so far proved a profitable field for Communist endeavours. The 1932 attempt in El Salvador to stir up a peasant rebellion was suppressed with the loss of thousands of lives. The Comintern plan to send Luiz Carlos Prestes from Moscow to head a rising in Brazil three years later proved almost as costly a failure. More effective have been the subtler methods of infiltrating labour organizations and weak political parties. Popular Front tactics brought the Communists a share of power in Cuba (1943–4) and Chile (1946–8, and again from 1970). Infiltration of President Arbenz's regime in Guatemala aroused fear of an eventual Communist take-over and led to the mounting of the right-wing coup which ousted him. The Communists have even found it possible and advantageous to co-operate on occasion with ostensibly anti-Communist regimes (whilst generally maintaining a clandestine apparatus in opposition), offering some degree of tacit or overt support in return for certain limited advantages such as a free hand in the labour organizations; accommodations of this type were made with Vargas, Perón, Odría, and Batista. The Communists' most telling card is perhaps their exploitation of nationalist sentiment. 'Anti-imperialism' is a cry which can unite all shades of left-wing and nationalist opinion, and may ensure Communist backing even for a military government which, like General Velasco's in Peru, plays the popular game of expropriating United States-owned companies. Castro's blend of communism and nationalism constitutes the driving force behind the Cuban Revolution and enables it not only to defy the United States but to preserve a certain freedom of manoeuvre within the 'Soviet camp'.

The present Cuban Communist Party differs from its Latin American counterparts not only in being the sole one to have gained full power but in its functional structure. Before the advent of Castro, it had developed along standard lines, being founded and controlled by the Comintern, gaining a hold over the labour movement and doing opportunistic deals with the Batista dictatorship. It had stood aloof from Castro's guerrilla movement until the eleventh hour, when it backed his take-over of power and was accepted by him as an ally, its identity being finally merged with that of his own followers in a new party which Castro proclaimed to be Marxist–Leninist and of which he himself assumed the First Secretaryship. Its Central Committee, made up largely of his former guerrilla officers, seldom meets and appears to take its cue without question from its First Secretary. Though the Revolution is more than ten years old, the Party has not yet met to hold its constituent assembly, and the 1968 purge of a 'microfaction' of old-guard Communists who wanted to bring it under more direct Soviet control ensures that it remains less a vehicle of collective leadership than a power apparatus at the disposal of a charismatic revolutionary leader. In his background, temperament, and style, Castro stands in striking contrast to the bosses of the other Latin American Communist parties. Some of them, like the late Vitorio Codovila of Argentina and Prestes of Brazil, have remained at the head of their parties for more than three decades and have become establishment figures of a revolution which shows little signs of dawning. Their parties seem generally to have lost their dynamism and to be wedded to the tactics of infiltration and accommodation. The Soviet Union, reluctant to jeopardize its diplomatic and commercial links with the regimes which the Communists are ostensibly pledged to overthrow, seems, in recent years at least, to have hesitated to encourage their effective revolutionary role. (See page 343.) This has contributed to the sterility of the orthodox Communist parties and left added scope for competing Socialist, Trotskyist, pro-Chinese, pro-Cuban, and other extremist groups.

'Socialist' parties, as the term is understood in Europe and the United States, have seldom carried much weight in Latin America. Only in Argentina, largely as a result of the influx of workers from Europe around the turn of the century, did they establish a party of national importance which, under the leadership of their founder Juan B. Justo and the respected writer and university rector Alfredo Palacios, succeeded in controlling the major working-class organizations in the inter-war period until their influence paled before the rise of Peronism. The chief theatre of Socialist activity has subsequently been in Chile, where the Socialists allied themselves with the Communists to contest the presidential elections. Unlike their Communist comrades, the Chilean Socialists have been under no obligation to adjust themselves to the shifts of policy of the Soviet Union, and have even criticized the latter on occasion. In their advocacy of revolutionary violence and their support of Fidel Castro they have shown themselves more extreme than the Communists, and thanks to the personal popularity of President Allende, won more votes in the 1971 municipal elections than any other party except the Christian Democrats. Outside Chile and Argentina, the term 'Socialist' has come to denote, or conceal, a bewildering range of political tendencies. In Brazil, the Social Democratic Party is actually of the extreme Right; in Mexico, the Popular Socialist Party is a small Marxist group formed from the personal following of the late Lombardo Toledano, which has followed a course parallel to that of the Communists. Elsewhere, particularly where a Communist Party is banned, a 'Popular Socialist' party may be actually no more than a cover-name for that party itself; this was for many years the case in Cuba. Or the term may be used, especially where coupled with the epithet 'revolutionary', to denote one of the innumerable and ephemeral factions which make up the revolutionary extreme of Latin America's political spectrum.

(v) *Other revolutionary groups*. A full enumeration of Latin America's small, extremist revolutionary groups is hardly possible. They proliferate amoeba-like, splitting off from the parent party under younger, more radical and impatient men, or forming around cells of Trotskyist, Maoist, or Fidelista inspiration, regrouping in fresh 'fronts', changing their names, tactics, and leaders, issuing manifestos, launching terrorist attacks and guerrilla raids. Wiped out by police or army, they reappear in fresh guise as symptoms of Latin America's continuing malaise, the frustrations caused by its anachronistic social structures, its population and economic pressures, the anarchic violence of the *caudillo* tradition, or a naïve belief in the magic formula of 'instant revolution'. They are fed by the endemic banditry of the countryside and the idealism of restless students. Though generally little more than froth on a deeper revolutionary brew, they cannot always be lightly blown aside; a hand-ful of such unlikely desperadoes once turned Cuba upside down and changed Latin America's political pattern. But though they have given the world the myth of Che Guevara, it seems unlikely that they can give their continent any practical solution for its ills.

The oldest are the Trotskyist groups, which have existed in Latin America ever since individual Marxists came under the personal influence of Trotsky (who met his death in Mexico) or felt the attraction of his ideas. In no country, however, did a coherent Trotskyist movement succeed in establishing itself. Sooner or later, the groups died out, fragmented into splinters, or became absorbed by the larger left-wing parties. Only in Bolivia did they manage, during the 'forties and early 'fifties, to grow into a significant force (POR), only to be reduced to insignificance again as a result of internal dissensions. Small Trotskyist groups, linked uneasily in the 'Fourth International', still exist in Bolivia, Argentina, Uruguay, and a few other countries, and individual Trot-skyists emerge from time to time as revolutionary leaders, as Hugo Blanco emerged to organize Peru's militant peasant *sindicatos* in the 'sixties. The Cuban Revolution has presented the Trotskyists with something of a dilemma. Fidel Castro's attitude towards them has been ambiguous, since he has im-prisoned the leading Cuban Trotskyists and attacked their doctrines, though individual Trotskyists from other Latin American countries appear to have received training and moral stimulus from Cuba. Trotskyists have sometimes joined and influenced guerrilla groups, such as that led by Yon Sosa in

Guatemala, but it seems probable that those who are more interested in revolutionary action than in ideological polemics will become increasingly absorbed into the pro-Chinese or pro-Cuban ranks.

Castro's success in Cuba gave impetus to a wide range of revolutionary groups throughout Latin America which operated for the most part outside the framework of the orthodox Communist parties, or in conjunction only with their more militant elements and youth organizations. Some received support in arms, funds, propaganda backing, training, and even personnel from Havana; others sought inspiration from Cuba's example and trusted to their own exertions. In the months of revolutionary euphoria following Castro's advent to power they expected—as Castro himself seems to have done—that at least the less stable governments in Central America and the Caribbean would be quickly toppled. A number of revolutionary ventures were mounted against them from Cuba, a major effort being directed against the Dominican Republic. A mixed Cuban–Dominican expedition was crushed in June 1963, but its survivors and sympathizers, assuming the name of the '14 June Movement' as Castro's followers had assumed that of the '26 July Movement', continued their attempts to overthrow the Dominican government until, by the end of the 'sixties, their revolutionary impetus was spent and they survived as only one of several small, unco-ordinated extremist groups sporadically active in that country.

Colombia, by virtue of the endemic *violencia* which afflicted the countryside, seemed a promising field for guerrilla action. The Communists adopted an ambivalent attitude towards it and made vacillating attempts to give a more specifically political orientation to this rural unrest. Various pro-Castro revolutionary groups waxed and waned. By the end of the 'sixties three distinct groupings had emerged which sometimes competed amongst themselves but seemed to pose little serious threat to the government: the Communist Party's Colombian Revolutionary Armed Forces (FARC), the People's Army of Liberation (EPL), controlled by the pro-Chinese Marxist–Leninist Communist Party of Colombia, and the pro-Cuban guerrillas of the Army of National Liberation (ELN).

In Guatemala, guerrilla action reached serious proportions by the mid-'sixties but was checked by the army's field operations and the counter-terror of right-wing organizations such as the White Hand. Two main groups were in the field: the Movement of 13 November (MR-13) led by Yon Sosa, an ex-officer of partly Chinese descent who seems to have been influenced by Maoist and Trotskyist ideas, and the Rebel Armed Forces (FAR) led by the pro-Cuban Turcios Lima, killed in 1966. These two groups diverged from a common stem, competed for a while, merged, and then separated once more. The Guatemalan Communists, as in Colombia, attempted at times to operate their own guerrilla units, and at others to control those of the pro-Cuban faction.

In Peru, after abortive attempts to infiltrate small bands of Cuban-trained guerrillas, a concerted rising was launched in 1965 by groups in different parts of the country operating under the command of the pro-Castro Movement of the Revolutionary Left (MIR), but was crushed by the army. In Brazil, the Peasant Leagues formed in the desperate backlands of the north-east by

Francisco Julião, a fervent admirer of Castro, ceased to loom as a threat after the 1964 coup which brought the military to power. Ambitious plans to establish a base in Bolivia from which revolutionary operations could be conducted against strategic parts of the continent were frustrated by the much publicized annihilation of the Cuban guerrilla nucleus and the death of Guevara in 1967. Three years before, a prelude to this venture had been attempted on the Argentine–Bolivian side of the frontier by another Cuban-trained Argentine, Jorge Massetti, and had likewise failed. Guerrilla risings had also been suppressed early in the decade in Paraguay and Ecuador.

By the end of the 'sixties, the guerrilla recipe for revolution thus seemed to have been discredited. Counter-insurgency forces had proved themselves more than a match for the *barbudos* and the latter were losing something of their appeal to Latin America's impatient youth. New revolutionary tactics were clearly called for and were already being applied. The urban guerrilla was coming to the fore. Precedents for this form of struggle were also to be found in Cuba. Batista had once nearly been brought down by desperate men who stormed the presidential palace and battled with his police in the streets, but their memory had been eclipsed by the glamour of the *barbudos*. The rebels of Guatemala and Venezuela aimed at combining rural with urban guerrilla action, switching emphasis to the latter by acts of spectacular terrorism—raids on police stations, arsenals, and public buildings, the murder or kidnapping of selected victims or attempts to undermine government authority by indiscriminate bomb attacks. In Brazil, commandos of two urban terrorist groups kidnapped the United States Ambassador (1969) and the German Ambassador (1970), holding them hostage until the release of a number of imprisoned revolutionaries. Even in Chile, with its tradition of orderly government, the Frei administration was harassed by MIR militants. Uruguay had its 'Tupamaros'—called after the Peruvian rebel leader Tupac Amaru—who came to public attention in the mid-'sixties through a series of raids on arsenals, banks, and casinos, and the abduction of prominent figures who were then released after making sizeable 'donations' to left-wing causes. The Tupamaros took pains to cultivate a Robin Hood image by posing as champions of the poor—wealthy bankers and shady business firms were favourite targets—but their violent methods inevitably involved innocent victims and cost them much of the public's initial sympathy.

Urban guerrilla actions of this nature, with or without a parallel recrudescence of guerrilla activity in the rural areas, are likely to persist throughout the 'seventies. Latin America's cities are vulnerable to explosions of mob violence, as the *Bogotazo* of 1948, and Argentina's lesser but more politically motivated *Cordobazo* of 1969 demonstrated. With their snowballing populations and lagging public services, the half-assimilated, half-employed multitudes from the shanty-towns, and their nuclei of radical students, intelligentsia and labour leaders, the cities may well appear to the extremist revolutionary groups as more promising soil than the *pampas*, jungles, and *cordilleras* postulated by the romantic nihilism of the Guevara mythology as the setting for the hoped-for 'Vietnamization' of Latin America.

5 Patterns of Thought and Culture

We have now outlined some of Latin America's salient social, institutional, economic, and political features; but what of the attitudes and assumptions underlying those forms, the indigenous beliefs and the external influences which have helped to shape them? Should we regard Latin America merely as a peripheral part of our Western civilization, a reflection—or at best an extension—of European culture? How 'Latin' can be these lands which no Roman ever trod, and where numerous native communities remain unassimilated and virtually untouched by western ways? Yet 'Indo-America', which has sometimes been suggested as an alternative designation, would be no less inappropriate when applied to countries like Argentina or Uruguay which have almost nothing Indian about them. As Simon Bolívar put it: 'We are mankind in microcosm—neither Indians nor Europeans, but something intermediate between the rightful owners of the land and the Spanish usurpers.' A century and a half ago, the Creoles took up arms in their resolve to be no longer considered as Spaniards; today, the emphasis is on being something other than North American, free of 'Yankee' tutelage and the cult of the 'American way of life' (though not of its material benefits). Moreover, the Latin American is becoming increasingly aware that he is different not only from the European and the North American, but from his own neighbours. He is a Brazilian, a Mexican, an Argentine first, and a Latin American second. But though the flood of cultural nationalism flows strong, there still remains the sense of a shared historical and cultural background and a destiny in common. If much of what it has so far achieved in letters, learning, and the arts seems derivative, there is now a new confidence that Latin America may be starting to move out of the stage of cultural as well as economic under-development. The vast untapped resources of the sub-continent have their counterpart in the realm of the mind. Latin America seems to be in the process of exploring and harmonizing its diverse potentialities, re-discovering its past, and incorporating that still living structure into its personality. In some fields of endeavour such as imaginative literature, the exciting moment of mental take-off has already been reached.

The Indian strands

Though the pre-Columbian civilizations had no true system of writing, and consequently no written literature, some of their poetry, legends, and sacred lore have survived in oral tradition or in the translations made by curious scholars in the years following the Conquista. One of the most remarkable treasures to be saved for posterity in this way is the *Popol Vuh* or *Book of the People*, which enshrines the creation myths held by the Quiché Indians of Central America and probably widely shared by other Amerindian peoples. The *Popol Vuh*, in a strange blend of biblical sublimity and nursery-tale fantasy, gives the Indians' version of the creation of Man and his place in the universe. It relates how the gods made a number of false starts, shaping creatures first out of mud and then out of wood, and succeeding only in fashioning Man by kneading him out of maize-dough, the staff of life. The human beings thus created spend their lives in an endless struggle to placate or outwit the malevolent gods. The chief protagonists are a pair of semi-divine twins who have to undergo a series of ordeals, including a round of the ceremonial ball-game in which the stakes are life or death, before triumphing at last by their superior magic and ascending into the sky to become the Sun and Moon. That the Indians of today still move in the twilight world of the *Popol Vuh*, where every river, rock, and animal has a living spirit, is apparent from such novels as *Hombres de Maíz* by the Guatemalan Nobel prize-winner, Miguel Angel Asturias (b. 1899) and the brilliant evocations of Quechua life by the Peruvian novelist José María Arguedas.

The Indians of the Andean *altiplano* were great lovers of poetry, music, and the dance. Survivals of the latter, though adulterated with later elements, are still to be seen in such colourful *fiestas* as the elaborate and grotesquely masked devil-dances of Oruro. Inca poetry contained many moving invocations of Pachacama, the great deity of the coastal regions, and to Viracocha the Creator, 'root of all being, God ever near', in whose cult the early missionaries thought to discern a mysterious foreknowledge of the Christian revelation. They encouraged their converts to sing the old songs, with Christian words, and to take part in pageants and dramatic representations designed, after the fashion of the medieval mystery-plays, to convey the lessons of the gospel story. The Indians had, too, their own tradition of secular drama. One precious survival, written partly in Spanish and partly in Quechua, is the tragedy of the *Death of Atahualpa*, probably composed only a few years after the Conquest, which curiously depicts Pizarro falling dead at the King of Spain's rebuke for the murder of the last Inca. Another is the famous romance of *Ollontay*, known to us only in a Spanish version of the eighteenth century, which tells of an Indian brave who fell in love with an Inca princess, rebelled, was captured, and finally pardoned by a magnanimous Inca. *Ollontay* is known to have been performed in the presence of Tupac Amaru II, and after the suppression of the great Indian rebellion the Spaniards banned 'the representation of dramas as well as other festivals which the Indians celebrate in memory of their Incas'.

A century was to elapse before there appeared the first Indianist novels, written under the influence of the romantic revival. The note of social protest was soon added, and by the middle of our century had swollen to a passionate chorus. The Bolivian Indians of Alcides Arguedas's *Raza de Bronce* (1919) are no longer Rousseau's noble savages, but peons driven by oppression to burn down the *hacienda* over their *patrón*'s head. The Peruvian village in Ciro

Alegría's *El Mundo es ancho y ajeno* (1941) is an idealized Indian community evicted by an avaricious landowner. The Ecuadorean Indians of Jorge Icaza's *Huasipungo* (1934) are shown as defenceless peons destroyed by the unholy alliance of landowner, priest, political boss, and *gringo* capitalist. These give us the white man's interpretations of the Indian mind, hardly a glimpse of that mind itself. For this we must wait until such novels as *Yawar Fiesta* and *Los Ríos Profundos* by José María Arguedas (1913–69), who was himself brought up with the Indians and shared their vision of the world. The translations from the Quechua, both traditional and contemporary, made by such scholars as José María Arguedas and Jesús Lara, attest the vitality and self-awareness of the indigenous mind. Some even claim that we are on the threshold of a 'Quechuan renaissance' (see page 220).

In Mexico, the Indian seems to have come again at last into his own. He gazes proudly over the discomfited and repellent figures of conquistadores, priests, and foreign capitalists from the spectacular scenes depicted by Rivera, Orozco, Siqueiros, and the other muralists who found a powerful inspiration in the Mexican Revolution. He speaks through the *Sinfonía India* and other folkloric compositions of Carlos Chávez, through the splendid translations from ancient Nahuatl poetry made by scholars like K. Angel Garibay and Miguel León Portilla and through the rich autobiographical material gathered by social anthropologists in such works as *Juan Pérez Jolote* by Ricardo Pozas (b. 1910) and Oscar Lewis's *Pedro Martínez*. The artistic achievements of his vanished civilizations and the varied aspects of his contemporary way of life stand magnificently revealed in the unique collections of Mexico's Ethnographical Museum. Politicians name their sons after Cuautémoc and other Aztec heroes, denounce the centuries of Spanish rule and claim that the Revolution has righted the many wrongs suffered by Mexico's indigenous population. Yet in the remoter parts of the republic, these Indian communities are still to be found living in the greatest backwardness and poverty. Though they may pay tribute to their Indian past, few Mexicans seriously believe that the Indian ethos has much to contribute to the modern development of their country. Some, like the poet and thinker Octavio Paz (b. 1914), hold that the Mexican mind is still scarred by the Aztecs' deeply rooted obsession with violence and death and by the traumatic experience of the Spanish conquest.

The Iberian strands

When the conquistadores and early colonists laid aside the sword for the pen, it was to send back reports of their discoveries and conquests, as in the vigorously written *cartas-relaciones* of Hernán Cortés. There soon followed more ambitious attempts to compose fuller accounts of the unfolding story of the Conquista and the wonders of the newly discovered lands—histories based on old soldiers' memoirs, like Díaz de Castillo's incomparable *History of the Conquest of New Spain*, or the compendium of military campaigns, natural history, and Indian customs compiled by the first official historiographer of the Indies, Fernández de Oviedo y Valdés (1478–1557), or the shapeless, passionate polemical works of Bartolomé de las Casas (1474–1565), the tireless champion of the Indians. Most remarkable of all is the work of Garcilaso de la Vega, whose *Comentarios Reales*, a poetic evocation of Inca history and customs, marks the first flowering of an authentically Latin American literature. Himself the offspring of an Indian princess and one of the conquistadores of Peru, Garcilaso was prompted to compose his work 'not only for the honour and renown of the Spanish nation which has accomplished such great things in the New World, but no less for those of the Indians . . . for they too appear worthy of the same praise'. Another great seminal work, composed by a Spanish friar with the help of Indian collaborators, is the monumental *Historia General de las Cosas de Nueva España* by Bernardino de Sahagún (d. 1590), an indispensable source for our knowledge of Mexican antiquity and the corner-stone of the future science of ethnography.

Since the Conquista was itself an epic, it is not surprising to find a number of attempts to celebrate it in the form of epic poems. One of these, *La Araucana* of Ercilla y Zúñiga (?1533–94), 'often penned on hides for lack of paper, and on scraps of letters so small that there was scarce room for six verses together', has won a worthy place in Spanish literature. The Portuguese, too, practised this genre with assiduity, from Bento Teixeira Pinto's *Prosopopéa* (1601) to Santa Rita Durão's *Caramurú* (1781), which aimed to celebrate the achievement of the Portuguese in Brazil much as the great Camoëns celebrated their achievement in India. Side by side with these formal commemorations of Iberian exploits in the New World, which often depict the conquered races too in a highly idealized light, there developed a mordant criticism of colonial society in the satirical poems of the Brazilian Gregório de Mattos (1633–96), described by his contemporaries as '*boca do inferno*' and by a later critic as 'the first native voice to be heard in Brazilian politics', and the Peruvian Juan del Valle Caviedes (?1652–?1697), the disreputable, sharp-tongued shopkeeper of Lima.

Amongst the most remarkable figures of the colonial period are the Brazilian Jesuit Antonio Vieira (1608–97) and the Mexican nun, Sor Juana Inés de la Cruz (?1651–95). For much of the seventeenth century Vieira played a dominant part in the councils of his King, João IV, and the public events of the day. Through his letters and reports, and especially through the stormy eloquence of his sermons, he helped to break the Dutch command of the ocean and their strangle-hold on north-east Brazil by urging the organization of a system of armed convoys. He campaigned tirelessly against the colonists' attempts to enslave the Indians, amongst whom he spent many years of arduous evangelization and into whose tongues he translated the Gospel. Though quick to denounce the faults of his countrymen, he was inspired with a messianic faith in the mission of the Portuguese nation which, he believed, was destined to constitute a world empire 'conquering and subjugating all the regions of the earth under one sole empire, so that all, under the aegis of the Crown, may be gloriously placed beneath the feet of the successor of St. Peter'. No wonder that to his contemporaries the fiery Jesuit seemed, as his monarch once observed of him, 'the greatest man in the world'.

For the Mexican nun, the avenues of public life were barred by her sex and her lack of fortune. But the cell in the convent where Sor Juana Inés de la Cruz spent her days, surrounded by her books and musical and scientific instruments, became the centre of Mexico's literary and intellectual life. Learning and poetry came to her as naturally as gossip to women of lesser calibre. Allegories, sonnets, plays sacred and profane, autobiography, verse in Latin and in Spanish, mostly couched in witty and highly rhetorical vein but sometimes poignant in its simple lyricism, poured from her pen. From crossing swords with the formidable polemicist Vieira, she would turn to the convent kitchen to deduce scientific principles from the frying of an egg or the spinning of a child's top. Then one day, reproved for the vanity of such pursuits, the nun fell silent, sold her books and instruments, and devoted the rest of her life to penitence and humble service to her community.

In an age when prudence enjoined orthodoxy, a brilliant and enquiring mind could be a dangerous possession, and the creative urge could find its safest vent, if not always the fullest satisfaction, in ingenuities of form. It is thus not surprising that the Baroque should be the most characteristic expression of Latin America's colonial age. Its literature, written for an élite for whom the Spanish master of *culteranismo*, Luis de Góngora, was the greatest of poets, abounded in elaborate metaphors, conceits, classical and contemporary allusions, and stylistic virtuosity. Fashionable society was addicted to the literary contest, in which aspiring poets would present their own elaborate but ephemeral compositions, whilst for the masses there were the bullfights and tournaments, the processions and sumptuous ritual of the Church, the *autos sacramentales* and other features of the Baroque culture of the great cities. The same spirit informed painting, the minor arts, and above all, sculpture and architecture, in which the local and popular elements added by *mestizo* craftsmen contributed to give to Latin American Baroque its distinctive character. Nowhere does the spirit find more striking expression than in the work of Brazil's 'Little Cripple', O Aleijadinho (Antônio Francisco Lisboa, 1730–1814), whose carvings adorn the wonderful churches of Vila Rica de Ouro Prêto ('The Rich Town of Dark Gold') and other once flourishing centres of Brazil's mining region. In O Aleijadinho's work—exquisitely carved portals, pulpits and medallions and especially the moving figures of his prophets, saints, and Christs—some critics see the expression of a Baroque genius akin to that of El Greco, whilst others stress its character of revolt against purely Portuguese artistic traditions and its embodiment of a deeply 'Brazilian' conception of art.

The African strand

One clue to the originality of O Aleijadinho's work may lie in the hybrid origins of its creator. Here the fusion is not that between European and Indian, which has produced the *mestizo* of Spanish America, but the fusion between European and African which colours the racial and much of the cultural character of Brazil and the Caribbean. In Haiti, where the European component is not

Portuguese but French, the blend has produced an overwhelmingly African stock and a vigorous and distinctive culture, particularly in the fields of painting and poetry. The African element is also important in Cuba, as the researches of Fernando Ortiz and the poetry of Nicolás Guillén, with its effective use of African rhythms and imagery, has shown.

In Brazil, the African influence has been profound, though the stigma of negro slavery long obscured recognition of this vital strand in the national genius. It was not until the second half of the nineteenth century, after the public conscience had been stirred by such moving poems as *The Slave Ship* and *Voices of Africa* by Castro Alves (1847–71), the passionate, short-lived 'poet of the slaves', that Brazil was prepared for the abolition of slavery (1888) and a gradual recognition of the social rights and cultural values of the negro. For the mulattos too, who in the words of an English traveller 'seem to unite the vices of savage and civilized life', the way to full acceptance has been long and hard. Calabar, the brilliant but unscrupulous half-breed who offered his services to the Dutch, remained for long the classic figure of mulatto treachery. The proverb that 'Brazil is a hell for blacks, a purgatory for whites, and a paradise for mulattos' has not always proved true. The offspring of Portuguese father and coloured slave-woman were indeed frequently brought up with the whites and fully accepted by them. But not always so; Aluízio Azevedo's powerful novel *O Mulato* tells the story of one such youth, carefully educated in Portugal, who returned to his native Maranhão (a part of Brazil traditionally less given to racial tolerance), only to be murdered when he tried to take his place in white society. It is curious that the most gifted of Brazilian novelists, Machado de Assis (1839-1908), the son of a negro father and a white mother, should have drawn the material for his penetrating and pessimistic studies almost exclusively from upper-class life and held aloof from the burning controversy over negro emancipation. But the polished and humane character of Machado de Assis's own work itself testifies to the enrichment brought by the African strain to Brazil's national genius.

The value of this African contribution was not, however, fully recognized until the 1930s, after the publication of Gilberto Freyre's *Casa-Grande e Senzala* (translated under the title of *Masters and Slaves*) with its glorification of Brazil's mixed heritage as 'one of the most harmonious unions of culture with nature, and of one culture with another, that the lands of this hemisphere have ever known'. The germinal institution of Brazilian life, in Freyre's view, was the *casa-grande* of the great patriarchal slave-owning families, with its adjacent *senzala* or slave-quarters which housed the negro labourers of the sugar estates: 'the social history of the plantation manor-house is the intimate history of practically everything Brazilian; of its domestic, conjugal life, under a polygamous slave-holding regime; of the life of the child; of its Christianity reduced to a family religion and influenced by the superstitions of the slave-quarters.' As time went on, there developed what Freyre calls 'zones of fraternization between conquerors and conquered, between masters and slaves', which resulted in a gradual fusion of cultures, a softening of the once sharply opposed economic, social and racial forces to produce what is most characteristic in the Brazilian character and way of life, so that now one has 'the impression that they have grown up together fraternally, and that rather than being mutually hostile by reason of their antagonism, they supplement one another with their differences'. Though stressing the positive results of miscegenation, Freyre is also aware of the deleterious effects which may have stemmed from this master–slave relationship—the exercise of arbitrary power tending to produce a strain of sadism in relationships not only between superiors and inferiors but those between the dominant male and the passive female, even perhaps in the social and political field 'where the dictatorial tendency has always found ready victims on which to exercise its sadistic qualities'. But on the whole, once freed from the degrading conditions of slavery, the negro element has endowed Brazil with many of its most attractive and distinctive features. We find it pulsating through the African rhythms and folklore themes in the music of Villa-Lobos (1887–1959) and inspiring the compassionate, proletarian paintings of Cândido Portinari (1903–62), and in Brazil's rich literature of poetry and fiction, particularly in such novels as Lins do Rêgo's *Sugar-Cane Cycle*, a sort of fictional counterpart to Freyre's sociological researches.

Cultural emancipation and the quest for identity

For the last century and a half, Latin American thinkers and writers have been much concerned with the problem of freeing themselves from the stultifying influence of the past and achieving what they feel to be their true and distinctive spiritual identity. 'The body has won freedom but not the mind,' wrote the Argentine poet and radical social thinker Esteban Echeverría (1805–51) soon after the wars of independence. 'We are independent, but we are not free: the arms of Spain no longer oppress us, but her traditions still weigh us down.' The political revolution carried out by the liberators needed to be completed by a mental and social revolution, and 'the social emancipation of America can only be achieved by repudiating the heritage bequeathed by Spain'. In Chile, José Victorino Lastarria (1817–88) tirelessly repeated the same theme and urged the Latin Americans to 'destroy completely the resistance offered by the old Spanish system embodied in our society'. His compatriot Francisco Bilbao (1823–65) went even further and attacked Catholicism itself as the basis of the old order: 'Either Catholicism triumphs and monarchy and theocracy rule America, or Republicanism triumphs with free reason and the religion of law dominating the conscience of every man.' Though the Liberals were ready to attack the Church as a reactionary institution, Bilbao's denunciation of the Christian faith itself struck his contemporaries as blasphemous and seditious, and he was forced into exile. The Conservatives believed with Andrés Bello (1781–1865), the Venezuelan who had been tutor to Bolívar and friend to Bentham and Mill before settling in Chile to endow that country with a new educational and legal system, that not only Catholicism but the best elements of the Spanish past should be retained as the surest foundations for the young republics. Not a few distinguished Latin Americans have continued to emphasize the principle of continuity and *hispanidad* which their countries share with Spain. A notable champion of this view was the Mexican educationist and philosopher José Vasconcelos (1881–1958), author of *La Raza Cósmica*, the famous paean to Latin American destiny based on a universal fusion of the races. After sharing the *indigenista* aspirations of the Mexican revolution and encouraging the work of the great muralists, Vasconcelos reverted to a faith in Catholicism and the Hispanic past. 'We shall never be great,' he wrote, 'until the Spanish American feels himself to be just as Spanish as the sons of Spain.' As for the Indian, he has 'no road other than that which has been traced out by Latin culture'.

Those Latin Americans who, unlike Vasconcelos, repudiated the cultural heritage of their mother countries, could nevertheless find another source of inspiration in Europe. Even in colonial times, French taste and French litera-ture, and the daring thought of the *encyclopédistes* had powerfully attracted Latin America's élite. Rousseau, Chateaubriand, Marmontel, and Bernardin de Saint-Pierre had aroused their romantic interest in the American Indian. In the nineteenth century French taste prevailed in painting, sculpture, and architecture, and the Positivist creed of Auguste Comte in the thinking of their enlightened statesmen and philosophers. Paris was the Latin American's Mecca, and few leading writers, even those of such original genius as the Peruvian poet César Vallejo (1892–1938) and the Chilean Pablo Neruda (b. 1904), failed to live and work in France at some time of their lives. 'We lived off Europe, off its science and literature,' wrote the Argentine historian Juan B. Tarán: 'we sought the help of its men; we absorbed its ideas and adorned ourselves with its culture. America was the satellite of Europe.' The Latin American capacity for eclectic absorption and adaptation could indeed reach such a pitch that it became itself a title to originality. Contemporary Spanish letters were in turn enriched and vitalized by that amalgam of many -isms and influences known as *modernismo*, which stemmed from the work of the Nicaraguan poet Rubén Darío (1867–1916) and became Latin America's first contribution to world literature. Some twenty years later a movement of the same name but differing inspiration stirred Brazil. Beneath the effer-vescence and eccentricities of the work of Mário de Andrade (1893–1945), author of a celebrated poem on the *Hallucinated City*, and other exponents of the movement, a serious purpose could be discerned: the search through this multiplicity of cultural components for a valid national identity, the quest for *brasilidade*.

'Civilization and Barbarism'

The challenge to Latin America was not simply to discard alien influence in order to discover her true self; that self, in the view of some of her thinkers, was as yet untamed and barbarous and needed first to be refined by the spread of more civilized ways. Such was the message of Argentina's great writer and statesman, Domingo Faustino Sarmiento (1811–88). His *Civilización y Bar-barie*, more popularly known as *Facundo* after the *caudillo* who forms its frightening central figure, is an extraordinary compound of biography, contemporary history, political diatribe, sociological interpretation, and essay in national psychology—'a chunk of rock hurled at the head of a tyrant', as Sarmiento himself described it. He saw the *pampa* roamed by bands of *gauchos*—'the source and symbol of the wretchedness, the savagery, and the poverty of the people'—who took the law into their own hands and terrorized the towns. Between the latter and the rough *gauchos* yawned a vast gulf. 'Implacable is the hatred which civilized men inspire in them. They seem to be two entirely different societies, two nations alien to each other.' Sarmiento believed that the gulf could only be bridged by better communications, which would break down the brutalizing solitude of the *pampa*, by education and by immigration, and after his election to the Presidency he worked tirelessly for these ends. Another distinguished compatriot, Juan Bautista Alberdi (1810–84), the chief architect of the Argentine Constitution, popularized the slogan *gobernar es poblar* ('to govern is to populate') and pressed for Anglo-Saxon immigrants, since he believed that they alone possessed the political maturity needed if democratic institutions were to take root. 'Liberty', he declared, 'is like a machine which, for its proper functioning, needs not only steam but engineers of English origin as well.'

Sarmiento's thesis of civilization and barbarism seemed relevant to other parts of Latin America besides Argentina. The Venezuelan classic *Doña Bárbara*, by Rómulo Gallegos (1884–1969), another writer who became President of his country, tells the story of a woman brutalized by the harsh life of the *llanos* and confronted by a man who represents the civilized values of the city. Brazil too has its epic of rural violence in *Os Sertões*, by Euclides da Cunha (1866–1909), an engineer who worked in the wild backlands and witnessed the closing scenes of the tragedy he movingly describes. The rebellious fanatics of Canudos, loyal to their half-crazed prophet Antonio the Counsellor, defied the forces sent against them by the Republic and held out until they were destroyed to the last man. Da Cunha's work, like Sarmiento's, defies classification. It is a blend of biography, vivid reportage, and sociological and ecological analysis which its admirers have variously compared to the Bible, *Don Quixote*, the *Divine Comedy*, the *Seven Pillars of Wisdom*, and *War and Peace*. Although imbued with the Positivist outlook of the day and expressing the now discredited thesis that 'an intermingling of highly diverse races is, in the majority of cases, prejudicial . . . Miscegenation, carried to extreme, means regression', *Os Sertões* is a penetrating, compassionate, and grandiose work which grapples honestly with the problems of Brazil's untamed hinterland. It is the first and greatest of the many fine works, such as João Guimarães Rosa's *Grande Sertão—Veredas* (1856), which deal with Brazil's intractable north-east.

Towards the end of the nineteenth century, when immigration, education, and railways were beginning to transform the *pampa*, there set in a reaction in favour of its vanishing ways of life. *Martín Fierro*, the eponymous hero of the famous poem by José Hernández (1834-84), relates in pithy, vivid verse the story of his untrammelled life before the coming of 'civilization', the suffering and injustices endured when he fell into the clutches of the press-gang for the wars against the Indians, the tavern brawls and brutal knife-fights, and his eventual flight to the freer life of the wild Indians. This poem and its sequel, *The Return of Martín Fierro*, in which the hero tries to come to terms with civilization, established the *gaucho* myth and quickly entered into Argentina's folk-lore. It fathered a host of *gaucho* novels, South America's equivalent of the Westerns, the finest of which is Ricardo Güiraldes's *Don Segundo Sombra* (1926), a tale of the cowboy who preserves his integrity by refusing to adapt himself to the new ways and finally rides off to lose himself in the immensity of the *pampa*.

The continuing cult of the *gaucho* seems to answer the psychological needs of an increasingly urban population. As Jorge Luis Borges (b. 1899), the distinguished Argentine novelist who moves in a very different world of ironic and scholarly fantasy, has put it: 'The civilized inhabitants of the modern cities of the River Plate now compensate themselves for what they have missed: the physical dangers, the barbarous duels with flashing knives, the nights spent in the open air with saddle as pillow, the drunkenness, rape, and violent death.' The *gaucho* cult has also stimulated writers like Ricardo Rojas (1882–1957) and Ezequiel Martínez Estrada (1895–1964) to an exploration of the moral values and material resources of their country, which they believe to have suffered from the imposition of alien modes of life and foreign exploitation. 'In the present state of our country,' wrote Rojas, 'it is the *campo* which is the seat of civilization on account of its valiant labour which sustains the cities, the moral health of those who live in it, and because its landscape and traditions are the inspiration of its nascent art, whereas the cities are parasites of bureaucracy, commerce, slothful sensuality, cosmopolitan rootlessness—in short, of barbarism. The terms of the problems posed by Sarmiento have been reversed.' In his *Radiografía de la Pampa* (1933), Martínez Estrada argues that the foreign influences which Sarmiento and Alberdi so warmly welcomed have not in fact enriched the country but have led to the exploitation of its resources in the interest of the overseas market and the foreign capitalist. The assumption that a 'barbarous' Latin America could be redeemed by more highly civilized influences from outside has given way to the belief that, on the contrary, its backwardness is the result of its exploitation by 'economic imperialism'.

The shadow of the Colossus

By the end of the nineteenth century the Latin American republics had been outstripped by the dynamic growth of the United States and felt themselves threatened by the ambitious and alien spirit of the 'northern Colossus'. 'Formerly it was a struggle against Spain,' wrote the Mexican philosopher Leopoldo Zea (b. 1912), 'now it is a struggle against our new mother country, the United States, for we are still a colony. It is always the same—a struggle for our independence. At one time it was a political struggle against Spain: then it was a spiritual struggle against Spain's habits and customs, and later an economic struggle against the bourgeoisie of which we are only the tools.'

In one corner of the Caribbean—the islands of Cuba and Puerto Rico— these stages of struggle overlapped, and many Cubans feared, and a few even wished, that they would break free from Spain only to be annexed (as proved to be the fate of Puerto Rico) by the United States. The dilemma was clearly discerned by José Martí (1853–95), the Cuban patriot and writer who spent much of his life in exile in the United States. Few foreigners have written with greater admiration and insight than Martí of the republic of Washington, Jefferson, and Lincoln. But Martí was keenly conscious of the differences be- tween Anglo-Saxon and Latin America, both in the nature of their genius and in their material strength. He feared that Cuba might be absorbed by a United States avid for fresh markets and new fields for investment. 'Economic union will lead to political union,' he warned in words which might be taken to heart by the present rulers of Cuba, who have broken free from the embrace of the Colossus of the North only to fall into that of the East. 'A nation which wants to die sells to a single country; a nation which wants to live sells to more than one. Excessive influence by one country on the trade of another becomes political influence.' A tireless champion of the underdog, Martí eloquently denounced the tyrannous exercise of power, whether by states or *caudillos*, and affirmed that 'in the last analysis, the greatness of nations rests on the independence of individuals'. In his distrust of the established Church as a tool of the repressive tyranny of Spain, Martí is in the anti-clerical tradition of Latin American liberalism. 'Christianity has perished at the hands of Catho- licism' is a characteristic Martian apophthegm. But in his freedom from hatred and bitterness, his conviction that 'the future must be conquered with clean hands' and a better social order built by those whom he calls 'fanatics of love' rather than by revolutionaries who are 'fanatics of hate', Martí occupies a place of his own amongst Latin America's political thinkers and men of action, and rightly deserves the name of the Apostle by which he is widely known and loved.

Many different explanations have been advanced by Latin American writers as to why their countries failed to progress to the same extent as the United States. Sarmiento and his compatriot Carlos Octavio Bunge (1875–1918) ex- plained it mainly as the result of miscegenation. The Chilean historian Francisco Encina, in his *Nuestra Inferioridad Económica* (1912), put the blame on inherited Hispanic character defects. The *Pueblo Enfermo* of Alcides Arguedas attributed the malady to a mixture of innate *mestizo* incapacity and harsh national environment. The diagnosis offered by the Uruguayan José Enrique Rodó (1871–1917) was more reassuring: Latin America was not sick but simply young and immature. His *Motivos de Proteo* and his shorter and more famous *Ariel* (1900) are a series of meditations, in polished and mannered prose, on the spiritual essence of man's nature and the need to preserve and nourish it. In *Ariel*, the sage exhorts the young of Latin America to eschew vulgarity and cultivate the nobility of mind, good taste, and delicacy of feeling which he sees to be lacking in their more materially successful cousins of North America. Rodó's unflattering allusions to the latter were only marginal to his main theme, but they soon won an astonishing popularity for *Ariel*, which became the credo of a whole generation and the apologia for an idealistic, spiritual Latin America in contrast to the crudely materialist Anglo-Saxon Caliban of the North. In the *Ariel* myth, Latin Americans found what one of their writers has described as 'the justification of their racial characteristics, the compensation for their practical backwardness, the claim to spiritual superiority over the Titan of the North'.

The propagation of the *Ariel* myth has served to deflect attention from that Achilles heel of Latin American culture—its neglect of science and technology. Spain's indifference to these pursuits, despite the stimulus which Enlightened Despotism had briefly attempted to provide, was a major factor in her decay. Apart from the initiative of a few early enthusiasts and the later pretensions of Positivists and *científicos*, the ruling élite of the independent republics did little to make good this lack. In recent times some honourable exceptions spring to mind: Carlos Finlay in Cuba, who discovered the link between yellow fever and the mosquito, Argentina's Nobel prizewinner Bernardo Houssay, characteristically dismissed by the Perón regime for 'incompetence', or the other Nobel prizewinners, Carlos Saavedra Lamas and Luis Federico Leloir. But in general, Latin America's contribution to the advancement of scientific knowledge has been of the most modest. Only now are the Latin Americans beginning to realize that they can never escape from under-development and dependence on the larger powers so long as they lag so far behind in science and technology. Native intelligence and, in the larger republics at least, material resources are not lacking. Several countries can already boast of fully automated factories and experimental atomic plant. There are those in Brazil who are seriously working for the day when a Brazilian satellite will be launched from a Brazilian rocket. But solid foundations for such advances have still to be laid in mental attitudes and in the curricula of Latin American universities, which continue to produce quantities of lawyers and arts graduates and only a trickle of scientists, engineers, agronomists, and technicians (see page 246). In 1962, less than one thousand students graduated in natural sciences for the whole of Latin America: the corresponding figure for the United States was 56,712. Caliban has grown up into a computerized colossus. No comforting myth of Latin America's superior concern for spiritual values can explain away the grave disparity in technological levels. In an age of communication satellites and space travel even Ariel may find himself obsolete.

New perspectives

In other fields of intellectual and artistic endeavour, however, the scene is one of vigour and variety. Architects of the stature of Oscar Niemeyer and Roberto Burle Marx in Brazil, Carlos Rafael Villanueva in Caracas, Mario Pani and Enrique del Moral, Juan O'Gorman and Felix Candela in Mexico, have endowed their cities with modern buildings whose daring forms are conceived as consonant with Latin America's distinctive spatial, social, and topographical context. In painting, the range is even wider, for there are still artists doing good work of traditional inspiration, or in the vigorous Mexican indigenist spirit or preoccupied, as in Cuba, with a consciously revolutionary style, whilst elsewhere the influence is predominantly surrealist or abstract. Here the urge is to transcend limitations of locality and period and to produce work whose character is universal rather than specifically Latin American. In the canvases of Roberto Matta, Wilfredo Lam, Jesús de Soto, or Rufino Tamayo, one is aware of sophisticated talents of a high order, rather than of any distinctively Chilean, Cuban, Venezuelan, or Mexican inspiration on the part of their respective creators. The musical spectrum is no less wide, ranging from the rich local colour of such compositions as the Mexican Silvestre Revueltas's snake-song *Sensemaya*, based on a lyric by the Cuban Nicolás Guillén, to works of 'pure' and experimental music in the contemporary idiom.

Literature is marked by the dividing line of language. The Spanish- and Portuguese-speaking parts of the population are sadly ignorant of each other; how many Spanish-American readers so much as know, for instance, the name of Cabral de Melo, who is probably Brazil's most distinguished living poet? We cannot therefore speak of any 'Latin American' literature proper, nor indeed of specifically Colombian, Mexican, or Argentinian literatures. Each Spanish-speaking country contributes its own strand. Together with the rich literature of Spain, these strands make up a single whole and constitute, in turn, one of the components of our wider Western culture.

In poetry, there is the towering figure of Pablo Neruda, whose *Canto General* is a grandiose attempt to explore the nature of his native Chile, and through it that of Latin America and of Man himself. In the field of fiction, half a dozen novelists of the first rank are at work. Cuba's social revolution has given a platform to several young writers of talent, but the great figures remain those of an earlier generation: Lezama Lima, whose *Paradiso* presents a protean world which owes little resemblance to the revolutionary ferment around him, and Alejo Carpentier, whose *Explosion in a Cathedral* is a historic evocation calling in question the nature of all revolutions and their effect on the human personality, and who recounts, in *The Lost Steps*, one man's quest to rediscover the cultural origins of his race. Mexico has its Carlos Fuentes and its Juan Rulfo, unsparing dissectors of contemporary society, and conscious of the background of violence and tragedy which has given it birth. Mario Vargas Llosa, in his fierce indictment of Lima society and the prevailing military ethos (*The City and the Dogs*), and J. M. Arguedas, with his subtle exploration of the other indigenous world, probe beneath the surface of contemporary Peru. Julio Cortázar, though he chooses, like so many of his contemporaries, to live and work in exile—for almost all write in protest against Latin America's present power and value systems—remains obsessed with the great city of Buenos Aires, not in a strictly documentary sense, but as a palimpsest of differing levels of time and experience. One of his short stories treats of a man undergoing an operation after a street accident in Mexico, who finds himself lying not on the operating table but over a sacrificial stone in an Aztec temple waiting for the stroke of the obsidian knife. This interaction of past and present, of the real and the fantastic, is a hallmark of the contemporary Latin American novel. In his *A Hundred Years of Solitude*, García Márquez writes of the remote Colombian village of Macondo, where the striking workers on the banana plantations are callously massacred (see page 146) but where the dead also walk and talk with the living, and a girl is caught up to heaven whilst hanging out the washing. The reader too may be swept off his feet by the sheer imaginative force and zest, the mingled tragi-comedy, of such writing. In this sphere at least, Latin America has passed far beyond the dependent and derivative to create something of irresistible originality.

6 Inter-American and International Relations

The Latin American republics, like other countries in the world today, are guided in their international relations by what they conceive to be their state interests and by the powerful promptings of nationalism. The latter is a somewhat ambivalent force. Towards each other the republics act with the assertiveness of the nation-state, conscious of the things which divide and differentiate them from one another. But in their relations with the great northern neighbour and with non-American states, this nationalist stance tends to broaden out into a sense of more generalized solidarity, almost to a sort of Latin American, continental supra-nationalism, stemming from an awareness of their common linguistic, cultural, and historical origins and certain shared customs and attitudes. In this two-tiered concept of nationalism they resemble the Arab states. Chileans and Argentines, Bolivians and Paraguayans, Peruvians and Ecuadoreans may be conscious of the differences, at times bitter and deep-rooted, which set them apart, but in their dealings with the non-Latin American world they tend to feel and act as members of the same community. Though bent on pursuing what they believe to be their immediate national interests, they nevertheless preserve a sense of higher regional loyalty and aspire, however falteringly, to closer integration and perhaps some form of ultimate union. A century and a half of independence has moulded the ex-colonies into fully differentiated nation-states; now they are finding themselves drawn more and more tightly together by improved communications, mutual economic advantage, and the need for enhanced security and influence. In the tensions created by these contrary pulls the Latin American republics have steered a troubled course.

Territorial and other disputes

Broadly speaking, the borders of the new republics were drawn on the principle of *uti possidetis* and followed the former administrative divisions of the old Spanish empire. The demarcation between them often ran across uncharted deserts or mountain ranges and was left vaguely defined and uncontested until some new economic or strategic factor aroused interest and competing claims. Thus, in the second half of the nineteenth century, the discovery of rich nitrate deposits in the hitherto disregarded Atacama desert and the lucrative rubber boom in the vast Amazon basin led respectively to the War of the Pacific between Chile and Peru and the Bolivian–Brazilian dispute over Acre. The suspected presence of oil is reputed to have been a cause of the Chaco

War between Bolivia and Paraguay. Nor do natural features such as rivers always make obvious and undisputed state boundaries; the silting-up of navigation channels, the possession of islands in mid-stream, and the control of the waters for irrigation and hydro-electrical purposes may all give rise to dispute, as has proved to be the case in the River Plate Basin. Demographic pressure from over-populated states such as El Salvador and Haiti may also lead to open or undeclared war against a neighbour. Disparity of size, population and resources is not, however, in itself a threat to peace, though the smaller states who live under the shadow of the 'big three'—Mexico, Argentina, and Brazil—may be excused from thinking so when a regime with aggressive hegemonic designs, such as that of Perón, takes over. Latin America contains within itself a balance of power system which is long established and has proved remarkably stable. Any serious attempt to upset it would still no doubt call forth strong counter-action, as when Chile went to war to foil the ambitions of the Peruvian–Bolivian Confederation (see page 156). Ideological differences alone, though they may lead to subversion and attempted coups engineered from neighbouring countries, have caused no radical change in the overall balance of power. Dictatorships continue to coexist with democracies, and (since the advent of Castro) Communist with anti-Communist regimes.

Some disputes, though officially, or at least unilaterally, regarded as closed, have nevertheless left scars which are apt to reopen in moments of stress. Bolivia has never reconciled herself to the loss of her maritime province and continues to demand some compensatory outlet to the sea. This grievance has prevented the use of the waters of the River Lauca, which are jointly owned by Chile and Bolivia, to the mutual benefit of both countries, and resulted in 1961 in the severance of diplomatic relations between them. Ecuador no less stubbornly refuses to recognize Peru's *de jure* title to the formerly Ecuadorean territory on the Upper Amazon which was seized in the war of 1940–1 and awarded to Peru by the Rio Protocol of the following year. Peru, for her part, harbours resentment against Chile for the latter's acquisition of Tacna following the War of the Pacific, and against Colombia for foiling Peruvian attempts to gain a foothold on the Amazon at Letitia (see page 146). Chile, in turn, is apt to remain resentful and suspicious of her more populous neighbour Argentina, though the long-standing territorial quarrels between the two countries have now been narrowed to the Beagle Channel linking the Atlantic and the Pacific south of Tierra del Fuego and to the question of sovereignty over the islands lying south of it. Colombia and Venezuela cannot agree on the demarcation of their maritime frontier in the Gulf of Venezuela, where rich submarine oil deposits may await exploitation, and relations are further strained by the large numbers of unauthorized immigrants from Colombia who have settled in Venezuela. In Central America, the chief source of tension remains the demographic pressures within El Salvador and the presence of a large body of unauthorized immigrants over the Honduran border which led to the brief 'football' war between the two countries in mid-1969. Elsewhere in Central America, along the once disputed borders of Costa Rica with Nicaragua and of Nicaragua with Honduras, settlements appear to have been reached. But he would be a bold optimist indeed who could claim that any frontier in Latin America which had once been in dispute had been safely 'settled' for good.

Pan-Americanism and the Inter-American system

In the wider context of inter-American solidarity, grounds for optimism have nevertheless not been lacking. Despite the setbacks repeatedly inflicted by aggressive local nationalism, Bolívar's vision of American union may have faded but it has never completely vanished from men's minds. In the years between Independence and the close of the nineteenth century, the republics fought at least five full-scale wars amongst themselves (Brazil against Argentina, 1825–8; Argentina against Uruguay and then Brazil, 1842–52; Paraguay against Brazil, Uruguay, and Argentina, 1864–70; Chile against Peru and Bolivia, 1836–9 and 1879–83); but in the same period, following the abortive Congress of Panama convened by Bolívar (see page 76), representatives of the American states also met together on seven different occasions to find solutions for commercial, legal, and medical issues of common concern.

In 1889/90 they met again for the first of a new series of official International Conferences. The inter-American system which emerged was of 'Monrovian' rather than 'Bolivarian' inspiration, and aimed less at drawing together the Latin American republics than associating them with the United States. It grew up under the wing of Washington, where the 1889 Conference was held and an Inter-American Bureau established. The latter was at first virtually an organ of the United States government. Its annual reports were submitted direct to Congress, and the Secretary of State named the chairman of its governing board and appointed its director and staff. During the 1920s, a series of measures was taken to give the Latin Americans, who naturally resented this United States tutelage, more say in the organization which nominally represented their governments. The latter began to accredit ambassadors direct to the organization instead of simply instructing their diplomatic representatives in Washington to attend its sessions; the chairmanship of the governing body no longer went automatically to the Secretary of State but was open to annual election; and the precedent was set of electing a Latin American to be its Secretary-General.

During the following decade, thanks to Roosevelt's Good Neighbour policy (see below, page 334) and the rising threat of Nazi Germany, inter-American co-operation acquired a new meaning and a new urgency. Non-intervention—the principle so vigorously championed by the Latin Americans and hitherto so often disregarded by the United States, that no state has the right to interfere in the internal affairs of another—received increasing recognition at a series of inter-American conferences and agreements (1933, 1936, 1938). The threat to their mutual security drew the American countries together, and three weeks after the outbreak of World War II in 1939, their Foreign Ministers met together in Panama to devise a neutrality zone for the western hemisphere and to set up machinery to mitigate the unfavourable effects of the war on their economies. The following year, in Havana, they worked out emergency plans for taking over European colonies in the area in case of need, and passed a resolution to the effect that any attack against one American state would be considered an act of aggression against all of them. After Pearl Harbor, the Foreign Ministers met again at Rio (January 1942) and recommended that, since such an act had been perpetrated, all the American republics should break off relations with the Axis powers; some did so forthwith, and a few went further and declared war. At the beginning of 1945, the Foreign Ministers met again in Mexico to take fresh stock of the problems of war and peace and to devise machinery which would put post-war inter-American co-operation onto a sounder basis (Act of Chapultepec). This paved the way for the important 1947 Inter-American Treaty of Reciprocal Assistance (Rio Treaty), establishing a system of collective security for the Western Hemisphere, and the foundation of the Organization of American States (OAS).

The Organization of American States

The OAS was conceived as an organ, under the United Nations, for the pacific settlement of regional disputes, collective security and the furtherance of economic, social, cultural, and political co-operation. Its membership included the United States and the twenty Latin American republics, and was later extended to Trinidad–Tobago (1967), Barbados (1968), and Jamaica (1969). (Canada has so far declined to join, and Guyana is excluded under the terms of the 1964 Act of Washington which disqualifies any country against whom a member state may have a territorial claim.)

The structure of the OAS originally comprised: (a) the Council, its executive organ, composed of one representative from each member state, each having equal voice and vote (but no right of veto); (b) the Pan-American Union, its permanent secretariat, with headquarters in Washington; (c) the Inter-American Conference, its supreme organ, scheduled to meet once every five years; (d) the Meeting of Consultation of Ministers of Foreign Affairs, summoned at the request of any member state to deal with urgent problems of common interest such as alleged violations of the principle of non-intervention or subversive activities; (e) specialized conferences concerned with technical matters or with developing specific aspects of inter-American co-operation; (f) specialized organizations dealing respectively with problems of Public Health, Indian Affairs, Geography and History, Agriculture, Children and Women, together with agencies and commissions on Human Rights, Statistics, Defence, Nuclear Energy, the Inter-American Peace Committee, and the Inter-American Development Bank.

In February 1970 a revised Charter came into force which introduced several important changes in the structure and character of the OAS. The quinquennial Inter-American Conference had been in abeyance since 1954 owing to Ecuador's insistence, and Peru's refusal, to place on the agenda an item calling in question the Rio Protocol by which Ecuador had lost her Amazonian territories to Peru. It was now replaced by an annual General

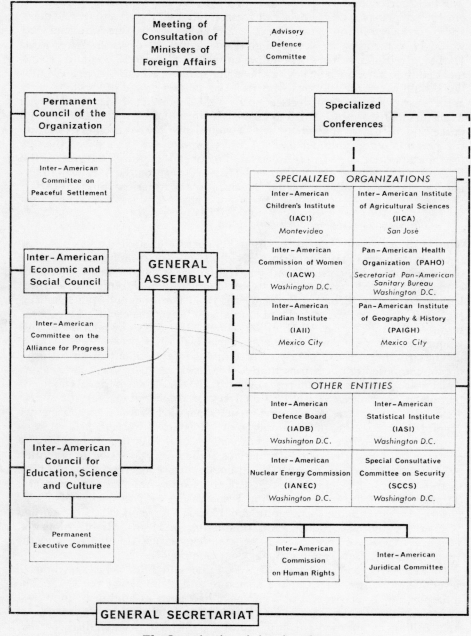

The Organization of American States

Assembly. The Executive Council was superseded by three parallel bodies: the Permanent Council dealing with political questions, particularly with the peaceful settlement of disputes, the Inter-American Social and Economic Council, and the Inter-American Council for Education, Science, and Culture. The OAS thus now has the organization shown in the diagram.

Though it has established itself as a useful forum for inter-American consultation and has a number of achievements to its credit, the OAS has been hampered by the divergent attitudes and interests of its members. The United States has been primarily concerned with hemisphere security which, since the onset of the Cold War, it saw threatened by international Communism and has been determined to oppose, preferably by collective but if necessary by unilateral action. The Latin American countries, on the other hand, have been preoccupied with upholding the principle of non-intervention in their internal affairs, and latterly with the need to accelerate the rate of their economic development, which they believe can best be done by strengthening their bargaining position *vis-à-vis* the United States. The Charter of the OAS was drafted with a view to reconciling these differing viewpoints. Articles 15 and 17 reaffirmed the pledge to renounce unilateral action, whereas Article 19 declared that 'measures adopted for the maintenance of peace and security' did not constitute a violation of this principle.

Much controversy has developed round the interpretation of these clauses. Washington's thesis has been that the threat of Communist subversion was tantamount to external aggression, and that appropriate measures of collective action against it were justified. This view received reluctant Latin American endorsement at the Tenth Inter-American Conference at Caracas (1954) when a Declaration was drawn up to the effect that 'the domination or control of the political institutions of any American State by the international Communist movement . . . would constitute a threat to the sovereignty and political independence of the American States'. Following the establishment of Castro's avowedly Marxist–Leninist regime in Cuba, a meeting of the OAS was held at Punta del Este in 1962 and a resolution passed, despite some initial Latin American opposition, that the adherence of any member state to Marxist–Leninist ideology was incompatible with the Inter-American system and that Cuba had consequently placed herself outside the OAS. At a further meeting, held two years later to consider Venezuelan charges of Cuban subversion, it was recommended, by 15 votes to 4, that member states should break diplomatic relations and suspend all trade and sea communications with Havana. The United States thesis seemed to have prevailed. But some Latin American states hesitated to implement their resolution to break with Cuba, and Mexico declined altogether to do so.

If the Latin Americans were loath to approve the principle of collective action against a Communist regime, the United States seemed no less unwilling to renounce the right of unilateral intervention. This was soon illustrated by two events which caused consternation in Latin America. The first was the abortive Bay of Pigs invasion of Cuba (1961), the second President Johnson's decision to intervene in the Dominican Republic (1965). (See pages 133 and

123.) The President declared that this course had been taken 'to save the lives of our citizens and all people', and furthermore that it was 'in keeping with the great principles of the Inter-American System, to prevent another Communist State in this hemisphere'. Washington's action, taken without prior consultation with her allies, was brought retrospectively within the framework of inter-American procedures by the setting up of a Committee of Mediation and an Inter-American Force which would take over from the United States command. Brazil was the only Latin American country to make an effective contribution to the International Force, though others sent token contingents. A Resolution passed by Congress on 20 September reasserting the right of the United States, or any other OAS member, to intervene to prevent the establishment of a Communist regime aroused strong criticism in Latin American countries and revealed the wide gap which still separated their standpoint from that of the United States. In helping to settle disputes between the smaller Latin American countries (e.g. that between El Salvador and Honduras in 1969) the OAS has subsequently proved able to play a useful role, but Washington has been unable to secure Latin American agreement for the setting up of a permanent Inter-American Peace Force.

The Latin Americans, for their part, have had more success in pressing for higher priority to be given to the economic aspect of inter-American co-operation. Though the proposals they put forward in 1948 were not adopted, a comprehensive programme of social and economic goals was formulated in the Act of Bogotá (1960), and at the same time, the Inter-American Development Bank began operations. Washington had at first objected to the foundation of the IADB, but later agreed to supply 40 per cent of the capital. The following year, in response to the appeal made in 1958 by President Kubitschek of Brazil for an 'Operation Pan-America' which would do for Latin America what the Marshall Plan had done for Europe, President Kennedy launched the Alliance for Progress (see below, page 335). The setting up (1963) of an Inter-American Committee (CIAP) to advise on its objective and operations went some way towards giving the Latin Americans more say in the working of the Alliance. But they pressed for more: a re-structuring of the OAS machinery—achieved with the entry into force of the revised Charter in 1970—so as to give higher priority to its handling of economic questions, and increased solidarity amongst the Latin American countries themselves *vis-à-vis* Washington. In May 1969, the Latin American countries formulated their standpoint in a document known as the Consensus of Viña del Mar which called for a radical revision of the United States' economic policies (and those of other developed countries) towards Latin America. They demanded an increase in the volume and efficacy of aid, preferably through multilateral bodies, a relaxation of the 'tied loan' requirement which confined Latin American purchases to the high-priced North American market, United States preferences for imports of Latin American manufactured and semi-manufactured goods, reduced interest rates, and the easing of the burden of debt servicing, a pledge that no new tariff restrictions would be imposed on Latin American goods entering the United States and that there would be no 'dumping' of United States products which might harm Latin American exports, and a promise of Washington's support for a new round of negotiations on primary products at GATT. The following year a Special Committee for Consultation and Negotiation was set up within the OAS framework where these and other economic issues between the Latin American countries and the United States could be further pursued. In April 1971, the first General Assembly under the revised OAS charter was held at San José and passed (the United States abstaining) a resolution reiterating the call for improved conditions of trade and aid from the industrialized nations. The confrontation between the Third World and the developed countries, between the 'Bolivarian' and the 'Monrovian' concept of inter-American relations, seemed likely to remain a continuing theme of the 'seventies.

Economic integration

(i) *The Latin American Free Trade Association (LAFTA)*. Latin America, like Europe (though starting from more unpromising positions), has become increasingly committed to the difficult process of regional economic integration. The need for action along these lines is now generally recognized by her leaders both as a means of strengthening their position *vis-à-vis* the United States and other trading nations and as a prerequisite for their own economic development. Their own national markets are too small to support the industrialization which they see as their best means of escape from underdevelopment, and consequently it suffers from high production costs and idle capacity. Even the large republics can scarcely hope to build up a viable heavy industry such as iron and steel without access to wider markets. Nor can new industries be established without the risk of wasteful duplication unless national development plans are co-ordinated in schemes of wider regional development. Though it offers no panacea for all Latin America's economic ills, the case for progressive integration is thus a strong one.

An important move in this direction was made in 1960 when seven countries (Mexico, Argentina, Brazil, Chile, Paraguay, Peru, and Uruguay) signed the Treaty of Montevideo establishing the Latin American Free Trade Association (LAFTA). Colombia and Ecuador joined in 1961, and Venezuela and Bolivia in 1966 and 1967 respectively. With the long-term objectives of preparing the ground for a Latin American common market and the immediate aim of progressively reducing trade barriers amongst its members, LAFTA began to operate through the parallel methods of annual bilateral negotiations for item-by-item tariff reductions and triennial negotiations for a 'common list' of products, which should account for at least 25 per cent of the value of their intra-zonal trade, to be irrevocably freed from tariff and other barriers. In this way it was envisaged that 50 per cent of trade within LAFTA would be free by 1967 and the entire intra-zonal trade by 1973. During the first five years of its existence, LAFTA did achieve a useful degree of trade liberalization as the result of annual negotiations covering more than 9,000 items. The volume of Latin America's intra-zonal trade rose from 6 per cent of her total in 1961 to over 11 per cent in 1965. By that year, however, the integration process had begun to lose momentum, and the difficulty of reaching agreement on the first 'common list' and the postponement of implementation until 1973 augured ill for the future. On the initiative, therefore, of President Frei of Chile, whose government had ardently espoused the cause of economic integration, a new blueprint for an eventual Latin American common market was worked out and a meeting of Foreign Ministers convened to consider measures to boost the integration process. This was followed, at the beginning of 1967, by a meeting between President Johnson and Latin American heads of state at Punta del Este, at which the goal of achieving a Latin American Common Market by 1985 was set. There followed a meeting of LAFTA delegates (Montevideo, 1968) to negotiate the second 'common list' through the elimination of duties on wheat and petroleum which accounted respectively for 15 and 13 per cent of intra-zonal trade. After four months of negotiating, however, the delegates dispersed without reaching agreement. The terms of the Caracas Protocol (1969) provided further evidence that the process of economic integration was running into the sands. The proposed freeing of all intra-zonal trade was postponed from 1973 to 1980 and no deadline at all was set for achieving the goal of a common market.

The obstacles in the way of effective integration are indeed formidable. Topography and history have combined to produce a pattern of road, rail, and sea communications which generally make it easier to send cargoes to Europe or North America rather than across the continent. To modify this pattern, an immensely costly infrastructure of new communications (of which the unfinished Pan-American Highway and the Andean Carretera Marginal are examples) is called for. Such industry as Latin America possesses has largely grown up as a result of import substitution in zones separated by wide areas of under-development and behind the protection of high tariff walls. Governments fear the effect of tariff reductions on industries so unused to facing competition. Still more loath are they to renounce their hopes of attracting new industries in the interest of wider regional development, nor are they required under the Treaty of Montevideo to co-ordinate their national plans with any wider scheme of intra-zonal development. The LAFTA countries, moreover, differ enormously amongst themselves in economic resources and productivity. At one end of the scale are the 'big three' who stand to gain most through their relatively advanced economies. At the opposite pole are Ecuador, Paraguay, and Bolivia whose manifest under-development entitles them to certain concessions. The other LAFTA countries form an intermediate group which tends to complain that they enjoy neither the advantages of their stronger partners nor the compensations of an under-developed status. The LAFTA countries also show the most marked differences in their tariff levels and trade policies and in monetary conditions, which range from the stability of Mexico to the galloping inflation of others. They also differ widely in the policies adopted towards foreign investment capital. The latter gravitates towards areas which offer the advantages of an already developed infrastructure and availability of skilled labour. Unless wisely handled, integration may thus stimulate the polarization into rich and poor areas instead of contributing towards a more even level of development.

(ii) *The Central American Common Market (CACM)*. One means of overcoming some of the difficulties outlined above may be to concentrate on groups of countries not too dissimilar in their economic structures and interests. One such area (though Guatemala far exceeds the others in population, El Salvador in entrepreneurial drive, and Costa Rica in democratic maturity and *per capita* income) is Central America. In 1960, after a good deal of groundwork, the five republics (Panama, whose policies and institutions differ completely from those of her Central American neighbours in that she has low tariffs, a currency tied to the US dollar, no central bank, and a higher standard of living, has so far remained outside) signed the General Treaty of Central American Economic Integration which envisaged the creation of a common market within six years. A number of supporting organizations and agencies were brought into being: a General Secretariat for Economic Integration, a Bank for Economic Integration, a regional clearing house, and institutes for technological research and training and for public administration, together with a number of specialized bodies dealing with such matters as transport and telecommunications. Between 1960 and 1965 regional trade showed a sevenfold increase, and the area seemed well on the way towards its goal of the complete freeing of intra-regional trade, uniform external tariffs, and a common customs administration. Progress was slower, however, towards meeting the area's basic needs for the acceleration of economic growth and industrialization. It was hoped to promote the latter by means of 'integration industries' which qualified for special privileges and incentives throughout the area and were to be selected with a view to promoting the balanced overall growth of the region, but it proved extremely difficult to reach agreement amongst the competing claimants for such industries. Nevertheless, CACM probably represents the most successful experiment of its kind in integrating the economies of the under-developed countries and has proved a more flourishing concern than LAFTA, with which it is one day expected to merge.

From these hopeful beginnings to the full economic integration of Central America is, however, still a long step. The process of tariff elimination and conflicting claims for exemptions and concessions give rise to constant friction. Governments feel the strain on their balance of payments through the need to make heavy imports of capital goods for the expansion of infrastructure and the establishment of new industries. Since these capital goods are generally exempt from import duties, and tariffs on intra-regional trade have all but vanished, they suffer too from a shortage of accustomed revenue. Honduras and Nicaragua, the most under-developed of the member states, complain that they have not yet received their fair share from the benefits of integration, and all five republics show misgivings lest their small local industries should be ousted by larger, more efficient foreign-owned concerns attracted by the growing regional market.

Nor are the obstacles to integration only economic. National sovereignty still inhibits the free movement of labour, without which population pressure may build up and lead to large-scale illicit migration and eventual conflict with a neighbouring state. The brief 1969 war between El Salvador and Honduras, which stemmed from such a cause, was a grave set-back to the integration process; two years later, Honduras was still refusing to resume her place in the Common Market. Historical rivalries and resentments, and suspicions arising from present differences of political outlook, pose constant dangers. Costa Rica, wary lest her civic liberties and democratic institutions should suffer from closer formal ties with her neighbours, has been slow to ratify the instruments of integration. Guatemala,with her large population and her tradition of authoritarianism, tends to inspire alarm when she speaks too enthusiastically of the need for closer ties: her predominance would be still further assured could she make good her territorial claims against British Honduras (see below, page 339) or establish a 'special relationship' with that country. Frontier disputes, albeit pronounced settled, are liable to re-open, and the activities of guerrillas and political exiles in neighbouring countries to cause bad blood. The republics have their own political machinery—the Organization of Central American States (ODECA), set up in 1962 with the aim of promoting concord and working towards the reunification of Central America. But ODECA and its constituent organs, such as the Legislative Council and Council of Central American Defence, have hitherto shown themselves little more than paper organizations.

(iii) *New subregional groups.* Another promising initiative in regional cooperation was taken by Chile, Colombia, Bolivia, Ecuador, and Peru, who signed an Andean Subregional Integration Agreement (the 'Cartagena Agreement') in 1969. Venezuela also showed interest but declined to adhere for fear of the adverse effects on her high-cost economy through the anticipated influx of cheaper goods from the other five. The Agreement aims at achieving free intra-zonal trade and a common external tariff by 1980, with special interim concessions for its economically weaker members, Ecuador and Bolivia. Member states are also pledged to adopt a common policy in respect of foreign investment (see page 278). Though the Andean Group has less than a quarter of LAFTA's population, its promoters are confident that it will develop much more rapidly and in time constitute a unit which will rank with Latin America's 'big three'. A Commission composed of government representatives, supported by a supra-national secretariat and other appropriate institutions, will guide the fortunes of the new group.

A grouping of a rather different kind has been formed between Argentina, Bolivia, Brazil, Uruguay, and Paraguay, whose representatives met at Brasília in April 1969 to sign a treaty for the joint development of the River Plate basin (Cuenca del Plata). This treaty is primarily concerned with co-operation for the regulation and better technological exploitation of the immense natural resources of the region in such matters as improving communications and port installations, the navigation and control of waterways, the efficient use and equitable allocation of water resources for irrigation, hydro-electric works, etc., and the establishment of new industries. Though these are primarily technical matters, some delicate political issues are involved, such as the demarcation of Brazil's frontier with Paraguay, the aspiration of that country and of Bolivia for access to the sea, and the smaller countries' fear of the expansionist pressures of Brazil and Argentina.

Another grouping which is beginning to interest some Latin American states is the Caribbean Free Trade Association (CARIFTA). Established in 1968 with the aim of promoting intra-zonal trade amongst the Commonwealth Caribbean countries and ultimately developing into an economic union, CARIFTA has already made sufficiently encouraging headway to prompt an application for membership from the Dominican Republic. British Honduras may also join both the Central American Common Market and CARIFTA after independence. This suggests a gradual drawing together of the Commonwealth Caribbean and Latin America which have traditionally belonged to entirely different political, cultural, and economic systems.

(iv) *Other organizations*. An important role in furthering the integration process and creating a climate of opinion favourable to it has been played by the United Nations Economic Commission for Latin America (ECLA). This was set up in Santiago in 1948 as a United Nations organ for the purpose of carrying out research and initiating appropriate measures to promote economic development in the area. Under the influence of the distinguished Argentine economist Dr. Raúl Prebisch, who was its Secretary General from 1950 to 1963, ECLA formulated a body of ideas which has become almost the creed of a generation of Latin American intellectuals. Rejecting the traditional assumption that international trade between industrialized countries and those which are mere suppliers of raw materials works to their mutual advantage, the ECLA thesis argues that the centre inevitably grows richer and the periphery poorer; the only escape from the under-development to which the Latin American countries are condemned through the progressive deterioration in the terms of trade is through their industrialization and the elimination of 'bottlenecks', both external and internal. The latter are due largely to antiquated and unjust social structures and to the fragmentation of their economies. Hence their need both for radical agrarian, fiscal, and other reforms and the strengthening of their economies and mutual trade by integration.

ECLA has sought to give concrete application to this diagnosis by producing a series of detailed research studies and development plans for the countries and regions of Latin America. LAFTA owes much to its work (though ECLA would have preferred to see a more decisive approach towards a free trade area). CACM is still more completely its brain-child, and the newer subregional groups will also no doubt depend on it heavily for guidance. Since 1961, ECLA's training and advisory functions have been channelled through a special Latin American Institute for Economic and Social Planning. Many of the economists and administrators who today play a leading part in the economic development of their own countries and in the regional organizations have at some time worked in the Institute or at ECLA, or have at least come under the latter's pervasive influence.

The Inter-American Development Bank (IADB), founded at the end of 1959 by the United States and the Latin American countries (except Cuba) for the purpose of promoting their individual and collective growth, has also given a keen stimulus to economic integration. From resources contributed by its member states and raised on the capital markets of the United States and Europe, the Bank has assisted in the preparation of national economic and social plans and helped to obtain global finance for their implementation. Through its Fund for Special Operations it also makes loans for approved projects at low interest rates and repayable in local currencies. The Bank's operations have been used to assist projects of social importance in such fields as housing and education, and priority has been given to measures likely to contribute directly to the integration process, i.e. the improvement of the Central American highway network. Another important activity has been its financing of exports of capital goods amongst the Latin American countries, with a view to making them less dependent on foreign suppliers and stimulating their local industries.

The IADB has also established and financed the Institute for Latin American Integration in Montevideo. The Institute is concerned with studying the integration process and recommending ways of promoting it, and offers its training and advisory services to that end. Another institution which may one day have a part to play in a more unified continent is the Latin American Parliament, founded in 1964 'to promote and guide the political, social, economic, and cultural integration of the Latin American peoples, the overall development of the Latin American community and . . . to eliminate all forms of colonialism'. Its membership is composed of legislators from a number of countries, in not a few of which parliamentary institutions have themselves been extinguished. The 'Parliament', which aims to meet annually and passes resolutions mostly aimed against 'Yankee imperialism' and in favour of Latin American solidarity, seems unlikely to achieve anything more practical until democratic processes become better established in the individual republics which it claims to represent.

The role of the United States

Implicit or explicit in the moves towards integration and the different aspects of inter-American relations which we have been considering has been the evolving role of the United States. The first half of the nineteenth century had seen no lack of goodwill on either side. Latin Americans had looked to the northern republic as an encouraging example for their own emancipation struggle and had acquired there arms, ships, and some volunteers. Washington had refrained from offending Spain, from whom it was hoping to purchase Florida, by openly assisting the rebel colonists. Agents and consuls had however been sent to stake out a claim, in competition with the British, in what seemed likely to be a promising new field for trade, and in 1822 the United States became the first foreign power to extend diplomatic recognition to Mexico, Gran Colombia, and the United Provinces. In the latter country especially she continued to find warm admirers in men like Alberdi, who based his draft for an Argentine constitution on that of the United States, and Sarmiento, who extolled her political institutions and system of popular education.

The conviction that the United States had a special role to play in the western hemisphere which no extra-continental power might challenge began to take shape at an early date. In 1811, when Spain was rumoured to be considering selling Florida to England, Congress adopted a 'no-transfer resolution' declaring that the United States 'cannot without inquietude see any part of the said territory pass into the hands of any foreign power'; ten years later she had secured it for herself. The famous message which President Monroe sent to Congress on 2 December 1823 was a still more explicit hands-off warning to foreign powers that 'we should consider any attempt on their part to extend their system to any portion of this hemisphere as dangerous to our peace and safety'. This enunciation of the Monroe Doctrine was little heeded at the time in the Latin American republics; their security from external aggression was then far more dependent on the attitude of Britain, whose navy controlled the seas, than on any pronouncement in Washington. But by the middle of the century, with the election of President Polk (1845) and the growing consciousness of the United States' 'manifest destiny', the annexation of Texas and the acquisition of further territory from Mexico, the doctrine acquired a new and more militant significance. It underlay the forward policies pursued by Washington in the Caribbean and Central America, where a British challenge was parried by the conclusion of the Clayton–Bulwer Treaty (see page 98). The Spanish reoccupation of Santo Domingo (1861–5) and Maximilian's short-lived Mexican empire were clear violations of the Monroe Doctrine; that they failed was due to the efforts of the Latin Americans themselves rather than to those of the United States.

By the end of the century the United States was moving towards frankly interventionist policies which President Theodore Roosevelt claimed were the logical extension of accepted doctrine. There had been frequent cases of European powers exerting force against a Latin American state in order to secure settlement of its financial claims (e.g. the British–German–Italian blockade of Venezuela in 1902). To put an end to the misgovernment which invited such actions, President Roosevelt argued that the United States must herself assume the 'international duty' of intervening, since adherence to the Monroe Doctrine 'may force the United States, however reluctantly, in flagrant cases of such wrong-doing or impotence, to the exercise of an international police force power'. The Latin Americans took the contrary view, formulated by the Argentine jurist Calvo (1824–1906) and elaborated by the Argentine Foreign Minister Drago in a note addressed to Washington two years before the 1904 pronouncement of the 'Roosevelt Corollary', that debt collection was no justification for foreign intervention. Underlying the United States' attitude was the compelling need to protect communications across the isthmus linking her western and eastern seaboards and to ensure that the approaches to this vital route remained in friendly hands. From these considerations stemmed a whole series of United States interventions: the 1898 involvement in the Spanish–Cuban war, the continuing American presence in Cuba and the retention of the right to intervene embodied in the Platt Amendment; the annexation of Puerto Rico (1901); the creation of Panama (1903) and the acquisition of sovereign rights in the Canal Zone; interventions in Haiti (1915–34), Santo Domingo (1904, 1912, 1916–24), and Nicaragua (1909–33); sporadic meddling in Mexico's revolutionary troubles between 1913 and 1917. These interventions often attained the immediate goals of enforcing law, order, and financial solvency but aroused passionate nationalist resentment and left dictators of the stamp of Trujillo and Anastasio Somoza as the testamentary legatees of United States rule.

With the apparent disappearance of any threat from Europe after World War I, the growing maturity of the Latin American states and their insistent pressure to secure Washington's recognition for the principle of non-intervention, the tactful diplomacy of Ambassador Dwight Morrow in Mexico and the more liberal spirit in international relations expressed in the 1928 Briand–Kellogg Pact outlawing war as an instrument of policy, the Roosevelt Corollary seemed to have become outmoded and the Monroe Doctrine was pronounced to be, in the words of Secretary Kellogg, 'simply a doctrine of self-defence'. The stage was set for Franklin D. Roosevelt's 'Good Neighbour' policy which led to the abrogation of the treaty with Cuba, with its hated Platt Amendment, and the abandonment of other treaty rights entitling the United States to intervene in Central America and the Caribbean. But if 'non-intervention' had become generally accepted as a concept, its observance was far from easy in practice. So great now was the economic power of the United States and so pervasive her influence that her every action, however free from malice, might be taken as 'intervention'. Not to give speedy recognition to a new government, for instance, might be enough to cause its fall. To maintain normal relations with a government, on the other hand, strengthened its chance of survival, and since arbitrary and tyrannical government was traditional in not a few Latin American republics, the United States incurred the odium of 'bolstering up' dictatorships.

World War II and its aftermath offered Washington and the Latin American governments a common interest in safeguarding the hemisphere against extra-territorial aggression and so provided a temporary respite from the dilemma. The 1939 Declaration of Panama, declaring a neutrality zone round the western hemisphere (see page 323), could be seen as a reassertion of the 'no-transfer principle', and the inter-American system itself as a means of applying the Monroe Doctrine along collective lines to preserve hemisphere security from the perils of the Cold War. So at least it appeared to Washington, but not all Latin Americans saw matters in this light. Perón's government in Argentina had its own designs for hegemony in South America, and by an opportunistic swing from a pro-Axis to a neutralist stance, presented a challenge to which Washington responded by policies fluctuating between intimidation and appeasement. The United States' preoccupation lay elsewhere. When the left-wing government of President Arbenz of Guatemala fell in 1954, his overthrow was widely attributed to the machinations of the CIA and to Washington's equation of radical social reform with the spread of 'international Communism'. The United States seemed, in effect, to have reverted to the policy of the 'big stick'. The hostile demonstrations which greeted Vice-President Nixon on his 1958 tour of Latin America indicated the deterioration of inter-American relations since the days of the Good Neighbour policy. There was clearly an urgent need for a new approach both in form—'an *abrazo* for the democratic leaders but a formal handshake for dictators'—and in content.

The Alliance for Progress

The upshot was the 'Alliance for Progress' announced by President Kennedy in March 1961 and formalized the following August in the Declaration of the Peoples of America and the Charter of Punta del Este, to which the governments of the United States and all the Latin American republics except Cuba adhered. Incorporating theses long championed by ECLA and advocated three years before in President Kubitschek's proposed Operation Pan-America, the Alliance was conceived as something far more than just another American aid programme; it represented nothing less than an unprecedented commitment by the United States to the social revolution by which alone Latin America could escape from under-development—'a vast new effort unparalleled in magnitude and nobility of purpose, to satisfy the basic needs of the American people for houses, work, and land'. The changes envisaged radical agrarian reform programmes and a revision of fiscal structures so as to shift the burden of taxation squarely onto the shoulders of the rich. The target was an annual overall increase in *per capita* income of 2·5 per cent, and of the hundred billion dollars which this vast transformation was estimated to cost over the next decade, 80 per cent was to be raised by the Latin American countries themselves and the remaining 20 per cent from other sources, the United States government providing half that quota.

Though it could claim success in some sectors, the Alliance sadly disappointed the high hopes which had been placed in it. By the end of the decade, Latin America's *per capita* economic growth rate was nearer 1·5 per cent than the 2·5 per cent aimed at. On the United States side, progress had been impeded by bureaucratic delays and difficulties and hamstrung by congressional cuts in aid. The extreme Left denounced it from the outset as merely a covert form of Yankee imperialism, whilst those Latin Americans of more moderate opinion complained that they had to pay excessive prices for the goods they could only purchase in the United States under the terms of tied aid, and accused Washington of dictating the objectives and controlling the whole operation of the Alliance. The setting up of an advisory panel of Latin American experts (the 'Nine Wise Men') and, in 1964, of CIAP (see page 326), only partially silenced these criticisms. Washington, for its part, found that only a few Latin American governments were willing or able to produce the national master-plans for economic development required of them, and that some had no serious intentions at all of implementing the social reforms to which they paid lip-service. Two of the countries which seemed most promising—Chile and Colombia—lost the momentum of reform under mounting domestic opposition, and the Chilean government constituted itself the spokesman of a prickly new Latin American nationalism. Brazil, under President Goulart, seemed heading for a Marxist rather than a democratic revolution until the military intervened, as they did too in Argentina to oust the more amenable President Illia. Nor did a military take-over mean any longer that things would be easier for Washington, as Generals Velasco and Ovando were to demonstrate in Peru and Bolivia. The 'democratic Left', to whom the New Frontiersmen had turned as their natural partners, proved broken reeds. The Alliance for Progress looked, in short, like finding itself an alliance with no allies and very little progress.

United States policy was complicated by the problem of Cuba. Though it could scarcely be said, as the Cubans liked to boast, that their Revolution had shamed Washington into launching the Alliance as a sham panacea for Latin America, the Cuban Revolution no doubt underlined the need to find a speedy solution for the continent's ills along democratic lines. Nor was the charge justified that the United States was everywhere hostile to socially progressive regimes. Washington's aid had underwritten Bolivia's revolution in the 'fifties despite its radical and even Marxist colouring. The United States was against Castro's Cuba, as it had been against the Arbenz regime in Guatemala, because it appeared to threaten hemisphere security by offering a foothold to a hostile foreign power. The half-hearted backing given to the abortive Bay of Pigs invasion (an operation inherited by President Kennedy, and watered down by him, from the previous administration) showed the danger of renouncing the United States' practice of unilateral action without the substitution of an alternative system of collective security. With the installation of Soviet rockets in Cuba the following year Washington's worst forebodings proved justified, and the situation was only restored (and with it, the United States' prestige in Latin America) by President Kennedy's forceful and brilliant resolution of the crisis. But the heavy-handed American action during the Panama incidents of 1964 and the intervention in the Dominican Republic the following year seemed to indicate that, under President Johnson, the United States had again taken up the 'big stick'. By the end of the 'sixties, a position of stalemate appeared to have been reached. Cuba had not succeeded in exporting her revolution, and her faltering economy was making her an object-lesson rather than a show-window for Communism in the hemisphere. Neither had the policies of diplomatic isolation and economic sanction which Washington applied against her, and induced the Latin American governments to apply, brought Castro to his knees. Only Mexico had declined to toe the line and still retained her ties with Havana, and it was perhaps a measure of Washington's greater tolerance that, despite this show of independence, United States–Mexican relations had never been warmer.

In the late 'sixties, United States policies were faced by a new challenge.

Relations with Peru had already come under strain during President Belaúnde's administration through Lima's determination to turn to Europe for the purchase of sophisticated arms which Washington considered should be acquired in the United States or not at all, and through the Peruvian claim to exercise jurisdiction over a 200-mile-wide zone of territorial waters where United States vessels were accustomed to fish. The military regime which ousted President Belaúnde (see page 160) sharpened the confrontation with Washington. The expropriation of the IPC, a subsidiary of Standard Oil of New York, seemed likely to provoke a suspension of all United States aid as envisaged under the Hickenlooper Amendment. Peru's defiance evoked an enthusiastic response throughout Latin America and set a precedent for similar action against the United States-owned Gulf Oil Company in Bolivia (October 1969). In the face of rising anti-American feeling, which led in some countries to the cancellation of a visit by his special envoy Governor Rockefeller and in others to hostile demonstrations, President Nixon sought a new formula for policy towards Latin America. In a speech of 31 October 1969, drawing largely on Governor Rockefeller's recommendations but also claiming to take into account the views formulated in the Consensus of Viña del Mar, he defined the guide-lines of his policy—'no grandiose promises, no panaceas', but emphasis on trade rather than aid, and the untying of the latter to permit goods to be purchased, if preferred, in Latin America rather than the United States, private investment where desired and attracted by the prospect of fair treatment, more Latin American say in settling development priorities and mapping out programmes, and a promise of good offices in persuading all industrialized countries to reduce barriers against goods from the under-developed countries. A pragmatic formula of 'Action for Progress' was to supersede the visionary goals of the Alliance. But the 'low profile' which Washington was now anxious to maintain south of the border seemed nevertheless likely to remain a major target of the militant nationalism which had many Latin American countries increasingly in its grip.

Great Britain

During the nineteenth and the early part of the present century Britain's influence was as dominant throughout Latin America as that of the United States is today. Her interests were first and foremost economic; and since she was the leading commercial nation and chief capital market of the day, she believed that these could best be served by upholding the principle of Free Trade. 'For herself, Great Britain asks no exclusive privileges of trade, no invidious preference,' Canning wrote in 1824, 'but equal freedom of commerce for all.' Britain was well placed to seize the opportunities offered by the eagerness of the new republics to build up viable national economies. In their struggle to gain political independence she had been unable to intervene officially, for Spain was for a time Britain's ally in the wars against Napoleon. But many British volunteers had given invaluable service to the patriot cause (see pages 64, 68, and 71). Britain would have liked to see a reconciliation between Spain and her rebellious colonists, but when this proved impossible, she made it clear that Spain must be left to settle her own difficulties and that the ships of other powers would not be permitted to intervene to help the mother country reimpose her rule. The British navy, too, conveyed the Portuguese court to the safety of Brazil (see page 63), and British diplomacy later helped to avert an armed conflict between Brazil and Portugal by inducing the latter to recognize the independence of her former colony. Britain also played a crucial role in ending the rivalry between Brazil and Argentina for the possession of the Banda Oriental and sponsoring the creation of an independent Uruguay (see page 69).

By the late 1820s, Brazil already figured as the third largest market for British manufactures, inferior in importance only to the United States and Germany. The Anglo-Brazilian Treaty of 1827, which ensured that British goods imported into Brazil should pay no duty greater than the 15 per cent traditional in Anglo-Portuguese trade, ushered in the period of British commercial pre-eminence in Brazil. For more than half a century, that country remained the major recipient in Latin America of British investment, more than half of it in government bonds, which enabled Brazil to take the first steps away from a plantation system towards a modern economy. Imported machinery gradually rendered slave labour anachronistic and provided an economic inducement to face the enormous social and psychological changes stemming from the abolition of slavery. By the end of the century, the main flow of investment had shifted to Argentina, where British capital and technical enterprise furnished the country with the greater part of its railway network and of its tramways, telephones, telegraphs, gas, and electricity, much of its vital meat-packing industry, and of its bloodstock, wire-fencing, and other technical innovations which were opening up the vast agricultural potential of the *pampa*. To Britain Argentina looked for its banking, insurance, and financial machinery, even for its fashionable clubs and sports. In other countries, thanks to men like North, the 'Nitrate King' of Chile, and Pearson, the most dynamic of the *entrepreneurs* in the Mexico of Porfirio Díaz, British commercial influence was often considerable, if not so pervasive. By 1914, British investments in Latin America were estimated at nearly £1,000 million, and their value continued to rise, despite setbacks occasioned by World War I and the growing economic challenge of the United States, to a peak of some £1,200 million in the late 1920s.

The Great Depression and the Second World War marked a watershed in Britain's fortunes in Latin America. With the breakdown of the traditional system of multilateral trade and the introduction of Imperial Preferences, an attempt was made to extend the spirit of the Ottawa Agreements to the faltering Anglo-Argentine trading relationship. Under the Roca–Runciman Pact of 1933, Britain undertook to continue her imports of Argentine beef at a given level, and Argentina to use the proceeds from the sale for further purchases of British goods. The implementation of this pact was resented by a public opinion increasingly sensitive to suggestions of economic dependence, and intensified the demands for the nationalization of the British-owned utilities.

The opportunity to achieve this aim came with the aftermath of World War II, when Perón was able to use for this purpose the balances of blocked sterling which had accumulated in London through the sale of Argentine meat at high prices during the needy war years. The post-war period also saw a settlement of Britain's dispute with the Mexican government over compensation for the assets of the British oil companies expropriated in 1938. The dwindling of Britain's stake in Latin America was matched by a weakening in her trading position. By the mid-'sixties, Britain was taking about 9 per cent of Latin America's exports and supplying no more than 5 per cent of her imports—less than half the proportions recorded in 1938, and a mere fraction of the 40 per cent which had been her share of Brazil's imports in 1909.

During her period of commercial pre-eminence in Latin America, Britain had seldom sought to turn economic influence into political pressure. Only in Brazil did she intervene persistently and deliberately during the first half of the nineteenth century to enforce compliance with the ban on the importing of slaves. British warships entered Brazilian ports to destroy or to carry off the slavers to face trial in British admiralty courts. Such high-handed actions put an end to the slave trade but outraged Brazil's national pride. When the Anglo-Brazilian Treaty expired in 1844 it was not renegotiated.

Britain harboured no designs of territorial aggrandizement in the western hemisphere. Having burned their fingers over the unauthorized venture against Buenos Aires in 1806 (see page 65), British statesmen confined their objectives to a broadly commercial field. Of the forty or so cases on record during this period of 'gun-boat diplomacy', when pressure was brought to bear by means of naval demonstrations, blockades, bombardments, or troop landings, the motives were to enforce respect for the claims of British subjects, to protect property or to restore order, not to acquire territory. For a time it looked as if Britain, by exercising a protectorate over the Mosquito coast (1844–60), wished to secure a new foothold for herself at the expense of Nicaragua. But the protectorate was given up, and Britain was left with her three colonies of the Falkland Islands, British Honduras, and British Guiana, the title to which, she maintained, was securely established before the American republics had won their independence. The status of these three territories still remains a matter of dispute. The Falkland Islands, lying 400 miles off her coast, are claimed by Argentina on geographical and historical grounds, though the 2,000 or more islanders have made it clear that they have no wish to give up their British nationality. British Honduras, once a settlement o reluctantly tolerated log-cutters, has grown up into a colony possessing internal self-government and now ready for full independence. In 1859, Guatemala signed a treaty recognizing the boundaries of the colony, but later withdrew this recognition, claiming that the treaty had lapsed because of the non-fulfilment of an article which provided for both sides 'to use their best efforts, by taking adequate means for establishing the easiest communication' between the Atlantic coast and the capital of Guatemala. The frontier between Venezuela and British Guiana appeared to have been settled by an arbitral award of 1899 (see page 138), but in the early 1960s Venezuela revived her claim on the grounds that the award had been rigged. British Guiana became the autonomous state of Guyana in 1966, and feared that an enforcement of the Venezuelan claim would strip her of nearly two thirds of her territory. A Mixed Commission was set up in the same year with a view to finding some basis for a settlement of the dispute, and under the 1970 Protocol of Port-of-Spain, Venezuela and Guyana agreed to 'freeze' their differences for a period of twelve years.

Since the early 1960s, Britain's trade with Latin America has shown a modest increase. Her exports amounted in 1970 to £283 million, and her imports from it to £325 million. But though she continues to invest in the area, her economic stake there is only about one seventh that of the United States. In spite of this decline in Britain's power—or perhaps because of it, for nationalist feeling now has little cause to fear the hand of 'British imperialism'—her influence remains an important factor in Latin America's foreign relations. It was to Britain, who had arbitrated a similar dispute in 1902, that Argentina and Chile turned for the settlement of a troublesome frontier issue in 1966. Two years later, the state visit of Queen Elizabeth II to Brazil and Chile—the first ever paid by a reigning British monarch to Latin America—marked the revival of interest which Britain was beginning to take in the sub-continent.

The EEC countries

France, too, had a considerable economic stake in Latin America and her investments there were nearly as extensive as Britain's before World War II. She had also once looked to the area as a possible field for political expansion until the tragic end of Maximilian's Mexican adventure dispelled Napoleon III's imperialist dreams. But France's real influence in Latin America has traditionally stemmed from her cultural and intellectual prestige. The writings of her *libres penseurs* prepared the soil for political emancipation. Her poets, novelists, painters, and architects set the tone for Latin America's cultured élite, and Paris was the Mecca for all travellers to Europe with any pretensions to taste or fashion. Despite her eclipse in World War II and her subsequent preference to channel capital resources towards her EEC partners and Africa, France still casts a powerful spell over Latin America's educated classes. This was demonstrated by the enthusiastic reception given to President de Gaulle during his 1965 Latin American tour. The General's readiness to voice criticism of the United States no doubt enhanced his popularity, and the French were quick to seize the opportunity of selling sophisticated arms (tanks to Argentina, Mirage jets to Peru) in place of those which Washington, anxious to discourage an arms race between governments needing to husband their resources for economic development, was reluctant to offer. France's own defence policy, which prompted her to carry out a series of nuclear tests in the Pacific in the 'sixties, led to difficulties with those Latin American republics who feared they might be exposed to the dangers of fall-out. But apart from friction on this account, and the more trivial incidents of a sporadic 'lobster war' with Brazil over fishing rights in the Atlantic, France's relations with the Latin American countries remain generally good.

Germany, from the time of Humboldt's travels and monumental researches, has taken a keen interest in Latin America. Well-organized colonies of German settlers, tenacious of their language and customs and exemplary in their good farming techniques, hard work, and enterprise in manufacturing, business, and the professions, did much to promote the development of their adopted countries, especially in Brazil and Argentina. In the 'thirties, Hitler attempted to use these German minorities not only for the economic penetration of Latin America but also to spread Nazi ideology and to further his schemes of political domination. The entry of the Latin American countries into World War II on the side of the Allies led to the confiscation of much German property and a setback to German influence. The latter rapidly reasserted itself in Argentina with the rise of Perón but waned again with his fall. Throughout Latin America as a whole, Federal Germany has concentrated in the post-war period on rebuilding her commercial position. In most countries she has outstripped Britain as a furnisher of exports and now ranks (though well behind the United States) as Latin America's second most important trading partner. Latin America now also receives some 40 per cent of the private capital investment which Germany sends abroad.

Italy, too, has been showing renewed interest in Latin America as a field for trade and investment and has benefited from the manifold connections stemming from the massive Italian emigration, particularly to Argentina and Brazil, of the last century. Of all the EEC countries, she has proved most insistent on the need to strengthen the Community's relations with the Latin American countries and to ease the difficulties created for the latter's trade through the preferences extended by the Community to their African competitors. Latin American misgivings over the EEC's Common Agricultural Policy and trading practices were voiced in the Declaration of Buenos Aires, drawn up by CECLA in 1970, and prompted Argentina to start negotiations which led to the conclusion of a non-preferential trading agreement with the Six. The latter may well find it advisable to take some steps to co-ordinate their policies, rather than to pursue purely national objectives in Latin America, in such fields as trade, technical co-operation, and financial aid.

Spain

Spain can claim a special relationship with her ex-colonies which she is anxious today to turn to political and economic account. Standing outside the EEC, as they do too, she offers an attractive market for their products which are hit by the Community's agricultural policies. In 1965, Madrid launched a vigorous trade drive with the ambitious offer of 1,000 million dollars' worth of credit, spread over a ten-year period, and despatched a series of trade missions to the Latin American countries which she hoped would take it up. Though having less to offer than the more technologically advanced countries, Spain can count on the sentimental regard felt by many Latin Americans, now that they have nothing to fear from her, for their former *madre patria*. More students from Latin America are to be found in Spain than in all the universities of the United States, the Soviet bloc, and the other countries of Europe combined.

After their victory in Spain, the militants of the Falange strove to extend their ideology and organization to Latin America. Franco had, and still has, his admirers in Argentina, for instance, during the Onganía regime—but the creed of *Hispanidad*, which stresses the community of language, culture, race, and outlook between the Spanish-speaking peoples, has a deeper and more pervasive appeal than the narrowly political slant given to it by the Falangists. It has helped to promote close commercial and other relations, for example, between Spain and Mexico, which gave asylum to some 30,000 Spanish republican refugees and still refuses to extend diplomatic recognition to Franco, and between the avowedly anti-Communist Franco regime and Castro's Cuba. Nor is the flow of ideas, any more than the flow of goods, merely one way. 'We Spaniards must understand that in order to save Hispanic culture we must work with the Latin American peoples as equals,' wrote the great Spanish thinker Unamuno. 'We must accept from them, and not content ourself with merely giving to them.' In the field of literature and the arts, Latin America is already showing herself more vigorously creative than contemporary Spain. Will she also offer Spain, once Franco goes, a choice of political ideologies and institutions—a Hispanic brand of Communism on the Cuban model, the Mexican formula for a one-party state, or the experiments in Christian Democracy tried out in Chile and Venezuela?

The Soviet Union

Before World War I only two Latin American countries established full diplomatic relations with the Soviet Union, and then only for a short time (Uruguay, 1934–5; Mexico, 1924–30). Uruguay broke off relations on account of the suspected involvement of the Soviet Legation in Montevideo in the 1935 Communist-led rising in Brazil, Mexico because of the support which her Communist Party was believed to be receiving from Soviet diplomats in Mexico City. These incidents revealed the basic dilemma facing Soviet policy in Latin America: that of reconciling support for the revolutionary Communist movement of which the USSR claims to be the head and the maintenance of good relations with governments which the revolutionaries are pledged to overthrow. During World War II, when the Soviet Union was allied with western democracies and was clearly destined to become one of the world super-powers, most Latin American countries thought it expedient to enter into some form of relationship with her. The onset of the 'cold war' and further cases of suspected Russian instigation of subversion led to further vicissitudes, but by mid-1970, Moscow was in diplomatic relations with Mexico, Cuba, and all the Latin American republics of South America except Paraguay. The Soviet Union has become more sophisticated and circumspect in her attitude to foreign affairs, and more discreet in her links with the local Communist parties. Incidents nevertheless recur from time to time and revive fears of Soviet instigation of subversion, e.g. Mexico's expulsion in 1971 of the *chargé d'affaires* and other members of the Soviet Embassy suspected of encouraging an anti-government guerrilla movement. The Soviet Union cannot escape the fundamental ambivalence of her position as the avowed spearhead of world revolution and at the same time a well-behaved member of international society who wishes to keep on good terms with Latin America's 'oligarchic' and 'reactionary' governments and professes regard for their cherished principle of non-interference in domestic affairs.

Though Moscow cannot remain indifferent to countries whose manifest social and economic stresses mark them as ripe for revolution, her main interest in the area probably stems from its proximity to the United States. Latin America is no longer Washington's 'back-yard', the exclusive preserve for the exercise of her political and commercial influence. The appearance of Castro's self-proclaimed Marxist–Leninist regime, though they did nothing to bring it to birth and must now pay heavily to keep it alive, has been a windfall for the Russians. They overplayed their hand, in October 1962, by attempting to exploit this new foothold in the western hemisphere in a way which might have tilted the world balance of power in their favour. Khrushchev's enforced withdrawal of his missiles demonstrated the limitations imposed on Soviet strategy in a distant area which, though it had now assumed new interest in Soviet thinking, nevertheless placed the USSR at a serious logistic disadvantage. Moscow's repeated attempts to get regional problems, such as the 1954 Guatemalan and the 1965 Dominican crises, dealt with in the Security Council rather than by the OAS, where Washington's influence remained paramount, also met with no success.

What does the Soviet Union hope to achieve in Latin America, and what do the Latin American countries expect from the development of their relations with her? Trade and aid have so far been on a modest scale. Between 1954 and 1964 only 5·4 per cent of the aid offered to the developing countries by the entire Soviet bloc was allocated to Latin America (excluding Cuba), compared with 18·1 per cent to Africa, 40·5 per cent to Asia, and 36 per cent to the Middle East. The Soviet share of the region's total trade (Cuba again excepted), during the first half of the 'sixties, did not even reach one per cent. Individual countries may do important deals with the Soviet Union—a substantial purchase of Ecuador's bananas or Costa Rica's coffee, for example, may be decided upon for partly political motives, as with Cuba's sugar, and give a temporary boost to weak Latin American economies—but the general picture is not likely to change greatly. A limited increase in their economic and political links with the Soviet Union may continue to be welcomed by the Latin American countries as a means of demonstrating their independence from the United States. The Soviet Union, for its part, is likely to press on with the cultivation of such relations, especially where a 'Socialist' government is in power, as in Chile, and also where military regimes, such as that installed at present in Lima, follow radical and nationalist policies little to the liking of Washington. But Moscow is likely to show caution in supporting revolutionary movements or assuming commitments to underwrite the economies of 'revolutionary' regimes which may turn out to be as burdensome as those which she has assumed *vis-à-vis* Cuba. But there always remains the possibility of the rich prize which would fall to the Socialist camp should a Communist-controlled government come to power, preferably by the *via pacifica*, in any major Latin American country.

Japan

Japan is another power—the world's potential third super-power—whose role in Latin America is likely to grow. Like Germany's, this role was already becoming important when interrupted by World War II. Like Germany, too, Japan had sent her sons overseas to form large, self-contained communities of industrious settlers, and co-ordinated her emigration, investment, and trade policies to further her political as well as her economic ends. Latin America's raw materials, particularly her minerals, were sought after for building up the Japanese war industries. Since the war, when many of her valuable assets and properties were confiscated, Japan has resumed her trade drive with equal persistence and ingenuity, but greater circumspection. From the mid-'fifties the value of her imports from Latin America increased at a cumulative annual rate of over 9 per cent, and by 1970 they represented about 7 per cent of the region's total exports, as compared with only 2·9 per cent in 1956/8. Japan imports from Latin America considerably more than she exports to it, and has already become the major customer, after the United States, of important countries like Mexico and Peru, whilst in Brazil, where her colonists now number more than 600,000, she has developed a massive network of interlocking investments and joint enterprises which will give her an increasing stake in that great country's future. So far, her energies have gone into building up these formidable economic interests, but the time may come when she will aspire to exert a commensurate political influence.

Latin America and the world

For many years to come, Latin America is likely to remain preoccupied with her own pressing internal problems, the process of economic integration, and the difficult relationship with her great northern neighbour. Her relations with the extra-continental powers may well be marginal to these overriding concerns. Yet slowly the sub-continent is ceasing to be the passive recipient of alien influences, a mere field for foreign conquest, colonization, economic exploitation, or cultural and political pressures, and is learning to tread the international stage in her own right. The League of Nations offered the first international forum where, in the absence of the United States, the Latin Americans could speak as the voice of America. But nobody seemed very interested, membership dues were expensive, and they lost interest and withdrew. In World War I most of the republics had remained neutral; in World

War II, all at least nominally declared for the Allies, whilst Mexico sent pilots to the Philippines and Brazil an expeditionary force to Europe—the first time in history that a Latin American army had been despatched overseas. After the war the twenty republics took their seats in the United Nations where, until the influx of new Afro-Asian states in the mid-'fifties reduced the relative strength of the bloc, their votes gave them an influential position in the General Assembly.

The emergence of these recently independent Asian and African states, all militantly anti-colonialist, resentful of great power tutelage, and loud in their demands for a larger slice of the world's cake, caused the Latin Americans to take fresh stock of their own position. Did they belong, by virtue of their historical origins, their religion, institutions, and general outlook, to the western world, now locked in Cold War conflict with the Communist camp? Or had they more in common with what was coming to be termed the Third World, which declined alignment with either bloc and was primarily concerned with safeguarding national independence and overcoming economic and social backwardness? They wished to move further out of Washington's orbit without falling into that of Moscow. Some—Haiti, Brazil, and Cuba—were conscious of the racial and cultural elements in their make-up which linked them with Africa. Brazil, in the early 'sixties, made efforts to strengthen her commercial and diplomatic ties with the independent African states, whilst revolutionary Cuba cultivated a special relationship with Ben Bella's Algeria, sent guerrilla instructors to help the African freedom-fighters, and played host to the Tricontinental Conference. But though they have taken a common stand in the UN and UNCTAD on issues such as colonialism and aid to the poorer nations, the Latin Americans in general have not felt fully at home in the Third World. Their longer experience of international institutions and their traditional respect for legal forms cause them to keep their distance from the often brash tactics of the Third World militants. Their own position is more complex. Countries like Brazil, Mexico, and Argentina include within their national territories areas which are highly industrialized and others which are grossly backward. They constitute, in short, if we may paraphrase a passage in Bolívar's famous Letter from Jamaica (see page 306), a world of their own, neither developed nor under-developed, but something intermediate between the Western and the Third World.

This ambiguity need not disqualify Latin America from playing a distinctive and useful role in world affairs. Some republics have taken their obligations under the United Nations seriously enough to contribute to its peace-keeping operations; Colombia even sent troops to take part in the operations in Korea. On some international issues, such as the claim for an extension of territorial waters and fishing limits from the usual twelve miles to 200 miles, the initiative has been taken up by a group of Latin American countries acting together. The most significant joint move of this nature has probably been the signing of the Treaty of Tlatelolco (1967), negotiated largely on Mexico's initiative, declaring Latin America to be a nuclear-free zone where the manufacturing, receiving, storing, or testing of nuclear weapons is forbidden. Though the Treaty has not yet been signed by Argentina, Brazil, or Cuba, and will largely depend for its efficacy on the readiness of the nuclear powers to respect its provisions, it represents the world's first instrument of denuclearization on a multi-national basis. In this field, vital for the prospects for man's survival, Latin America has set a valuable precedent which other regions of the world would do well to follow.

The Treaty of Tlatelolco does not of course preclude the use of atomic power for peaceful purposes, and it is indeed through a technology of such advanced nature that the Latin Americans hope to see the eventual physical transformation of their countries. The cutting of a new inter-oceanic sea-level canal in Central America or the opening up of the immense Amazon basin are examples of what nuclear energy may one day accomplish. Latin America has never lacked its seers. Vasconcelos saw it as predestined by geographical environment and the process of miscegenation to become the cradle of the 'Cosmic Race' of the future. 'The great civilizations began around the tropics, and the final civilization will return to the tropics,' he wrote, and to Latin America would fall 'the great enterprise of initiating humanity's universal era'. But the immediate challenge is nearer home; to find solutions for Latin America's clamant social, economic, and political problems. Only then can the classic lands of *mañana* hope to see their day dawn.

Table of Basic Data

Country	Area (sq. miles)	Estimated population (thousands) 1970	Estimated population (thousands) 1980	% of urban population	Annual rate of population growth	G.D.P. per capita (1970) dollars	G.D.P. growth per capita (% p.a.) (1961–9)	% of literacy
Argentina	1,072,068	24,352	28,218	78·9	1·6	895	1·9	91·5
Bolivia	424,163	4,931	6,456	29·3	2·6	210	2·6	39·8
Brazil	3,286,473	92,238	121,574	47·6	2·8	380	1·9	71·0
Chile	292,257	8,836	10,054	74·2	1·3	560*	1·7	89·6
Colombia	439,513	21,116	28,924	57·7	3·2	325	1·5	72·9
Costa Rica	19,653	1,766	2,493	49·0	3·5	530	2·3	84·4
Cuba	44,164	8,553	10,000	60·0	1·7**	n.a.	n.a.	96·1
Dominican Republic	18,703	4,012	5,287	40·0	2·8	320	−0·8	53·1
Ecuador	104,506	6,093	8,473	45·7	3·4	220	1·1	69·7
El Salvador	8,083	3,515	4,904	38·8	3·7	280	2·2	49·0
Guatemala	42,040	5,170	6,913	30·8	3·1	335	1·9	37·9
Haiti	10,714	4,867	5,988	17·3	2·0	75	−0·6	22·0
Honduras	43,277	2,582	3,661	32·2	3·4	250	2·0	47·3
Mexico	759,530	48,313	66,843	58·7	3·3	455*	3·2	83·7
Nicaragua	53,668	1,982	2,818	39·7	3·5	405	3·4	49·8
Panama	29,208	1,415	1,865	47·1	2·8	565	4·3	76·7
Paraguay	157,047	2,374	3,456	36·0	3·1	250	1·4	74·4
Peru	494,293	13,586	18,527	51·9	3·1	630	2·3	61·1
Uruguay	72,172	2,886	3,251	79·9	1·3	690*	−1·1	90·5
Venezuela	347,029	10,399	14,870	74·9	3·5	980	1·1	73·9

* 1969   ** 1953–65   n.a.: not available

Sources: Socio-Economic Progress in Latin America, Inter-American Development Bank Social Progress Trust Fund, 10th Annual Report, 1970: IMF reports: UN Monthly Bulletin of Statistics.
For Cuba: Boletín Estadístico, 1967: Compendio Estadístico de Cuba, 1968: Gramma, 5 February 1970 and 31 December 1970: World Bank Atlas, 1970.

Main Events 1945-1971

1945

February–March	Mexico	Inter-American Conference on Problems of War and Peace. Signature of Act of Chapultepec advocating hemispheric solidarity and reciprocal assistance
March	Guatemala	Arévalo, first democratically elected President, takes office
October	Brazil	Pres. Vargas deposed
,,	Venezuela	Pres. Medina ousted by coup organized by reformist officers and Acción Democrática

1946

February	Argentina	Perón wins presidential elections
July	Bolivia	Pres. Villaroel lynched

1947

September	Brazil	Signature of Treaty of Reciprocal Assistance (Rio Pact)
March	Paraguay	Col. Franco makes unsuccessful bid to seize power and starts civil war

1948

February	Chile	Establishment of United Nations Economic Commission for Latin America
March–May	Colombia	Ninth International Conference of American States. Gaitán's assassination sparks off large-scale riots in Bogotá. OAS Charter and Pact of Bogotá signed
October	Peru	Gen. Odría seizes power
November	Venezuela	Acción Democrática government ousted by military *junta*

1950

October	Brazil	Vargas re-elected President

1951

October	El Salvador	Organization of Central American States established

1952

March	Cuba	Batista reassumes power through a coup
April	Bolivia	MNR takes power with a revolutionary programme
November	Venezuela	Pres. Gallegos deposed by military *junta*

1953

June	Colombia	Pres. Gómez deposed. Rojas Pinilla imposes dictatorship
July	Cuba	Castro launches unsuccessful attack on Moncada barracks, Santiago de Cuba
August	Bolivia	Agrarian Reform Law enacted

1954

March	Venezuela	Tenth Inter-American Conference. Declaration of Caracas against intervention of international Communism
June	Guatemala	Arbenz regime overthrown
July	Paraguay	Gen. Stroessner's assumption of presidency confirmed by elections
August	Brazil	Pres. Vargas commits suicide

1955

September	Argentina	Pres. Perón forced to resign

1956

January	Brazil	Kubitschek installed as President
June	Argentina	Peronist revolt crushed and ringleaders executed
December	Cuba	Castro returns from Mexico and begins guerrilla revolt in the Sierra Maestra

1957

March	Cuba	Unsuccessful attempt to kill Batista in the presidential palace
May	Colombia	Rojas Pinilla forced to resign
July	Chile	Christian Democrat Party founded
October	Haiti	Duvalier assumes presidency

1958

January	Venezuela	Pérez Jiménez ousted by *junta*
„	Peru, Ecuador	Serious damage caused by earthquake
February	Argentina	Frondizi wins presidential elections
September	Chile	Jorge Alessandri elected President
December	Venezuela	Acción Democrática wins presidential elections

1959

January	Cuba	Batista flees; Castro enters Havana
April		Inter-American Development Bank founded
May	Cuba	Agrarian Reform Law promulgated
June	Dominican Republic	Unsuccessful invasion attempt from Cuba
November	Panama	Flag incident in the Zone sparks off riots

1960

February	Cuba	First commercial treaty with USSR signed
April	Brazil	Dedication of Brasília as the new capital
June	Uruguay	Signature of Treaty of Montevideo setting up LAFTA
August	Costa Rica	OAS passes Declaration of San José condemning threat of extra-continental intervention
November		International Court of Justice assigns disputed frontier zone to Honduras; Nicaragua accepts decision
December	Nicaragua	Treaty of Central American Economic Integration signed with view to establishment of Central American Common Market

1961

April	Cuba	Castro describes his Revolution as 'Socialist'. Abortive Bay of Pigs invasion attempt by Cuban exiles
May	Dominican Republic	Trujillo assassinated
August	Brazil	Pres. Quadros resigns
,,	Uruguay	Alliance for Progress launched on signature of Charter of Punta del Este

1962

February		Cuba excluded from OAS
March	Argentina	Pres. Frondizi deposed
May	Venezuela	Left-wing military rising crushed
July	Peru	Military intervene to annul elections and prevent Haya de la Torre assuming presidency
October	Cuba	Soviet missile crisis
December	Dominican Republic	Bosch wins presidential elections

1963

March	Guatemala	Pres. Ydígoras deposed
May	Peru	Hugo Blanco, chief organizer of peasant invasions of *haciendas* in the sierra, arrested. Infiltration of Cuban-trained guerrillas foiled
July	Peru	Belaúnde inaugurated as President
,,	Argentina	Illia wins presidential elections
,,	Guatemala	Diplomatic relations with Britain broken off on account of British Honduras dispute
,,	Ecuador	Pres. Arosemena deposed by military
September	Dominican Republic	Pres. Bosch deposed by military
October	Honduras	Pres. Villeda Morales deposed by military

1963

| December | Venezuela | Guerrilla action and urban terrorism fail to prevent holding of presidential elections which are won by Leoni |

1964

January	Cuba	Long-term Sugar Agreement with USSR signed
,,	Panama	Flag incident in the Zone causes riots and rupture of relations with USA
April	Brazil	Pres. Goulart deposed; Marshal Castelo Branco installed as President
July		OAS recommends severance of links with Cuba
September	Chile	Frei wins presidential elections
November	Bolivia	Pres. Paz ousted by Gen. Barrientos

1965

| April | Dominican Republic | Civil War followed by United States intervention |
| June | Peru | Start of unsuccessful guerrilla rising |

1966

January	Cuba	Tricontinental Conference held in Havana
February		Venezuela and Guyana agree to set up Mixed Commission to seek a settlement of their frontier dispute
June	Argentina	Pres. Illia ousted by Gen. Onganía

1967

January	Nicaragua	Opposition rally in Managua shot down
February	Mexico	Signature of Treaty of Tlatelolco setting up Latin American Nuclear-free Zone
February	Uruguay	Punta del Este Summit Conference of Latin American Heads of State
July	Chile	Agrarian Reform Bill promulgated
July–August	Cuba	OLAS Conference held in Havana
October	Bolivia	'Che' Guevara killed and guerrilla rising suppressed

1968

February	Cuba	Trial of 'Microfaction'
August	Mexico	Riots in Mexico City on the eve of the Olympic Games
,,	Colombia	Visit of Pope Paul VI
October	Peru	Pres. Belaúnde ousted by Gen. Velasco; IPC expropriated
,,	Panama	Pres. Arias ousted by Col. Torrijos
November	Chile, Brazil	State visit by the Queen
December	Venezuela	Christian Democrats win presidential elections

1969

April	Bolivia	Pres. Barrientos killed in helicopter accident
May		Agreement to establish Andean Group signed at Bogotá
,,	Argentina	Riots in Córdoba and other cities
,,		Consensus of Viña del Mar formulates Latin American demands for more favourable treatment by developed nations
June	Peru	Agrarian Reform Law enacted
July	El Salvador, Honduras	Outbreak of 'Football War'
September	Bolivia	Pres. Siles ousted by Gen. Ovando
October	Bolivia	Bolivian Gulf Oil Co. expropriated

1970

April	Guatemala	German Ambassador kidnapped and murdered by terrorists
May	Peru	Earthquake causes heavy damage and loss of life
,,	Cuba	Castro announces that the sugar harvest, though a record, has failed to reach the 10-million-ton target
June	Argentina	Pres. Onganía deposed; *junta* proclaims Gen. Levingston President
September	Chile	Dr. Allende, heading a coalition of Socialists and Communists, wins the presidential elections
October	Bolivia	Pres. Ovando deposed by Juan José Torres

1971

January	Uruguay	Tupamaros kidnap British Ambassador (released following September)
March	Argentina	Pres. Levingston deposed by Gen. Lanusse
August	Bolivia	Pres. Torres deposed by Col. Hugo Bánzer

Abbreviations

AD	Acción Democrática—Democratic Action (Venezuelan political party)
ADELA	Atlantic Community Development Group for Latin America (investment company)
ALALC	Asociación Latinoamericana de Libre Comercio—Latin American Free Trade Association (LAFTA)
ANAP	Asociación Nacional de los Agricultores Pequeños—National Association of Smallholders (Cuba)
ANAPO	Alianza Nacional Popular—National Popular Alliance (the party of ex-President Rojas Pinilla, Colombia)
APRA	Alianza Popular Revolucionaria Americana—American Revolutionary Popular Alliance (party founded by Haya de la Torre, Peru)
ARENA	Aliança Renovadora Nacional—National Renewal Alliance (official pro-government party, Brazil)
ARPEL	Asistencia Recíproca Petrolera Estatal Latinoamericana—Association of Latin American State Petroleum Agencies
BID	Banco Interamericano de Desarrollo—Inter-American Development Bank (IDB, IADB)
CAEM	Centro de Altos Estudios Militares—Centre for Advanced Military Studies (Peru)
CARIFTA	Caribbean Free Trade Association
CDR	Comite(s) de Defensa de la Revolución—Committee(s) for the Defence of the Revolution (Cuba, Peru)
CECLA	Comisión Especial de Coordinación Latino-Americana—Special Commission on Latin American Co-ordination
CECON	Comisión Especial de Consulta y Negociación–Special Commission for Consultation and Negotiation (of OAS)
CELAM	Consejo Episcopal Latinoamericano—Latin American Episcopal Council
CEPAL	Comisión Económica para América Latina—(United Nations) Economic Commission for Latin America (ECLA)
CEPE	Corporación Estatal Petrolera Ecuatoriana—Ecuadorean State Petroleum Corporation
CGT	Confederación General del Trabajo—General Confederation of Labour (Argentina)
CIAP	Comite Interamericano de la Alianza para el Progreso—Inter-American Committee of the Alliance for Progress (ICAP)

CIDOC	Centro Intercultural de Documentación (Mexico)
CIES	Consejo Interamericano Económico y Social—Interamerican Economic and Social Council (of the OAS) (IA-ECOSOC)
CIPEC	Conseil Intergouvernemental des Pays Exportateurs de Cuivre —Inter-governmental Council of Copper-exporting Countries
CLASC	Confederación Latinoamericana de Sindicalistas Cristianos— Latin American Confederation of Christian Trade Unionists
COB	Central Obrera Boliviana—Bolivian Labour Centre
COFIDE	Corporación Financiera de Desarrollo—Financial Development Corporation (Peru)
COMIBOL	Corporación Minera de Bolivia—Mining Corporation of Bolivia
CONADE	Consejo Nacional de Desarrollo—National Development Council (Argentina)
COPEI	Comite de Organización Política Electoral Independiente— Venezuelan Social Christian Party
COR	Comision(es) de Orientación Revolucionaria—Revolutionary Orientation Committee(s) (Cuba)
CORA	Corporación de Reforma Agraria—Agrarian Reform Corporation (Chile)
CORDIPLAN	Oficina Central de Coordinación y Planificación—Central Office of Co-ordination and Planning (Venezuela)
CORFO	Corporación de Fomento de la Producción—Production Development Corporation (Chile)
CSTAL	Confederación Sindical de Trabajadores de América Latina— Trade Union Confederation of the Workers of Latin America
CTAL	Confederación de Trabajadores de América Latina—Confederation of Latin American Workers
CUTCh	Central Única de Trabajadores de Chile—Single Centre of Chilean Workers (Chilean Trade Union Confederation)
CVF	Corporación Venezolana de Fomento—Venezuelan Development Corporation
CVG	Corporación Venezolana de Guayana—Guayana Development Corporation (Venezuela)
CVP	Corporación Venezolana del Petróleo—Venezuelan Petroleum Corporation
DESAL	Centro para el Desarrollo Económico y Social de América Latina—Latin American Centre for Socio-economic Development (Chile)
DIGEPOL	Dirección General de Policías—General Directorate of Police (Venezuela)
DSE	Departamento de Seguridad del Estado—Department of State Security (Cuba)
ECLA	See CEPAL
ECOPETROL	Empresa Colombiana de Petróleos—Colombian Petroleum Company

ELN	Ejército de Liberación Nacional—Army of National Liberation (Bolivia, Colombia)
ENAMI	Empresa Nacional de Minería—National Mining Company (Chile)
ENAP	Empresa Nacional del Petróleo—National Petroleum Company (Chile)
EPF	Empresa Petrolera Fiscal—State Petroleum Company (Peru)
FALN	Fuerzas Armadas de Liberación Nacional—Armed Forces of National Liberation (Venezuela)
FAR	Fuerzas Armadas Rebeldes—Rebel Armed Forces (Guatemala) Fuerzas Armadas Revolucionarias—Revolutionary Armed Forces (Cuba)
FARC	Fuerzas Armadas Revolucionarias de Colombia—Revolutionary Armed Forces of Colombia
FEDECÁMARAS	Federación Venezolana de Cámaras y Asociaciones de Comercio y Producción—Association of Chambers of Commerce and Industry (Venezuela)
FEU	Federación de Estudiantes Universitarios—Federation of University Students (Costa Rica, Cuba, Guatemala, El Salvador, Honduras)
FLN	Frente de Liberación Nacional—National Liberation Front (Peru)
FMC	Federación de Mujeres Cubanas—Federation of Cuban Women
FRAP	Frente (Revolucionario) de Acción Popular—(Revolutionary) Popular Action Front (Chile)
FSTMB	Federación Sindical de Trabajadores Mineros de Bolivia—Bolivian Mineworkers' Federation
IADB	Inter-American Development Bank
IBC	Instituto Brasileiro do Café—Brazilian Coffee Institute
IBRD	International Bank for Reconstruction and Development
ICAITI	Instituto Centro-americano de Investigación y Tecnología Industrial—Central American Research Institute for Industrial Technology
ICAP	Instituto Cubano de Amistad con los Pueblos—Cuban Institute for Friendship with Peoples
ILPES	Instituto Latino-Americano de Planifacación Económica y Social—Latin American Social and Economic Planning Institute
INCORA	Instituto Colombiano de Reforma Agraria—Colombian Institute for Agrarian Reform
INRA	Instituto Nacional de Reforma Agraria—National Institute for Agrarian Reform (Cuba)
JUCEI	Junta de Coordinación, Ejecución e Inspección—Co-ordination, Execution, and Inspection Board (Cuba)
JUCEPLAN	Junta Central de la Planificación—Central Planning Board (Cuba)
JUDCLA	Juventud Demócrata Cristiana Latino-Americana—Latin American Christian Democratic Youth

LAFTA	See ALALC
MAPU	Movimiento de Acción Popular Unitaria—Unitary Popular Action Movement (Chile)
MDB	Movimento Democrático Brasileiro—Brazilian Democratic Movement (opposition party)
MEP	Movimiento Electoral del Pueblo—People's Electoral Movement (Venezuela)
MINCEX	Ministerio de Comercio Exterior—Ministry of Foreign Trade (Cuba)
MINFAR	Ministerio de las Fuerzas Armadas Revolucionarias—Ministry of the Revolutionary Armed Forces (Cuba)
MININT	Ministerio del Interior—Ministry of the Interior (Cuba)
MINREX	Ministerio de Relaciones Exteriores—Ministry of Foreign Relations (Cuba)
MIR	Movimiento de Izquierda Revolucionaria—Movement of the Revolutionary Left (Bolivia, Ecuador, Peru, Chile, Venezuela)
MLN	Movimiento de Liberación Nacional—Movement of National Liberation (Mexico, *et al*)
MNR	Movimiento Nacionalista Revolucionario—National Revolutionary Movement (Bolivia)
MR–13	Movimiento Revolucionario de 13 de Noviembre—Revolutionary Movement of 13 November (Guatemala)
OAS	See under OEA
OCLAE	Organización Continental Latino-americana de Estudiantes—Continental Organization of Latin American Students
ODCA	Organización Demócrata-Cristiana de América—Christian Democratic Organization of America
ODECA	Organización de Estados Centroamericanos—Organization of Central American States
OEA	Organización de Estados Americanos—Organization of American States (OAS)
OLAS	Organización Latinoamericana de Solidaridad—Latin American Solidarity Organization (LASO)
OPANAL	Organismo para la Proscripción de las Armas Nucleares en la América Latina—Agency for the Prohibition of Nuclear Weapons in Latin America
OPEC	Organization of Petroleum Exporting Countries
ORIT	Organización Regional Interamericana del Trabajo—Regional Inter-American Labour Organization
OSPAAL	Organización de Solidaridad de los Pueblos de Asia, Africa y Latino-América—Afro-Asian-Latin American Peoples' Solidarity Organization
PAN	Partido de Acción Nacional—National Action Party (opposition party, Mexico)
PC	Partido Comunista—Communist Party
PCA	Partido Comunista (Argentina)

PCB	Partido Comunista (Boliviano, Brasileiro, etc.)
PEMEX	Petróleos Mexicanos—Mexican Petroleum
PETROBÁS	Petróleo Brasileiro S.A.—Brazilian Petroleum Corporation
PGT	Partido Guatemalteco de Trabajo—Guatemalan Labour (Communist) Party
POR	Partido Obrero Revolucionario—Revolutionary Workers' Party (Bolivia)
PPS	Partido Popular Socialista—People's Socialist Party (Mexico)
PRI	Partido Revolucionario Institucional—Institutional Revolutionary Party (government party, Mexico)
PRIN	Partido Revolucionario de Izquierda Nacionalista—Revolutionary Party of the Nationalist Left (Bolivia)
PSD	Partido Social Democrático—Social Democrat Party (Brazil)
PTB	Partido Trabalhista Brasileiro—Brazilian Labour Party
SIECA	Secretaría Permanente del Tratado General de Integración Económica Centro-americana—Secretariat of the General Treaty on Central American Economic Integration (Secretariat for the Central American Common Market)
SMO	Servicio Militar Obligatorio—Compulsory Military Service (Cuba)
SNA	Sociedad Nacional de Agricultura—National Agricultural Society (Chile)
SUDAM	Superintendência do Desenvolvimento da Amazonia—Superintendency for the Development of Amazonia (Brazil)
SUDENE	Superintendência do Desenvolvimento do Nordeste—Superintendency for the Development of the North-East (Brazil)
UDN	União Democrática Brasileira—National Democratic Union (Brazil)
UP	Unidad Popular—Popular Unity (Chile)
URD	Unión Republicana Democrática—Democratic Republican Union (Venezuela)
YPF	Yacimientos Petrolíferos Fiscales—Government Oil Deposits (Argentina)
YPFB	Yacimientos Petrolíferos Fiscales Bolivianos—Bolivian (Agency for) Oil Deposits

Glossary

Adelantado (S) Governor of a frontier province

Agregação (P) Practice of seconding military officers to take up civilian appointments (Brazil)

Alcabala (S) (from Arabic) Tax levied on saleable articles in colonial Spanish America

Alcalde (S) (from Arabic) Mayor, president of a municipal council; magistrate

Alpaca (Q) Small cameloid animal found in the Andes and bred for its fine wool

Altiplano (S) High plateau, specifically that of the Andean regions of Peru and Bolivia

Amauta (Q) Sage, wise man; influential left-wing journal of that name edited by J. C. Mariátegui in the 1920s

Amparo (S) Writ issued by Mexican courts to protect individual or constitutional rights

Andino (S) One who lives in the Andes; particularly in the Andean provinces of Venezuela

Aprista (S) Member of APRA (Alianza Popular Revolucionaria Americana) founded by Haya de la Torre. *Aprismo* —movement or ideology of the same (Peru)

Arielismo (S) The body of ideas expounded by the Uruguayan writer Rodó in his *Ariel* (1900), stressing the spiritual and cultural values said to characterize Latin America, and especially its youth, in contrast to the materialism of North America

Asentamiento (S) Land expropriated from large estates under Agrarian Reform and made over to the rural labourers working it (Venezuela, Chile)

Asiento (S) (1) Mining area (Mexico); (2) (*asiento de negros*) monopolistic right granted by the Spanish authorities for the import of African slaves

Audiencia (S) Spanish colonial institution serving as High Court of Justice and also exercising certain administrative and legislative functions

Auténticos (S) Members of the Cuban political party led by Grau San Martín and Prío Socarrás

Ayllu (Q) Native clan or kinship group; rural community derived from such

Aymará (aimará) Tribe of Andean Indians; language spoken by them

Azules (S) 'Blues'; faction of Argentine armed forces composed chiefly of army and air force officers opposed to the *Colorados* (*q.v.*)

Bandeirante (P) Member of an exploring, prospecting, or slave-raiding band in the interior of Brazil

Bando (S, P) Official edict

Barbudos (S) 'Bearded ones'; name applied to the guerrilla followers of Fidel Castro

Barriada (S) Shanty-town (Peru)

Barrio (S) Town district; shanty-town (Venezuela)

Blancos (S) 'Whites'; the Conservative faction in Uruguay

Bogotazo (S) The riot which destroyed a large part of Bogotá in 1948

Boleadoras (S) Weighted leather thong thrown at an animal's legs to bring it down (Argentina)

Bracero (S) Seasonal agricultural worker; especially one migrating from Mexico to the United States

Brasilidade (P) 'Brazilianness'; qualities and ethos held to be specifically Brazilian

Cabildo (S) Town Council; *cabildo abierto*—meeting of the same enlarged by the inclusion of other prominent citizens

Caboclo (P) Native farmer; rustic, hillbilly; Indian or crossbreed between Indian and white (Brazil)

Cacique Native chief; local political boss

Cafuso (P) Offspring of Indian and Negro parents (Brazil)

Callampas (Q) 'Mushrooms'; shanty-town (Chile)

Campesino (S) One who lives in the *campo* (country); peasant; euphemism for Indian

Cangaceiro (P) Bandit of north-eastern Brazil

Capitânia (P) Fief, corresponding to a province, in colonial Brazil

Carioca (P) A citizen of Rio de Janeiro

Carretera Marginal (S) Highway under construction along the eastern glacis of the Andes

Castas (S) Persons of mixed blood; *mestizos*

Caudillo (S) Leader; political boss. *Caudillismo*—rule by *caudillo*

Cédula (S) Royal decree or warrant

Chasqui (Q) Indian messenger or courier

Chicha (Q) Alcoholic drink, generally made from maize

Chinampas 'Floating gardens'; system of cultivation on plots formed from alternating layers of lake mud and aquatic plants (Mexico)

Cholo Term used in Andean countries for *mestizo* or to denote any lower class person of Indian or mixed blood

Científicos (S) Group of politicians and businessmen imbued with the ideas of Comte and Spencer which they attempted to apply for the development of Mexico under the rule of Porfirio Díaz

Cimarrón (S) Runaway negro slave

Coca (Q) Narcotic plant grown in the Andes

Co-gobierno (S) Student participation in university administration

Colorado (S) Literally, 'Red'. (1) Member of the Liberal Party (Uruguay); (2) member of the government party (Paraguay); (3) faction of the Argentine armed forces opposed to the *Azules* (*q.v.*)

Compadre (S, P) Godfather; sponsor, protector. *Compadrismo*—political system of oligarchic nepotism and patronage

Comunidad (S) Traditional (Indian) community or group

Conscientização (P) Term brought into use by left-wing Catholic circles in Brazil to denote 'the awakening of consciousness', particularly amongst the underprivileged classes, of the need for social change

Consulado (S) (1) Merchant guild, chamber of commerce; (2) consulate

Continuismo (S) Perpetuation of a president or political party in power, usually through unconstitutional means or rigged elections

Cordillera (S) High mountain range; used particularly of the Andes

Cordobazo (S) Riot occurring at Córdoba, Argentina, in May 1969

Coronel (P) 'Colonel'; title given to powerful landowners in rural Brazil

Corregidor (S) Spanish colonial official in charge of a district (*corregimiento*)

Criollo (S) Creole; person of European descent but born in Spanish America; (adj.) of indigenous inspiration or strong local colour (lit.)

Cristero (S) Mexican rebel or bandit professing fanatical devotion to 'Cristo Rey' and traditional Catholicism

Cuartelazo (S) Barrack-room revolt; military rising in general

Curaca (Q) Indian chieftain

Curandero (S); **Curandeiro** (P) Indian witch-doctor; unqualified medical practitioner

Descamisados (S) 'Shirtless ones'; applied especially to the workers in Perón's Argentina

Ejido (S) Common land adjacent to town or village; inalienable plot of land under the Mexican Agrarian Reform

Encomienda (S) Originally a grant of Indians 'entrusted' by the Spanish Crown to a conquistador or settler; by extension, the usufruct of an estate worked by such Indians. *Encomendero–* one in possession of an *encomienda*

Engenho (P) Large plantation in Brazil; sugar mill on such a plantation

Entreguismo (S) Betrayal of the national interest; subservience to foreign political or economic pressure

Estancia (S); **Estância** (P) Large estate; cattle ranch. *Estanciero–*owner of an *estancia*.

Favelas (P) Shanty towns (Brazil). *Favelado–*one who lives in the same

Fazenda (P) Ranch or large farm in Brazil. *Fazendeiro–*owner of a *fazenda*

Febreristas (S) Followers of Col. Rafael Franco who seized power in Paraguay in February 1936

Fidelismo (S) Political ideology or movement inspired by Fidel Castro

Finca (S) Large estate or farm

Flota (S) The fleet sailing regularly in armed convoy to convey bullion from the Indies to Spain and Spanish goods to the Indies

Frigorífico (S) Meat-packing plant (Argentina, Uruguay)

Fuero (S) Right or privilege granted by law or tradition

Fundo (S) Large estate or farm

Gamonalismo (S) Term to denote the exploitation of the Andean Indians by the *gamonales* (large landowners), and lawyers, officials, etc. held to be in league with them (Peru)

Gaucho (S); **Gaúcho** (P) Cowboy or herdsman of the *pampa* and Southern Brazil

Getulismo (P) Ideology or movement inspired by Getúlio Vargas (Brazil)

Gobernación, Ministro de (S) Key post in the cabinet, roughly corresponding to Minister of the Interior, with responsibility for police, public order, etc.

Golpe (S) *Coup d'état*; military coup. *Golpista–*one who carries out such a coup

Gorillas (S) Insulting term to denote members of right-wing military regimes

Gringo (S) Slang expression for foreigner, particularly British or North American

Guajiro (S) Worker on sugar plantation (Cuba)

Guano (Q) Bird excrement used as fertilizer (Peru, Chile)

Gusano (S) 'Worm'; derogatory term for an opponent of, or exile from, Fidel Castro's regime (Cuba)

Hacienda (S) Cattle ranch; large farm or estate. *Hacendado–*owner of a *hacienda*

Hispanidad (S) The hispanic spirit or tradition; those attitudes and values which Spain and other Spanish-speaking countries are held to have in common

Huaca (Q) Sacred object or place; archaeological site. *Huaquero*—one who rifles such sites for treasure

Huasipungero One who works a *huasipungo* (subsistence plot) allowed him on a large estate by its owner in return for labour

Huaso Chilean cowboy or herdsman

Inca (Q) Ruling caste of ancient Peru; supreme head (*sapa inca*) of this caste

Indigenismo (S) Intellectual and literary movement (especially in Mexico and the Andean countries) exalting Indian values, culture, and modes of life. *Indigenista*—adherent of such a movement

Inquilino (S) Tenant; labourer on a Chilean estate

Integralismo (P) Ideology of the Brazilian Fascist group, Acção Integralista Brasileira. *Integralista*—member of this group

Intendencia (S) Spanish administrative district on the French model which superseded the traditional jurisdictions in the late eighteenth century. *Intendente*—governor of such a district

Itamaraty (**Itamaratí**)(Tupi-guaraní) 'Palace of stone'; name applied to Brazil's Ministry for Foreign Affairs

Juicio de residencia (S) See under *Residencia*

Junta (S, P) Directorate, governing board; frequently one composed of officers

Justicialismo (S) Political ideology professed by the followers of Perón

Ladino (S, P) (1) Indian who speaks Spanish and has abandoned the native way of life; (2) slave with some knowledge of Portuguese and the white man's ways; (3) *mestizo* (Guatemala and Southern Mexico)

Latifundio (S) Latifundium; large estate worked by servile labour

Léperos (S) City riff-raff (Mexico)

Letrado (S) An educated person, particularly one with legal training

Ley fuga (S) The execution of a prisoner on the pretext that he had tried to escape

Llama (Q) Commonest of the cameloid animals of the Andes

Llanos (S) Plains; particularly in Venezuela. *Llaneros*—people of the plains

Llautu (Q) Fringed head-band worn by the *sapa inca*

Macumba Fetish cult based on African beliefs and practices fused with Catholic elements (Rio de Janeiro)

Mambises Derogatory term applied by the Spaniards to the Cuban rebels, and later adopted by the latter, in the nineteenth century

Mameluco (P, from Tupi-guaraní) (1) Offspring of white and Indian; (2) by extension, any person of mixed blood (Brazil)

Mandato de Segurança (P) Writ issued by Brazilian courts to protect individual or constitutional rights

Mestizo (S); **Mestiço** (P) Half-breed; one of mixed Indian and European parentage

Milpa Maize-plot

Mineiro (P) Resident of Minas Gerais

Minifundio (S) Dwarf holding

Minka (Q) Communal labour performed voluntarily by Indians

Mita (Q) Forced labour imposed by rota on Indians as a form of tribute

Mitimaes (Q) Forcible transplanting and resettlement of population under the Incas

Modernismo (S) Literary revival, the outstanding exponent of which was the Nicaraguan poet Rubén Darío, of the late nineteenth century; (P) *Avant-*

garde Brazilian literary movement developed in São Paulo in the 1920s

Momio (S) 'Mummy'; abusive term for a member of the traditional ruling class (Chile)

Montaña (S) Forested foothills; specifically those on the eastern side of the Andes

Montanera (S) Band of rebel horsemen or mounted guerrillas. *Montanero* —member of such a band

Mordida (S) 'Bite'; slang term for bribe (Mexico)

Oidor (S) Magistrate serving on an *audiencia* in the colonial period

Orejón (S) 'Big-ears'; term applied by Spaniards to denote Inca nobles who wore ear-discs to denote rank

Oriental (S) Uruguayan; i.e. a resident of the República Oriental del Uruguay, so called because it lies on the east bank of that river

Ortodoxos (S) Members of Cuban reformist, anti-Batista political party

Pampa (Q) Low-lying grassy plain; specifically of the River Plate basin

Participacionista (S) One favouring co-operation with the government in power; section of Argentine labour movement of this nature

Patrón (S) **Patrão** (P); Master of an estate; head or boss of a firm

Patronato real (S) Right of the Crown to present nominees for episcopal and other church offices

Paulista (P) Resident of São Paulo

Pelucones (S) 'Bigwigs'; nickname given to the Conservative faction in post-independence Chile

Peninsulares (S) Term used during the colonial period to denote persons born in Spain

Peón (S) Agricultural labourer, generally of Indian or *mestizo* stock, tied to an estate through debt peonage, i.e.

until he or his family pay off debts contracted to the *patrón*. *Peonaje*—forced labour as a result of indebtedness

Peronismo (S) Juan Perón's political movement or ideology (Argentina)

Personalismo (S) Government based on the personal authority of the ruler

Peruanismo (S) Type of nationalistic, reformist government characteristic of General Velasco Alvarado's military regime in Peru

Pipiolos (S) 'Greenhorns'; nickname given to the Liberal faction in post-independence Chile

Plaza de armas (S) Central square of a town or city

Poderoso do Sertão (P) 'Powerful one of the backlands'; owner of a large estate in north-east Brazil

Pongaje Compulsory domestic service exacted from the Andean Indians. *Pongo* (Q) —Indian liable for such service

Porfiriato (S) The regime of Porfirio Díaz in Mexico

Porteño (S) An inhabitant of 'the port', i.e. Buenos Aires

Procurador (S) Delegate, emissary

Pronunciamiento (S) Formal repudiation of government authority; signal for a military revolt

Puros (S) 'Pure ones'; nickname given to the extreme Liberal faction in post-independence Mexico

Quechua Indian race mainly inhabiting the Andean *altiplano*; language spoken by this race

Quilombo Settlement of runaway slaves (Brazil)

Quinto (**real**) (S) The Royal Fifth due to the Spanish Crown as a proportion of the booty taken during a campaign or of the produce of a mine

Quipu (Q) Mnemonic device, used in Inca times, consisting of knotted and differently coloured cords

Reajuste (S) Official yearly 'readjustment' or raising of wage levels at rates fixed by law, generally in proportion to the annual rise in the cost of living (Chile)

Reducciones (S); **Reduções** (P) 'Reductions'; Indian settlements or villages placed beneath the supervision of royal or ecclesiastical authorities in the colonial period

Regidor (S) Alderman; member of a municipal council

Repartimiento (S) (1) Allocation of Indians to a conquistador or settler; (2) system of forced labour by Indians (Mexico); (3) forced sale of European goods to Indians

Residencia (juicio de residencia) (S) Enquiry conducted into an official's conduct of affairs, generally at the end of his tenure of office

Rosca (S) Literally, the thread of a screw; derogatory term for the former wealthy ruling class in Bolivia

Roto (S) Literally, broken or ragged; term used in Chile to denote someone of the poorer classes

Rurales (S) Mexican rural police force during the Díaz regime

Saladero (S) Factory for the preparation of dried and salted beef (Argentina)

Sertão (pl. sertões) (P) The Brazilian backlands. *Sertanejo*—inhabitant of the same

Sierra (S) Mountain range; often used to denote the Andean regions of Ecuador, Peru, and Bolivia

Sinarquismo (S) Movement of the extreme Right, expressing fanatical devotion to Spanish and Catholic traditions (Mexico)

Sindicato (S) Trade union

Taclla (Q) Foot-plough; metal-tipped pole with handle and footrest

Tahuantinsuyu (Q) 'The Four Quarters'; the Inca empire

Tambo (Q) Caravanserai; storehouse; barracks (Inca period)

Tapada (S) Lady wearing the veil in the traditional Lima style leaving one eye exposed (Peru)

Tapado (S) Literally, 'one who is kept covered', i.e., whose identity is not generally known; the presidential candidate chosen by influential sponsors before formal adoption by the PRI National Assembly (Mexico)

Tenentes (P) 'Lieutenants'; young officers taking part in an insurrectionary movement of nationalist and radical inspiration in the 1920s (Brazil)

Tonton-macoutes Bogey-men of Haitian folk-lore; President Duvalier's bodyguard of armed thugs

Trabalhismo (P) The political ideology professed by the supporters of Getulio Vargas (Brazil)

Tupamaros (S) Urban guerrillas or terrorists in Uruguay, taking their name from Tupac Amaru, leader of the Indian rebellion in eighteenth-century Peru

Tupí Guaraní-speaking Indian, especially from the coastal area between Bahia and the Amazon

Turco (S, P) 'Turk'; person of Lebanese, Syrian, or other middle-eastern extraction (i.e. from the former Ottoman empire)

Unitarios (S) Advocates of strong centralized government, but bitter enemies of the Rosas dictatorship, in post-independence Argentina

Vaquero (S); **Vaqueiro** (P) Cowboy, gaucho

Vecino (S) Householder; resident of a Spanish town possessing traditional rights and status

Vicuña (Q) Cameloid animal of the Andean Cordillera prized for its fine wool

Violencia, La (S) Endemic rural banditry and unrest (Colombia)

Viracocha (Q) The Creator-God venerated in Inca and pre-Inca times; lord, respectful term of address

Visita (S) Tour of judicial and administrative inspection carried out by Viceroy or other senior colonial official

Yanacunas (Q) Servile sub-stratum of the Inca empire

Zafra (S) (from Arabic) The harvesting and grinding of the sugar crop (Cuba)

Zambo (S) One of mixed Indian and negro stock

Bibliography

The Amerindian World
Middle America
Bernal, Ignacio, *The Olmec World* (University of California Press, 1969)
Burland, C. A., *The Gods of Mexico* (London, 1967)
Caso, Alfonso, *The Aztecs: People of the Sun* (University of Oklahoma, 1958)
Coe, Michael D., *The Maya* (London, 1966)
—, *Mexico* (London, 1963)
Morley, Sylvanus G., *The Ancient Maya* (revised by G. W. Brainerd, 1956)
Séjourné, Laurette, *Burning Water: Thought and Religion in Ancient Mexico* (New York, 1956)
Soustelle, Jacques, *Daily Life of the Aztecs* (London, 1964)
Thompson, J. Eric S., *The Rise and Fall of Maya Civilization* (University of Oklahoma, 1954)
Vaillant, George C., *The Aztecs of Mexico* (revised edition, New York, 1962)
Wolf, Eric R., *Sons of the Shaking Earth* (Chicago, 1959)

South America
Baudin, Louis, *Daily Life in Peru under the last Incas* (London, 1961)
—, *A socialist empire: the Incas of Peru* (Van Nostrand, 1961)
Bennett, Wendell C. and Bird, Junius B., *Andean Culture History* (American Museum of Natural History, New York, 1949)
Bushnell, G. H. S., *Peru* (Ancient Peoples and Places Series, London, 1956; New York, 1957)
Falk Moore, S., *Power and Property in Inca Peru* (New York, 1958)
Lanning, Edward P., *Peru before the Incas* (Prentice-Hall, 1967)
Mason, J. Alden, *The Ancient Civilizations of Peru* (Penguin Books, London, 1956)
Means, Philip Ainsworth, *Ancient Civilizations of the Andes* (London and New York, 1931)
Métraux, Alfred, *The Incas* (London, 1965)
Rowe, John H., *Inca Culture* (Washington, 1946)
von Hagen, Victor W., *Realm of the Incas* (New York, 1957)
—, *The Desert Kingdoms of Peru* (London, 1964)

The Iberian Imprint
Conquest and Colonial Period
Boxer, C. R., *The Golden Age of Brazil, 1695–1750* (University of California Press, 1962)

Diffie, B. W., *Spanish American Civilization: Colonial Period* (Harrisburg, Pa., 1945)

Gibson, C., *Spain in America* (New York, 1966)

Hanke, L., *The Spanish Struggle for Justice in the Conquest of America* (Philadelphia, 1949)

Haring, Clarence H., *The Spanish Empire in America* (New York, 1947)

—, *Empire in Brazil* (Cambridge, Mass., 1958)

Hemming, John, *The Conquest of the Incas* (London, 1970)

Kirkpatrick, F. A., *The Spanish Conquistadores* (London, 1934)

León-Portilla, M., *The Broken Spears: the Aztec Account of the Conquest of Mexico* (London, 1962)

Madariaga, S. de, *The Rise of the Spanish Empire* (London, 1947)

—, *The Fall of the Spanish Empire* (London, 1947)

Merriman, R. B., *The Rise of the Spanish Empire in the Old World and the New* (4 vols., New York, 1918–34)

Parry, J. H., *The Spanish Seaborne Empire* (New York, 1966)

Prestcott, W. H., *The History of the Conquest of Mexico* (various editions)

—, *The History of the Conquest of Peru* (various editions)

   Independence Period

Clissold, S., *Bernardo O'Higgins and the Independence of Chile* (London, 1968)

Masur, Gerhard, *Simón Bolívar* (revised enlarged edition, 1968)

Nicholson, Irene, *The Liberators: A Study of Independence Movements in Spanish America* (London, 1969)

Pilling, William (after B. Mitre), *The Emancipation of South America* (London, 1893)

Robertson, W. S., *Iturbide of Mexico* (Durham, N. Carolina, 1952)

—, *Life of Miranda* (2 vols., Chapel Hill, 1929)

Street, J., *Artigas and the Emancipation of Uruguay* (Cambridge, 1959)

Trend, J. B., *Bolívar and the Independence of Spanish America* (London, 1946)

Webster, C. K. (ed.), *Britain and the Independence of Latin America, 1812–1830* (Oxford University Press, 1938)

The Twenty Republics

   1 *Mexico*

Alba, Victor, *The Mexicans: the making of a nation* (New York, 1967)

Cheetham, N., *A History of Mexico* (London, 1970)

Cline, Howard F., *Mexico. Revolution to evolution, 1940–60* (New York and OUP, 1962)

Cumberland, C. C., *Mexico's Struggle for Modernity* (New York, 1968)

Lewis, Oscar, *The Children of Sanchez: the autobiography of a Mexican family* (New York, 1961; London, 1962)

Nicholson, Irene, *The X in Mexico: growth within a tradition* (London, 1965)

Parkes, Henry B., *A History of Mexico* (revised edition, Boston and London, 1966)

Simpson, L. B., *Many Mexicos* (3rd edition, University of California Press and CUP, 1952)

Tannenbaum, Frank, *Mexico. The struggle for peace and bread* (New York, 1950)

Womack, Jr., *Zapata and the Mexican Revolution* (New York, 1969)

2 *Central America and Panama*

Biesanz, John and Biesanz, Mavis, *Costa Rican Life* (New York, 1944; London, 1952)

Cox, Isaac J., *Nicaragua and the United States, 1909–27* (Boston, 1927)

Jones, C. L., *Guatemala, past and present* (University of Minnesota Press and OUP, London, 1940)

Martz, J. D., *Central America: the Crisis and the Challenge* (Chapel Hill, 1959)

Osborne, Lilly de Jongh, *Four keys to El Salvador* (New York, 1957)

Parker, Franklin D., *The Central American Republics* (OUP and New York, 1964)

Raynolds, D. R., *Rapid Development in Small Economies—the example of El Salvador* (London and New York, 1967)

Schneider, Ronald M., *Communism in Guatemala, 1944–54* (New York, 1958)

Silvert, Kalman H., *A Study in Government: Guatemala* (New Orleans, 1954)

Stokes, William S., *Honduras: an area study in government* (University of Wisconsin Press, 1950)

Whetten, Nathan L., *Guatemala: The Land and the People* (New Haven, Conn., 1961)

Biesanz, John and Biesanz, Mavis, *The People of Panama* (OUP and Columbia University Press, N.Y., 1955)

Dubois, J., *Danger over Panama* (Bobbs-Merrill, N.Y., 1964)

Howorth, David, *Panama* (New York, 1966)

Liss, Sheldon B., *The Canal, Communism and Chaos: Aspects of U.S.–Panamanian Relations* (University of Notre Dame Press, 1967)

McCain, William D., *The United States and the Republic of Panama* (Duke University Press, Durham, 1937)

Padelford, Norman J., *The Panama Canal in Peace and War* (New York, the Macmillan Company, 1942)

3 *Haiti and the Dominican Republic*

Diedrich, Bernard and Burt, Al., *Papa Doc: the truth about Haiti today* (New York, 1969)

Leyburn, James, *The Haitian People* (Yale University Press, 1941)

Logan, Rayford W., *Haiti and the Dominican Republic* (OUP and New York, 1968)

Rodman, Selden, *Haiti; the Black Republic* (New York, 1954)

Bosch, Juan, *The Unfinished Experiment: democracy in the Dominican Republic* (London, 1966)

Crassweller, Robert D., *Trujillo: the Life and Times of a Caribbean Dictator* (New York, 1966)

Rodman, Selden, *Quisqueya—a History of the Dominican Republic* (University of Washington Press, Seattle, 1964)

Welles, Sumner, *Naboth's Vineyard; the Dominican Republic, 1844–1924* (2 vols., New York, 1928)

Wiarda, Howard J., *The Dominican Republic: Nation in Transition* (London and New York, 1969)

4 *Cuba*

Barnett, Clifford R., *Cuba: its people, its society, its culture* (New Haven, 1962)

Boorstein, Edward, *The Economic Transformation of Cuba* (New York, 1968)

Draper, Theodore, *Castro's Revolution: Myths and Realities* (New York, 1962)

—, *Castroism: Theory and Practice* (New York, 1965)

Goldenberg, Boris, *The Cuban Revolution and Latin America* (London and New York, 1965)

Karol, K. S., *Guerrillas in Power: the Course of the Cuban Revolution* (London, 1971)

Nelson, Lowry, *Rural Cuba* (University of Minnesota Press and OUP, 1950)

Scheer, Robert and Zeitlin, Maurice, *Cuba: an American Tragedy* (New York, 1963; London, Penguin, 1964)

Smith, Robert F., *Background to Revolution: the Development of Modern Cuba* (New York, 1966)

Thomas, Hugh, *Cuba: or the Pursuit of Freedom* (London, 1970)

5 Venezuela

Alexander, R. J., *The Venezuelan Democratic Revolution: A Profile of the Regime of Rómulo Betancourt* (New Brunswick, N.J., 1964)

Lieuwen, Edwin, *Venezuela* (Oxford University Press, 2nd edition, 1965)

Martz, John D., *Acción Democrática: evolution of a modern political party in Venezuela* (Princeton, N.J., 1966)

Morón, Guillermo, *A History of Venezuela* (London, 1964)

6 Colombia

Dix, R. H., *Colombia: the Political Dimensions of Change* (Yale, 1967)

Fluharty, V. L., *Dance of the Millions: Military rule and social revolution, Colombia, 1930–56* (University of Pittsburg Press, 1957)

Galbraith, W. O., *Colombia: a general survey* (2nd edition, Oxford University Press, 1966)

Martz, John D., *Colombia, a contemporary political survey* (Chapel Hill, N.C., 1962)

7 Ecuador

Blanksten, G. I., *Ecuador: Constitutions and caudillos* (University of California Press, 1951)

Linke, Lilo, *Ecuador, Country of Contrasts* (3rd edition, OUP and New York, 1959)

8 Peru

Bourricauld, F., *Power and Society in Contemporary Peru* (London, 1970)

Ford, Thomas R., *Man and Land in Peru* (Gainesville, Flor., 1962)

Marett, Robert, *Peru* (London and New York, 1969)

Owens, R. J., *Peru* (London and New York, 1963)

Pike, Frederick B., *The Modern History of Peru* (London and New York, 1967)

9 Bolivia

Alexander, R. J., *The Bolivian National Revolution* (Washington, 1965)

Klein, H. S., *Parties and Political Change in Bolivia, 1880–1952* Cambridge University Press, 1969)

Osborne, Harold, *Bolivia: A Land Divided* (3rd edition, OUP and New York, 1966)

Zondag, C. H., *The Bolivian Economy, 1952–65: the Revolution and its aftermath* (New York and London, 1966)
Zook, D. H., *The Conduct of the Chaco War* (New York, 1960)

10 Chile

Butland, Gilbert J., *Chile: an outline of its geography, economics and politics* (3rd edition, OUP and New York, 1956)
Galdames, Luis, *A History of Chile* (Chapel Hill, 1941)
Gil, Federico, *The Political System of Chile* (Boston, 1966)
McBride, G. M., *Chile: land and society* (New York, 1936)
Pike, Frederick B., *Chile and the United States, 1880–1962* (University of Notre Dame Press, 1963)
Silvert, K. H., *Chile, yesterday and today* (New York, 1964)

11 Argentina

Alexander, R. J., *An Introduction to Argentina* (New York, 1969)
—, *The Perón Era* (New York, 1951)
Blanksten, George I., *Perón's Argentina* (Chicago, 1953)
Ferns, H. S., *Britain and Argentina in the nineteenth century* (Oxford University Press, 1960)
—, *Argentina* (London, 1969)
McGann, G. W., *Argentina: the divided land* (Princeton, 1966)
Pendle, George, *Argentina* (3rd edition, OUP and New York, 1963)
Rennie, Y. F., *The Argentine Republic* (New York, 1945)
Scobie, J. R., *Argentina: a City and a Nation* (New York, 1964)
Whitaker, A. P., *Argentina* (Englewood Cliffs, N.J., 1964)

12 Paraguay

Pendle, George, *Paraguay: a riverside nation* (3rd edition, London and New York, 1966)

13 Uruguay

Alisky, M., *Uruguay: a contemporary survey* (New York, 1969)
Fitzgibbon, R. H., *Uruguay: Portrait of a Democracy* (New York and London, 1956)
Pendle, George, *Uruguay: South America's first welfare state* (3rd edition, OUP and New York, 1963)
Taylor, Philip B., *Government and Politics of Uruguay* (New Orleans, 1962)

14 Brazil

Bello, J. M., *A History of Modern Brazil, 1889–1964* (Stanford, Calif., 1966)
Freyre, Gilberto, *The Masters and the Slaves: a Study in the Development of Brazilian Civilization* (New York, 1946; abridged edition, 1964)
—, *New World in the Tropics* (New York, 1959)
Furtado, Celso, *The Economic Growth of Brazil: A Survey from colonial to modern times* (Berkeley, Calif., 1963)
—, *Diagnosis of the Brazilian Crisis* (Berkeley and Los Angeles, 1965)
Graham, R., *Britain and the Onset of Modernization in Brazil* (Cambridge, 1968)

Haring, Clarence H., *Empire in Brazil: A new world experiment with monarchy* (Cambridge, Mass., 1958)
Livermore, H. V. (ed.), *Portugal and Brazil: an introduction* (Clarendon Press, 1953)
Manchester, A. K., *British Pre-eminence in Brazil; its rise and decline* (Chapel Hill and OUP, 1933)
Poppino, Rollie E., *Brazil: the Land and the People* (New York, 1968)
Schurz, W. L., *Brazil, the infinite country* (New York, 1961)
Skidmore, T. E., *Politics in Brazil, 1930–64* (New York, 1967)
Smith, T. Lynn, *Brazil: People and Institutions* (3rd edition, Baton Rouge, 1963)
Wagley, C., *An Introduction to Brazil* (5th edition, New York, 1966)

The Latin American Scene

1 *The Social Structure*

Adams, Richard N. (*et al*), *Social Change in Latin America today: its implications for United States Policy* (New York, 1960)
Hauser, Philip M. (ed.), *Urbanization in Latin America* (UNESCO, 1961)
Johnston, John J., *Continuity and Change in Latin America* (Stanford, Calif., 1964)
Lambert, J., *Latin America: Social Structure and Political Institutions* (University of California Press, 1967)
Landsberger, H., *Latin American Peasant Movements* (Cornell, 1969)
Lipset, S. M. and Solari, A., *Elites in Latin America* (New York, 1961)
Stycos, J. M. and Arias, M. (eds.), *Population Dilemma in Latin America* (Washington, 1966)
Tannenbaum, Frank, *Slave and Citizen: The Negro in the Americas* (New York, 1947)
Veliz, Claudio (ed.), *Obstacles to Change in Latin America* (OUP and New York, 1967)

2 *Institutions*

Alba, Victor, *Politics and the Labor Movement in Latin America* (Stanford, 1968)
Alexander, R. J., *Labor Relations in Argentina, Brazil and Chile* (New York, 1962)
—, *Organized Labor in Latin America* (New York, 1965)
Burnett, B. G. and Poblete Troncoso, M., *The Rise of the Latin American Labor Movement* (New York, 1960)
Busey, J. L., *Latin America: Political Institutions and Processes* (New York, 1963)
Johnston, John J., *The Military and Society in Latin America* (Stanford, 1964)
Landsberger, Henry A. (ed.), *The Church and Social Change in Latin America* (Notre Dame, 1970)
Lieuwen, Edwin, *Arms and Politics in Latin America* (New York, 1961)
—, *Generals vs. Presidents: Neomilitarism in Latin America* (New York, 1964)
Mecham, J. L., *Church and State in Latin America* (revised edition, Chapel Hill, 1966)
Pike, F. B., *The Conflict between Church and State in Latin America* (New York,1964,
Smyth, T. Lynn (ed.), *Agrarian Reform in Latin America* (New York, 1965)
Veliz, Claudio (ed.), *The Politics of Conformity in Latin America* (OUP and New York, 1967)

3 *Economic Problems*

Baer, W. and Kerstenetzky, I., *Inflation and Growth in Latin America* (Irwin, Illinois, 1964)

Benham, F. C. and Holley, H. H., *A Short Introduction to the Economy of Latin America* (Oxford University Press, 1960)

Bernstein (ed.), *Foreign Investments in Latin America: Cases and Attitudes* (New York, 1966)

Brandenburg, F., *The Development of Latin American Private Enterprise* (Washington, 1964)

Cole, J. P., *Latin America: An Economic and Social Geography* (London, 1965)

Economic Commission for Latin America, *Development Problems in Latin America* (Austin, 1970)

Edel, M., *Food Supply and Inflation in Latin America* (New York, 1969)

Frank, A. G., *Latin America: Underdevelopment or Revolution* (New York and London, 1969)

Furtado, Celso, *Economic Development of Latin America—A Survey from colonial times to the Cuban Revolution* (Cambridge, 1970)

Gordon, Wendell, *The Political Economy of Latin America* (New York, 1965)

Griffin, Keith, *Underdevelopment in Spanish America* (London, 1969)

Hirschman, Albert O., *Journeys towards Progress: Studies of Economic Policy-making in Latin America* (New York, 1963)

James, Preston E., *Latin America: an Economic Geography* (3rd edition, New York, 1959)

Lauterbach, Albert, *Enterprise in Latin America. Business Attitudes in a Developing Economy* (Ithaca, 1966)

Nisbet, Charles (ed.), *Latin America: Problems in Economic Development* (New York, 1969)

Rippy, J. Fred, *British Investments in Latin America, 1822–1949* (revised edition, Hamden, Conn., 1966)

Urquidi, Victor L., *The Challenge of Development in Latin America* (New York, 1964)

Vernon, Raymond, *How Latin America Views the U.S. Investor* (New York, 1966)

Withers, W., *The Economic Crisis in Latin America* (Free Press of Glencoe, 1964)

4 *Political Forces*

Alba, Victor, *Nationalists without Nations: The Oligarchy versus the People in Latin America* (London and New York, 1968)

Alexander, R. J., *Communism in Latin America* (New Brunswick, N.J., 1957)

—, *Latin American Politics and Government* (New York, 1965)

Debray, Regis, *Revolution in the Revolution: Armed and Political Struggle in Latin America* (New York, 1967)

Edelman, A. T., *Latin American Government and Politics: the Dynamics of a Revolutionary Society* (New York, 1965)

Gott, R., *Guerrilla Movements in Latin America* (London, 1970)

Horowitz, I. L. (ed.), *Latin American Radicalism. A Documentary Report on Left and Nationalist Movements* (New York, 1969)

Mercier Vega, L., *Guerrillas in Latin America. The Technique of the Counter State* (London, 1968)

Needler, Martin C., *Latin American Politics in Perspective* (Princeton, 1963)

—, *Political Systems in Latin America* (Princeton, 1964)

Poppino, R. E., *International Communism in Latin America: a history of the movement, 1917–63* (Free Press of Glencoe, 1964)

Stokes, William S., *Latin American Politics* (New York, 1959)

Williams, E. J., *Latin American Christian Democrat Parties* (Knoxville, Tenn., 1967)

    5 *Patterns of Thought and Culture*

Anderson Impert, E., *Spanish American Literature—a History* (Wayne State University, Detroit, 1963)

Arciniegas, Germán, *Latin America: a cultural history* (London, 1969)

Azevedo, Fernando de, *Brazilian Culture: An Introduction to the Study of Culture in Brazil* (New York, 1950)

Castedo, Leopoldo, *A History of Latin American Art and Architecture: from pre-Columbian Times to the Present* (New York and London, 1969)

Clissold, S., *Latin America: a cultural outline* (London, 1966)

Crawford, W. R., *A Century of Latin American Thought* (Harvard, 1961)

Cruz Costa, J., *A History of Ideas in Brazil: the development of Philosophy in Brazil and the Evolution of National History* (Berkeley, 1966)

Franco, Jean, *The Modern Culture of Latin America: Society and the Artist* (London, 1967)

—, *An Introduction to Latin American Literature* (Cambridge, 1969)

Henríquez-Ureña, P., *Literary Currents in Hispanic America* (Cambridge, Mass., 1945)

—, *A Concise History of Latin American Culture* (New York, 1966)

Picón-Salas, M., *A Cultural History of Latin America, from Conquista to Independence* (Berkeley, 1962)

Putnam, S., *Marvellous Journey; Four Centuries of Brazilian Literature* (New York, 1948)

Torres-Rioseco, A., *The Epic of Latin American Literature* (Paperback—University of California Press, 1959)

Verissimo, E., *Brazilian Literature—an Outline* (New York, 1954)

Whitaker, A. P., *Latin America and the Enlightenment* (2nd edition, New York, 1961)

    6. *Inter-American and International Relations*

Astiz, C. A. (ed.), *Latin American International Politics: Ambitions, Capabilities, and the National Interest of Mexico, Brazil and Argentina* (Notre Dame, Ind., 1969)

Bailey, Norman A., *Latin America in World Politics* (New York, 1967)

Ball, M. Margaret, *The OAS in transition* (Durham, N.C., 1969)

Bemis, S. F., *The Latin American Policy of the United States: an Historical Interpretation* (New York, 1943)

Castillo, C. M., *Growth and Integration in Central America* (London and New York, 1967)

Clissold, S. (ed.), *Soviet Relations with Latin America, 1919–1969* (Oxford University Press, 1970)

Connell Smith, G., *The Inter-American System* (OUP, London and New York, 1966)

Dell, Sidney, *A Latin American Common Market?* (OUP and New York, 1966)

Dozer, Donald (ed.), *The Monroe Doctrine: Its Modern Significance* (New York, 1965)

Drier, John C. (ed.), *Alliance for Progress: Problems and Perspectives* (Baltimore and OUP, 1962)

García Robles, Alfonso, *The Denuclearization of Latin America* (New York, 1967)

Harrison Wagner, R., *United States Policy towards Latin America: A Study in Domestic and International Politics* (Stanford, 1970)

Houston, John A., *Latin America in the United Nations* (New York, 1956)

Mathews, Herbert L., *The United States and Latin America* (2nd edition, New York, 1963)

Nystrom, J. Warren and Haverstick, N. A., *The Alliance for Progress: key to Latin America's Development* (Princeton, 1966)

Rippy, F. J., *Globe and Hemisphere* (Chicago, 1955)

Stoetzer, O. Carlos, *The Organization of American States: An Introduction* (New York, 1965)

Urquidi, Victor L., *Free Trade and Economic Integration in Latin America* (University of California Press, 1962)

Wionczek, Miguel S., *Latin American Free Trade Association* (New York, 1965)

Whitaker, A. P. and Jordan, D. C., *Nationalism in Contemporary Latin America* (New York, 1967)

Index

gl = glossary

Acção Popular 236
Acción Democrática 140–3, 298–9
Acción Popular 159–60, 209, 296
Acre 165, 320
Action for Progress 337
Adams, John Quincey 125
Adelantados 40, *gl*
Africa 47, 115, 168, 268, 281, 310–12, 345
Agency for International Development (AID) 278
Agrarian reform—*see* land reform
Agriculture (*and see under individual countries*): pre-Columbian 5, 12, 14, 17, 23; colonial period 47, 53, 55; current problems 219, 225, 249, 255–62
Alamán, Lucas 80
Alamo, siege of the 81
Alaska 3
Alberdi, Juan Bautista 182–3, 224, 272, 314
Alcaldes 39, 51, 58, *gl*
Alegría, Ciro 216, 308
Aleijadinho, O (Antônio Francisco Lisboa) 60, 223, 310
Alemán, Miguel 94
Alessandri, Arturo 175, 295
Alessandri, Jorge 176–7
Alfaro, Eloy 153
Aliança Renovadora Nacional (ARENA) 298
Alianza Nacional Popular (ANAPO) 149
Alianza Popular Revolucionaria Americana (APRA) 158–62, 248, 253, 296
Allende, Miguel de 73
Allende, Salvador 177–9, 302
Alliance for Progress 121, 149, 207, 229, 245, 285, 326
Almagro, Diego de 31–3, 38–40
Almagro, Diego de (the Younger) 49
Alpacas 17, *gl*

Alvarado, Pedro de 31, 34, 48
Alvear, Marcelo 185
Alves, Castro 311
Amadis de Gaula 30
Amautas 20, *gl*
Amazonas, Department of 15
Amazon River 34, 36–7, 57, 146, 165, 204, 269, 271, 320–1, 346
Anaconda Company 267
Anáhuac 73
Anarcho-syndicalists 249–50, 252
Anchieta, José de 59
Ancón, Peace of 157
Andean civilization 17–24
Andean Group 141, 149–50, 278, 284, 330
Andean Mission 220
Andes, Army of 70
Andrada e Silva, José Bonifácio de 63, 199
Andrade, Mário de 313
Angostura (Ciudad Bolívar) 68
Antillia 28
Antioquia 217
Antofagasta 166, 223, 270
Antonio the Counsellor (Antônio Maciel) 203, 314
Apure River 271
Aramayo family 268
Aramburu, Pedro 189
Arana, Carlos 101–2
Arana, Francisco Javier 99
Aranda, Count of 60, 62
Aranha, Oswaldo 206
Araucanians (Mapuches) 19, 24, 34, 38, 172, 174, 178
Araújo Lima, Pedro de 199
Arawaks 28, 43
Arbenz, Jacobo 99–100, 301
Arbitrations 158, 175, 340

Arce, Aniceto 166
Arce, Manuel José 97
Architecture: pre-Columbian 4–6, 8–9, 14–15, 18, 23–4; colonial 51, 59; modern 317
Arequipa 156–7, 159–60
Arévalo, Juan José 99
Argentina: agriculture 183–8, 229, 258; army 185–6, 188–90, 240–1; and Brazil 181, 194, 199, 202, 206; and Britain 65–6, 182, 184–7, 261–2, 338–9; and Bolivia 168, 170; and Chile 175, 188, 321, 340; Church 188, 236; constitution 182, 188, 287; culture and education 184, 245–7, 314–15, 318; discovery and conquest 33; economy 183, 185–90, 257, 272–4, 276; foreign policy 181–2, 186, 188, 192–3, 341; history (pre-Columbian) 19, 22; (colonial) 52; (19th century) 75, 180–4, 293; (20th century) 184–90; immigration 183–4, 223, 340; independence 69, 75; inflation 279; labour 185–90, 249–54; livestock 261–2, 338; and Paraguay 183, 188, 192, 322; petroleum 188–9, 263, 265; political problems 180, 188–90; population growth 224–5; railways 187, 270; trade 281, 338; and United States 175, 185, 188, 206, 333–4; and Uruguay 194, 196, 202, 322
Arguedas, Alcides 216, 307
Arguedas, Antonio 170
Arguedas, José María 216, 307, 318
Arias, Arnulfo 112
Arica 157–8, 166, 174, 266, 270
Armed forces (and see under individual countries): political role of 160–3, 237–45
Arms race 244, 337, 340
Arosemena, Carlos Julio 153
Arosemena, Otto 153
Arrães, Miguel 209, 292
Arroyo del Río, Carlos 153
Art: pre-Columbian 4–6, 8–9, 11, 15–18, 23–4; colonial 59–60; modern 91, 317–18
Asiento system 47, gl
Asturias, Miguel Angel 290, 307
Asunción 35, 39, 49, 76
Asylum, right of 292
Atacama 34, 156–7, 320

Atahualpa 19, 32–3, 40, 47, 222, 307
Atrato River 113, 269
Audiencia 52, 57, 192, gl
Austin, Stephen 81
Auténticos 129, gl
Autonomy, university 247–8
Avellanada, Nicolás 183
Aviation 271
Avila Camacho, Manuel 94
Axis powers 176, 186, 195, 205
Ayacucho, Battle of 72
Ayala, Eusebio 192
Ayllu 18–19, 21, 221, 296, gl
Aymará 18–19, 220, 223, gl
Azevedo, Aluízio 311
Azopardo 250
Aztecs 10–13, 29–31, 41, 50
Azuay 154

Báez, Buenaventura 119
Bahamas 27
Bahia 35, 54, 63, 199
Balaguer, Joaquín 123
Balboa, Vasco Núñez de 28, 31, 37
Ballivián, José 164
Balmaceda, José Manuel 174, 293, 393
Balmis, Francisco Javier 57
Bananas 96, 104–5, 108, 151, 154, 258, 343
Banda Oriental (see also under Uruguay) 69, 181, 194, 199, 202, 338
Bandeirantes 54, 58, gl
Banks 81, 278
Bánzer Suárez, Hugo 171
Barbados 323
Barbosa, Ruy 201–2
Baroque 59–60, 310
Barriadas 218–19, 296, gl
Barrientos, René 169–70, 236, 251, 268
Barrios, Justo Rufino 97–8
Batista, Fulgencio 128–30, 133, 251, 288, 301–2, 305
Batlle y Ordóñez, José 195, 249
Bay Islands 195, 249
Bay of Pigs (Playa Girón) 133, 324, 336
Beagle Channel 321
Belalcázar, Sebastián de 34, 50
Belaúnde, Fernando 160–1, 291, 294, 296, 337
Belgrano, Manuel 69–70
Belize—see British Honduras

Bello, Andrés 67, 75, 312
Belo Horizonte 198, 203
Beltrán, Pedro 290
Belzú, Isidro 164
Benavente, Toribio de (Motolinía) 55
Benavides, Oscar 159
Beni 169
Bentham, Jeremy 312
Beresford, W. C. 65
Betancourt, Rómulo 121, 140–2, 247, 297, 299
'Betancourt Doctrine' 143
Bilbao, Francisco 312
Bimini 28
Birth control 226–7
'Black Legend' 45
Blanco, Hugo 222, 253, 303
Blancos 194–6, 202, 295, gl
Bobadilla, Francisco de 28
Bogotá 24, 34, 57, 60, 67–8, 72, 110, 147; Act of 326
Bogotazo 147, 305, gl
Bográn, Luis 104
Bolívar, Simón 46, 65, 67–9, 72, 75–6, 124, 172, 306, 312, 322
Bolivia: agrarian reform 168–9, 232, 296; army 166, 169–71, 240, 243; and Brazil 320; Chaco War 166–7, 192; and Chile 157, 165–6, 320–2; Church 236; constitutions 286; education 246–7; economy 165, 167–70, 255, 257, 278–9; foundation 72, 155; guerrillas 134, 170–1, 301, 303; history (19th century) 155–7, 164, 170; (20th century) 166–71, 297; immigrants 223; Indians 49, 166–8, 220–2, 307–8; inflation 279; labour 251; and Paraguay 166–7, 192, 321–2; and Peru 155–7, 164, 170; petroleum 166–7, 263–6; revolution (1952) 167–71, 216; tin 164–5, 168–9, 265; and United States 167–71, 268, 336–7
Bolivian Gulf Oil Company 170, 266, 337
Bonampak 5, 8
Bonilla, Policarpo 104
Borges, Jorge Luis 315
Bosch, Juan 121–2
Bougainville, Louis Antoine de 57
Bourbon dynasty 57–8, 60–1
Boves, José Tomas (Rodríguez) 68
Boyacá, Battle of 68

Boyer, Jean Pierre 115
Braceros 94, gl
Brasília 207, 209, 270, 271, 274, 330
Bravo, Nicolás 73
Brazil: agriculture 257–61; and Argentina 182, 188, 199, 202, 206, 244, 322; army 202–3, 205, 209–12, 240–4; and Bolivia 165, 170, 192, 202, 320–2; and Britain 63, 200, 203–4, 231, 338–9; Church 60, 202, 211–12, 233, 236–7; coffee 201, 204, 206, 258–9; and Colombia 202; communications 269–71; communism 206, 209, 212, 237, 301–2; constitutions 199, 203–4, 210–11, 287, 294; culture and education 58, 245–6, 310–12, 314, 317–18; discovery and conquest 35; and Dominican Republic 326; economy 53–4, 58, 63, 201–12, 256, 272–4, 276, 279, 340, 344; foreign investment 203, 206–8, 210–12; history (pre-Columbian) 22; (colonial) 47, 49, 53–4, 58, 61, 63; (19th century) 199–204; (20th century) 204–12, 297; immigrants 49, 63, 203–4; independence 63–4; Indians 59, 221–2, 309; industrialization 201–2, 205–7, 211–12; inflation 206, 209–11, 279; labour 249, 251–3; land reform 212, 229, 230; and Paraguay 192–3, 202, 322, 331; Peasant Leagues 304–5; petroleum 263–5; political problems 198, 211–12; population growth 224–5; and Portugal 63–4; racial composition 49, 198, 201, 310–12, 222–3, 341, 344; slavery 47, 49, 53, 199–202, 222–3, 310–12, 338–9; social conditions 203, 212; trade 63, 201, 211, 283; and United States 205–7, 212, 226, 258; and Uruguay 194, 196, 199, 202; and Venezuela 202; in World War II 345
Britain (see also under individual countries): colonial possessions 97–8, 339–40; communities 223; independence movement 64–9, 71, 75, 337–8; investments 75, 81, 83, 85, 91–3, 106, 138–9, 187, 276–9, 338–9; navy 63, 65, 200, 338; and Portugal 63, 338; and Spain 38, 61, 64–6, 338; trade 61, 63–5, 75, 282, 337–40
British Guiana (see also under Guyana) 64, 138, 339–40

British Honduras 5, 64, 97–8, 330–1, 339
Brizola, Leonel 208–9
Bryan–Chamorro Treaty 103
Bucaram, Asad 154
Buccaneers 64
Buenos Aires: British attacks 65–6; colonial period 60, 62, 67; foundation 34–5; modern 155, 181–4, 218, 273, 318
Buenos Aires, Declaration of 341
Bulnes, Manuel 156, 173
Bunau-Varilla, Philippe 110–11
Bunge, Carlos Octavio 316
Burgos, Laws of 43
Burle Marx, Roberto 317
Busch, Germán 167
Bustamante, José Luis 159

Caamaño Deñó, Francisco 122
Cabeza de Vaca, Alvar Núñez 38–9
Cabildos 51–2, *gl*
Cabot, Sebastian 34
Cabral, Pedro Alvares 35
Cabral de Melo Neto, João 318
Cáceres, Andrés 157
Cáceres, Ramón 119
Cadiz 57, 61, 67, 74
Cajamarca 17, 32
Cakchiquels 8
Calabar 311
Caldera, Rafael 143
Calderón Guardia, Angel 108
Calendar, pre-Columbian 4, 6–7
California 31, 57, 81, 85, 98, 102
Callao 71–2, 156, 158
Calleja del Rey, F.M. 73–4
Calles, Plutarco Elías 90–1, 298
Calmecac 12
Calpulli 12
Calvo, Carlos 333
Câmara, Helder 234, 237
Canada 323
Candela, Felix 317
Canning, George 337
Canudos 314
Cape Verde Islands 35
Capitanias 35, *gl*
Capitulations 39–40, 48, 50
Captaincies-General 39, 52, 60
Carabobo, Battle of 69

Caracas 66–8, 72, 138, 143, 219, 248, 292; Declaration of 100, 325; Protocol 328
Carbajal, Francisco de 39
Cárdenas, Lázaro 91–4, 298
Carías, Tiburcio 105
Caribbean Free Trade Area (CARIFTA) 112, 331
Caribbean Legion 108
Caribs 43
Carlota, Empress 83
Caroní River 141, 273
Carpentier, Alejo 318
Carranza, Venustiano 88–9
Carrera, José Miguel 70–1
Carrera, Rafael 97–8, 289
Carretera Marginal 160, 271, 328
Cartagena 53, 233; Agreement 330
Carúpano 142
Casa de Contratación 53
Casas, Bartolomé de las 43–7, 233, 309
Caseros, Monte, Battle of 182
Castelo Branco, Humberto de 209–11
Castilla, Ramón 156
Castillo Armas, Carlos 100
Castillo, Ramón 186
Castlereagh, Lord 64
Castro Alves, Antônio de 311
Castro, Cipriano 138–9
Castro, Fidel 101, 124, 129–36, 162, 239–40, 248, 251, 288–9, 292, 298, 301–5
Castro, Raúl 130, 242
Catavi 167
Cattle-raising 180, 182–4, 261
Cauca 148, 151, 269
Caudillismo 75, 136–8, 215–16, 288–90, 294, *gl*
CECLA 327, 341
Central America (*see also under individual countries*) 96–109; Common Market 97, 106, 109, 112, 284, 329–31; discovery and settlement 28, 31, 40; population growth 224; pre-Columbian 3–8; United Provinces 75–6, 96–8
Central Intelligence Agency 100, 170, 335
Centralism 287, 295
Centro Bellarmino 234, 300
Cepeda, Battle of 182
Cereal production 183–4, 187, 258
Cerro de Pasco 162
Céspedes, Carlos Manuel de 125

Céspedes, C. M. de (President) 128
Chacabuco, Battle of 70
Chachapoyas 15
Chac-Mool 9
Chaco 166; War 166, 192, 266, 320
Chamorro, Emiliano 103
Chancas 19
Chan Chan 17
Chapultepec, Act of 323
Charles III, King 60
Charles V, Emperor 34, 40
Chasquis 22, *gl*
Chávez, Carlos 308
Chávez, Federico 193, 240
Chavín de Huántar 14
Chibchas 24
Chicha 23, *gl*
Chichén Itzá 7, 10
Chichimec 10
Chihuahua 85
Chilam Balam 7
Chile: agriculture and agrarian reform
  177–8, 230, 232, 258, 261; and Argen-
  tina 175, 188, 321, 340; and Bolivia
  165, 173–4, 244, 320–1; and Britain
  175, 340; Church 234; communism
  175, 177–9, 300–5; constitution 175,
  294; copper 177–9, 266–7; culture and
  education 177, 226, 247, 318; discovery
  and conquest 33–4, 37; economy 173–
  4, 176–9, 256, 272–3, 276–7, 279;
  history (pre-Columbian) 19; (19th
  century) 156–8, 172–5; (20th century)
  175–9, 295, 298–300; immigrants 223;
  independence 70–1; inflation 176, 279;
  labour 175–7, 179, 249, 251–3; and
  Peru 156–8, 164, 173–4, 244, 320–1;
  petroleum 263, 266; political problems
  172, 178–9; population growth 227;
  and United States 175–7, 267, 336
Chilpancingo 73
Chimbote 273
Chimor, Kingdom of 16–17, 19
Chimú culture 16–17
China 28, 178
Chinampas 12, *gl*
Chinchas Islands 156
Choco 269
Christian Democrats: in Chile 176–8,
  234, 248, 251, 279, 285, 298–301, 342;
  labour organization 251–2; in Peru

160, 299; in Venezuela 141–3, 298–
  300, 342
Christophe, Henri 115
Chubut 183, 223
Chuquicamata 267
Chuquisaca 70
Church (*see also under individual coun-
  tries*): colonial period 40–1, 43–4, 57,
  59–60; independence movement 73,
  75; 19th century 79–80, 82, 85, 295,
  312, 316; today 96, 226, 233–7, 299–
  300
Científicos 84–5, 272, 284, 317, *gl*
Cinnamon, Province of 40
Cities: pre-Columbian 5–6, 8–9, 17, 30;
  colonial 51, 54; modern 218–19
Ciudad Bolívar (Angostura) 68, 271
Ciudad Trujillo (Santo Domingo) 120
Civilistas 156–7
Claver, St. Pedro 59, 233
Clayton–Bulwer Treaty 98, 110, 333
Cleveland, Grover 138
Cleveland, Richard 62
Coal 262
Cochabamba 168–9
Cochrane, Thomas 63, 71
Codovila, Vitorio 302
Coffee (*see also under individual countries*)
  96, 99, 108, 258–9, 281, 283, 343
Cohuacán 11
Colhua—*see under* Mexico
Colombia: agriculture and land reform
  146, 148, 230; army 148; Church 144–
  6, 148–9, 236; coffee 146, 149, 258–9;
  communism 304; Conservatives and
  Liberals 144–9; constitutions 145–6,
  294; culture and education 245–7,
  318–19; discovery and conquest 28, 34,
  38, 40, 43, 50; economy 113, 145–6,
  148–50, 259, 272–3, 279; history (pre-
  Columbian) 24; (colonial) 52, 57; (19th
  century) 76, 144–5, 151; (20th century)
  143, 146–50, 295, 345; independence
  68–9, 72, 75; labour 144, 146, 150; and
  Panama 110–11, 145; and Peru 146,
  321; petroleum 263, 265; political
  problems 144, 149–50; population
  growth 224, 227; trade 281–2; and
  United States 145, 333; and Venezuela
  321; *Violencia* 147–8
Colón 112–13

380 INDEX

Colorados gl; in Paraguay 193; in Uruguay 194–6, 202, 295
Columbus, Bartolomé 28
Columbus, Christopher 27–9, 38, 40–2, 47, 50
Columbus, Diego 28, 50
Comintern 301–2
Comité de Organización Política Electoral Independiente (COPEI) 142–3, 299
Commission on International Development 285
Commodity agreements 258–9
Communications and transport 268–71
Communism (*see also under individual countries*) 249–54, 299–305, 325–6, 342–4
Communitarianism 300
Comte, Auguste 84, 202, 313
Concepción 266
Concón, Battle of 174
Condamine, La, Charles-Marie de 57
Condorcanqui, José Gabriel—*see* Tupac Amaru II
Confederación General del Trabajo (CGT) 185, 187, 250
Confederación Latino-Americana de Sindicalistas Cristianos (CLASC) 252
Confederación Revolucionaria de Obreros Mejicanos (CROM) 90–2, 250–1
Confederación de Trabajadores de América Latina (CTAL) 252
Confederación de Trabajadores de Méjico (CTM) 92, 231
Conquista: in Mexico 29–31; in Peru 31–3; in other areas 31, 33–5; strategy and tactics 35–8; social, legal, and religious aspects 38–46
Conservatives (*see also under individual countries*) 295, 312–13
Constant, Benjamín (Botelho de Magalhães) 202–3, 284
Constitutions (*see also under individual countries*) 42, 286–8
Consulado 53, gl
Contraband 53, 60–1, 64
Cooperatives 132, 161, 220, 232
Copacabana 15
Copán 8
Copper (*see also under* Chile *and* Peru) 112, 154, 165, 266–8, 281
Córdoba 180, 190, 236, 247, 248, 250

Cordobazo 305, gl
Coricancha 23–4, 32
Coro 66
Corporación Minera de Bolivia (COMIBOL) 268
Corregidores 52, 56–7, gl
Corrientes 181
Cortázar, Julio 318
Cortés, Hernán 29–32, 36–9, 47–8, 50–1, 308
Cortés, Martín 49
Costa Rica (*see also under* Central America) 96, 97, 102, 107–9, 224, 227, 230, 258, 259, 270, 321, 330, 343
Costa e Silva, Artur da 211, 293
Cotton 53, 58, 84, 93, 156, 259–60
Council of the Indies 52
Cowdray, Lord—*see under* Pearson, Weetman
Creole (dialect) 114, 117
Creoles 49–50, 59–63, 65, 67–9, 72–5, 124, 307, gl
Crespo, Joaquín 138
Cristeros 91, gl
Cruz, Sor Juana Inés de la 60, 309–10
Cruz, Ramón 106
Cuajone 162, 266
Cuautémoc 31, 222, 308
Cuba: agriculture and land reform 131–3, 135, 230, 232, 257–8; army 241–2; communism 128–34, 136, 242, 301–5, 325, 342; constitutions 126, 129, 131, 136, 288, 290; culture and education 131–2, 136, 226, 242, 246, 311, 316, 318; discovery and conquest 27–9; economy 126–8, 131–2, 135–6; foreign investments 126, 133; guerrillas 125, 130, 134, 160, 243, 303–5; history (colonial) 47, 124; (19th century) 124–6; (20th century) 126–36; human rights 288, 292; immigrants 127; independence 125–6; labour 127–32, 135–6, 249, 251–3; missile crisis 134, 336, 343; petroleum 263–4, 266; political problems 124, 135–6; revolution 130–6; slavery 47, 124–5; and Soviet Union 124, 131–3, 136; and Spain 124–6, 342; sugar 124, 126–7, 132, 135–6, 201, 259–60; and United States 124–8, 133–6, 259–60, 316, 325, 336
Cunha, Euclides da 203, 314

Cusi Yupanqui—*see* Pachacuti
Cuyo 70
Cuzco 19–24, 32–3, 57

Darien 29, 112, 271
Darío, Rubén 313
Daza, Hilarión 165
Debts, foreign 276
De Gaulle, Charles 340
Descamisados 187–8, *gl*
Dessalines, Jean Jacques 62, 114–15
Development questions, 284–5
Díaz, Adolfo 103
Díaz, Porfirio 83–7, 272, 284, 287, 289, 338
Díaz del Castillo, Bernal 30, 36, 41, 308
Díaz Lanz, Pedro Luis 133
Díaz Ordaz, Gustavo 94
Dolores 73
Dominican Republic: agriculture and land reform 120, 230, 259–60; army 241; constitution 287; Church 236; communism 304; economy 120–3, 279; and Haiti 119, 121, 224–5, 321; history 119–20; independence 119; post-Trujillo 121–3, 134; and Spain 119; Trujillo period 120–1; United States intervention 119–20, 122, 325–6
Dorticós, Osvaldo 132
Drago, Luis María 333
Drake, Francis 64
Duarte, Juan Pablo 119
Durão, José de Santa Rita 309
Dutch 35, 54, 64, 309, 311
Dutra, Eurico 205
Duvalier, François ('Papa Doc') 117–18, 122, 239, 287
Duvalier, Jean-Claude 118

Earthquakes 67, 153, 162
Echeverría, Esteban 312
Echeverría Alvarez, Luis 94
Economic Commission for Latin America (ECLA) 281, 331–2, 335
Economy (*see also under individual countries*): colonial 53–7, 61; contemporary problems 255–85; pre-Columbian 12–14, 17, 20–1
Ecuador: agrarian reform 230; bananas 151, 154, 258, 343; Church 152–3; constitution 152, 287; culture and education 247; discovery and conquest 34; economy 151, 154, 278; history (pre-Columbian) 17, 19, 22; (colonial) 49; (19th century) 151–3, 295; (20th century) 153–4, 228; independence 68; Indians 49, 151–2, 154, 220–2, 308; and Peru 153, 159, 321, 323; petroleum 151, 153–4, 263–5; political problems 151–2, 154
Education (*see also under individual countries*): colonial 245; contemporary 225–6, 245–9; pre-Columbian 12, 20
Eisenhower, Dwight D. 133
Ejidos 82, 88–9, 93–4, 229, 232, *gl*
El Baúl 5
El Chocón 273
El Dorado 34, 37
Electric power 273
Elizabeth II, Queen 340
El Mutún 262
El Salvador (*see also under* Central America) 5, 97–8, 106–7, 225, 230, 241–2, 287, 299, 301, 321, 326, 330
El Teniente 267
Encina, Francisco 316
Encomiendas 43–5, 48, 50, 57, *gl*
English (*see under* Britain) 38, 54, 173
Enlightenment, the 57–8, 83
Entre Ríos 181–2
Erasmus 44
Ercilla, Alonso de 309
Escalante, Aníbal 133, 135
Escambray 130
Esmeralda, the 71
Esmeraldas 265
Espaillat, Ulises 119
Estado Nôvo 204–6
Estimé, Dumarsais 117
Estrada Cabrera, Manuel 99
Estrada Palma, Tomás 128
Estremadura 38
European Economic Community (EEC) 258, 282–3, 340–1
Exótica mine 267

Facundo 181
Falange (Chile) 234, 299
Falkland Islands (Malvinas) 64, 339
Farrell, Edelmiro 186–7
Fascism 167, 192, 204–5, 249, 252, 296–7
Febreristas 193, *gl*

Federalism 287, 295
Federmann, Nikolaus 34, 50
Feijó, Diogo Antônio 199
Ferdinand II, King 41
Ferdinand VII, King 66–9, 74
Fernández de Oviedo, Gonzalo 308
Fernández Pradel, Father 234
Figueres, José 104, 108–9
Finlay, Carlos 126, 317
Fishing 262, 341, 337
Flag discrimination 270
Flores, Juan José 151–2
Florida 28, 37–8, 40, 332–3
Fonseca, Manoel Deodoro da 203
Football 107, 212
Foot and mouth disease 261–2
Foreign investments 275–9
France: and Argentina 182, 340; and Brazil 62–3, 340; cultural influence 299, 313, 340; and Haiti 114–6, 233; and Latin America 340–1; and Mexico 83, 340; and Panama 110; and Peru 245, 340; and Spain 66–7
Francia, José Gaspar Rodríguez de 69, 191, 289
Franciscans 44, 57, 233
Franco, Guillermo 152
Franco, Rafael 192–3
Frei, Eduardo 176–7, 234, 294, 299, 300, 328
Freire, Ramón 172
French (see also under France) 35, 54, 64, 81, 243, 311
French Revolution 62, 286
Frente de Acción Popular (FRAP) 176, 299
Frente Amplio 196
Freyre, Gilberto 172–3, 222, 311–12
Frezier, A. F. 57
Frigoríficos 184–5, gl
Frondizi, Arturo 189, 265
Frontier disputes 320–2
Fuentes, Carlos 318
Furtado, Celso 208

Gaitán, Jorge Eliécer 146
Gallegos, Rómulo 140, 314
Gálvez, Juan Manuel 105
Gamarra, Agustín 156
Gamonalismo 215, gl
García, Calixto 125

García Godoy, Héctor 123
García Márquez, Gabriel 318
García Moreno, Gabriel 152–3, 289, 295
Garcilaso de la Vega ('el Inca') 48–9, 309
Garibay, K. Angel 308
Garrastazú Médici, Emilio 211, 241, 293
Gauchos 181, 184, 314–15, gl
Geffrard, Fabre 116
Germans 38, 48, 81, 102, 184, 203–4, 223
Germany 89, 116, 139, 168, 178, 211, 268, 299, 322, 341
Gestido, Oscar 196
Getulismo 205, gl
Godoy, Manuel 66
Gold: pre-Columbian 15, 23, 24; Conquista 28, 32; colonial production 54–5; current production 262
Gómez, José Miguel 128
Gómez, Juan Vicente 138–9, 247, 289
Gómez, Laureano 146–9
Gómez, Máximo 125
González, Manuel 83
González, Paniagua 49
González Videla, Gabriel 176
Good Neighbour policy 334
Goulart, João 206–9, 237, 252, 274, 298, 336
Granada 102–3
Gran Colombia 68, 72, 75, 137, 144, 151
Grau San Martín, Ramón 128–9
Grito de Dolores 73
Grito de Yara 125
Grito de Ypiranga 63–4
Growth rates 255–6, 285, 335
Guadalupe, Virgin of 73
Guairá falls 193
Guanabara 208
Guanajuato 55, 73
Guano 14, 156–7, 165, 262, gl
Guantánamo Bay 126
Guaraní 24, 35, 49, 58, 191
Guardia, Tomás 108
Guatemala (see also Central America): agriculture and land reform 99–100, 258, 261; and British Honduras 5, 64, 97–8, 330–1, 339; communism 99–101, 304–5; conquest 31, 44; economy 99, 102; guerrillas 101; history (pre-Columbian) 4–8, 14; (colonial) 48, 67, 96, 98; (19th century) 97, 99; (20th century) 99–102, 134; immigrants 223;

Indians 96, 98, 220, 243; political problems 98, 101, 330; and United States 99–100
Guayana 141, 269, 273
Guayaquil 34, 69–70, 151–5
Guerrero, Vicente 73–4, 80
Guerrillas 125, 130, 134, 160, 243, 303–5
Guevara, Ernesto ('Che') 130, 134–5, 170, 208, 303–5
Guido, José María 189
Guillén, Nicolás 311, 318
Guimarães Rosa, João 314
Güiraldes, Ricardo 315
Guiteras, Antonio 129
Gutiérrez, Teodoro 221
Guyana (see also under British Guiana) 143, 323
Guzmán Blanco, Antonio 137–8

Habsburgs 60, 83
Hacienda 56, 87, 93, 107, 228–32, 257, gl
Haiti: agriculture and land reform 114–16, 118, 230; constitutions 115, 117, 293; culture and education 117, 246, 310–11; discovery and conquest 27–8; economy 114, 118, 255–6; and the French 62, 114; history (colonial) 16; (19th century) 68, 114–16; (20th century) 116–18, 134; independence 62, 114, 124; political problems 114, 118; population growth 225; and Santo Domingo 115, 121–2, 321; slavery 47, 62, 114; and United States 116–18, 334; Voodoo 116, 233
Havana: Second Declaration of 134
Haya de la Torre, Víctor Raúl 158, 160, 248, 292
Hay–Bunau Varilla Treaty 110–11
Hay–Pauncefote Treaty 110
Hernández, José 314–15
Hernández Martínez, Maximiliano 106
Heureux, Ulises 119
Hickenlooper Amendment 161, 337
Hidalgo, Miguel 73–4
Hispanidad 312–13, 342, gl
Hispaniola (Española) (see also under Haiti and Dominican Republic) 27–8, 47, 114, 118
Hochschild, Mauricio 268
Honduras (see also Central America):

agriculture and land reform 105, 230; army 105–6, 240; constitutions 105; economy 256, 329; and El Salvador 106–7, 224–5, 321, 326, 330; exploration and conquest 28, 31; history (pre-Columbian) 5; (19th century) 97, 102–3; (20th century) 100, 103–4, 293; political problems 102, 104
Houssay, Bernardo 317
Houston, Sam 81
Huaca 18, 23, gl
Huachipato 273
Huari 18
Huáscar 32–3
Huascar, the 157
Huasipungeros 230, gl
Huayna Capac 19, 32, 33
Huerta, Victoriano 88
Huitzilopochtli 11, 30
Human rights 287–8
Human sacrifice 11, 13, 23, 30
Humboldt, Alexander von 57, 60, 341
Hurtado, Alberto 234
Hydro-electric power 273
Hyppolite, Florvil 116

Ibáñez, Carlos 175–6
Icaza, Jorge 216, 308
Iguala, Plan of 74
Illia, Arturo 189, 265, 336
Illiteracy 246
Immigration (see also under individual countries) 216, 223–4
Import substitution 272–5, 298
Incas 18–24, 31–3, 40, 46, 50, 156, 160, 307, 309
Independence movement 60–76
Indians (see also under individual countries): arms and tactics 36–8; art and culture 5–9, 11–12, 14–19, 22–4, 306–8; conversion and civilizing 41–5, 58; labour 43–4, 55–6, 58, 222; legislation 42, 45–6, 55; miscegenation 46–50; pre-Columbian civilizations 3–24; risings 56, 73, 221–2, 216; situation today 220–2, 296
Industry (see also under individual countries) 225, 271–5, 281
Inflation 279–81
Inquisition 60, 73–4

384 INDEX

Integralismo 204, *gl*
Integration: economic 327–32; political 76, 320, 322–7; racial 46–50, 198, 220–3, 346; Institute for Latin American 332
Intelligentsia 218
Intendencias 57, *gl*
Inter-American Conferences 322–7; Committee of Alliance for Progress (CIAP) 326; Development Bank (IADB) 332; System 322–37
International Monetary Fund (IMF) 280–1
International Petroleum Company (IPC) 159–62, 337
International Bank for Reconstruction and Development (World Bank) 276, 278, 285
Inti 23
Intransigent Radical Party 189
Investments (*see also under* Britain, United States, Germany *and* Japan) 275–9
Iquique 174–5
Irigoyen, Hipólito 184–5, 295, 297
Iron 165, 262, 273
Irrigation 17, 23, 47, 158, 160, 330–1
Isabella, Queen 27–8, 42
Isle of Pines 126
Italians 38, 223
Italy 139, 203, 299, 341
Iturbide, Agustín de 74, 79, 96
Iturrigaray, José de 72–3
Izapan 4–5, 9

Jackson, Geoffrey 196
Jaén 155
Jaguars 4, 15
Jalisco 91
Jamaica 28, 127, 323
Japan 28, 259, 344
Japanese 14, 204, 223
Jérez, Francisco de 36
Jesuits 35, 45, 57–8, 60, 152, 191, 233–4, 300, 309
Jews 53, 223
Jiménez de Quesada, Gonzalo 34, 38, 40, 50
João IV, King 309
João VI, King 63, 199
Johnson, Lyndon B. 111, 226, 328, 336

Joint ventures 277–9
Joseph (Bonaparte), King 66–7
Juan, Jorge 56, 59–61
Juárez, Benito 81–3, 89, 289
Julião, Francisco 253, 305
Junín, Battle of 72
Justicialismo 154, *gl*
Justo, Agustín 185
Justo, Juan B. 302

Kaminaljuyú 5, 9
Kennecott Copper Co. 267
Kennedy, John F. 134, 230, 245, 335–6
Khrushchev, Nikita 343
Knorosov, Yuri 7
Korean War 159, 168, 195, 243, 268, 279, 345
Kotosh 14
Kubitschek, Juscelino 206–7, 252, 274, 294, 326, 335
Kukulcán—*see* Quetzalcóatl

Labour (*see also under individual countries*): colonial period 43–4, 55–6, 58, 222; legislation 287–8; organizations 249–54; rural 219, 229, 231–2; urban 218–19
La Brea-Pariñas 160
Lacandones 8
Lacerda, Carlos 206, 208
La Convención 160, 222
La Guaira 68
Laguna 93
Lakas, Demetrio B. 112
Lam, Wilfredo 318
Landa, Diego de 7
Land tenure and land reform (*see also under Encomienda, Ejido, and separate countries*): colonial 228–9; current 229–32, 256–7, 335; pre-Columbian 12, 21–2
Lanusse, Alejandro 241
La Paz 70, 156, 166, 222
La Plata (town) 183
La Plata, Viceroyalty of 52
Lara, Jesús 308
Larraín, Manuel 234–5
Larrazabal, Wolfgang 141
Lastarria, José Victorino 312
Latifundios (*see also under Hacienda*) 127, 132, 140, 168, *gl*

Latin American Free Trade Association (LAFTA) 141, 196, 270, 284
Latin American Institute for Economic and Social Planning 331
Latin American nationalism 326–7, 345–6
Latin American Parliament 332
Latin American Solidarity Organization (OLAS) 135
Lauca River 321
La Venta 4
Law 41–2, 292
Laws of Burgos 43
Laws of Reform 82
Lead 262
League of Nations 146, 344
Lechín, Juan 169–70
Leclerc, Victor Emanuel 62
Leguía, Augusto B. 157–8, 248, 289
Leloir, Luis Federico 317
León 102
Leoni, Raúl 141–2, 247
León Portilla, Miguel 308
Lescot, Elie 117
Lesseps, Ferdinand de 110
Letitia 146, 321
Letrados 50–1, *gl*
Levingston, Roberto 190, 250
Lewis, Oscar 95, 308
Ley Juárez 82
Ley Lerdo 82
Lezama Lima, José 318
Liberals 74–5, 79–80, 97–8, 102, 104–6, 295, 312
Lima 33, 53, 59, 60, 67, 70–2, 156–7, 173, 217, 219, 223, 270, 292, 297
Linares, José María 164
Liniers, Santiago 65
Lins do Rêgo, José 312
Lisbon 53, 63
Literature 306–19
Littoral Provinces 281
Livestock 261–2
Llamas 17, 20, 37, 55, *gl*
Llanos 34, 68, *gl*
Llautu 21, 33, *gl*
Lleras Camargo, Alberto 148–9
Lleras Restrepo, Carlos 149, 282, 294
Lobitos Co. 266
Logia Lautarina 71
Lombardo Toledano, Vicente 92, 251–2, 302

Lonardi, Eduardo 189
Loncomilla, Battle of 173
Londrina 231
López, Carlos Antonio 192, 289
López, Francisco Solano 192
López, Narciso 125
López Arellano, Osvaldo 105
López Contreras, Eleázar 139
López de Gómara, Francisco 41
López Mateos, Adolfo 94
López Michelsen, Alfonso 149
López Pumarejo, Alfonso 146
Los Patos pass 70
Lott, Henrique 206
Luiz, Washington 204
Lull, Ramón 42
Luque, Fernando de 40

Maceo, Antonio 125
Machado, Gerardo 128
Machado de Assis, J. M. 223, 311
Macumba 233, *gl*
Madeira River 165
Madero, Francisco 87–9, 287
Magdalena River 34, 269
Magellan, Ferdinand 29, 34, 38
Magellan Straits 29, 34, 173
Magloire, Paul 117
Maine, U.S.S. 125
Maipú, Battle of 71
Maize: pre-Columbian 5, 14, 17; present cultivation 93, 257–8
Malaria 47, 116
Malinche (Malitzín, Doña Marina) 30, 48–9
Malvinas—*see* Falkland Islands
Mamoré River 165
Managua 104
Manaus 269
Manco, Inca 33
Manco Capac 19
Manufacturing 272–5
Mapuches—*see* Araucanians
Maranhão 311
Mariana, St., of Quito 59
Mariátegui, José Carlos 158, 221, 296
Maritain, Jacques 234, 299
Marmontel, Jean-François 313
Martí, José 125, 316
Martín Fierro 314–15
Martínez, Tomás 103

Martínez Estrada, Ezequiel 315
Marxism 133, 178–9, 221, 296, 299
Massetti, Jorge Ricardo 305
Matarazzo, Francisco 217
Matilde mines 171
Matos, Hubert 132
Matta, Roberto 318
Mattos, Gregório de 309
Mauá, Baron of (Ireneu Evangelista de Souza) 201–2
Maule River 19
Maximilian, Emperor 83–4, 340
Maya 5–8, 31, 84, 88
Maynas 155
Meat production 183–4, 186–7, 261–2
Medellín 149, 235
Medina, Bartolomé de 55
Medina, Isaías 139–40
Meiggs, Henry 156
Melgarejo, Mariano 164–5
Mella, Julio Antonio 128, 248
Méndez Montenegro, Julio César 101
Mendieta, Carlos 128
Mendieta, Salvador 97
Mendoza 70, 180, 265
Mendoza, Antonio de 31
Mendoza, Pedro de 34–5, 48
Menocal, Mario García 128
Mesilla valley 81
Mestizos 46–50, *gl*
Mexico: agriculture and land reform 73–4, 81, 85–7, 89, 93–4, 225, 232, 257–9, 261; army 240–1; art 91, 308, 317; and Britain 338–9; Church 44, 73, 79, 82–3, 86, 88, 91–2, 236; communism 301, 303; conquest 29–31, 39; constitutions 82, 88–9, 92, 94, 287–8, 293; and Cuba 325; culture and education 82, 86, 91, 245–8, 317–18; economy 81–3, 84–6, 90, 93–5, 256, 272–3, 275–7, 281; foreign policy 81, 83, 89, 92–3, 342; history (pre-Columbian) 4, 8–13; (colonial) 45, 52, 55–6; (19th century) 76, 79–86; (20th century) 84–91; independence 72–5; Indian question 55–6, 73–4, 84–8, 91–2, 308; industry 56, 85, 94; labour 84, 88–90, 92–4, 249–54, 287–8; literature 59–60, 308–10, 313, 315, 318; mining 55–6, 80, 85, 88, 94, 226; oil 92–3, 263–5, 339; politics 94–5; population growth 224–

5; revolution 86–91, 216, 221, 281, 287; and Soviet Union 342–3; and United States 80–3, 85, 89, 92–3; in World War II 345
Mexico City, 60, 83, 86–7, 91, 218, 270
Michoacán 13, 44, 93
Middle classes 217–18, 223
Mill, John Stuart 312
Milpas, 5, *gl*
Mina, Francisco Javier 74
Minas Gerais 54, 60, 203, 206, 209, 270
Minerals, 54–5, 262–8
Minifundios 132, 149, 169, 232, 257, *gl*
Mining: colonial 54–5, 57; modern 80–1, 165–8, 262–8
Miranda, Francisco de, 668
Miró Quesada, Antonio 159
Misiones 183
Missile crisis 134, 336, 343
Missionaries 42–6, 57–8, 233
Mita 55–6, 152, *gl*
Mitimaes 22, *gl*
Mitre, Bartolomé 182–3
Miztecs 13
Moche valley 16
Mochica 16–17
Modernismo 313, *gl*
Monagas family 137
Moncada, José María 103
Moncada Barracks 129–30
Monclova 273
Monetarists 279–81
Monroe Doctrine 83, 134, 138–9, 333
Montalvo, Juan, 152
Monte Albán 4, 9
Monte Caseros, Battle of, 182
Monterrey 217, 273
Montes, Ismael 166
Montesinos, Antonio de 42–3
Montesquieu, Baron de 60
Monteverde, General 68
Montevideo 62, 65–6, 69, 155, 182, 194–6, 202, 218, 295, 332; Treaty of (1960) 327
Montezuma (Moctezuma) 10, 29–30, 47
Montt, Manuel, 173–4
Moraes Barros, Prudente José de 203
Moral, Enrique del 317
Morazán, Francisco 97, 104
More, Thomas 45
Morelos 85, 88–9

Morelos, José María 73–4
Moreno, Mariano 61, 69
Morillo, Pablo 69
Moríñigo, Higinio 192
Morla, Francisco de 41
Morones, Luis 90, 92, 251
Morrow, Dwight W. 334
Mosquera, Tomás Cipriano de 144
Mosquitia 64, 97–8, 339
Motolinía—*see* Benavente, Toribio de
Movimiento de Acción Popular Unitaria
    (MAPU) 177
Movimiento Democrático Brasileiro (MDB)
    211
Movimiento de la Izquierda Revolucionaria
    (MIR) 178, 248, 305
Movimiento Nacional Revolucionario
    (MNR) 167–71, 222, 251, 266, 296
Mujal, Eusebio 129, 131
Mulattos 62, 114–18, 311
Municipalities 51–2
Music 312, 318
Mutis, José Celestino 57

Nabuco, Joaquim 201
Napoleon (Bonaparte) I, Emperor 62, 66,
    337
Napoleon (Bonaparte) III, Emperor 83–4
Narváez, Pánfilo de 30, 38, 47
National Front (Colombia) 148–50
Nationalism 75–6, 298, 320, 336–7
Nationalizations 92–3, 168, 178, 264, 267,
    277–8, 298, 300
Nazca 15–16, 18
Nazis 176, 297, 341
Negroes: in Brazil 49, 53–4, 200–2,
    222–3; colonial period 46, 49, 53–4; in
    Cuba 124–5, 311; culture 310–12; in
    Haiti 62, 114–18
Neruda, Pablo (Neftalí Reyes) 313,
    318
New Castile—*see* Peru
New Granada—*see* Colombia
New Laws for the Indies 45
New Mexico 81
New Spain—*see* Mexico
Nezahualcóyotl 11
Nicaragua, Lake 102, 103, 113, 339
Nicaragua 64, 96–7, 100, 102–5, 108, 134,
    230, 261, 287, 293, 321, 329
Nicaragua, Lake 102, 103, 113, 339

Nickel production 262
Niemeyer, Oscar 317
Nitrates 156–7, 173–4, 262, 320
Nixon, Richard 113, 284, 337
Nóbrega, Manoel de 59
Non-intervention 322, 325–6, 333–5
Norsemen 27
North, John Thomas 338
Nuclear energy 113, 273, 317
Nuclear Free Zone 345
Núñez, Rafael 145

Oaxaca, 4, 82, 85
Obando, José María 144
Obrajes 56, *gl*
Obregón, Alvaro 88–91
Ocaña 72
O'Donojú, Juan 74
Odría, Manuel 159, 297, 301
O'Gorman, Juan 317
O'Higgins, Bernardo 70–2
Oidores 52, *gl*
Oil (*see also under individual countries*)
    320–1, 262–6, 281
Olaya Herrera, Enrique 146
Ollontay 307
Olmecs 4–6, 8–9, 14
Onganía, Juan Carlos 190, 248, 250
Ongaro, Raimundo 250
Operation Panamerica 207, 326, 335
Orejones 20, *gl*
Orellana, Francisco de 34, 37
Organización Inter-Regional Latinoameri-
    cana de Trabajadores (ORIT) 252
Organization of American States (OAS)
    97, 118, 153, 323–7, 343
Organization of Central American States
    (ODECA) 330
Organization of Petrol Exporting Coun-
    tries (OPEC) 264
Orinoco River 28, 68, 138, 140, 269, 271,
    273
Orozco, José Clemente 91, 308
Ortiz, Fernando 311
Ortiz, Roberto 186
Ortiz Rubio, Pascual 90
Ortodoxos 129, *gl*
Oruro 268, 307
Ospina Pérez, Mariano 146–7, 149
Otumba, Battle of 30
Ouro Prêto 54, 310

Ovando, Alfredo 169–71, 243, 251, 266, 336
Oviedo, Gonzalo Fernández de 33

Pachacama 307
Pachacuti (Cusi Yupanqui) 19, 21
Pacheco, Jorge 166, 196
Pacific Ocean 14–17, 29, 31, 102, 110, 113, 340
Páez, José Antonio 68, 72, 137
Pais, Frank 130
Palacios, Alfredo 302
Palenque 5, 8
Pampa 35, 38, 180, 261, 314–15, *gl*
Panama: agriculture and land reform 230, 258; economy 266, 270, 328; exploration and settlement 28, 53; history and politics 109–13, 145; independence 110, 145; and United States 110–13, 334, 336
Panama, Congress of 76, 322
Panama, Declaration of 323, 334
Panama Canal 109–13, 158
Panama City 223, 271
Pan-American Highway 271, 328
Panamericanism 322–3
Pan-American Union 323
Pando, José Manuel 166
Pani, Mario 317
Pará 199
Paracas 15
Paraguay: agriculture and land reform 230; and Argentina 69, 183, 188, 192–3; army 240; and Brazil 166–7, 192–3, 202; Chaco War 166–7, 192; Church 193, 236; communism 301; conquest and settlement 35, 48–9; constitution 293; economy 193; history 24, 39, 49, 191–3; immigrants 223; independence 69; Jesuit missions 58; Paraguayan War 192; petroleum 264, 266; political problems 191, 193
Paraguay River 35, 167, 191–2, 269
Paramonga 17
Paraná 231, 259
Paraná River 58, 193, 269, 273
Paranaguá 271
Pardo, José 157
Pardo, Manuel 156
Partido de Acción Nacional (PAN) 90, 248
Partido Obrero Revolucionario (POR) 303

Partido Revolucionario Institucional (PRI) 90, 95, 298
Partido Social Democrático (PSD) 206–7, 297
Partido Trabalhista Brasileiro (PTB) 206–7, 297
Party systems 261, 273
Pastrana Borrero, Misael 149
Patagonia 273
Patiño tin interests 169, 268
Patrocínio, José de, 201
Patronato Real 59, 152, *gl*
Paul VI, Pope 235
Paz, Octavio 90, 308
Paz Estenssoro, Víctor 167–9, 297
Paz del Río 273
Pearson, Lester 285
Pearson, Weetman (Lord Cowdray) 85, 338
Peasant Leagues 209, 237, 304
Pedro I, Emperor 63–4, 199
Pedro II, Emperor 200–2
Peixoto, Floriano 203
Pelé 223
Péligre 118
Peñaranda, Enrique 167
Peonage 56
Peralta Azurdia, Enrique 101
Pérez Jiménez, Marcos 140–1, 143, 247, 292, 299
Pernambuco 54, 63, 209
Perón, Juan 180, 186–9, 216, 250, 253, 265, 274, 289, 292, 297, 301, 321, 339, 340
Perón, Eva Duarte de 187–8
Peronismo 176, 186–90, 250, *gl*
Pershing, John J. 88
Peru: agriculture and land reform 161–2, 229, 232, 259, 262; APRA 158–62, 248, 296; army 156, 158, 160–3, 242–3; art 14–18, 23–4; and Bolivia 156–7, 320; and Chile 156–8, 320–2; and Colombia 146, 321; communism 158–62, 222, 296, 301, 304; conquest 31–3, 40; constitutions 287, 294; culture and education 24, 49, 245, 247–8, 309, 318; economy 156, 158, 160–3, 256, 258; and Ecuador 159, 320, 323; history (pre-Columbian) 14, 24; (colonial) 49, 53, 55–7; (19th century) 76, 152, 155–7; (20th century) 157–63, 299; immigrants

223; independence 71–2; Indian question 49, 71, 155, 158, 160, 220–2, 308; industry 158, 160, 163; mining 266, 273, 278; petroleum 263, 266; politics 155, 162–3; trade 281, 283, 344; and United States 158, 160–2, 337
Petén 5, 7–8, 98
Pétion, Alexandre 115
Petroleo Brasileiro (PETROBRAS) 206
Petroleos Mexicanos (PEMEX) 265
Petroleum—*see under* Oil
Philip II, King 29
Philippines 46, 125, 345
Picado, Teodoro 108
Pichincha, Battle of 69
Piérola, Nicolás 157
Pisco 15, 156
Pitt, William 66
Pizarro, Francisco 31, 36, 38–40, 43, 47, 50
Pizarro, Gonzalo 33–4, 36–7, 39–45
Pizarro, Hernando 33
Placilla, Battle of 174
Plate River 65, 166, 269; discovery and early settlement 29, 34–5, 52–3; modern development of Basin 193, 196, 269, 321, 330–1
Platt Amendment 126, 128
Playa Girón—*see* Bay of Pigs
Plaza, Leónidas 153
Plaza Lasso, Galo 153, 291
Pochteca 13–14
Political parties 294–305
Polk, James K. 81
Pombal, Marquis of 58
Ponce Enríquez, Camilo 153
Ponce de León, Juan 28
Popayán 50
Popham, Sir Home 65
Popol Vuh 5, 7, 307
Popular Front 175–6, 267, 301
Population: age structure 225; birth control 226–7; composition and growth rate 224–6, 256; decline following conquest 46–7; economic consequences of rapid growth 114, 224–6; foreign communities 223; individual countries (table) 347; immigration (*and see individual countries*) 216, 223–4; marginal 218–19; over-population 114, 225; pre-Columbian 3, 46; shift to towns 218–19; under-population 224–5

Populism 296–8
Porres, St. Martín de 59, 233
Portales, Diego 172–4, 295
Portes Gil, Emilio 90
Portinari, Cândido 312
Porto Bello 53
Port of Spain, Protocol of 340
Portugal 35, 53–4, 58, 61–3, 66, 69, 199, 203, 233, 311
Portuguese 29, 38, 47, 49, 53–4, 60, 309
Positivism 84, 157, 184, 200, 202, 313–14, 317
Potatoes 17, 257
Potosí 55
Pozas, Ricardo 221, 308
Prado, Manuel 159, 290
Prebisch, Raúl 281–5, 331
Prestes, Luíz Carlos 204, 209, 301–2
Prieto, Joaquín 172
Prío Socorrás, Carlos 129
Privateers 60
Promoción Popular 298
Protestantism 226, 233
Puebla, Battle of 83
Puerto Cabello 67, 142
Puerto Ordaz 273
Puerto Rico 124–5, 316
Pueyrredón, Juan Martín de 69
Punta del Este: Charter of 335; Summit Conference 244, 328

Quadros, Jânio 207–8
Quechua 18–20, 220–2, 307–8
Querétaro 83
Quetzalcóatl (Kukulcán) 7, 9–11, 29, 44
Quiché Indians 8, 307
Quipus 19–20, 22–3, gl
Quiroga, Facundo—*see* Facundo
Quiroga, Vasco de 45, 57, 73
Quito 19, 22–3, 31–2, 34, 36, 37, 69, 72, 151, 154

Race—*see* Indians, Negroes, *Mestizos*, Mulattos
Radicals 295; in Argentina 184–7, 189; in Chile 175–7
Railways 156, 158, 183, 187, 270–1
Ramírez, Pedro 186
Rancagua 267; Battle of 70
Ray, Manolo 133
Raynal, Abbé 60

Rebel Armed Forces—*see* Guerrillas
Recabarren, Luis Emilio 175
Recife 54, 237
Reconquista 27, 41
Reducciones, 57, *gl*
Regency, Council of 67
Regidores 38–9, 50–1, 58, *gl*
Reid Cabral, Donald 122
Religion (*see also* Church, Voodoo): pre-Columbian 9–12, 14–16, 18, 20, 23
René Moreno, Gabriel 220
Repartimiento 41, 43, 55, 65, *gl*
Requerimiento 42, 46, 286
Residencia (*juicio de*) 52, *gl*
Revueltas, Silvestre 318
Revolutionary Armed Forces—*see* Guerrillas
Reyes, Rafael 145
Rice production 258
Río Blanco 267
Río Grande 89,
Rio Grande do Sul 199, 204, 208–9
Rio de Janeiro 54, 63, 198–9, 203, 209, 216, 218–19; Protocol 321, 323; Treaty 323
Río Negro 269
Rivadavia, Bernardino 69, 181–2
Rivera, Julio Adalberto 107, 242
Rivera, Diego 91, 308
Roads 268–71
Roca, Julio 183
Rocafuerte, Vicente 151–2
Roca–Runciman Pact 186, 338
Rockefeller, Nelson 337
Rodó, José Enrique 316–17
Rodríguez, Abelardo 90
Rodríguez Lara, Guillermo 154
Rojas, José 168
Rojas, Ricardo 315
Rojas Pinilla, Gustavo 148–9
Rondón, Cândido Mariano 243
Roosevelt, Franklin D. 92, 117, 129, 322
Roosevelt, Theodore 110
Rosas, Manuel de 181–2, 202
Rose, St., of Lima, 59
Rousseau, Jean-Jacques 60, 313
Royal Fifth, 38, 40–1
Rubber 165, 204, 320
Ruiz Cortínez, Adolfo 94
Rulfo, Juan 318
Rumiñavi 222

Russia—*see* Soviet Union
Russians 66, 223

Saavedra, Bautista 166
Saavedra Lamas, Carlos 317
Sacasa, Juan Bautista 103
Sacsahuamán 24
Sahagún, Bernardino de 59, 309
Saint-Pierre, Bernardin de 313
Salamanca, Daniel 166
Salaverry, Felipe Santiago 156
Salomon, Lysius 116
Salta 33
Sam, Vilbrun Guillaume 116
San Antonio 81
Sánchez Cerro, Luis 158–9
Sánchez Hernández, Fidel 107
Sandino, Augusto César 103
San Jacinto River 81
San José 327
San Juan River (Colombia) 269; (Nicaragua) 102–3, 113
San Lorenzo 4
San Luis Potosí, Plan of 87
San Martín, José de 70–2
Santa Anna, Antonio López de 80–1
Santa Cruz 169, 171
Santa Cruz, Andrés 156, 164, 173
Santa Fe 181
Santa María 27
Santana, Pedro 19
Santander, Francisco de Paula 72, 144
Santiago (St. James) 41
Santiago (Chile) 34, 48, 67, 70–1, 175, 218, 234–5
Santiago (Cuba) 129–30
Santo Domingo 28, 42, 119–20, 122
Santos, Eduardo 146
Santos Dumont, Alberto 271
São Paulo 54, 198, 203–4, 207, 209, 216, 218, 259, 270
Sapa Inca 19–23
Sarmiento, Domingo Faustino 183, 289, 313–15
Schick, René 104
Schmidl, Ulrich 48–9
Schomburgk, Robert 138
Science and technology 317
Seregni, Liber 196
Seville 29, 41, 52, 57, 61, 67
Shanty towns 218–19, 296–7, 300

Sheep 183, 194, 261
Shipping 269–70
Sica-Sica 266
Sierra, Justo 84
Sierra Maestra 130, 132, 134
Siglo Veinte mine 268
Siles Salinas, Luis Adolfo 170
Siles Zuazo, Hernán 167, 169
Silver 54–5, 156, 165
Siqueiros, David Alfaro 91, 308
Slavery: in Brazil 53–4, 58, 200–2; emancipation 114, 152, 155, 202; in Haiti 62, 114; pre-Columbian 12, 22; in Spanish colonies 28, 43, 46, 66, 124; in Texas 80
Slave trade 47, 61, 200–1
Smallpox 31, 47 ,57
Socialism 300–3
Socialist parties 175–6, 177–9, 300–3
Social security 287–8
Social structure (see also individual countries): colonial 38–41, 49–54, 60–1, 215; contemporary 215–27; post-independence 215–20, 223; pre-Columbian 12–13, 16, 19–24
Solís, Juan de 34
Somoza Debayle, Anastasio ('Tachito') 104, 239
Somoza Debayle, Luis 104
Somoza García, Anastasio ('Tacho') 103–4, 289
Sonora 88, 266
Sorí Marín, Humberto 133
Soto, Hernán de 37–8, 40
Soto, Jesús de 318
Soto, Marco Aurelio 104
Soulouque, Faustin Elie 116
Soviet Union: and Bolivia 268; and Brazil 208, 342; and Chile 175, 343; and Cuba 131, 133–6, 259–60, 342–4; and Guatemala 100, 343; and Latin America 301–2, 342–4; and Mexico 342; and other countries 109, 342–3; trade 343
Spain: colonial regime 38–62; conquest and settlement 27–38; and Cuba 124–5; cultural influence 308–10; loss of colonies 66–76; and Portuguese America 35; relations with ex-colonies 83, 173; reoccupation of Santo Domingo 119; trade (colonial) 61–2; (current) 341–2

Spanish–American War 110, 125
Spencer, Herbert 84
Spice Islands 31
Standard Oil Company 159, 166–7, 337
Steel production 273
Stroessner, Alfredo 193, 239
Structuralists 279–81
Suárez, Inés 48
Suárez, Nicolás 165
Sucre 245
Sucre, Antonio José de 69, 72, 164
Sugar production 53, 62, 124, 126–8, 132, 156, 201, 259–60, 283

Tabasco 4
Tacna 157–8, 174, 321
Tahuantin-suyu 20
Talara 161
Talavera, Hernán de 42
Tamayo, Rufino 318
Tambos 22, 32, 37, gl
Tarán, Juan B. 313
Tarapacá 157, 175
Teixera Pinto, Bento 309
Teller Amendment 125
Tenochtitlán 11–13, 29–31, 37, 47
Teoponte 170
Teotihuacán 8–11
Terms of trade 282–5
Terra, Gabriel 195
Territorial waters 161, 337, 345
Texaco 263, 265
Texas 80–1
Texcoco 11
Tezcatlipoca 10–11
Third World 327, 345; priests of 235
Tiahuanaco 16–19
Tierra del Fuego 3, 261, 266, 321
Tikal 8
Tin 165–70, 267–8, 283
Tinoco, Federico 108
Titicaca, Lake 15, 18
Tlacaélel 11
Tlaloc 9
Tlatelolco, Treaty of 345
Tlaxcala 13, 30
Tlaxcalans 13, 29–31, 37
Toledo, Francisco de 52, 55
Tollan—see Tula
Toltecs 8–10
Tomic, Radomiro 177, 299

Tonton-macoutes 117–18, 239, *gl*
Topa Yupanqui 19, 21
Topiltzín 10
Tordesillas, Treaty of 35
Toro, Daniel 167
Torre Tagle, Marquis of 71
Torres, Camilo 236
Torres, Juan José 171
Torrijos, Omar 112
Toussaint L'Ouverture, Pierre Dominique 62, 115, 119
Trade (*see also under individual countries*):
Britain 61, 63–5, 75, 282, 337–40; with EEC 340–1; foreign (general) 281–4; inter-American 284, 327–31; with Japan 259, 344; Portuguese colonial 53–4; pre-Columbian 13–14; with Soviet Union 343; Spanish colonial 61–2; with United States 61–2, 259, 282–3, 332, 337
Trade unions—*see* Labour
Transport 268–71
Tres Zapotes 4
Tricontinental Conference 135, 345
Trinidad 28, 61, 323
Triple Alliance 192
Trotskyists 302–3
Truando River 113
Trujillo 17, 158–9
Trujillo Molina, Rafael Leónidas 117, 120–1, 142, 216, 289
Tucumán 69, 180, 250
Tula (Tollan) 9–10
Túmbez (Tumbes) 17, 32, 155
Tupac Amaru II (José Gabriel Condorcanqui) 56, 307
Tupamaros 196–7, 305
Turcios Lima, Luis Augusto 304
Turcos 223, *gl*
Tuzutlán 44
26 July Movement 130, 132, 298
Tzotzil Indians 221

Ubico, Jorge 99
Ucureña 168
Ukrainians 223
Ulate, Otilio 108
Ulloa, Antonio de 56, 59, 61
Unão Democrática Brasileira (UDN) 207
Unión Cívica: in Argentina 184; in Dominican Republic 121

Unión General de Trabajadores (UGT) 251
Unión Republicana Democrática 140–2
Unitarios 181–2, *gl*
United Fruit Company 96, 99, 104–5, 108
United Nations 108, 227, 331, 345
United Nations Commission for Latin America (ECLA) 331–3
United Nations Conference on Trade and Development (UNCTAD) 283–4, 345
United Provinces of Central America 96–7
United Provinces of River Plate 69, 180
United States: aid 226, 248, 278–9, 335, 337; Alliance for Progress 335–7; and Argentina 175, 185, 188, 206, 333–4; arms supplies 244–5; and Bolivia 167–71, 268, 336–7; and Brazil 205–7, 212, 226, 259; and Central America 97–8, 333–4; and Chile 175–7, 267, 336; and Colombia 68, 145, 333; and Cuba 124–8, 133–6, 259–60, 316, 325, 336; and Dominican Republic 119–20, 122, 325–6; and Guatemala 99–100; and Haiti 116–18, 334; and inter-American affairs 76, 332–7; interventions 102–3, 116–17, 119–20, 122–3, 125–6, 333–5; investments 92–3, 158, 276–9, 337; and labour 253; and Latin American independence 62, 137, 332; and Mexico 80–3, 85, 89, 92–3; missionaries 233; and Nicaragua 102–3; and Panama 110–13, 334, 336; and Peru 158, 160–2, 337; and Puerto Rico 334; and Spain 332–3; Texas 80–1, 333; trade 61–2, 259, 282–3, 332, 337; and Venezuela 138, 264–5, 333
Universities 158, 245–9, 292, 317
Upper Peru (*see also* Bolivia) 69–70, 72, 155, 192
Uriburu, José Félix 185
Urquiza, Justo José de 182
Urubupangá 273
Uruguay (*see also* Banda Oriental): agriculture 194–6; and Argentina 69, 182, 188, 192, 322; and Brazil 69, 192, 322; communism 301, 304; constitution 290, 293; culture and education 246–7, 316; economy 195–7, 256, 261; history since independence 194–6; inflation 279; labour 195–6; origins 69, 338;

politics 194, 196–7, 293, 295, 297; population growth 224; social services 195–6
Uruguay River 58, 69
Uspallata pass 70
Utopia 45

Valdivia 71
Valdivia, Pedro de 34, 39, 48, 50
Valencia, Guillermo León 149
Valle Caviedes, Juan del 309
Vallejo, César 313
Valparaíso 71, 155, 175, 266
Valverde, Vicente 32
Vancouver, George 57
Vanderbilt, Cornelius 102
Vandor, Augusto 250
Vargas, Getúlio 204–6, 253, 287, 297, 301
Vargas Llosa, Mario 318
Vasconcelos, José 91, 313, 346
Vecinos 51, gl
Vekemans, Roger 234
Velasco Alvarado, Juan 161, 243, 245, 336
Velasco Ibarra, José María 153–4, 161
Velásquez, Diego 29, 30, 39, 47
Venezuela: agriculture and land reform 140, 142, 230; army 140–3; and Britain 138–9; *caudillos* 137–9; Church 138, 143; and Colombia 321; communism 301, 305; conquest and settlement 28, 34, 38, 43; constitution 286–7; and Cuba 325; culture and education 226, 247–8, 314–15; democratic governments 140–3; economy 139, 141–3, 255–6, 272–3, 276–7, 281; foreign relations 138–9, 143, 300; guerrillas 134, 142, 305; and Guyana 138, 143, 339–40; independence movement 66–9; industry 139–43, 273; labour 139–42; petroleum 133, 137–8, 140–3, 263–5; politics 137, 143, 298–9; population growth 224; and United States 138, 264–5, 333
Venezuela, Gulf of 143
Vera Cruz 4, 29–30, 39, 53, 80–1, 88–9
Vera Paz 44
Vespucci, Amerigo 27
Viceroyalties 52, 57, 60
Vicos 220
Victoria, Guadelupe 73

Vicuñas 21, gl
Vieira, Antônio de 59, 309–10
Vietnam War 267
Villa, Pancho 87–8
Villa-Lôbos, Heitor 312
Villanueva, C. R. 317
Villaroel, Gualberto 167, 171, 297
Villeda Morales, Ramón 105, 240
Villegagnon, Nicolas Durand de 54
Viña del Mar, Consensus of 326, 337
Vincent, Sténio 117
Vinto 265
Violencia, La 147, 304
Viracocha 18–19, 23, 44, 307
Virgins of the Sun 23
Vitoria, Francisco de 45
Vives, Fernando 234
Voltaire 60, 191, 313
Volta Redonda 250, 273
Voodoo (Vodun) 116–17, 233

Walker, William 98, 102, 108
War of the Pacific 157, 165, 174, 320–1
Washington, Act of 323
Wellesley, Arthur, Duke of Wellington 64, 66
Welser family (bankers) 40
Welsh 183, 223
Wessín y Wessín, Elías 122
Weyler y Nicolau, Valeriano 125
Wheat 257–8
Whitelocke, John 65
Wilson, Woodrow 89
Wool 195, 260
World War I 153, 185, 204, 249, 272, 338, 344
World War II 94, 139, 153, 159, 168, 186–7, 195, 205, 249, 274, 298, 322–3, 338–40, 342, 344–5

Yanacunas 22
Yaquis 84
Ydígoras Fuentes, Miguel 101
Yellow fever 47, 62, 126
Yeroví, Clemente 153
Yon Sosa 303
Yucatán 7, 10, 13, 81, 84, 88
Yugoslavs 223
Yungay, Battle of 164, 173

Zacapa 102
Zacatecas 55
Zanjón, Pact of 125
Zapata, Emiliano 87–9, 93, 231
Zapotecs 4, 13, 82

Zayas, Alfredo 128
Zea, Leopoldo 315
Zelaya, José Santos 97, 103
Zinc 171, 262
Zumárraga, Antonio de 44